ALL the KING'S HORSES

BARRY MILAZZO

CREATION HOUSE

All the King's Horses: Finding Purpose and Hope in Brokenness and Impossibility by Barry Milazzo
Published by Creation House
A Charisma Media Company
600 Rinehart Road
Lake Mary, Florida 32746
www.charismamedia.com

Design Director: Justin Evans
Cover design by Nathan Morgan

Visit the author's website: www.AllTheKingsHorsesMinistry.com.

Library of Congress Cataloging in Publication Data: 2014956293
International Standard Book Number: 978-1-62998-419-3
E-book International Standard Book Number: 978-1-62998-420-9

15 16 17 18 19— 9 8 7 6 5 4 3 2
Printed in the United States of America

CONTENTS

ACKNOWLEDGMENTS

Thank you to my three wonderful children, Janelle, Bryson, and Tim; my daughter-in-law, Emily; and son-in-law, Miguel: each of you have made me proud to be called "Dad."

Thank you to Theresa Brotherton, a servant of Christ: your sharp eyes and tireless efforts caused this book to become far better than this author could have made it on his own.

Thank you to the BCS men: your generosity made the publishing of this book possible.

It is said that a man is wealthy if he finds just a few loyal, trusted friends during his journey through this world. Thank you, my friends, for making me wealthy.

A special thanks to my lifelong friend Phil Mandato. You refused to allow me to give up and quit, which I felt like doing many times as I sought to finish this work.

Thank you to Allen Quain, Berta Coleman, Ann Stoner, and the staff at Creation House. You guided me through this process with professionalism and grace.

A special thanks to Diana and Steve Richardson, a beautiful married team of God. You made this manuscript professional and sound and you loved, encouraged, and prayed for me and Bryson throughout the process.

A special thank you lifted up toward heaven for the life and memory of my counselor and dear friend, Dave Wanner. I stand among many who miss your joyful smile, your laugh, your wise and biblical counsel, and your warm embrace at the top of those stairs in Hoboken. Thank you for being God's vessel to guide me through the darkest hours of my life.

Thank You most of all to Jesus: it is for Your glory this book has been written. I pray that every man and woman who reads this story will come to know You as the magnificent God and King You truly are, and that those with shattered, Humpty Dumpty lives will come to know that in You, and only in You, their broken lives can be restored, and hold together forever.

> For by Him all things were created, both in the heavens and on earth, visible and invisible, whether thrones or dominions or rulers or authorities—all things have been created through Him and for Him. He is before all things, and in Him all things hold together.
>
> —Colossians 1:16–17

SPECIAL THANKS

SPECIAL THANKS TO the following individuals for their generosity in granting permission to use portions of their songs within this book:

BOB DYLAN

BILLY JOEL

GORDON LIGHTFOOT

The penetrating questions and introspection about life which you've posed within your own works have helped me to delve beneath the shallow surfaces of human experience in the telling of my own story.

Introduction
SITTING ON THE WALL

Humpty Dumpty sat on the wall,
Humpty Dumpty had a great fall.
All the king's horses and all the king's men
Couldn't put Humpty Dumpty together again.

HENRY THOREAU CONCLUDED that most people lead lives of quiet desperation.[1] Dan Allender declared: "Desire so often proves fruitless. Disappointment has answered hope so many times that it seems utterly absurd to hunger and yearn for anything any longer."[2] Scottish hymn writer Horatius Bonar began his classic book, *When God's Children Suffer,* with these words:

> It is no easy matter to write a book for the family of God.... They may not be found unsuitable for the younger brethren of the Man of sorrows. For the way is rough, and the desert blast is keen. Who of them can say anything regarding their prospects here, save that tribulation awaits them in every place as they pass along?[3]

You don't need another book telling you life is hard, a reminder that it is far from what you once hoped and planned. You know that song all too well, don't you? You've faced your unbeatable foes, your unreachable goals. Indeed, you've fallen embarrassingly short of the unreachable star.

Maybe you've picked up this book because you've suffered a "great fall" that has *so* decimated your dreams that the notion is now laughable that all the king's horses and all his men, or even God Himself, could put them back together again.

Others reading these pages may wonder what I'm talking about. You're among the fortunate, as I once was. Oh yes, I was among the notorious "1 percenters," wealthy in every resource valued in this world. As I looked down from my privileged perch atop the wall of prosperity, I thanked God for my place way up there. Cries from those far below rarely reached my ears.

Images of war, catastrophe, and squalor on other continents are easily dismissed. We can entertain ourselves to distraction as another car bomb obliterates life and as tsunamis sweep it away as if it were cheap. Mercifully, those images quickly fade from our minds. But as they edge closer to home, they become harder to block. Man's mightiest towers in Manhattan come crumbling down, taking thousands with them. Hurricanes, floods, and tornadoes whisk away entire communities. Fires kill innocent children. Auto accidents result in a mommy or daddy never again coming home. Murders by the thousands. Children abused and neglected. Suicides at an alarming rate. Women savagely enslaved and raped.

Millions do battle daily with less sensational dramas behind the walls of our homes. Strokes, heart attacks, and degenerative diseases of myriad description decimate once healthy bodies. Children are born handicapped, retarded, blind, and deaf. Many plunge from able-bodied strength to quadriplegia in an instant. Families watch helplessly as loved ones fade into the nebulous world of dementia and Alzheimer's.

Millions more are immobilized with emotional and psychological disorders every bit as debilitating as physical disease. Countless others suffer the pain of human relationships that are unhealthy and abusive. The anguish of being trapped in a bad marriage demoralizes an untold number, as does the pain of children and spouses left behind by divorce. Layoffs, financial reversals, and bankruptcy represent a "great fall" for countless families. Innumerable others suffer the mundane yet crushing agony of unending loneliness.

The above list scratches only the surface. It's not a pretty picture, and frankly, not a pleasant way to start a book. I don't mean to be pessimistic, yet I will take this one step further. Anyone willing to face reality must admit that, irrespective of your youthful strength or the vastness of your personal resources, *all* efforts to remain permanently seated atop that prosperous wall of pain-free security in this world is a laughably losing battle.

The odds of being tossed into the ring against an "unbeatable" foe make this a foregone conclusion. Important dreams and aspirations in the lives of every human being (and yes, every Christian) will ultimately lay scattered on the ground. You want better news? Buy a less honest book. But ignorance is never bliss.

Larry Crabb states it this way: "Live long enough, and dreams important to you will shatter. Some will remain shattered. God will not glue together the pieces of every Humpty Dumpty who takes a great fall in your life."[4]

Shattered dreams are often marked by futile efforts to pray, plead, and claw our way out. Despite our best efforts, crushing problems wedge their way deeper. Pitching a tent, they take up residence in our lives for the long haul. Exhausted from fighting and praying, many give up hope of feeling "normal" ever again. The notion that God cares is nice, but not very practical. Frankly, to those who are honest, God has not come through for us. Not in the way we expected or hoped.

Yet there remains an ache deep inside, a near dormant desire to fight back against the indignity and frustration of it all. We hunger for the happy ending, yearn for the underdog to rise up and achieve victory before the final curtain falls—Come on Rocky. You can do it! Get up off that canvass. But what do we do when we've fought our hearts out, given every last ounce of what was in us to give, and we've got no fight left? What do we do when all that remains is an overwhelming sense of hopelessness, defeat, and despair?

Many choose to blame God for their broken dreams. An understandable response. After all, if He's as powerful and good as He's *supposed* to be, why didn't He simply prevent our tragic circumstances? Some choose to blame others: If only that offender hadn't caused the accident, or that abuser treated me cruelly, then I'd be happy and free. Still others blame themselves. They could have done better in the midst of their battles, and they know it. When the going got tough, they didn't get going at all. They wimped out and compounded their problems by making *all* the wrong choices. They deserve what they've gotten, and they know God is "ticked" at them to boot.

I can't condemn those who find themselves playing the blame game. Frankly, I've struggled badly through all three of the above perspectives during my lifetime, and not just once. Were it not for the fact that I ultimately found something better, something worth living for, there would be no good reason to write this book.

Understandably, brokenness is not a popular theme in our culture, even within Christian circles. We'd rather hear about getting our best life now. Yet one of the clearest, most consistent themes in Scripture reveals something startling. God has extraordinary purposes in mind for those who find themselves desolate and broken by life's circumstances. If the truth be fully told, God has *always* chosen to perform His most powerful works through vessels that have been deeply and irreparably broken. These are the sons and daughters who have learned that the greatest privilege we could ever attain in this world is not to grab for our best life now but to give our best away for the benefit of others, as a Spirit from another realm flows through our brokenness.

Jesus' first words from the mount are aimed at desperate souls who face devastating brokenness.

> Blessed are the poor in spirit, for theirs is the kingdom of heaven. Blessed are those who mourn, for they shall be comforted.
>
> —Matthew 5:3–4

Beautiful teachings; even poetic. "*But come off it, Jesus!* You don't expect us to believe that the circumstances that have tortured and brutally twisted our lives are something to be *happy* about, *do You?*" Indeed, talk is cheap. But not from Jesus, nor from His Father!

When it came time for God, peering into the eyes of a serpent, to push His chips to the middle of the table, the most shocking wager in history was revealed for all creation to see. How would God choose to handle the issues of sin, brokenness, pain, and human defeat? He staked the whole world, the fate of every son of Adam and every daughter of Eve, on a peculiar hand indeed. He chose brokenness and death for His very own Son. What kind of strange gamble was *this?*

All the King's Horses will pose a question to be considered by every person whose dreams have been shattered, whose life has been broken beyond repair: Could it be possible that God intends to use your brokenness—the crushing circumstances which symbolize defeat, death, and shame in your life—to produce victory and abundance in and through you that is higher than you could ever have dreamed? Does not the question itself remind us of something? Strange indeed!

This is not a "how-to" book, concerning suffering. It contains no easy-to-follow steps for the time when an "impossible" battle arises in your life (and arise it will). Pious platitudes and simplistic outlines sound useful until the heat gets turned up. When your distresses come to a boil, class is in session for the Master to teach us things about Himself and about ourselves that we couldn't, or wouldn't, receive before.

This book centers around the life of one of the most beautiful little boys God ever created. He was born on Mother's Day, May 11, 1986. His features were gorgeous, his body healthy and vibrant. Surely he'd be an athlete, as his father had been. Suddenly, this boy's brain was damaged beyond all hope of recovery, his life broken beyond repair. Not only would he be unable to compete in athletics, it was predicted that he would never walk or even speak. His parents were advised to consider placing him in an institution. Welcome to hell, my son.

I suppose if there were ever a story to cause someone to doubt that God is good, or whether He exists at all, this boy's tragedy would rank among those to be debated for that purpose. The way he was "broken" in particular is one of the most heartbreaking injustices you will ever learn of. Yet studying this boy's life through a period of decades has led me to some strikingly different conclusions about life, and about God.

For the benefit of those seeking genuine hope, I will be honest and blunt in this book, even as God has been brutally honest in His Word, the Bible. You deserve no less, particularly those of you who sit among the smoldering ashes of dreams gone up in smoke.

Frankly, you are about to read a story written by a man who has been often depressed, powerless, angry, hopeless, and frightened, not in years gone by, but even as I have written this book. I borrow, once again, from Horatius Bonar as he reveals something of the "fear and trembling" I feel as I dare to pass along *anything* of value to any other suffering individual:

> It is written in much weakness, and with many sins to mar it.... It is written by one who is seeking himself to profit by trial, and trembles lest it should pass by as the wind over the rock, leaving it as hard as ever; by one who would in every sorrow draw near to God that He may know Him more, and who is not unwilling to confess that as yet he knows but little.[5]

In the chapters to follow, you will learn of a child whose life was radically altered through severe brain injury. His courage and determination to come back against enormous odds is inspirational even for me as an author, and as his father. But this is hardly a story of continual triumph. You'll have no trouble finding one of those at your local bookstore.

This is a story about God working in His mysterious way to lift my son from one level of achievement to the next, amidst many crushing and protracted reversals. It is also a story about a King who, without condemnation, lifted this author from the dirt of abject failure and anger and fear. This King never stopped loving me, even when I was tempted to raise my puny fist against heaven. Indeed, He forgave me, again and again, after I had done precisely that.

This story will inspire you, even as it causes you to rejoice, and to cry. Yet I've written this book knowing that your pain, like mine, is far too deep for spurious claims of healing and victory. Your soul yearns for something higher, something that will transform your life and cause you to persevere in true victory, as heaven defines it. Clearly, you don't need embellished tales about my son in order to do that. You were born to learn of and receive the highest victory, the victory which comes only from an intimate connection with God's Son.

God knows, could I reverse some of the circumstances in the chapters to follow, I would do so. But the bitter cup from which we must sometimes drink is from a wine list of His choosing, carefully fermented in heaven. We would all do well to remember that the wine Master uncorked a particularly bitter vintage to be swallowed by His own precious Son.

Inscrutably, fellowship with this Son, King Jesus, is never made more intimate than from the willing sips we trustingly learn to take from the bitter cup in our hands, as the One who drank the bitterest cup sits lovingly by our side.

Because of the pain involved, this has been a difficult book for me to write. Yet through this story of brokenness, I pray that you will see your own story as you press on through this battleground world. Above all, I trust that this story will give you the courage and hope you need to continue on with a greater sense of the purpose and privilege of brokenness, in the strength of a King who will enable you to fight the impossible battles that rage in your own life.

> When you go out to battle against your enemies and see horses and chariots and people more numerous than you, do not be afraid of them; for the LORD your God, who brought you up from the land of Egypt, is with you. Now it shall come about that when you are approaching the battle, the priest shall come near and speak to the people. And he shall say to them, "Hear, O Israel, you are approaching the battle against your enemies today. Do not be fainthearted. Do not be afraid, or panic, or tremble before them, for the LORD your God is the one who goes with you, to fight for you against your enemies, *to save you.*"
>
> —DEUTERONOMY 20:1–4, EMPHASIS ADDED

Chapter 1

AN AMERICAN DREAM

Present day Christianity has redefined spiritual maturity… The mature among us are now thought to be the successful, the happy, the effective people on top of things and doing well.… It seems that our highest ambition has been producing people whose circumstances are pleasant enough to praise God.[1]

Larry Crabb

The Question

It was a dreary March day in 1986. My wife, nearly seven months pregnant, was busy making our daughter's bed. We knew that this child, due in May, was to be a boy. Our two-and-one-half-year-old princess, Janelle, had just moved into her new chambers down the hall, making room in the royal nursery for the pending arrival of the new prince. Excitement and anticipation were intensifying throughout the Milazzo kingdom.

As she continued working on the bed, my wife wondered about the plans God had for this new life growing within her, and she began to pray for him. She ended her prayer with the simple request, "Lord, what I want most for my baby is for him to be healthy." A reasonable request, I think you'll agree.

Suddenly, her prayer was interrupted by a startling question. It was as if God had stepped in to respond. The question in her mind that day was more significant than either of us could have realized then. The voice simply said, "What if the child isn't healthy, as you have prayed? Would you still accept him as a gift from Me?"

She was so startled by this "voice" that she sat down on our daughter's bed and began to cry. God seemed to be asking, "Would you love and accept this baby you're carrying just the same if it turns out that My plans for him are contrary to your hopes and dreams?" She was shaken and trembling. Was God communicating that something was wrong with our soon to be born son? Was this just a test? Could saying "yes" to God actually mean that something horrible might happen? This was just too much to take in.

I don't know what my answer would have been if God approached me with His question at that time. Would I be willing to sacrifice the life of my own son for God's glory, as Abraham was willing to do with Isaac? Does it even matter what my response would have been? I mean, I don't remember being asked to cast a vote on many circumstances that have drastically affected my life. To be honest, my ballot would differ greatly from God's "vote" many times. As you've no doubt noticed, we haven't exactly been born into a democracy. We've been created in the image of God, a pretty high rank in this world. But God alone is God, and He has no term limits. To be honest, there have been times I've yearned for much more of a say in His government, times when I've even yearned for that top spot—not to rule everything, just my own life. Is that too much to ask?

DAMNED FOR *WHAT?*

Martin Luther once said that we must get to the point in our Christian walk where we would be willing to be damned for the glory of God. "I don't mean to be flippant, Marty, but would you mind running that one by me again? As a young father and an executive in New York, I don't have a whole lot of time to dwell on *that* kind of thinking. And if you don't mind my saying so, your standard is just a bit too dire and depressing for me. I've seen a painting of you somewhere or other and, to be honest, you *look* like the kind of man who *would* say something like that. Talk about *dour*—my *goodness*! Did you guys suck lemons while having your portrait done in those days? In any event, if your life's dream is to die at the stake, *go for it man*! Sure my faith is real, Marty; but frankly, it's talk like *yours* that scares the daylights out of people and gives Christianity a bad name. Look, Marty, this is not a day when people go around wanting to be 'damned' for things. We live in a day that is all about getting our best life *now*! What's wrong with that?

"I don't mean to be harsh with you, Martin. You seem like a reasonable man, albeit a tad gloomy. I'm sure we can come to some sort of 'meeting of the minds' here. We're more alike than you might think. Just like you, I'm grateful Christ has saved me from my sins and that I'm going to heaven. And I'm *certainly* not opposed to setting high standards for myself. I'll have you know I've sacrificed a *lot* for my family and I'm a very involved member in my church. I give a good percentage of the money the Lord has blessed me with back to the cause of Christ, and I'm beginning to be recognized for leadership positions in the Christian community. Furthermore, I've been asked to join the Board of Directors of a *very* influential Christian organization in the New York area. I *even* teach the adult Sunday school class now and then. And I'll have you know that as I've done all these good things for the Lord, God has added many wonderful blessings to my life.

"Don't you get it, Marty? This is the way things are *supposed* to work. Me and God, we've got a good thing going. Life is hard enough without killjoys like you dampening the party. *Damned for the glory of God? Let's get real!* Things are going quite well for me right now without wishing such morbidity on myself. Frankly, you'd be an embarrassment if you tried to come into many of our churches today.

"What's that you say, Martin? You think I should read something from the *Old* Testament. Why am I not surprised that you're stuck in ancient, outdated thinking? I want you to know that I'm more comfortable spending my valuable time in the New Testament, at least the parts of it that I like. Okay, okay, Marty. I'm a reasonable man too. I'll read it."

> Though the fig tree should not blossom, And there be no fruit on the vines, Though the yield of the olive should fail, And the fields produce no food, Though the flock should be cut off from the fold, And there be no cattle in the stalls, Yet I will exult in the Lord, I will rejoice in the God of my salvation.
>
> —Habakkuk 3:17–18

"What in the *world* is this guy talking about, Marty? Why *should* we rejoice when God allows lousy things to happen in our lives? This kind of poetry may be of value for monks to meditate on or perhaps for the good Sisters of Mercy, or some such order. But let's get real here. *Our* society places *no* value whatsoever on fig trees which don't blossom, or fields which produce no food. Exulting in failure may be *your* idea of a good time, but not mine. Honestly, it sounds like a mantra for *losers*! Sentimental drivel! Unless…Habakkuk knows something that we also need to know? *Nah!*"

Life is Good

Those of you who remember the late 1980s probably remember a popular beer commercial which claimed: "When you enjoy the cold, great taste of [that particular brew], *life* is good." Though I enjoyed a few cold ones while watching sports in those days, I chuckled when I saw this ad. As ridiculous as this claim was about life being good because of the taste of their beer, I have no doubt the ad worked very well in the marketplace. Why? I think there's a place inside all of us that's a bit gullible about the things that will bring true happiness and contentment to our lives.

Many of us spend a great deal of time and energy chasing things almost as shallow as that commercial. We believe we can make life "good" by obtaining or achieving all sorts of things. Presumably, you've set your sights a bit higher than the taste of a particular beer. But even the higher things on our list never truly satisfy. Not for long, anyway.

My own advertisement, if I had to write one a few months before the birth of our firstborn son, would go something like this: "When you're thirty-one years old and have a beautiful wife and gorgeous little girl, life is good. When you're making plenty of money as a managing director for one of the most powerful commercial real estate organizations in the United States, life is good. When you're expecting your firstborn son to be a pal, a sports enthusiast just like you, life is good." I could go on, but you get the idea. Lots of good stuff was happening for me, and I was happy about it.

I wasn't particularly materialistic and there wasn't anything wrong with the way my life was going as a Christian. I had received many blessings given by God to be enjoyed. Looking back, I can honestly say I was thankful to God in a sincere way. I really wanted to serve Him the best way I knew how. But there were circumstances ahead, rolling out there somewhere like a tsunami, which God was going to use to teach me things He evidently wanted me, like Habakkuk and Martin Luther before me, to know.

THE PURSUIT OF HAPPINESS

Ask the serious student what she wants, and she may tell you that if she could only get into a particular college, she will be happy. The young college man is convinced that, if only he can get that special girl to marry him, he'll have it made. Later, after they become a couple, they arrive at another conclusion. They just know that they will live happily ever after when they can afford their dream home. Some years go by and they reach this goal. But something is still lacking. She concludes that once she is able to successfully complete furnishing and decorating their lovely home, she will relax and be happy.

A few more years go by and the home is splendidly furnished, but an emptiness remains. They realize that having children will make them *truly* happy. They have one and then another. They love their kids; but somehow, something is still missing. He knows what it is. After working so hard all these years, he's going to buckle down and get it done. He just *knows* that when he achieves that corner office, and all the perks that go with it, he will finally have it made. Life will be *good*.

That day finally arrives and there is a great deal of satisfaction, at least for a while. In a few years, though, he becomes bored with his success. There *must* be something more. A younger woman catches his eye. He dearly loves his wife and family. But, after all, doesn't he have the right to be happy? Having this affair will provide what is lacking.

From a distance, the next desire is *always* the missing piece of the puzzle. Happiness and fulfillment are always around the *next* corner. Of course, the pot of gold at the end of the rainbow is never found. There *must* be a better way.

In his excellent book *Waking from the American Dream*, Donald McCullough highlights many of the things people strive for to fill their longing for significance and meaning. He groups man's attempt to find fulfillment into three general categories which he labels as the "false gods" of materialism, power, and (interestingly) religion. Instead of condemning those who pursue such "false gods," he makes an interesting observation:

> When we resort to the false gods of materialism, power and religion in an attempt to fill the cup of longing, we err not because we desire too much but too little. We need more than we want.[2]

What is your next goal? Do you *really* believe it will achieve for you what the last one failed to provide? How many more "corners" do you intend to turn in your pursuit of happiness in life? Is there *any* human achievement, anything at all that we can gain and hold onto in this world that will finally cause us to be permanently content?

Could it be possible that men like Luther and Habakkuk understood some things we also need to know if we ever hope to satisfy the void deep inside?

Interesting postulations! But listen, I was thirty-one years old and my life was on the rise. Fig trees that don't blossom? Damned for the glory of God? Can these guys get *any* more depressing? I think I'll pass!

A Star Is Born

That evening, my wife told me about the voice she heard as she prayed that day. I had just commuted to our New Jersey home from Manhattan. I had struggled through a hard day and I was stressed and tired. I tried to listen and understand the importance of what she was attempting to describe through her tears. I prayed with her, and then gently assured her that our son was going to be completely fine. I reminded her that our doctors had given no indication otherwise. Again, she cried, as I quietly held her. As far as I was concerned, the matter had been dealt with, and I put it out of my mind. It would be much later before either of us would remember it again.

On May 11, 1986, Bryson James Milazzo was born, and any lingering concerns regarding voices and dreams were gone. He was one of the most beautiful babies God ever placed on this earth, a little cherub of a boy, with a turned up button nose no less. Better still, Bryson was *completely* healthy. All the tests doctors use to measure vigor and aptitude were at the very *top* of the charts! It *couldn't* get any better than this. Truly, life was good!

Bryson, alert and in perfect health at two months old

Chapter 2
WAKING FROM THE AMERICAN DREAM

God has created the world for His reasons and not for ours. That is the very bad news.[1]

Stephen Brown

A Good Start

People often remarked about how alert Bryson was for an infant. His eyes were straight and sharp. His hands were relaxed. He had lifted his head up off the bed, to see what was going on, at two weeks of age. He had already displayed a wonderful smile and a contagious giggle. He was able to turn over from his back to his stomach at five weeks. This boy was going to be the next Michael Jordan or Derek Jeter. (Okay, I know this is sickening, but don't try to tell me that you were different with your first son.)

On August 4, 1986, it was time for another one of his "well baby" visits to the doctor for his three-month examination. He was also scheduled to receive his first set of "routine" childhood vaccinations. Once again, Bryson's doctor found him to be very healthy, having achieved all normal developmental milestones.

Indeed, we were thankful that God had blessed us with our second beautiful and healthy child. Janelle was now two and one-half years old; and even though she now had to share mom and dad, she was enjoying having a baby brother. My wife and I were continuing to adjust to the added responsibility a second child brings. All in all, there wasn't much to complain about in the Milazzo household. We had two healthy children, my career was going well, and we belonged to a good church. God had blessed us beyond measure.

You probably remember the commercial in which four scraggly guys, fishing and drinking beer on the dock, start getting all sentimental saying: "It just doesn't get any better than this." My wife and I could have said the same thing. By the way, I realize I've now quoted beer commercials in each of the first two chapters. You teetotalers will be happy to know I gave up drinking alcohol many years ago, for reasons I'll explain later in the book. But getting back to those scraggly guys on the dock, they've *got* to be *kidding*. If my life ever gets to the point where the best I can do is sit around fishing with three guys badly in need of a shower, I'm checking-out of this world.

Hopefully someone just laughed. To be honest, I could use a laugh right now as I prepare to write what I must tell you next. It's still tough after all these years to think about it. The next few chapters may not be much fun for you either. But there will be some better news ahead, if you'll "hang in there" with me. Isn't that what much of our hope in this life is really based upon: better news ahead? Isn't this the reason we use the term "Good" Friday? Well, anyway, here we go.

"Surviving" a Scare

Our daughter had been through her early vaccinations without much difficulty, so we didn't have strong concerns about Bryson's first set of shots. We had heard, however, that some children were known to experience reactions from the pertussis portion of the DPT and from the oral polio vaccine. My wife had earlier asked Bryson's doctor about this and told me what he had said. His smug answer was that millions of babies receive these injections every year, and that he had "never heard of a single serious reaction in all his years" of being a pediatrician. Looking back, I wish I had considered his cocksure answer to be a warning that there was indeed something to be concerned about.

Bryson began crying immediately after he received his oral polio vaccination and the DPT injection. There was nothing unusual about that. But the crying began to intensify once my wife brought him home. He continued to cry louder until, about two hours after the injection, it had gotten to the point where he was screaming nonstop. It seemed as if he was in intense pain. His fever shot up to 105 degrees. My wife had called the doctor and was told by the nurse that this was a "normal," reaction, and that she should give the baby Tylenol and tepid baths to reduce the fever. She called me in New York and asked me to come home right away.

The high-pitched screaming and fevers lasted for days. As we held Bryson in our arms to comfort him, he began to forcefully extend his writhing body backward in an "arching" pattern so that it was difficult even to hold him. He was experiencing vomiting and diarrhea with a very peculiar type of mucous secretion that had a horrible smell. Numerous calls were made to the doctor to report these intense symptoms. We continued to be told to treat Bryson at home and to concentrate on lowering his fever. The other symptoms were ignored as unimportant.

Three days of providing Bryson with cool baths, Tylenol, and very little sleep left both of us drained. At the end of those three days, it appeared that Bryson had gone through the worst. The fever and symptoms began to subside. Bryson took long periods of sleep, presumably to make up for the trauma of the past several days. When he was awake, he was extremely sluggish. There was a noticeable contrast to the sharp baby he had been up until this time. The strange arching behavior continued periodically. It almost seemed as if Bryson were attempting to stretch out tight muscles in his back. Although his lethargy lasted a few weeks, we were relieved because we believed that we had weathered the storm. We were unaware that our nightmare was only just beginning.

We took Bryson to his doctor for a full examination. He examined Bryson and declared him to be fine. We described all of the terrible symptoms and their intensity to the doctor, but he was unfazed. Looking back on this now, we are amazed that a licensed pediatrician failed to see more. At the time we were simply relieved that the doctor put us at ease that Bryson was now "okay."

We then had a long consultation with the doctor regarding the safety of the vaccinations. We were determined not to vaccinate Bryson again. We were taken off guard as the doctor began using guilt tactics to convince us to change our minds. He informed us that we would be putting "all the other kids" at risk of disease, even those who were vaccinated, if Bryson did not become fully vaccinated. Though we were largely ignorant of these issues at that time, this didn't make much sense to us. If the other kids were vaccinated, then why would *they* be at risk? The doctor did admit that babies sometimes have adverse reactions, though in his view, with no serious consequences. He implored us to stay on schedule with Bryson's immunizations, but since Bryson had suffered such a strong reaction, he conceded to remove the pertussis serum from all subsequent inoculations. We agreed to continue on this basis, albeit with reservations.

During the following weeks, it appeared that things were getting back to normal for Bryson. Once again he was laughing and eating well, generally enjoying being a part of our home. Yet the sluggishness, which began after we "weathered the storm" of his first injections, still appeared to be with him. He also began to experience several ear infections and had a bout with bronchitis. My wife brought him to the doctor several more times. During those visits she attempted to get the doctor to validate the concerns which were growing inside her about Bryson's overall development. The doctor continued to insist that there was nothing wrong with him.

That fall, after a touch football game, several of my friends came to our house to watch some college football on television. Bob Boylan, one of my closest friends, pointed to Bryson, remarking that he truly was "a Milazzo." There was Bryson on the rug in front of the TV, in sort of a wrestler's neck bridge, his back arching up in the air, with only his head and his feet touching the floor. We had become accustomed to this arching, and it did not appear that Bryson was in any discomfort. We all chuckled at this seemingly precocious behavior from a six-month-old baby. Little did we know at the time that this behavior was anything but precocious. We had no idea that this was a type of seizure called a rainbow arch in which babies arch backward in this manner.

A One-Two Punch

On January 10, 1987, Bryson (now eight months old) received the DT shot (diphtheria and tetanus without the pertussis) and his second oral polio vaccination. Incredibly, Bryson began, once again, to experience all the *same* symptoms he had gone through after his initial (three-month) injections. For the rest of my life I will recall this with great sadness. I later came to believe that Bryson's first two sets of vaccinations (at three and eight months) had acted as a "one-two" punch against our son. It was as if the three-month injections stood Bryson up, and the subsequent series knocked him out permanently.

I also believe that Bryson's body had been trying, during the months since his initial injections, to make a comeback from the first devastating blow. Attempting to be diligent by keeping on track with his immunizations (as urged by the doctor), I later realized that we were allowing the second devastating blow to be delivered. Some in the medical establishment share my opinion. Some do not. I will elaborate on this in later chapters.

We again contacted the doctor repeatedly as we struggled with Bryson's severe symptoms during the next several days. We were treated by his staff like "the boy who cried wolf." They merely repeated their automaton-like instructions regarding how to care for an "irritable" baby. As Bryson writhed in pain, we prayed for him to escape with no serious consequences, as we mistakenly believed he had done after the three-month inoculations. Once again, Bryson appeared to "pull through" the trauma after about three days. We were initially unaware of just how devastated our child was. The truth would soon be revealed. In many respects, our son's life had already been destroyed, and the Milazzo family would never again be the same.

This Can't Be Happening!

We became increasingly concerned during the following weeks regarding Bryson's sluggishness. His eyes were turning in and his legs seemed unresponsive, as if numb. My wife brought Bryson to the doctor to determine why his developmental progress had stopped. In many ways, he had even regressed. In the ensuing months his legs, which were once able to zoom around in his baby walker, had stopped functioning. His attempts at crawling resulted in his crashing down, flat on his face. He tried to stand and cruise the furniture but his feet could not step sideways. Oddly, he sometimes seemed to "stand" on his ankles as he held onto furniture, almost as if he couldn't feel his feet any longer.

He no longer possessed the balance to sit up without falling over. Yet even in the face of this obvious regression, the doctor only seemed interested in treating the ear infections and bronchitis he was now regularly suffering. My wife was scolded for being an "unfair mother," expecting this child to be as advanced as our now three-year-old daughter had been. The doctor declared that he, himself, had never even walked until nineteen months of age. He was "tired" of parents' expectations that all their children should be "advanced."

The Safety Net

My wife was somewhat alone during this period. I just didn't see everything she saw. Perhaps I didn't want to see. Don't get me wrong, I was a "hands-on" father involved in diapering and taking care of our kids with the best of them. But I was also dealing with an enormous amount of stress and pressure in a fiercely competitive business in New York. Just as my wife was unsuccessful in getting the doctor to acknowledge her fears about our child, she also found it difficult getting me to fully share in her concerns.

We had a very successful and popular local doctor. He seemed a bit arrogant;

but as far as I was concerned, this doctor was an expert. He had seen thousands of babies through the years. I didn't think it was possible for him to miss something as serious as my wife now feared to be happening to our son. Besides, the alternative to my temporary denial was simply too frightening to consider.

We had grown up in an era in which doctors were viewed with a certain reverence and awe. Don't hear me saying that doctors do not deserve our respect. I believe the majority to be dedicated professionals who do all they can to alleviate disease, death, and pain. But the idea that modern medicine and doctors always have the answers for every ill, or even the capability to accurately diagnose every problem, are myths which die hard. We live in the most advanced civilization in the history of mankind. But false expectations of modern science and medicine can be the cause of great disillusionment. We are still, after all, only human. The "safety net," which we expect will be solidly in place for us in the medical field when we desperately need it, sometimes has gaping holes in it.

In our case, we all should have been listening to Bryson's mother much sooner. She knew her son as only a mother can know her child, and she knew something was seriously wrong. What a shock when I finally caught on.

The Nightmare of a Lost Baby

A real-life nightmare was being lived out in our home. In this nightmare, it's as if Bryson is trapped behind a thick wall of glass bricks. We see his blurry image, but are unable to get to him. Incredibly, no one seems to understand that our baby has been separated from us. I bang on the glass in a futile attempt to rouse someone's attention, anyone on the other side of that glass wall who might be able to help. But no one responds. It's as if an impenetrable chasm separates us. A terrifying reality then begins to dawn. To my horror, I realize that our baby is slowly beginning to fade away. I continue banging away, as the dream ends. Waking in a cold sweat, I fear I might never see my son again.

There could be no more denial, no further explaining away of his condition on the basis of a slower pace of development. Our son was in deep trouble and we both knew it now. He continued staring listlessly for long periods, aroused only with great effort. We still didn't understand the full horror of it; but the healthy, sharp-minded baby sent from heaven to live with us a brief time, was already gone.

Chapter 3

THE NIGHTMARE

The rope's breaking is not the central problem we face. Our real problem is the seeming meaninglessness of the breaking ropes.[1]

STEPHEN BROWN

As BRYSON TURNED one in May 1987, there could be no more denying that there was something seriously wrong with his development, though incredibly, our pediatrician *still* could not (or would not) see it. My wife and I took him to the pediatrician together and presented a list of the developmental milestones Bryson had previously achieved, which he could no longer do. He reluctantly referred us to a local pediatric neurologist.

We were now hoping and praying that Bryson would be found to have a simple disorder, something which could be routinely treated and cured, finally bringing life back to normal in the Milazzo household. Countless people joined us in this hope, and there was an active prayer chain going on.

The neurologist reviewed Bryson's history. He examined him for a mere five minutes, and then asked us to get him dressed and meet him in his consultation room. I was never more shocked in my life than when the doctor informed us of his findings. It wasn't as if I hadn't been aware of our son's symptoms. But having an expert reveal the significance of these symptoms was, for me, like being awakened from a deep sleep by receiving electric shock treatment.

He calmly noted that Bryson was drooling excessively, and he pointed to his right eye that was now facing squarely toward his nose. He indicated that our now twelve-month-old child did not possess even the most primitive of reflexes. He noted that his hands were tightly clenched into fists and that he was unable to even sit up on his own. He commented on his lack of responsiveness and awareness to his surroundings. As we endured the doctor's commentary regarding Bryson's symptoms, we anxiously awaited the cause, but more importantly, the *cure* for his condition.

When the diagnosis finally came, I was literally stunned. I thought I was prepared for anything the doctor might say, but the words "global brain damage" stabbed me in the heart. He continued speaking, but I heard him as an echo through a tunnel now, and the room began to spin. A sickening numbness began to overtake me, and I thought I might vomit right there on the consultation room floor. "Global," he continued, "means that extensive damage has occurred throughout every region of your son's brain."

After he finished speaking, I recovered from my shock enough to inquire regarding the cause and cure for this "global brain damage." He seemed surprised that I was inquiring about a "cure." Naturally, if his diagnosis was correct, our son's condition was permanent and irreversible. The cause, according to the doctor, *was* a matter of some urgency. In view of Bryson's pattern of developmental regression, a "progressive" cause for the brain damage could not be ruled out. "Perhaps a brain tumor, or series of tumors. Possibly a degenerative nerve disease." He ordered a series of tests to narrow down the cause, providing us with a prescription for these to be performed at several outpatient clinics, beginning with a full MRI (magnetic resonance imaging) of Bryson's brain.

We soon found ourselves back in the reception area, with more unanswered questions than before we came. Neither of us said much during the car ride home. So many things were racing through our minds now. How could Bryson's pediatrician have been completely unaware that something was so seriously wrong? What if Bryson's condition had no cure? What did this mean for his future? More frightening still, what if there was a tumor growing in our child, or a progressing disease of some kind? Could our beautiful son be dying? It was sickening even to think about the roadblock Bryson's pediatrician had been to us. Yet there was no time to deal with what we were both feeling now. Our son's life was on the line.

I immediately called Tom Kaufman, a close friend and business partner whose father was a highly regarded eye physician in Manhattan. He responded quickly with the name of one of the most respected pediatric neurologists in the nation. Because of the referral we received, the chief of pediatric neurology at one of New York's world-renowned hospitals agreed to see us at 7:00 a.m. on Monday morning before his normal office hours began. We were grateful to have an opportunity to see one of the foremost experts in the world. Now, we hoped, our son would finally be getting the help he needed.

A Theory

It was overcast and still dark as we set out early toward Manhattan on that Monday morning in June 1987. We had risen before 5:00 a.m. in the hope of beating some of the commuter traffic to New York. Neither of us had much sleep, but we were way too anxious to feel tired. Adrenaline was flowing, but neither of us felt like saying more than a few words. The trip was solemn and the day dreary as we approached our destination of hope and fear. It began to rain as we approached the George Washington Bridge.

The Upper Manhattan neighborhood was ugly and foreboding. But there was only one thought on my mind. The best doctor in the world was going to help our son. He *had* to! We were praying silently even now. We arrived at the doctor's waiting area at about 6:30 a.m. It seemed an eternity passed as we awaited the doctor's arrival. A few minutes before 7:00 we were ushered into his office.

This eminent neurologist was quite charming and considerate of our anxiety. He listened closely as we answered his questions. Taking notes as we spoke, he kept one eye focused on Bryson the entire time. Our session was interrupted by one phone call. Incredibly, Bryson's pediatrician was on the phone. As we listened in to the only side of the conversation we could hear, the neurologist began to ask about the immunizations that Bryson had received. After the call, the doctor proceeded with an examination, which was far more thorough than the first neurologist had done. Finally, he turned his attention toward us. It was time to receive the verdict.

He declared that he was extremely concerned about the seriousness of our son's condition. He was alarmed that Bryson had met many appropriate milestones early in his young life, yet had regressed so rapidly to a primitive state of neurological function. Based on the phone call, we asked him if he believed the problem was caused by the reaction to the vaccinations. He responded that he did not rule out the immunizations as a cause, but that he suspected something else. He suspected that Bryson might be suffering from a serious degenerative condition, perhaps an acute form of leukodystrophy, which was causing deterioration in his brain. If this theory was correct, Bryson was dying.

Making a diagnosis is often very difficult even for the best doctors. A good physician takes into account all available clues, and then pieces the "puzzle" together like any good detective does in police work. I have always believed that this neurologist did his best to diagnose our son's problem. But I later came to believe he had been persuaded by our pediatrician that the vaccinations were not the cause of the damage. If the doctor "on the case" didn't perceive that our son's problems arose at the time of his vaccinations, then it was logical for this neurologist to move on to other clues. This led us all down a rabbit trail in pursuit of the truth.

Perhaps the pediatrician was attempting to "save face" regarding something which should have been obvious to any professional, particularly one who specializes in childhood development. Then again, maybe he truly believed what he told us, that immunizations were *never* the cause of serious damage to a child. If you are not open to the truth, then even your own eyes will deceive you. His failure to acknowledge the problems pointed out by Bryson's mother after the first vaccinations made it nearly impossible for him to be open to truth now. He had dug in his heels early on, and forced himself into a position from which he felt compelled to cover up his arrogance, and his incompetence.

Before going further, I would like to make clear that the purpose of this book is not to debate the risks involved in childhood vaccinations. The purpose of this book is to deal with the pain and brokenness which one little boy and his family have suffered, and not to debate its cause. I do not consider myself an expert concerning how pervasive the vaccination problem is today. All I can tell you with certainty is that I am convinced that through his "routine" vaccinations, my son suffered serious and permanent damage which changed his life forever. I also believe that the issue of the safety and efficacy of immunizations is a vital topic deserving extremely careful study, with a far different approach than that which has been taken in the research that has been conducted thus far.

As mentioned previously, some within the medical establishment share my conviction about what happened to my son through his "routine" vaccinations;

some do not. The uncertainty and confusion of this issue reaches far beyond my family story. It is one of the most pervasive healthcare issues in our society. Beyond question, there are ample grounds for healthy debate and for extensive *independent* studies to be conducted. I believe that truly independent studies would reveal difficult truths that not all within the medical or financial communities will be ready or willing to accept. I do not believe that the truth will *ever* be revealed by relying upon entities that have a vested financial interest in the outcome of the debate, or in the research that must be performed.

After all my family has been through, it is easy for me to feel angry and judgmental of a system I believe to be fraught with bias toward the risks involved. Yet the sad truth is that even I was willing to remain somewhat in denial and in support of the "system" during this early stage. It was simply too frightening to fully embrace that there was a connection between the vaccines and Bryson's brain injury. The specter of my son being permanently damaged in this way represented the most traumatic scenario I could conceive. Would God allow our precious baby to be destroyed by something that was intended for his good? It would all seem so senseless, so unfair, so meaningless. Bottom line: it would also be too late. The damage would be permanent, and there'd be no hope for a cure. This, I was simply not ready or willing to accept.

With a world-renowned neurologist now leading the way, we remained intent to move forward in the pursuit of *any* cause, *as long as it had a cure*. We could still cling to hope of healing and recovery if a disease or even a tumor were found. There could still be a happy ending. And, of course, there was the matter of our own guilt waiting in the wings. How could we ever deal with the guilt of sharing in our own baby's destruction? The pediatrician had removed the pertussis vaccine from Bryson's second series of injections. Should we have done more? Should we have stopped the vaccinations altogether? The fear and confusion we were experiencing at this time is beyond my ability to describe. I was actually relieved to hear the doctor suggest another theory, and I was content to remain in denial a bit longer about what I believed in my heart.

We left the doctor's office with greater confidence than we had after seeing the first neurologist. We agreed to admit Bryson to the hospital for four days of extensive testing to discover the cause of his problems, once and for all. We would return to the hospital in a few days when all the tests, and a room, had been arranged. Though a four-day stay in a Manhattan hospital was a stressful thought, the idea of doing intensive testing as quickly as possible made much more sense to us than making appointments one by one at outpatient clinics. There was no time to lose.

A GLANCE

It was only 8:30 a.m. as we crossed back over the George Washington Bridge to New Jersey. The sun was breaking through the clouds as we drove on Route 80 West. It had been such a whirlwind arranging and preparing for these doctors' appointments during the past several days that I hadn't yet processed the reality we were now facing. As we sped along the highway, I happened to glance at my son in the rearview mirror. Until the day I die, I'll *never* forget what I saw.

Our adorable son with the turned up button nose sat quietly, limply, in his child seat. He was thirteen months old now, the time when most children are walking and getting ready to run, yet this child couldn't even sit up. His head was tilted to one side and he was drooling profusely. He didn't even attempt to refocus his blank stare onto any object, either inside or outside of the car. This once sharp, perfectly healthy child appeared *so* far away. Perhaps it was only in my mind, but as I gazed at him in that mirror, I got the powerful impression that he was very sad. For the first time that I can remember, a great wave of grief swept over me for my helpless son.

Powerful emotions and terrifying thoughts flooded my soul: "What was happening to our son? Could it be possible we were losing him? Was it already too late? Would the Lord allow such a thing to happen to us?" As I continued gazing in the mirror at my limp little boy, a nursery rhyme forced its way into my mind:

> Humpty Dumpty sat on the wall,
> Humpty Dumpty had a great fall.
> And all the king's horses and all the king's men
> Couldn't put Humpty Dumpty together again.

The tsunami swept in fully now, along with that cursed rhyme, and horror consumed me. I quickly looked away from the mirror, trying to grab positive thoughts from somewhere; from anywhere: "Our ship isn't sunk *yet!* Help is on the way! We have one of the *best* doctors in the world on the case now. The best cure that medical science has to offer will soon deliver our son back to us and…'all the king's horses and all the king's men.' *Oh no!* I *couldn't* keep it out!" My head was swimming.

I glanced again in the mirror, and started pleading with my boy as though my thoughts could somehow be transmitted to him: "Bryson, this is your daddy. It's time to wake up now, son. Listen to your daddy. Please, Bryson, wake up! Listen to me, my boy! For God's sake, WAKE UP! PLEASE!"

Maintaining a calm exterior as I drove, my soul was gasping for air. I spoke not a word of this to my wife. Being strong for her was going to require a great deal of acting on my part. But tears filled my eyes at that moment, even as they do now as I type these words, so many years later. I began praying a silent prayer.

> *Lord God in heaven, I know You can heal our son and bring him back to us, just as healthy as he once was. Maybe all the king's horses and all the king's men can't deal with this seemingly hopeless, impossible situation; but I know You can, Lord.* ***Please!***

Chapter 4
MORE THAN WE CAN HANDLE?

We hear a lot about the necessity for "brokenness," but it seems that some of us have a hazy understanding of what we must be broken from. God seeks to destroy our Lord-of-the-Ring ways. They are harlotry! Often He has to allow suffering that our flesh can't handle to come into our lives in order to break us.[1]

Bill Gillham

I WAS CHOMPING AT the bit to get him to that hospital, so we could discover once and for all the cause of his regression. We revealed the neurologist's theory to family and friends, now asking for prayers that a specific, curable cause would be identified. Arrangements were made for Janelle to stay with my wife's mother for four days.

Two days prior to the hospital admittance, Bryson's condition took a turn for what appeared to be the worst. His lungs filled with fluid, and he spiked a high fever. As he lay on the pediatrician's examining table, his body trembling, the pediatrician called the neurologist. We were informed that he would be treated with antibiotics, and the New York hospital visit would be postponed if his condition did not improve. If his condition worsened, he would be admitted to a local hospital.

If our bus was shaky before, it now seemed that the wheels were flying off. I was dejected. How could this be happening *now* when time was so precious? Was God going to allow our son to die without even giving us the opportunity to fight a good battle on his behalf? I knew that God was good, but things were getting very confusing.

Life sometimes makes me feel that I am out on a limb, alone. Clinging to that limb and praying that things will get better, I begin to hear the rumblings of a storm in the distance. I think to myself, "What else can happen *now*?" Clinging tightly to the branch, I brace myself for the impending storm, fearing the worst.

When I see that Jesus has arrived, I breathe a sigh of relief. At *last*, He is here! I notice He has something in His hand and I suppose it to be a rope to lower me to safety. He comes closer, and I am puzzled to see that the item in His hand is not a rope, but a saw. He has taken a seat between me and the trunk of the tree, and begins to saw off the branch. I am stunned and baffled. As the creaking branch gives way and the free fall of my descent begins, I think to myself, "With a Friend like this, who needs enemies?"

God is often deafeningly silent, seeming to disappear when we need Him most, and as life falls apart piece by piece. Until now, there was no question in my mind God would come to our rescue. As our raft drew close to the edge of the waterfall, it was beginning to seem that God's cavalry was late. But I reasoned: "If this is the way God wants to test our faith, to see how we'll respond as we flirt with disaster, so be it!" I could deal with this delay. I could deal with it, that is, *if* God did *His* part, as He is *supposed* to do.

As Bryson grew weaker, it seemed that God had not only forgotten His obligatory role in our play, but now He was even taking away our oars, our only means to row away from that waterfall. We weren't being given a fighting chance. It didn't seem fair. I began to get angry. If God wasn't willing to help us, maybe He could just leave us *alone* for awhile so *we* could do what needed to be done to save our son.

The Scriptures tell us it is okay to be upset, even angry, but in our anger we are commanded not to sin (Eph. 4:26). I'd love to tell you I displayed flawless faith and obedience during these life and death tests. That wasn't true of me back then, and quite honestly, it's still not true as I write these words. The purpose of this book is not to proclaim how faithful I have been, pointing to my performance as somehow being "victorious." Far too many books take that angle. We can all slant and embellish our stories to make ourselves look good.

The truth that I hope exudes from this book is that God *alone* is good, *irrespective* of our circumstances. Paul was very clear in saying that we are not to preach *ourselves*, but *Jesus Christ* as Lord (2 Cor. 4:5). Frankly, sometimes my anger was righteous, and sometimes it was sinful. But I know God was calling me higher, and He began teaching me that He *always* wants me to come to Him when I am hurt and angry.

God won't strike us down for being honest. He is far too big for that. Mercifully, our Father sits on a throne of grace, not of condemnation. We can throw all our doubt, our exasperation, and even our anger right into our Daddy's lap. At least that would mean we are where we belong: in His lap. This is the place He can teach us, and change us. Even when our attitude is dead wrong, He doesn't slap us around, as a cruel father might. Nor does He affirm our error. As a good Father, He remains intent on turning our minds and hearts toward what *is* right, and transforming our character toward the image of our elder Brother, His firstborn Son. No, the danger isn't in coming to His throne with a "bad" attitude. The danger is in staying away. Greg Laurie, whose family has gone through indescribable grief from the tragic death of his son Christopher, put it this way:

> You need to know that it's not wrong to tell God exactly how you feel.... Sometimes we get the idea that it's irreverent or even sinful to express our real fears or the doubts of our heart, even to God....Sometimes we allow trouble and trauma and hardship to cause us to be angry with God, so that we withdraw from Him and don't want to talk to Him. No, my friend, that's when you need Him more than ever! Cry out to Him with your pain. He will patiently, lovingly, hear you. He might set your crooked thinking straight as you seek Him, but He wants you to pour out your pain. He loves you![2]

> so that we *despaired even of life*; indeed, we had the sentence of death within ourselves in order *that we might not trust in ourselves, but in God* who raises the dead; who delivered us from so great a peril of death, and will deliver us, He on whom we have set our hope. And He will yet deliver us.
>
> —2 Corinthians 1:8–10, emphasis added

Paul was brutally honest, but we often prefer to fall back on clichés, such as, "God will never give us more than we can handle." You can believe that if you want to, but then don't get ticked off at God when crushing circumstances invade your life that you *cannot* handle, circumstances that make you despair of life. Take a closer look with me at the scripture that appears to teach that God will never give us more than *we* can handle.

> No temptation has overtaken you but such as is common to man; and God is faithful, who will not allow you to be tempted beyond what you are able, but with the temptation will provide the way of escape also, that you may be able to endure it.
>
> —1 Corinthians 10:13

God will sometimes place us under the waterline of life. Try quoting the above scripture when you cannot breathe. This scripture was never intended as a protection against circumstances which God may choose, in His wisdom, to utilize in breaking us to the point of full dependence upon Him. Throughout the Old and New Testaments, God routinely brought circumstances into the lives of His chosen people that they had *no way* of handling. He did this to bring deep and irreparable brokenness into their lives, brokenness that they could not *possibly* handle or manipulate in their own strength.

It's closer to reality to say that God will *always* give us more than we can handle, than to say that He will never do so. If you buy into the lie that God will never give you more than you can handle, you will ultimately come to a very confusing place. As you sit amidst the smoldering ashes of a difficult trial that has thundered mercilessly beyond your ability to "handle," you will be tempted to become bitter against God, or to accuse Him of being unfaithful to you. The Bible is consistent and clear that the Lord's plan for us will *often* involve circumstances which are *far* more than *we* can handle. But those circumstances will never be more than *He* can handle.

Nancy Leigh DeMoss has been ordained by God to teach biblical truth to women in these dark days. The following quote from her series on the life of Joshua and the next quote from Spurgeon within it contain vital truth that we all need to come to grips with as we encounter circumstances that are more than we can handle:

> *God knew that the task to which He had called Joshua was bigger than He could handle*. God knew the task was not humanly possible....Joshua needed to learn, as do we, that we are to be strong and courageous, not in our own strength or ability, but in God's strength. We face powerful enemies and

> we have no chance of resisting them successfully, much less overcoming them...if we are dependent on our own strength.... When we go forth armed in His strength, we cannot lose. *The enemy, no matter how fierce, is no match for Christ.*[4] (emphasis added)

> Be not dispirited as though your spiritual enemies could never be destroyed. You are able to overcome them. Not in your own strength. The weakest of those enemies would be too much for you in your own strength. But you can and shall overcome them through the blood of the Lamb.[5]

God never designed us to be self-sufficient. To put it bluntly, we couldn't take our next breath if the Lord didn't give it to us. As Spurgeon taught, our weakest enemies will defeat us if we do battle in our own strength. Foolishly, I am *constantly* tempted to approach my life and my Christian walk with a false sense of self-reliance. Our propensity to "handle" things on our own, to the exclusion of God, is precisely what we all need to be broken from.

Hannah Whitall Smith, who experienced more than her share of suffering and pain, learned to press on through the discouragement of her circumstances. This was hardly because she found that God would never give her more than *she* could handle. Hannah came to realize that there was *much* in her life that she was utterly incapably of handling:

> There would be ample cause for discouragement—if we were called upon to fight our battles ourselves. We would be right in thinking we could not do it. But if the Lord is to fight the battles for us...this puts an entirely different face on the matter! If this is the case—and indeed it is—then our inability to fight becomes an advantage instead of a disadvantage. For we can only be strong in the Lord when we are weak in ourselves. In reality, in the life of the spirit, our human weakness is our greatest strength.[6]

In the same letter in which Paul admitted despairing even of life, he ultimately heard the Lord say: "My grace is sufficient for you, for power is perfected in weakness..." (2 Cor. 12:9). Paul responded by boasting about his weaknesses. But this seems ridiculous. Why would the great apostle boast of such a thing? He gives us his answer in the very same verse: "...so that the power of Christ may dwell in me." Finally, Paul makes a truly astonishing declaration: "...for when I am weak, then I am strong" (v. 10).

Why is there no wiggle room here? Why is God such a stickler about the sufficiency of grace? Why do we have to be weak? Life would be so much more comfortable if we were given only tasks and assignments that *we* could handle. God refuses to allow us to walk in the puny power of our own might. He has something much grander in mind for us: the life and power of His Son. Yet something has to be taken out of the way to unleash His power. What might that be? Just us! Just our own arrogant self-confidence, thinking that we can live good Christian lives in our own strength, without Christ.

In his excellent book *Release of the Spirit,* Watchman Nee describes the necessity of our being "broken" from our propensity to try to *handle* things on our own:

> Anyone who serves God will discover sooner or later that the great hindrance to his work is not others but himself.... His outward man and his inward man are not in harmony... basically because their outward man has never been dealt with. For this reason, revival, zeal, pleading and activity are but a waste of time.... There is just one basic dealing which can enable man to be useful before God: brokenness.[7]

The Lord's method has always been to bring life out of brokenness and death. It is the way He does things. If you doubt that pattern, take a look at our Lord at Calvary on Friday afternoon, and then look at Him again on Sunday morning. But what does this have to do with us? God wants to do a similar work in our lives as well. A "broken rope," or a dead end, almost certainly means that God is at work in your life. He wants to bring life out of death for us too. He wants His power to be perfected in our weakness.

If your life has been devastated by circumstances which seem utterly impossible, even cruel, your future is brighter than you may realize. God is going to use the brokenness He has allowed to invade your life to give you a valid reason to "boast." He will give you power that can only be perfected when you are broken and weak. You don't feel up to the challenge? Good! You are in position for the Lord to take over, to do *His* work.

As for me, I'd have avoided God's course on weakness and brokenness if I could have. Frankly, I would have chosen *anything* else. I had countless other things I wanted to do with my life rather than go through the very long ordeal, decades long, which has now become the subject of this book. But God's classroom was in session, and the curriculum was going to be fraught with lessons about brokenness and reliance upon the sufficiency of something I knew far too little about. Something called grace.

> God is in the business of putting His children in holes so deep they can't possibly get out without His help. What is your need right now? Whatever it is, rejoice. That's God's hole, and while you're in it, He's going to teach you how to believe.[8]
>
> —Steve Brown

Two Knocks at the Door

The prayers of many focused intently on Bryson's recovery, but he continued getting weaker, and his trembling intensified. The next day, his fever broke and his trembling body stabilized. The doctors soon confirmed that Bryson was well enough to be admitted to the hospital for the tests. To this day I believe God answered the many prayers which were being offered up on my son's behalf, so we could get to that hospital. But I mistakenly thought this was a sign that God had opened the door to a miraculous healing.

Our trip would entail being at the huge Manhattan hospital for four days. We wondered about the things we would face there. We were told that we could take turns sleeping on a cot in Bryson's room. Would the tests be painful for Bryson? We had never spent time away from our three-year-old daughter, Janelle. Would she be okay?

The day before our trip, the anxiety meter in our home began to build to red-alert level. But the Lord sent two knocks on our door that afternoon and evening that couldn't have been more welcome if the hands of angels were knocking. First, our good friend and associate pastor of our church, Tom Clark, paid a visit to pray with us. If you knew Tom, you'd know his life is full of godly gestures like that one. His prayer was short and his stay brief, but his simple act of love in visiting us was a tremendous encouragement. Shortly after Tom's visit another unexpected knock came. It was Ed Stapp, and he had a basket of "cheer" in his hands, prepared by his wife, Patrice. The basket was full of lotions, bags of tea, and other comforting items to make our stay at the hospital more tolerable. My wife and I looked at each other with tears in our eyes, overwhelmed that anyone would be so thoughtful.

I learned a lesson from receiving these acts of kindness. Now, when the Lord prompts me to make a phone call, write a note, or pay someone a visit, I am more likely to understand the impact these "little" acts can have. There are times when our simple acts of obedience to the Lord's prompting will result in more encouragement to hurting people, and more glory to God, than we can conceive.

It certainly seemed God had performed a miracle when Bryson's trembling suddenly stopped the day before. But the anxiety and anticipation for this trip to the hospital had been intense, and we now wanted to get on with it. The next morning, we drove toward our "city of hope," praying that God's miracles would continue.

Chapter 5
WHEN WAVES TURN MINUTES TO HOURS

Does anyone know where the love of God goes, when the waves turn the minutes to hours?[1]
Gordon Lightfoot

Rude Awakening

We were in awe of our surroundings at this world-renowned institution. The hospital had many of the most respected doctors in the country on staff. It consisted of a large complex of mostly old buildings in a poor, upper Westside Manhattan neighborhood. We had come in the hope that our son's life might be saved. It seemed that those at the registration office couldn't have cared less why we had come. The place was very busy, and the staff seemed overly stressed. We were treated almost as if we were an annoyance, another of their volume of burdensome cases to be "dispensed" with.

We spent close to an hour filling out forms and waiting. Then we were sent to another building, which we thought would be our home for the next four days. When we arrived, we were told that a mistake had been made, that the ward was "overfilled." We would have to be sent somewhere else. After more waiting, we were finally sent to a wing on another floor that was specifically for terminally ill children. As we approached the nurses' station, a busy staff member, barely looking up, blurted out a room number to us and pointed down the hall with her pen. We pushed Bryson's stroller down the hall, alone, to try to find our way. Not exactly a welcome that soothed our anxieties.

By the time we arrived at the room, we had already observed much despair and suffering throughout the ward. The pain on the forlorn faces of numerous children and their parents is something I will never forget. Bryson's roommate was anxious to meet us. He was a three-year-old boy who had been born without much of his stomach and intestines. He was hooked up to numerous devices, including a large feeding tube attached directly into his midsection. The tubes allowed him only a few feet of freedom to stand and move around his crib, which, like the one assigned to Bryson, was made of stainless steel bars. Its appearance was like that of a cage. This boy lived permanently at the hospital, a great majority of the time right in that mini-jail. We later learned that his parents visited seldom. He was not expected to live too many more years.

As you might expect, this child had severe behavioral problems. He yelled almost incessantly to get attention from the busy staff members, but they were unable to scratch the surface of this child's enormous emotional needs. We soon found that he would be calling upon us to meet many of his "mommy" and "daddy" needs, and he quickly began calling out to us for attention. We felt very sad for this poor little boy. We were also, to say the least, overwhelmed in the settling down of our own son. Bryson clung to us in this bustling, daunting environment. The next few hours were consumed with filling out yet more paperwork, more waiting, and much comforting of our now anxious son.

Finally, a female medic in a white uniform, who barely spoke English, entered with what appeared to be dozens of vials on her tray for the drawing of blood. We soon learned that this woman didn't have a clue regarding how to draw blood from a baby's tiny arm. Bryson began squealing in pain, and after she made several aborted attempts to get the needle into his vein, I had seen enough. I demanded that this woman get out, and I went down to the nurse's station to request someone who knew what they were doing. Another staff person soon arrived to take over, and another attempt was made to draw our son's blood; but the process was not a whole lot smoother. We felt helpless as our screaming, thirteen-month-old child kept looking at us as if to ask, "Who are these people, and why are you allowing them to hurt me like this?"

After it was over, Bryson's little arm began to turn black and blue. Our son was now terrified of his strange new surroundings. He clung to us tightly, and he sobbed for a very long time. We tried not to show it, but we were just as traumatized as our son.

Unusual Perseverance

That night, as we placed Bryson in his cage-like steel crib, we quickly learned what the next three nights would be like. There was one cot and a chair for my wife and me to take turns sharing. But there was no way Bryson was going to allow himself to be separated from us even a few feet in this scary place. Each time we placed him down in the crib, the same thing would occur, which was amazing under the circumstances. He could sit up only with great effort, and for only a few seconds at a time before falling over.

Once placed in a lying position in the middle of the crib, he would struggle mightily to squirm toward the side. Each time he made it successfully to the steel bars, he tenaciously attempted to pull himself up to a standing position by latching onto them. He wanted to pull himself to the top to call out to us (he was unable to use any words, he would merely whine) to come pick him up out of the crib. Each time he neared the top, a wave of imbalance overtook him, sending him sprawling back to the bottom of the crib. After he fell, we kept placing him back in the middle of the crib and patting him for comfort, hoping he would give up and stay down. But as many times as we placed him down, he went *right* back to work on his quest to reach the top.

This happened over and over and over again. I was amazed. Due to his lack of motor control and balance, his effort to climb up those bars was a harder challenge than that of a mountain climber straining to hang onto the cleft of rocks on the way up to the peak. With remarkable willpower, our son stayed at his task until finally, if ever so briefly, he stood triumphantly at the top, before tumbling down again. This went on for *hours*. He never gave up, but we did. When he began to hurt himself by falling against the steel bars, we decided to take turns holding him in our arms in the tiny cot until morning. The first of his difficult tests was scheduled to begin at 8:00 a.m.

We had come to this place seeking hope, but in our hearts we already knew that our son was in deeper trouble than these doctors could cure. Some realities in life are so stunning, so dreadful, they numb you against full acceptance until the passing of time. Indeed, our son had already been robbed of so much life in this world. The weeks and months ahead would slowly reveal that the odds stacked against our son were higher than we knew.

But that night we began learning something every bit as important as the results of all the tests to ensue during the next four days. That first night in the hospital we began to learn that while much had been taken from our son, the Lord had left some very precious gifts within him. His sheer willpower and personal determination, his relentless perseverance, his absolute *refusal* to give up on a task until he, somehow, painstakingly accomplished it, would cause us to marvel in the years ahead.

INFERNO

If Bryson's refusal to remain in his crib wasn't enough to keep us from sleeping, our roommate with the tube in his stomach and his beeping machines certainly was. The door to our overly lit room constantly swung open as one nurse after another came to attend to him *all* night long. At about 3:00 a.m., one nurse with a rolling table replete with medicines came in to change the dressing for the large tube entering his stomach. The boy struggled with the nurse, and after she subdued him, he began to scream bloody murder! It was obvious that she was hurting him in some way.

Finally, after the screaming child had woken half the ward, a senior nurse came in to see what was happening. We were horrified and sickened when we realized what had been taking place. The senior nurse began berating the other nurse. Apparently, the child had every right to be screaming. The first nurse had unknowingly used the wrong solution in changing the dressing, and had been inflicting burning pain into the child's wound. Our confidence in this place had already been shaken. We were now on high alert.

We were bleary eyed at 8:00 a.m. as one of the medics came to lead us to the first of Bryson's countless tests of the day. We rode an elevator down, down, down for an unusually long time. We *finally* arrived at our destination, and the door opened to reveal an eerie, poorly lit, subbasement corridor. All sorts of pipes, ducts, and conduits were exposed below the ceiling; and though it was June, the subterranean catacombs we entered were as cold and damp as if it were a rainy November day. If Dante had seen this place, he may well have used it to depict one of the lower levels of his *Inferno*.

We followed our guide through this gloomy tunnel (which connected various buildings in the hospital complex) for what seemed to be miles. In reality, we were traveling the distance of city blocks below the streets of Manhattan. After the previous day's debacle drawing blood, we had a great deal of anxiety about what awaited us. This dank passageway didn't calm our nerves. We walked in silence, finally arriving at another elevator, which we rode up to the place Bryson would undergo the first of his tests.

The test was a simple EEG. It involved laying Bryson on a table for an hour, as numerous electrodes were attached to his head to take readings of his brain waves. After this, we were led to another building, once again through the bowels of the subbasement, to perform an MRI scan of his brain. We learned that our son would need to be fully sedated before the scan, since he would be encased inside the loud, dark MRI cylinder. The MRI machines of the 1980s made a banging sound that could wake the dead and were far darker inside the tube than modern MRI machines that are more open to the light.

We got Bryson to drink some medicine to "put him out." Forty-five minutes had passed when the attendant came to get Bryson to put him inside the tube. But there was a slight problem. Bryson was drowsy, but *not* asleep. We refused to allow him to be put inside that dark, deafening environment until he was fully conked out. After some debate about our not allowing our child to be taken, the nurse realized I was resolute and returned with more sedative for Bryson to drink. Another half hour passed, and Bryson was still "hanging in there." It took yet *another* dose and twenty more minutes for him to finally doze off.

I was close to being frantic when they put him inside that tube. Even from behind the glass where we observed, the noise was as intense as rapid fire from an AK-47 machine gun. We were petrified that Bryson would be awakened, finding himself trapped in a hellish tomb. Several times I felt like bolting into the room to pull my son out of there, but the attendant inside the glass kept assuring us that Bryson was sound asleep.

My wife and I clung to each other as we saw numerous color images of our son's brain on the lighted screen inside the technicians control room. We saw a dark image, like a tumor, near the center of his brain. We whispered to each other and both began to cry. After the test was completed, and our still sleeping child was handed to his mother, we asked the technician if what we had seen was a tumor. He had not been aware that we could see his screen from where we were sitting. He told us that he was not able to comment on the tests, that we would have to speak with our doctor. Unfortunately, we were not scheduled to see the doctor for *two* more days.

For *whatever* reason, each separate department required new samples of blood. Some technicians were more adept at drawing it than others, and we had several more traumatic experiences with medics who were not good at drawing blood from such a young child. I began to confront those who were incompetent. It seemed to me that some of them simply didn't care, and I actually had a shouting match with one of them. If Jesus could take a whip of cords when He was rightfully angry, I felt the least I could do was to step forward to protect my son. But I can't honestly tell you that my anger was "righteous." Frankly, I was becoming so exhausted and stressed in this place that I didn't much care. It may have been a moral victory that I didn't wind up in jail.

Another Sleepless Night

That night wasn't much different than the previous one. We thought Bryson would finally be tired enough to fall asleep in the crib, but there was no way he was going to allow himself to be separated from us now. We again took turns holding him as we snoozed. Our unfortunate roommate had another fitful night, and we were continually awakened as the staff kept coming in to attend to him. We had such pity for this child. He was effectively an orphan, living out his entire life in this place we had so quickly come to hate. The hospital staff was his "family." His prognosis was to be kept alive as long as possible, until his physical condition would ultimately end his life.

At 1:30 a.m. I realized that sleep wasn't coming anytime soon. I whispered to my wife that I was going to walk down the block to the parking garage to check on our car, which had been there for two days. This wasn't the brightest idea I've ever had. The hospital was located in a relatively unsafe area of the city. Due to the late hour, all the main hospital entrances were now closed, and a custodian sent me in the direction of the emergency room entrance. I found my way through the labyrinth until I came to the ER.

I was shocked at the incredible volume of late night activity in the waiting room. Scores of people, mostly minority and poor, were sitting and waiting with various injuries and illnesses. Some had been injured in accidents; some appeared to be there as a result of gang fights. The place looked like a war zone. It was obvious that many of the patients had been waiting a very long time. The look of resignation and hopelessness on many of those faces is something that I will never forget.

As I walked out into the street, I noticed the general squalor of the neighborhood, which I hadn't focused upon the day we arrived. When I returned from the garage and made my way back through the ER, I panned the forlorn faces again. It occurred to me that this night in 1987 was probably no different than any other night in this place. I have no doubt that if I went there tonight, decades later, the look of despair and hopelessness on the faces would be the same.

The first test the next morning involved laying Bryson on a table as very long needles were stuck into all the muscles of his arms and legs. This electromyography (EMG) would provide a reading of whether Bryson's muscles were interacting properly with his neurological system. Bryson cried in pain as the needles were moved to various locations on his little body. From the relatively low intensity of his cries, I could tell that this procedure was not quite as painful as some of the others. However, since our arrival Bryson's body had been poked and probed in so many invasive ways that he was now paranoid, ready to scream out as anyone prepared to touch him. As we watched the large needles being pushed into his arms and legs, *we* were wincing, forcing back the tears ourselves.

That afternoon, we were resting back in our room when a diminutive, arrogant male medic burst in. Without greeting us or even informing us who he was, he abruptly announced he was "taking Bryson Milazzo" for his spinal tap. As I got up to carry my son, this individual put his hand up to my face as to make a "stop" sign, then bluntly informed me that "no parents" were permitted to be present for the procedure. I stood there with my son in my arms, amazed that anyone could be so rude. Then he thrust out his hands to "take" Bryson in order to put him onto his cart.

I handed our son to my wife and stepped up close to this medic. I had now had enough of the callousness and insensitivity of this place. It was all I could do to keep from picking up this punk (whoops, I forgot this is a Christian book). It was all I could do to keep from picking up this dedicated young medic by the lapels of his uniform (is that better?). In no uncertain terms and with direct eye contact (good communication skills, you understand) I made it *unmistakably* clear that I required his undivided attention. I told him if we could not accompany our son to the spinal tap, then there would *be* no spinal tap. I was almost hoping he would challenge me again, just itching for it really. I hadn't had any satisfying physical contact with anyone since playing football in college. The truth is, I was so angry I wanted to wipe the floor with this guy. But catching my drift (and possibly noticing the smoke emanating from my ears) he scurried out of the room.

I don't say these things to romanticize my anger, nor to excuse it. My desire to protect my son was legitimate and good. But through the years the Lord has been teaching me that it is *very* easy to cross the line from justifiable, righteous anger into fear-based responses and actions that are sinful. The truth is I had a lot of growing in Christ to do in those days, and I still have plenty more to do as I write these words many years later. Looking back on this incident, I realize I could have done better by speaking firmly yet calmly to this medic while standing as firm as necessary to protect my son.

The medic returned a few minutes later. He had checked with someone who told him it was okay for *one* of Bryson's parents to come. My wife and I decided I would be the one. I followed him, carrying my son to the lab room. One of the two medics there instructed me to lay Bryson on a cold, steel table. He was extremely anxious and frightened. I kept patting his back to calm him, but I was at least as scared as he was.

One of the medics attempted to put him in a curled up position, like a ball, which was the necessary position for the spinal tap. Bryson began to writhe and scream, and the medic was unable to keep him in position. After several more failed attempts, the medic finally asked me to get on that table with him and hold him in position. It was then that some of the most hellish moments of my life began to play out.

I nearly fainted when I saw the size of the needle to be inserted into my tiny son's spine. As I cradled him into position we were face-to-face. He looked at me with a horrified expression, as if he could not believe that his own daddy was betraying him. As was predictable in this place, the medic began having trouble inserting the needle into the right spot, and Bryson began to scream with all the fury his little lungs could unleash. My son was screaming directly into my face, and his tears began to flow. I choked back my own tears and maintained a calm exterior, but my soul was screaming just as loud.

It was as if time was standing still. I knew it was not fear causing him to scream now, because he never saw the needle. The pain must have been excruciating. The second hand on the clock continued moving at glacial speed as I kept holding my son in position. The procedure took perhaps all of ten minutes. It seemed an eternity had passed.

Does Anyone Know Where the Love of God Goes?

In the 1970s, Gordon Lightfoot wrote and sang a provocative song about the tragic, final journey of a ship named SS *Edmund Fitzgerald*. In this ballad, the ship set out across Lake Superior, one of the Great Lakes, only to come upon a great November storm. The crew fought courageously for days against fierce winds and waves. The men realized they were doomed as the waves finally began to overtake them and the ship slowly began to sink. In the refrain to the song, Lightfoot asks a striking question: "Does anyone know where the love of God goes, when the waves turn the minutes to hours?"[2]

I've considered Lightfoot's question as I've looked back on the trauma I shared with my son during his spinal tap. I was wearied from the whole ordeal at that hospital, no less from the sleepless nights there. For that matter, I was exasperated from being trapped in a nightmare for six months now, being forced to watch helplessly as my son's life slowly began to sink. He was a vibrant, perfectly healthy child, and he had deteriorated right before our eyes. No, it wouldn't have been a good time to ask me what I thought about the love of God just then, especially after seeing my son tortured on that cold table. I don't know what I would have told you, but it would likely not have been pretty.

There may be no more difficult issue in this world in which to reconcile the love of God with the reality of pain than when an innocent child suffers. Such times seem to support the cruelty of God, but definitely not His love or goodness. After all, He's the One in charge, right? Isn't it reasonable for us to expect His protection against pain and injustice? Even Christians are tempted to join the chorus of angry scoffers as the children they love are forced to endure senseless pain. At this time in my life I just didn't understand why God wasn't stepping in.

Through the years I've come to understand that it is *precisely* when we are tempted to doubt and accuse God that we have an opportunity to discover something important—not only about God, but also about ourselves. As we shake our fists toward the heavens, ignorantly lashing out against Him, God often remains exasperatingly silent. He ignores our demands to know why He allows pain and evil to win so many battles in this world, and His silence can make us even angrier. But while He doesn't yield to our angry demands, neither does He get His "nose" bent out of shape or assume a defensive posture when we go on the attack against Him. The truth is, He does not need to defend anything. He is God. It is *we* who have misunderstood.

Secular culture foolishly attempts to bring God down to a human level in an effort to understand Him, going as far as to project human frailties onto Him. But if we seek to truly know God, one of the first things to understand is that He is *vastly* higher than anything we can come to know by looking within ourselves. The Bible indicates that God is "holy," which essentially means "set apart," "sacred," or "high above." But have you ever asked yourself, "High above what?" I think God's "holiness" means, in part, that God is high above our puny expectations of Him. God's thoughts and ways are immeasurably higher than ours (Isa. 55:8–9). In fact, God is so much higher than our thoughts and imaginations of Him that He doesn't begrudge us our doubts.

If I could have held a conversation with God that day in the hospital, I would have asked Him why He had allowed such pain and difficulty in my innocent son's life, and why He allows so much evil, cruelty, and suffering in this world at all. I've envisioned that the conversation might have gone something like this:

> **Barry:** "Didn't You *see* the horror on my son's face, Lord? Didn't you know he was in excruciating pain? There he was, a terrified child, pleading with me not to allow those people to do those awful things to him. And I was praying to You as hard as I could. You did *nothing* to help us! Why, Lord? Tell me *why*!"
>
> **God:** "That certainly was a rough moment. It still hurts Me to think about it."
>
> **Barry:** "I don't understand You at all, Lord. You could have *done* something! Maybe I'm on thin ice here. I mean, You could strike me down for what I'm about to say…but I think you *owe* me an explanation. What kind of God allows such injustice, such cruelty in His world? What kind of God would allow an innocent baby like mine to have his entire life ruined through a senseless brain injury before he's even had a chance to taste life a little? And what kind of God would put a father like me in the helpless position of not being able to stop excruciating pain from being delivered to my own son as we lay down on that cold table?"
>
> **God:** "First of all, I'm not going to strike you down. In fact, I'm glad you asked such a direct question."

Barry: "You *are?*"

God: "Have you ever heard of a place called Gethsemane?"

Barry: "Sure I've heard of it. But I hope You don't' start using the tactic of evading my question by asking *me* a question. But okay, I'll bite. Gethsemane was the place where *Your* Son pleaded with You to... Uh... He pleaded with you to... take away... *His* cup... of pain. O Lord! *What are You telling me?*"

God: "It's a tough position to be in, isn't it?"

Barry: "Whoa! I guess You *do* understand how I feel. You must have endured immense pain as a Father as Your Son suffered on the cross. I'm taken aback and a bit overwhelmed here, Lord. I mean, I *never* thought of there being any parallel between your Son's sufferings and my son's sufferings. But can I ask You another question?"

God: "What is it?"

Barry: "The Bible says that Jesus suffered and died for the sins of the world. Why then, does my son Bryson also have to suffer? For that matter, why does *any* human being have to suffer anymore? Didn't your Son say, 'It is finished?' just before he died? Why aren't things settled? I mean, why is there still *so* much suffering and injustice in the world? What exactly was finished?"

God: "You sons of Adam think you know so much, but you can't see the spectrum of history from My vantage point. I see it all, right in front of Me, unbound by space and time. Nothing escapes My notice. As I look out, I observe the rise and fall of kingdoms and powers, of saints and tyrants. But I don't just see the people that *you* consider significant. I also see *every* mundane moment ever lived by every descendent of Adam. I know every *detail* of every life, and of every human tragedy that's ever occurred. Not even a sparrow that falls to the ground escapes My notice.

"When I finished my work of creation, it was completely perfect; and I was pleased. I created you in My image, giving you a free will, the ability to choose. That was a great gift, but you misused it. You could have soared to the loftiest heights, abiding in My love forever in a perfect world. But Adam and Eve rebelled against Me, and distress and carnage came into this world, grieving Me deeply. The entire human race has been infected with sin ever since. Because of your sinful choices, you have brought great harm upon yourselves, upon each other, and upon all of creation.

> "If the earth consisted merely of breathtaking landscapes, roaring oceans, and soaring mountain peaks, I might have destroyed it all, and started over. But because of My intense love for you I vowed to redeem this broken world, to purchase it back from the serpent that first tempted you toward evil, though I knew the cost would be supreme. My Son willingly came to this world to redeem it back to Me. He was tortured and hung on a cross for you, taking upon Himself the horrors of every sin ever committed in this world. My Son said, "It is finished," as He died because His work of paying for human sin was finished. He paid the penalty of death that I require for sin. He did so for every last son of Adam, and every last daughter of Eve.
>
> "Scoffers and fools will continue to blame Me, as if I don't care about the suffering in the world, or claiming that I don't possess the power to deal with evil. The truth is I haven't yet crushed all the evil that you continue to bring upon yourselves because I am a longsuffering God who yearns for every son of Adam and every daughter of Eve to have the opportunity to embrace My Son's finished work on the cross, His wondrous gift of grace that brings forgiveness and salvation to all who will believe on Him. Yes, My Son said, "It is finished," but He also told you that I would leave the ninety-nine and go searching after the *one* lost sheep out of one hundred.
>
> "Suffering must remain in this world due to sin until the very last person destined to accept My Son's gift of grace has done so. Then I will sum all things up well. I will bring this world to an end, and I will bring every person who has accepted My Son as their Savior home, and they will live with Us forever. And as it was destined from the beginning, I will be their God, and they will be My people."

Barry: "I am speechless, Lord. I have nothing more to ask."

In a world that blames God for the sorrows and pain we have caused for ourselves as a race that has chosen sin, don't *ever* believe that God is indifferent, impotent, or uncaring. His love is far higher than the flimsy, shallow thing we call love. Too often, we merely speak about love with our words. When God speaks love, He speaks through powerful actions, even through the death of His own precious Son on the cross.

To this day, I still shudder when I look back at that episode in the hospital. Tears still come for my precious baby boy if I dwell on it, even as they came as I typed this chapter. But with all my heart I believe now that there weren't just two of us on that cold table that day. Jesus was right there with us, sharing in our pain.

I can't prove this to you, but there isn't a question in my mind about it. He was right there on that table, shedding tears with us. He is right there with you too, dear reader, as you suffer in pain, seemingly alone. He is just waiting for you to believe in Him and trust in His perfect love for you. I pray that each hurting soul who reads this book will come to understand more about His immense love for you, and how near He is to you right now. Horatius Bonar says it far better than I could:

> Jesus weeps with us. "In all our affliction He is afflicted." He knows our sorrows, for He has passed through them all, and therefore He feels for us. He is touched with the feeling of our griefs as well as of our infirmities. Man—very man—man all over, even in His glory, He enters most fully into the fellowship of our burdens and sorrows whatever these may be, for there is not one which He did not taste when He "dwelt among us" here. His is sympathy, deep, real and true. It is no fiction, no fancy. We do not see His tears falling upon us; neither do we clasp His hand nor feel the beating of His heart against ours. But still His communion with us in suffering is a reality. We may not understand how it can be. But He understands it; and He can make us feel it, whether we can comprehend it or not.[3]

To be honest, I still have many questions I'd like God to answer. Perhaps He will answer them when I get to heaven. Perhaps He won't. Perhaps when I see Him as He really is, it will become obvious that my questions are irrelevant. But as to the question at hand in this chapter, just where *does* the love of God go when waves turn minutes to hours?

Perhaps we should be asking another question. What kind of Creator stoops down to die for a world that shakes a fist at Him, that blames Him for all of our own, self-imposed evils? Truly, we see only through a glass darkly now. But a day is coming when we will see Him face-to-face. No accusations will be lifted up against Him on that great day, just awe. Every knee will bow, and every tongue will confess that Jesus Christ is Lord. Along with many of you who are suffering right now, I long for that great day.

> For I consider that the sufferings of this present time are not worthy to be compared with the glory that is to be revealed to us.
>
> —Romans 8:18

> And He will wipe away every tear from their eyes; and there will no longer be any death; there will no longer be any mourning, or crying or pain.
>
> —Revelation 21:4

Run That By Us Again?

Due to the stresses involved, my wife had gone home to regroup, leaving me alone in the hospital with our son for a night and a day. She had now returned for the final day, when we were scheduled to meet the chief neurologist in our room at 2:00 p.m. To say we were anxious would be a ridiculous understatement. As we tried to keep Bryson amused, we kept hearing footsteps coming down the hall, thinking it was him. But he was delayed for what seemed an eternity.

It seemed we couldn't possibly wait one more minute to hear the doctor's verdict. At the same time, we were terrified, almost not wanting to know. The black mark we saw on the MRI screen of Bryson's brain was very much on our minds. We had already prayed that if this really was a tumor, it would be found to be operable.

At last the doctor arrived with "good news." *All* of the tests were negative! Bryson had a condition known as "static encephalopathy," a brain injury that was not degenerating toward something worse. We should be relieved that our son's condition, pending the outcome of some "long shot" metabolic tests that hadn't yet come back from the lab, was not going to deteriorate further. We could be certain now, that Bryson would live.

He then leaned forward, and in a hushed tone the doctor advised us that some families take advantage of an "option" for their brain-injured children. "Often," he continued, "these children are placed in institutions for their care."

Neither of us could *believe* what we were hearing. Stunned, we quickly answered that this would never be an "option" we'd consider for our son. He would continue to live with us, not as an orphan in some "institution." Bryson had lost so much already. It was a horrifying thought that we would allow his family to be taken away from him too.

The meeting lasted no more than ten minutes. After four days of tests, we had expected so much more information, so much more hope. As the doctor rose to leave, we were dumbfounded. "Just a minute, doctor," my wife said. "You told us that all the tests were negative. What *is* the cause of our son's brain injury?" Before he could answer, I blurted, "We saw a black mark on the MRI screen. We thought that our son had a tumor."

The doctor seemed surprised. No, the MRI showed Bryson's brain to be completely free of any malignancy whatsoever. He explained that it takes a trained professional to know what all of the shadings from the scan mean. As we pressed him for an answer regarding the *cause* of our son's condition, it was obvious that he didn't want to be pinned down. He repeated that Bryson had a "static" encephalopathy (brain injury) that wasn't progressing toward death. He did offer though, that it was evident from Bryson's presenting symptoms that his brain had been very profoundly and deeply damaged. Yes, the condition was permanent. No, there was no particular cure; and no, he did not know how a perfectly healthy child had come to be so profoundly brain damaged. The meeting was over. We were shocked, disappointed, and bewildered.

We had just been through the most traumatic four days imaginable. We were exhausted. We were utterly *flabbergasted* not only by the doctor's diagnosis, but by the complete lack of direction he offered regarding the cause of our son's demise. We were now being discharged knowing nothing more about what had happened to our son than the day we arrived. Hope for a cure seemed nothing more than pure fantasy at this point.

Chapter 6
A VOICE IN THE DARK

The light of God goes beyond understanding scriptural doctrines. His light is meant to dawn within you, so that you embrace with your heart the truth of God.[1]

John of the Cross

Twilight Zone

I toss and turn. It is nearly dawn, and I am almost conscious. In my final dream of the evening I find myself waking alongside my wife. We are not in the comfort and safety of our bed, but in a damp, dimly lit alley somewhere in the city. We have been beaten and can hardly move. As I gain consciousness, the throbbing pain becomes more real. Am I really dreaming? Very weak now, I drift back into unconsciousness.

When I awake again, it is in a local hospital. Fortunately, someone found us just in time. The authorities tell us we are very fortunate. We had been left for dead. They have no idea how we came to such an unfortunate plight. They've searched our home and found everything in perfect order. All the doors were securely locked. Even the security system was still armed and intact. They don't know how we could possibly have been captured and taken away. We are shocked and bewildered. We are even more astonished as they inform us there will be no investigation. They remind us we are fortunate to be alive. We ought to be grateful. Weak and in pain, I plead with the authorities to do their job and find out what has happened to us. The detectives coldly respond that we must simply accept it, and move on with life.

Frightened and confused, we return home. But how can we move on? How can we ever feel safe again? Our lives have been literally turned inside out. Yet no one is able, or willing, to tell us what really happened. My dream ends in confusion and fear.

The above dream falls short of depicting the appalling nightmare in which we were now trapped. We were grateful to learn that our son was not dying. His brain injury was "static." Yet this did not diminish the horror of our predicament. The doctor's attitude at that world-renowned hospital was particularly galling given the dearth of information he provided regarding the *cause* of our son's brain injury. Our son's life had been brutally and permanently altered. How could we possibly "accept" what happened to him and move on with life when we didn't even know *what* had happened?

Bryson spent the first several months of life developing beautifully. He was a *completely* healthy baby. All the doctors knew this. Their records had consistently indicated it. Yet none of them were willing to venture an educated guess regarding what had caused our son's brain injury. "Etiology unknown" was the term doctors were now using. How comforting! I expected Rod Serling to emerge from the shadows with his classic, sick grin and explain to the TV audience that the Milazzo family was this week's featured guests, trapped somewhere in the *Twilight Zone* (bring up the music).

The only thing we knew for sure was that the perfectly healthy baby boy we brought home fifteen months before was now profoundly and irreversibly brain injured. In the weeks after returning from the hospital, we tried to regain our equilibrium, but it seemed we were tumbling through space. We had been to one of the world's best medical institutions with high hopes of finding the cause of our son's decimation, and more importantly, the cure. Our hopes had been crushed, stamped out, regarding both. Perhaps our son could live in an "institution," the doctor had suggested.

Bryson's once good muscle tone was now gone and the muscles throughout his body sagged (a condition called "central hypotonia"). The motor controls in his brain were virtually destroyed, resulting in an absence of balance and coordination. As mentioned in the last chapter, he was no longer able to sit up for more than a few seconds before awkwardly falling over. He didn't even possess the primitive reflex action to hold out his arm to prevent his head from slamming into the floor as he toppled over, and we were told that our son was permanently crippled.

The notion of "getting on with life" was a joke. Our daily experience was stressful to the hellish point. Bryson's tenacity and inner drive continued to amaze us, and he kept trying to achieve tasks that his misfiring brain would not allow. He awkwardly crept and crawled throughout the house, finding *endless* new ways to injure himself. He wobbled precariously with each movement, and his body collapsed to the ground without warning, countless times per day. The danger was greatest, and the crashes most painful, as he relentlessly pulled himself up and attempted to cruise around furniture.

Again and again, every day, all day long, the crashes came. The stress level in our home was tantamount to a war zone, listening for the next bomb to hit. Several times each day he'd scream out in excruciating pain from another "direct hit" of his head and body onto hardwood floor. We quickly installed wall-to-wall carpeting throughout the house, with a thick underlying foam pad. We did this even in our newly constructed family room in which we had just installed hardwood flooring. We watched him like a hawk, but there was no *possible* way to prevent every painful injury as he continued to fall against walls, floors, and furniture.

It was absolute agony to watch helplessly as our precious, innocent child was being maimed. I still wince at the memory of it, decades later. His little body often quivered with pain, and he began to wear cuts and contusions all over. We comforted him the best we could, but we were being tortured right along with him. And yes, Gordon Lightfoot, as I think of his quivering pain, I am still tempted to wonder where the love of God goes when the waves turn the minutes to hours. But if I believed God had no good answer to this question, I'd never have written this book.

Ripple Effects

We began actively pursuing other medical and therapeutic avenues to seek help for our son. With so much time devoted to him, I was scrambling now to keep up with my career as a managing director of a major commercial real estate company in Manhattan. Our schedule was filled with doctor and therapy appointments for Bryson, with Janelle in tow. Our nearly four-year-old daughter required some of our attention too. It seemed as if she were regressing somewhat, emotionally going back to the days of her "terrible two's," as her brother's needs consumed most of our attention.

No doubt, our little family was struggling now, and so was our marriage. We had been married for five years, and I loved my wife dearly. But the backdrop of exhaustion and stress was making it increasingly difficult to summon the kind of energy required to resolve our marital conflicts in a healthy way. Our marriage had been difficult from the start, well before the onset of Bryson's tragedy. By this time we were painfully aware that we were two very different people from two extremely different backgrounds. It was amazing how radically our perspectives differed concerning so many things.

If you are married, or have been, I don't need to tell you how hard marriage can be. Gary Thomas, in his excellent book *Sacred Marriage*, states the following:

> Anyone who has been married for any length of time should be able to understand how truly difficult marriage can be, and how, even among Christians, tensions can rise so high and hurt can be so deeply embedded that reconciliation would take more energy than either partner could ever imagine possessing in ten lifetimes.[2]

The subject of our marital discord will come up again in this book, and I hope to be helpful to some of you who think you are alone in your marital struggles. Honestly, I've often thought God could have made life a whole lot easier for everyone if He hadn't made men and women so different from each other. Then again, perhaps ease and comfort weren't on top of His agenda when He created the institution of marriage. Again, Gary Thomas points out something that God values higher than the ease and comfort we cherish so highly in our society:

> The beauty of Christianity is in learning to love, and few life situations test that so radically as does marriage.[3]

A Desperate Search for Answers

At first glance Bryson looked the same as always, save for his low muscle tone and turned in eye. He was so adorable it was almost inconceivable he could be so injured inside. As you observed his functional limitations things became clearer, and it also became evident that his intellect had been diminished. He no longer cuddled with us as he had once done, and he often seemed very far away, as if he was in his own little world.

We still believed he was "taking in" a whole lot more than he was able to give out, and we continued to talk to him as if he understood every word we said. It sometimes seemed as if our son was a prisoner locked up inside a malfunctioning body. This was a foolish notion as far as the professionals were concerned. They were now telling us he was profoundly retarded. But he still had the best giggle I had ever heard, and I could swear I saw glimpses of the "old" Bryson when we were able to get him laughing. And there was something in his eyes, even in his badly drooping right eye, which cried out that there was more going on inside him than the doctors were indicating.

Bryson was now classified as having "cerebral palsy." It was painful to hear the experts tell us our son would never walk, but I could have learned to live with that. The horrifying prediction that he would never speak intelligibly caused me to grieve far more deeply. The inability to communicate with our own child was almost too much to bear, often bringing us to tears. Teaching him sign language was not an option, since the motor controls governing his hands were virtually destroyed. The anguish we felt for our son is beyond my ability to describe. But we had precious little time to grieve. Our child was lost. Somehow we had to break through to his darkened, brain-injured world and find him.

We clung to *any* small hope that a cure might be found. But without knowing the *cause* of his devastating brain injury, how could we possibly find a cure? We needed to educate ourselves. If Bryson was ever to come back to us, we needed to become the foremost authorities regarding our son's degeneration. The hellish aftermath of both of Bryson's immunizations kept coming back to mind. Still, we'd remain in denial a little while longer. Perhaps our search would lead us to a cause that was easier to deal with, a cause that might offer hope for a cure.

A Voice in the Dark

> Then you will call, and the Lord will answer; You will cry, and He will say, "Here I am." . . . Then your light will rise in darkness and your gloom will become like midday.
>
> —Isaiah 58:9–10

Being in such a vulnerable position can make you susceptible to various forms of suggestion, even ones that make no sense. In late August 1987, several weeks after we had returned home from the hospital, I saw a television special about balance disorders. The program revealed that a major cause of once healthy individuals losing the ability to maintain their balance is a malfunctioning of the vestibular apparatus in the middle ear.

I began to wonder if perhaps this could be the cause of Bryson's balance difficulties. Ignoring all his other symptoms, including his intellectual distance, his low muscle tone, his clenched fists, his turned in eye, and all the rest of it, I began to think that my son might merely have developed a problem in his middle ear. I even began to speculate that the Lord may have provided our long sought answer by virtue of my seeing that program. It was insane, and I should have known it. I suppose immense pressure can make you temporarily insane. The next thing we knew, we were on our way to Manhattan again. This time we were scheduled to have the functioning of Bryson's middle ear tested at one of the foremost centers for balance disorders in the United States.

The staff advised us to prepare Bryson for a demanding test known as sinusoidal harmonic acceleration (SHA). It involved strapping the patient into a chair inside a vertical cylinder that measured approximately four feet in diameter and resembled a mini rocket ship. The patient was connected to electrodes to monitor the movement of his eyes during the test. Once the door was sealed, the inside of the SHA cylinder was pitch black. Slowly, the chair would begin to spin, rapidly picking up speed until you were spinning inside that dark cylinder at great velocity. The chair was guided by a computer and was programmed to spin alternately, in both clockwise and counterclockwise directions.

From the eye movement during the test, the doctors would be able to tell if the patient's inner ear was functioning properly. If the test revealed a malfunctioning of Bryson's inner ear, then this could be the cause of his problems. We could finally have the problem "fixed," and our nightmare could be over. The test was scheduled for early the following week. But first, we needed to determine how we could possibly put our now sixteen-month-old child in such a dark and foreboding environment. The doctor's staff decided that it would be best for me to go into the cylinder, with Bryson strapped onto my lap.

This solution caused me no small trepidation. In my childhood I was one of those kids who *always* got carsick. To this day I hate amusement park rides, particularly ones that spin or swing back and forth. Even playing on swings had always made me nauseous. I had never outgrown this condition. At the doctor's office that morning, I swallowed the maximum dose of Dramamine I could safely ingest.

The test was scheduled to last ninety minutes. Once inside the cylinder, I realized how necessary it was for Bryson not to be alone in there. The tiny, pitch black, completely enclosed compartment was disconcerting to say the least. Interestingly, the rapid speed of the chair spinning inside the cylinder was not as difficult to endure as I had feared. You simply could not guess how fast you were spinning due to the total absence of light. Still, the whirring sound of the rapidly spinning chair was unnerving.

My sixteen-month-old son was not able to speak at all, but he was able to make sounds. From the darkness I began to hear his worried little voice calling upward in my direction. Over and over again he began to utter a frightened question: "Eh? Eh? Eh?" His meaning was perfectly clear to me: "What's going on, Dad? Are you there, Dad? Is it going to be okay, Dad?" He kept repeating these questions through his one-syllable sounds. He needed reassurance that he hadn't been abandoned in the darkness. He needed to know that his daddy was still there, spinning in the darkness with him.

I spoke words of comfort to my son. "Daddy is here, Bryson. It's okay, my boy. You're *not* alone, son. Your daddy is right here." Over and over I repeated this message to him. "Everything is going to be all right, son. Your daddy is here." All it took to ease my son's fears was for him to hear my voice reassuring him that his daddy was still with him in that dark, scary place. As I kept repeating that message, I felt his tense body begin to relax into my arms as if he didn't have a care in the world. He no longer feared the darkness or the whirring sounds. He had all that he needed. His daddy was with him.

But as I listened to myself reassuring him, I began welling up with tears. If only it were *really* true. If only I *could* make everything "all right" in his broken little world. As I sat there spinning in the darkness considering my son's reality, I realized I was lying to him. I would emerge from the darkness in another hour. He would not. His entire world would continue to be a place of brain-injured darkness, and deep inside I knew it.

Simplicity

> Spiritual life is the life of a child. We are not uncertain of God, but uncertain of what He is going to do next.[4]
>
> —Oswald Chambers

My brain-injured son couldn't possibly understand the things that had occurred to devastate his life, and he didn't have the slightest idea why he was sitting in that dark, spinning cylinder. But even we clear thinking adults can misunderstand what is actually occurring in our lives when times of darkness come. Crushing circumstances and devastating sorrows almost always arrive suddenly. When God turns out the lights, our well-ordered plans disappear just as quickly, even as our neat little sayings begin to fall short. As fear and confusion arise, and it seems we are utterly alone, spinning in the darkness, the last thing we need is doctrinal complexity. What we need is simplicity.

I believe this is what Jesus meant, in part, when He said we must become like a little child (Matt. 18:3). Jesus foresaw the future, both ours and His own. He warned us that we would have severe troubles in this world (John 16:33), and He knew that our strength needed to be drawn from the very same Source He drew His confidence from during His time of living and dying in this world. You can bet that during His darkest hour, praying in anguish at Gethsemane, Jesus didn't take the time to review every lesson He learned in Hebrew school. I believe He chose simplicity as He cried out to "Abba," His Daddy.

Jesus suffered intense anguish, sweating great drops of blood even as He prayed. He pleaded for the bitter cup that had been placed in His hands to be passed from Him. But Jesus already knew the answer to His request, even before uttering it. After all, He was God the Son, and He knew this bitter cup was His very purpose for coming into the world. That same week He chastised His dear friend as "Satan" because Peter was too worldly-minded to accept what He had just revealed to him about His own plight, this cup: His imminent crucifixion. If Jesus knew the score in advance (and, of course, He did), why then did our Savior waste His breath in prayer that night, requesting the passing of the cup? I believe He made this request in order to teach us something.

Obviously, the Father didn't answer Jesus' prayer in the affirmative regarding the passing of the cup. Had He done so, Jesus would have been minus one "cup," the world would have been minus one Savior, and every soul in this dark world, including yours and mine, would be in more trouble than we could fathom. But while the Father did not take away the cup, He *did* respond to Jesus' prayer that night. We are told that an angel from heaven appeared after Jesus prayed, strengthening Him (Luke 22:43). This makes me wonder, just exactly how did the angel strengthen Him?

Did he strengthen Jesus by bringing Him food and water? I doubt it. Jesus had just eaten the Passover supper with His disciples, during which He said, "I shall never again eat it until it is fulfilled in the kingdom of God" (v. 16). And after fasting for forty days and forty nights in the wilderness, Jesus had rebuked Satan who was tempting Him with bread, saying, "MAN SHALL NOT LIVE ON BREAD ALONE, BUT ON EVERY WORD THAT PROCEEDS OUT OF THE MOUTH OF GOD" (Matt. 4:4). No, I hardly think it was bread the angel brought.

The rebellion of the human race that began with Adam and Eve in the Garden of Eden hardly took God by surprise. But at Gethsemane, the pivot point of all history had now arrived. God was about to reveal His plan to redeem the world back to Himself, a plan that was conceived before the Fall, and before the dawn of time. That entire plan now hinged totally on what Jesus would accomplish after rising from His anguished prayer. I am not sensationalizing the point in the least in saying that the entire universe, and the fate of life as we know it to be, literally hung in the balance that night.

In view of all that was now at stake for our Savior and for the world, with all of creation and the entire human race literally hanging in the balance, just how did the angel strengthen Jesus? I believe the angel brought a message proceeding directly from the mouth of God, a message that instilled Jesus with renewed courage, strength, and endurance as He began His final march against the powers of sin and hell on our behalf.

So then, what was the message from the Father that the angel brought to the Son? Did He lecture His Son, as fathers are known to do, rebuking Jesus for His apparent vacillation? After all, Jesus did seem to equivocate regarding the "cup." A good scolding might be just the thing to get Him back on track. Or perhaps the Father took a more positive approach, appealing to His Son's sense of heritage, reminding Him of His glorious position as a member of the triune Godhead. Then again, maybe the Father chose to inspire His Son by engaging Him in challenging discourse, getting Jesus' theological juices flowing through the revelation of paradoxical truths and doctrinal mysteries that only Father, Son, and Spirit could *begin* to understand.

I hardly believe the Father chose any of the above methods to strengthen His Son. As Jesus cried out from that mountainside, I believe the angel brought a message that was as simple as it was powerful as it rang in the ears of our Savior that night. We'll never know the exact words, because Scripture doesn't record them. But I believe Jesus received a very simple message from His Abba, His Daddy; and I believe that message brought Jesus back to the place of simplicity, as a Son.

Just as Bryson needed to hear the voice of his daddy from the darkness of that spinning SHA cylinder, I believe our Savior was strengthened in His darkest hour by words from His Daddy which were powerful, not because of their profundity but in their simplicity. Again, we'll never know the exact words, but I believe Jesus heard: "I am here, Jesus. Everything is going to be all right, Son. Everything will unfold just as we planned together before the beginning of time. Your Daddy is still right here with You, Son. Your Daddy loves You always."

The reason I've written this book is that many of you reading it right now have dreams that have been decimated, sorrows that have crushed you, lives that have turned out to be far from what you've planned. What's worse, many of the painful things that have thwarted you seem to be random and meaningless. There doesn't seem to be any redeeming value, any good that could ever come from it. As far as religion is concerned, you've been there, done that, and *still* your world keeps spinning out of control. As you sit in the darkness, you can hardly summon the energy to move a muscle, no less the optimism required to exercise hope or faith in anything anymore.

If I had all the specific answers for you, I would certainly tell you. The truth is, I don't have answers for many of my own problems, no less for yours, even as I write this book. But I do wish to remind you of something very simple.

As my deeply wounded son sat in that dark, spinning cylinder, he didn't need to hear sophisticated explanations nor understand all the implications of his medical condition. He needed something far simpler. I'll never forget the way Bryson relaxed into his daddy's arms after he heard my reassuring voice. Though he was still spinning in the darkness and *nothing* in his circumstances had really changed, his tense little body sank restfully into mine. He was able to sit back and experience complete peace, with his daddy's strong arms wrapped firmly around him. He didn't need explanations. He needed to know his daddy was with him. And, of course, so do we all.

For many of us, it is only during times of trouble that we are disposed to cry out to God. But whether you've kept up with God during the busy pace of your life or not, God has kept up with you. He knows where you are this very moment, and He understands your sorrows and your problems far better than you do. And of this I'm certain: Your Daddy is waiting, right now, for you to call out to Him.

Don't think you need to figure out an eloquent prayer before you can cry out to Him. My son was able to make only primitive sounds from the darkness of that spinning cylinder. Your most polished prayer will be just as crude and just as welcomed by your Daddy. And don't bother trying to get your act together before crying out to Him. The Physician knows you *can't* get your act together from where you sit in the darkness, and He heals only those who know they are sick (Matt. 9:12; Mark 2:17; Luke 5:31).

You may believe you are lost forever in the darkness. But can you really be lost if Daddy knows where you are? Cry out to Him. He will come and find you in *His* time and provide any answers you need. Some day you will come to understand that He *is* your answer. Daddy is an ever present help in time of trouble (Ps. 46:1). Cry out to Him *now* from your dark, scary place. Lean back and rest into His arms. Let Him wrap His strong arms around you.

> There is none like the God of Jeshurun, Who rides the heavens to your help,
> And through the skies in His majesty, The eternal God is a dwelling place,
> And underneath are the everlasting arms.
>
> —DEUTERONOMY 33:26–27

BACK TO REALITY

We anxiously awaited the results of the SHA test, clinging to the faintest of hope that, just maybe, fixing the vestibular apparatus in Bryson's inner ear would solve our son's problems, at least his physical problems. When we came back to New York the following week, our hopes were quickly dashed as the head doctor at balance clinic informed us that the functioning of Bryson's vestibular was completely normal.

Sensing our distress, the doctor spent a long time with us; and we relayed our ordeal of watching our completely healthy child deteriorate, inch by inch, and we informed him of all the tests that had already come back negative. He was especially moved by our plight of not knowing what had happened to our son. He suggested that we have a complete "brain mapping" study done at the Boston Children's Hospital. We were grateful for his time and for his referral to Boston.

Our unrealistic balloon had been popped. But I didn't consider the SHA test a waste of time. In a peculiar way, I had enjoyed it. I came away knowing I had "conversed" with my son in a meaningful way. Despite what the experts were telling us, perhaps he could learn to communicate more fully with us one day. At the very least, I thought it was intellectually significant that Bryson had the presence of mind to call out to me from the darkness of that cylinder. Certainly, he had understood my response.

I still didn't want to admit it, but all the signs now pointed to the frightening reality that our son was permanently lost in the dark and confusing world of his profound brain injury. But can a child really be lost if Daddy knows where to find him? We knew our journey couldn't end here, and we clung to the belief that there was hope out there, somewhere. There just had to be! We'd soon be on our way to Boston to find it.

Chapter 7
THE YELLOW BRICK ROAD

The greatest human tragedy is to give up the search.... To lose heart is to lose everything. And if we are to bring our hearts along in our life's journey, we simply must not, we cannot abandon this desire.[1]

JOHN ELDREDGE

HAVING STRUCK OUT badly in all we had tried thus far, we had no choice but to continue exploring every available avenue to find help for our deeply injured son. Not unlike Dorothy (and Toto too), we believed there *had* to be a great wizard, somewhere over the rainbow, who would give us the answer we were seeking, so that we could all get back to a life of normalcy and peace in Kansas...ahem—make that Glen Rock, New Jersey. There just *had* to be a way to get our son back. Some way, somehow, we would find it.

But as it tends to do, the yellow brick road sometimes comes to a fork. Though we were scheduled to go to Boston Children's Hospital for brain mapping in September 1987, we decided to first go to the JFK Institute at John's Hopkins University Hospital in Baltimore, Maryland, for three days of testing and evaluation. The head of the department at JFK specializing in rare metabolic diseases was able to see us right away, and told us that she would do the best she could to determine the cause of our son's problems.

We were treated with more respect at both JFK in Baltimore and Boston Children's Hospital than we had been at the mammoth New York institution, and we found the staffs far more pleasant to deal with. The testing at JFK focused on finding a possible metabolic cause for Bryson's condition. This meant numerous additional blood tests. Thankfully, their staff was far more proficient at drawing Bryson's blood than the nightmarish episodes in New York. After three days of testing at JFK, every known metabolic cause and all the rarest known diseases were ruled out as the cause of Bryson's brain damage.

In Boston we had the benefit of staying at the home of some friends, the Erdmanns, who were my wife's classmates at Wheaton College. They cared for our three-year-old daughter, Janelle, during each of the three days we spent at the hospital for tests on an outpatient basis. It was particularly encouraging to be with uplifting friends each evening after stress-filled days at the hospital.

The brain mapping was disappointing to us. It was essentially a very sophisticated EEG exam in which Bryson's brain waves were studied in each area of his brain, under varying types of stimuli. After four hours of testing (with Bryson sedated), we expected decisive news regarding our son's brain injury. Unfortunately, this exam seemed more geared toward benefiting the research effort than in helping our son. We were told that Bryson had abnormal brain wave activity throughout his brain, but the research had not progressed to the point at which the data could provide meaningful benefit for our son. We were exhausted and demoralized, but still resolved to leave no stone unturned.

After visiting these major institutions, we sought the opinion of several respected neurologists in the New York area. Each week brought us to the steps of a new emerald palace, where we hoped and prayed we'd find the "wizard" who could work miracles. Week after week, month after month, our hopes were dashed, as each wizard turned out to be just a little man behind the curtain. It wasn't their fault. They were dedicated professionals. I didn't want to admit it, but it was becoming clear that our problem wasn't the lack of the right wizard. Our problem was the hopelessness of our son's injury.

He was only eighteen months old, but his Humpty Dumpty life was so shattered it seemed no power on earth could ever put him back together again. Exasperatingly, no one could even tell us how he'd become so broken. After all the testing and evaluations in New York, Baltimore, Boston, and *everywhere* in between, Bryson had been seen by the foremost experts in the world. Pressure was mounting on us to accept the inevitable.

This brought us to one of the most important forks in the road we'd come to thus far. We were at the crossroads of the Boulevard of Acceptance and the Path of Hope.

FALSE HOPE?

We were offered no reason to believe that our son could ever "come back" from his devastating brain injury, but we were given many sound medical reasons why the damage was irreversible. The consensus was that Bryson would never walk, would never speak intelligibly, and would only be educable to a very rudimentary level. Hope for a cure was inconceivable. Some well-meaning professionals informed us that our relentless pursuit of our son's healing would cause unnecessary emotional distress in our lives because we were investing in false hope.

After several days of tests at the JFK Institute in Baltimore, we were asked to meet with one of their social workers. She advised us that we needed to say "good-bye" to the perfect, healthy baby who was part of our family for a brief time. We needed to accept that this child was gone forever, that we would never be able to find him again. We had to allow ourselves to properly grieve the great loss we had sustained. We must accept this sad reality and move on, even as parents need to do after the death of a child.

We thanked this professional for her advice. Yet trying to grieve the loss of a child who wasn't dead put us in a very strange predicament. I felt like screaming, "Don't talk to me about grieving my 'loss.' My son is still alive!" I kept thinking, "What if this were my life? What if my entire future was ruined by a profound brain injury just as my life was beginning?" I would hope my parents wouldn't give up on me, even if every last person in the entire world advised them to accept my "loss."

Don't get me wrong. I didn't want to live in delusion, nor in emotional turmoil. I didn't want to become bitter or insane. Part of me desperately wanted to "move on." I wanted peace for myself and my family. I wanted all these things. But I *couldn't* give up searching for a cure, or at least for substantial improvement for our son. No doubt, we needed a miracle now, not just a cure. But whatever you call it, I wanted it. Simply put, I couldn't live without hope. By the way, neither can you.

Dr. Bernie S. Siegel, in his fascinating book *Love, Medicine & Miracles,* described how critical it is to maintain a sense of hope during a desperate medical crisis:

> Even if what you most hope for—a complete cure—doesn't come to pass, the hope itself can sustain you to accomplish many things in the meantime. Refusal to hope is nothing more than a decision to die.[2]

But forks in the road require a decision. Did taking the road called "hope" mean we had to abandon the road of "acceptance?" Was it necessary to ignore reality and live in denial to cling to our hopes and dreams for our son? Clearly, we needed to properly accept reality. That was a no-brainer. But on the other hand, we couldn't live without hope. Frankly, neither road seemed acceptable if taking one path meant we had to completely abandon the other. Pressure was mounting on us to make a decision, and we desperately needed wisdom. We needed the kind of wisdom that is sought by those in twelve-step groups, such as Alcoholics Anonymous:

> God grant me the serenity to accept the things I cannot change, The courage to change the things I can, And the wisdom to know the difference.[3]
>
> —Reinhold Niebuhr

But the serenity prayer seemed a bit too black and white. Many real-life situations seem to reflect more of a shade of gray. We had a child who desperately needed us to engage in difficult battles that he couldn't possibly fight for himself. If accepting his condition meant abandoning this responsibility, then acceptance was an unacceptable option. We needed to somehow accept what couldn't be changed in his life in a manner that wouldn't rob us of the courage to battle for positive changes. Before wisdom comes, sometimes you just need to keep moving forward, step by step, until the situation becomes bright enough to see the next step. You simply don't know what to accept and what to courageously fight for until you begin moving forward.

As Christians, we can feel pressure to move prematurely into the "acceptance" mode before our situation is even clearly understood, thinking that this is what honors God. We can then tie up all the loose ends, nice and tidy, assuring ourselves that we have humbly obeyed God by "accepting" our circumstances. Don't hear me saying that we are not to surrender to the Lord in the face of difficult trials, or that we are to refuse to bear the cross that He requires us to bear. The Bible teaches unequivocally that we must fully surrender our lives to the Lord, and that our surrender must always include our willingness to say, "Your will be done, Lord, not mine."

But we need to be careful. There is a danger of surrendering when the Lord requires us to battle our way out of a trial. Our "surrender" can look pretty spiritual, but in reality our choice to accept our difficult trial might be more cowardly than holy.

In his book *When Your Rope Breaks,* Steve Brown addresses the issue of acceptance in saying: "Whenever something comes into your life that you cannot change or avoid, accept it as coming from the hand of your loving Father."[4] However, he also addresses the necessity to fight when the Lord lays a battle before us:

> The Bible is not a passive book. Scripture challenges us to run the race, to fight the fight, to wrestle with angelic powers (1 Cor. 9:24, 27; Eph. 6:12). The "let go and let God" philosophy may be good in some situations, but in others it is absolutely wrong. We need to be still sometimes, but sometimes we simply need to get busy and do what needs doing.... There are, of course, times when you can do nothing more about your broken rope.... However, you must be very sure that there is nothing more you can do before you decide not to act.[5]

Margaret Clarkson says something similar in her book *Grace Grows Best in Winter:*

> To those hedged in by illness or crushing sorrow, to find peace is literally essential to survival. Without it, in many cases, life simply could not be tolerated.... "Just how much of this do I accept, and from how much do I seek to free myself?" The answer would seem to be something of a dichotomy: "You accept everything, even the worst, completely and permanently; and then you use every possible resource, both human and spiritual, to effect a solution."[6]

Nowhere in the Bible are we instructed to avoid all warfare and conflict in life, nor to retreat into false modes of "acceptance." There are times when, even if it is with our teeth chattering and knees knocking, we must engage the enemy in battle. In our case, we couldn't even *begin* to accept our situation until we discovered what in the world had happened to destroy our son's life. But given the lack of information and direction we had received from the doctors up to this point, setting out to do battle on his behalf was a doubly difficult task. We still didn't even know where the field of battle *was.*

Yet even if what all the professionals had told us was true, even if everyone believed our son would be permanently crippled, have unintelligible speech, and be essentially uneducable, we *still* couldn't give up on our search for something much higher. I didn't care what others thought about the apparent obsessiveness of our search. If "accepting our loss" meant giving up on our son, failing to fight the necessary battles on his behalf, or giving in to laziness or cowardice, then "acceptance" was simply unacceptable.

Furthermore, no one had ever satisfactorily explained to me the concept of "false hope." Isn't the term "false hope" an oxymoron? The Bible reveals something intriguing, yet profoundly simple, about hope. It is so simple, in fact, that it is easy to miss. Listen to this teaching from two different passages:

> Hope that is seen is not hope; for who hopes for what he already sees? But if we hope for what we do not see, with perseverance we wait eagerly for it.
>
> —Romans 8:24–25

> Now faith is the assurance of things hoped for, the conviction of things not seen.
>
> —Hebrews 11:1

Duh! How *simple! Who in the world would ever hope for what he already sees?* How could I have *missed* this? Since we couldn't *see* any reason to hope, the *last* thing in the *world* we should do is give up hope. Circumstances that *appear* hopeless are *precisely* what God designed hope to be *for! Of course!* If you can *see* the solution to your problem, if you have it all figured out, then you are disqualified as a candidate to *hope*. You may have a plan, even a pending resolution to your problem. Praise God for that. But *until* then, when we have no apparent reason to hope, God asks us persevere in hope.

G. K. Chesterton embellished this point:

> As long as matters are really hopeful, hope is mere flattery or platitude. It is only when everything is hopeless that hope begins to be a strength at all. Like all the Christian virtues, it is as unreasonable as it is indispensable.[7]

Hope is so vital to us that it is on God's "short list" of just three things that will remain when He closes this planet down at the end of time (1 Cor. 13:13). Remember, hope is best exercised in truly "hopeless" situations, not promising ones. Hope is designed precisely for situations in which we can see no possibility whatsoever of victory. Hope has *nothing* to do with whether you *feel* hopeful. Our emotions will almost always point us to despair when things are bleak. God designed hope to be an *indispensable* source of strength, an ally for us precisely when we see and feel *nothing* to be hopeful about, when our emotions plead with us to give up and give in to despair.

Hope placed in God is the great equalizer for all hopeless situations. Yes, I meant to say *all* situations. No, I am not trying to sugarcoat suffering, either mine or yours. It isn't lost upon me as I write these words that there will be some reading this book who would love to be in the shoes that I was in at this time, even considering the hellish, life-destroying brain injury that my son had sustained. At least I still had my son with me on this earth. Many are not so fortunate. You have lost spouses or other dear family members through death. Some of you may have even experienced the unthinkable, the death of one of your children. What about these situations? Is hope null and void here?

I'm going to allow Greg Laurie to answer this question. He is more qualified to do so than I. For many years, Greg has powerfully declared life giving, biblical truth without apology in this day of lukewarm compromise within the church.

And how has the Lord repaid him? Greg and his family suffered the tragic loss of his dearly loved, thirty-three-year-old son Christopher in the summer of 2008. Is he bitter? Is he at peace with his son's death? Does he simply pretend that all is "fine?" Does hope matter? Here are Greg's words:

> People will sometimes ask the question, "Are you at peace with your son's death?" At peace? Of course not! Don't ever ask someone that. We should never be at peace about anyone's death. Death is an enemy. The Bible says, "The last enemy that will be defeated is death." Having said that, God is a friend, and I am at peace with Him.... For the believer... death is not the end of the road. It's only a bend in the road... a path that Jesus Himself has walked. And because of what He accomplished on the cross for us, the grave is not an entrance to death but to life, because death has been swallowed up in victory (2 Corinthians 5:1–5).[7]

If hope is going to matter to us in any practical sense, we must stop thinking of hope as a substance that can be placed in a test tube to be analyzed. We must think instead of what, or more precisely, to whom, hope points us toward. Biblical hope points us to Jesus Christ, whose resources toward us through His Spirit are immeasurable, unending, and invincible over *every* last foe we will ever have to face—even the foe of death.

Am I just playing "mind games" with you, trying to put a positive "spin" on your hopeless, impossible situation? Don't hear me saying you should jump for joy when there is nothing in your circumstances that *appears* hopeful. No sane person would choose to be stuck in an apparently hopeless situation. Nonetheless, when you've run completely out of options, when it is clear for all the world to see that your life has been completely decimated, thwarted to the point of making it laughable to believe you could recover in any meaningful way, or ever see any good come from your impossible situation, then, my friends, you are blessed (Matt. 5:4). You are God's candidate to walk in hope.

If what I have just said is not true, then you are a fool to be reading this book. But if what I am saying, if what the Bible is saying, holds water, then you don't have to give up and wallow in defeat. You have an important decision to make. If you choose to trust fully in the God of hope, He will see to it that you are filled with all the resources at His disposal. Without minimizing your sorrows, your grief, or the impossible nature of your problems, suffice it to say that your hopeless situation is no match for the mighty power available to you from the God of hope.

> Now may the God of hope fill you with all joy and peace in believing, so that you will abound in hope by the power of the Holy Spirit.
>
> —ROMANS 15:13

THE ROAD TO THE EMERALD PALACE?

As we sought to persevere in hope for our son, we prayed for some tangible, effective things we could do to help him. This put us at somewhat of a loss, since we had seemingly come to the "end of the line" in terms of finding hope from the medical field. We began to seek out private therapists and early intervention programs which might help us with some of Bryson's developmental needs.

In November of 1987, at eighteen months of age, Bryson was enrolled at The Child Center in Paramus, New Jersey. This was an "early intervention" center operated under the auspices of the Association of Retarded Citizens (ARC). Initially, after reviewing his medical reports, we were told that Bryson was too "neurologically involved" (too brain injured) to be accepted into this program. But when the staff finally met our gorgeous son, they fell in love with him, and the decision was made to admit him.

There were seven children enrolled in the program, which took place for two hours each weekday morning. The purpose of the program was to stimulate and educate these children, according to their individual needs. Since Bryson was unable to walk, he was handed to a staff member each morning, who carried him inside. He no longer possessed enough balance or motor control to sit up by himself, so he was strapped into a specially designed seat to prevent him from slumping over and falling out. The teachers and therapists were compassionate and very dedicated in their care of our son.

For all his problems, Bryson was the most adorable little boy you could imagine. Though he now had cuts and bruises from continuous falling, his little button nose with light freckles and his soft skin made you want to pick him up and squeeze him. His loosely defined cheeks (due to his lack of muscle tone) made him even more cherub-like. He was a gorgeous child, and we believe this gave him an "advantage" of sorts in causing teachers and therapists to enjoy working with him. We were glad for every advantage Bryson had going for him. Certainly, much had been taken away.

Through The Child Center, we were put in contact with private physical, speech, and occupational therapists. Bryson began to attend these private therapies three times per week, for a total of nine therapy sessions, in addition to attending The Child Center program. Our lives became frightfully busy getting him to all these sessions.

Our now four-year-old daughter was healthy, intelligent, and beautiful. Most little girls are very sensitive, and Janelle was no exception. We realized that her life had been greatly affected by having a multiply handicapped brother. Not only had we needed to visit numerous hospitals, doctors, and therapists as she stayed home with Grandma, but so much of our time and energy at home was now devoted to her brother too.

We also realized that Janelle had suffered another very deep loss. When Bryson was born, Janelle had high hopes of having a brother she could be close to and share fun activities with. Unfortunately, her much anticipated pal was not much of a playmate. Unable to speak at all, and drooling profusely, he could not even sit with her on the floor for very long without falling over.

We began talking and praying about how this problem had affected our daughter's life. We decided we would help each other schedule times of play, one-on-one, with Janelle. I would take care of Bryson while my wife took her shopping, read her stories, or played games with her. My wife would take care of Bryson while I took Janelle to the park or did other fun activities with her.

My favorite was when I got to take my daughter on "dates." I would dress up in good slacks and a sport jacket, while Janelle's mom helped her into one of her prettiest dresses. I would take her to a *My Little Pony* movie (or whatever was "hot" at the time), and we would end up at the ice-cream parlor or at McDonalds. I had so much fun that I continued these activities with Janelle through her teen years. I took her to breakfast regularly prior to my dropping her off at junior high and high school. Janelle is such a sensational kid. If I had missed an opportunity to spend time getting to know her, I would have missed one of the great opportunities of my lifetime.

CANDLES OF HOPE

We began receiving reports from The Child Center and from our private therapists that Bryson's physical and mental functioning was not progressing as meaningfully as we had hoped. His crippled body was now referred to under the heading of "cerebral palsy," which simply means a condition in which the motor controls in the brain are severely damaged. Since Bryson's intellect was also damaged, the overall label used to identify him was now "multiply handicapped."

Observing his hour-long physical therapy session one day, I watched as Bryson was placed on a large mat and asked to crawl across the room toward an enticing toy. With each placement of his hands and knees on the mat he would lose his balance and either fall flat on his face or roll completely over onto his back. He had more control over his arms and upper body than he had in his legs. This was not a good sign for his future. His therapists began to confirm our fears that he would never be capable of walking.

But as I continued to watch him closely, I was impressed, once again, by his shear tenacity and determination. Each time he found himself flat on his face or his back, he would simply roll himself over and push himself back up to a crawling position to start over again in his quest to reach the awaiting toy. I needed to turn away, not only so my tears would not be noticed by the therapist, but so that they could not be seen by my son. I only wanted him to see me smiling at him, cheering him on. I was so proud of my son's courage I could scream.

As much as we hoped Bryson would one day walk, it was our greater hope that Bryson's mental capacity would develop to be higher than what was predicted. Professionals calculated his IQ rating to be about 50. But we began to notice something interesting. Though he had difficulty focusing his eyes, there seemed to be an increasing level of brightness in those eyes. The professionals did not share our opinion regarding the brightness we believed was there.

Near the end of the spring term at The Child Center, we met with Bryson's main teacher for a conference. She reminded us that Bryson was a "borderline" case even to participate in this early intervention program. In her opinion, Bryson's cognitive abilities were as severely impaired as his physical functioning, and it would never be possible for Bryson to be educated in a normal school setting.

In May 1988 we experienced a bittersweet moment of joy and sadness as we attended Bryson's two-year-old birthday party at The Child Center. Strapped into his special chair with a birthday hat on his head, a cake with two candles was placed in front of him, and the other children and teachers began to sing "Happy birthday." His limp body remained very still, and one could wonder if he was even "tuned in" enough on this day to know there was a cupcake in front of him, no less that it was his birthday.

He appeared so detached, so sad. My mind drifted to thoughts of what might have been had my son's life not been so cruelly altered. He would have been in a different place, a happier place, running around the room with healthy kids. He would be free, not only from the constraints of his special chair, but also from the prison of his mind and body. But as I blinked away the tears, I began to notice something that startled me.

As the birthday song neared its final stanza, although no one had yet instructed him to do so, Bryson began attempting to purse his lips to blow out the candles. He must have remembered this from another child's party. He was trying extremely hard to blow, but he was unable to get more than a tiny bit of air to come through his severely uncoordinated lips. Intrigued, I focused in on him. As usual, he displayed such an incredible spirit of determination as he went about his futile task. Finally, after numerous unsuccessful attempts to blow, one of his teachers helped him blow the candles out.

I turned to my wife. Through our tears, we both had the same reaction. It was as if our son was making a statement. We understood all the reasons for the dire predictions about his future. But he was doing a darn good impersonation of a child who knew how to imitate appropriate behavior, if not a child with an IQ far in excess of 50.

The teachers and therapists were all wonderfully dedicated people, and we came to love them for what they were attempting to do for our son. But how could *anyone* predict our son's future for certain? It had only been a year since it was suggested to us that it might be best to place him in an institution. Now, here he was, attempting to blow out his candles like a "normal" child. Maybe he could go farther than anyone believed?

Much of our son's physical and mental ability had been stolen. No one disputed that. The most optimistic observer couldn't claim to see the emerald palace anywhere beyond the rainbow, or honestly, any tangible evidence pointing to a bright future for him. Maybe we were just grasping at straws. Maybe we were clinging to every faint reason we could find for hope. But this wouldn't be the last time we would have a reason to consider the possibility that there might be much greater intelligence and ability locked up inside the prison of his injured brain. Indeed, this was only the beginning.

And while God had allowed much to be taken, He also left some vital qualities behind, weapons for him to fight with. His relentless pattern of perseverance and tenacity was becoming evident to those with eyes to see. And from what God had taught us about hope, there wasn't a reason in the world why we shouldn't remain solidly behind our son as he fought the desperate battles looming ahead. No, we would never give up on him. We would continue to hope for more. *Much* more!

> "For I know the plans I have for you," declares the LORD, "plans for welfare and not for calamity to give you a future and a hope."
>
> —JEREMIAH 29:11

Chapter 8

TOUCHED BY AN ANGEL

See that you do not despise one of these little ones, for I say to you that their angels in heaven continually see the face of My Father who is in heaven.

MATTHEW 18:10

MY FATHER WAS a first generation American citizen, the son of Italian immigrants. He grew up in the Little Italy section of Lower Manhattan. His shoeshine box still sits in my office, a testament to a man who was willing to sacrifice for his parents and siblings, to help them through the Great Depression. After fighting for our country in World War II, he raised his own family in the New Jersey suburbs, working two jobs to support a wife and four children. Laboring as a painter, he went to school at night to get his real estate license. Together with my mother, also a person of great sacrifice, he built a residential real estate business that was successful enough to put the four of us through college.

Somehow, I wound up working for Harry B. Helmsley, who owned much of the Manhattan skyline, including the Empire State Building. In 1977 I became connected with one of the top brokers in New York, Jack Vickers. Jack was one of a kind in selflessly teaching skills to young beginners, and he propelled me toward a very successful career. I made my mark in overseeing the successful renovation and leasing of the famous old Knickerbocker Hotel on the corner of Broadway and 42nd Street. In 1981 I became a vice president of that prestigious Helmsley firm, at the ripe old age of twenty-six.

In 1984 I joined the Edward S. Gordon Company (ESG), one of the most powerful commercial real estate firms in the United States. By the time Bryson became injured in late 1986, I had become one of the top producers in their Wall Street office, specializing in relocating corporate headquarters within the canyons of Manhattan skyscrapers.

The stakes are high and the competition fierce in the world of Manhattan real estate. Being on the alert to defend your turf, even within your *own* firm, is a major aspect of the job description. You need to be energized and mentally focused for the contentious negotiations and challenges of each day. As in the theory of "natural selection," those who are weak should expect to become extinct from the business pretty quickly. Being out of the office to take care of personal matters, as was required for Bryson's unending medical needs, can cause you to be placed on the endangered species list.

Yet kindness and encouragement can be found in surprising places, even in the high stakes world of Manhattan real estate. I'll never forget the day Ed Gordon, founder and Chairman of ESG (since merged with other firms and now known as CBRE) called me into his office, not to discuss a deal, but to inquire about my son.

He informed me that he had made arrangements for me to visit with Cardinal John O'Connor, head of the Archdiocese of New York, to offer up prayers on behalf of my son. I declined Ed's gracious offer, already feeling spiritually well cared for. But I was deeply touched by his compassion in attempting to help me in this way.

I knew where Ed's empathy came from, and it was hard earned. His adult daughter had died tragically the year before. Grief gains you membership to a club you'd rather not belong to, but it is a club that creates bonds between people of varied backgrounds. I shouldn't have been surprised that Ed, being Jewish, could arrange a meeting with the cardinal. Being a powerful business leader in New York has its privileges.

The Ed Sullivan Show

I began spending a lot of time taking Bryson to therapy sessions to relieve my wife a bit, and continued attending all his doctor appointments. I did my best to play "catch-up" on my full days at work, often rising at 4:30 a.m. to take the 5:35 a.m. train from Glen Rock. After long, exhausting days in New York, my first task upon arrival back home was to check the emotional status, which was often very needy. Days fraught with caring for a brain-injured child were far more exhausting than my days in the Manhattan jungle. Naturally, my wife required lots of help when I walked through the door. After dinner and some play time with the kids, we got them to bed; but this was not the time to relax.

I dreaded picking up the mail. There were always *stacks* of doctor bills and insurance forms to administrate. The insurance company routinely rejected coverage for seemingly *every* medical and therapeutic service our son required. For families with long-term illnesses, fighting with insurance companies is an unending, exasperating part of life.

I felt like one of the performers on *The Ed Sullivan Show* from days past. Some of you who are old enough may remember this act. The guy begins spinning dishes on top of vertical sticks that look like pool cues. Soon he's got about a dozen dishes spinning, and he's running frantically back and forth to keep all the wobbling plates from smashing down to the ground. At this point in my life I had too far too many wobbly plates. When I finally shut my eyes and tried to sleep, those plates kept right on wobbling in my mind. The balancing act was beginning to wear me down. Way down!

Physicians and therapists were now addressing a myriad of problems. Bryson had severely crossed eyes that would require surgery, and there was a need for braces on his feet. He continued suffering from repeated inner ear and respiratory infections. We later learned that his immune system had been suppressed as a related consequence of the original assault on his neurological system.

One doctor suggested that Bryson be fitted for an orthopedic helmet to protect him during the endless daily crashes he experienced, as he attempted to cruise around the furniture. He crashed painfully to the floor several times per day, without possessing the reflexes necessary to enable him to reach out and cushion his falls. He fell like a dead weight into whatever hard or dangerous object might break his fall. He often had welts, bruises, and cuts on his cherub face and body, and he began to bash out teeth.

The stress level on all of us, including Janelle, was enormous. Imagine living in a nightmare in which you suddenly realized your wobbly toddler was not at your side, but teetering precariously at the edge of a high cliff. Your heart is thrust to your throat as you realize he is falling. In terror, you rush toward him, but this is one of those nightmares in which you can't move your limbs fast enough to get where you need to go. Screams and tears fly as you realize in horror that you will not arrive before his body is smashed on the rocks. This hellish nightmare was our daily reality, day after injury-filled day.

I have now met several families with children whose motor control and balance mechanisms have been destroyed through brain injury. The feeling of stress inside parents' chests as they live through this daily horror defies description. The following is an excerpt from a letter I wrote a few years later to my now retired pastor, Dr. Earl Comfort, on April 27, 1993, after Bryson had suffered through *years* of this torture:

> Other points of stress include Bryson falling several times per day. He tries to do a lot more than his degree of balance and impaired reflexes allow for, and therefore he often falls hard. He always has bruises all over his body (including his still gorgeous face) and he has smashed out teeth on two separate occasions. This is something a parent never gets used to, no matter how many times it happens. We are typically "on edge" since he has about 10 near falls for every actual one, and he has about two very hard crashes each day, replete with screaming and the need to be comforted.

Bryson was nearly seven years old (several years beyond where we currently are in his story) when the above letter was written. His then larger body fell no more softly into hard objects than in previous years. Many times I had rushed home from Manhattan after Bryson suffered a particularly traumatic accident that only "daddy" could comfort. There were bashed out teeth, the regular spilling of his blood, the time he nearly lost an eye. I could continue, but you get the idea.

As I write these words many years later, the memories cause me to flinch. I used to joke with my wife about this, saying that we should donate our nervous systems to science to be studied when we die. Joking aside, it has occurred to me that things deep within my soul have been twisted from this protracted torture. Things I don't pretend to understand.

I am not a psychologist (although my now grown children think I need one), but I can tell you from experience that your emotional and spiritual health will largely be determined by what you decide to do with your long-term misery and your feelings of anger about the situation. You can deny your rage (I've been there), thinking it will just go away if you try hard enough to be a good Christian. Trust me on this: it will not go away. If you suffer the agony of repetitive, circumstantial torture and exhaustion that continues on and on for months or years, you will be tempted toward rage and despair, and tempted to withdraw from God and sink into despondency.

The world has its own remedies for escape and temporary relief; everything from alcohol, drugs, illicit sex, and a trillion dollars worth of other idols. Step right up and choose your poison. But if we're serious about not being conformed to this world, what then is God's prescription for the pain of long-term, torturous circumstances? Are we to pretend that we don't bleed or feel the pain because we are Christians? Does it give glory to God when we stuff our anger while raging on the inside? Is this true spiritual maturity? As mentioned in an earlier chapter, we need to have some honest discussions with God.

Relax! I'm not going to advocate some secular (and foolish) "get in touch with your anger" campaign. But for those who feel it would be disrespectful to bring your angry feelings to God, I would ask the following: Is it honoring to God to pretend that your anger doesn't exist? Does is glorify God when we relegate the working out of our anger under the guidance of a psychologist who never opens the pages of the Bible, a therapist who treats us as victims and tells us that we *deserve* to be angry? How does the anger ever get resolved?

Scripture informs us that it is possible to be angry without sinning, and that one of the keys to settling conflicts with our neighbor is speaking the truth in love before the sun goes down, so the devil is given no opportunity in our lives (Eph. 4:25–27). So how about speaking truth to God? Should we treat Him with less regard than our neighbor? Will the devil ignore our failure to resolve our conflicts with God?

Scripture is consistently clear that God *wants* us to come to Him with our feelings, even our anger. He can handle it. If He were the kind of god who would strike us down for exhibiting the emotions He created us with, we'd all be in bigger trouble than we know. Philip Yancey addressed this in his excellent book *Disappointment with God*:

> One bold message in the Book of Job is that you can say anything to God. Throw at him your grief, your anger, your doubt, your bitterness, your betrayal, your disappointment—he can absorb them all. As often as not, spiritual giants of the Bible are shown contending with God. They prefer to go away limping, like Jacob, rather than to shut God out. In this respect, the Bible prefigures a tenet of modern psychology: you can't really deny your feelings or make them disappear, so you might as well express them. God can deal with every human response save one. He cannot abide the response I fall back on instinctively: an attempt to ignore him or treat him as though he does not exist.[1]

Jesus is the ultimate example of what it means to be a truly healthy, functioning man. He is the only man who ever lived a perfect life, yet scripture reveals several glimpses of His times of righteous anger and grief. We are told that when He got alone with God to pray, His prayers were sometimes filled with emotion and passion:

> In the days of His flesh, He offered up both prayers and supplications with loud crying and tears to the One able to save Him from death.
>
> —Hebrews 5:7

God requires those who worship Him to do so in spirit and truth (John 4:24). Pretending I am not angry so I can appear more respectable as I pray is not truthful, nor is it helpful, either to me or to those around me. How ridiculous would it be to refuse to go to the doctor's office until we were well? The truth is we will *never* get our act together enough or be well enough to come to Him. We are welcomed right now, *just* the way we are, and we must learn to run to Him when we are angry and hurting.

When we go to see the Great Physician, we will discover something amazing. He has given His throne a title. His throne is not a throne of indifference. He knows *exactly* what we have been going through. It is not a throne of condemnation. It is not a throne of "how dare you come here disheveled and stinking the way you do." Praise God, His throne is a throne of grace (Heb. 4:16). Because Jesus paved the way for us to come to the throne, the Father waits with an ample supply of healing mercy and grace.

> For we do not have a high priest who cannot sympathize with our weaknesses, but One who has been tempted in all things as we are, yet without sin. Therefore let us draw near with confidence to the throne of grace, that we may receive mercy and may find grace to help in time of need.
>
> —Hebrews 4:15–16

I don't know about you, but my time of greatest need is almost always when I have failed the worst, including my angry failures. Praise God that He is ready and willing to lavish every child with healing mercy and grace. We can stay away to our peril, or we can come to Him. We can only receive His healing when we come.

If you are still a bit timid about approaching His throne just the way you are, read through the psalms and the prophets, one chapter per day. The honesty of these servants of God will encourage you to approach God boldly, even as they did. In their anguish, they wail and rage their frustration at God, aiming blistering doubts and accusations against God's wisdom, judgment, and even His love for them. Though these emotional outbursts might make a lesser god blush, our Father does not hide them from us. He is not embarrassed by our frailty. He knows we are but dust. He proudly features these outbursts of emotion in His Word, carefully recording even the most scathing railings against Him; not to teach us to do better, but to encourage us to do likewise, so we can be healed.

> I pour out my complaint before Him; I declare my trouble before Him.
>
> —Psalm 142:2

> What profit is there in my blood, if I go down to the pit? Will the dust praise You? Will it declare Your faithfulness? Hear, O LORD, and be gracious to me; O LORD, be my helper.
>
> —PSALM 30:9–10

> Why has my pain been perpetual And my wound incurable, refusing to be healed? Will You indeed be to me like a deceptive stream with water unreliable?
>
> —JEREMIAH 15:18

> You have held my eyelids open; I am so troubled that I cannot speak.... Will the Lord reject forever? And will He never be favorable again? Has His lovingkindness ceased forever? Has His promise come to an end forever? Has God forgotten to be gracious, or has He in anger withdrawn His compassion?
>
> —PSALM 77:4, 7–9

> In dark places He has made me dwell, like those who have long been dead. He has walled me in so that I cannot go out; He has made my chain heavy. Even when I cry out and call for help, He shuts out my prayer.... He is to me like a bear lying in wait, like a lion in secret places He has turned aside my ways and torn me to pieces; He has made me desolate. He bent His bow And set me as a target for the arrow. He made the arrow of His quiver To enter into my inward parts.
>
> —LAMENTATIONS 3:6–8, 10–13

> For the enemy has persecuted my soul; He has crushed my life to the ground; He has made me dwell in dark places, like those who have long been dead. Therefore my spirit is overwhelmed within me; My heart is appalled within me.
>
> —PSALM 143:3–4

The next time you are "appalled" at what God has allowed to occur into your life, when it seems that God has set you as His "target," when He seems to be relentlessly hunting you down like an animal, you will be faced with a choice. You can withdraw from God in anger, declaring that you've "had enough." This reaction is understandable, but be aware that this choice will make your heart hard and bitter. As you judge the One who truly loves you to be uncaring and cruel, you will be handing your heart over to a truly cruel slave master whose intention is to wreck your life (1 Pet. 5:8). This is a fool's choice. God has given us a better option.

Bryson screamed out his tortured pain to us every day, and we never admonished him for bothering us. Each time, we picked him up and gave him as much comfort as a parent can give a hurting child. How much more does our heavenly Father know *exactly* how to comfort us? Come to His throne and let Him minister mercy and grace to you.

As for Bryson, the spirit of tenacity he was now well known for continued to exhibit itself. No matter how many times he failed and fell, nor how intense his pain, he continued to relentlessly pull himself back up and try to ambulate around the house, clinging to objects and furniture. I marveled at his fortitude. Being a former college football player who was weaned on the Vince Lombardi "never give up" ethic, I was both intrigued and inspired. I continued to hope toward the day when that tenacious spirit might be rewarded, but his therapists were becoming even more pessimistic that he would ever walk on his own. We were advised to place him in a wheelchair.

Touched by a Truly Great Man

Among the dreams that were dying in our struggling little family, we laid aside our dream of having another child. We knew Bryson's needs would be extraordinary for years to come, and we were already overwhelmed with stress and fatigue. It would be unwise to add the responsibility of another child. I may be dumb (and ugly, depending on who you ask), but I'm not crazy. There was no way I could handle another *ounce* of stress.

You can imagine, then, how stunned we were to discover that we were expecting our third, very unplanned child. The baby was due to arrive in November 1988. We had no alternative but to trust that the Lord knew what He was doing. Frankly, during my weaker moments, I had my doubts, and there was great trepidation about how we were going to handle this. And, of course, there were nightmares and fears about the health of the new baby. Once you've had a tragedy with one child, you simply cannot presume that it will not happen again. Ready or not, we began to brace ourselves for what we soon learned would be a baby brother for Bryson and Janelle.

At two and one-half years old, Bryson was drooling profusely and still unable to utter a word. His eyes were badly crossed (the medical term for this is "bilateral alternating strabismus"); but we continued to see what we believed to be awareness in those eyes, and an increased responsiveness as we spoke to him. He began to turn and point toward things in the room as we talked to him about them. His teachers and therapists did not share our opinion regarding the intelligence we believed was locked inside him, and our comments laid on the table like a lead balloon each time we brought up the subject.

We often spoke to Bryson and Janelle about the fact that the time was drawing near for their baby brother to arrive. We told them that the baby would belong to them, as much as to us. Janelle was indignant; making her feelings known that she wanted a sister, *not* another baby brother. My recollection is that she called the new baby "Stephen" for about six months after he was born (not his name) to register her displeasure. As far as Bryson was concerned, there was no way to know for sure how much, if anything, he comprehended about the pending arrival of his brother.

On November 10, 1988, Timothy Robert Milazzo was born into our family. His middle name, Robert, was taken from one of the greatest men I've ever known. Bob Boylan and I had known each other since the little league days. I was the quarterback on the football team in high school, and he was my receiver. The truth is I couldn't shine Bobby's shoes as an athlete. I always knew that he was the only guy to throw to in the clutch. Yet, as much as I learned from my friend as a champion athlete, I learned much more from him about sacrificial, compassionate friendship. In the early days of Bryson's tragedy, this strong man listened to my anguished sobbing on the phone and gently said, "Steady now."

Several years later, it was my turn to comfort him as he courageously battled against a cancer that had ravaged his magnificent body. Though he fought gallantly for three years, it became evident that his battle had taken a turn for the worst, and his fight would soon be over. He would be leaving Karen, his wonderful wife, and their child, Bryan (the same age as Bryson), behind. Though it was now my turn to give comfort to Bobby, this giant of a man was not yet finished teaching me. Shortly before Timothy Robert's birth, as he lay dying at age thirty-three, Bobby taught me something I will be reminded of every day until my own death. My friend had this to say from his bed at Mount Sinai Hospital in Manhattan:

> I don't want you, or anyone else feeling sorry for me. Even if you live to be 83, Barry, the extra 50 years God will give you is just a blink of an eye compared to the eternity that is prepared for both of us. I'll just be going there a little sooner, and I'll look forward to seeing you when you get there.[2]

One of the most solemn privileges of my lifetime was to give the eulogy for Bobby, my hero, at his funeral service. He was too big a man for mere words, and mine were woefully inadequate. One of my highest prayers from that day forward has been to respond to the disappointments and tragedies of my lifetime with the dignity, faith, and courage he lived out for all to see. And there's not a doubt in my mind I will see him again, just as he said. It is my hope and prayer that all who read this book will believe in Jesus Christ, so that the eternal life Bobby spoke of will be yours as well.

Touched by an Angel

We thought that having another child would be irresponsible, imprudent, and impossible to deal with. God often overrules our faulty judgments and sends us good gifts despite our ignorance and foolishness. Sometimes He even sends "angels."

Timothy Robert was born a completely healthy, beautiful baby. The bad news is that he broke his mother's tailbone on his way into the world. Her pregnancy had already been very painful, with a herniated disc in the middle of her spine. I was deeply concerned. I thought perhaps my humor would help, especially some of my favorite Ralph Kramden jokes from *The Honeymooners*. You know, like when Ralph says to Alice: "Honey, I hate the fact that you carry that heavy basket of laundry up *three* flights of steps with your bad back. If I've told you once, I've told you a thousand times: take *two* trips."

Okay ladies, don't slam the book shut. I was just kidding. I became immediately concerned about how my wife would be able to care for a newborn and a crippled toddler as I was at work, and I began planning to bring live-in help into the home. I'll tell you more about that in the next chapter.

A day after the delivery it was time to bring Bryson and Janelle to meet their baby brother, and God was about to reveal one of the most surprising and joyful experiences we've ever encountered as a family. It was also an event which reinforced our belief that Bryson was much brighter than he was being recognized for. After greeting mommy in her room, the four of us set out down the hall to the nursery to meet Timothy Robert. As I held Bryson (two and one-half years old) and Janelle (five) in each arm up to the glass window of the nursery, my wife pointed in the direction of Timothy Robert, sleeping in his little crib.

It happened so fast I was startled. Bryson immediately tried to leap out of my arms in the direction of his new brother. I attempted to balance both children back into my arms, but Bryson continued to lunge toward his brother, banging his uncoordinated hand against the glass. He had an enormous smile across his face as he tried to wriggle from my grasp to move closer to his little brother. Unable to speak, he squealed and giggled with sheer delight. We had never seen him more animated, or happier, as he continued pointing at his brother and banging on the glass.

Even as Elizabeth, mother of John the Baptist, was startled as her unborn child leaped in her womb in the presence of his unborn cousin Jesus, we were startled by Bryson's attempt to leap toward his newborn brother. There could be no doubt that Bryson had understood the things we had told him about the playmate who would be arriving to live with us, and his reaction indicated something important. Most two and one-half-year-olds do not have a deep understanding of the implications involved in having a newborn sibling. As we looked back on this later, we realized that our brain-injured child had a deeper grasp of the impact this baby would have on our family, and on his own future, than we did.

Despite our shortsighted attempts to plan out our lives, God had given us clear new evidence of His wisdom and sovereignty. Don't ask me how Bryson intuitively knew about the goodness of God's gift. As he continued banging on the glass of that nursery with unbridled enthusiasm, I realized that he had grasped something that I had failed to "get." In fact, I missed it by a country mile. But there's not a doubt in my mind Bryson understood that this baby brother would loom large in his future, as large as any guardian angel ever could. Indeed, Tim has loomed very large for our entire family.

This baby would become Bryson's greatest ally in the years ahead. He would mean the difference between years of loneliness and joyful companionship. He would be his teammate, one who would "push" Bryson to strive for normal behavior and higher achievements. He would stand up with and for his weaker brother. All these things, and more, Timothy Robert has accomplished. In a world lacking enough real men, this little baby has grown to become a man of integrity and strength. He is a young man as I write this, decades later, and his life has been far from easy. Yet he has demonstrated, time and again, the character and courage to do what is right, rather than what is easy. I can unequivocally say that there's never been a father who has ever been more proud of a son than I am of Timothy Robert. Bob Boylan would have respected him greatly.

The professionals continued to tell us Bryson was barely educable. But we viewed Bryson's reaction to his newborn brother as another piece of evidence that there was far more intelligence locked inside him than he was being given credit for. Perhaps we were just being unrealistic. After all, who were we as mere parents to think that we knew something the professionals could not see? Either way, as time moved on the debate was beginning to appear meaningless. It seemed, more and more, that there was no power on earth that could ever unlock his prison door.

But despite the unyielding opinion of the professionals and the seeming impenetrability of his prison walls, this was no time to give up on our son's future. Clearly our tenacious son had not given up. Despite all his brain-injured limitations, somehow he knew how to celebrate the important things in life. And something else was becoming clear for those with eyes to see.

As wearying, frustrating, demoralizing, and infuriating as those days often were, we had seen firsthand that the King sometimes stoops down, without warning, to intervene in our lives. As I look back, perhaps we should all have been banging on that glass. The great King had taken notice of a struggling little family, and with His mighty hand He reached down from heaven, and touched us with an angel.

Janelle and Bryson enjoying baby Tim

"A brother is born
for adversity"
(Proverbs 17:17)

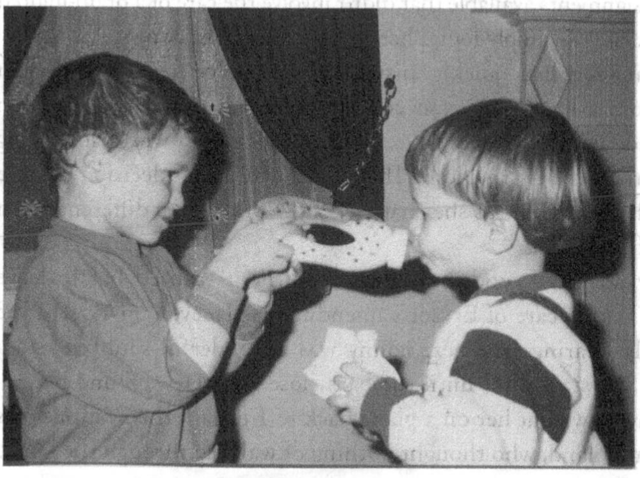

Chapter 9
THE SOUND OF A MIRACLE

Before a thing can be made useful, something must be broken.... Before there can be life, there must be death. Before there can be joy, there must be weeping.... Our Lord Jesus stated the principle of brokenness in these words: "Unless a grain of wheat falls into the earth and dies, it remains alone; but if it dies, it bears much fruit" [John 12:24]. This is the law of life.... There is no making without breaking.[1]

Dr. M. R. DeHaan

The Hand that Rocks the Cradle

With tremendous relief and gratitude we returned home from the hospital with our third child. But the old adage is often true that there is no rest for the weary. With my wife suffering from a painful back, I tried the best I could to take up some of the slack in our home. I was getting busy at work again. My largest client in New York asked me to represent them on deals in Atlanta, Cleveland, Charlotte, Philadelphia, Hartford, New Orleans, and other cities. I arranged some ridiculous round trips to these cities to get back home the same day, flying out early in the morning and returning home at night; but some overnight stays were unavoidable. We soon hired some live-in help to give my wife a break from the demands of an infant and a multiply handicapped three-year-old.

Anyone familiar with nannies or live-in "mother's helpers" will tell you that this can lead to good and bad experiences, and we had both. The bad experiences were not as intriguing as in the 1992 horror film *The Hand that Rocks the Cradle*, but they did make life a bit more interesting. The first one left us high and dry without notice. There were easier assignments available that didn't involve the care of a brain-injured toddler and a newborn. We simply found her room empty after two weeks.

We thought that God had quickly answered our prayer for a replacement when a student from a local Christian college arrived at our door. We soon found her to be moody and irresponsible. She left her own dirty dishes lying around and her clothes all over the floor. The last straw was her decision to leave Tim alone on the changing table as she chatted on the phone in a different room. We fired her after five days.

The next helper was very good, but "Bryson burnout" caused her to leave after two months. Taking care of Bryson's unending needs, even on a part-time basis, was extremely wearing. The next nanny was a wonderful soul but had a drinking problem. She stayed out until the bars closed. After we found bottles of liquor in her drawer, we put her on a plane back to Ireland. The next one was a beautiful girl from Poland, who thought nothing of walking through the house wearing only a towel. I didn't see the problem with this (yeah, right!), but my wife thought it best to let her go.

Just when it seemed almost too much trouble to try again, we met a wonderful gal from the Bronx name Geraldine, who was studying to be a nurse. She was an intelligent, hard working girl, who had a great deal of common sense and resourcefulness. She was good with all three children, and my wife began to feel at ease leaving Tim and Janelle at home with her while she drove Bryson to his unending therapy sessions. Gerry was even a Yankee fan (how could it get any better). She remains a lifelong friend to this day.

Didn't God Know?

Even with help, taking care of a newborn baby, a multiply handicapped toddler, and a five-year-old (going on fifteen) daughter was a tall order for us. Our family life was not exactly "normal," whatever *that* is. Patsy Clairmont once wrote a good book called "*Normal Is Just a Setting on Your Dryer,*" indicating that there really is no such thing as a "normal" family.[2] Any way we chose to look at it, *normal* was not a word which described our family experience. Probably not yours either.

We kept praying that Bryson would make a dramatic recovery. Countless people from churches throughout our area prayed for him too. He was now in therapy every day but not making much progress. At three years old he still couldn't sit for more than a few seconds before falling over. He drooled profusely, and he still couldn't speak. Where was this dramatic recovery that we could all praise God for? Didn't God know that He needed to answer our prayers in the affirmative to bring glory to Himself?

As reality continued its relentless assault it seemed God had left for a long vacation, neglecting to leave a forwarding address. C. S. Lewis shared a similar view after his wife died of cancer:

> Meanwhile, where is God? This is one of the most disquieting symptoms. When you are happy, so happy that you have no sense of needing Him...you will be—or so it feels—welcomed with open arms. But go to Him when your need is desperate, when all other help is vain, and what do you find? A door slammed in your face, and a sound of bolting and double bolting on the inside. After that, silence. You may as well turn away. The longer you wait, the more emphatic the silence will become.[3]
>
> —C. S. Lewis

It's a good thing that the Bible tells us to walk by faith and not by sight. The stress and exhaustion wore us down again and again, and it remained difficult to *see* or *feel* a whole lot to be positive about. My faith often resembled Peter's experience as He took His eyes off the Lord and began to sink into the waves. As the raging storm intensified, the waves captivated my focus, and my attention.

WHEN TROUBLES MULTIPLY

As mentioned earlier, I used to believe the myth that God never gives us more than *we* can handle. The enemy has done a pretty good job passing this deception along in American Christian culture. Too often we seek a "faith" geared toward success in life by our own fleshly effort, without God. God's definition of success is quite different. Knowing and loving God and trusting and obeying Him, these are the values of success Scripture exhorts us toward as followers of Christ. These values are fostered through the study of God's Word, and by persevering through tests and trials the Lord brings our way in order to bring us to the point of total dependence upon Him.

When this story began, I was a young, hotshot real estate executive. I was living the Christian life the best I knew how, but with a great deal of ignorance about God's methods and ways. As I write this book, I can assure you that I still have a long way to go in my Christian walk. But having tasted that the Lord *is* good, and that His ways *are* right, I wouldn't ever turn back to ignorance. The lessons have been extremely painful, but Scripture couldn't be clearer that this is the way the Lord told us it would be.

> The refining pot is for silver and the furnace for gold, But the LORD tests hearts.
>
> —PROVERBS 17:3

> Behold, I have refined you, but not as silver; I have tested you in the furnace of affliction.
>
> —ISAIAH 48:10

As those "tests" ensued in my life, God seemed to be responding to my prayers, not with solutions I sought but by giving us even *more* problems to deal with. It was almost as if God were saying, "Now let's see. The Milazzos are struggling pretty badly. Perhaps I'll overwhelm them with a few more problems. That's it! I'll hit them while they're down." Don't tell me you haven't felt this way. The fact that most of you (at least the honest ones) *have* felt this way is the reason I've written this book. C. H. Spurgeon expressed this same sentiment with more eloquence than I just did:

> When troubles multiply, and discouragements follow each other in long succession, like Job's messengers, then too, amid the perturbation of soul occasioned by evil tidings, despondency despoils the heart of all its peace. Constant dripping wears away stones, and the bravest minds feel the fret of repeated afflictions.... Accumulated distresses increase each other's weight; they play into each other's hands, and like bands of robbers, ruthlessly destroy our comfort. Wave upon wave is severe work for the strongest swimmer. The place where two seas meet strains the most seaworthy keel. If there were regulated pauses between the buffetings of adversity, the spirit would stand prepared; but when they come suddenly and heavily, like the battering of great

hailstones, the pilgrim may well be amazed. The last ounce is laid upon us, what wonder if we for awhile are ready to give up the ghost![4]

Over time, who among us has not felt "ready to give up the ghost," especially when we are hit by new waves of suffering before we've been able to get up from the last that swept our legs out from under us? This is real life for Christian and non-Christian alike. If we Christians have no answer for this other than to smile and pretend we are always "fine," why should the world listen to us? Don't misunderstand what I'm saying. We don't need to be glum sad sacks, *always* down in the mouth about something. But Like Lewis and Spurgeon, we do need to be honest about our pain when we are crushed by life's sorrows.

My wife began to come down with illnesses and infections which kept her sick for extended periods. Even when she was "well," she often suffered from migraine headaches, dizzy spells, and nausea. The doctor diagnosed her as having "chronic fatigue syndrome." He told us he could even feel the warmth from her inflamed joints. A doctor from our Glen Rock neighborhood was good enough to pay us an emergency visit one evening at midnight, after she had a severe bout with pain and vomiting. It took two injections to relieve her nausea and pain and help her sleep.

I began to experience severe stomach pain which required medical intervention after I awoke on the floor of the bathroom one evening in a pool of my own blood. The pain had caused me to pass out and hit the floor in a free fall, and the impact caused me to remain unconscious for about an hour. A thorough GI series revealed nothing serious. Stress, sleep deprivation, and diet were considered the culprits. Soon thereafter I began to suffer from a painful skin condition, which, although the doctor thought had been brought under control through medication, recurred three separate times over a twelve-month period. This condition, along with baby Tim's colic, kept sleep at a minimum. Coach Vince Lombardi of the Green Bay Packers taught his players that "fatigue makes cowards of us all."[5] I felt well qualified to test his theory. As I sought to keep up with work while addressing all the medical needs cropping up in our family, deep fatigue was setting in.

Just when we thought it was safe to go back to sleep (bring up the *Jaws* music), Bryson began to suffer what was described to us as "night terrors." He would go to sleep fine, but in the middle of the night blood-curdling screams came from his room. Was he in pain? Did something bite him? Not able to speak, he couldn't tell us. But he was clearly traumatized and terrified as we scooped him out of his crib. As we held him, he kept shrieking and staring at the wall as if something awful was lurking there. Some nights his screaming continued for half an hour. We became worried about what was going on inside his injured mind, and we were grieved that he couldn't tell us.

These episodes often awakened Janelle and Tim. After nearly an hour of comforting all three of them, we usually had the troops back asleep. But getting ourselves back to sleep was almost always more difficult. Bryson's "night terrors" continued nearly every night, sometimes twice per night, for about two *years*.

To this day one of our favorite family stories (definitely not *my* favorite) is about the night that I went flying into Bryson's room as he screamed and unceremoniously broke my big toe on the dumb pop-up toy someone left out on the floor. You know the toy I'm talking about: the hard plastic kind with Mickey, Donald Duck, Goofy, and their friends who all pop up when you hit their button. My foot hit that stupid toy so hard that Mickey was never again found (calling all physics majors: can a toe obliterate Mickey at the molecular level?). Suffice it to say that my wife took care of Bryson as I hopped around the room, barely maintaining my "Christianity" (verbally speaking). And no, don't even go there! God was *not* paying me back for my Ralph Kramden jokes.

Between the medical ailments, Bryson's night terrors, baby Tim's colic, and one very swollen, purple toe, there seemed to be a conspiracy against sleep in our home. It seemed God wanted us to deal with the "waves" He was sending our way as sleepwalking zombies. But, brace yourselves men, things got *worse*! One night, my wife *actually* failed to have dinner ready and on the table when I arrived home from work! "*Bang, Zoom,* to the *moon,* Alice!" Okay ladies, I couldn't help it, and I'm sorry. I promise to be good for a chapter or two. But I can't promise you I won't do some boasting.

Boasting about *What?*

I began to see a pervasive theme in Scripture that I had somehow missed during all my years of being a "success" for Christ. Maybe I just wasn't ready to see things clearly until now. Maybe I hadn't been desperate enough. But now I was enthralled by the teachings of Paul, whose bold honesty captivated me down to my core. In Paul I found a passion that was fueled by something I desperately needed at this time. My guess is that some of you reading this right now need some of this same "fuel" in your lives too.

In the Book of 2 Corinthians, Paul took the time to catalog some of the great sufferings he had been through. When I noticed he had listed "sleepless nights" among his great sufferings, I felt an immediate kinship with him. Sleepless nights were significant enough for him to list along with beatings, hardships, imprisonments, starvation, stonings, lashings, being shipwrecked, and facing many other horrific dangers (see 2 Corinthians 11:23–27). Paul went on to reveal some precious truths regarding the *reason* God allowed that litany of trials, including sleeplessness, to come into his life.

Paul evidently knew that he would be perceived of as odd by those reading his letter, and he didn't try to hide the peculiarity of his message. Instead, he underscored it. In the same chapter in which Paul details his litany of hardships, he admits that he is speaking "foolishness" (v. 21). But he then approaches the level of absurdity as he begins to "boast" about something that makes no sense whatsoever.

> If I have to boast, I will boast of what pertains to my weakness.
>
> —2 Corinthians 11:30

"Paul, have your sufferings driven you mad? Our faith is *not* supposed to be about weakness, it's supposed to represent *victory*. Placing our faith in Christ gives us *power* to *overcome*! Let me straighten you out here, Paul. Perhaps all those beatings, lashings, and stonings have impaired your reasoning? *You* are the great apostle. *You* are the one to whom Jesus appeared from the sky. *You* are responsible for planting and growing a great number of the early churches. *You* wrote more books of the New Testament than anyone else. *You* spread the gospel of Christ throughout the known world. It was all *you* man!

"Don't give us this nonsense about *weakness*. Tell us about your great accomplishments. Tell us about your victories. Tell us that God wants us to be giants of the faith, *not weaklings*! Give us *hope* that we can follow in your footsteps and accomplish great things for God! Wake up, man, and stop talking like a fool! Give a struggling family like mine and those reading my book some reason to hope that we can, *somehow*, live happily ever after. We need some inspiration here, Paul, not all this drivel about weakness!"

But as Paul continues his peculiar oration, he comes *right* back to his most embarrassing boast, and He dares even to use the very words of Christ to reinforce his bizarre claim:

> And He has said to me, "My grace is sufficient for you, for power is perfected in weakness." Most gladly, therefore, I will rather boast about my weaknesses, so that the power of Christ may dwell in me. Therefore I am well content with weaknesses, with insults, with distresses, with persecutions, with difficulties, for Christ's sake; for when I am weak, then I am strong.
>
> —2 Corinthians 12:9–10

I found these words mind-blowing. For *so* long, as a Christian, I missed the *central* point. I actually thought that this Christian life of mine was all about *me*! *I* was to be strong. *I* was to be good. *I* was to overcome the world. *I* was to be victorious. But as troubles overwhelmed me to the point of incompetence, and I visited Vince Lombardi's world of fatigue and cowardice, the words of Christ began to ring loudly in my ears.

> In the world you have tribulation, but take courage, *I* have overcome the world.
>
> —John 16:33, emphasis added

Of course! This life God has given me is not primarily about *me*. It is about *Christ*. *He* has overcome the world. But I just couldn't see this until now.

A Different Way of Thinking

> "For My thoughts are not your thoughts, Nor are your ways My ways," declares the Lord. "For as the heavens are higher than the earth, So are My ways higher than your ways And My thoughts higher than your thoughts."
>
> —Isaiah 55:8–9

> *Okay, Lord, I'm listening and trying to understand. But this is strange indeed, and I'm at the end of my rope here. I have a brain-injured son, a stressful career, and a family so stressed and exhausted we're in danger of falling apart. I'm willing to admit that I don't have a clue about Your ways. The truth is, I don't even know which way is up anymore! So if Paul has something to say to me and to my readers, bring it on. Why did You bring him to the point where weakness was the only thing he dared to boast of? And again, Lord, what does all this have to do with me? I'm just a guy trying not to curse in front of my children as I hop around the room holding my toe! Please bring it down to my level.*

The dramatic events in Paul's life, including the beatings, shipwrecks, imprisonments, the sleepless nights, and all the rest of it, accomplished something *inside* of Paul that God values highly. God values our personal recognition of our limitations and weakness. Our awareness of our weakness leads to something far better, something more "victorious" than being "strong" in ourselves ever could. It leads to our reliance upon Christ.

How hard it is for God to take strong-willed lumps of clay like me, and you, and cause us to rely upon the infinite power of the grace of Christ. I would rather have God make *me* strong so that I can rely upon *my* own gumption, *my* own intellect, *my* own drive, *my* own resources of every kind. It's a hard pill to swallow; but the truth is that even when we're at our *very* best, we are still pathetically inept by God's standards. God wants to accomplish higher things *through* our lives than we could ever achieve, even on the strongest day of our lives.

Even if I could work everything out in accordance with my will, my desires, and become the strongest Christian in the history of the world, I would still wind up bringing glory only to myself, *not* to God. Indeed, it takes quite a bit of "breaking" to correct my stubborn delusions about who is weak and "Who" is strong.

Paul ultimately came to terms with reality. Clearly, he was not the one who was strong. Christ was. He was not the one who was wise. Christ was. He was not the one who could accomplish *anything* important in life. It was Christ all along. Christ came to set us free from our self-reliance and arrogance. Coming to terms about who is weak and "Who" is strong is a critical juncture in experiencing the freedom Christ came to provide for us. We must recognize the throne of our lives belongs only to Christ.

SIN THAT PRECEDES TIME

Our desire to sit on God's throne is as old as time. In fact, this sin precedes time:

> How have you fallen from heaven, O star of the morning, son of the dawn! You have been cut down to the earth, You who have said in your heart, "I will ascend to heaven; I will raise my throne above the stars of God, And I will sit on the mount of assembly in the recesses of the north. I will ascend above the

> heights of the clouds; I will make myself like the Most High." Nevertheless you will be thrust down to Sheol, to the recesses of the pit.
>
> —Isaiah 14:12–15

But what does Lucifer's sin have to do with you and with me? In essence, the rebellion he had the audacity to attempt against God is the *same* core sin that needs to be dealt with in our own hearts. When Adam and Eve took a bite into that fateful apple in the Garden of Eden, it was as if Satan stuck a syringe full of his own poisonous rebellion directly into the vein of all mankind.

But what does this have to do with the weakness Paul is talking about? "And I ask You again, Lord, what does all this have to do with me and my struggling family?" Interestingly, this question brings us right back to the same chapter in which Paul was exulting in his newfound weakness. Paul began this chapter by expressing his *central* fear about what would happen to the believers in the early church if they fell prey, once again, to the lie from our age-old adversary:

> But I am afraid that, as the serpent deceived Eve by his craftiness, your minds will be led astray from the simplicity and purity of devotion to Christ.
>
> —2 Corinthians 11:3

Self-sufficiency *still* runs in our veins. The serpent knows this better than we do. The subtlety of his deceptions against the church has always been geared to appeal to our natural propensity to rely on our flesh, instead of upon Christ. Even after we have been devoted to Christ for years, this core sin of self-sufficiency *still* pulls us like the weight of gravity toward independence from God. Many honest saints have lamented wasted years heading in the wrong direction as they sought to serve God. Theresa of Avila speaks of her own "mistake," which took eighteen years to correct:

> I would pray for help over and over again, it is true. But I made a mistake all that time, which deadened my poor efforts. I did not place my whole trust in His Majesty. Oh, that I had totally and utterly distrusted myself—but I did not. If only I had despised and suspected the conniving, secretly clinging self hidden within me. Yes, I certainly did seek help from the Lord during all those years. But I did not understand: It is of little use to seek God's help until we root out every bit of confidence we place in ourselves—our opinions, our understanding, our personal strengths. Our prayers are pathetic, indeed, until we place all confidence, once and forever, absolutely, in God.[6]

What Brings You Down Will Bring You Up

> For we do not want you to be unaware, brethren, of our affliction which came to us in Asia, that we were burdened excessively, beyond our strength, so that we despaired even of life; Indeed, we had the sentence of death within ourselves *so that we would not trust in ourselves, but in God* who raises the dead.
>
> —2 Corinthians 1:8–9, emphasis added

What circumstance, dear reader, has the Lord allowed to occur that has stopped you dead in your tracks, causing you to despair even of life? What enemy are you battling that you know, deep down, you don't have the *slightest* possibility of conquering? What dreams lay at your feet, shattered into such tiny pieces that even all the king's horses and all the king's men wouldn't have a prayer of putting together again in your life?

You can choose to believe God has abandoned you. Deep inside, you know that isn't true. God *never* gives up on a struggling child any more than you would give up on your own child. Maybe you'll never understand the reasons why your life has become so hard. But if you belong to Christ, you can be certain that God still has a plan. An important part of that plan is to transform your life to make you more like His precious Son. The transformation process often requires pain and suffering, tools that God uses to instill deeper levels of personal brokenness, weakness, and dependence upon Him.

If you had cancer inside you, you would expect your surgeon to "hurt" you, to cut it out and get rid of it. The Great Physician will do no less, but we must not underestimate the task He has undertaken in our redemption. God's work of bringing brokenness and dependence into our lives is by no means a onetime event, but an ongoing process. Watchman Nee gives keen insight into what is going on behind the scenes of our lives:

> The basic lesson we must learn is to be transformed into a vessel fit for the Masters use. This can only be done by the breaking of the outward man. God is at work in our lives unceasingly. Many years of sufferings, trials, hindrances—this is the hand of God, daily seeking to carry on His work of breaking us. Do you not see what God is doing in this endless round of difficulties? If not, you should ask Him, "O God, open my eyes that I may see Thy hand."[7]

As you stand amidst smoldering ashes of dreams that have gone up in smoke, realize that you are on hallowed ground. God may have brought you low, but He intends to bring you to a higher place (Matt. 5:3–4; Ps. 30:5). During your painful, lonely time of wilderness travel, you may not be given an answer to every question nor a solution to every problem. But God will cause you to rely on a Source of power that will never wear down. His name is Jesus; and by the sufficiency of His grace He will live in and through you for God's glory in this dark world, and you will ultimately learn to boast in Him.

THE JOY OF LAUGHTER

As our three-year-old son sat quietly fumbling with a toy, he seemed to have thick mittens on his uncoordinated little hands. He just couldn't get them to work the way he wanted them to. Undaunted, he'd keep struggling to pick it back up. Often without warning, as if a wave swept into the room, he simply fell over, his head hitting the floor. The professionals kept reminding us he was crippled for life and that he would never speak. Yet his brain injury had not been able to rob him of his *wonderful* personality. His smile was irresistible, and as he looked up attempting to focus his badly crossed eyes on you, his smile could melt a heart of steel. At the same time, that smile seemed to have a trace of sadness. Maybe this was just the projection of my own sad soul onto my son.

I often lifted him up for a bit of rough play, to get him laughing. His favorite was being thrown high into the air (our family room had a high cathedral ceiling) and catching him as he squealed in delight. Yes, much had been lost, but praise God, laughter had not been taken away. His laugh was as normal as could be. Better than normal! His giggles were the most irresistible sounds God ever created. He would laugh hysterically as I lifted him high up overhead with outstretched arms, knowing what would happen next. Down he came so that I could put an enormous "bite" into his midsection, wiggling my nose in his ticklish tummy. In those moments there wasn't a "normal" child *anywhere* more thrilled with life than my crippled son. I cherished his laughter more than I can tell you.

We continued to cling to every hopeful sign we saw. We reminded each other about his attempt to blow out the candles on his birthday cake the year before. His surprising reaction to his newborn brother, banging on the glass, bore much repeating. His recognition of objects and things, evidenced by his pointing to them as we spoke about them, became one of our favorite topics. But as the months wore on, our son's lack of progress, especially his inability to speak, began to depress us once again.

It would be one thing if he had just one or two areas of "brokenness," but his brain was damaged in *so* many areas. "Fixing" him was like taking on the renovation of a ramshackle house at the risk of collapse. *Everything* was needy, yet only one area could be "renovated" at a time. Our "subcontractors" (doctors/therapists) kept reporting to us that the foundation, framing, roof, walls, plumbing, and electrical systems were all failing. As skilled and dedicated as these professionals were, they continued to offer little hope that Bryson would ever reach a meaningful level of recovery.

His physical therapist reaffirmed that Bryson would never walk. His cognitive therapist and teachers still believed he was educable to only rudimentary levels. His speech therapist continued to warn us that it was unlikely for him to develop intelligible speech. She instructed us to learn sign language in the hope that Bryson's cognitive and fine motor development would one day improve to the point where he could communicate this way. We continued praying for a miracle. The miracle didn't come.

My son's life had been smashed to bits; and, so it seemed, were my dreams for him. Occasionally that cursed nursery rhyme pried its way into my mind: "All the king's horses and all the king's men couldn't put Humpty together again." As mentioned earlier, I never shared these thoughts with my wife. There was no need to create such a disturbing image in her mind. I tried my best to block it out of my own mind, but this riveting imagery was nearly impossible to erase once it got rolling in my head.

The Pain of Silence

On a "bad" day Bryson would whine and cry for long periods, adding tension to our already stressed household. We tried everything parents normally do to distract hurting children. On some days nothing relieved the misery, for Bryson or for us.

Who wouldn't whine in misery if they were suffering like our son? I'd be a basket case in ten minutes if I were constrained by his limitations. *Nothing* in his body responded to what his injured brain told his body to do. His arms, legs, fingers, hands, lips, and tongue were all dysfunctional. Then there were all the injuries and the pain to deal with. It's easy to talk about smashed out teeth and nearly losing an eye. My son experienced excruciating pain every day.

Nor could he compensate intellectually by reasoning things out as a clear thinking adult, like you reading this book can do. His injury was sustained as a baby. He had no recall of how things were *supposed* to be. All he had was the darkness of an injured, garbled young mind. Perhaps worst of all, he had no means of venting his pain and frustration. He couldn't talk! No wonder he whined. Forget ten minutes. Bryson had no relief *ever*, and every day was the same! My son was a brain-injured prisoner, and I knew it.

The thought of him being trapped inside a silent world of his own was torture for me, far more painful than I could describe here. My greatest fear for my son was not that he would never walk. My greatest fear was that he would never speak. I can't convey the longing we felt to communicate with our son. There was no way to know for sure how much he understood or what he was thinking. No way even to know if he understood how loved he was as a member of our family. For me, his silence was the most unbearable cross the Lord had asked us to bear.

In February 1989 Bryson's speech therapist came to us with "exciting" news. She showed us a catalogue for a new electronic communication device made for individuals who couldn't speak. The idea was to keep the device strapped to his lap as he sat in a wheelchair. Someday he could learn how to push corresponding buttons on the board for the things he needed, such as, "I want cookies," or, "I want juice," etc.

She believed we needed to equip Bryson with electronic communication not only because it was unlikely he would ever speak intelligibly, but also to relieve his frustration. She was a wonderful, dedicated professional. However, I feared that this approach might create a self-fulfilling prophecy, that our son might never achieve real speech if he learned to rely on machines. His whining made me want to climb the walls, but something inside told me that his frustration might ultimately work in his favor, causing him to strive harder for real speech.

I understood where the professionals were coming from. I knew the odds stacked against our son were high; and frankly, I was tired of hearing about it.

He was a profoundly brain-injured, crippled child who would probably never do much in this world. I got all that. But in my mind he was far too young to concede that these things were permanent. Therefore, buying a wheelchair was out of the question. This would keep him crippled and become just another self-fulfilling prophesy, even as an electronic voice would keep him speechless. Maybe hope was all we had; but as mentioned, that was all the more reason to cling to hope. Without hope, we might as well curl up and die.

A Call from a Friend

At about this time we received a call from the Erdmanns, the couple we stayed with when we brought Bryson to Boston Children's Hospital during the fall of 1987. They informed us of some friends who had received help for their brain-injured child from an organization called The National Association of Child Development (NACD).

We had heard about NACD a year earlier from another friend, John Gilmour, who gave us brochures and information. But when John approached us, our schedule was over full with early intervention programs, therapists, and doctors. We put the information he gave us into a file, not thinking of it again until we heard from the Erdmanns. The timing was now right; and frankly, we had nothing to lose.

We called Barbara Frey, director of the New York metropolitan area branch of NACD. She informed us that the NACD, founded by Robert Doman, was dedicated to the recovery of brain-injured children. Interestingly, Barbara told us that the brain is the most resilient organ in the body. If a brain-injured individual is given appropriate input and stimuli, delivered with extreme levels of intensity, repetition, and duration, they can progress significantly over time. She indicated that many children served by their organization had experienced great improvement. Some had even learned to walk and speak after conventional doctors and therapists failed to help them to achieve this.

Barbara cautioned that she could make no promises regarding Bryson. He would need to be evaluated by Bob Doman to determine the extent of his injuries and his current level of function in each developmental area. I had little idea what she was talking about in terms of intensity, repetition, and duration. But there was no way we could ignore the hope laced throughout her message. We scheduled Bryson to be evaluated by the NACD on the next available appointment date, April 12, 1989.

The Sound of a Miracle

In the view of most professionals, Bryson's brain was far too injured to achieve any meaningful recovery. They thought we were wasting our time and frustrating our son further by our lack of acceptance of his condition. Were we just setting ourselves up for yet another painful crash by listening to theories about the resiliency of the brain? Honestly, I had no idea. When you dare to hope, you risk the pain of crashing down hard if your balloon bursts. We had already experienced some pretty painful crashes, but I still hoped that our son would one day speak, walk, and regain everything he had been robbed of. All of it! I couldn't share this hope with others. It was just too preposterous. Being honest, I sometimes felt foolish for hoping these things, and I was seemingly alone.

But something changed that winter. It happened without warning. There are people who can explain away what happened. These kinds of things happen all the time, and they categorize such things as misdiagnosis or even spontaneous healing. But I see it differently. I believe God took great delight in preparing a long awaited gift for us. And I think, too, that angels watched intently as the King carefully prepared His gift.

When I first heard it, I couldn't believe my ears. Bryson began making sounds we hadn't heard before. It almost seemed like he was trying to *say* something. Then it happened. It was just a few, barely intelligible words: Da (dad) and Ma (mom). But our tenacious, irrepressible little boy had *done* it. He had broken through.

It didn't matter that he struggled like a stuck butterfly, painstakingly attempting to free itself from a cocoon that was too tight. It didn't matter that his lips barely cooperated nor that he drooled profusely as he strained to offer each sound. And it certainly didn't matter that each syllable was slurred and barely intelligible. None of these things mattered, not at all! But I'll tell you what did matter. Those beautiful sounds were coming from our son's lips, not from some machine.

And I can tell you that the sound was the most breathtaking music I had ever heard, or expect to hear, ever again. It was like the voice of God, telling us not to despair but to keep trusting, to keep walking along the path He had now made available to us.

Despite the skeptics, our appointment with the NACD on April 12, 1989, was now riveted in my mind. I thought of it every day, almost every hour, for the next three months. Balloons that offer hope do burst. I understood that. But the dreadful agony of silence had been lifted from our son, and from our shoulders, forever. It was time to invest heavily in balloons once again. We had just heard the sound of a miracle.

> How blessed are the people who know the joyful sound! O LORD, they walk in the light of Your countenance.
>
> —PSALM 89:15

Chapter 10
FOOLISH THINGS

But God has chosen the foolish things of the world to shame the wise, and God has chosen the weak things of the world to shame the things which are strong... so that no man may boast before God.

1 CORINTHIANS 1:27, 29

SURVIVAL OF THE WISEST?

A PRIVATE JET CARRIED four passengers: the richest man on earth, a biochemist reputed to have the world's greatest intellect, an old priest, and a lowly drifter. The pilot's shrill voice suddenly came from the loudspeaker with shocking news: "This plane is leaking fuel and we are going to crash in five minutes! We have only three parachutes for the four of you. You must decide which one of you will not survive!"

The wealthy man jumped up and said, "I must survive or the world will never see new versions of the vital technology I've created." He grabbed a parachute and leaped from the plane.

The biochemist then rose, cleared his throat, and declared, "I am the wisest man on earth. My intellect is superior to every other being on the planet, and my research is crucial to the advancement of mankind." He too, strapped on a pack, and dove out.

With a calm smile, the elderly priest turned to the drifter and said: "Go ahead, son. I'm an old man and I've had a good life. Take the last parachute. Save *yourself*."

With a smirk the drifter replied, "Don't worry, Father, there are still two parachutes left. The smartest man on earth just jumped out of the plane with my knapsack."

A FOOLISH PLACE

To anyone who didn't know of my son's personal war to break free from his brain-injured prison, his speech sounded like piteous garble, as he strained to offer each one syllable word. To us, the sounds were breathtaking; and the fact that he was speaking at all made us all the more resolved to never again settle for meager predictions.

As in the case of a child anticipating Christmas, our three-month wait for his evaluation by The National Association of Child Development (NACD) seemed unbearable. *Finally* the day arrived; and as we drove to the NACD's New York branch in April 1989, I felt the tingling of pre-game sensations I hadn't felt since my days quarterbacking my high school and college football teams. Those of you who have been involved in competitive sports know the feeling. You sit in the locker room awaiting the coach's command to run out onto the field. The clock moves at glacial speed, and the butterflies in your stomach remind you that you are about to engage in a battle that is more important than anything else on the planet. As we arrived at our destination, it was game time.

During the previous three years we had been to some of the most renowned medical institutions in the world. *None* of them offered us hope for more than a meager future for our son. Still, there was something comforting about those huge edifices. The enormity of those complexes that made me feel as if we were giving our son his best shot, the very best mankind could offer. They were staffed by esteemed professionals, and they featured the most advanced technologies on earth. The "New York" branch of NACD wasn't even in New York, but in Mountain Lakes, New Jersey. As we arrived I was struck by the stark difference between this place and all those distinguished institutions. Frankly, it was a bit disconcerting arriving in the parking lot of St. Peter's Episcopal Church where the NACD rented space for its quarterly evaluations.

Was it possible to find hope for our son in a foolish place like *this*, hope that all those prominent institutions failed to provide? As I picked Bryson up out of the car, I thought I heard the hissing of air seeping out, just a bit, from yet another balloon. I fought back the negativity, remembering Barbara Frey's hopeful words. She had mentioned the resiliency of the brain, using words like *intensity*, *repetition*, and *duration*. As I carried my son into the fellowship hall of the church, serving as NACD's reception area, I silently prayed, "Oh Lord, we can't afford to have our hopes dashed again. We just *can't!*"

We were put at ease by a smiling Barbara Frey, director of the local branch. The facility was staffed predominantly by volunteers, most of whom had brain-injured children of their own. We had already mailed in exhaustive developmental history forms, including Bryson's voluminous medical files from all those other institutions. Upon arrival, we were asked to fill out additional forms, detailing Bryson's most recent developmental progress. These were brought to Bob Doman's office as we waited. My stomach was churning. "Coach, let us out on the field!" In about ten minutes, we were ushered into his office. I don't think I could've waited another *minute*.

But I'm going to ask you to wait just a bit longer, before I tell you what happened in that office. First, I need to speak to you about something rather foolish.

God's Surprising Foolishness

As we struggled through the battles of raising a brain-injured child, the Lord was reshaping my thinking, teaching me that the things that pass for wisdom in this world are radically different than His wisdom. He often delighted me with treasures I had missed for so long in my Christian walk. But I have to admit, God's ways often seemed downright foolish compared to my deeply ingrained ways. God had begun teaching me what it *really* means to "lean not" on my own understanding, but in my utter weakness to rely upon Christ alone (Prov. 3:5–6; 2 Cor. 1:8–9).

Pulling ourselves up by our bootstraps is a revered human value, particularly in America. So revered, in fact, we attempt to import this ethic into our Christian walk. But relying on our own resources, intellect, and willpower in the spiritual realm is tantamount to being on the wrong road, headed in the wrong direction. God loves us enough to use painful trials to teach us how inadequate and sinful our self-reliant resources truly are. God paid a monumental price to bring us from spiritual death into life in Christ Jesus. He did this knowing that our new life in Christ was everything we would ever need in this dark world, and all we would need to live in fellowship with Him for eternity. Because He is a good Father, He is determined to break us from reliance upon *anything* other than Christ.

Ben Patterson illustrates the nonnegotiable severity of God's requirement to trust in Him alone by reminding us of the way He tested Abraham. Abraham was asked to sacrifice something he cherished, his precious son Isaac (Gen. 22:2). This was not because God is cruel. It is because God's love cannot help but to move us toward the best He can give us:

> It is not that God is a sadist who likes to dangle us over the abyss. He isn't a bully who wants to cow us into submission by constantly holding over us the possibility that he may one day take from us the things and people we most dearly love. It is just that none of the things we love are worthy of our complete trust. One day, in death, everything will be taken away from us: spouse, children, home, health, car, career—everything. Then all we will have will be God and his promise. But that is all we ever have. Our trust should never be in what God gives us, but in the God who gives. That is why Moses prayed, "Teach us to number our days aright, that we may gain a heart of wisdom" (Psalm 90:12). God asks what he asks of Abraham, and all of us, mercifully. He desires not to tear from us our loves, but to push us back to our life—Him.[1]

After Adam and Eve's rebellion, their attempt to "be like God" (Gen. 3:5), Cain followed *right* in his parents' footsteps. God had no regard for the hard work and sweat represented by Cain's self-sufficient offering. But God did have regard for Abel's offering. Why? Because God will only accept *His* work, *His* best, *His* sacrifice for us; He will never exalt ours. God provided the perfect lamb for Abel's sacrifice, and He intended that sacrifice to be offered *exactly* as provided, without the embellishments of those, like Cain, who would substitute human effort in the place of God's perfect sacrifice.

God knows our sinful nature, and He understands the deepest motives of our hearts. He knows we will inexorably move away from Christ, the spotless Lamb, and attempt to substitute our own religious efforts and sweat as our sacrifice to Him in Christ's stead. Then, like Cain, we will expect more merit from God, and we will arrogantly expect Him to exalt us higher than our brothers and sisters. From a human standpoint, Cain's sacrifice seems far better because he worked *harder* at it. But only Abel was found to be the obedient son. Why? Because he was willing to simply *receive* the sacrifice God had provided, without adding his own pretentious, arrogant, self-righteous works to it.

Do God's methods seem a bit foolish? You bet they do! But why should we be surprised? Pick any section of the Bible where God did something significant throughout human history and give it the "foolishness" test. God routed a mighty army through Gideon and his outnumbered troops by having them foolishly smash empty pitchers. He brought down the impenetrable walls of Jericho by having Joshua and his followers foolishly blow trumpets, after spending a foolish week marching foolishly around the city. Time after time God confounded and amazed His followers by making *certain* they recognized that His ways were vastly different than their own humanly-wise ways.

When you get right down to it, God chose to visit this world in a foolish manner. Born in a stable with animals? A poor carpenter? Brought to dishonor? No place to lay His head? God's own Son beaten and murdered by arrogant men? Can a story purported to be about the King of the universe *possibly* get more foolish? I doubt it. But what relevance does God's foolishness have for me, or for you, as we face our impossible battles and the troubles that threaten to destroy us here?

In order to successfully battle through the pain and grief involved in parenting a brain-injured, multiply handicapped child, my efforts couldn't be based on my puny resources any longer. I needed something *far* better and stronger than the sleep-deprived guy I saw shaving in the mirror each morning. If God couldn't prove Himself to be sufficient in my weakness, then frankly, my family was in big trouble (2 Cor. 12:9). But as I started stepping in the direction of God's counterintuitive, foolish wisdom, so many scriptures began to jump out at me concerning the biblical theme of *full* reliance upon God. I began to see scriptures I had known for many years in a brand-new light.

> "Not by might nor by power, but by My Spirit," says the LORD of hosts.
>
> —ZECHARIAH 4:6

> Trust in the LORD with all your heart, and do not lean on your own understanding, In all your ways acknowledge Him, And He will make your paths straight.
>
> —PROVERBS 3:5–6

> But Jesus, conscious that His disciples grumbled at this, said to them, "Does this cause you to stumble?...It is the Spirit who gives life; the flesh profits nothing."
>
> —JOHN 6:61, 63

> I am the vine, you are the branches; he who abides in Me and I in him, he bears much fruit, for apart from Me you can do nothing.
>
> —JOHN 15:5

> I can do all things through Christ who strengthens me.
>
> —PHILIPPIANS 4:13, NKJV

If you are facing a battle right now that appears absolutely impossible, and there are no solutions anywhere in sight, you need something far greater than this author can give you, far greater than *any* book can give you. You need Jesus Christ. Your life might be an absolute train wreck. He is still God's only answer to every human problem, and no problem poses even the slightest challenge to His power. I pray that God will use the story that is unfolding in this book to open your eyes to the reality of who Jesus Christ really is, and to cause you to trust in Him *alone*. Does that sound foolish? I suppose so. But God's Word does not apologize for God's foolishness, nor will I.

Before I continue on with my story, I want to say something to those of you who have never trusted Christ as your Savior. Maybe your heart leaps a little as you read this story, particularly when I tell you that Jesus can help you to deal with your broken dreams and guide you in your impossible battles. Maybe you'd like to know Him the way I am suggesting it is possible to know Him, but you fear it's too late for you. You've made *far* too many mistakes in your life, and there's no way you can fix them now. There's no use kidding yourself, you don't fit the religious mold. Honestly, you never have. You'd never be able to clean up your act and make yourself acceptable enough for God, and you know it. You've got far too much history, and you've messed things up *way* too badly.

Besides, your life is *so* hard right now. The last thing you have time for is becoming "religious." You suspect that turning to God will mean He'll require you to jump through countless religious hoops, and this will make your life that much harder. No, now is not the time to think about becoming religious. Now is the time to survive. You've already failed at so much in life. You may as well be honest with yourself and forget all this Jesus stuff, and avoid failing at religion on top of everything else you've botched in life.

If what I've just said in the above paragraphs mirrors some of your thoughts as a nonbeliever, then I have some pretty foolish but *excellent* news for you. The fact that you recognize that you're *not* good enough, that you *don't* have what it takes, indicates that you are already very close to the kingdom of God. *No one* who has ever lived, save Jesus Christ, was good enough either. One of the clearest descriptions of the gospel message I've ever heard came from Phillip Yancey's book *Disappointment with God*, as he quotes from Will Campbell's *Brother to a Dragonfly*.

> We're all bastards, but God loves us anyway.[2]

That pretty much nails it! It may be hard for you to believe, but in God's eyes you are in no lesser position than all the other bastards, including the most religious person you've ever met. *Every* person on this earth is a dreadful, ugly sinner who, without Christ, is worthy *only* of hell. What's more, any effort that anyone makes to prove themselves good enough to be saved without Christ is like a filthy rag in His sight. He doesn't want our efforts to be good. He wants our humble admission that we are *not* good.

God *knows* your life is hard. He is *not* seeking to add "religion" to the already heavy burden you are carrying. The good news of the gospel is that God *loves* sinners. He loves you *already*, right now, far more than you can possibly understand. He has loved you since before the day you were born, and He has loved you every day since. He is ready to forgive you for every sinful thing you have ever done and accept you completely, *just* the way you are, even with your history of past failures.

Pompous religion be damned! False religion is more foolish to God than it is to you; and frankly, arrogance and phony religion made Jesus furious as He walked the earth. He longs to give you something *far* better than religion. Any attempt to clean yourself up to be worthy and presentable before coming to Him will only mess things up more. The truth is that you will *never* be good enough, and you don't have to be.

God is opposed to the proud but gives grace to the humble (James 4:6). He *hates* the pretentiousness of those who *think* they are good enough, and He exalts those who know they aren't. The Physician can only heal those who are sick, not those who think they are well. If you are ashamed that your life is a total mess, then you are finally getting somewhere in God's foolish economy. The forgiveness and salvation He holds out to you is *not* based on any efforts that you can ever achieve. He holds forgiveness and eternal life out to you as a gift, through the provision of the spotless Lamb who died for you, His Son, Jesus Christ.

The gifts of the forgiveness for your sins and of eternal life, is *completely* free to you. God asks *only* that you *receive* His awesome gift, and respond. You respond by telling Him that you know you don't have what it takes to clean up your act, but that you are grateful for Christ's loving sacrifice on the cross which makes this gift free to you. You determine in your heart to turn from your selfishness and sin and to allow Jesus Christ to take over your life from this point forward. His Spirit will come to live inside of you, and for the first time in your life you will become fully alive and fully free to be the man or woman He created you to be. And with regard to all of your insurmountable problems, remember that God runs a universe. Your problems are *no* challenge whatsoever to the power of Jesus Christ. Hand your problems, and yourself, over into His good hands.

But maybe you are already a believer in Christ as you read this story, yet you've still come to the point of extreme disappointment in life. You've tried so hard to follow Christ; but frankly, God hasn't exactly gone out of His way to keep your cherished dreams from shattering. You were once excited about the Lord, but now your life has become so complicated and so hard that being a "good" Christian doesn't exactly rank at the top of your list anymore. You're discouraged in your faith, disappointed in yourself, and you're pretty sure God must be disappointed in you too. There's not a whole lot you can do about it anymore. You're just trying to survive the latest storm. Being a "better" Christian will have to wait until the pressure is off, *if* that day ever comes.

Sadly, this is the experience of countless Christians, even as it was for me. For many years as a Christian I missed the *central* point of the Christian walk as I traveled from storm to storm. Finally, when the big storm hit and my son's life was decimated before my eyes, God began to open my spiritual eyes to see that my self-sufficiency needed to be laid aside. As I was gasping for air, I needed something far different, something foolish. I needed to rely totally and completely on the sufficiency of Jesus Christ.

My mistake was that I allowed God's grace to do only half the job God had intended. I allowed Christ to save me and forgive me of my sins; but from that point onward I was going to live out my Christian life from the resources of my own willpower, wisdom, and strength. Like Cain, I insisted on adding my own sweat and efforts to the process. My deeply ingrained desire to control my own life, to the exclusion of Christ, caused me to miss out on the vast riches God freely provides in Christ to live in this world.

God does not ask us to place our faith in the perfect sacrifice of Christ for our initial salvation only, and then ask us to live for Him in the power of our flesh. Jesus Christ is our wisdom, our righteousness, our *sanctification*, and our redemption (1 Cor. 1:30). He is the Alpha and the Omega, the beginning and the end (Rev. 1:8). Jesus is the *whole* nine yards. The world was created by Him and for Him, and in Him all things hold together (Col. 1:16–17). Certainly, our salvation holds together *only* in Him. Any part of our salvation that we attempt to live out apart from Him is doomed to fall apart and fail.

Charles Trumbull was a teacher at Moody Institute and editor of *The Sunday School Times* during the first half of the twentieth century. There weren't endless Christian radio and television programs, blogs, and websites in those days. *The Sunday School Times* was one of *the* publications in the Christian world. In his book *Victory in Christ*, Trumbull admits that he had fallen into an error over a period of *decades* as a national Christian leader. His mistake is similar to the mistake that many Christians continue to make today.

> Jesus makes two offers to everyone.... Every Christian has accepted the first offer. Many Christians have not accepted the second.... They mistakenly think, as I did... that their efforts, their will, their determination, strengthened and helped by the power of Christ, is the way to victory. And as long as they mistakenly believe this they are doomed to defeat.... While all true Christians know that they can have their justification only by faith, most of us have been brought up to believe that "for sanctification," we must paddle our own canoe. And that is why so many justified Christians are so pathetically, miserably disappointed in the matter of a satisfying, personal experience of sanctification, or walking "in the newness of life."... Jesus Christ does not want to be our helper; He wants to be our life. He does not want us to work for Him. He wants us to let Him do His work through us.[3]

Andrew Murray spoke in similar terms about the cause of failure in the Christian life. God requires us to grow in our Christian life through faith in

Christ alone. Our efforts are the cause of our failure because they focus us on ourselves, and not on Him.

> Could they but understand that their very efforts are the cause of their failure—because it is God alone who can establish us in Christ Jesus—they would see that, just as in justification they had to cease from their own working and to accept by faith the promise that God would give them life in Christ, so now in the matter or their sanctification, their first need is to cease from striving themselves to establish the connection with Christ more firmly and allow God to do it.[4]

Teachings like these from Trumbull and Murray helped to reinforce what I was seeing everywhere in Scripture now. As I found myself below life's waterline as the head of a desperately hurting family, I could not afford to have a faith fraught with miserable futility. I needed a faith grounded on the grace and power of Jesus Christ. So do you, dear reader, especially if your life is full of the grief and pain of an impossible situation.

Hannah Whitall Smith came to cling to Christ as her sufficiency as she suffered years of intense sorrow. When a saint's life is tested in the furnace of affliction, self-sufficiency simply doesn't cut it. Only a faith grounded in Christ from start to finish can withstand the heat. This is how Hannah describes authentic faith that looks to Christ alone:

> You have trusted Him as your dying Savior; now trust Him as your living Savior.... He has come to live your life for you. You are as utterly powerless in the one case as in the other. You could as easily have got rid of your own sins, as you could now accomplish for yourself practical righteousness. Christ, and Christ only, must do both for you; and your part in both cases is simply to give the thing to Him to do, and then believe that He does it.[5]

TRULY FOOLISH

I realize that all this talk about the grace of Christ may sound not only to be foolish, but threatening to some who fear that this may cause believers to become lazy and uncaring in their work for the Lord. But embracing the foolishness of the gospel sets us free to get out of God's way and allow Christ to do greater works in and through our lives than we can ever accomplish on our own. Listen to the incredulous apostle Paul as he sets the record straight about what is *truly* foolish as we seek to serve the Lord:

> You foolish Galatians! Who has bewitched you? Before your very eyes Jesus Christ was clearly portrayed as crucified. I would like to learn just one thing from you: Did you receive the Spirit by observing the law, or by believing what you heard? Are you so foolish? After beginning with the Spirit, are you now trying to attain your goal by human effort?
>
> —GALATIANS 3:1–3, NIV

There's not a person who's ever been saved by his efforts to make himself sinless enough to be acceptable to God. And there's not a person who's ever grown in love and service for God by the sweat of his efforts to do so. In the same manner that he addressed the church in Galatia, Paul's letter to the Colossians addresses the issue of living the Christian life, making it clear that this is to be done in a radically different manner than the principles of the world. *Just* as we received Christ for our initial salvation, we are to continue to walk in Him.

> Therefore, as you have received Christ Jesus as Lord, so walk in Him, having been firmly rooted and now being built up in Him and established in your faith, just as you were instructed....See to it that no one takes you captive through philosophy and empty deception, according to the tradition of men, according to the elementary principles of the world, rather than according to Christ.
>
> —Colossians 2:6–8

It's easy for us to read these passages and look disparagingly upon the foolishness of those early Christians who were so easily taken "captive" away from their faith. But is it possible that we have integrated the "traditions of men" and the "elementary principles of the world" into our own walk with the Lord? Have we largely become a Christian culture that holds to a form of godliness (2 Tim. 3:5) while denying the power of Christ?

Charles Trumbull was asked to reveal the most dangerous heresy of his day. After naming several common heresies, he zeroed in on the heresy he considered most dangerous. If he was still alive, I believe he'd put his finger on this very same heresy:

> Any one of these things is dangerous enough. But none of these, I believe, is the most dangerous heresy of today. For the most dangerous is the emphasis that is being given, right in the professing Christian church itself, on *what we do for God*, instead of on *what God does for us*....Oh, I hope God will make that very plain to us!...The subtle, almost all-pervading presence of that thing: the emphasis in the church, and in Christian organizations, on what we do for God as the great thing, as the most important thing; instead of just the opposite—the emphasis as we ought to place it, on what God does for us.[6] (emphasis added)

As for me, I already had too many impossible battles taking place in my life. My attempt to live the Christian life could no longer be an impossible battle too. I could no longer follow "elementary principles" that were robbing me of the riches and power found only in the grace of Jesus Christ. I needed to embrace something far more foolish. I needed to allow Christ to do what His Word *promises* He would do in my life. These many years later, there is still much work remaining for Him to do in me; but I can rest now, knowing that He is the One who is able to do it.

> For I am confident of this very thing, that He who began a good work in you will perfect it until the day of Christ Jesus.
>
> —PHILIPPIANS 1:6

INVALUABLY FOOLISH

With a comforting smile Bob Doman got up from behind his desk, greeting us warmly. Once again, I was struck by the difference between this place and the prestigious hospitals where we had previously sought hope. Bob didn't wear a white coat, and he sported a pair of cowboy boots. He asked us to take off Bryson's clothes, leaving his diaper on, and have him sit on his mother's lap in a chair, so that he could observe him. Sitting on her lap was necessary, not only to keep Bryson calm, but because he still did not have the balance to sit independently without slumping over and falling to the floor.

The examination itself did not appear different from the ones performed by numerous neurologists. Bob examined him from head to toe, looking deeply into Bryson's eyes with a penlight. He examined his joints and reflexes with various medical tools. He spoke with Bryson as he examined him, asking him many questions, to which Bryson offered a few one-syllable answers and some drool. He then asked us to place Bryson on the rug so that he could watch him as he crawled across the room to an awaiting toy. As Bryson awkwardly crawled toward the toy, one of his arms immediately gave way and he fell face-first into the rug, continuing to roll completely onto his back. He tenaciously righted himself, and continued undaunted to the toy.

Bob then observed Bryson as he "walked," with his hands held overhead, firmly clasped in mine. His crippled legs were rubbery and loose, and all of the effort was mine as I literally pulled him across the room. He was able to perform something akin to a walking motion, but each leg "scissored" in front of the other. Interestingly, each foot slammed awkwardly into the ground, almost as if he could not perceive where the floor was. Bob then asked us to get Bryson dressed and join him at his desk to discuss his condition. This was the moment we had so anxiously awaited. I felt like I could hardly breath as I waited to hear what Bob was going to say about our son's future.

After reviewing Bryson's exhaustive medical records, his developmental history, and observing him as he attempted to perform several developmental functions, Bob told us that he now had a good understanding of Bryson's condition. What he said next, as we sat nervously in front of his desk, wasn't particularly comforting. He told us that Bryson was indeed severely brain injured, even as we had been told at all the other places. Damage had occurred in *every* area of his brain, including his motor controls, his audio and visual pathways, his speech centers, his frontal lobe which controls the emotions, and in his upper cortex where information is processed and higher learning occurs.

My eyes welled with tears as Bob told us he could offer no miracle for Bryson. But then he began teaching us about the "neuroplasticity" of the brain. He told us that many doctors of that day (1989) still treated brain injuries as if they were irreversible. Many conventional doctors still incorrectly presumed that injured tissue in the brain could never be replaced, and that new passageways could not be opened. He told us that based on the research that the NACD was founded upon (and had followed since the 1950s) the brain was *a great deal* more resilient than was widely believed.

He told us he had little use for labels, such as "cerebral palsy," "multiply handicapped," or "autistic," since these were merely descriptive of various types of symptoms. The purpose of the NACD was to help brain-injured children to sequentially achieve higher levels of function in each developmental area. He told us that most people develop only a small percentage of their brain's capacity. The NACD was going to provide us with the tools necessary to methodically "recircuit" Bryson's brain around the damaged lesions through stimulation that would actually create new, healthy tissue. Bryson's advancement would be achieved by systematically delivering vast quantities of appropriate input and stimuli to "teach" his brain to achieve higher levels of function.

He told us it was of no value to ask Bryson to provide us with "output" or function that his damaged brain couldn't generate. We were going to retrain his brain from the outside in, through appropriate *input*. This input would be delivered with extraordinary levels of *repetition* and *intensity*, over a long period of time (*duration*). Methodically and gradually, greater levels of output and function would come. His brain would be retrained, or recircuited, to perform those higher functions.

Bob went on to describe some of the intricacies of cellular growth in the brain, using words such as synapses and dendrites and other terms, which, frankly, went over my head. My wife had been a pre-med major, and she caught quite a bit more from that part of the discussion. I had something very simple on my mind, and I could hardly wait to ask it. Sounding as intelligent as I could (which isn't so great) I asked if the output ultimately coming from his brain would result in the "higher level of function" known as *walking*.

I knew he heard my question, but Bob didn't answer. Instead, after a long pause he reached across the desk, grabbed my arm, and began to squeeze. I mean *hard*! Bob is a fairly large man and he had a powerful grip. As he continued to squeeze, I began to feel pain. Just when all the intriguing things Bob had said were beginning to make sense, just when I was beginning to think we were receiving a reason for hope in this foolish place, Bryson's evaluation had taken a radical turn toward utter foolishness; and I mean *weird*. Finally, Bob let go, and he sat back in his chair looking at me.

"Mr. Milazzo, how did that feel?" I rubbed my arm, now being careful to keep one eye on him. Finally, I replied that it had hurt. "Well, Mr. Milazzo, just a few minutes ago during his examination I squeezed your son's leg *just* as hard, and he didn't even look up at me." My wife and I looked at each other, intrigued, then listened intently as Bob continued.

"Bryson's legs are no longer able to feel deep pressure sensation. His brain has been injured to such a degree that his neurological system no longer recognizes the signals being sent back and forth between his legs and his brain. His lack of deep pressure sensation is similar to the lack of sensation that you and I experience when our feet fall asleep. By the way," he continued, "one of the reasons Bryson has such difficulty speaking is due to the *same* condition.

"In addition to the fact that the speech processing centers in his brain have been damaged, his lips and tongue are essentially asleep. He cannot feel them. Imagine if you attempted to speak with a sleeping tongue and lips, such as when you have had Novocain at the dentist's office. The absence of feeling in Bryson's mouth is much more profound than that. The deep pressure sensation in his mouth, his limbs, and throughout his entire body will need to be reawakened, so that his brain can communicate with each part."

He then returned to the issue of walking, telling us that walking is a very complex neurological function, involving the sending and receiving of messages between the brain and various parts of the body. It requires visual input to the brain through the eyes, and communication between the brain and the balance center in the middle ear. Each of these systems had been significantly impaired in Bryson's brain.

Bryson's ability to perceive the location of his various body parts within a room spatially (called "proprioception") had been extremely damaged. This, coupled with the absence of deep feeling sensation, was the reason his feet kept awkwardly slamming into the floor when I walked him across the room. His brain simply did not know where his "sleeping" feet were, nor did he know where the floor was due to his damaged visual-spatial perception. In fact, his brain didn't have the slightest idea where any of his body parts were in relation to the objects around him. His entire system was disoriented.

He then told us that, due to the extent of his brain injury, he was not surprised that the other professionals thought that walking would be impossible for our son. Nonetheless, the NACD would establish walking as one of Bryson's long-term goals. He told us he could not guarantee it, and he made it clear that if this goal were to be achieved one day, it would need to be attempted from this point forward by remediating the *cause* of the problem in his central nervous system, not by attempting to alleviate the symptoms.

Bob informed us that it was useless to work only on his muscles and skeletal structure with conventional therapies and braces, since his muscles and bones were as healthy as the day he was born. The only thing that had been altered was his brain's ability to receive, process, and send organized neurological information back out to his body. Even his "central hypotonia" (loose muscle tone throughout his body) was a neurological issue, not a physical one. He repeated that working on the symptoms instead of the cause of our son's problems would be of little value. His brain was injured, not his body. Bob addressed many other concerns for which we had never received reasonable answers.

Some of the discussion regarding the extensive damage to our son's brain was difficult to take. A parent never gets used to rehashing the tragic realities concerning a child. At the same time Bob's message was laced with hope, and we rejoiced in the fact that at long last, there was something meaningful we could do to improve our son's life.

We had been to some of the most respected medical institutions the world had to offer. Now, at long last, we were *finally* being given a reason to hope, and a fighting chance, in a church basement. Oh, how wonderfully, invaluably foolish.

One of the Most Foolish Mistakes in Life

Bob would not allow us to leave until he was certain we understood the commitment we would have to undertake to truly help our son. He informed us that what we had been doing for him thus far was "not even an opportunity" for Bryson to improve significantly. His brain required *enormous* amounts of input and stimuli to reach higher levels of function in his mobility, language, manual competence, auditory and visual function, and tactility. He was going to provide us with a program to be delivered to our son under which his brain would receive input specifically designed to improve his function in each of those developmental areas.

To reinforce his point regarding the demands of the program, Bob used the analogy of a fledgling pianist who desires to play at Carnegie Hall one day. This type of mastery requires thousands upon thousands of repetitious hours of intense work over a period of many years. But once mastery is accomplished, the pianist can sit and play almost as effortlessly as he is able to breathe. Yet it's not his hands or fingers that have learned to play. His brain has been trained to perform through those fingers.

Bob also used the example of an Olympic gymnast. The repetition, intensity, and duration required to train an athlete's body to perform at so dramatic a level would be the same kind of effort Bryson would need to exert to perform the feat of walking, speaking with fluency, processing information, and performing many other basic functions in life. Bob emphasized that our work on his behalf would be more difficult than we could imagine.

A master pianist! An Olympic gymnast! After all our crushing disappointments, I was *so* excited now that I shrugged Bob's warning off. We were great parents, and I was sure we had what it took to handle this program of recircuiting our son's brain. I *knew* that through our commitment, willpower, sweat, and sacrifice we could do *whatever* was necessary to bring our precious son back to us. I just couldn't *wait* to start.

Being too sure of yourself is one of the most foolish mistakes you can ever make. Neither my wife nor I had *any* comprehension of the anguish, the exasperation, the abject failure, and disillusionment that loomed, just ahead.

Chapter 11
THE WINGS OF THE WIND

He rode upon a cherub and flew; and He sped upon the wings of the wind.
Psalm 18:10

I cringe when I think what my son's life would have been like had we placed him in an institution. As mentioned, much had been stolen from him, but the Lord had left much behind as well. His personality was *1,000* percent intact. The little smirk on his face made this clear. Unable to walk, my now four-year-old son would crawl from one family member to another trying to stir something up. He'd steal Timmy's (now eighteen months old) pacifier, snatch one of his sister's dolls, or giggle as he latched onto her hair (boy did she *love* that). I loved every minute of our family interactions that brought us back to some semblance of "normal," even chaos and fighting among siblings.

In a world which scoffs at God's gender specific design, Bryson was *all* boy. His fondest activity was playing with little trucks and cars, and I began to bring them home to him regularly. He'd sit for hours pushing them back and forth. He wasn't able to hold onto them easily, since the motor control governing his hands was poor. He often seemed far away, staring with an absent gaze for long periods. But when you came to engage him with play, he tuned in immediately. He fought hard to latch onto one of his treasures, displaying a broad smile as he held up a favorite vehicle for you to see.

Baby Timmy had long ago advanced far beyond Bryson's levels of function, having begun walking at eight months old. We rejoiced over Tim's abilities, but our joy was tempered by the fact that Bryson could not take his rightful place in leading the way for his little brother. Since he could only crawl, the entire family spent a lot of time on the ground crawling with him. Hide-and-seek throughout the house on your knees is an interesting experience. I often took all three of our kids on tours through the house on my shoulders. Bryson absolutely loved this. If we were walking through the neighborhood as a family, Bryson was always up there. It was as if he was walking too.

His speech remained arduous and primitive, yet he had now developed a few more words. As I carried him into church on Sunday mornings, he'd greet everyone (and I mean *everyone*) *with* a salutation of "Pa Pa" (my father was known to my children as "Pop Pop," which he could not pronounce). He knew it was Sunday, and he wanted everyone to know that it was his day to go to Pop Pop's house. He knew that Pop Pop would have a special plate of macaroni and meatballs waiting for him, and that he would pick him up and march him around the house with him in one arm, with a look on his face that made it clear that he was

Pop Pop's pride and joy. He also knew that his cousins and siblings, all nine of them ranging from nine to one in age, would be raring to play.

Family events were among the few places in his life where he was totally accepted and loved, one of the few places where he would not be stared at and laughed at by other children for crawling instead of walking and for uttering barely intelligible sounds. He fought so hard to break through his debilitating limitations in order to be just like all the others. If his cousins were doing something, he insisted on doing it too. He tirelessly raced after them on his hands and knees as they ran through the house.

His passion to be just like others was an enormous asset. This would later propel him to break through his limitations to levels of function that few professionals thought was possible. This passion would also prove to be a double-edged sword, piercing him with loneliness all his life, as the higher development of his peers brought them to places he could no longer go. But on those wonderful early Sundays of his life his irrepressible desire to connect with the others kept his mom and me on the move as he attempted to pull himself upright onto furniture to be "eye to eye" with his cousins. He'd often fall and hurt himself, so one of us had to be with him *constantly* for his protection and to wipe away the tears. Sundays were no day of rest. We were always on guard, always on edge.

Another place where Bryson was loved and accepted was in my in-law's home, which was a much quieter place than "Pop Pop's." "Gramps" sat in front of the fire with Bryson on his lap, and together they would throw wood onto the fire, which Gramps had chopped himself. Gramps would always make Bryson think that it was his own strength that heaved the wood into the fire, placing Bryson's uncoordinated little hands on the logs as they were thrown. "'ood" (wood) became one of the first words in Bryson's vocabulary, which he repeated incessantly while he was at Gramps' house.

We tried hard to find places Bryson could fit in beyond our extended families, but this often proved to be an enormous challenge. People with busy lives and families of their own just didn't know what to do with a brain-injured, crippled child who could barely speak. It wasn't their fault. Our son was a square peg in a world of round holes.

With significant anxiety, I carried my four-year-old son to the toddler's class at Grace Church in Ridgewood one Sunday morning to see if it might be possible to integrate him into this setting. It seemed wise to try to fit him in with children who were younger, but I was fully prepared to understand if they were unable to deal with my son. They had numerous "normal" children under their care. As I stood at the door stammering to describe Bryson's difficulties, the teacher, Donna Rourke, cut me short. Her eyes had already seen what I was tripping over myself to say. She did not care how extensive Bryson's problems were. She simply held out her arms for him with a compassionate smile. She and Robyn VanYperen, who had also come to the doorway smiling broadly, warmly and joyfully accepted my son. I told them I could stay to help, but they insisted that I go to the church service and relax, assuring me that Bryson would be just fine.

They probably didn't notice my tears as I turned away quickly, but the lump in my throat was pretty thick. I found it hard to believe, even in church, that people could be so good. From that point on, Bryson became an accepted and loved member in another place beyond family, crawling around, playing with others, and enjoying cookies and juice. Best of all, he was being taught stories about his King, the One who loved him more than he could possibly know. Through the sacrifice of these wonderful servants Donna and Robyn, *this* big kid, Bryson's dad, was learning something about the King's love too.

PREPARING FOR BATTLE

As I write these words in 2012, it is well known that the human brain is a very resilient organ, and that new brain cells continue to be generated throughout one's lifetime. In 1989 the NACD's emphasis on improving function in the brain through the input of appropriate stimuli with extreme "repetition, duration, and intensity" was ahead of its time. The NACD knew that, even as it would be a waste of time to enlist a team of body repair mechanics to fix a broken engine, conventional therapies designed only to improve muscular or skeletal function were of little value to our brain-injured son.

The NACD's repair strategy was tantamount to the repair of a computer with a damaged processing chip. We had to navigate around damaged lesions in his brain and reload a functional "operating system." With an injured brain, there is no "broadband" downloading of software. The process is infuriatingly slow, and only tiny bits of "data" can be "downloaded" (inputted) at a time. There are many exasperating "fatal errors" to be dealt with throughout the process since the processing chip (brain) has been damaged in terms of its ability to receive data. Computer analogies aside, the NACD trained us to deliver a program of appropriate stimulation and input to our son, with *endless* repetition and high intensity, over a very long duration of time. This was a daunting task; but it was Bryson's only hope for a meaningful recovery, and we were determined to do it.

Have you ever been called upon to fight a battle you instinctively knew was ridiculously beyond your ability? I think Joshua felt this way when God put him in charge of a task that even the revered Moses was unable to complete: to bring the Israelites into the Promised Land. Attempting to fill the shoes of Moses, through whom God parted the Red Sea, was a tall order indeed.

Evidently God knew that Joshua needed confidence for the task. Notice how many times in the following passage that God exhorted Joshua to be "strong and courageous." He was now in charge of this huge throng of people that had wandered in the wilderness for *forty* years. They had heard rumors of giants in the land, and you can bet Joshua had doubts and fears about moving them toward it. But notice also the specific *kind* of courage God commanded Joshua to take up.

It had *nothing* to do with Joshua's natural ability and strength. It had *everything* to do with God's promised provision and presence.

> Moses My servant is dead; now therefore arise, cross this Jordan, you and all this people, to the land which I am giving to them.... Every place on which the sole of your foot treads, I have given it to you.... No man will be able to stand before you all the days of your life. Just as I have been with Moses, I will be with you; I will not fail you or forsake you. *Be strong and courageous,* for you shall give this people possession of the land which I swore to their fathers to give them. Only *be strong and very courageous;* be careful to do according to all the law which Moses My servant commanded you; do not turn from it to the right or to the left, so that you may have success wherever you go... Have I not commanded you? *Be strong and courageous!* Do not tremble or be dismayed, *for the* Lord *your God is with you* wherever you go.
>
> —Joshua 1:2–3, 5–7, 9, emphasis added

Perhaps you are facing a mountain right now that you know you can't climb, or an "impossible" battle is looming squarely in front of you, and you're afraid to move forward. I can offer no simple formula for taking on that monumental challenge. Based on my experience, the battle God has set before you may turn out to be even *harder* than you now realize, even as Bryson's battle would prove to be for us. Now is not the time to deny the realities of war or to sugarcoat them. Now *is* the time to remember that when the battle proves to be too hard for you, it will *still* be no challenge for God.

When King Jehoshaphat was besieged and surrounded by several armies that had allied against him to invade his kingdom (Judah), he was so absurdly outnumbered that he realized his kingdom was doomed unless God stepped in. He gathered the leaders together and uttered a simple, yet powerful prayer:

> Our God, will You not judge them? For we are powerless before this great multitude who are coming against us; nor do we know what to do, but our eyes are on You.
>
> —2 Chronicles 20:12

This great scripture goes on to detail how God miraculously routed those "invincible" forces arrayed against Jehoshaphat, causing them to rise up against one another and slaughter each other. But what does this have to do with my impossible battles or with yours as you read this story? The Lord is the One who holds my unique battle plan, and yours, even as He held Jehoshaphat's. There are times when His battle plan will make sense to no one, not even to you. Our task is to keep our eyes on our King, to keep trusting Him as we wait for Him to reveal His plan. But waiting for Him to show up can be a problem if we think that He will arrive in a timely manner. God's timing is often preposterous, as any veteran of His wars will attest. Nonetheless, true faith and character is burned into the soul of a weary soldier, as he or she learns to wait for Him.

In the meantime, the enemy will throw every arrow of doubt, fear, and confusion in your direction. Count on it, and expect it. He will tell you lie after lie. That is what a liar does. His methods involve slipping in his deadly lies amidst insidious half-truths. He will tell you the task is too big, and he's definitely right about that. He will then tempt you to believe it is all up to you to win this impossible battle and that you are all alone as you attempt to do so. He is definitely lying to you about that. If his discouraging lies are flying fast and furious in your direction, perhaps the enemy realizes even more than you do the importance of the task God has set before you. Don't turn back. Keep at it.

For Joshua, the goal was clear: take the land for Israel. For us, victory represented bringing our son back from the prison of his brain injury to a life of full function and freedom. I will not reveal until later in the book whether or not we ultimately achieved that goal. Many times, though, I have misunderstood what true "victory" is in the battles God assigns. It seems that God places a higher value not on our preconceived notions of victory but on *why* and *how* we fight the battles He sets before us.

In Randall T. Wallace's epic feature film *Braveheart*, William Wallace (played by Mel Gibson) made a speech on horseback to a ragtag throng of Scottish soldiers, many of whom did not want to be on that battlefield at all. Intriguingly, Wallace didn't promise them victory over England's mighty army. He chose instead to reveal something that lay dormant and forgotten underneath layers of resignation and fear, deep within their hearts. It is a matter that also lays dormant in many hearts today. Wallace called on them to fight the battle set before them in the same manner that God called upon Joshua to fight his battles: with courage and valor. He knew that dying for the cause of freedom was far superior to living the half-dead existence of acquiescence to tyranny.

> Aye, fight and you may die. Run and you'll live, at least awhile. And dying in your beds, many years from now, would you be willing to trade all the days from this day till that for one chance, just one chance to come back here and tell our enemies that they may take our lives but they'll never take our freedom![1]

After three tortured years grieving the "loss" of our profoundly brain-damaged son, it sounded just too good to be true when Bob Doman informed us there was something we could actually *do* to bring him back. We were *finally* being given a key to his prison door, a shot at bringing our precious son back to life.

I knew in my heart that God was pointing us toward a battlefield on which the war for my son's life would be won or lost. Like that ragtag Scottish army, I was impassioned by the cause, and there could be no turning back. I would have died for my son if necessary. That would've been far better than seeing him languish in his hellish prison. But despite my desire to throw myself into this all-important war, we soon faced battles that were *so* fierce and *so* discouraging they made me want to lay down my weapons and die.

Quickly Overmatched

Reality struck quickly as we began the exhausting regimen Bob Doman prepared for us. The program of neurological input to stimulate Bryson's brain consisted of twenty activities to be delivered to him two to four times each day (depending on the activity), six days per week. This added up to more than fifty program activities to be performed periodically throughout each day. If you do the math, you'll understand that every day consisted of battle after endless battle. I'll describe only a few of the program activities in the ensuing chapters, as describing them all would be a book in itself.

Our lives immediately became consumed with the realities of repetition, intensity, and duration. Repetition is self-explanatory. The twenty activities had to be repeated several times each day. Duration is also a simple concept. Each activity had a specific duration, some only a few minutes, some longer. Intensity, as you might guess, meant that each activity had to be performed at the *maximum* level of energy and vigor possible, both by the one delivering the input (us), and the one receiving it (Bryson).

It's one thing for an aspiring Olympian or musician to decide they want something badly enough to push themselves through years of pain and sacrifice to reach their goal. But can you imagine asking even a healthy four-year-old to perform extremely demanding tasks which pushed him to his neurological, mental, and physical limits every day, all day long? Now try to imagine, if you can, asking a brain-injured four-year-old to perform in this way. Imagine that, before you even begin, he is already frustrated beyond description due to his extreme limitations. Imagine that the child is crippled, dizzy, disoriented, and essentially unable to communicate. Consider what it would be like to successfully deliver a program of more than fifty intense activities every single day to such a child.

Imagine what this child's disposition would quickly become. Imagine what would happen to your own life and schedule as the frustrated "patient" began taking up nearly all your waking focus, often lashing out at you in anger. Imagine the strain on your marriage as you reached levels of fatigue and frustration you never dreamed existed. Imagine what would happen to your other children. Imagine what would happen to every other pursuit of your life. I could go on, but you get the idea. Your life would be consumed with war.

The NACD suggested we read a book entitled *What to Do about Your Brain-Injured Child*. The book featured research done through an organization called the Institutes for the Advancement of Human Potential, out of Philadelphia. The Institutes are not associated with NACD, but their philosophy regarding the resiliency of an injured brain is similar. The book chronicled the case histories of several families who had success retraining their brain-injured children. I was struck by a quote from one father who described the anguish of delivering the exasperating regimen to his child:

> There is only one thing in the whole world worse than this damned program, and that is having a little girl whom you love who can't do what other kids do. I must say that the worst day on The Institutes' program is better than the best day we had before we began this lousy program.[2]

This father's experience reflected my sentiments precisely. Though the task was excruciating and nearly unbearable, quitting was inconceivable. Clearly, the program was wreaking havoc on our lives. But it was also beginning to bear fruit for our brain-injured son. The bottom line was that the prospect of failing to help our son to recover from his brain injury, to help him achieve some of the basic functions of life, was a fate far worse than losing our daily comfort. Like those Scottish soldiers, failing to give our best to this battle would have been a fate worse than death.

Thirteen years of organized football had taught me the necessity of going back to the drawing board on Monday after getting the daylights beaten out of me on Saturday, and I suppose that was good training. But the monumental amount of failure involved in working with a brain-injured child made those gridiron days seem like a day at the beach. No matter how hard we battled, we kept finding ourselves beaten down to the point where there was simply nothing left to give.

Yes, giving up would have been a fate worse than death; and I'd like to tell you I had what it took to summon new resources from within to battle on victoriously for my son. But way back in the introduction to this book I promised to be honest with you. The truth is that as I continued to get knocked down, I finally reached the point at which I was unable to get back up. I was beaten.

It was one thing for God to exhort Joshua to be "strong and courageous." But talk is cheap. We needed God to *do* something for us. I began to get angry with Him again. He responded by asking me to consider some of the war stories from His Word. The soldiers He directed me toward were not what I expected.

Models of Failure

The Lord mercifully led me to scriptures which, if nothing else, made me realize I was in good company. Several of His soldiers found themselves in situations which made them feel as if they couldn't *possibly* continue on in their God-assigned battles. Listen to the words of the prophet, who obviously knew the reality of being beaten down.

> Why do you say, O Jacob, and assert, O Israel, "My way is hidden from the Lord, And the justice due me escapes the notice of my God"? Do you not know? Have you not heard? The Everlasting God, the Lord, the Creator of the ends of the earth, Does not become weary or tired. His understanding is inscrutable. He gives strength to the weary, And to him who lacks might He increases power. Though youths grow weary and tired, And vigorous young men stumble badly, Yet those who wait for the Lord Will gain new

> strength; They will mount up with wings like eagles, They will run and not get tired, They will walk and not become weary.
>
> —Isaiah 40:27–31

I don't know about you, but I consider it a good thing this passage doesn't say that only those who are performing at a high level of proficiency with a good attitude can come to God for "new strength." If proper attitude *was* the requirement, it would have been a waste of my time to come to Him. Frankly, I didn't have the best attitude in those days. To be honest, I often felt like sulking and quitting. But since the only qualifications God cared to list in this passage met with my experience, namely stumbling badly and being weary and tired, I thought coming to Him was worth another shot.

As I "waited" on the Lord, He reminded me of several servants who didn't quite fit the description as "heroes" of the faith. Wimps maybe, but certainly not heroes. I was reminded about Abraham, the great "father" of faith. But was it not Abraham, in his cowardice, who attempted to give up his own wife (not once, but embarrassingly, *twice*) to kings he feared? Ben Patterson provides some perspective regarding the failures of Abram, including his outrageous betrayal of both God and his wife, for the *second* time.

> If we were making a film epic of Abram's life, we are no longer sure how we would cast him. Based on the first nine verses of Genesis, chapter 12, it would have been Charlton Heston. But now, who would it be? Pee Wee Herman, I think.... When we look at Abram we see a person who, like us, struggles with waiting, and who sometimes fails pathetically. It was a great triumph of faith for Abram to leave his home for a land that God would show him. It was a wretched failure for Abram to go down to Egypt in fear and attempt his tawdry little deception of Pharaoh. But triumph and failure always go together in the wait of faith. They are the head and tail of the same coin. Show me a person who has had no struggle with waiting, whose faith has known no swings between victory and defeat, and I'll show you a person who has never really trusted God with his or her life. To wait on God is to struggle and sometimes fail. Sometimes the failures teach us more that the successes. For the failures teach us that to wait on God is not only to wait for his mercy, but to wait by his mercy.[3]

I was reminded of the blunders of Peter, who pledged his unfailing allegiance to the Lord, declaring that even if *everyone* in the world abandoned Jesus, he never would. But where was Peter in Jesus' time of greatest need? He cowered like a frightened little kitten at the words of a lowly servant girl (Luke 22:56–57). Some allegiance!

I was reminded of the mighty prophet Elijah, who lost his nerve and ran for his life from Jezebel, *immediately* after God had just completed the most miraculous display of power of Elijah's entire life (see 1 Kings 18–19). You want to talk attitude? How's *this* for attitude? Elijah didn't want to go on living. He wanted to die rather than to continue on in battle:

> And he was afraid and arose and ran for his life....But he himself went a day's journey into the wilderness, and came and sat under a juniper tree; and he requested for himself that he might die, and said, "It is enough; now, O Lord, take my life, for I am not better than my fathers."
>
> —1 Kings 19:3–4

And of course, Elijah was right. He was, indeed, no better than those who came before him. Nor was he better than the bumbling, stumbling servants who would come after him, including you and me. He was just a frail human being like *every* servant God has ever chosen to perform His work in and through in this battleground world. The ones He chose for some of His mightiest works were consistent as much in their failures, foolishness, and cowardice as in their faithfulness. But as you follow the story of each servant, you'll realize that God was also consistent. He was consistent in showering His erratic servants not with the shame they deserved, but with vast quantities of mercy and grace that ultimately transformed them from wimps into warriors of the faith.

God has a long-term view, and many of those servants needed to be brought to the depths of humiliating, abject failure before they were ready for their assigned tasks. Oswald Chambers encourages us to persevere in hope when we are thwarted and disappointed, even by failure, knowing that God can use all the delays to purify our motives in His time, so that we will approach the battle in the spirit of perseverance that honors Him.

> If our hopes seem to be experiencing disappointment right now, it simply means that they are being purified. Every hope or dream of the human mind will be fulfilled if it is noble and of God. But one of the greatest stresses in life is the stress of waiting for God. He brings fulfillment, "because you have kept My command to persevere" (Revelation 3:10).[4]

How about you, dear reader? Do you think God has forgotten you? Is He woefully late in coming to your rescue? Legendary Yankee Yogi Berra put it this way: "It ain't over till it's over."[5] Far be it from me to correct Yogi. Yet in the context of our most difficult battles in this world I would only add: "It ain't over till *God* says it's over." The only thing that can defeat you is your refusal to believe, and the resulting decision to stay down after you've been knocked down. If we are going to rise again, we *must* persevere in *faith,* even when there is no logical or visible reason to believe, and even after we've suffered defeat after defeat. God is worthy of that trust, and He will reward it.

Although we were only at the beginning of the NACD journey, Bryson was showing signs of significant progress. Giving up on the program was obviously not an option, but pressing on with the demands of the regimen seemed absolutely impossible. It's hard to describe how discouraged we felt knowing that our physical and emotional resources were failing just when our brain-injured, crippled son needed us to persevere on his behalf. Like Jehoshaphat we had no idea what to do. But we knew our eyes had to remain on the great King. There was simply no other good alternative.

We also had to realize that trusting in God doesn't necessarily require continuing to do the same things that aren't working without changing them up. Sometimes God will speak wisdom to us that may seem as if He is asking us to turn back. In reality, He may simply be asking us to get to the destination via a new and different road, a road we may not have been ready or willing to take prior to the failures that drove us to our knees. In our case, the One who walks on the wings of the wind was about to define wisdom and power on His own inscrutable terms.

Bryson's Army

> The king is not saved by a mighty army; A warrior is not delivered by great strength. A horse is a false hope for victory; Nor does it deliver anyone by its great strength. Behold, the eye of the Lord is on those who fear Him, On those who hope for His lovingkindness, To deliver their soul from death And keep them alive in famine. Our soul waits for the Lord; He is our help and our shield. For our heart rejoices in Him, Because we trust in His holy name. Let Your lovingkindness, O Lord, be upon us, According as we have hoped in You.
>
> —Psalm 33:16–22

I called Barbara Frey at the NACD and discussed the fact that we were failing in our attempts to deliver a consistent program to Bryson. I told her that we were beginning to see some signs of life and growth from our globally brain-injured boy, but we knew that we could not continue to maintain any semblance of personal or family health while continuing to meet Bryson's therapeutic needs all day long, every day.

Barbara was a woman of courage who had been through the wars with her own extremely handicapped son. She not only knew the problem, but she was ready with a solution that she now knew we were ready to hear. She told us that there was no way, based on Bryson's vastly diverse needs (cognitive, speech, physical, etc.), that it was realistic for us to deliver the entire program to him alone. She advised us to solicit the help of volunteers. She even sent us samples of certificates the NACD had prepared to acknowledge the participation of those who had volunteered in the programs of other NACD children. The mere suggestion that there was a hopeful direction for us to proceed in encouraged us tremendously, and we began to pray about who the volunteers could be.

The previous year we had switched churches from a church which was thirty minutes away to Grace Church in Ridgewood, a little church that was only ten minutes from our home. We didn't realize it at the time, but by obeying the

VOLUNTEERS NEEDED

Four-year-old Glen Rock boy with cerebral palsy needs volunteers to provide home therapy to help him learn to walk and speak. Two hours per week for each volunteer. Parents will provide necessary training. Volunteers should be in able physical condition (Adults or high school age). Good experience for those considering physical therapy or working with the handicapped as a career.

Chapter 12
THE AWAKENING

I was asleep but my heart was awake. A voice! My beloved was knocking.
SONG OF SOLOMON 5:2

BRYSON'S BRAIN INJURY had placed him into a deep neurological "sleep" in terms of his ability to function in this world. Awakening his mind was precisely what our battle for his freedom was centered upon. But awaken his mind with what? Bryson's Army consisted of some of the finest people we'd ever met. They had awfully big hearts, but no professional training. "Global brain dysfunction" (just one of our son's myriad medical labels) denotes that lesions of irreparable damage have occurred to every region of the brain. His motor, speech, and intellectual impairments were considered permanent; and our battle to "awaken" our son was naïve and absurd to those in the know.

That was the impossible battle we were facing. What is yours? To be sure, your circumstances are different. But certain aspects of our God-assigned battles in this world are constant. When you are called to do something against the odds, and against the grain of conventional wisdom, there will be no lack of critics determined to discourage your efforts. But when the Lord calls you into battle, does it really matter that your goal is impossible in the eyes of men, or that your weapons seem foolish and weak? Did it matter to David that he faced Goliath with only a slingshot and a few stones (1 Sam. 17:40)? Did it matter that Gideon and his paltry 300 troops carried only pitchers and trumpets (Judg. 7:16)?

God sometimes calls on us to move forward in hope when our circumstances are anything but hopeful. In his excellent biographical book on the life of Jeremiah the prophet, *Run With the Horses*, Eugene Peterson challenges those faced with seemingly impossible circumstances to move forward in hope by taking tangible steps to follow God's leading, particularly when doing so is anything but "practical."

> All acts of hope expose themselves to ridicule because they seem impractical, failing to conform to visible reality. But in fact they are the reality that is being constructed but is not yet visible. Hope commits us to actions that connect with God's promises. What we call hoping is often only wishing. We want things we think are impossible, but we have better sense than to spend any money or commit our lives to them. Biblical hope though, is an act. Hope acts on the conviction that God will complete what He has begun even when the appearances, especially when the appearances, oppose it…
>
> It is, of course, far easier to languish in despair than to live in hope, for when we live in despair we don't have to do anything or risk anything. We can live lazily and shiftlessly with an untarnished reputation for practicality…
>
> We have to get practical. Really practical. The most practical thing we

> can do is hear what God says and act in appropriate response to it.... Hope-determined actions participate in the future that God is bringing into being.... These acts are rarely spectacular. Usually they take place outside sacred settings. Almost never are they perceived to be significant by bystanders. It is not easy to act in hope because most of the immediate evidence is against it.... It takes courage to act in hope.[1]

Despite the risk of ridicule, it was time for us to swim upstream. Vital aspects of our son's ability to function in this world were locked up inside his sleeping brain. We had done the best we could to awaken him under the guidance of the professionals of this world. It was time to begin knocking much harder at his door; and we had an army of soldiers ready, willing, and able to knock with us. It was a foolish army, to be sure, but an army with an unseen Commander as its troops began to march forward.

THE AWAKENING

During the months prior to the volunteers' arrival, we had already seen the NACD program beginning to pay dividends for our son. We had delivered endless hours of deep pressure massage all over his body, and his deep pressure responses were slowly improving. Bob Doman had been pleased with his overall progress during Bryson's quarterly reevaluation in July 1989. His brain was beginning to recognize the signals being sent back and forth from his arms and legs. This was a positive milestone, fueling our hopes that our crippled son might one day walk. We were also encouraged that he seemed to be slowly becoming more responsive and alert.

Bryson was four years old when the volunteers joined us, and they arrived none too soon. We organized them into teams of two, and began to train them for "battle." Sometimes there were two adults together, sometimes two teens, and sometimes one of each, working *wonderfully* together. Some teams came during the morning hours, and some in the afternoon. No matter the combinations, these selfless troops gave us the infusion of hope, enthusiasm, and momentum we desperately needed.

But their arrival was not joyfully received by our son. Just as you would not appreciate being forcibly awakened in the middle of your night's slumber, Bryson did not appreciate our collective efforts to awaken him *at all*. As relentless quantities of vigorous input began to stimulate his sleeping mind, his tenacious spirit rose up against our efforts, exhibiting itself in sharp, angry resistance against our efforts.

Nonetheless, thousands of hours of input were provided to our son during those early years, through both active and passive methods. There was always classical music playing in the background (passive). We began to expand his brain's ability to process information through activities geared to increase his ability to receive that information. The following is an example of one activity, known as "visual digit spans," which was designed to increase Bryson's visual processing and short-term memory.

He was seated at a table in front of a long piece of white construction paper with large circles drawn on it. Objects were placed on those circles, and then taken away after he had viewed them for several seconds. Bryson was required to remember the *order* of the objects, placing them back into the same circles from which they had been removed. We started by using only one object. A little plastic replica of "Big Bird" was placed into one of the circles, and kept there for three seconds for him to see. Then Big Bird was taken from the circle and placed down directly in front of Bryson. He was then exhorted to pick up Big Bird and place him back into the *same* circle.

This activity was not only geared to improve Bryson's memory, but also to increase his fine motor function. The motor controls in his brain had been virtually destroyed. Although he was nearly four, he couldn't use his fingers individually at all. Like someone with thick mittens on, he used his entire hand, and he did so very ineffectively. Picking up small objects was excruciatingly difficult. But our goal was not to make things easy for our son. We exhorted him to do countless activities which were quite unreasonable, knowing that his advancement would only come as he worked his way through exasperating, repetitious failure. Any goal that wasn't significantly beyond current levels of function was of little value to our son in terms of pressing toward the reality of one day functioning normally in this world.

Bryson tried *so* hard to pick that object up and place it where we exhorted him to place it. We kept urging him on until Big Bird landed, often unceremoniously on his head, into that circle. When he finally got the object into the circle, a very important element of the program would then ensue: we would go absolutely bananas. I mean it! We not only congratulated him, we went *nuts*! We'd yell and scream and dance and carry on as if our son had just accomplished the most amazing feat in the history of mankind. The enthusiasm of the teenagers was a major help in this, causing an amused and delighted Bryson to *want* to achieve things that would cause this reaction.

Bryson worked agonizingly hard on so many tasks, all day long. The NACD advised us to give him at least twelve positive, energetic reinforcements for every negative act of discipline that was required. Placing Big Bird inside that circle was a major accomplishment, and we wanted our son to feel pride in it. It was vital for him to feel great about his progress, in order to give him a hunger to reach higher.

In the ensuing months Bryson was asked to place objects into *two* circles, and then three. Big Bird would be placed in the first circle and one of his prize matchbox cars in the second. Then those objects were removed and placed down in front of him *randomly*. His task was to place them back into the *exact* circles they had been taken out of. This task was exasperatingly slow and monumentally frustrating, as objects continued to slip out of his uncoordinated hands and onto the floor, and as his mind struggled to recall what circle each object was taken from. Endless hours of this (and similar activities) began, ever so gradually, to improve his level of touch, fine motor control, and memory.

As months and years wore on, the number of digits his mind was able to receive, process, and then give back out expanded to higher and higher levels. His short-term memory and his ability to process information were slowly, but surely, beginning to awaken.

BALANCING LOFTY GOALS

Crawling was his main mode of ambulating as a four-year-old, and this was still very awkward and unstable. His balance remained so poor that he continued to periodically fall over, even while sitting. He would occasionally "wipe out" while crawling, crashing face first to the floor. We did our best to keep him in padded, protected areas, and we kept a close watch on him. But there continued to be constant tension, pain, injury, and tears in our home. Oh, how agonizing it was to see our child suffering unending pain! The following is an entry from my journal from that time:

> Last night, I knelt by his bed and watched him sleep. I was near tears as I counted ugly bruises on his beautiful face, nose and head.... We must find a way to bring our son back to us. Somehow, we must awaken his mind.[2]

I would gladly have stepped into my son's place to take his pain. Our Father feels for us just as deeply, as we suffer the consequences of sin in this world. But the Father's love is never just a feeling. He didn't sit back and helplessly sympathize with us. His love acted decisively on our behalf. God had a plan, and He fulfilled that plan by placing the consequences of our sin upon His Son, as our Savior hung on the cross. While I couldn't remove my son's pain in the same way, my love for him also had to be more than a feeling. The Lord had called us to act.

To treat my son as a victim would be to keep him trapped as a victim. Loving him properly required firm, loving actions that would set him free from his debilitating limitations. When exhaustion, failure, and doubt came (and these visited us *regularly*), we had to fall back on what the Lord had *already* taught us. We had chosen our path. We now had to stand firm in it. If we couldn't maintain our confidence in the NACD system in the midst of monumental amounts of failure, then we were wasting our time, and exasperating our son for no reason. We could not be double-minded. We had to maintain our confidence as we provided the input his brain desperately needed.

Even as we exhorted Bryson to strive beyond his failures and limitations, the Lord exhorted us not to give up on ourselves in disgust and frustration. Just as Bryson continued to fail and fall, we needed to look beyond the stumbles and failures of our sinful flesh. The Lord requires all of us to maintain confidence in His long-term system of "input" to our souls: His grace. There are times when we must remain confident that He is making changes in our hearts that our eyes simply cannot see (Phil. 1:6). Our confidence must often be sustained in the midst of periods of darkness and exasperating failure. We need to trust in the work His Spirit is doing within us as we keep receiving grace, even when logic tells us we've sinned too many times.

We all need to crawl before we learn to walk, but crawling properly didn't come easily for our son. The NACD asked us to begin spending significant periods of time on the ground with Bryson, teaching him to crawl in a "cross pattern." Crawling in a cross pattern is a significant developmental milestone. It involves moving your right arm and left leg simultaneously, and your left arm and right leg simultaneously. This cross pattern crawling must be mastered prior to making any realistic strides toward walking. This was *backbreaking* work, and we were more grateful than ever for the help of our volunteers.

Bryson's brain also needed to begin to learn what it was like to be in an upright position. His legs were like rubber, having no ability to support him whatsoever. Nonetheless, we were asked to lean his limp body up against the wall, and catch him as he fell. Our initial goal was to get him to lean against the wall for just one second. This may seem a modest goal, but leaning against a wall for one second is an eternity for a crippled child. We propped his crippled body up against the wall again and again and again. Each time he fell *instantly*. Anyone observing this may have considered us cruel, but we kept to the system, doing this day after day, month after month, catching him each time. And each time the volunteers joked, cajoled, bribed, and pleaded with Bryson to give it another try.

The logic was that if he could find it within himself to lean against that wall for just one second, he could ultimately lean against the wall for progressively longer periods of time. And while leaning his limp body up against the wall appeared ludicrous, even the failures involved in this activity were accomplishing much on an *unseen* level. Vital areas of his brain were being stimulated and awakened. Some professionals thought this was crazy. But it wasn't crazy at all. Let me illustrate.

There's no way the small bottoms of your feet should support the size and shape of your body to make it stand. If you were to put this book down right now and stand on your two feet, you'd actually be performing a very complex neurological function. Your eyes send input to your brain regarding where your body is spatially in relation to your surroundings. At the same time your brain is receiving input from the liquid balance center (vestibular apparatus) in your middle ear. The brain then processes and organizes all this information (which is received as electronic messages) and sends electronic signals back through your nerves to muscles all over your body. For each second that you stand, *millions* of signals are sent back and forth between your brain and the various muscle groups throughout your body. These muscle groups are instructed to make adjustments to maintain your balance. If your neurological system ceased functioning for even a split second, you'd plop to the ground like a storefront mannequin.

The above description of the neurological system is, of course, a great oversimplification. The point is that much of Bryson's central nervous system (his brain) was seriously damaged. His brain needed relentless, appropriate input to "relearn" basic functions, and new passageways had to be developed around lesions of damage to carry out those functions. Leaning Bryson against the wall was just one of the numerous activities in our regimen to provide him with the kind of input that would stimulate and awaken critical motor and balance functions in his brain.

Eventually he reached his goal of leaning against the wall for a single second. And if anyone thought we were nuts for the things we did when he got Big Bird into the circle, they'd conclude we were truly insane when Bryson reached this one-second goal. We jumped around hooting and hollering and looking sillier than Ralph Kramden doing the mambo. We praised that precious boy as if he had just scored the winning touchdown in the Super Bowl. As far as we were concerned, he had accomplished something far more glorious. My son was teaching his father, who once thought sports were so important, the real meaning of the word *champion*. I was so proud of him I could scream.

Of course, there were a myriad of other program activities ongoing each day which were geared toward the goal of one day standing independently. But having reached that goal of leaning him against the wall for one second, we established a radically new and different goal. Our new goal was to get him to lean against the wall for *two* seconds. After we reached that goal, you'll never guess what our next outrageous goal became? (You're catching on to this.) Our new goal became to stand him up against the wall for three full seconds. With every attempt he made, successful or not, we continued going fanatically wild, treating my son like the champion he truly is.

A Sleeping Tongue

Bryson's simple words remained deeply slurred and agonizingly enunciated, making him very difficult to understand. Similar to his arms, legs, hands, and fingers, Bryson's mouth and tongue were "asleep," lacking the ability to feel. It was as if his tongue was imprisoned in a dark dungeon, from which it was desperately calling out to be rescued: "Hey, up there!...This is your tongue calling!...It's dark and lonely down here!...Does anyone know that I'm down here?...Hello!...Does anyone up there hear me?"

Our task was to get his brain to begin to call back to that dungeon by massaging his mouth, teeth, lips, and tongue several times per day with an electric toothbrush. As he began to feel more sensation in and around his mouth, his drooling diminished significantly. As his tongue began to awaken further, it was as if his brain began to hear his tongue's desperate calls for help. I envisioned his brain responding by calling down to his tongue in that dark dungeon: "Hey, man!...Don't worry, I hear you!...Everything is going to be okay!...Man, this is so cool!...I have a tongue!"

As Bryson's brain became more acquainted with his newfound friend (his tongue), his speech, *very* slowly, began to improve. As time passed he began expressing his thoughts in brief sentences. His ability to enunciate remained painstakingly arduous for many years, and his sentences continued to be broken up with lots of missing words. Nonetheless, remarkable progress was made in the ensuing years in his ability to make himself understood. The input was *working. He was communicating!*

Pouring It On

We spent time each day shining specially designed lights into Bryson's eyes at various timed intervals, delivering specific stimulus and input to his brain through the visual passageways. He also spent several minutes, several times each day, in my home-office swivel chair as we spun him three times in one direction and three in the other. This disturbed and stimulated the balance mechanism in his middle ear. A properly functioning vestibular is a key element of maintaining one's balance. Repetitious stimulation of this system over a period of months and years was needed for his brain to recognize and interpret the signals that his vestibular apparatus was attempting to send. Bryson hated this activity, because it made him dizzy. But the volunteers cheered him through, rewarding him by making him laugh when it was over.

Although we had been told Bryson was uneducable beyond rudimentary levels, we began delivering exhaustive quantities of academic information to him. We flashed large cards to him as we repeated the names of colors and objects. He listened to tapes and watched videos about counting, naming plants, animals, and things, all with unending repetition.

I prepared an academic video with the help of Bryson's wonderful sister, Janelle. As I watch this video today, I remember how *gorgeous* my then six-year-old daughter was. Today, she is a sensational young woman, beautiful inside and out. It wouldn't be possible to say too many wonderful things about her. Frankly, I'm hoping she reads the words I have written about her here…and decides *never* to get married. Alright, I admit that was thinly veiled, weak, and just plain wrong. But you fathers out there who have daughters know where I'm coming from. You understand the father who described the day his daughter got married as being like handing over a priceless Stradivarius to a gorilla and…Okay, I'll stop while I'm behind. (Note: By the time this book was published, my daughter had married the greatest young man in the world. She and Miguel now serve Christ together through an international human rights organization based in Washington, D.C.)

Including Bryson's sister in the video was geared to give the information more interest for Bryson, particularly since he had to watch it so often. As this video rolled, Bryson would see his sister Janelle on my lap. We both greeted him with big smiles. I would ask a series of questions for Bryson to answer as he watched the video. About three seconds after I asked each question, Janelle would state the answer. For spontaneity, I let Janelle make up her own versions of the answer. Her method of emphasizing things and her born theatrical ability was a big plus. It went something like this:

Dad: "Bryson, what does a sheep say?"

Janelle: "Baaah…baaah"

Dad: "What do ducks say?"

Janelle: "Quack, quack, quack, quack, quack."

Dad: "What do you hit a baseball with?"

Janelle: "A *bat*!"

Dad: "How does dad travel to work?"

Janelle: "In a *choo choo* train."

Dad: "What does mommy drive?"

Janelle: "A *car*."

Dad: "What do you color with?"

Janelle: "A *crayon*!"

Dad: "Who made you, Bryson?"

Janelle: "*God*."

Dad: "Who is God's Son?"

Janelle: "Jesus."

Dad: "Does Jesus love you?"

Janelle: "EEEYESS" (Janelle emphasized the pronunciation, in order to teach Bryson how to say "yes." At this time he could only pronounce it as "ESS.")

Our son's mind continued to be bombarded with "wake up calls." He received, listened to, and saw, thousands upon thousands of units of information, over and over and over again, through a myriad of methods and techniques.

Backward Thinking

Though we were now headed in the right direction, I often became discouraged when I realized how long the journey ahead truly was and how slow we were progressing. I remember staggering, physically and emotionally drained, toward the end of each day. Each time we reached a breakthrough in his ability to function, we celebrated. Yet it was like reaching the top of a huge mountain only to peer over that peek and find, not the promised land of health and wholeness for our son, but an intimidating view of new mountain ranges that also needed to be conquered. Skeptics continued to point out the insurmountable challenges before us. Technically, they weren't wrong. The challenges ahead *were* too much for us, just as they are in your life.

In the feature film *Anna and the King*, Anna (played by Jodie Foster) is asked by one of the King's wives, Lady Tuptim, (played by Bai Ling) how she made it through the days of grief following her husband's death. Her response doesn't sound particularly spiritual, but her words reveal an honest aspect of any long and painful journey:

> **Lady Tuptim:** "How did Ma'am's husband die?"
>
> **Anna:** (after a long pause) "In my arms, actually."
>
> **Tuptim:** "How did Ma'am survive?"
>
> **Anna:** (Slowly, with tears filling her pain-filled eyes): "The same way you would—one awful day at a time."[3]

What keeps us going when the monotony and pain of life becomes so intolerable that we are forced to walk "one awful day at a time"? We are told that for the joy set before Jesus, He endured the cross, pressing on through the pain and the shame (Heb. 12:2). But no matter how far we progress in our journey with the Lord, there are times of drudgery when the very *last* thing our senses can perceive is anything resembling joy. Sometimes we see only a myriad of new and additional problems looming ahead, mountains that spell disaster or doom, but certainly not joy.

Our Lord maintained His determined focus on the joy set before Him, our redemption. Similarly, our focus must not be on the mountains that stand in our way. Those mountains, like the cross, need to be endured but not focused upon. We are not to fix our eyes on our insurmountable problems nor even on the solutions to those problems. Our focus must continue to be fixed on the Savior who travels with us, step by step, on the long, long road leading us through those mountains.

This sounds so simple, but let's be honest. There are many days when we feel thwarted, not only because our problems cry out so loudly for our attention, but also because all evidence of God's goodness is nowhere to be found. What do we do then? I wish I had an easy answer, for you or for myself. I can only say that there are days when we need to trust that the Lord is good, not because we can *see* or *feel* His goodness but because we *remember* that He has been good to us in the past. Since He is the same yesterday, today, and forever (Heb. 13:8), though I can't see His goodness now, it's a good bet that He's still good.

During those difficult days I couldn't trust in my fickle *feelings*. I needed to recall what was really true about God's faithfulness according to His Word. This is true for all of us. Our personal experiences and our feelings can change like the wind. As we learn to cling to His Word as our first and foremost resource, it's also a pretty good idea to do some backward thinking to bring God's goodness back into focus. Yes, you heard me right. I said *backward* thinking.

Don't hear me telling you to live in the past. Paul wisely taught us to forget what lies behind and press on toward our upward call in Christ (Phil. 3:13–14). Indeed, we dare not wallow in our failures nor rest on our laurels. Yet there are times when, instead of focusing toward the treacherous mountains ahead, we must do an about-face in our effort to find the Lord. We are so pitifully forgetful. God's faithfulness needs to be brought out of the recesses of our memory to remind us just how faithful the Lord has *always* been to us personally. We must look *backward*.

Like Anna, we all come upon periods of monotonous, plodding, "awful" days when we are not able to see or feel the goodness of the Lord. If we're not careful, we can begin to believe the lie that it is not only our circumstances that are awful but perhaps the God who allowed such painful circumstances is a bit on the awful side too. Forgetfulness leads to complacency, and sometimes to fearful, mistrustful rebellion.

The enemy has been destroying souls in this world for a long time, and he knows full well about our forgetfulness. His lies are often geared toward causing us to forget God's faithfulness in the past as we struggle with current trials and difficulties. Embracing the serpent's false accusations against God can lead to feelings of victimhood, entitlement, self-pity, bitterness, and hardness of heart. When we can't see the Lord in our present, learning to find Him faithful in our personal past is a powerful tool to keep us pressing on through the awful present, as we reject the enemy's lies.

During the early years of Bryson's NACD program we had many "awful" days, weeks, and months fraught with exasperating setbacks as we sought to awaken our son. I've envisioned having the following conversation with the Lord on some of those "awful" days in which He might remind me of the importance of recalling His past faithfulness:

> **God:** "Barry, do you remember when I commanded Joshua to be strong and courageous?"
>
> **Me:** "Sure. In Joshua 1:9 You asked him not to tremble or be dismayed, because You would be with him wherever he went."
>
> **God:** "Do you know that this command wasn't enough for Joshua?"
>
> **Me:** "*Not enough?* How is it *ever* possible that *Your presence* is not *enough?*"
>
> **God:** "Pay closer attention to what I am telling you, Barry. I didn't say My *presence* wasn't enough. I said the *command* I gave to Joshua to be strong and courageous wasn't enough, even though I promised that I would always stay with him."
>
> **Me:** "So, what more was needed?"
>
> **God:** "Mustering up strength in your flesh to follow my commands to move forward in battle will never be enough. Human flesh is far too weak and prone to deception. You try to obey my commands, but as time moves on you tend to look only at the

difficult battles looming ahead and you forget to look for *Me*. Sometimes you need to remember what I've *already* done for you. Joshua and My people needed a tangible reminder of My faithfulness in the past."

Me: "Is that why you commanded him to build a monument of stones for You, in Joshua chapter 4, after you held back the waters of the Jordan River, allowing the people to cross on dry ground?"

God: "You have it partly right. But what makes you think that monument was for Me?"

Me: "Well, I just assumed…"

God: "I design vast galaxies as easily as I build great mountain ranges. The last thing I need is another pile of rocks. That monument was intended as a memorial for the benefit of Joshua and My people so they could look back and remember a specific time when I stepped into their lives to perform a miracle."

Me: "Well, Father, I think I see your point. We still have quite a long road ahead of us to fully awaken Bryson. It's pretty hard not to become intimidated as we walk in the shadow of all those mountains ahead that still need to be conquered. Do you want us to build a monument of stones, like the one You commanded Joshua to build?"

God: "A physical monument is not necessary. You need only to build such a monument in your mind."

Me: "You mean that I should meditate about a bunch of stones?"

God: "Man, sometimes I wonder what your wife sees in you! Just think back to a time when you were in a *really* difficult spot. Take a minute to remember how I worked things out for you there. If you think hard enough, you'll remember *many* times throughout your life when you've received the help you desperately needed. Take the time to think through those situations, and you'll begin to understand that I've been more involved in your life, all along, than you've realized. If you discipline yourself to remember Me in this way, then those frightening mountains ahead will begin to look a little different."

Me: "Lord. I don't know why my memory is so short."

God: "Don't worry. My memory is *not* short. I remember that I made you from dust. I remember that I loved you even before the day you were born. I remember that My Son's great sacrifice covers *all* your shortcomings, even your short memory. But Barry, there is one more thing."

Me: "Yes, Lord?"

God: "Ralph Kramden looked a *whole* lot better doing the mambo."

Me: "Ouch, Lord. But thanks for letting me know that it's okay to envision laughing with You. Your gift of laughter, and even remembering that I have laughed in the past when I'm too discouraged to laugh in the present, has often helped me maintain my sanity."

God: "Humor was one of my favorite gifts to mankind. I wish all my children would stop to enjoy it more. But as you laugh, Barry, remember to look for Me in your personal past, especially when you're tempted to forget that I am still with you in your difficult present. My servant David had this 'backward thinking' thing down pretty good. Listen to His words."

> I shall remember the deeds of the LORD; Surely I will remember Your wonders of old. I will meditate on all Your work and muse on Your deeds. Your way, O God, is holy; What god is like our God?
>
> —PSALM 77:11–13

MONUMENTS AND MOUNTAINS

These many years later, there are so *many* monuments to lift up from this difficult time of life. An exhausted family? Clearly. Huge, insurmountable problems? You bet! Our firstborn son had suffered a tragedy that changed his life, and our lives, forever. But praise God, he had not been taken back into heaven's arms prematurely, as we once feared might occur. Nor had we made the unspeakable mistake of placing this precious child in an institution, as had been suggested. And how could I forget the wondrous monument of hearing our precious son speak to us through his lips, and not through a machine. And, of course, there was the awesome monument of Bryson's Army, bringing the finest people in this world into our lives. There was *so* much good to remember.

I decided to write regular letters to Bryson's Army to commemorate some of those good things. I wrote a letter once every three months, after Bryson's quarterly reevaluations by the NACD. This was usually a time when we were all feeling somewhat "burned out" from all our hard work. The letters were geared not only to encourage the troops, amidst our ongoing failures, but also to help us regain perspective by taking stock of all that had been accomplished during the previous quarter. The letters themselves became yet another tangible monument to God's faithfulness, and could be reread when things got rough again, as they always did. The following is my very first letter to Bryson's Army.

November 16, 1989

Dear Members of Bryson's Army,

We cannot express how grateful we are that you have chosen to become a member of Bryson's Army. Each one of you is making a contribution to Bryson and to our family, the proportion of which you may never fully realize during this lifetime.

Why do we refer to you as "Bryson's Army?" Well, as you get to know Bryson more you will share our perspective that he truly is fighting a war. Some professional therapists and doctors have recommended a special talking computer to place on his lap so that he can push buttons in the event he never speaks intelligibly. Almost no one believes he will attend school with "normal" kids. We, of course, have no intention of taking such measures. War has been declared. The battle is on.

We refuse to limit Bryson's potential with fearful and puny expectations. Our hopes are now sky high (although they had been sagging a bit) and you, through the sacrifice of your time and energy, are the reason our hopes are soaring. There is so much which needs to be done, but there was no way we could do it all ourselves. We needed reinforcements, fresh troops, and you responded to the call.

A long battle lies ahead, but there is no question about the outcome of this war. God, our great Commander, is all powerful and He is in control. We know that God could issue a simple command, and in a split second, Bryson would be completely healed. Yet God often chooses to do His "miracles" over time through the efforts of people. He expects us to fight as if the outcome of the battle depends on us, and pray knowing that the results will come from Him. We could not take our next breath if He didn't will it. The praise always belongs to Him.

Thanks for becoming part of the battle. Your role is important, whether it is in providing therapy, rides to school, or being a prayer warrior. Your efforts are deeply appreciated, and will never be forgotten.

Love, Barry Milazzo
Your Partner in the Battle[4]

There wasn't a doubt in our minds now that the Lord had placed us on the right road. The daily grind remained just as hard and the mountains up ahead loomed just as tall. But something was changing. We were knocking on Bryson's door very loudly now, and bit by precious bit, his door was creaking open. The healthy child who was cruelly taken from us years before was slowly beginning to awaken, and return.

Awake, sleeper, And arise from the dead, And Christ will shine on you.

—Ephesians 5:14

Chapter 13
STANDING FIRM

To his own master he stands or falls; and he will stand, for the Lord is able to make him stand.
ROMANS 14:4

WE PRAISED GOD that our son was beginning to awaken, but oh those mountains looming ahead! At four and one-half he remained a profoundly brain-injured, crippled child with barely intelligible speech. The NACD believed there's only one thing to do as you face mountains: keep climbing. One of our most difficult challenges as we strove toward those peaks was to keep standing firm in our conviction that we were still on the right road.

After all I've written about Bryson's awakening, it may seem odd to you that maintaining our faith in the NACD program was still an issue. The truth is, in the midst of such exhilarating progress, we still suffered gut-wrenching weeks and months when absolutely *nothing* was accomplished. During those periods, we were tempted to wonder if we had really seen progress, or if we just *thought* that we had. Our quarterly reevaluations with NACD always revealed that progress had indeed been made. We needed all the reminders we could get that in the midst of agonizing, outward regression, real advancement was still occurring *inside* our son that could not be seen.

His personality continued to shine through his handicaps, and when he wasn't fighting against us tooth and nail as we delivered his daily regimen, he was often full of grins and smirks. His gorgeous appearance had always been one of his strengths, and we were determined to make the most of it. His hair was cut short, with a thin, curly "tail" coming down the back of his neck. Our goal was to present Bryson to everyone as a cool dude.

The NACD encouraged us to raise him as "un-handicapped" as possible, wanting him to participate in as many venues with healthy children as we could arrange. Bob was confident that Bryson would make tremendous gains by imitating the actions and behaviors of his peers. We didn't think this was possible with respect to schooling. When we asked Bob Doman about this, without flinching he asked us why we hadn't already signed him up for the *same* nursery school that our daughter Janelle had attended.

I nervously called Pat Jacquin, director of Care-A-Lot Christian Nursery School in Wyckoff, New Jersey, fully prepared to understand that she'd need to decline my request. It was one thing for Bryson to participate in Sunday school at our church, but a nursery school open to the public couldn't possibly take on the responsibility of handling Bryson's needs. As a businessman, I understood the issues of risk and liability. Tears welled in my eyes as I listened to Pat's response. In a nonchalant manner, as to provide me some dignity, she indicated that Bryson would be as welcome as any other child in her school. She went on to say she would enroll him in her own class, just as had been done for his big sister. Not too many things in life cause me to become speechless, but I thanked her and hung up the phone, trying not to weep.

It is impossible to describe how much this opportunity benefited our son. He was right at home in the wonderfully positive atmosphere Pat fostered for all the children. He loved the academic learning times. He loved the songs and the snacks. He loved being close with the other children, all sitting gorgeously on the rug as Pat taught them about Jesus. As the other children ran around the playground, Bryson crawled right after them, sporting a cool pair of red kneepads to protect his bruised knees.

His tenacity and courage were evident to all now. Whenever he faced a new opportunity, he went right after it. I mean he dove in headfirst, seeming not even to notice the obstacles. I marveled at his courage, sometimes stepping back from my role as his dad to try to view him as a separate individual. This was the same child considered too "neurologically involved" to be included in an early intervention program for *handicapped* children, just a few years before. Now he was fitting in with healthy peers in his own unique way, with a *little* bit of help from some friends of course.

God's humble servants are simply that. They are friends for hurting people in this world, just as Jesus was. Friends don't make a big production of what they do, considering it official "ministry," and they rarely make their efforts known. Pat Jacquin didn't consider it anything special to provide *all* the extra care that was needed to ensure our son's safety. She never even mentioned that she carried our son, now thirty-five pounds, to special activities throughout the building and across the parking lot to the playground. In fact, she never acknowledged *any* of the endless care she provided for our son. To her, these were just *little* things that God's friends do. Through her efforts I was reminded that *little* acts of loving friendship strike the fiercest blows against the darkness in this world.

Reading today's newspaper will remind you that we live in a world of deep darkness, where people do horrifying things to each other. People all around us are desperately hurting, though most have become so good at putting on their masks that their pain remains well hidden. Some of you reading this book don't need to be convinced. You've been "through the wringer." You've suffered excruciating pain and crushing sorrow. You understand that Jesus wasn't blowing smoke when He warned us there's an enemy who seeks to steal, kill, and destroy (John 10:10). You know that this enemy is savvy enough to come in for the kill when you, or someone you love, is down.

It's probably never been the grand programs of the world or of the church that have been your lifeline. For me, it has always been the *little* acts of friendship and kindness that came when I was gasping for air. And I've come to realize that God's closest, most intimate friends have been through life's wringers themselves.

They've become the kinds of vessels God can mightily use: broken ones. Broken friends of God, wounded healers some might call them, have eyes and ears attuned to the needs of others. Their ears have been trained to hear *little* things from the Lord that others simply cannot hear:

> Although the Lord has given you bread of privation and water of oppression, He, your Teacher will no longer hide Himself, but your eyes will behold your Teacher. Your ears will hear a word behind you, "This is the way, walk in it," whenever you turn to the right or to the left.
>
> —Isaiah 30:20–21

Of course, even after you've been though God's wringers, it's easy to dismiss the Teacher's voice, since He tends to whisper and speak mostly of *little* things. We'd rather involve ourselves in something grand. Yet we're seldom privy to what the Teacher may do through our *little* acts of friendship. He may use our obedient response to His whisper simply to brighten someone's day. Then again, those *little* acts He whispers into our ears just might bring someone's life back from the brink of hell and destruction. Do you think He only breaks and multiplies loaves and fishes? Sometimes He multiplies the *little* acts of obedience from His broken friends. But what the King chooses to do with our *little* acts of kindness is His business. Our part is obedience to His still small voice.

If you possessed a healing power within you that could cure all human disease, this power would *easily* be worth trillions of dollars. We who belong to the King have been inhabited by a *far* more brilliant power. Jesus Christ *Himself* dwells in us through the Holy Spirit, and we are vessels of His awesome Light and Love in this dark world! There is only one appropriate response to such an awesome truth:

> Work out your salvation with fear and trembling; for it is God who is at work in you, both to will and to work for His good pleasure.
>
> —Philippians 2:12–13

Many of our churches are chock full of programs and activities that aren't making the slightest dent against the darkness and evil in our world. We need to consider that even Jesus didn't choose His own path of service here. He said: "I can do nothing of My own initiative…because I do not seek my own will, but the will of Him who sent Me" (John 5:30). Perhaps our best prayer each day might be:

> *Open my eyes, Lord. Cause me to see the little things that You've prepared in advance for me to do for others today. I believe that You live inside of me, and that You desire to work in and through me for the benefit of hurting souls that only I will be in the position to touch as a friend in this dark world today. Help me to hear Your voice and to see the good works that You've prepared in advance for me to do this day. I trust in You to lead me and to do the work that You alone, friend Jesus, can accomplish through me. Amen.*

> For we are His workmanship, created in Christ Jesus for good works, which God prepared beforehand so that we would walk in them.
>
> —Ephesians 2:10

I could never properly thank Pat Jacquin, nor our selfless volunteers, nor the teachers, nor all the therapists and doctors, nor all the others who did such wondrous *little* things for my son through the years. We've been blessed with many good friends in this world, and I am confident that what God's Word says about them is true:

> And whoever…gives to one of these little ones even a cup of cold water to drink, truly I say to you, he shall not lose his reward.
>
> —Matthew 10:42

Standing in Confidence

> It was for freedom that Christ set us free; therefore keep standing firm and do not be subject again to a yoke of slavery.
>
> —Galatians 5:1

As mentioned at the outset of this chapter, even after all the evidence we had seen regarding Bryson's growth and awakening from the NACD program, maintaining our faith in the NACD system still required faith and perseverance against the backdrop of regression and failure. Similarly, even after all God had been teaching me regarding His foolish plan for our growth toward maturity in Christ, maintaining my faith in His plan of grace was *still* a struggle. As periods of regression and sudden outbreaks of sinful failure continued to arise in my soul, I sometimes wondered if I was making any progress at all.

Praise God that against the backdrop of our continued failures, our merciful Father never treats us as though we are handicapped. In His eyes we are dearly loved children who are complete in Christ. The Father doesn't give up on us when we fall and fail anymore than I would have given up on Bryson due to his failures and periods of regression. His Word makes it clear that there is *no* condemnation for those who are in Christ Jesus (Rom. 8:1) and exhorts us to press on in the path of grace, remaining confident that *He* will complete the work that He has begun in us.

> For I am confident of this very thing, that He who began a good work in you will perfect it until the day of Christ Jesus.
>
> —Philippians 1:6

Those who are confident in Christ's ability to perfect us refuse to give up during the heat of battle. They refuse to believe that even our most grievous failures limit His ability to complete His work in our lives, over time. They continue getting back up, acknowledging even more deeply the vast difference between self-sufficiency and Christ-sufficiency, between our lack and His wholeness, between our weakness and His strength, between our sinfulness and His perfection, between our wretched failure and His victory. Our success in fighting His ordained battles always hinges on our learning to rely, more and more, on *His* adequacy, *His* goodness, and *His* power, not our own.

Sadly, much of our focus in the American church can often be boiled down, in essence, to two words: "Do better." This teaching is well-intended, and sounds quite spiritual. After all, who wouldn't want to do better, to stop failing, to give one's all for God? But chasing a better performance for God is tantamount to a dog chasing its tail. It is the wrong goal. Our goal must be to relinquish control to God's Spirit, so *He* can perform better in us and through us. In order to give Christ a shot at "doing better" through us, we need to get our fleshly efforts and false piety out of His way, and trust Him completely.

David Hazard has given the world a wonderful gift through his series of devotional books entitled *Rekindling the Inner Fire*. The series brings to life the writings of many ancient saints from throughout the centuries. John of the Cross, one of God's bright lights from the sixteenth century, reaffirms Paul's teachings that our confidence must *always* be in the continuing work of God's Spirit within us, not in our ability to perform on our own:

> You must never make the mistake of rushing out of God's presence to try to do good, or to find freedom from sin on your own. You will fail. Let the Guide of your poor blind soul lead you first to Himself. There you will receive His empowering grace....Do you think it impossible that you, with all your flaws, can be changed into His likeness? God offers to take you with His loving hand and lead you where you cannot go by yourself...along a way that no human eye can see, and that is the way of the Holy Spirit.[1]

In the Sermon on the Mount, Jesus stated God's requirement very simply: "you are to be perfect, as your heavenly Father is perfect" (Matt. 5:48). How ridiculous it would be to conclude that mustering up our next recommitment to "do better" for God might somehow result in the perfection He requires. Oh, how we have underrated the goal Jesus has called us to, and overrated our ability to reach it.

My problem, as I attempted to provide for the enormous needs of a struggling young family was that I constantly found myself hitting a brick wall in my attempts to "do better." Being "perfect" was an outright joke. I wasn't exactly the poster child for Christian "victory." As I stumbled through grief, anger, emotional ups and downs, and sins of various kinds, my failures were as painfully evident to me as my son's handicaps. Even a small degree of honesty and self-awareness revealed my propensity to fail. What could I *possibly* do with Jesus' command to be perfect even as my Father in heaven was perfect? I was tempted to cover up Matthew 5:48 with black permanent marker!

There *had* to be a better way than endless, exhausting, self-sufficient attempts to "do better." Praise God, there is. Through painful lessons of personal failure, God kept driving me back to the matchless grace of Jesus Christ. He alone has the power, by His Spirit working within us, to transform us over time. Our task is to stand firm in the Lord, even when we must do so against the backdrop of humiliating failures and demoralizing periods of actual or apparent regression.

> Therefore...stand firm in the Lord, my beloved.
>
> —PHILIPPIANS 4:1

> You therefore, my son, be strong in the grace that is in Christ Jesus.
>
> —2 TIMOTHY 2:1

As we seek to stand firm in the Lord, being strong in His grace, we need to understand the foundational relationship into which we have been called. God's love for us is our *unshakable* foundation. The words of Steve Brown are helpful in reaffirming this.

> Many Christians say "I'm going to be holy and righteous even if it kills me." And it usually does. But, here is the exciting thing: holiness and righteousness have already been achieved for you by Christ. When you stand before the Father, He sees you as holy and righteous because of the blood of His Son. You are, in fact, justified before God because of the cross. That is a cold hard fact; you don't have to try so much anymore to be holy and righteous. You are now free to fail and, more importantly, free to allow Him to love you and to love Him back. You enter a relationship, not between a criminal and a policeman, but between a loving Father and His child. When you enjoy that relationship something wonderful happens: you find holiness and righteousness comes tagging along behind...you are in a process that makes you increasingly more holy and righteous.[2]

STANDING UNDER GOD'S BANNER

Bryson was straining *so* hard to comply with so many impossible things, and he was constantly exhorted to perform tasks that his waking brain could not yet successfully accomplish. The NACD had taught us that when the method and the input are appropriate, intense repetition eventually promotes the development of brain circuitry that can perform higher levels of function.

He was a "daddy's boy," and I knew that my influence over his life, for good or bad, was very powerful. In order to keep him from becoming discouraged to the point of giving up, monumental amounts of failure had to be anticipated. As his father I understood this. As a brain-injured child, Bryson did not understand it. Therefore, I wanted to make sure that each time he looked up at me in the midst of his unending failures, he'd be strengthened by the image of a daddy who believed he would one day succeed. If he was ever going to develop confidence in himself, he needed to know I believed in him.

This caused me to wonder, did my Father anticipate my failures as I strained to follow and obey Christ? Was He confident that Christ's image would one day be fully formed in me (Gal. 4:19)? Was He pleased to call me His son only when

I *succeeded?* Was He shocked and disappointed when I failed? What did He think of me as a person who continued to stumble and fall?

Put this book aside for a moment and look up to your Father. What do you see? Does He have an angry scowl on His face? Perhaps His look is one of disappointment. You've failed Him so many times that you don't really blame Him. You've earned His disdain, and you know it. As a Christian, at least you can take solace in the fact that the Bible says He won't kick you out of His family. But He probably wishes He *could* kick you out, based on your performance in life. He sent His Son *all* the way to die on the cross for your sins, and now you're *still* not able to get your act together. He is utterly disgusted with you. You don't have to be told. You *see* it written all over His face.

My now retired pastor, Dr. Earl Comfort, helped me to correct my understanding regarding God's love for His "impaired" children. He grew up in a poor ghetto of Philadelphia, and he came to envision God as a great Policeman in the sky with an intimidating nightstick in his hand, just waiting to whack him when he stepped out of line. What a joy when he finally came to know the true disposition of his Father. What a relief to learn that his Father wasn't angry at him, that all of His anger was satisfied at the cross of Christ, that his Father loved him more than he could conceive.

The Bible asks a critical question in Romans 8:31: "If God is for us, who can be against us?" (NKJV). If we have trusted Christ for the forgiveness of our sins and have sincerely surrendered our lives over to His control, then God is truly *for* us. As any good father will, our Father will discipline us, sometimes severely, to protect us from evil paths that will destroy us. Even so, God is not angry at you, or me, any more than I could have been angry at my own impaired son as he continued to fail and fall, time after time.

I truly believe that the Father doesn't care as much about the fact that we fail as often as we do, as He cares about where we turn after we have failed. We will only turn to Him if we see Him as He *really* is. God is not angrily waiting to destroy us. He wants us to come to Him so He can cleanse us, change us, and heal us from the sin that is *already* destroying us. Once Earl came to know his Father's true disposition toward him, he began to look up often. To his amazement, he learned that God indeed had something in His hand, but it wasn't an intimidating nightstick. Incredibly, the object in his Father's hand was an enormous banner with "Earl" scrawled boldly across it.

If you forget everything else written in this book, *please* remember that your Father holds a banner for you. He doesn't cheer for you to succeed in a shallow, temporal sense. His banner represents a vast supply of undeserved love and grace, which is what you need to *truly* succeed in life, despite your obvious flaws and continuing failures. God forbid that we would ever use that banner as a license to deliberately continue in our sin. The banner is soaked in the blood of our Savior, the Father's beloved firstborn Son.

Bryson continued to struggle and fail countless times each and every day during those exasperating years. When he became discouraged I wanted him to look up and know beyond question that I still stood with him, that I still loved him, that I would never stop working toward his success, no matter what the cost. I saw my son's many handicaps, imperfections, and failures. I knew he might never perform perfectly in this world. But each time he fell, I wanted him to look up and be empowered to get up and try again, if for no other reason than for the loving and proud look he saw on his daddy's face.

If like my son's life, and my life, your life is fraught with stumbles and falls, then I challenge you to look up and see your Daddy for who He *really* is. He is not angry with you. His anger has been *fully* satisfied by the death Jesus died for you on the cross. Just a glimpse will empower you and motivate you to obey and serve Him. Yes, there is something in His hand. Look up and see.

> He has brought me to his banquet hall, And His banner over me is love.
>
> —Song of Solomon 2:4

Wise Counselors

On November 3, 1989, my wife called my Manhattan office to tell me Bryson had a very bad fall in the bathroom, knocking out one tooth, loosening three others, and painfully injuring the front of his mouth. She had tried to calm him, but through breathless tears, he continued screaming for "daddy." It was 1:00 p.m., and there wasn't another train to Glen Rock, New Jersey, until 2:30. I jumped in a taxi in Hoboken, and had the driver take me all the way home, my stomach churning all the way. When I finally arrived, Bryson clung to me and sobbed deeply. I carried my precious boy with me for the rest of the day.

There is no adequate way to describe my emotions from the *many* days like that, when such deep pain was inflicted on my son. I was the leader of our struggling family, the one who was supposed to steady our family ship. I'd love to tell you that I was mature enough, "spiritual" enough to handle it all well. The truth is that my emotions sometimes seemed like a ping-pong ball, batted back and forth between anger to despondency. I often feared the Milazzo ship was on its last voyage, in the middle of the ocean with a gaping hole in the hull. God often seemed nowhere to be found, as I wrote in my journal:

> Last Friday Bryson fell and knocked out one tooth and damaged three others. It is incredibly hard for us to see our handicapped son's beautiful face being maimed. Nobody (but God) truly understands this. We have deep concerns for Bryson's future, and it's always with us...a deep, long-term stress. Add to this two other children with needs...a stressful job in New York City...you can believe that the combination of stress and fatigue produces anger, arguments, and sometimes a sense of hopelessness...a feeling that God is absent.[3]

A few days after this accident, I sat in the Park Avenue office of Edward Gordon, explaining why I was resigning from my position as managing director in the firm's Wall Street branch office. The Edward S. Gordon Company (since merged with CBRE) was one of the most successful commercial real estate firms in the United States. The company had been good to me, and Ed had become a trusted friend. I had consistently been one of the top producers in his Wall Street office, but I had no illusions about being irreplaceable. ESG was a very dynamic organization and Ed had plenty of talented people. Frankly, it would have been a small loss for him had I left.

Yet he urged me to reconsider my decision, telling me to take whatever time I felt was necessary to care for my son, but not to leave. He said he'd arrange as much help for me as possible so that I could stay with the company. There wasn't a doubt in my mind that Ed was more concerned for my family than he was for his wallet. His concern for my family had been consistent since the time my son was first injured. Looking back, I realize that leadership like Ed's was one of the key reasons his firm was so successful.

I wasn't sure what to do after I left that meeting. I realized that Ed was making sense. At thirty-four years old, you simply don't throw away a promising career. On the other hand, I was already spending *so* much time out of the office working with Bryson and his army of volunteers. The volunteers were wonderfully dedicated. But due to Bryson's tenacious resistance to the work (we couldn't make *all* of it fun), it was becoming more necessary for me to be present as the "enforcer," getting him to cooperate with his difficult regimen.

There are only so many hours in a day. Something had to give. Either I would step away from a rewarding career, or live with the greater agony of diminishing the effectiveness of the life-giving program that was literally saving my brain-injured son. I was torn. There didn't seem to be an acceptable answer. As I went back to my knees to pray, I was reminded to remain open to the wisdom the Lord might give through trusted people:

> For by wise guidance you will wage war. And in abundance of counselors there is victory.
>
> —PROVERBS 24:6

The reference to war was fitting, since this was exactly what we faced daily. If wise counsel was important, I knew where to turn. The next day, I sought the advice of a Jack Vickers, my longtime mentor and friend from my days in the Helmsley organization. Jack had become like a second father to me. He reminded me that I was just at the beginning of the long and costly process of providing many years of care for Bryson. He strongly recommended that I reconsider my decision to leave ESG, particularly since I didn't have a solid plan for what to do next. He told me I needed to work smarter, not necessarily harder or longer, in order to find the time to spend with my son.

It often appears (and feels) like we are wrestling with our problems and decisions alone. The Bible informs us that God is not only deeply concerned, but deeply involved in our lives, promising to accomplish *all* that concerns us, as we trust Him to do so. He *never* forsakes the works of His hands. *We* are the most valuable works His hands ever made.

> The Lord will accomplish what concerns me; Your lovingkindness, O Lord, is everlasting; Do not forsake the works of Your hands.
>
> —Psalm 138:8

I soon met with Ed Gordon again. He supported my plan to implement a rather odd schedule, significantly reducing my work hours. I would rise early, about 4:30 a.m., and arrive at my Manhattan office at about 6:30 a.m. I would leave at 1:00 p.m. to return home and participate in my son's program. In order to make my day more efficient, Ed arranged to have my secretary administer Bryson's unending medical insurance filings. Val was terrific, and this took a great burden off my shoulders.

Ed also arranged for me to lighten my schedule by allowing me to terminate my position as the senior leasing agent for Exchange Place Centre, a development on the Jersey City waterfront which was the tallest office tower in New Jersey at that time. We agreed that I should focus on my strength: representing tenant-clients in the relocation of their corporate headquarters. This aspect of the business afforded me more flexibility in arranging meetings and negotiating sessions, and it fit within my reduced hours.

Ordinarily, when you work on fewer projects in the real estate business, you make less money. But after making the decision to reduce my hours and responsibilities, each succeeding year became more lucrative. There is no way I can explain this except to say that the Lord accomplished what concerned me (Ps. 138:8). He blessed the decision my wife and I made to make our son's recovery a priority over finances. I hasten to add that I don't believe in formulas that obligate God to provide blessings or financial rewards to those who presumptuously "name it and claim it." Nonetheless, the Lord did choose to bless us greatly during these years. As I look back, I realize He was providing resources for some very fallow and distressing years that lay ahead.

It is an emotional matter for me to write about some of these events in view of Ed Gordon's untimely death from cancer in the autumn of 2000. He is remembered as a dynamic force that swept through the New York real estate community in the 1980s and '90s. I remember him for his integrity and kindness, and for his friendship.

He *Will* Stand

Inch by painstaking inch, my son's progress came. There continued to be about twenty NACD activities to perform each day, focusing on motor, speech, and cognition. Most activities had to be repeated at least twice each day. The volunteers often had great ideas regarding how to make this grueling routine fun for Bryson. After completing each activity, he'd often be thrown in the air, or swung around by his ankles, or given horsy rides as volunteers held him on the "horse's" back to keep him from falling off.

He could now speak in five to six word sentences, but his speech was still arduous and slurred, with many words missing from his sentences. We later learned that there are regional processing centers for speech located throughout the brain, each one specializing in the recollection of certain types of words. He had particular trouble retrieving articles like "the" and "a." Therefore he formulated sentences such as: "I have cookie" instead of "I have a cookie," and "Give me car" instead of "Give me the car."

Bryson had achieved *remarkable* progress in his ability to lean against the wall, and we were now coaxing him to do so, not for seconds, but for minutes at a time. He loved anything having to do with balls and sports, and to make things interesting, we handed him rubber balls to throw as he stood leaning against that kitchen wall. Lacking the motor control to properly throw a ball in any specific direction, he squealed with delight as they bounced *all* over the kitchen. Delighted, he tried to clap as we ducked out of the way of the careening balls, but his uncoordinated hands rarely found each other.

We began helping him to strengthen his wobbly legs by doing deep knee bends. We held him by the hips to keep him steady as he bent down to the ground to pick up one of his matchbox cars, and then guided him steadily upward as he strained to reach the homemade ramp we had positioned at the height of his reach. He would continue going up and down for twenty minutes at a time, being delighted as his cars sped down the ramp. We were still doing most of the pushing for him as we held his hips, and we did *all* the balancing. Nonetheless, we were getting him to exert the maximum effort possible.

He was laid face down on a table to do "leg curls" with ankle weights strapped to his feet. Robyn VanYperen, one of our dedicated volunteers, brought us a tambourine to make this exercise into a game. As Bryson strained to lift the leg with the weight attached, we'd position the tambourine so that his foot would bang into it at the top of his leg's motion. He *loved* making that banging noise. Bryson was still spinning in my office chair several times per day, and he continued receiving deep pressure massage. We also began doing several new types of eye exercises to improve his visual-spatial perception.

We pressed ahead with much more work than I could detail here, as he neared five years old. We understood clearly now that Bryson needed to attempt feats that far exceeded his grasp. Even so, my jaw nearly dropped at our next quarterly NACD evaluation when Bob Doman informed us it was time for Bryson to stand *on his own*.

Similar to the goal of training him to lean up against the wall, we were asked to break this new goal down into the tiniest increments possible. We established an initial goal for him to stand in the middle of our family room for just *one* second. Even so, this goal was preposterous to ask of a crippled child. He still wasn't even able to lean against the wall without being closely spotted to prevent a crash.

Yet, as outlandish as it was to ask a crippled child to stand in the middle of a room with no supports, the Lord was now asking me to surrender areas of my life to Him that would have seemed impossible to do just a few years before. And though I couldn't take it as a direct promise that my son would *ever* stand on his own physically, it meant a lot to me that the following verse did not say "he *might* stand," but that "he *will* stand."

> To his own master he stands or falls; and he *will* stand, for the Lord is able to make him stand.
>
> —Romans 14:4

I placed my son in the middle of our carpeted family room, my hands firmly clasping his shoulders from behind. He staggered immediately when my hands were removed, even an inch. I quickly grabbed him to keep him from crumbling to the floor. A few seconds later, after steadying him, my hands were removed again, with the exact same result. This went on day after day, and month after month.

It seemed cruel to put our child through such exasperating, fruitless failure. But something was going on behind the scene of those failures that couldn't be observed with the naked eye. Bryson's brain was being bombarded by the relentless input of *millions* of life-giving, neuron-generating, electrical messages coming from all over his body. Thank God we never gave up just because we couldn't *see* what was happening.

One day without warning, right in the middle of all the frustration and failure, a miracle occurred. It lasted only one second, after which his body crumbled into my arms once again. After a stunned pause, when I finally realized what he had done, I scooped him up and carried him through the house celebrating wildly with his volunteers. Yes, it was only one second. But that victorious second came from one very courageous, crippled child, standing *alone*. We couldn't have kept a lid on that eruption if we tried.

I'd like to tell you that the miracle continued on seamlessly and gloriously, and that my five-year-old son soon began to walk. But that victorious moment faded into months of continued, excruciating effort and exasperating failure. Yet out of those failures one second ultimately became two, then two seconds became three, three became four, and on it went. Praise God! Our son was beginning to stand!

The mountains ahead remained just as tall; yes, seemingly invincible still. The NACD reminded us there's only one thing to do when facing impossible mountains: just keep standing firm in the truth and keep on climbing. But there's not a person reading this story right now who will not face treacherous and impossible mountains. By His grace, God will bring about a purpose-filled future for you that you cannot yet see, *if* you do not turn back from Christ. Our marching orders are clear.

> ...and having done everything...stand firm.
>
> —Ephesians 6:13

Chapter 14
THE MIGHTIEST DUCK

At long last, Bryson is running in the park with the other children.
It is a warm spring day, and I'm content to sit and watch my son play.
His speech is now perfect, his eyes straight and sharp.
Maybe he'll turn out to be the athlete he was born to be after all.
Maybe he'll become a motivational speaker, God's
living model of overcoming the impossible.
Never again will my son return to that cruel prison of his brain injury.
Warm rays filter through the leaves onto my face.
Intense joy fills my soul; joy that words cannot express.
Tears well up in my eyes; I thought I'd never live to see this day.
Utter elation. He is free! My precious son is free!

I ROLL OVER, CLINGING desperately to the joy. But as the morning fog fades, the joy slowly drifts away. These many years later, I cannot forget that dream. I sometimes wonder if joy that intense could ever exist in this world. You know the old adage, if it sounds too good to be true, it isn't. Still, somewhere in my mind there is a remnant, a notion that such joy *did* exist somewhere. An ache deep inside reminds me of it. One thing is sure, trying to grasp onto anything that promises such joy in this world is as futile as holding a fistful of pure spring water. Oh, that I could find it and claim it, and remain in it forever. Nothing else would be worth pursuing. *Nothing!* If heaven is even remotely as joyous as that dream, only a fool would not make certain of his future there (Ps. 27:4).

It is 4:30 a.m. I'd love to roll back over for desperately needed sleep. But somewhere in the background is a clock relentlessly ticking away the time left in our son's childhood. He will not run in the park today, at five years old. Despite all his triumphs, he will still crawl awkwardly through our home. He will injure himself, as he does every day. He has come so far, but the journey remains so long. Many scoff at what he has accomplished. Learning to stand under tightly controlled conditions doesn't constitute walking. In their view, he will never walk. After nearly three years of his intense program, he is not able to take *one* single step, and his brain-injured mind *still* doesn't possess the clarity even to comprehend that he is handicapped. He has missed *so* much of his childhood already. That cursed clock keeps ticking. It's time to rise and take on today's battle against it.

I needed to arrive at my Manhattan office by 6:30 a.m. to accomplish enough work to return home in time for his afternoon program. I can still smell the best coffee in the world, from the Essex coffee shop, across from the Twin Towers of the World Trade Center. As I got my order to go, the owner, Johnny Costalas, often inquired about my son. This was a strong man, a man who built a fortune rising each day at 3:00 a.m. baking fresh doughnuts. In his thick Greek accent he would come up, shake my hand, and ask, "How's your boy?" Sometimes there were tears in his eyes as I told him of Bryson's latest feat, such as standing in the middle of the room for longer periods of time. Even in a tough city like New York, tender hearts can be found everywhere.

I'm not really sure what brought out the tenderness in people, or why so many wanted to know how our son was doing. Perhaps we're all yearning to regain something that has been lost. It seemed almost as though my son's battle to regain pieces of what had been shattered in his life might somehow prove there was still hope out there, somewhere. Hope that God still reaches down to perform miracles in the midst of all the despair and tragedy in this world. Whatever the reason, it was good to have friends who stood with us as our son fought his personal war, and as we fought ours.

My work in Manhattan remained fiercely competitive. The stakes at the bargaining table were high, and the negotiations were often contentious. I took the trust placed in me by my clients seriously, since the effectiveness of my work had a significant impact on their corporate bottom line, and since the work was entrusted to me by the Lord. But as I sat on the 1:30 p.m. train each afternoon for the trip home, I knew I needed to gear up for my greatest battle of the day. I couldn't allow fatigue to cause me to fail my son. As I rode the train home, I often pleaded for some of Isaiah's "Eagle Power."

> He gives strength to the weary, And to him who lacks might He increases power. Though youths grow weary and tired, And vigorous young men stumble badly, Yet those who wait for the Lord Will gain new strength; They will mount up with wings like eagles, They will run and not get tired, They will walk and not become weary.
>
> —Isaiah 40:29–31

God was faithful, not always to make me *feel* rested or good, but to give me the grace and strength to keep moving forward, as I continued to "stumble badly" into occasional fits of self-pity, exhausted anger, and depression.

Discipline for Both of Us

As soon as I arrived home, I threw off my suit and jumped into a pair of jeans just prior to the volunteers' arrival at 3:00 p.m. We always told Bryson which pair of volunteers were coming and tried to get him excited. The teenagers often wore silly costumes or brought interesting things for him to see. They brought remote control racing cars, silly hats, and all sorts of stuffed animals. I'll never forget Bryan Egan, a senior at Glen Rock High School, showing up with an enormous pair of Bullwinkle moose slippers. I don't think they realized that their silliness and enthusiasm encouraged and perked me up as much as Bryson. He loved them all. Still, their arrival was not always met happily.

He knew they'd soon be asking him to do difficult things. Some of the tasks they coaxed him to perform were more than difficult. They were impossible. It wasn't fair that my young son had to work so hard each day, and he began to let us know how unfair this was through strong displays of anger, and his well-known tenacity began to exhibit itself in stubborn resistance against us, and by a refusal to cooperate with his program.

It meant nothing to him that we were all there for his welfare. He was five years old. If I was him, I'd throw tantrums and throw things on the floor too. Yet, as his father, I had to be equally tenacious, meeting his resistance with whatever means necessary to overcome his will. Sometimes there were "time-outs" sitting on a chair in his room. Sometimes favorite toys were taken away. Sometimes the discipline involved spanking and tears (his and mine). I *hated* it. Part of me (a big part) just wanted to leave this struggling kid alone.

After all, he was *right*. So much in his life *was* unfair. It was patently unfair that he had to work so hard and long for such tedious, minute gains. There was nothing fair about his having to endure such an excruciating, long-term struggle just to get his tongue, his fingers, his legs, his eyes, and his intellect to function. It was grossly unfair that he was monumentally frustrated all day, every day, and that his darkened mind couldn't even understand why his body refused to cooperate with the tasks he wished it to do. I despised disciplining this fragile child. But the one thing I hated more was to leave him imprisoned inside a body that wouldn't permit him to function in this world, or allow him to pursue the dreams that were locked inside that prison with him.

As our Father in heaven does for us, I had to love our child enough to discipline him toward freedom. And like our Father, I'm very proud and pleased to tell you that I *always* disciplined my son wisely and compassionately, without *ever* losing my cool. I had been up since 4:30 a.m., rushed through a stress-filled day in Manhattan, hurried home to take on the impossibly exasperating task of working with a brain-injured child, a child who often appeared to be regressing instead of progressing, all against the ticking of that cursed clock in the background. When Bryson stubbornly brought our efforts to a screeching halt, I *always* exhibited flawless self-control and Solomon-like wisdom in dealing with the situation. I tell you that you are reading a book written by a spiritual *giant*! And if you're buying any of this, perhaps I can interest you in purchasing a wonderful bridge that connects Brooklyn to Manhattan.

Giant or midget (and aren't we all a mixture of both), I began to see that the Lord is the perfect model for the fathering I *wanted* to do for my son. Our Father loves us far too much to allow us to stay in such a limited, sinful prison. Similar to my son, I don't like it one bit when my Father's discipline is applied to me. It often comes as a hardship or difficulty of some kind, replete with pain and sorrow.

Yet *His* discipline, though it often seems unfair, is *always* measured perfectly and full of compassion. He knows *exactly* what hardships and difficulties will get us moving toward the freedom He desires for us as His children. Dr. Charles Stanley speaks plainly of God's persistence and His goal as He disciplines us.

> God is not about to let up on a believer until He has accomplished what He has set out to do. If a man or a woman refuses to give in, God will just turn up the heat. Remember, His ultimate goal for you and me is not ease, comfort, or pleasure. It is conformity to the image of His Son. And He is willing to go to great lengths to accomplish His purpose.[1]

Oswald Chambers issued a similar sentiment, pointing out that the Lord wants to bring us to the place where we will put our complaints aside, as legitimate as they seem, and recognize that He has placed us on earth for something higher than personal comfort. When we come to understand even a bit about the sin and self-centeredness from which He has saved us (we can't fully grasp it) and the heights of freedom to which He is calling us, we will thank Him for the discipline He sees fit to bring into our lives.

> "Whom the Lord loves He chastens..." (Hebrews 12:6). How petty our complaining is! Our Lord begins to bring us to the point where we can have fellowship with Him, only to hear us moan and groan, saying, "Oh Lord, just let me be like other people!" Jesus is asking us to get beside Him and take one end of the yoke, so that we can pull together. That's why Jesus says to us, "My yoke is easy and My burden is light" (Matthew 11:30). Are you closely identified with the Lord Jesus like that? If so, you will thank God when you feel the pressure of His hand upon you.[2]

The writer of Hebrews goes on to inform us that when the sorrow of the Lord's discipline has served its purpose, we will rejoice at what God has accomplished in us.

> For [our earthly fathers] disciplined us for a short time as seemed best to them, but He disciplines us for our good, so that we may share His holiness. All discipline for the moment seems not to be joyful but sorrowful; yet to those who have been trained by it, afterwards it yields the peaceful fruit of righteousness.
>
> —Hebrews 12:10–11

As I faced the daily frustration of imperfectly disciplining a stubborn, confused, multiply handicapped child toward freedom, the Lord continued perfectly and compassionately disciplining me toward freedom, helping me to win at least *some* battles with my frustration, impatience, and self-pity. Even after all these years I know I still resist Him. Yet I am learning to accept His discipline, even to welcome it, trusting that His goal for me is the same goal I had for my own son during this difficult time. He is *always* working to bring us to higher levels of freedom and righteousness. Real love never does less.

LADDERS, SKATEBOARDS, AND CROSS PATTERNS

We continued working on Bryson's balance, strength, and coordination, performing about twenty routines and exercises daily, all designed to build new milestones of developmental circuitry in his brain. As always, the regimen was grueling, and since his love for everything having to do with sports continued to grow, we used balls, bats, gloves, and videos of some great athletic achievements to motivate him forward.

There was great power in Bryson's passion to aspire to his heroes, and he began to immerse himself in his fantasies. We bought him a Christian video called *Colby, the Talking Computer,* which featured André, the world's reigning skateboard champion. Bryson immediately became enthralled with André. Though he could barely stand independently, I purchased a brand-new skateboard for him. Darned if our little champion didn't go *right* to work imitating André!

Bryson asked us to replay that video *countless* times, particularly where André did a "360" on his board. We'd place his skateboard on the floor in front of the couch. Immediately, Bryson went at it! He painstakingly climbed up onto that board and stood on it while leaning against the couch. He'd struggle and fall, struggle and fall, struggle and fall, over and over and over again. One day, holding onto the couch the whole time, he *finally* completed his own 360-degree turn. His ability to block everything out as he fantasized was intriguing. As André, his body was anything but handicapped. In his mind, his 360 was flawless. He was the *best* in the world. He was free.

The physical side of his NACD program was designed to move him through each developmental milestone that had to be mastered before walking could be possible. We kept relearning the painful lesson that though we had come so far, the journey was so *very* long. A key component in building the neurological circuitry for walking is the development of a successful "cross pattern." Walking in a cross pattern is a highly developed neurological achievement, with only human beings and some higher primates possessing this ability. Cross-pattern walking occurs when you swing one arm forward together with the *opposite* leg. The cross pattern can be clearly observed as a short distance runner sprints down the track, pumping each arm with the opposite leg.

We were still training Bryson how to *crawl* in a cross pattern. Developmental neurologists know that children who don't learn to crawl in a cross pattern are likely to have many other developmental difficulties. For kids with profound brain injuries, the development of cross-pattern crawling is *essential.* So we got on the floor with him to teach him to crawl correctly. We pushed one of his legs forward with the *opposite* arm. We always had a toy or a prize of some kind waiting for him at the other end of the carpeted room, and he often giggled wildly as he neared his destination, particularly since one of our teen volunteers also waited to tickle him there. This was tedious work for us as well as for Bryson, whose legs and arms did not easily learn the cross pattern.

During this same period my brother-in-law Jim Schwarz built an "overhead ladder," designed by the NACD, for Bryson to train on. This device was about twelve feet long and had vertical supports at each end, with ladder rungs above for Bryson to grab onto. The overhead ladder routine was geared to get Bryson's arms and legs working together in a cross pattern as he grabbed onto a rung of the ladder with one arm, while stepping forward with the *opposite* leg. Through immense repetition, this routine was designed to provide vital neurological input, training his brain to perform cross-pattern walking by providing input from his bodily movement. But, as always, the NACD had designed a routine that was *absurdly* above our son's current level of development. In reality, Bryson was still working on standing. He wasn't even close to being a walker yet.

So we all got down under that ladder with him. One volunteer held Bryson's body upright by his hips as another very slowly moved one of his arms toward the closest rung of the overhead ladder. Bryson didn't possess either the motor control or the strength in his hands to grab onto the rungs, so we closed his fingers around each rung for him and then held his hand securely in place as we *simultaneously* picked up the opposite foot and moved it forward. This was *back-breaking* work, not only because we were leaning down under the ladder moving his hands and legs, but because his spastic legs kept moving his feet out of place each time we placed them down. Each foot needed to be patiently placed back *exactly* where it belonged and held there as we moved Bryson's opposite hand toward the next rung. We moved him forward in this manner, ever so slowly, until he reached the end of the ladder, where a volunteer waited with some fun.

There was no way he was ever going to walk across that ladder without stronger hands, so we began numerous routines designed to strengthen his hands and fingers, and to increase his fine motor control. My brother Ray volunteered for us at this time, and his father-in-law, Dave Cassels, built a wooden hanging bar in the doorway of our bathroom. When we held Bryson up to the bar and asked him to hang on, he screamed and cried, terrified he'd fall. We assured him that we wouldn't let go of him, and for the first several weeks I held him firmly by the hips as he slowly acquainted himself with just *touching* the bar. Eventually we were able to coax him to grab it as we still held him firmly.

As always, we established a simple goal initially. We wanted him to clasp the bar and support his weight for just *one* second. We kept at this task for many months, and then *years*, increasing his hanging time one precious second at a time. Eventually, we stood by with a stopwatch encouraging him: "Wow, you are so strong, Bryson. You are incredible." And, of course, we went wild each time he broke a new record.

There were numerous other "cross-pattern" routines ensuing now. One of them involved Bryson seated in a chair with a red and blue glove on either hand, and a corresponding red and blue kneepad on the *opposite* knee. Bryson was slowly and rhythmically trained to reach across and tap the opposite knee (with the matching color) as he raised that knee, simulating a cross pattern. In the early months of this routine, we moved his hands and legs for him, not only because he didn't have the coordination to lift each leg at the right time, but also because he'd miss the knee completely with his hand due to poor depth perception and lack of eye-hand coordination.

It was vital to continue awakening his brain's capacity to feel deep pressure sensation from *all over* his body, but particularly from his feet and legs. Bryson's favorite (and easiest) part of the program was to receive deep pressure massage, and he always asked for it when we neared the end of the session. He'd look at me, or Charlotte Anderson, one of his favorite volunteers and say, "Sage now?" With his limited speech, this was his way of abbreviating the sentence: "Is it time for my massage now?"

Stop Signs and Green Lights

Our district school psychologist came to our home to "test" Bryson. The difference between the NACD methods, which are based on appropriate input, and those of our school district, based on conventional methods, became quickly evident. Our five-year-old son didn't possess the motor control to properly hold a pencil. He held it with his entire hand wrapped around it and was able to make only crude marks on the paper in front of him. Obviously this had *nothing* to do with cognition. And although Bryson was a visual learner (his audio passageways were severely damaged), a test was given only with *auditory* instructions with no visual cues whatsoever.

As the test questions were quickly recited to him, he wasn't given an adequate amount of time to attempt his answers with his slow, slurred speech. The psychologist simply assumed that Bryson didn't understand the tasks he was being asked to perform. Quite simply, this *professional* (and I use the term advisedly) didn't believe in Bryson's capacity to learn. The testing process lasted about ten minutes, after which the psychologist labeled Bryson with an IQ in the 50 range, which is essentially uneducable.

Bob Doman laughed when he heard of the methods used to test Bryson's intelligence. In reality, our son's *handicaps* had been tested, not his abilities. Bob taught us many valuable things through the years, but nothing more valuable than the understanding that we must *never* place an artificial ceiling on our son's capacity to learn. Certain standardized tests, if given appropriately, can provide *some* value in measuring *current* levels of function. But they must never be used to limit a child's potential.

Once it is presumed that a child cannot learn, then appropriate opportunities to achieve higher levels of function are rarely pursued with sufficient vigor, and pronouncements of the child's inability to learn often become a self-fulfilling prophecy. For *any* person, whether brain injured or mastermind, learning is a dynamic process. The most important thing is to provide appropriate, repetitious input designed to help him or her reach the *next* higher level of function in each developmental area.

Even so, we were surprised when the NACD informed us it was time for Bryson to read. Since significant damage had occurred in the auditory passages of his brain, his ability to process auditory information was extremely limited. Therefore learning to read through phonetic methods was impossible. But Bob Doman told us that any child who can learn what a stop sign means, or a green light, can also learn to read. Each word is merely a different sign. For Bryson, reading would just be a matter of recognizing more signs.

We had to teach him to read through visual input, by flashing word cards (signs) for him to recognize. He needed to see the same words thousands and thousands of times, over a period of many years. We introduced two new words to his reading vocabulary each day, flashing them on 3 by 5 cards. We flashed the new cards four times per day for one minute, along with a set of ten review cards. The cards were flashed as rapidly as our fingers could flash them, as we verbally pronounced each word. Even an injured brain is much faster than your fingers at taking a "snapshot" of each card, and his mind was slowly learning to recognize the snapshots. He was not asked to repeat the words or to give us any feedback (output) whatsoever. As always, Bryson's brain was bombarded with *input, input, input*.

One Small Step

The NACD kept pushing Bryson, and us, to achieve things he was *far* from ready to accomplish. They now informed us it was time for Bryson to attempt his first *independent* step. Neil Armstrong, the first man to set foot on the moon, said: "This is one small step for a man, one giant leap for mankind."[3] Bob Doman believed that if Bryson could just take that first independent step on his own, this would represent his giant leap. Once that *first* step was conquered, then no matter how long it might take, other steps would follow. But somehow, our crippled son had to accomplish that first small step.

We were asked to place Bryson on a mattress, holding him firmly from behind by the shoulders. Then we were to let go and plead with him to move one foot forward, as we had painstakingly taught him to do with the overhead ladder. The reason for the mattress was not only to cushion his fall, but to help him overcome the intense fear of falling that all crippled individuals have. Someone suggested purchasing some foam rubber padding that carpet stores use under wall-to-wall carpet. This would be flatter and easier to walk on than a mattress, and we could use a double layer for adequate cushion. The manager of the Faber Brothers carpet store, once he understood the reason we were buying padding with no carpet, insisted on *giving* it to us, refusing to take our money.

Walking is the act of "falling forward." The trick is to "fall forward" without falling down. Even after years of intense work, Bryson still had only a tiny bit of strength in his crippled legs, and his balance was near nonexistent. It took a long time just to steady him in a standing position on that foam. Countless times his spastic legs involuntarily moved, requiring us to reset his feet. When he was *finally* ready to make an attempt, our son *immediately* fell flat on his face. This went on day after day, month after month, with *no* discernible progress toward that first step.

We tried to hide our anguish from him as he went down, again and again and again. Together with the volunteers, we praised him wildly just for making each attempt. He was thrown in the air and "raspberries" were blown in his tummy. Everything you can think of. We made it seem as if he, merely by trying, had just accomplished the most magnificent feat in the history of the world.

Amidst such futility, we needed to somehow fight off the discouragement ourselves. We'd remind each other how long it had taken Bryson to finally stand for that first second against the wall, and then once again in the middle of the room. I wrote quarterly letters to Bryson's Army with verbal encouragements that, despite appearances to the contrary, progress was indeed being made, especially inside his brain. We'd offer reminders to each other that failure was merely the doorway to success, and we'd share encouraging scriptures about falling and walking, such as the following:

> For a righteous man falls seven times, and rises again.
> —Proverbs 24:16

> Do not rejoice over me, O my enemy. Though I fall I will rise.
> —Micah 7:8

But when his daily program ended and the volunteers had all gone home, Bryson reverted to crawling through the house, which was still his only way of independently ambulating. Caring for three young children in a state of exhaustion, we'd sometimes succumb to doubt and fear. The professionals had warned us. Why should we be surprised? In their view we just were being cruel to our son and wasting our time. My son was nearly six years old, and nowhere *near* walking. I always tried to stay positive, for everyone's sake. But in my private moments, I wondered if the skeptics just might be right.

More Forks in the Road (Are There Never Spoons?)

Sorry about the "spoons" thing, but it's been a couple of chapters since I told a bad joke, and things were getting a little heavy as I described my discouraging moments. In any event, there are undoubtedly individuals reading this book who are just as exhausted and discouraged as I was at this time. Perhaps you've endured for so long and tried so hard to make progress in your impossible battle. Not only are you discouraged *again*, but it also seems that God has vanished, yet *again*, and your circumstances have turned out to be just the *opposite* of what you *begged* Him for. What in the world does God want from you? Does He want you to grovel? It hardly seems to matter anymore. You've had it!

I must remind you that this is not a "how to" book. The truth is, I don't have answers to many of my own problems, no less to yours. But if I've accomplished what I've set out to do, this is very much a "Who to" book, pointing you to a King. This King will not always grant us what we request. Sometimes He will allow absurd, seemingly evil events to unfold in our lives. But in the face of the most discouraging times of your life, when your dreams have been shattered, His path of victory is still *very* near. This is why our choices are so critical as we stand at the fork of discouragement.

I know I've said this somewhere in this book (and I hope I have the good sense to say it several more times before the conclusion) that we are to walk by *faith*, not by sight (2 Cor. 5:7), and certainly not by our feelings. This is particularly important when everything in our line of sight goes black. During times of discouragement we simply cannot trust our feelings. Bill Gillham communicates this in a refreshing, practical way, urging us to keep believing what the King has taught us in His Word:

> God is committed to training you to walk in the Spirit by faith, and a critical part of that training is to teach you that you cannot trust your 'feeler,' but you can trust Him. At times, He'll give you all the zingy feelings you can handle, but He will not permit you to build a tabernacle there. Sometimes it'll feel as though He's gone to Mars for a summer vacation. He will withdraw all experiential evidence of His presence in order to train you, indeed, to box you in and force you to walk by what you know rather than what you feel.... But has He left you in those times?... Your job is to keep believing... keep operating by what you know.[4]

For me, it is critically important to cling hard to this truth in order to keep from doing something *really* stupid during my exhausted, self-pitying, dejected times. If I operate by what I see and feel, I'm quickly in trouble. I suspect the same is true for you. Our feelings tell us to chuck it all, to take our ball and go home. Sometimes we are tempted to go somewhere even more dangerous than "home."

During deeply discouraging times, we can be tempted to seek relief through addictions, secret sins, and all manner of "harmless" comforts this world offers to anesthetize us from the emptiness and despair. We think we're just taking the pressure off, just easing up on the gas pedal a bit as we engage in our idol of choice (alcohol, pornography, gambling, spending, shopping, overeating... the list is endless). But taking this fork in the road, even when it appears to involve only harmless distractions, is a deadly trap.

The trap is that we become quickly enslaved, not only to these idols, but to the cruel slave master who holds out the bait. We think we won't be controlled. Ed Welch and Steve Gallagher have written excellent books which wisely caution otherwise: *Addictions: A Banquet in the Grave*[5] and *At the Altar of Sexual Idolatry*.[6] There's an old adage: The devil will take you farther than you want to go, he'll keep you longer than you want to stay, and he'll cost you far more than you ever dreamed you'd have to pay.

There's a much better alternative, a life-enhancing road to take at this fork. To be sure, it is a narrower, less traveled road, even in Christian circles. This less traveled road was spoken of by two demons in C. S. Lewis' classic work, *The Screwtape*

Letters. The demons, one whose name is Wormwood, refer to God as the "Enemy." Their conversation got my rapt attention, particularly since they spoke of a subject near and dear to my heart at this time, that of learning how to walk.

> He [God] wants them to learn to walk and must therefore take away His hand; and if only the will to walk is really there He is pleased even with their stumbles. Do not be deceived, Wormwood. Our cause is never more in danger than when a human, no longer desiring, but still intending, to do our Enemy's will, looks round a universe from which every trace of Him seems to have vanished, and asks why he has been forsaken, and still obeys.[7]

Something stirred in my heart as I read this demonic perspective. If the forces of evil are never more in danger than when I stand at the fork of affliction and unanswered prayer, and *still* choose to obey, this is reason enough to choose God's narrow path. Yet I believe there's something more at stake. God can handle the forces of evil without my help or yours, thank you, and He will one day prove this convincingly (Phil. 2:10–11). So what *else* is at stake in our choices? Something that our Father desires deeply, something that brings us back to a discussion of what any good father wants for his child.

The Lord sometimes removes not only the blessings of life, but seemingly also *Himself* from us, to get us to pursue the only joy that can ever last: our relationship with Him. Everything that is truly good and lasting is wrapped up in knowing and loving God. *Everything!* He is our joy. He is our freedom and our abundance. He is the attainment of our most deeply ingrained desires. Who do we think put those desires in us anyway? Darwin? Our intimacy with Him is, without overstating it, the reason we've been born. We were born to know Christ, to experience a depth of love from Him that surpasses knowledge. Any father worth his salt would do *anything* to keep his son from missing the reason for his existence. Why would we expect the Father to do any less for us?

Our Father's discipline seems unnecessarily harsh. I often conclude that He is allowing my trials to go on and on, my pain unabated, with no satisfactory endgame in sight. But how much more harsh would He be if He allowed us to languish in the false, temporary idols and comforts we would settle for and die with in this world? It's hard to choose the road of obedience when we come to the fork of discouragement, especially when everything appears black and our choices seem to be just as meaningless as our pain.

Like my brain-injured son, we've all been wounded and twisted by this world in ways that are impossible to fully comprehend, no less to untangle. We don't need introspective psychoanalysis to free us from the wreckage. We need Light. Periods of darkness and confusion are opportunities for seeing Light for who He really is. Larry Crabb indicates that God is up to something when He removes blessings from us, and when He allows intense sorrow and pain. Sometimes the Lord will even remove Himself, so that we will finally be awakened from the trance of seeking the idols of this world and seek Him.

> He is taking away good food to make us hungry for better fare. But then He doesn't seem to give it. The table stays bare. Those who claim otherwise most often are feeding on their own resources or on their remaining blessings, mistaking them for God.... When the pain of shattered dreams helps us to discover our desire for God, God seems to disappear. Or at least His absence becomes obvious. And then we feel our desire for God as throbbing agony. We discover how badly we long to know Him. It is the frustration of our desire for God that deepens it. Only by not revealing God to us, at least for a while—sometimes a long while—can the Spirit put us in touch with a desire that eventually displaces every other desire.[8]

God intends to ignite a passion within us to pursue *Him,* not just to enjoy the comforts of this world. Jesus didn't even have a place to lay His head. Please don't hear me wrong. I love comforts and pleasures. I think Jesus enjoyed them too. Above all men, He lived life to the full. But He knew how to enjoy the blessings of life as an extension of His relationship with the Father, not as a *replacement* for it. We are talking here about those times when God gives us a grand opportunity to come up higher as dearly loved children. Those times require a response of willing surrender, and a determination to seek Him.

Many of you reading this right now have lost battles in life you never expected to lose. It's not as if you were fighting the wrong battle. If you were, then you could understand. But you just wanted your marriage to survive, your body to be kept from being riddled with cancer, your finances from being destroyed after *decades* of hard work. Now many of your long held, cherished dreams have been decimated. Don't hear me telling you not to feel horrible about that. It would be cruel to tell someone to deny their pain. But for God's sake, and yours, please don't move forward with your feelings as your guide. You need a better battle plan than that, and a much better Commander.

> But thanks be to God, who always leads us in triumph in Christ, and manifests through us the sweet aroma of the knowledge of Him in every place.
>
> —2 Corinthians 2:14

Your personal war is not over; your life is not over, until God says it is over. You wouldn't still be here if God didn't have a plan to redeem what has happened to you for His glory and for your good. His Word says that He can even make up for the years that the locust has eaten (Joel 2:25). Go ahead and grieve your dreams. But realize this: our shattered dreams are not even the slightest challenge to His power and ability to replace those dreams with new ones, and to move us forward with a higher sense of purpose, as we turn to Him through the anguish of our broken dreams and our unfulfilled desire.

Hannah Whitall Smith lived a pain-filled life, replete with broken dreams. Her words inspired me not to give up during times of discouragement, or after lapses into personal sin and failure. Intriguingly, she also used the analogy of a child learning to walk. I couldn't take her words literally in terms of my son walking one day, but she reminded me to keep getting up again after a fall, and to never abandon this dream for my son.

> From whatever cause we have been betrayed into failure, it is very certain that there is no remedy to be found in discouragement. As well might a child who is learning to walk, lie down in despair when he has fallen, and refuse to take another step, as a believer, who is seeking to learn how to live and walk by faith, give up in despair because of having fallen into sin. The only way in both cases is to get right up and try again.[9]

THE MIGHTIEST DUCK

Bryson's passion for sports and his escape to freedom into the fantasy world reached something of a crescendo when he saw the Disney movie *The Mighty Ducks*. He was absolutely enthralled by it, and he wanted to see it every day, continually asking us to fast forward or rewind it to his favorite parts. One Saturday I went to the local sports store and bought him a hockey stick, which he went absolutely nuts over. He immediately crawled to the couch and stood with the stick, leaning against the couch. Clearly, he had embarked on a proud career as a member of the Mighty Ducks.

One day as I hurried into the house after the 1:30 p.m. train home, my wife asked me to come into the family room before rushing upstairs to change clothes for the program. What I saw there made my jaw drop. Not only was Bryson standing in the *middle* of our family room, but he was attempting to move across the "ice" using the stick to support him. The stick, together with his two legs, formed sort of a tripod. Every attempt to move either leg forward resulted in his crashing to the floor. Though we had installed thick padding under the carpet, I winced each time he wiped out, his body hitting the floor as the hockey stick went flying. But in typical relentless Bryson fashion, each time he merely reached for his stick, crawled back to the couch, and slowly began dragging himself back up to get ready for another breakaway toward the goal.

He fell and crashed, fell and crashed, over and over and over again. It didn't bother him that he made almost no progress in a forward direction. In his *mind* he was skating down the ice to score a goal, as any self-respecting Mighty Duck would. I stood there in awe. Oh, how I delighted in this child. I was reminded of the words of King David:

> The steps of a man are established by the LORD; And He delights in his way.
> When he falls, he shall not be hurled headlong, Because the LORD is the One who holds his hand.
>
> —PSALM 37:23–24

Imagine! The awesomely powerful Creator of the universe actually *delights* in the path of failing, stumbling men and women like David, like Bryson, like you, and like me. My heart stirred, and I wondered since the *steps* of a man are established by the Lord, would He answer our desperate prayers to establish some physical "steps" for our little man? God's silence had been the only answer to our pleadings for *so long* now.

By the time we saw Bob Doman again for our quarterly reevaluation, Bryson still had not taken his first independent step. To state the obvious, we were discouraged. Bob exhorted us to keep pressing forward. He was convinced that the years of exhaustive input had provided circuitry in Bryson's brain that would ultimately make that first step possible. He was delighted to hear of Bryson's hockey playing and he encouraged him to keep it up, knowing this provided him tremendous inspiration, and also that picking himself up off the ground was an excellent, self-motivated exercise.

As the months went by, Bryson slowly began reaching for the rungs of his overhead ladder by himself. His hands were stronger now, from hanging on the bathroom bar and from all his other hand exercises. His hands were doing as much of the work as his legs. We had known for years that he had superior control over his upper body, as compared to his legs. This was not a good sign for ever being able to walk independently. But the determination on his face to get to the end of the ladder was astounding. He was exhibiting the same resolve away from the ladder now too, out on that foam padding. He was no longer afraid, but he wasn't showing signs of improvement yet either.

As usual, his feat came suddenly one afternoon. It was late 1991, and to the extent that Neil Armstrong's step was an awesome spectacle, my son's step was no obvious wonder. In fact, you had to pay close attention, or you'd have missed it. The "step" was merely a fleeting second of his weight suspended on one leg, before flopping down again onto that foam padding. To the skeptics, I suppose Bryson's first step could be written off as a glorified stumble. But it was a *full* second, and it belonged to my son!

When we saw it we *knew* it was the miracle we had prayed and pleaded for. We went insane, as much from relief as from exultation, celebrating wildly as always. With so many doubters in the world, it was up to us to make him feel like the greatest champion, the Mightiest Duck alive. No headlines were made by Bryson's miracle that day, and only his volunteers and the members of my struggling little family shared in the joy of this achievement. But I'll never forget the proud look on Johnny Costalas' face, nor the tear in his eye, when I told him of Bryson's triumph the next morning.

I haven't spoken to him in many years now. I heard he somehow survived the destruction of his store as the World Trade Center's Twin Towers crumbled just across the street, on September 11, 2001. But as that humble owner of a coffee shop helped me to understand, we're all yearning to find something that has been tragically lost in this world.

When Bryson was born, the thought of him taking his first faltering step at six years old could only have entered my mind in a nightmare. Now, this milestone was the fulfillment of a long-cherished dream, and I was more grateful for it than words could express. Still, my mind often drifted to thoughts of how different life had turned out to be from what I expected, or what I wanted. I remember the sheer joy in that dream of Bryson running free in the park, playing with the other children. I couldn't hold onto that dream; nor, as it turned out, would my son ever fully escape the cruel realities of his brain-injured prison.

But no one will ever convince me that the joy in that dream wasn't real. An ache deep inside reminds me of it still. I'm determined to find it, more convinced than ever that God will bring it to pass one day. Until then, those with eyes to see know that He still performs miracles in this world. His miracles are random and mysterious, and they rarely make headlines. For a while yet they must be seen as through a mist. But a day is coming soon when all will be made clear, when every longing conceived for us in the heart of God will be fulfilled, when pain and sorrow will be remembered no more.

For now we see in a mirror dimly, but then face to face.

—1 CORINTHIANS 13:12

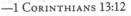

The fantasies are so real.

Always reaching forward

Chapter 15
THE WASHINGTON CAPER

Consider it all joy, my brethren, when you encounter various trials.

James 1:2

I DOUBT COURTROOM TRIALS were on James' mind as he wrote his epistle. Nonetheless, we were about to encounter a courtroom trial that to this day remains difficult to put in the same sentence with the word "joy." This trial would fit better in a sentence with the word agony or misery, but certainly not with joy. Let me back up a bit and tell you about it.

My Uncle Nick was a gracious, humble man who cared for others without fanfare. By the time he died in 2004, he had served as a Roman Catholic priest for over fifty years, running a church and school in a poor section of the Bronx, New York. He never received worldly acclaim for his life of service, and he wanted none. We may never have found out about the National Childhood Vaccine Injury Act (NCVIA) had it not been for Uncle Nick handing us a tiny article he clipped from *The New York Times*. He brought it to a family gathering at my father's house (Bryson's beloved "Pop Pop") in the spring of 1989.

The article indicated that the NCVIA was designed to help families with children who were injured through reactions to vaccines. We filed a claim later that year, but it wasn't until the spring of 1992 that our claim finally came to trial. During the two-year interval between filing the claim and going to trial, we faced numerous legal procedures and filings. Some of these procedures involved gut-wrenching depositions, requiring us to revisit the horrifying events from the time Bryson was first injured. We'd sometimes wake in anguish in the middle of the night after reliving those awful days and hours.

Yet it was with high hopes that we drove toward Washington, DC, for our trial as petitioners against the United States Department of Health and Human Services. We left our three children in the capable hands of my wife's mother who stayed with them in our Glen Rock home. Our trip was scheduled for three days, and the trial lasted for two of those days. We believed, at long last, justice would be served for our brain-injured son, and that the practical economic needs for his future would be provided.

We were also passionate about registering Bryson's brain injury among the numerous cases then being filed under the NCVIA, hoping that the sheer volume of these cases would create an outcry for a safer vaccination system for all children. It is my conviction that this outcry continues to fall on deaf ears these many years later, as I write this book.

We soon came to believe that the National Childhood Vaccine Injury Act, drafted by the United States Congress in 1986, was a politically compromised

an injury has occurred, to pinpoint the *single* vaccine from numerous vaccines administered *simultaneously* to their child.

Another practical difficulty posed to families filing under The National Childhood Vaccine Injury Act was the limited compensation afforded to the attorneys representing children like Bryson. The maximum allowable fee to attorneys under the Act at that time was $30,000. These cases typically required *years* to prepare and bring to trial. A fee of $30,000 is nowhere *near* the compensation required by top malpractice attorneys. We had a very fine young attorney representing us. However, we sensed that the deck was stacked against us as soon as we entered that Washington, DC, courtroom. There were not one, but *three* government attorneys opposing us. They were all experienced at arguing these cases, while our attorney was about to argue his very first case under the NCVIA.

The government attorneys requested that the court sequester me in another part of the building as my wife testified the first day. She was cross-examined by those attorneys for several hours without my presence. Their reasoning was to later cross-examine me without my directly hearing my wife's testimony. We were treated like suspects in a crime investigation who needed to be interrogated in separate rooms to try to catch us in an inconsistency, any slightly differing recollection of some minute detail that they could seize upon in order to win their case. Several years had passed since the events that we were being cross-examined about. Nonetheless, the details were actually easy to remember, particularly for my wife, who was home with Bryson the entire time.

One fact weighing heavily in our favor was that Bryson's medical history was clear that he was *completely* healthy at birth. This was confirmed at several "well-baby" visits to the pediatrician. Bryson was a bright, bubbly, extremely alert baby during his first several months of life. Everyone in our extended family, including both sets of grandparents, had rejoiced with us over the health of the firstborn Milazzo son coming from my generation. And everyone in the family watched his radical decline in horror.

As described in earlier chapters, our son was subjected to rigorous medical testing at some of the finest institutions in the world. His medical file was voluminous. Every known prenatal or postnatal cause for our son's brain injury had already been considered and ruled out. So even though there were doubts about whether Bryson was injured only by his three-month vaccinations, or by his eight-month vaccinations, or by both, we believed our case was solid. We believed it would be obvious to the court that the vaccinations were the *only* reasonable explanation for our son's brain injury.

The facts of our case posed a problem for those government attorneys, and they knew it. So they developed a theory of their own regarding how our perfectly healthy son became profoundly brain damaged. In my view, the theory they developed was a whopper. They seized on the opinion of a *single* doctor who, like Bryson's pediatrician, did not believe that vaccinations ever caused neurological damage. This doctor postulated that Bryson's injury *could possibly* have been prenatal, and simply missed at birth. The attorneys embellished their case by suggesting that Bryson may have been injured by a very rare, prenatal disorder that had not been considered.

Our attorney objected to this absurd theory since the specific disorder suggested by the opposing attorneys had not been brought forward in the discovery proceedings. Our attorney was quickly overruled. He then raised questions concerning this rare disorder, and the government attorneys were forced to admit that there were only a tiny number of cases of it ever identified in recorded medical history (my recollection is seven). Furthermore, this disorder did not fit the profile of Bryson's symptoms nor of his brain injury at all, which is why none of the myriad doctors or institutions that had examined him had even considered it. Their theory was preposterous, and when I heard that this was the best theory the opposing attorneys could come up with, I rejoiced, thinking it was a slam dunk that we had won our case.

But *amazingly,* when it came time for the special master (under the NCVIA the judge is known as the special master) to rule on the case via a telephone conference three months later (we were in our attorney's New Jersey office, the special master and lead government attorney were in his chambers in Washington), he opined that the theory of the government attorneys was "plausible." He ruled that we, as petitioners, had not met our burden to overcome the *preponderance of the evidence.*

We sat in shocked disbelief as the special master pronounced that our case was now closed. We began to protest. Our attorney held up his hand, signaling us not to speak. He thanked the special master, and hung up the phone. In the eyes of the law, justice had been served. In our eyes, injustice on top of tragedy had been heaped upon our son's life.

Our lawyer reminded us that our case had flaws from the court's perspective. The contemporaneous medical records (the pediatrician's records) did not indicate that Bryson had suffered neurological damage *within* seventy-two hours after his immunizations, as required by the statute. Further, the government attorneys had pointed out that we ourselves had not *strongly* asserted in the early stages of Bryson's degeneration that we believed he had been injured by his vaccines. They tried to portray us as opportunists who came up with our theory about the vaccines years later for the purpose of gaining a monetary award for our son from the NCVIA system.

To *every* doctor we had seen from the beginning, we had specified the violent reactions that occurred after Bryson's vaccinations. Still, I wish we had been bolder in stating that it was our firm belief that the vaccinations were the *definitive* cause of our son's injury. Looking back, I realize I was personally too intimidated to assert this. I was afraid to appear foolish, suspecting that those doctors would scoff at our opinion, even as our pediatrician had done. Further, I wanted to be cooperative with these doctors so that they would help our son. I believed that the cause would ultimately become irrefutably clear through all the evaluations and tests, without the need for me to forcefully assert my personal opinion that the vaccinations were the definitive cause.

As stated in an earlier chapter, it's not as if we *wanted* the vaccines to be found to be the cause. We *desperately* hoped that the doctors could identify another cause, a *curable* cause, so our nightmare could end. It wasn't until after every other conceivable cause for our son's degeneration was ruled out that it became *inescapably* clear to us that there *couldn't* be any other cause. The *last* thing on our minds throughout the entire, horrifying process was to document our concerns regarding the vaccines with a view toward future litigation. We never dreamed we would wind up in court to settle this matter. Our sole focus in seeing all those doctors was to save our son's life.

From a legal standpoint, I suppose our battle against the *preponderance of the evidence* was a slam dunk for the United States Government, not for us. I hasten to add that I consider our legal system to be the best in the world. Yet I have become painfully aware that justice is not always received in any worldly system. We never received a penny of compensation for our son's enormous expenses, nor for his future. More sadly, Bryson's case will never be included in the statistics used in the analysis of the safety of vaccines. All evidence indicating that his brain injury was caused through his vaccinations will continue to be disregarded by the professionals of this world as "anecdotal." I believe that there are *countless* other families in the same boat, skewing the official statistics.

Will I ever be able to prove in a court of law that my son was damaged through his vaccines? Probably not. But in my mind there is no question that the "routine" childhood vaccinations administered to my once perfectly healthy son were the cause of his injury.

Why Not Ask the Questions?

It is my understanding that, to this day, 80 percent of the cases filed under the NCVIA fail. This means there are an awful lot of families who believe their children are autistic or brain injured due to vaccines, whose stories are also considered "anecdotal." In my view, such statistics represent a travesty. In any event, my son's trial is over, and I now have nothing to gain by offering my opinion in this regard.

I don't take a position regarding whether parents should vaccinate their children. But I urge parents to become educated concerning the benefits and risks associated with each of the numerous (and growing number of) immunizations being offered, even *mandated* today. We began our childbearing years with no predisposition whatsoever regarding vaccinations. Our oldest child, Janelle, went through all her immunizations without a hint of a problem. My perspective changed solely because of our tragedy with Bryson.

As Christians, we are called to be good stewards of the world God created, protecting the environment by paying close attention to the substances we allow to be released into our air and water. Is it not *just* as important to pay rigorous attention, to be *absolutely certain* of the safety and efficacy of each and every substance we release *directly into the bloodstream* of our children? I believe it is reasonable to ask (particularly in view of today's *skyrocketing* incidences of autism, brain injury, hyperactivity, ADD, learning disorders, and neurological and autoimmune diseases, etc.) if the health of our nation's children is being put directly and unnecessarily at risk as a consequence of today's accepted vaccination regimens.

These are scary and difficult issues, and they can make us want to bury our heads in the sand. But the stakes are far too high to not to ask some very hard questions. We owe it to our nation's children to invest heavily into comprehensive, *independent* research in order to clarify not only the immediate risk of injury from vaccines, but also the long-term health effects of the products and procedures now in place. Further, I believe that parents should *always* retain the right to make informed decisions concerning the safety risks they are willing to accept for their own children.

This issue cuts across party and socioeconomic lines like no other. We all have children. We live in a day when *intense* lobbying pressure is being exerted toward our legislators geared toward the limitation of parental rights in general, and specifically with regard to the vaccine issue. This is occurring even as numerous new vaccines continue to be introduced (and seemingly rushed) into the marketplace together with mega marketing campaigns to vaccinate. Do we, as a society, want the role of parents to become so diminished that we will have no say regarding whether these vaccination regimens are forced upon our children? Do parents have the right to determine the risks that are acceptable for their own children? Or are we willing to relinquish that role to big corporations (making big profits) and to big government bureaucracies who "know" better than we do as "mere" parents what is best for the welfare of our children?

This has become a very emotionally charged issue, with many accusations being hurled by both sides about the motives and even the sanity of the other side. But it is *far* too vital an issue to be settled through a shouting match between opposing sides' experts and websites. The side with the most money will always be able to shout louder. Obviously, decisions concerning an issue of this magnitude ought *never* to be made by those with a vested financial interest of *any* kind.

All truth will ultimately come to light on that great day when God dries every tear from the eyes of those who belong to Him. There may be some surprises then. But nowhere in Scripture are we told to ignore the truth right now as we await our presence with the Creator. I believe we are to fight to see that truth and justice prevail in this world, *particularly* when we know, or even if we suspect, that the innocent and the helpless among us are being harmed. I do not believe that truth has yet prevailed on this issue.

> If you are slack in the day of distress, Your strength is limited. Deliver those who are being taken away to death, And those who are staggering to slaughter, Oh hold them back. If you say, "See, we did not know this," Does

He not consider it who weighs the hearts? And does He not know it who keeps your soul? And will He not render to man according to his work?

—PROVERBS 24:10–12

CONSIDER IT *WHAT??*

Consider it all joy, my brethren, when you encounter various trials.

—JAMES 1:2

I don't think I will ever feel joy when I look back on some of the trials I've encountered in life, particularly that extremely painful trial we endured in Washington, DC. But is James really asking us to *feel* joy when we go through trials?

In previous chapters we've discussed the need to choose obedience to God's Word even when our feelings conflict with what Scripture says. I don't want to minimize feelings. We men are pretty good at that, I'm told. God created us with emotions and it is important to try to understand what we are feeling. However, feelings change like the direction of the wind; and while emotions can be a good indicator that something needs attention in our minds and hearts, we need to be careful not to place our confidence in what we may be feeling in any given moment.

The real battleground, as we seek to follow and obey the Lord, is the battleground of our minds, not of our emotions. If we really want to understand what we are feeling, we need to take a look *underneath* those feelings, to discover what we are *thinking*. James seems to be indicating that correct *thinking* can lead us to the reality of joy.

If we are asked to *consider* something, we are not necessarily being asked to *feel* something. Rather, we are being asked to reflect on something, to probe a matter, to mull something over in our minds. James is asking us to *consider* something about the trials we experience, knowing that such consideration will ultimately result in joy. Look at the next few verses from James to gain insight into what he is actually asking us to consider.

Consider it all joy, my brethren, when you encounter various trials, knowing that the testing of your faith produces endurance. And let endurance have its perfect result, so that you may be perfect and complete, lacking in nothing.

—JAMES 1:2–4

James is exhorting us to *think* in a certain way about the trials that come into our lives. He wants us to reflect on what the Lord is using those trials to accomplish *within* us. Obviously, no one *feels* joyful about grievous trials. But as we consider the Lord's good work being accomplished in us through those trials, we can reach the rational conclusion that those trials are indeed something to be joyful about.

Who among us wouldn't want to be "perfect and complete"? Who wouldn't want character that is "lacking in nothing"? James is saying that when unwanted trials come into our lives God is at work, moving us toward higher levels of maturity and perfection.

Praise God that He sees wretches like us as perfect and complete right *now* in Christ (Col. 2:10). Some theologians refer to this as our "positional" righteousness. Yet His grace does more. God is continually working to move us toward practical maturity in our character through His grace. James reveals that He is moving us toward being "perfect and complete," toward "lacking in nothing." These are very lofty aspirations. Jesus Christ is the *only* One who is perfect and who lacks nothing.

Jesus commanded this same thing of us when He said: "You are to be perfect, as your heavenly Father is perfect" (Matt. 5:48). So the goal is clearly enough stated in Scripture. But can we talk privately? I don't know about you, but this scares the *daylights* out of me. I'm no spring chicken anymore; and frankly, I'm still *ridiculously* far from perfect. As I consider the limited time I have left in this world, along with all the weakness and evil I still see in my flesh, it has occurred to me that I'm just not going to make it to sinless perfection. If you are honest, neither will you.

So what about these commands to be perfect? Is God toying with us? Does He relish our being stuck in a no-win situation? Is He trapping us into some kind of double bind? Of course not! We are His dearly loved children. But if we are ever going to make *any* progress toward perfection, toward being conformed to the image of Christ, we need to understand that this is a process God *alone* can successfully work into our lives.

As discussed in earlier chapters, our self-righteous desire to be independent from God is our core sin and must be purged from our souls. John of the Cross reveals that God is working through our inner trials to correct this deep darkness that dwells inside all of us. It should come as no surprise that this inner darkness compels us to attempt to purify and perfect ourselves without relying upon God.

> The Lord Himself allows these inward trials. It is His way of causing us to see that our own fallen understanding of the spiritual way is bound up in our attempts to purify and perfect and to be strong in ourselves.... When we are overwhelmed by these attacks, we finally cast ourselves in total dependence upon His benevolent wisdom.... Our fleshly strengths must be proven to be weakness; our present understanding must be proven to be blindness. Then we can walk in wisdom...and strength in the Spirit.... These greater trials of the soul are measured out by the loving hand of God. And He only permits them to come upon us to the degree of self-dependence and self-righteousness that must be purged from our soul.[1]

Andrew Murray, the great Scottish missionary to South Africa in the 1800s, described the journey from self-righteous striving to dependence upon God in similar terms, placing the emphasis on the work of the Spirit of God to bring about our growth. He makes it clear that we are never to rely on the feeble working of our self-exalting flesh:

> In a parable about seeds, Jesus teaches us two of the most important lessons on the growth of the spiritual life.... The truth is, all we can do is *let* the life of the Spirit grow within us. We can do nothing to force ourselves to grow in spirit. It is from within that the power of spiritual life must come—in order to be true spiritual growth, and not self-righteous striving, our growth must come from within, from the Life and Spirit planted in us. We do not hold the power to create new spiritual life, and so we can contribute nothing to this side of it. It shall be given to us to grow.[2] (emphasis added)

Notice the passive language Murray uses: "*let* the life of the Spirit grow within us." Is he advocating "easy believism"? Is he giving us permission to be lazy, telling us that we are not responsible to do a *blessed* thing to move forward in our Christian walk? Before you take Murray to task, did you notice that James used similarly passive language to describe our journey toward perfection? James asks us to "*let* endurance have its perfect result, so you may be perfect and complete, lacking in nothing" (James 1:4).

It almost seems as if we are being asked to become inactive observers of a process we have nothing to do with, that we are to stand aside and behold the unfolding of God's handiwork in our lives. But James is not advocating irresponsibility, nor is John of the Cross, nor is Murray. As passive as our part in God's work *appears* descriptively, our role is *vital*. But it is a *different* role than we often think it is.

In John 6 the disciples were growing a bit antsy with Jesus regarding this very same issue. They were fed up with Jesus concerning His lack of direction, and they asked Him point-blank about the works they could accomplish for God (John 6:28). Jesus answered that our work is to "believe in the One Whom He has sent" (v. 29, AMP). They were hardly satisfied with His answer. In fact, after Jesus went on to tell them that the flesh profits *nothing* (v. 63), many of those indignant disciples refused to follow Him any more (v. 66).

In their arrogance, they had no intention of yielding to God and His ways, and they certainly didn't want their role relegated to believing in the One whom He has sent. They were exasperated by what Jesus was telling them, not because they loved God but because they wanted to control their own religion. They wanted to "work the works of God" (v. 28) on their *own* terms, and they wanted full credit for doing so. They wanted to be recognized and rewarded. If you are over the age of ten, you've undoubtedly noticed that God never bows to our terms. We must surrender to His.

According to God's foolish ways, the works of our flesh profit *nothing*. Make that nada, zip, zilch. God is the *only* One who has life. He is the *only* One who is able to give life (John 6:63). This is true for our initial salvation, and it is true for *any* and *all* of our growth toward perfection. There is one Author. There is one Perfecter. *All* life and growth comes from the Spirit of the living God. But don't think for a second that Jesus didn't intend for these disciples to do hard work, nor that He was giving them permission to be lazy. Jesus calls each of His followers, including you and me, to the obedience of faith at the heart level. The obedience of faith is the heavy lifting of the Christian walk.

Earlier I mentioned that our real battleground as we seek to follow and obey the Lord is the battleground of our minds. Our daily effort to choose truth amidst the lies flying fast and furious in our direction is a knock-down, drag-out battle. It is a ferocious war to maintain our faith, to choose truth over expedient, self-serving equivocation. Those arrogant, self-focused disciples didn't realize that Jesus was asking something of them that was excruciatingly hard. They wanted to "do" religious works so that they could be blessed by God and look good in front of one another to boot. Jesus was presenting them with something far higher. They didn't want it, and they didn't want Him. In their arrogant minds their religion was working for them just fine, without His grace.

But what was this higher offer Jesus was extending to them? Our task is exactly what Jesus said it was: we are to believe in the One Whom He has sent (John 6:29, AMP). Without faith, it is *impossible* to please God (Heb. 11:6). He was calling them, even as Paul later called us, to the obedience of faith, the kind of heart obedience that leads to every other aspect of obedience that God will bring about in our lives (Rom. 1:5; 16:26). No doubt, believing in the One whom He has sent seems far too passive, even for us today.

Believing in the One whom He has sent involves believing what God's Word says in its entirety, desperately clinging to the truth for dear life at times. Believing in the One whom He has sent involves trusting that God is in full control of all that concerns us, even as our feelings pull us spiraling down like the weight of gravity toward despair, resentment, and self-pity. Believing in the One whom He has sent involves choosing to remain pure minded when it would be easier to simply place our faith aside for a while so that we can escape into sin and idolatry and enjoy the temporary relief it provides. Believing in the One whom He has sent involves rising up again and again when we have fallen into sin, humbly repenting and trusting in His ability to lift us back up in the power of His grace.

Insofar as James' teaching concerning trials, believing in the One whom He has sent involves considering our trials to be joy because of the perfecting work God is accomplishing in us through those trials. Believing in the One whom He has sent means refusing to give up ever, even when we are discouraged, grieved, exasperated, demoralized, and totally thwarted by life's trials.

Believing in the One whom He has sent involves trusting that He will come through for us, in His way and in His time, even if it becomes clear that we must wait until we see Him face-to-face to receive His provision. Believing in the One whom He has sent sometimes even involves looking up from crushing defeat, with tears streaming down our faces and broken dreams scattered at our feet, and *still* choosing to believe, to the bitter end if necessary, that our King, our Hero, our Savior, our Jesus can *never* be defeated.

This, and nothing less than this, is the battle of believing in the One whom He has sent. Don't try to tell me that faith isn't hard. You *know* it's hard. It is "work" that can *only* be accomplished through the enabling power of His Spirit ruling and working in us.

When I look back and consider my personal track record of grumbling, griping, raging, sulking, withdrawing, and complaining as God sought to do His marvelous work in me through various trials, I am ashamed. When I realize the precious time I've wasted, not joyfully surrendering but kicking and screaming, running from reality, anesthetizing myself to distraction against it, I must truly bow my head in shame.

How about you, dear reader? Praise God that He is merciful. He is the God of second chances. In my life He has proven to be the God of thousands of chances as I have responded with such opposition and disobedience. And all along my King kept patiently waiting for me, seeking to make a prince out of me as Christ's younger brother, to transform me into His image, if only I'd surrender. No doubt, I still have a long way to go. Yet I praise His holy name for His longsuffering patience with us all.

BACK TO REALITY

As we walked in the door after being away for three days, our kids clamored for the attention of their very stressed and emotionally worn and tired mommy and daddy. The needs of our three young children, the strain on our marriage, the demands of a stressful career, and the grueling daily regimen of Bryson's NACD program all loomed large in my weary mind, especially against the backdrop of that disturbing trial in Washington, DC. It would not have been a good moment to ask if I *felt* joy.

But *considering* this trial in Washington to be joy, and *considering* each and every trial the Lord ever allows to enter our lives to be joy, this is an altogether different matter. This is a choice, and we will be blessed if we make the choice to persevere under trial.

> Blessed is the man who perseveres under trial; for once he has been approved, he will receive the crown of life which the Lord promised to those who love Him.
>
> —JAMES 1:12

James realized there would be some reading his Epistle who believed it was too late for them. The trials they had personally endured had twisted and destroyed so much in their lives and families that it was now impossible even for God to redeem those trials for any good purpose. Perhaps this is why he ended his epistle by referring to Job. No one in history endured more grievous trials than Job. He lost his children, his wealth, his health, and even the respect of his friends. Yet, even in Job's case, God had the power to sum all things up well. Job gave God the chance to do this by enduring in his faith.

We can give God the chance to do this in our lives too, by making the choice to believe in Christ alone, the One whom He has sent. Daily the choice is mine.

Daily the choice is yours. Is there really any other choice in this world fraught with tribulations and trials that makes any sense?

> You have heard of the endurance of Job and have seen the outcome of the Lord's dealings, that the Lord is full of compassion and is merciful.
>
> —James 5:11

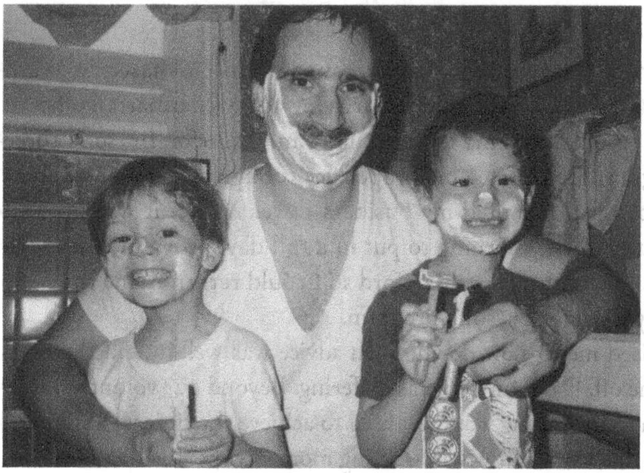

Two little shavers and one lucky Dad

Always a firm hand to steady my courageous boy

challenges and press on in their own lives.... But I think I hear where you're coming from, Lord. Maybe I wasn't being *completely* honest in my portrayal of how I 'pressed on' during those days. Perhaps I'd better clarify a few *small* details."

My Father: "*Details?* What makes you think it will be helpful to the people reading your book to make yourself appear to be Superman? Does the direction you're going in really give glory to Me—or to *you?*"

Me: "Well, you know, Father. I've already told them quite a bit about Your faithfulness, about how You were teaching me that I could count on You to be strong, even as I became more in touch with my weakness. I've also told them that the brokenness You allowed to come into my life made me more dependent upon You. Don't You think I need to move this story toward a victorious conclusion, telling the readers how I pressed on toward the goal, like the great apostle Paul did?"

My Father: "There will be people reading your book in the midst of their own seemingly impossible problems. If you suggest to them, by your slanted self-portrayal, that it's all up to them to work out some sort of Hollywood victory in their lives through their own resolve, then you won't really be pointing them to Me as their only source of hope, now will you?

"When they stumble and fall, and go through dry periods, when the great accuser points his arrows of doubt at them and convinces them I have abandoned them because their lives are such a grand mess, will the 'spiced up' version of your story do them any good? You've talked openly about your son's patterns of regression. What about your own regression?

"As for My servant Paul, you seem to be forgetting that he saw not only discouraging days, but *years* of discouragement as he sat in prison. He had *no* idea what I would ultimately do with his teaching, nor his writings. In fact, he feared that the serpent would snatch it *all* away from the young churches he had labored so hard to build up (2 Cor. 11:3).

"And if you're going to use Philippians 3:13–14 to instruct your readers about how I want My children to 'press on toward the goal,' then don't skip the part where Paul admitted he had not yet laid hold of it. Pressing on is an arduous, lifelong, often gut-wrenching process during which you will have many victories, but also many defeats. My grace *alone* was sufficient for Paul. I still work in the lives of My children the same way today. *Only* My grace remains sufficient to propel them toward victory, and to lift them back up as they stumble and fall. My power is made perfect in human weakness."

Me: "As always, Father, You're right. I should tell them that, though I kept pressing on the best I could, cracks were appearing in my life in some pretty personal and critical places. There were more times than I'd like to remember when my faith was very small. In fact, there were days when I was feeling completely beaten and numb, far too exhausted to catch that early train to New York. Days when I sat on the *late* train crying inside, just wanting to crawl under the seat to hide.

"Days when I thought, even with the marriage counseling we were seeking, that it simply wasn't *possible* for our marriage to survive. Days when I felt so depressed, so inept, I would have been ashamed to tell *anyone* how I was feeling for fear that my futility and incompetence would bring dishonor to Your name. Days that were so black that laughter bellowing from the pit of hell sounded more real to me than the sound of Your voice."

My Father: "That's more like it. But don't make it seem like this is all in the distant past just because you're writing a book. Keep going."

Me: "If you say so, Father. I'll also tell them that even now, many years later, I *still* have days when I feel disillusioned. I'll tell them I've often been frustrated even by the writing of this book; that it has taken me many years longer than I ever dreamed it would. That my efforts to make progress in life are still stalled and thwarted by circumstances that seem *so* absurd that, for the life of me, I can't understand why You allow them.

"I'll tell them that I *still* sometimes suffer from sleepless nights, followed by 'night of the living dead' days, as I've come to refer to them. I'll tell them that coming to Your throne to pray, even now, sometimes means dragging myself, discouraged and disheveled, to just sit there numb and exhausted, not even knowing what to say or where to *begin* in praying to You.

"But, Father, if I tell my readers all that, won't some of them get discouraged as they realize their own efforts to 'press on' may not result in all their problems being wrapped up, neat and tidy, the way they desperately hope?"

My Father: "A day is coming when every last problem will be resolved in a manner neither you, nor your readers, can comprehend. My Word says it this way:

"... EYE HAS NOT SEEN AND EAR HAS NOT HEARD, AND which HAVE NOT ENTERED THE HEART OF MAN, ALL THAT GOD

HAS PREPARED FOR THOSE WHO LOVE HIM" (1 Cor. 2:9).

"'For I consider that the sufferings of this present time are not worthy to be compared with the glory that is to be revealed to us' (Rom. 8:18).

"'For momentary, light affliction is producing for us an eternal weight of glory far beyond all comparison' (2 Cor. 4:17).

"In the meantime, you and your readers will press on more effectively if you are honest with one another about your common experiences of suffering (1 Pet. 5:9). Remember, I've chosen to accomplish My work in this world through earthen vessels. My work is never done by human might, nor by human power, but by My Spirit working in and through those who are weak (Zech. 4:6; 2 Cor. 12:9–10). Your sufferings and failures play a bigger role in this process than you understand. I use them to cause you to repent of your arrogance and independence, and to rely upon Me more deeply."

Me: "Father, if I'm going to tell them about my continued struggles, I must also tell them that as I look back on all the disappointment and the heartache, You've never failed me. Not even after the times I've doubted You, and been unfaithful to You. Every time I've crawled back to Your throne dirty, bloodied, and in great need from my battles in this world, I've found, not the condemnation I've deserved (Rom. 8:1), but grace and mercy I could never earn or deserve (Heb. 4:16).

"And, Father, though I still don't have answers for many of my own problems, no less for those reading this book, I wouldn't want to live *any* other way than to keep drinking in Your matchless grace and love, and to keep pressing on to know and serve You more."

My Father: "I'm glad we had this talk. This discussion will be more helpful to the readers than the thought of you in a gladiator outfit. Besides, with *your* legs, it was foolish to go there in the first place, don't you think?"

Me: "Ouch."

My Father: "I just thought you could use a laugh. Now, get on with your story."

The Gladiator—Take Two

If *anyone* was pressing on well, it was Bryson. So weak, so vulnerable, so deeply hurt. Yet he took on each new day with a clean slate. Forgetting the pain and the joys of yesterday, he pressed forward to the opportunities *this* day offered. I marveled at his ability to do this. My son continued to suffer more emotional and physical pain than anyone I've ever personally known. Yet he displayed such resiliency, such courage. Perhaps the most amazing thing was that he looked to *me* for hope and optimism. If he only knew how much courage and inspiration I received from him.

New slate or not, our little gladiator continued displaying tenacious opposition against his grueling program. We continued using both positive reinforcements and stern discipline to motivate him. I was sometimes shaken to tears by the things I had to make my son do. But a failure to keep him moving forward would have been far worse. And as draining as his opposition was to overcome, his fierce and manipulative attempts to defeat our efforts were proving that he was quite a bit smarter than he had been given credit for.

I began taking him to the "prize store" (he still called the local Five and Ten the "pwize" store) after the three-hour program was completed each day, to buy a Matchbox car. He now had hundreds of these little vehicles. We realized we were walking a fine line between motivating him and spoiling him. Frankly, I don't know how well we always tread this balance. But I know we were doing the best we could under unbelievably stressful conditions. I also know it is beyond my ability to convey to you how hard he worked, how hard we *all* worked, so that he could get to that "pwize" store each day.

We still performed twenty program activities per day, continuing to focus on his cognitive, fine and gross motor, speech, and visual deficiencies. His deep knee bends with padded weights on his shoulders had progressed to the point where he could now rise from a short stool, though he still needed to be closely spotted to prevent him from falling. We also taught him to slowly lower his body back onto that stool from a standing position. This was much harder than rising from it. It took many months to learn to control his body so that it would not immediately plop down onto the stool.

He was now able to do a "round-trip" back and forth through the twelve-foot overhead ladder, grabbing all the rungs by himself. He did twenty round trips per day, with each hand straining to reach and hold the next rung. He still fell to the padded carpet often. We scooped him back up, sometimes drying his tears, and we sent him back on his way across the ladder. He always received a big hug from dad or a volunteer after each round-trip, plus some rough play from the teen volunteers.

Beating the daylights out of the teen volunteers with a pillow (he called it a "powwow") was one of his favorite rewards. Our little gladiator couldn't wait to take a couch cushion and destroy his opponent. Countless hours hanging on the wooden bar together with numerous other finger strengthening exercises were slowly helping him to grab onto his "weapons" more securely. The "powwow" fights provided excellent fine motor work for his hands also. Once he had beaten his foes to the ground, he'd often dive on top of them to finish them off. The teens fought back with some of the fiercest tickling in any army's arsenal. Getting Bryson back to work after such battles was no easy task. We reminded him there would be no trip to the prize store until all his work was finished.

We strung Teflon coated steel cables along each side of the overhead ladder mechanism, at the height that he would naturally swing his arms. This enabled us to use this twelve-foot expanse to do another walking exercise. He grabbed onto plastic handles that slid along the cables and "walked," sliding his hands back and forth in a cross pattern (right hand moving with the left foot, and left hand moving with the right foot). The cables gave him the support he needed as he walked, but he needed to be closely spotted so that we could catch him as he faltered, to prevent him from falling onto those cables.

Bryson's speech continued slowly improving. During his "cable walking" Bryson could be heard saying, "I big" (I'm big), and, "Who doon har?" (What are they doing here?), referring to the volunteers. And, of course he incessantly asked his favorite question: "Pwize now?" The rascal inside of him became evident as he suddenly turned to Charlotte, one of our long-term volunteers and exclaimed, "Out my *face,* Charotte" (Get out of my face, Charlotte). Charlotte was hovering close as she spotted him, to insure that Bryson did not fall painfully onto the steel cables. Pleased with his ability to chastise Charlotte (whom he adored), "Out my *face, Charotte,*" could be heard repeatedly, with the gracious Charlotte breaking out in laughter each time.

Bryson's neurological system had no capacity to filter out visual or auditory stimulation, so we had to keep the environment as quiet and free of extraneous stimulation as possible. He lost his balance *immediately,* as if a wave knocked him off his feet, as soon as any sights or sounds distracted him. We learned this the hard way when we took the family to a carnival. Within minutes he was a "basket case," screaming loudly as he was bombarded with stimulation that he was unable to filter out of his mind. We quickly removed him from the scene and calmed him for a long time in a cool, quiet area.

With the strong hands of a volunteer grasping his shoulders, he was now able to "walk" through the house. We called this activity "assisted walking." This routine gave his brain vital motor memory and visual input, and he was slowly becoming more accustomed to where he was spatially, as he "walked." We began taking our hands away from his shoulders for a split second. As he began to falter, we would grab his shoulders again, pull him back up, and keep him moving forward.

Man, did he *love* assisted walking. Even though we had to cling to his shoulders, he was up on his feet like everyone else. And boy, was he ever bossy about where he wanted to "walk." With slurred speech he'd bark out commands, pointing in the direction he wanted to go. It didn't matter to us where we went, as long as we kept him moving forward for ten minutes during each set of assisted walking. We almost always had a game going as we walked him around the house. Sometimes he wanted to go looking for monsters in all the closets. He often had his cowboy holster on, and he'd shoot every monster he found.

As his legs grew stronger, we began "assisted walking" around the neighborhood. His legs were still so uncoordinated that they often "scissored" in front of him. And since the sidewalk outside was much more challenging than the flat surface in the house, we had to provide even more of his balance as we firmly held his shoulders, and more of the energy needed to keep him moving forward. We'd stop at all his favorite spots, including the enormous tree that had roots that looked like snakes ("nakes" as he called them).

As described earlier, Bryson had taken his first independent step on foam rubber padding. We had now taken this padding away. I leaned him against the family room couch as I stayed on my knees right in front of him. I would then take him firmly by the shoulders and pull his body away from the couch, steadying him in a standing position. Very slowly moving my hands away, I asked Bryson to walk toward me, as I remained on my knees.

Before he could take his first step in each set of this activity, we usually had to reposition his feet at least a half dozen times. Time after time his feet kept spastically moving out of the "toes forward—shoulder width apart" position we arduously placed them in. One of the volunteers held him steady as I placed each foot back into position. Without warning, a foot would again move, requiring the repositioning process to begin *all* over again. Frustration would build for Bryson, and for all of us, when several minutes ticked away getting him in position for a single walking *attempt*.

After trying *so* hard just to begin, each attempt was almost always just as frustrating. His legs were getting stronger, but his balance lagged far behind. The average number of steps he could take before stumbling into my arms was very low. Each time he gave it a try we would praise him. Then, we immediately began steadying his body and feet all over again, for the next attempt. Having a fixed focal point for his eyes was critical. From my knees in front of him, I pleaded with him to focus both of his eyes on me. I would repeat, over and over, "Look at Daddy…Look at Daddy…Look at Daddy."

His steps were often giant ones. He had a distorted sense of visual proportion, with no ability to measure short steps. As he fell into my arms time after time, we could all be heard reminding him: "Short steps, Bryson.…Real short and tiny now…Look at Daddy…Short steps…Short and tiny now…Keep your eyes on Daddy." This was so easy for us to say, and so hard for him to do with his lack of motor control, poor balance, and proprioception (awareness of where his body is).

Nonetheless, Bryson slowly continued breaking personal records. During the spring of 1992, his record stood at ten independent steps, and you'd better believe we all went nuts each time he reached a new milestone. But as exciting as these milestones were, there were *many* more days and weeks when records were not being broken.

Remember, walking is the act of "falling forward" *without* falling down. He was only able to get near his record of ten steps approximately once in every *fifty* tries. On all his attempts he lost his balance at some point and fell. Often he collapsed into my arms after only a few steps, sometimes before even taking a *single* step. His average number of steps *per attempt* remained very low. On many days, *all* fifty attempts yielded no success *at all*. These days were indescribably demoralizing. We constantly encouraged each other that we had actually *seen* good days. But exasperating weeks of regression could play with your mind, almost convincing you that the good days had never happened at all.

This is the up and down nature of a profound brain injury. Developmental advancement simply does not follow a typical sequential pattern. The recircuiting process is fraught with regression, disappointment, and endless, abject failure. Keeping Bryson feeling positive about himself in the midst of such monumental failure was indescribably difficult. Thank God for the teens who kept cheering our little gladiator on. They never knew they inspired me every bit as much as my son.

Digging for Treasure

We had worked hard to train him out of diapers when he had turned six. His damaged motor skills still kept him from dressing himself, and he still spoke in brief, slurred sentences fraught with omitted words. His hands possessed neither the coordination nor the dexterity even to hold a pencil. Placing him in a public school was a daunting goal.

Our volunteers encouraged us as we shared our concerns about his education. They had seen him surpass the predictions of professionals. They had seen him progress from needing to be strapped into a special chair to being able to tenaciously complete twenty round trips per day through his overhead ladder. They had helped him to develop a growing number of memorized words for his sight-reading vocabulary, and had taught him to learn all his numbers. They were even teaching him the basics of math.

These dedicated troops shared something with my wife and me that we held sacred: they believed in our son. They had now invested years of their own lives into our son's broken little life, and they had earned the right to have dreams of their own for him. Honestly, their eyes could sometimes see the future with greater clarity than ours, and some of their dreams were very powerful.

I'll never forget the words of Elaine Sullivan, a saintly woman who was one of the first Grace Church volunteers to join us. Elaine had experienced great sorrow in her own life, yet she faithfully came to our home each week to provide Bryson with exhaustive academic input. She flashed number and word cards and cards with objects and animals, as she stated their names. She patiently persevered as he incessantly asked his repetitive, relentless, daily question of her: "Pwize? I get pwize now?"

One day, Elaine turned to me suddenly as Bryson was pleading his case for a "pwize." Looking me straight in the eye she said, "I'm going to be there someday, in the *front* row, when Bryson is able to get up in front of the church and speak to us all about how *good* God is. You wait and see! *He'll* be up there, and *I'll* be there to see it!"

Maybe my eyes became teary because we had all been working too hard, and

I was tired. Maybe it was just because I'm an emotional Italian. Whatever it was, Elaine's words stopped me dead in my tracks. To this day I still look forward in hope to that great vision Elaine foresaw. It's a very powerful thing when someone chooses to believe in another human being. How powerful, too, not to keep such beliefs to ourselves, but to speak them out loud. The people around us need to hear uplifting words more than we often know.

> A man has joy in an apt answer, And how delightful is a timely word!
>
> —Proverbs 15:23

Sadly, some chose *not* to believe in our son. Most skeptics could be ignored. But we were about to meet up with some professionals in the educational community who could not be ignored, for they had the power to do great harm to our son. Amazingly, we met these individuals in a place where one would expect to find those whose job description *required* a belief in the possibilities of special needs children.

As stated in an earlier chapter, our local school psychologist had come to our home and performed some ludicrous tests to measure our son's potential. He had asked Bryson to perform tasks with his hands that he couldn't *possibly* accomplish, due to motor impairments. Bryson's speech and visual handicaps prevented him from answering the questions which were thrown at him quickly, without giving him adequate time to answer. Bryson's handicaps, not his intelligence or potential, had been tested. This psychologist's display of incompetence, combined with the fact that Bryson's daily regimen was full, had caused us to wait until Bryson turned six to meet again with our school administration to develop a plan for his education.

We thought they'd become enthused partners with us, particularly after seeing the progress he had made. But unlocking the treasures God places within an injured child is a privileged task. It can only be accomplished by those who believe that the treasure exists. No one goes to the effort involved in digging deep for treasure unless they believe it's there. We soon learned that some of the administrators in our school district didn't even own a shovel, and we were about to learn about the *needless* pain suffered by countless families in their quest to educate their special needs children.

Bryson's experience at Care-A-Lot Nursery School had been a *huge* success. Our son was a terrific copycat, and his ability to observe and copy the behavior of healthy children had proved to be a vital key to his overall development. Though his handicaps were obvious, the other children had learned to accept Bryson for who he was, and many of them wanted to take turns helping him with various daily tasks. This was a magnificent opportunity for the other children. It was a beautiful, "win-win" situation.

The NACD now advised us to arrange the same type of mainstreamed setting for Bryson's public schooling. Surprisingly, our local school administration began to fight us very hard on the issue of Bryson staying "in district." Unlike those nursery school children, some in our special education department seemed to focus only on Bryson's handicaps. They couldn't see our son's tenacity and inspiring courage, nor did they embrace the dreams we had for our son's future. It seemed more important for them to categorize him, to neatly fit him into one of their definitive bureaucratic labels such as "cerebral palsy," "neurologically impaired," and "multiply handicapped." Each label described our son in negative terms, and there seemed to be an absence of optimism regarding how they were going to help him to *overcome* his challenges.

Generally speaking, I am in favor of having as little government involvement in the lives of people as possible. Without getting into politics, I believe this is an aspect of freedom that has made our nation a great one. But we soon learned why it is necessary to have specific laws to protect the rights of the *truly* needy, including handicapped children and their families. By the late spring of 1992 our negotiations with the district were badly stalled, and we consulted an attorney. Unfortunately, many parents of handicapped children have neither the time nor the resources to become experts in the law, and they can't keep an attorney on retainer. As a result, they are often manipulated and exploited.

We didn't relish the idea of getting into a legal battle, particularly on the heels of our gut-wrenching case in Washington, DC. But battle lines were quickly drawn, and we prepared for one of the most important and difficult battles we'd ever fight on our son's behalf. We were fighting for a precedent that would loom over his entire educational future.

The law in New Jersey specifies that a child's education must take place in the "least restrictive environment." In our view, the least restrictive environment was the mainstreamed classroom in our neighborhood school. We had been warned by an educational support group that some school districts have hidden agendas, being awarded advantageous state funding *if* a certain percentage of children are sent "out of district." I don't believe this was what we were battling against in our district in Glen Rock, New Jersey. In my opinion, we were battling against good, old fashioned arrogance.

I had been in the business world long enough to meet people with varying approaches to negotiating. The type I least liked dealing with were ones who presented themselves as if they had *all* the answers. These individuals usually attempt to manipulate the proceedings with no higher apparent goal than maintaining the appearance of their own competency. The school administrator with whom we were dealing seemed intent on portraying herself as *the* expert. She confidently took charge as if she knew *exactly* what our son needed, though she knew little about him. It seemed that the members of the special services group under her were afraid to offer opinions that varied from hers.

She arranged for us to visit some "special" schools. After seeing them, we became more adamant than ever that our son belonged in our mainstreamed, local school. These "special" schools seemed to be glorified day care centers. The level of sensory stimulation was *incomparably* higher in the regular school setting, as compared to these self-contained schools for the handicapped. Bryson was a "sponge," ready to drink in everything around him. We wanted him in a stimulating environment where children were *expected* to learn, not where it was assumed that they could not learn.

Our administrator seemed to want us involved in as little of the planning process as possible. She didn't seem interested in the things that had helped him reach higher levels of development. It seemed to us that she feared any involvement by anyone she could not control. And she was absolutely *determined* not to have *any* contact with the NACD whatsoever. She claimed that state law wouldn't even permit her to do so. This was one of many statements that caused us to investigate the law thoroughly ourselves.

All sorts of regulations were tossed out at us during our planning meetings, seemingly to keep us off balance and intimidate us. She opposed us on so many issues in an arbitrary manner. At one meeting, the principal from our local elementary school turned to this obstinate administrator in the midst of a heated discussion, and asked, "Is what Mr. and Mrs. Milazzo are asking for *really* such an unreasonable request?" The livid administrator glared back at him with contempt. How *dare* he challenge her in front of us! The situation was getting bizarre. I thought Jack Nicholson might burst through the door any moment screaming, "You can't handle the truth!" Unfortunately, that principal seemed to be the person in this district who wasn't intimidated by this administrator.

Arguments even arose about our request not to place Bryson in a wheelchair. We didn't see why Bryson's aide couldn't help him with his assisted walking, even as our teen volunteers were able to do. The administrator told us this would be too risky and difficult. After all the thousands of hours of work, after all the progress he had made, it was absurd to make us fight to prove that a wheelchair would be detrimental to our son's ability to walk independently one day. But this administrator seemed pleased to negotiate with us in this manner, before ultimately conceding an issue or two as if they were bargaining chips. This made me very angry. Those bargaining chips involved my son's welfare.

I don't like conflict. I prefer to be liked by others, and as you know by now, spare time was not something I had an abundance of. But being liked simply cannot be at the top of your agenda when you are fighting for a defenseless child, and I came to believe we had no choice but to fight vigorously against this district. Even so, looking back, I realize there was too much fear in my heart as I fought those battles, resulting in unnecessary personal anger. In the years ahead, the Lord would teach me that "taking off the gloves" meant getting on my knees and trusting in Him more, and in myself less (Ps. 138:7–8).

After many months of emotional meetings, negotiating sessions, and letters, just about every issue was worked out, except one. The main issue remained whether Bryson was going to be accepted into our local, neighborhood school. We wanted him in. They wanted him out. They dug in. We dug in. Battle lines were drawn.

An Appeal to the Troops

There were times when the stress was so great that when I attempted to sleep at night, it seemed there was a barbell on my chest. With all that had happened that year, our battle in Washington, DC, followed by this gut-wrenching battle with our local school system, we needed all the help that God could send our way.

In June 1992 it was time to write another letter of thanks and encouragement to Bryson's Army. That quarter Bryson had progressed to a new record of fourteen steps, before regressing badly once again. This letter was as much a call for desperately needed emotional support for us, as it was to thank and encourage our troops. There was no need to pretend with these dear people. They knew we were run down, and I shared our reasons:

> This year has been one of the most stressful we have experienced as a family. We've traveled to Washington, DC, for hearings regarding Bryson's 2-½ year old federal case. We have worked through the arduous process of planning how to educate our son. This process has been fraught with difficult decisions and much anxiety. We have seen continued physical pain inflicted upon Bryson as he continues to fall (4 more loosened teeth, regular bumps and bruises on his beautiful face, etc.). We have shared Bryson's emotional pain and frustration at not being able to participate in activities with other children that require walking and running. Our own frustration is compounded by the up and down nature of Bryson's progress. Why is he suddenly able to progress to a record of 14 independent steps (a month ago), and then regress (yet again) to just a few steps at the time of this writing? After years of agonizing over this pattern of 3 steps forward–2 steps back, we just can't figure it out. It's accurate to describe us as physically and emotionally tired at this point.
>
> Having said this, I must clearly state that we continue to have very high hopes for Bryson's future. Our objective is to give him the best opportunity to reach his highest potential, whatever that may be.... I remain confident that Bryson will one day walk independently. On the cognitive side, we remain convinced that there is a higher degree of intelligence inside that mind of his (you can see it in his eyes), and we aim to give him every opportunity to work through his processing problems so that this intelligence can be unleashed. We sincerely believe that the future will bear out the validity of these hopes.... It is you who have given him the foundation from which he will grow in the years ahead. You have kept the process going and, at times, you have kept the parents going, even though you may not have realized that. We are grateful to you. We thank God for you.
>
> In His Grace, Barry[1]

Oh how those wonderful warriors responded! They just kept showing up every single day. One day, Bryan Egan Sr. showed up in the place of Bryan Jr., one of our fantastic teen volunteers for *three* full years. He explained that his son had taken a summer job, and that he intended to take his place until he could return in the fall. I protested, telling him I didn't want him to go to all the trouble. He cut me off in mid-sentence, *insisting* that this would be his privilege. Colleen, Bryan's teen daughter was also a fantastic, long-term member in Bryson's Army. His wife, Bonnie, and other son Ryan had also been a wonderful encouragement to Bryson. I was beginning to wonder if the Egan family might possibly have descended directly out of heaven, as angels in disguise.

Then there was the BMFC. Phil Mandato, my college roommate, had named his family the Bryson Milazzo Fan Club. Phil was an all-American defensive tackle on our college football team. He was an intimidating specimen physically, but his huge heart was always his most awesome feature. Phil began mailing Bryson funny and encouraging greeting cards *every* week. His fingers couldn't open the envelopes, but he sat on my lap as I opened each week's card, and listened intently as I read them to him. Each card had something to make us laugh, and there were always inspirational reminders about how much Phil admired his courage and determination, along with reminders to continue working hard with his dad. Bryson never said much in response, but he drank it all in. The BMFC kept those cards coming each week for many *years*.

To this day, I speak to Phil on the phone nearly every day. He is a giant of a man who continues to inspire me to keep pressing on even in the writing of this book, and encouraging me with his wisdom and faith. Anyone gaining anything from this book should thank him. It would never have been written without him.

Lights, Camera, Action: *The Gladiator*—Take 3

I'm not sure why I enjoyed the feature film *The Gladiator* so much. Maybe it's because it's a motion picture in which good and evil are clearly defined. Many of today's Hollywood productions portray good and evil in such a twisted manner. If a Christian is written into the plot at all, he is usually depicted as a bigoted buffoon, while characters with no regard for God, or for morality, invariably emerge as the heroes. Such portrayals remind me of a warning from the prophet of old:

> Woe to those who call evil good, and good evil; Who substitute darkness for light and light for darkness; Who substitute bitter for sweet, and sweet for bitter! Woe to those who are wise in their own eyes, And clever in their own sight!
>
> —Isaiah 5:20–21

Irrespective of how truth is often distorted today, the grand production of history is unfolding precisely in accord with the Word of the Executive Director of the universe. On the surface, it's sometimes hard to believe there is any redeeming value to this feature film, or that it could possibly have a happy ending. Right from the opening scene, the plot has been fraught with grievous, distressing events which would tempt any reasonable audience to flee from the theater. There have been rebellions and murders and wars, earthquakes and tsunamis, death camps and holocausts, disease and famine and squalor and floods.

Frankly, there have been endless scenes in this production when one might think there is a serpent seated in the Director's chair.

But a day is coming, not too long from now in the scheme of things, when the Director will close down the set for the last time. On that day, everyone will see that He has been working behind each scene all along, and has woven them all together to fulfill His grand purpose. On that day, the Director will finally be revealed as the magnificent King He truly is, and every knee will bow as the credits roll across the screen (Rom. 14:11; Phil. 2:10).

I was a young man when most of the events of this book unfolded. I am older now, and I've come to understand that some of the most difficult scenes from my family's part in His grand production were ones to be cherished, though I couldn't see it at the time. I'll never forget the scenes when our courageous little gladiator pressed on through countless, frustrating battles that led to our daily trip to his beloved "pwize" store.

Due to weariness, and often due to personal discouragement about that day's lost battles and regression, I often missed the richness of this scene at that local Five and Ten Cent Store. Impatient and irritated, I strained to hold onto Bryson from behind, trying to keep him from falling down right there in that store aisle. Exhausted, I sometimes pleaded with him to make a decision, so we could go home and have dinner. But he had worked far too hard for his "pwize," and he was in no hurry. He slowly pawed over car after Matchbox car, unable to make up his mind. When he finally made his choice and held it up, his eyes sparkled as if he held the most priceless treasure in the world in his uncoordinated little hand. What a *splendid* scene this had turned out to be after all!

But a scene was coming in the months ahead that would top every other scene from that difficult year in our lives. It was just after Labor Day 1992, and there were tears in the eyes of many parents arriving that day, as they snapped pictures. No one could have known the things that stirred our hearts behind our tears. As my wife snapped away, her tears were hidden behind the camera. There he stood, a cool backpack on his back, wearing a colorful sweat suit, with *no* diaper underneath (he had worked *so* hard at this).

At six and one-half, save for his badly crossed eyes, he looked just like any other child arriving that day. I stood him up carefully and then backed away, just out of range of the camera lens. With tears flowing, I stood poised to reach out and catch my son the instant he tottered and began to fall, which he did several times as we prepared to take each picture.

Our little gladiator had no idea what all the fuss was about, as he proudly posed for this memorable scene. He didn't understand that a great army had battled for years so he could stand here on this day. Those brave warriors were merely his beloved playmates. And just as he had never known that there were those long ago who thought he should be sent away from his family and placed in an institution to live, he had no idea that there were *still* some who thought he should be alienated and sent away from his neighborhood school. He just stood there, unaware of all these things, his uncoordinated thumb pointing triumphantly up in the air, mimicking our favorite sign for him as our champion.

As this scene rolled on, I was more grateful to the Director than words could possibly express. So many emotions were flowing now. I felt a combination of joy, pride, and fear; quite anxious about how this was all going to play out. No doubt, he was far more prepared to take on this new challenge in his life than I was, as his father.

Beaming a great smile, he kept his thumb pointing skyward. No one should have been surprised that he had climbed another mountain, beaten another foe. Soon a bell rang, and the door to our local, neighborhood kindergarten classroom swung open. Our little gladiator was led inside with all the other children. Fade out! That's a wrap!

> No man will be able to stand before you all the days of your life. Just as I have been with Moses, I will be with you; I will not fail you or forsake you. Be strong and courageous, for you shall give this people possession of the land which I swore to their fathers to give them.... Have I not commanded you? Be strong and courageous! Do not tremble or be dismayed, for the LORD your God is with you wherever you go.
>
> —JOSHUA 1:5–6, 9

My gladiator!

Chapter 17
THE GOAL OF OUR INSTRUCTION

The goal of our instruction is love from a pure heart and a good conscience and a sincere faith.
1 TIMOTHY 1:5

BRYSON'S EXPERIENCE IN our neighborhood kindergarten was *sensational*, in every sense worth the battle to secure his place there. After all the obstinacy and fear regarding his inclusion, our son *thrived* in this mainstreamed setting, and the other children benefitted tremendously too. Beyond this, the cost to the district was less than sending him away to a special school for the handicapped. This was clearly a win-win-win situation.

He had a one-on-one aide to ensure his safety and help him with his special needs. His outstanding teacher, Dianne Schlegel, had also been Janelle's teacher three years earlier. Mrs. Schlegel had the wisdom to treat our son the same way she treated all the other children. She knew there could be no cookie-cutter approach to achieving academic success for Bryson, nor for any child. She treated them all as unique individuals.

Like so many New York City area "type A" personalities, some parents came to the orientation program *demanding* to know exactly when the curriculum would transform their children into proficient readers. We had seen Mrs. Schlegel field anxieties from driven parents before, and there was wisdom behind her calm smile. Rather than outlining a rigid chronological curriculum, she unveiled a program that would provide these children with exciting opportunities to gain a fascination and a passion for learning.

She understood that each child has a unique learning style, replete with strengths and weaknesses, and a timetable all their own for making progress. She knew that even the best curriculum in the world would have little impact on a child's life if it remained an exterior program of study. A child's love for learning, once ignited, would prove more valuable in kindergarten and throughout their lives than any driven curriculum. Exterior goals come and go. The goal of a wise teacher's instruction is always deeper and higher. Passions that are kindled inside the heart of a child become part of who they are.

The NACD always reminded us to treat Bryson as "un-handicapped" as possible, and this is exactly how Mrs. Schlegel approached his needs. His full-time aide helped him to travel safely through the classroom and the playground. Still, Bryson's handicaps were obvious to his new little friends. He was a crippled child, unable to run and play with them, or even to get out from behind his own desk without the help of his aide. His words came too slow to converse much with his classmates. But under Mrs. Schlegel's wise leadership, the children were taught that each of them was unique, that they all possessed great value irrespective of their differences. The children responded beautifully, helping to make this a positive and cherished year.

When I stepped back to consider some of the things that were unfolding in our son's life, I was in awe. I sometimes had a sense that we were just along for the ride, characters in a story being written one chapter at a time. Obviously, I would never have chosen the tragedy that had so devastated my child's ability to function in this world. At the same time, I was gaining a sense of the privileged position the Lord had granted us as his parents. As I continued to observe him move forward through his life of difficulty, my admiration for my son continued to grow, as did my sense of wonder for the One bringing it all to pass.

Joy, Grief, and Anger

> Grandchildren are the crown of old men.
>
> —Proverbs 17:6

What pride and joy he had in all nine of his grandchildren. But there was a special place in Pop Pop's heart for Bryson. He would often cook our Sunday meals with his crippled grandson in one arm. For his part, we thought Bryson might drive people at church insane with his endless rendition of, "Pop Pop," "Pop Pop," "Pop Pop," over and over to anyone who would listen to him each Sunday morning. He wanted everyone in creation to know that he was going to Pop Pop's for macaroni and meatballs right after church. In view of his relentless mantra, every bit of creation Bryson touched certainly did know.

While this was a season of rejoicing over Bryson's good fortune in kindergarten, it became a season of grief for the Milazzo family. I wasn't surprised by the courage my father displayed as his body was ravaged with cancer at seventy-eight years old, because he had always lived courageously. This proud veteran of World War II continued to "carry on," even as his commanding officer aboard the navy destroyer USS *Hobson* had taught him to do as a chief petty officer, firing his Oerlikon 20 mm cannon against Japanese kamikaze suicide missions in the Pacific, and against the shores of Normandy.

Words can be cheap, but when my father looked me in the eye and reminded me to "carry on," his meaning ran deep. Giving up wasn't an option for my dad under fire, not when he wore the uniform of the United States of America. From his example I was reminded that giving up is not an option for we who bear the name of Christ the King. Our Commanding Officer is the same yesterday, today, and forever (Heb 13:8). He remains fully in control as we experience our greatest victories here, and as we suffer our most sorrowful seasons of defeat. He even remains in control when it becomes clear that our deliverance will not be realized until we see Him face-to-face, as my father was soon to do. Our mission is to carry on, fighting our assigned battles for His glory, until the end.

My father continued serving his family at our Sunday gatherings until God called him home in October of 1992, after a vicious battle with pancreatic cancer. This wicked form of cancer causes its victims essentially to starve to death, and this proud man wasted away before our eyes, suffering excruciating pain. Yet he knew that our King is worthy of praise even in the midst of intense suffering. There was joy and deep peace in his soul during that season of anguish that could *only* be attributed to the awesome, living God.

Bryson listened quietly as we told him he wouldn't be able to see Pop Pop again until we saw him in heaven. With all his profound problems, my simple child understood. He was happy that Pop Pop wouldn't be sick anymore. Like his Pop Pop, he carried on.

When my dad finally passed on into heaven, we were physically and emotionally drained. My siblings and I had pitched in to take care of him, taking him to see numerous doctors throughout the New York City area. We tried quite a few alternative medical treatments after it became clear that conventional medicine could offer nothing more than pain management. My sister Linda (having four kids of her own) selflessly provided most of the care necessary to abide by our dad's wishes to remain in the home he built for the family he loved, rather than in a hospital. These were months of intense strain on all of us, especially with my mother also recovering from colon cancer surgery.

I had begun working only in the afternoons in Manhattan, after performing the three-hour NACD program with Bryson each morning (he attended the afternoon kindergarten session). Bryson was in the midst of another exasperating pattern of physical regression that fall. I joined my siblings as much as possible after commuting home in the evening to help them in caring for my dad, and I was reaching levels of physical and emotional exhaustion I had not yet known. But I'm glad to tell you that as the mature Christian I had grown to be, I dealt with this stress remarkably well, experiencing only a *tiny* bit of irritability now and then…Perhaps I should refer to it as a *moderate* level of anger…*All right already!* This is a Christian book! I'll be honest.

As the stress and exhaustion kept coming, I found myself doing dysfunctional things that were out of character for an organized guy like me, like running out of gas. I was on my way to visit my dad, with no room for error in my schedule, as usual. I was stuck in the *left lane* of a busy New Jersey highway, nowhere *near* a gas station as the car sputtered to a stop. But this was hardly a problem. This mature Christian merely put on the flashers and calmly assessed my situation. I wisely discerned that this was a good time to conduct an important scientific experiment, one I had been meaning to perform for a while now.

I decided to test the strength of the steering wheel on my Mazda RX7. I was *amazed* it could actually remain attached to the steering column as I exerted superhuman strength to rip it off the dashboard. Also intriguing in this experimentation, upon which I had embarked, was the punishment a windshield can endure as fists are applied to it. Naturally, this wouldn't have been a true scientific sampling if the windshield was struck only once. It had to be *battered* repeatedly. This experiment needed to be methodically performed together with a variety of well-timed expletives screamed at the *top* of my lungs, all in the name of empirical scientific study, of course... Thank God I was alone.

You Didn't Come to Call the Righteous?

> It is not those who are healthy who need a physician, but those who are sick. But go and learn what this means: "I DESIRE COMPASSION AND NOT SACRIFICE," for I did not come to call the righteous, but sinners.
>
> —MATTHEW 9:12–13

I don't mind telling you about my meltdown in the car. This is chapter 17. If you haven't realized I'm a bit "off my rocker" by now, you're probably nuttier than I am. But I've included the above episode of rage for an important reason. People all around us, many who have learned to cover it up, are suffering mightily from carrying grievous, long-term problems on their backs that never come to an end. They are emotionally and physically battle weary. Their exhaustion, stress, and fears can sometimes result in periods of crankiness, outbreaks of anger, and other evidences of sin. This book has been written largely for them, but not from a superior position—for I am one of "them."

Sometimes it's good when ugly evidences of our flesh rise to the surface. I say this with hesitation, since sin is too lethal and too destructive to be excused or taken lightly. Yet the sins that bubble to the surface during times of prolonged stress can serve a purpose. Our failures can remind us just how hopeless we are without Christ's *continuing* healing power. And they can keep us humble as we encounter other failing, sinful people.

If you happen to observe someone in an angry meltdown, or engaged in some other aberrant behavior, be very, very careful before yielding to the impulse to judge that person or categorize them with a neat and tidy psychological label. The arrogance of thinking that we understand the trials of others, or that *we* would do better if we were in their shoes, is almost always the greater sin. This is not a time to judge them. It is a time to roll up our sleeves and do what we can to help them.

We must help them, not from a position of perceived superiority, but with a spirit of humility and gentleness, realizing that we may need to be the recipient of such help the next time (Gal. 6:1). We've *all* been there before, remember? Scripture is clear that there was only One human being on this earth who was truly good. All the rest of us are the beneficiaries of endless volumes of mercy and grace for our own foolish, sinful failures (Titus 3:3–5). For your sake, and for the sake of those around you whom you *say* that you love, I hope you do remember. I hope your own failures are fresh on your mind.

Most men need to deal with their anger. We are often guilty of expressing it in frightening ways, and there is no excuse for that. Yet it is politically correct and popular to point out, seemingly endlessly today, the problems men have with anger. But it is not politically correct to point out that there are some pretty angry women out there too. The emasculation of men and male bashing has become a favored sport in our society, sadly infiltrating many of our churches.

While anger is generally expressed differently by each gender, anger is not a male problem or a female problem. It is a human problem, and only God has the vantage point from which to condemn sinners—male or female. Ironically, though He is in the position to do so, He chooses *not* to condemn those who are in Christ Jesus (Rom. 8:1). Instead, He continues dispensing His prescription for change into our lives: His grace. As recipients of God's healing grace, it is required that we become dispensers of grace. Oswald Chambers had this to say about taking a superior position:

> The greatest characteristic of a saint is humility, as evidenced by being able to say honestly and humbly, "Yes, all those, as well as other evils, would have been exhibited in me if it were not for the grace of God. Therefore, I have no right to judge."[1]

I love watching ESPN's Top 10 lists. Someone has suggested that if we were all forced to walk around holding a sign with the top ten sins of our lifetime, no one would ever know about the sins of anyone else. We'd all be too busy trying to cover up our own sign. Taking a "snapshot" of someone's moment of failure, then arrogantly waving that photo around and judging them as if the photo characterizes their entire life (with our own photos hidden, of course) puts us on very thin ice in our own walk with the Lord.

I attended a Family Life marriage conference many years ago, and I still consider this organization to be the best at what they do. I've forgotten much of what was presented that weekend. But I do remember Dennis Rainey having the humility to reveal he was so frustrated and angry one day as he attempted to put up Christmas lights on his house during a time of duress in his schedule, that he threw his hammer clear through a closed window in a fit of rage, smashing it. Such vulnerability is rare in the Christian community. But Rainey's humility was the most helpful thing in that conference for me.

Sadly, being a Christian can sometimes make it harder to come into the light concerning the sin we *all* battle against in our inner lives. We want to live and love well, but when our behavior doesn't match up with Christ's, we're tempted to pretend we're better than we really are, fearing that we don't measure up to those who are walking well. We've learned how to wear our masks and hide from each other, for fear of being judged by the "righteous." I wonder, just who are these "righteous" ones whom we fear?

Jesus spoke of a Pharisee who proudly prayed, "I thank You that I am not like... swindlers, unjust, adulterers, or even like this tax collector" (Luke 18:11). Meanwhile, the tax collector wouldn't even lift his eyes to heaven, but was beating his breast saying, "God, be merciful to me, the sinner!" (v. 13). Jesus made it clear that only the tax collector went home justified (v. 14). Scripture consistently instructs us that God is opposed to the proud, but gives grace to the humble (1 Pet. 5:5; James 4:6).

It is a tragic thing when forgiven people fail to notice their own sin but focus on the sins and shortcomings of others. Jesus asked: "Why do you look at the speck that is in your brother's eye, but do not notice the log that is in your own eye?" (Matt. 7:3). Pretty good question! Why? What is the basis of our superiority? What righteousness have we ever achieved that hasn't been received from above? (1 Cor. 4:7).

It is often when we're the most eager to serve the Lord that we are in the greatest danger, in terms of humility. Steve Brown makes it a point to teach this to his seminary students when they are particularly critical of other Christians, their views, or their actions. He tells them they haven't lived long enough or sinned big enough to even have an opinion on that subject. Although common wisdom would conclude that the longer we walk with Christ, the better we ought to get (called sanctification); Steve believes that sanctification is reflected more in our awareness than in our goodness.[2]

We are *so* evil it took the blood of our precious Lord to save us. We must remain keenly aware of how desperately we *still* need the healing power of His grace working in us every hour of every day, because we *still* have no true goodness apart from Him. Does this prick your pride? I know it pricks mine, and it ought to! Our pride is our core sin, and it can kill us like no other sin. We must remain aware of how desperately we need Christ.

But if our hearts are as deceitful and wicked as Scripture indicates (and they are), how is it ever possible for us to reach the goal of our instruction, which is for love to come from a pure heart, and to have a good conscience and a sincere faith?

> The heart is deceitful above all things, and desperately wicked; who can know it?
>
> —Jeremiah 17:9, kjv

> The goal of our instruction is love from a pure heart and a good conscience and a sincere faith.
>
> —1 Timothy 1:5

Any intelligent estimation of the *enormous* gulf between our wicked, natural hearts and the heart of love and purity God has established as the goal of our instruction must conclude that this is a truly hopeless chasm. It would take an absolute *miracle* to bridge that gulf. Our Father realized that too, and He knew the only thing that could bridge that gulf was not a repair of the old life, but to provide the miracle of a brand-new heart.

> I will give you a new heart and will put a new spirit within you....I will put my Spirit within you and cause you to walk in My statutes.
>
> —Ezekiel 36:26–27

The life of Jesus Christ *is* that miracle. He is our brand-new, beating heart. But if Christ is *really* alive in us, why do we doubt His power to transform our behavior? Could it be that we have forgotten we are kindergartners? Mrs. Schlegel would never have condemned her students for being unable to master doctoral material. Nor would she condemn my brain-injured son for all his limitations as a student. She understood that each child has a unique learning style, replete with strengths and weaknesses, and a timetable all their own for making progress. She knew that *years* of advancement lay ahead for all of them; and above all, she knew that a passion had to be ignited from *within*.

God's matchless grace and love for us, as hopeless sinners, was the *only* thing that first lit our passion for Him. Sadly, many of us forget that His matchless grace and love for us is the only thing that *keeps* our passion burning, especially as we continue to stumble and fall. Learning the entire Bible by rote and committing it all to memory can still leave it as just an exterior curriculum that changes little in our lives. Getting to know the depth of God's love for us, in Christ, must remain our focus if we hope to grow as students.

> See how great a love the Father has bestowed upon us, that we would be called children of God; and such we are.
>
> —1 JOHN 3:1

> Do not fear, for I have redeemed you; I have called you by name; you are Mine! When you pass through the waters, I will be with you; And through the rivers, they will not overflow you. When you walk through the fire, you will not be scorched, Nor will the flame burn you... Since you are precious in my sight, Since you are honored and I love you.
>
> —ISAIAH 43:1–2, 4

How sad it must be for our Father, who has honored us and made us precious in His sight, when we disregard His grace and love toward us, in Christ, to seek a "higher" curriculum. His love is so great that it drove His Son from a lofty throne in heaven all the way to a lowly cross to be tortured to death for us in this dark and evil world. We could take the rest of our years on earth and all of eternity studying the depth of His love, and we would still not have mastered this central of all courses in His curriculum.

There is only one way that His beloved students can even *begin* to grow toward the goal of our instruction. Our passion, once ignited by His grace, must continue to receive the only fuel that can keep it burning: the love of God toward us in the grace of Christ.

LOOKING FOR NEW LIFE IN ALL THE WRONG PLACES

Many Christians believe in Christ for their initial salvation (justification) and the forgiveness of their sins, but not for their sanctification, or growth. They live defeated lives as they attempt to reach the goal of their instruction in the power of their flesh, apart from the grace of Christ. Watchman Nee reminds us that Jesus Christ now lives in us as our Source of growth in godly character and conduct:

> When we know the precious truth of justification by faith, we still know only half of the story.... God has something more to offer us, namely, the solution of the problem of our conduct.... Our eyes must be opened to see the finished work of Calvary.... The good news is that sanctification is made possible for you on exactly the same basis as that initial salvation. You are offered deliverance from sin as no less a gift of God's grace than was the forgiveness of your sins. God's way of deliverance is altogether different from man's way. Man's way is to try to suppress sin by seeking to overcome it...*we plead with the Lord to strengthen us* that we may exercise more self-control. *But this* is altogether fallacy; *it is not Christianity. God's means of delivering us from sin is not by making us stronger and stronger, but by making us weaker and weaker.* That is a peculiar way of victory...but it is the divine way...
>
> For years, maybe, you have tried fruitlessly to exercise control over yourself, and perhaps this is still your experience...once you see the truth you will recognize that you are indeed powerless to do anything.... God has done it all. Such a discovery brings striving and self-effort to an end.... *Do not be moved back on to your own ground. Never look at yourself as though you were not in Christ. Look at Christ and see yourself in Him...live in the expectation that he will complete his work in you.* It is for Him to make good the glorious promise that "sin shall not have dominion over you" (Rom. 6:14).[3] (emphasis added)

The enemy knows that we become highly dangerous to his dark kingdom in this world as we advance toward the goal of our instruction, and he will do his damndest to keep us ignorant of Christ's power within us. We must reject the enemy's lie that the grace of Christ is for our initial salvation only. We must not, as Nee warned us, be *moved back to our own ground,* attempting to live for Christ out of the power of the flesh. The flesh is the enemy's turf, and Satan will do anything he can to lure us back to it.

If we are foolish enough, either through ignorance or lack of faith in Christ's power within us, to keep striving to reach the goal of our instruction through the flesh (Gal. 3:1–3), we become devoid of Christ's power to heal us and change us. Nature abhors a vacuum, and Christians will often attempt to fill that power void by mixing worldly remedies in with their "faith" for their deliverance from sin. But trying to mix God's grace with worldly remedies is like taking pure spring water, mixing in some Tang, and then expecting to drink pure spring water. In reality, you're drinking Tang.

Paul warned that in the last days there would be those "holding to a form of godliness, although they have denied its power." He went on to warn us to "avoid such men as these" (2 Tim. 3:5). Sadly, instead of avoiding them, many of today's churches and struggling Christians have jumped right into the deep end of the pool with them.

Many in the Christian community are quick to outsource problems caused by sin to the world's experts. We classify them as psychological disorders, not spiritual problems. We place our faith in humanistic psychology to "fix" our inner problems without Christ. Many so-called Christian psychologists dispense the same humanistic wisdom as do their secular counterparts, without ever opening the pages of a Bible in their practices. They offer a "higher" knowledge. Paul had this to say about the world's wisdom:

> We preach... Christ the power of God and the wisdom of God. Because the foolishness of God is wiser than men, and the weakness of God is stronger than men.... Let no man deceive himself. If any... thinks he is wise in this age, he must become foolish, so that he may become wise. For the wisdom of this world is foolishness before God.
>
> —1 Corinthians 1:23–25; 3:18–19

I've met some wonderful Christian counselors and psychologists who teach the power of Jesus Christ as our only remedy and hope. Sadly, these faithful servants are the exception, not the rule. Many excuse personal sin, imploring their patients to forgive *themselves* instead of leading them to repentance and to the forgiveness of Christ. Then, rather than leading them toward freedom from paralyzing bitterness through extending forgiveness to those who have abused them in childhood (please note that I said *forgive* past abuses, not *excuse* them), these professionals specialize in fostering a self-focused sense of victimhood and entitlement to remain angry for those past abuses. Such victimhood brings no healing, but it does keep their cash registers ringing, even as it ruins current relationships.

Dr. Bill Gillham, a Christian psychologist, teaches the *full* gospel, emphasizing the power of Jesus Christ to live in and through us. Dr. Gillham has called the church to account for our current reliance upon psychotherapeutic methods that exclude Christ:

> Much of what passes for "Christian" counseling in most churches and seminaries is merely attaching Scripture to humanistic, self-help, psychotherapeutic models.... I was listening to a Christian radio station and heard some of these practitioners label Christians with an uncontrollable temper as "rage-aholics." They spoke of how common the "rage-aholic" problem is, and addressed one another as "Doctor" this and "Doctor" that, "What do you think, Doctor?" It sounded like General Hospital.... Nonsense! It's sin. These folks must embrace their true identity in Christ and learn how to let Christ overcome their temper for them. Learning to develop greater self-control through therapy is long-term, tedious, temporal, expensive, and will be burned up at the judgment seat of Christ.... God says we are to "put no confidence in the flesh" (Phil. 3:3)....
>
> Today the church abounds with well-meaning staff counselors, seminary-trained in psychotherapeutic techniques that seem to correlate with selected Scripture in order to "help strengthen" hurting Christians.... God

> seeks to lead Christians to abandon their trust in self and place all confidence in Christ, who indwells us (John 15:5).... Such counselors may be compassionate, godly Christians, but if they naively equip Christians to help them feel better, they are not only failing to do God's work, they actually hinder the work of the Holy Spirit by strengthening the flesh.... Learning how to abandon all self-reliance and cast ourselves upon Christ's sufficiency for us and through us is mandatory.... Trusting in oneself is folly. God is diligently working to bring us to the end of trusting in ourselves (2 Cor. 12:9). Godly counsel always takes our focus off self and places it upon Jesus Christ and His finished work for us.[4]

Scripture is clear that, in God's eyes, we are complete in Christ right now (Col. 2:10). But for all of us, a great gulf exists between our *experience* right now and the goal of our instruction, which is love from a pure heart, and a good conscience, and a sincere faith (1 Tim. 1:5). Clearly, we cannot bridge that gulf and remedy the problems of our souls by turning to the experts of this world to strengthen our flesh.

So then, how can we ever change our behavior? What do we need in order to grow? How do we bridge the enormous gulf between what we experience now and the goal the Lord has established for us? We grow by abiding in Christ and trusting Him alone to do His work in and through us by His mighty power. As Jesus taught us, we must stop honoring Him with our lips while embracing the traditions of men for the "real" issues of life:

> "This people honors Me with their lips, But their heart is far away from Me. But in vain do they worship Me, Teaching as doctrines the precepts of men." Neglecting the commandment of God, you hold to the tradition of men.
>
> —Mark 7:6–8

Unadulterated, biblical Christianity is pretty radical stuff. It teaches us that we have been crucified with Christ for our deliverance from sin. But God has not left us for dead on that cross anymore than His firstborn Son remains dead on that cross. He has risen and we have been raised up with Him. Our risen Lord living within us, Jesus Christ, will provide for our growth as we respond to His gracious presence in obedience, starting with the obedience of trusting Him to do what His Word declares He will do.

> I have been crucified with Christ; and it is no longer I who live, but Christ lives in me; and the life which I now live in the flesh I live by faith in the Son of God, who loved me, and delivered Himself up for me.
>
> —Galatians 2:20

> For if while we were enemies we were reconciled to God through the death of His Son, much more, having been reconciled, we shall be saved by His life.
>
> —Romans 5:10

Back to School

The gulf Bryson faced daily between the reality of his crippling limitations and his desire to function normally in this world was very wide. In fact, it was an impossible gulf. Still, he wasn't stressed about his advancement in his kindergarten classroom. He simply loved being there each day, with a wonderful teacher and classmates who accepted him for who he was as an individual. The gulf faced by his classmates was wide too, far greater than any of them could leap all at once. After all, they were kindergartners!

Mrs. Schlegel wisely understood there could be no cookie-cutter approach to learning in her classroom, because each student was unique, with strengths and weaknesses all their own. Yet I don't think any of the children in that wonderful classroom were stressed about their performance. Under the wise leadership of a teacher who accepted them where they were and astutely planned for their growth, they simply loved being there too.

Some driven, "type A" parents just didn't understand. It isn't possible to pressure young students, all on the same timetable, to achieve academic mastery. Mrs. Schlegel knew that an external curriculum held little value without first cultivating a passion and love for learning on the inside. Unless children gain a heart of passion, the best curriculum in the world will never take them across that great gulf.

Why do we, as God's children, sometimes view Him as if He were a cold, uncaring proctor, sitting stern and disinterested in the front of the classroom as we take His harsh exams? A good Teacher always devises a far better plan for His beloved students. He doesn't require quick, perfect performances from them. He knows each one intimately, delighting in them, even with all their unique weaknesses and obvious areas of lack.

In a sense we are all kindergarten students, and a huge gulf exists between what we are now and what our Teacher desires us to be. How can we ever get across that chasm? No one ever mistakes a seedling for the great oak tree it will one day become (1 Pet. 1:23). But oak is oak no matter the stature, and the Teacher asks us to patiently trust Him, remaining confident in His promise and power to finish what He has begun (Phil. 1:6).

I've walked with the Teacher a long time now, and I *still* don't fully understand His salvation, or His ways. A new heart? Alive and beating in *me*? No, I don't understand it all, not even now. Perhaps I never will. But I've come to realize that the Teacher has written something upon my heart, something that caused all my striving to cease. All that I once strove to do through devotion to an exterior curriculum now seems as dry toast compared to the banquet feast of love and truth written there. What a wise curriculum!

I must admit, I sometimes see little evidence of a new heart, even now. Yet one thing I know: my devotion is now to the Teacher, the One who sacrificed so much to give me His heart. My flame has been kindled, my passion is burning, and I am utterly captivated by His love! I can't help myself now, nor do I care to hold back! I tell you I'll follow Him *anywhere!* Just try and stop me! My heart is His, and His heart is mine.

> After those days…I will put My law within them and on their heart I will write it; and I will be their God, and they shall be My people.
>
> —Jeremiah 31:33

> I delight to do Your will, O my God; Your Law is within my heart.
>
> —Psalm 40:8

Focused on Dad

My irrepressible thumbs-up warrior!

Chapter 18

NOTHING WILL BE IMPOSSIBLE

And behold, you will conceive in your womb and bear a son, and you shall call Him Jesus.... Mary said to the angel, "How can this be, since I am a virgin?

Luke 1:31, 34

Oh, how hard it is to keep pressing on in life, yes, even after our hearts are aflame with passion, and after we've become convinced we will never again shrink back from following so great a King. Continuous battles make us weary. Monotony wears us down.

It's not that each step forward is so difficult, on its own. Most steps are, well, just steps. But after traveling mile after endless mile in your personal marathon and *still* seeing no finish line anywhere in sight, *this* is what makes an otherwise ordinary step so very hard to take. Your race has come to seem downright impossible, even absurd, not only to your doubters, but also to you. Honestly, you're not even sure you're on the right path anymore. The real battle you are fighting as you consider dropping out of the race is not just your battle against monotony and pain. Your hardest battle is to believe what is visibly impossible, as God remains silent.

Bryson had worked excruciatingly hard for four full years now. Others saw him merely as a disabled child who couldn't walk without being held upright. They wondered why he wasn't in a wheelchair. We observed our son's endless setbacks with eyes that saw way back to the beginning. We were grateful that he was even alive. We remembered his body shaking with seizures and writhing with fevers as a baby. We remembered that he couldn't even sit up on the floor without falling over as a three-year-old. He'd come such a long way; but he was nearly seven now, and still crippled. Despite the doubters and skeptics, we clung to our dream of seeing our son walk independently one day.

It would have been reasonable for us to ease up on him, to have him attend school and let him merely rest and play afterwards, like every other child. But every other child could run and play. Our son had to sit and watch them do it. If we quit now, the slow, steady progress he had fought for would begin to unravel, and the prediction of the skeptics would become a self-fulfilling prophesy. Frankly, this step in our marathon, the decision to stay with the NACD program wasn't that hard. What *was* hard was determining how to keep our own lives from becoming a shambles as we kept our son moving forward.

I had always performed his program together with our volunteers in the afternoon, after commuting home from the City early. Now that he was in school, we became concerned about the amount of energy he would need to expend there, even with the help of his personal aide. We concluded that there was no way he could take on the immense effort required for his physical regimen after school.

After praying, the answer became clear. We would perform Bryson's intense physical regimen during the *morning* hours, and send him to the afternoon kindergarten session.

Our gracious adult volunteers agreed to revise their schedules. Some of the teens who had served loyally for years had now gone on to college. Some who remained in high school began filling in on Saturdays. This proved to be a wise decision for our son, since he was always more energetic in the morning and more able to take on the demanding NACD regimen then. And he still had plenty of energy left over for the afternoon kindergarten session, simply because he couldn't *wait* to get there each day. He just loved it so much.

While this solved Bryson's problem, it created a significant new problem for me. He had become a real daddy's boy, responding well to my motivational style, which was a throwback to my days as a high school and collegiate athlete. During times of discouraging regression, I was often able to convince him to lift up his chin and carry on like the champion I knew he was. My wife and I agreed that it was vital for me to remain actively involved in the daily program, along with our volunteers. But to do this, my work schedule had to be flipped completely around, yet again.

Instead of commuting to Manhattan on the early morning "milk" train (as we called the 5:37 a.m. train from Glen Rock) and returning in the afternoon for Bryson's program, I would now commute to the City *after* his morning program. By the time the members of Bryson's Army arrived each morning, he had eaten breakfast and was ready to go. We performed the program between 9:00 a.m. and 11:30 a.m., and I then jumped into a business suit and was off to the station to catch the 12:00 p.m. train into the City. Oh, and of course, Bryson continued to receive his daily "pwizes" for his hard work. But now I had to buy them in advance, and we held his prize ceremony in the presence of his volunteers in our home, before I ran to the City each day.

Working half days was nothing new. I had done this for four years now, and Ed Gordon, the owner of my company and my friend, reaffirmed that he would support my new schedule. But arriving in Manhattan extremely early had been much easier for me. I am a morning person by nature, accomplishing my best work while the office was quiet, before the phone started ringing. Arriving at the office at 1:10 p.m. was a ridiculous time to start the business day, and I quickly began to feel behind the eight ball.

My terrific secretary, Val, was always there to "catch me up" with the stack of phone messages and work that was most urgent. Somehow, I kept up with conference calls, taxi and subway rides to appointments all over Manhattan, contentious negotiations of 100-plus page documents in attorneys' offices, and the delivery of presentations to clients in various boardrooms. I don't think I ever looked as ruffled or depleted on the outside as I often felt on the inside. But not a soul at those meetings had any inkling that I had expended the best of myself earlier that day in a pair of jeans.

My battle wasn't only against fatigue now. My new battle was with ineptitude. I wasn't on top of my game professionally, and I knew it. Because of the way a man is built, this bothered me quite a bit. God made men to be providers for our families. I was still providing, but I had a constant gnawing feeling. I just didn't feel satisfied at the end of many of these disjointed, frazzled days. I once felt so capable. Now I felt disorganized and inefficient.

Still, there was never a doubt in our minds that we made the right decision in diminishing my career to accommodate our son's needs. And somehow the Lord continued blessing my work. Each year brought a new record financially, even as I struggled personally. I couldn't understand that then, and I can't fully explain it now. But the Lord was providing for devastating circumstances ahead that couldn't be foreseen at that time.

When I became discouraged, I sometimes heard the voice of my father, Bryson's beloved "Pop Pop," ringing in my ears. His exhortation was simple, old school, and to the point: "Carry on!" As mentioned in the last chapter, he had heard those words endlessly from his commanding officer on the battleship USS *Hopson* during World War II. Somehow my dad knew when I felt like giving up. His words were so simple, so right, and his meaning was unmistakable: "Do what is necessary! Take that next step! Stop feeling sorry for yourself! Do it now!"

I now needed to hear those simple words "carry on" in my memory. Yet there was something even more powerful than my dad's words ringing in my memory. I remember the look on his face as he spoke them. It was a look of confidence, of expectation, a look of pride that I was his son. He *knew* I would succeed, even when I doubted myself. I now wanted to pass this confidence on to my own struggling son.

The memory of my father encouraged me, but something motivated me even more. If my brain-injured son could press on in his battle against impossible obstacles and setbacks in the hope of one day accomplishing things that we all just take for granted, things like walking and speaking, like bathing ourselves and tying our own shoes, then I could honor his courage by pressing on in the battle too. I could continue to believe even when there was no evidence worthy of belief. For his sake and for God's sake, I could forget what was behind, and "carry on" even when I felt like quitting (Phil. 3:13–14).

Getting "Hooked"

His limitations thwarted nearly every task his injured brain commanded his body to perform, yet somehow, my son didn't see himself as handicapped. In some ways he seemed disconnected from reality. Was this merely because his intellect was too limited to comprehend his circumstances? Perhaps he was simply petrified of his reality, unable even to consider it. One thing I am certain of: in his mind he was *anything* but handicapped. He was Andre, the great skateboard champion. He was Charlie, the star hockey player on the Mighty Ducks, who always scored the winning goal. These fantasies drove him. They impassioned him. They were part of him.

We constantly used these fantasies to motivate him, always going with the "hot" item of the month. If his latest passion was the Mighty Ducks, his assisted walking routine always ended with his hockey stick in hand, scoring the winning goal. When he was fascinated with Andre, we bought him the coolest skateboard around, and used it to break new records in the amount of time he could stand on it, as we held him from behind.

After a pizza deliveryman came to our door one day, Bryson decided this was the coolest thing in the universe. Our good friend John from John's Boy Pizza shop in Glen Rock supplied us with small pizza boxes for Bryson to carry as we did his assisted walking. Bryson became our friendly neighborhood pizza deliveryman as I held his shoulders from behind. Volunteers had to stand behind every closet door in our house accepting pizza boxes from Bryson, and counting out play money to pay him with. His hands didn't work well enough to take the money, so they stuffed it directly into his pockets.

Improvements to his balance and motor control remained exasperatingly slow. But as always, so much was going on that couldn't be seen. The circuitry in his brain was being developed, even as his muscles and visual pathways were receiving more stimulation than ever. One of Bryson's new regimens involved stair walking. Various muscle groups in his legs were exercised and his neurological system received tremendous quantities of input as he leaned forward and strained to push upward on the stairs in our home.

We started in the basement, climbing the "L" shaped stairs, stopping to rest at the landing, continuing up to the main floor and then on to the second floor of our split level home. I was able to take my hands off his shoulders for an instant at a time, quickly grabbing him again as he lost his balance. Waiting for him at the very top, was a blanket-covered treasure prepared by Bryson's four-year-old brother, Timmy, and a volunteer. Bryson couldn't *wait* to get up those stairs to rip off that blanket and see his treasure. There was always an assortment of his favorite Matchbox cars and trucks and some of his favorite stuffed animals and toys. After playing with them for a minute or two, he was lifted onto my back for a *fast* run down those flights of steps, as he squealed in delight. Then the arduous process of climbing started all over again, to seek out another treasure.

During this same year, the feature film *Hook* starring Robin Williams and Dustin Hoffman became such a smash hit in our home that it was destined to become a featured part of Bryson's program. We purchased the VHS version, which he watched *endlessly*. My wife made Bryson a gorgeous Captain Hook costume, complete with a plastic sword set and a feather in his cap. His volunteers and I had swords too. After Bryson completed a difficult exercise, he was rewarded by watching a brief section of the video, followed by acting out a sword fight with me or one of the volunteers.

I can't tell you how many times I died in swordfights during those days, but I'm confident I still hold the world record for being a giant, burping Crocodile after swallowing up Captain Hook. Bryson *loved* pretending to be Hook or Peter, depending on the scene he wished to act out. He got *such* joy from stabbing and killing each one of us. By the way, those of you who just smirked, assuming this must come from the Italian side of his family, will be reported to the Italian Anti-Defamation League. We *know* who you are, and you'll be having a little chat with my Uncle Tony. Try not to get him upset! His emotions are...how shall I say it? Tony is a bit fragile. Know what I mean?

The point I've been trying to make (and belaboring, no doubt) is that these fantasies were utterly *real* to my son. He was totally immersed in them. This helped us *immeasurably* in getting him through his brutal regimen. We all said our lines so many thousands of times we could have acted out those scenes in our sleep. And though he struggled to articulate his own lines because of his limited speech, we became quite impressed with Bryson's ability to memorize them. It was *amazing* what his injured mind was capable of when he engaged in activities of high interest, with extraordinary repetition.

Yet chief among his dreams, by *far,* was his passion for sports. When my son's now well-known tenacity connected with his ability to fantasize regarding sports, the sparks began to fly. He *knew* he'd one day hit homeruns in Yankee Stadium, score the winning touchdown at the Super Bowl, *and* hit the winning shot at the buzzer like Michael Jordan. In this respect he was just like any other child. The fact that his body kept toppling to the ground when he swung his Wiffle Ball bat, or each time he took a step toward the end zone with his Pixie football, never seemed to deflate him. He simply picked himself back up and set his sight toward the goal, again and again, expecting glory with that next attempt.

We bought a Fisher-Price baseball set, complete with bases for him to "run." I no longer needed to be the focal point of his eyes as when he walked toward me. His focus was now first base, then second, then third, and home. I stood behind him, grabbing him by the shoulders each time he faltered. Each base was placed about ten feet from the last, and on a successful attempt he could reach the next base without my needing to grab onto him. But successful attempts came only once out of every ten tries. And although his 90 percent failure rate was hard on all of us emotionally, this part of the program was *easy* compared to our newest goal: teaching him how to come to a *stop.*

I would *never* have conceived that stopping is such a demanding neurological feat. But as I've reminded you, walking is the art of "falling forward." The real trick is to fall forward without actually falling down. The NACD had warned us that training him to stop would require as much repetition as the walking. The thin plastic bases were ideal stopping points, since they were clearly defined and flat. I kept admonishing my son to take short steps: "Short steps, Bryson...short and tiny now...Look at the base...Look at the base, Bryson...Short steps, my boy."

When he was able to make it all the way to a base *and* stop without falling (we succeeded at this approximately once in *twenty* tries) pandemonium broke out in our house. He got thrown in the air or roughed up by one of the volunteers. As always, we wanted it to sink deep inside him that he was accomplishing something *sensational.* He faced such immense quantities of failure each day. I'd get down on his level, look him squarely in his eyes, and tell him he was a greater champion than Derek Jeter, and *all* of his TV heroes. Kids almost always know when you are lying to them. I can't tell you how good it felt to know that I was telling my son the truth.

Scrooged

During the previous spring, when Bryson had first reached ten steps in his independent walking, we established a very ambitious goal for him to reach twenty-five independent steps. He was promised that when he reached this goal he would receive his greatest "pwize" ever: a battery powered, Power Wheels Porsche. This vehicle, which he'd seen on TV, was *so* cool it made me want to be a kid again. He desperately wanted it.

My wife used her wonderful artistic ability to create a colorful drawing of an Olympic track, with Bryson standing at the place marked "10," for the number of steps he had achieved thus far. The finish line was marked as "25." I promised Bryson that the *very day* he reached the finish line I'd go out and buy him that Porsche. It was nearing Christmas now, and he *still* hadn't achieved his goal.

Each holiday season we had attempted to get Bryson excited about Christmas, but we weren't sure how much was registering. As a seven-year-old kindergartener, it was almost as if someone had drawn open the drapes allowing light to come flooding into his brain-injured mind. He was electrified with anticipation. Tim, now four, was enthralled too. Janelle loved Christmas, but she was nine now. She had decided *four* years earlier that there was no Santa Claus. Realizing how disappointed *I* was, she decided to humor me for another year, pretending that she still believed (it hasn't been easy for her, raising a dad).

I loved every bit of it, the Christmas movies and the cookies, the Advent calendars, the decorating, and, of course, reading *The Night Before Christmas* to the boys every night at bedtime (Janelle drew the line here, only sitting on my lap for epics like *The Story of Holly and Ivy*. And don't start acting shocked that someone writing a Christian book teaches his kids about Santa. I'll have you know that Saint Nicholas was a *real* person from a *real* place who lived in a *real* time in history and... All right, I know my position is weak. Let's just not have this argument, and I'll get on with the chapter, okay?

One of our favorite movies was Dickens' *A Christmas Carol* with George C. Scott as Scrooge.[1] It was *so* cool that we were together as a family watching this for the first time. We dimmed the lights and we were all snuggled in eating popcorn; and then, well, the mood suddenly changed. The story line about Tiny Tim not being able to walk brought my wife and me to tears as we looked across the room toward our own struggling child.

As mentioned, we were grateful that Bryson was no longer in danger of dying; but he was crippled far worse than Tiny Tim. And while Tiny Tim's mind and speech were clear and sharp, our son's intellect and ability to speak remained garbled and confused. I wondered if my son would ever run and jump into my arms as Tiny Tim ran to Scrooge at the end. As we watched that scene, part of me was afraid that he would view Tiny Tim's condition and suddenly realize that he, too, was handicapped. But as I glanced across the room, my son's inability even to comprehend his dilemma made me more sad than afraid.

He was now up to twenty-one steps on his colorful chart, edging ever nearer to the twenty-five steps he needed for that Porsche. But even on the "good" days, he *still* experienced only a few successful attempts toward his goal. Most times he fell after just a few steps. After *all* these years we still had no satisfactory answer for his frustrating patterns of regression, which seemed to recur each time momentum began to build toward independent walking.

Well, wouldn't you know it? It was December 11, 1992, and I remember it like it was yesterday, because there was an absolute *blizzard* in the northeast. This meant it was going to be a white Christmas, and I *love* white Christmases. But I remember this day even more vividly because this was the day our little champion crossed that finish line on his colorful Olympic track.

Since we always counted the number of his steps out loud, Bryson knew what he had done the moment his body remained upright as I mouthed, "Twenty-three...twenty-four...twenty-five"; but our champion *still* took three more steps, making it all the way to twenty-eight before falling into my arms. For an instant we were all stunned, and none of us said anything. Then, well, you already know what happened. Pandemonium broke out, along with our tears. I screamed for my wife to come in from the kitchen, and we hugged each other, and we hugged our volunteers, and we all took turns picking up and hugging our champion and throwing him in the air. The excitement went on for several minutes.

Bryson was excited, of course, but he was growing a bit impatient with all this. Sure, he was proud. He was the one who pressed on through month after month of exasperating failure. It had taken *seven months* to reach that finish line. Of course, he had received Matchbox cars and other "pwizes" along the way. But now, he realized he had *finally* earned the "pwize" of his life, and he wasn't going to wait a *minute* longer.

I tried my best to explain that we were smack in the middle of a snowstorm, and it would be necessary to wait until the next day. But after such an exultant moment, Bryson began to look at me as if I was Scrooge himself. And in view of his disappointment (and his pit bull tenacity—he simply wasn't taking "no" for an answer on this day), I soon found myself navigating through a blizzard in search of a Porsche.

I don't know how I ever made it in my 1986 Volvo, which had rear-wheel drive and was *terrible* in the snow. But the Tons of Toys store in Wyckoff was open, and Jerry the owner helped me get the oversized package strapped to the car. Somehow I made it home alive. After my wife and I maneuvered this monstrous vehicle through the doorway, Bryson sat in it for *hours* pretending he was Mario Andretti. He was kind enough to let Tim sit in it too, very proud that he could provide such a thrill for his younger brother. Even Janelle graced us with a try, stooping low from her *much* more mature play with Barbies. It would be springtime before we could bring that Porsche outside for a real ride. Bryson didn't seem to care. Ever the dreamer, the pretending was just so real.

Nothing Will Be Impossible

That Christmas season was a time to rejoice in so *many* things. Our champion's poster remained on the wall next to the Christmas tree, with the finish line *already* broken. It was by *far* our most prized decoration. Bryson's time in kindergarten was going wonderfully, better than we could have dreamed. And while my work situation was peculiar, it was more than meeting our needs. I was also thankful that the powers of hell that seemed to descend so viciously against our struggling marriage to destroy it had been denied, at least for another year. And what a joy it was to see Bryson, with all his mental challenges, develop a very simple love for the baby Jesus that Christmas season.

And for all you doubters, Santa *did* come to our house that year. In addition to leaving a great stash of toys, he took the time to decorate our little champion's prize Porsche. And before he ate his cookies and left, he was nice enough to leave a note, which I have kept all these years. Typing it here doesn't really do it justice, since it was a handwritten note. But it's just as well, since Santa's handwriting might possibly cause some of you readers to put an extra dose of rum (or two) in your eggnog, and neither Santa nor I would want to drive any of you nice people to drink. Anyway, with three kids sitting on my lap (after opening all the presents, of course) I read the letter. It was addressed to Bryson.

12/25/92

Dear Bryson,

I have been up in the North Pole, hearing about the wonderful progress you have been making in your walking. I am so proud of you, and I want you to know that by the time I come to your house again next Christmas, you will be walking all around—anywhere you want. You are getting stronger and someday you will run and play baseball and all the other sports you love. In the meantime, keep on working hard and obeying your dad. The exercises you are doing with him will make you walk better and better.

I wanted to surprise you by decorating your new Porsche. You earned this car by working hard. Walking 28 steps is a big, big accomplishment. I hope you are proud of yourself. We are all (including Mrs. Claus and the Elves) very proud of you. You are a terrific boy and you have a good mommy and daddy and a wonderful sister Janelle and a good buddy in your brother Timmy (I like him a lot).

Merry Christmas, Love, Santa

P.S. Thanks to you, Timmy and Janelle for the good cookies and milk. Your mom is a good baker.

All in all, this had turned out to be a *fabulous* Christmas. Yet, as joyous and memorable as it was, our champion did not again achieve that magical number of twenty-five steps that season. Unforeseen obstacles were about to appear in his rocky path in the months ahead that would derail his march toward freedom, including a very distressing period of illness and regression, the worst yet. Sadly, Santa's prediction of Bryson "walking all around" did not come true that next year, nor did it come true for several more Christmases to come.

Doubters abounded, as they always do when your chips are way down. The skeptics weren't the least bit surprised by his regression, and they wondered why we continued doing his foolish "home program" at all. His record of twenty-eight steps was now fading from view, and I couldn't deny that this cherished goal had been achieved under tightly controlled conditions with spotters all around. My son was growing older now. For his own good, and ours, some thought we should settle him into a wheelchair. Others thought he might walk with the assistance of a walker one day. But on his own? Crippled children run to their "Scrooges" at the end of feature films, but not in real life. There was no need to keep chasing unreachable fantasies, nor to keep pushing him so relentlessly.

Oh, how hard it is to keep pressing on, especially after traveling mile after endless mile of your personal marathon and seeing no finish line anywhere in sight. Still, each successive December continued to bring a magical quality into our home. One year soon, Bryson's little brother Tim left Santa behind, a very warm memory of his childhood, even as Janelle had done. With his much simpler mind, Bryson continued to believe well into his teenaged years. Santa *always* left him a note, which I read each Christmas morning as he sat on my lap, listening eagerly. These many years later, I now realize I needed to write those notes of encouragement to my son even more than he needed to hear them.

The letters always made it clear that Santa was very proud of him. They encouraged him to keep working hard, promising him that good days were coming. Sometimes I searched for something honest and encouraging to say to my boy, while groping for something to salve my own struggling soul. Ever the aging child on my lap, Bryson kept clinging to his cherished dreams, looking to his dad to lead him toward hope. I *never* let him know how badly I was struggling now, but the temptation to let go of my own dreams and give in to despair was immense. I wasn't even sure we were on the right path anymore. On my weaker days the whole blasted thing seemed so impossible—my son's progress, the saving of my struggling marriage and family, holding on to my career, *all* of it!

Through the years I've come to understand that we all need to be reminded of something we tend to forget when our chips are way down. It's always been this way, I think. Even the blessed mother Mary needed to be reminded, prior to the very first Christmas. The things spoken to her by the archangel nine months earlier had caused her to be perplexed: "How can this be, since I am a virgin?" Gabriel chose not to contend the point on her level; because on her level, he knew she was right. In human terms, the things he proclaimed to her that night were indeed impossible.

The angel had reassured her by saying, "Do not be afraid" (Luke 1:30), but nine months had now passed, and not much had happened to assuage Mary's fears. Joseph did not divorce her or have her killed for adultery, as could have occurred in those days. Finally, he did believe her about the pregnancy, after he was visited by the angel too (Matt. 1:20). But that had not prevented others from talking. They had both been disgraced.

A decree had gone out from Caesar Augustus, and a long, wearisome journey was taken, on a donkey no less, through a perilous land full of thieves. At long last, they arrived in Bethlehem, exhausted, as time for her labor drew near. She had every reason to be perplexed, ever since the Angel first visited, but now, who could have guessed *this*? No room in the Inn? She would be forced to deliver her child in a stinking, unsanitary stable. Mary's life, much like yours and mine sometimes, had taken a turn for the absurd.

She viewed her predicament from every angle. She couldn't *begin* to understand how this was all going to work out. As her pain intensified in that cold little barn, Mary groped to remember just *exactly* what the archangel had told her nine months before. What *reason* had he given her not to fear? She remembered him saying, "Greetings, favored one" (Luke 1:28). Some favor, indeed! Her life was now a wreck. Maybe the angel's visitation was just a dream after all. Either way, it didn't seem to matter anymore, as she writhed in the hay. Her life and her circumstances seemed more ludicrous and impossible than ever.

But I suppose if God intended to keep us imprisoned in the realm of the possible, He would never have sent that first Christmas at all. The angel's words were later recorded, but not for Mary. She has long since passed her test. It is now time to pass our test, and overcome our fears. Life ebbs away too quickly not to do so.

When our most cherished dreams have been shattered, and it seems the doubters of our lives just may be right, when it appears we'd be absolute *fools* to dare to take even one more step forward, we need to remember something that is easily forgotten. God chose to enter our world during Mary's darkest hour, even as the cry of a Baby pierced the blackness of that night. Mary finally did remember the angel's promise then. It is now time for us to remember, to lift our eyes to that Baby, and believe:

> The angel answered and said to her… *"For nothing will be impossible with God."*
>
> —Luke 1:35, 37, emphasis added

Two boys with big sis on a hayride

Brothers at the park—and together forever

So blessed by these treasures. Some things in life are worth fighting for.

Stylin' in a Porsche!

Chapter 19

THE EYES OF YOUR HEART

I pray that the eyes of your heart may be enlightened, so that you will know... the surpassing greatness of His power toward us who believe.

EPHESIANS 1:18–19

PLAYGROUNDS AND BATTLEGROUNDS

THE PATH OF least resistance would always have led to our son sitting passively alone. This we simply could not accept. We tried hard to maintain a "can do" spirit in our home, giving him every opportunity to follow his dreams. And our irrepressible child wanted to try *everything*. Janelle and Tim, both naturally smart and athletic, were sometimes hesitant to try new activities. Like most children, they wanted to be certain they could do something well before jumping in, particularly when others were watching. With all his limitations, Bryson always wanted to jump *right* in and try.

We needed to be creative in involving him in some activities. My wife brought him to a gymnastics birthday party, jumping on the trampoline with him, walking him across the balance beam, tumbling his body in somersaults along with the other kids. When we took our three kids to the park, it took thoughtful effort to include Bryson in games of Red Light, Green Light, Duck, Duck, Goose, and tag between the slides and monkey bars. I scooped his growing body up into my arms and ran with him, touching his feet to the ground every once in a while to make him feel as if he was running with the other kids. I look back on this in amazement, not because of how hard we tried to include our son, but because of his passionate desire to rise above his limitations. He often became frustrated, confused, and angry, but quitting *never* seemed to enter his mind.

We were still working toward walking in his daily NACD regimen. He had reached new heights the previous Christmas season in terms of taking twenty-eight steps. But, as mentioned, the process was fraught with enormous quantities of failure, and on most attempts he could still only manage a few steps prior to falling. He had entered another exasperating season of regression, and after *years* of excruciating effort, his main mode of ambulating through the house (or through a park) was still to crawl like a baby.

He wore a colorful pair of kneepads to cushion the constant pounding. Still, his knees were always deeply bruised now. It was hard for us to stay back and watch him crawl across that playground, trying *so* hard to keep up with the other kids. But just as there were times when he wanted us out there helping him to "run," there were other times he desired, if even on his knees, to strike out on his own. But when any of us, including you reading this book right now, attempt to break free in life, we inevitably find that stepping out into brave new areas of opportunity also presents bold obstacles. This was the case as Bryson strove to stake his claim to fame out on that playground.

We desperately tried to protect him from cruelty, but this was no easy task. The more he attempted to overcome his limitations by participating in normal activities, the more he experienced the brutality of others. We couldn't keep his ears from hearing every malicious comment, nor his eyes from seeing some children laugh and sneer at him as he crawled across that playground. "Look at that kid crawling. What is he? A *dog?*" The cruelty was exacerbated by his inability to understand why these things were being said.

At seven years old, his simple, injured mind remained unable to comprehend that he was handicapped. Still, he was slowly becoming aware that he was different. There was sort of a "disconnect" in his mind, an intensifying confusion between the reality of his circumstances and his ability to understand or deal with his limitations. Observing him experience such cruelty against the backdrop of his internal confusion was, in a word, hell. I *hated* what my son had to experience daily. He had suffered *immensely* all his life. Now, he was being abused just for being handicapped. It seemed God was allowing him to slowly bleed to death. I was tempted to doubt, to accuse God of indifference.

> How long, O LORD, will I call for help, And You will not hear? I cry out to You, "Violence!" Yet You do not save.
>
> —HABAKKUK 1:2

I desperately feared my son's day of reckoning, the day he'd finally understand just how far his cherished dreams and fantasies were from reality. It sometimes seemed those dreams were the only thing keeping him going. As described earlier, I heard a clock in the background, ticking relentlessly against his childhood. The ticking became thunderous as I watched my son facing such cruelty.

Oh, that I could wrap this tender child in my arms to protect him forever. It was as if a tidal wave named "reality" was rolling out there, somewhere, but not knowing when it would hit. I was terrified that when it finally hit his shores it would crush him, along with all his dreams, once and for all. This is part of what drove me so intensely in his program of development. What did I have to lose? Time? Money? Sleep? I'd have given my *life* to protect this precious child from that tsunami.

Oh, but giving our lives away for those we love is never quite that simple. The kind of surrender and sacrifice God requires is often very different than what we envision for ourselves. As well-intentioned as we may be, like Moses, the slaying of the Egyptian taskmaster (Exod. 2:11–12) never frees God's people in His way, or in His timing. His ways are far higher and different than our ways (Isa. 55:8–9). There is one solitary remedy that can ever elevate our motives, our plans, our actions, and our dreams into compliance with His higher ways. That one remedy is the road of brokenness, surrender, and death to self. It is not ours to fully understand His ways of surrender and death. It is ours to trust.

> We are afflicted in every way, but not crushed; perplexed, but not despairing; persecuted, but not forsaken; struck down, but not destroyed; *always* carrying about in the body the dying of Jesus, so that the life of Jesus also may be manifested in our body. For we who live are *constantly* being delivered over to death for Jesus' sake, so that the life of Jesus also may be manifested in our mortal flesh. So *death works in us*, but life in you.
>
> —2 CORINTHIANS 4:8–12, EMPHASIS ADDED

We think the Lord to be cruel for failing to help us fulfill our childlike dreams as we take on the playgrounds of life, as if *that* is what God exists for. Growing from childhood to adulthood requires seeing things more clearly. Don't hear me saying it is wrong to dream. If we lose our ability to dream, we will live out the remainder of our lives in this world as a death sentence. The death that "works in us," that Paul taught about is anything but a death sentence. It is our ticket to reality and freedom. Jesus said:

> If anyone wishes to come after Me, let him deny himself and take up his cross and follow Me. For whoever wishes to save his life shall lose it; but whoever loses his life for My sake shall find it. For what will it profit a man if he gains the whole world and forfeits his soul?
>
> —MATTHEW 16:24–26

Our eyes must be opened. The world we've been born into is not a playground, but a battleground. God's Word gives homage to an enemy, calling him the "ruler" of this world (John 12:31; 14:30; 16:11). Scripture goes so far as to say that "the whole world lies in the power of the evil one" (1 John 5:19). Jesus made it clear that the truth will make us free (John 8:32). Conversely, Satan has a vested interest in veiling the circumstances into which we've been born. He is satisfied to remain hidden, either as we ignore God as unbelievers, or as we redefine the gospel as believers, making it more palatable to our culture and our fleshly sensibilities, while living out our playground scenarios.

What small dreams we choose to invest our lives in, thinking they are the highest we can aspire to. Do you think you are a higher dreamer than the Truth? Hardly! But we need to keep from getting it backwards. God was not created for us. We were created for God. Through His gracious, awesome plan of salvation, we have been offered the opportunity to live out a dream of grander significance than any of our puny playground aspirations. But He will never conform His grand plan to fit in with our temporal dreams. Mercifully and magnificently, He remains willing to elevate our dreams to conform to His.

The road of brokenness, surrender, and death to self makes no sense whatsoever to those who remain insistent upon living in a fantasy world. Nor can they understand what Jim Elliot said: "He is no fool who gives what he cannot keep to gain what he cannot lose."[1] Any clear thinking person would immediately exchange their temporal dreams for God's eternal purpose. Jesus Christ came to open our eyes to the truth, and to set us free from lies, from sin, and from dreams that are far too small.

The Importance of the Eyes

We did our best to counteract the cruelty of others by giving our son torrents of affirmation and praise. He received constant reminders that he was fantastic, smart, handsome, and courageous. Nonetheless, the limitations that bound him, along with the rejection of those who were cruel, began to take a heavy toll. A deadly combination of frustration, anger, and fear was building inside him, and a costly payday was looming in the form of his growing self-hatred. This latent land mine, which will be revealed in later chapters, would not surface until his teen years; and it would then become one of the most powerful tsunamis to ever slam into the shores of his life, or mine.

But during those playground days more urgent, daily waves just kept rolling in. An orthopedic specialist informed us Bryson needed surgery on both of his feet. Due to his absence of balance he had been exerting extreme skeletal effort to stand independently, pressing hard into the ground through his ankles and feet. This resulted in his ankle bones protruding (pronation), and his feet becoming completely flattened (pes planus). The NACD advised us to avoid this surgery and the immobilizing leg braces the doctor recommended. They put us in touch with a doctor who provided him with rubber inserts or "wedges" to be worn inside his shoes to help strengthen his arches over time.

Intense exercises were added to his regimen geared toward building up his calf muscles, feet, and ankles. This work was demanding and painful. But choosing the NACD alternative once again seemed best. It helped us to avoid the uncertainties of surgery and the weakened, atrophied muscles and joints that the hard plastic leg braces would have caused. We remained determined not to yield to alternatives that would give our son immediate benefit while diminishing the possibility of his ever walking independently.

But there was one surgery looming that the NACD agreed needed to occur. Since Bryson had sustained more extensive damage to his brain's left hemisphere (which controls the right side of the body), his right eye drifted and was rarely being used. Both the NACD and Dr. Rudolf Wagner informed us years before that we needed to help his brain to keep his right eye "alive." He needed a vast amount of stimulation and input through his right eye so that his brain would not shut it off, blinding that eye permanently due to lack of use. Though he kicked and screamed about it, he needed to wear a patch on his left eye while he was at home, *forcing* him to use his weakened right eye, thereby saving it.

Depth perception and spatial awareness is one of the foundations of walking. A tremendous quantity of input to Bryson's brain had been accomplished through visual exercises during the previous four years, and his spatial awareness had slowly begun to improve. One of these exercises required him to keep his head still (held from behind) and follow one of his favorite toys with his eyes as I made the sign of a cross in front of him. I held the toy next to his nose, pulled it away eighteen inches, and then made a "cross" in front of him, eighteen inches high, eighteen inches low, eighteen inches to the right, and eighteen inches to the left. We'd then begin again at his nose. Sometimes we used a good tasting vitamin instead of a toy, and pop it in his mouth when the exercise was complete.

Four years of patching and visual exercises had saved the function of his right eye. But both his eyes continued to droop and move toward his nose on an alternating basis, almost as when a cartoon character gets walloped on the head. This condition is known as "alternating, bilateral strabismus." Unlike most children with this condition, Bryson's "drifting" was not a muscular problem. The muscles in his eyes were perfectly fine. His brain lacked the ability to direct and coordinate those muscles, and those eyes.

Dr. Wagner was one of the most accomplished pediatric surgeons in the nation, but we would never have known this by his demeanor. He was gentle and humble, listening patiently to our fearful questions, calmly answering them. We later found that he had spent vacations providing free surgery to needy children in places like Bangladesh. When this great man told us it was time for surgery on *both* of Bryson's eyes simultaneously, we were scared to death; but at the same time, we had full confidence in him.

The stress meter in the Milazzo household rose to red-alert level. Placing Bryson under general anesthesia was a *major* concern. No one, not even Dr. Wagner, could predict with certainty what the neurological implications might be for our son. Years of exasperation and thousands of hours of painstaking work had been endured to "awaken" our son's injured brain. Though he still crawled across playgrounds, we continued to believe he was on his way toward a bright future. The horrifying specter of incurring additional neurological damage at this time was dreadful. We spent much time in anguished prayer over this; but honestly, my trepidation did not fully subside as the surgery approached.

In very simple terms, we began to inform Bryson about the operation, including the fact that he would be separated from us as he was taken into surgery. Each bedtime we began to include this in our simple prayers with him, as all five of us said "good night" to the Lord. As always, Bryson was unable to say much, but we believed he understood more about what was going to happen to him than he was able to express. Not surprisingly, all our discussion and prayer about his eyes had convinced him that eyes were a *very* important topic, and his response resulted in something surprising one evening.

Bears, Buttons, and Kisses

I must tell you that the bedtime routine was never one of my favorite times of the day. In fact, there were nights when I didn't think I could make it through another *minute* before our kids were asleep. I've often wondered why God didn't make kids with "on/off" buttons, so they can simply be switched "off" when parents become too busy and exhausted to deal with them. I realize I just horrified some people. Obviously, those people don't have kids.

Anyway, it's good that I didn't have access to such a button. I might have used it *every* night to shorten the bedtime routine. Most times I could excuse myself for being cranky. I was drained and tired. I had rushed through a stressful day in Manhattan, *after* spending several hours working on the demanding morning program with Bryson. But I suppose there is little I could say to defend the fact that I tended to growl, something like a bear, when I became weary. No, I don't mean just in my head. I mean an audible growl. Usually I wasn't even aware of it. There were times when my wife looked at me (lovingly, *of course*) and asked, "What in the world was that?"

Wild animal noises aside, bedtime in our home was similar to bedtime in most homes. There were bedtime stories and brushing teeth and endless requests for one more cup of water from all three kids. But for Bryson the bathroom was a *highly* dangerous place. He was still falling numerous times per day, still suffering painful injuries. He tended to impulsively lunge to try to release himself from our grip. Our most crucial bedtime task was to keep him from hurling himself headfirst into the sink, tub, toilet, dresser, or bed frame, as he squirmed to get away from us and get into mischief. We clung to him firmly to prevent serious injuries that could occur in an *instant* as we worked our way through the bedtime routine.

It would be about ten more years before Bryson acquired the motor skill to use a toothbrush. At age seven he didn't possess the ability even to *hold* one without dropping it. Nor did he possess the skill to undress himself or put on his pajamas. His cups of water needed to be carefully and slowly delivered to his mouth (as *we* held the cup), since his lips were not coordinated enough to drink it neatly. And as for that *last* cup of water (you parents know the one I'm talking about, the one that you argue about not giving him until he wears you down and you finally give it to him), he would invariably spill it all over himself and the bed as he stubbornly grabbed at it with his uncoordinated little hands.

This was the last mile of our daily marathon, and as mentioned, I couldn't *wait* until it was over. One exasperating night (fraught with a few growls from yours truly), after *all* the stressful bedtime tasks were completed, after the bedtime prayer and after tucking him in for the seventeenth time, I was fit to be tied. Bryson began pointing at my face, beckoning me to come closer. I groaned, thinking: "What in the world does this kid want *now*!" But we had been praying about his pending eye surgery, and it was evident that the subject of eyes was *very much* on his mind. As I came closer he asked a question that melted the hardness and growls right out of my heart. As he kept pointing to my face, he asked, "Kiss eyes, Daddy? Kiss you eyes?" (He could not pronounce "your.")

My precious son wanted me to come close enough so that he could give each of my eyes a kiss, as I closed them. I came closer and let him give me a tender, gentle kiss on both eyes with his uncoordinated lips. Then, he wanted me to kiss his eyes; which, of course, I did. With that done, he was finally satisfied, and ready to go to sleep. He didn't quite understand what this surgery we had just prayed for was really all about. But he had heard enough to realize that fixing his eyes was *really* important. If eyes were *that* important, then he wanted to kiss his daddy's eyes every night. And after daddy had kissed his, he was satisfied that everything was going to be okay.

On a deeper level than this growling bear often grasped, our precious son was right. His eyes *were* more important than he could understand. It is the same for us though. Our eyes are far more important than we often understand, and our Daddy is deeply concerned about their condition. He wishes to kiss them and bless them, so they will be opened to see what He planned from the beginning for them to be able to see.

The Lamp of the Body

> The lamp of the body is the eye. If therefore your eye is good, your whole body will be full of light. But if your eye is bad, your whole body will be full of darkness.
>
> —Matthew 6:22–23, NKJV

Even as Bryson's right eye was in peril of being "shut off" through lack of use, the Lord admonishes us to keep our spiritual eyes clear lest they become "bad" in a way that floods our souls with darkness. Julian of Norwich, a saint from the thirteenth century, put her finger on a perilous mistake that can cause the eyes of our soul to become dead, ultimately causing us to "rot from within."

> Sin is this: to look for the spiritual food that re-creates your soul—that is, love and life and beauty and truth—in any created creature or thing. When we pursue our life in anything other than God, our soul becomes weak and failing. And if we are not careful, the eyes of our soul will close and become dead and dried. In this way, a man or woman can rot from within, and die, and yet think they live. What a tragedy! For then they cannot see Him who is our blessed life.[2]

What a tragedy, indeed! God created us with eyes that have the capacity to behold the most wondrous Light in existence: Him. When we forget or reject that we have been created *by* God and *for* God (Col. 1:16) and seek our fulfillment in the assortment of idols and substitutes for God in this world, our eyes become dead and dried, and we begin to rot from within. This is precisely the condition Satan desires for us: dead inside! But when we focus our eyes on what we have been born for, light comes flooding in.

> God is Light, and in Him there is no darkness at all.
>
> —1 John 1:5

> For with You is the fountain of life; In Your light we see light.
> —PSALM 36:9

> One thing I have asked from the LORD, that I shall seek: That I may dwell in the house of the LORD all the days of my life, To behold the beauty of the LORD.
> —PSALM 27:4

These scriptures seem to be telling us that we must maintain our focus upon God. As a Christian, this seemed right and good to me, and I really wanted to obey. Besides, the possibility of winding up being full of darkness as Jesus warned, or of being dead inside as Julian of Norwich warned, scared the day-lights out of me. But can this growling bear be honest with you? The notion of maintaining my focus on God seems a bit unrealistic, even a tad sanctimonious. Don't get me wrong, God is great and all, and the Bible is wise and true. But my life was no day at the beach at this point, and after *all* the difficult things we are commanded to do and to be aware of and to remain alert to, these are all things that, quite frankly, I'd rather *not* have to deal with *all* the time!

Things like being born onto battlegrounds and not playgrounds and *all* the rest of those *hard* teachings, and *now* what exactly is God asking us to do? He wants us to make *Him* our *entire* focus in life? Okay, so He's beautiful and full of light. I get it! And the Bible is important. Agreed! But *come on already!* Is God asking us all to become *so* hyper-spiritual that we focus *all* our attention on Him while placing no emphasis on what *we* want in the *real* world? Don't we ever get to live our *own* lives? I thought Christianity was supposed to give *us* some blessing and comfort in life! And I hate to be so crass as to ask God: "What's in it for me?" But, "What's in it for me, Lord?"

And even if I did decide to become *that* fanatical about my faith, isn't God too high and mysterious to really know anyway? I mean, it's impossible to look directly at the sun, right? Wouldn't it be accurate to say that it's even more impossible to look at the God, who is far more brilliant than the sun that He made? So what exactly is scripture asking us to do in exhorting us to "behold" God's beauty and "see" light in His light?

While God is immeasurably brilliant, awesome, and fearful, His Word makes it clear that He is far from unapproachable. He has not hidden His glory from us, nor has He wrapped Himself inside a riddle that cannot be solved. He desires us to know Him, and He has gone to astonishing lengths to provide a way for us to see Him and know Him with absolute clarity, in Christ. Everything we need to know about God is clearly laid out in His written Word, which reveals Jesus Christ His Son, the living Word.

> And the Word became flesh, and dwelt among us, and we saw His glory, glory as of the only begotten from the Father, full of grace and truth.... No

> one has seen God at any time; the only begotten God who is in the bosom of the Father, He has explained Him.
>
> —John 1:14, 18

> God, after He spoke long ago to the fathers in the prophets...in these last days has spoken to us in His Son, whom He appointed heir of all things, through whom also He made the world. And He is the radiance of His glory and the exact representation of His nature.
>
> —Hebrews 1:1–3

> He who has seen Me has seen the Father.
>
> —John 14:9

It is an enormous understatement to say God has done His part in revealing Himself. Jesus Christ, the radiance of His glory, has been lifted up for all to see. And to the extent that I think I "get it" about God's beauty, I should think again. When I catch even a glimpse of who He *really* is, I am *ruined* by the comparison between His righteous majesty and the vileness of my own sin (Isa. 6:5). Seeing Him clearly will drop any sane person to their knees in holy fear, and in adoration. And with respect to any lingering concern over being shortchanged as we ask, "What's in it for me?" the truth is that our eyes need to be opened. God has *already* made us vastly wealthy, in Christ.

> The kingdom of heaven is like a treasure hidden in the field, which a man found and hid again; and from joy over it he goes and sells all that he has and buys that field. Again, the kingdom of heaven is like a merchant seeking fine pearls, and upon finding one pearl of great value, he went and sold all that he had and bought it.
>
> —Matthew 13:44–46

> Guard, through the Holy Spirit who dwells in us, the treasure which has been entrusted in you.
>
> —2 Timothy 1:14

Why would anyone who has found the Pearl of great value continue to spend their time and energy trying to become wealthy in this world? From the moment we are born, we live inside of dying bodies that last about a blink of an eye compared to eternity. It's tragic when we who *say* we belong to Christ live no differently than those who are unsaved, failing to guard the great treasure that has been entrusted to us.

Many Christians are thankful to be saved from sin and hell, and they're looking forward to heaven one day. But in *this* world we often find ourselves living as paupers, remaining blind to our true wealth and inheritance. We are the picture of a poor recluse living in the squalor of a rickety shack, desperately attempting to eke out a living. How much sadder would this picture be if the pauper's shack sat atop the world's wealthiest oil reserve, and he never knew it? His ignorance would be his doom. Sadly, so is ours.

The good news in both cases is that the Source of wealth and power is *very* near. But somehow our eyes must be opened to it. This is what impassioned Paul as he dropped to his knees to bring this matter to the throne of God on our behalf. Clearly, he didn't want us to remain poor. Interestingly, his prayer has to do with the functioning of our eyes:

> I pray that the eyes of your heart may be enlightened, so that you will know what is the hope of His calling, what are the riches of the glory of His inheritance in the saints, and what is the surpassing greatness of His power toward us who believe. These are in accordance with the working of the strength of His might which He brought about in Christ.
>
> —EPHESIANS 1:18–20

Even as my brain-injured son didn't quite grasp the importance of the functioning of his eyes as we prayed for his surgery, Paul prayed that the eyes of our heart may be opened to see all of our *untapped* riches in Christ and His *surpassing* power toward those who believe. If we don't want to live out our *vastly* wealthy lives as practical paupers in a rickety shack, the eyes of our hearts must be opened, by faith, to what has *already* been accomplished *for* us and *in* us, in Christ. Similar to Paul, Watchman Nee implores us to open our eyes to the power of the Person who lives inside of us *right now*:

> Oh, that our eyes were opened to see the greatness of God's gift! Oh, that we might realize the vastness of the resources secreted in our own hearts! I could shout with joy as I think, "The Spirit who dwells within me is no mere influence, but a living Person; he is very God.... I am only an earthen vessel, but in that earthen vessel I carry a treasure of unspeakable worth."...All the worry and fret of God's children would end if their eyes were opened to see the greatness of the treasure hid in their hearts...there are resources enough in your own heart to meet the demand of every circumstance in which you will ever find yourself.... The reason why many Christians do not experience the power of the Spirit, though He actually dwells in their hearts...they have not had their eyes opened to the fact of His presence. The fact is there, but they have not seen it.... True revelation of the fact of the Spirit's indwelling will revolutionize the life of any Christian.[3]

Jesus Christ has already finished His work of making us wealthy. Our work is to *believe* in Him, to be confident in the life He now lives from within us (John 6:29). It is utter faithlessness to continue to search for meaning, purpose, success, or power in *anything* beyond what we *already* possess, in Christ. Who in their right minds would rummage through garbage pails when they have been seated at the banquet table of a King?

SIMPLE ENOUGH FOR A NINE-YEAR-OLD

God forbid that anyone should hear me saying that our eyes must be opened through the figuring out of complex, doctrinally sophisticated facets of our salvation. The enlightening of the eyes of our heart that Paul prayed for is *far* simpler than that. It exceeds the grasp of the proud and arrogant every time, but God made sure that perfect vision is a gift that can easily be received through the eyes of a child.

About the same time that Bryson was scheduled to have his eye surgery at seven years old, my daughter Janelle was nine and one-half. One day I asked her if she knew what the greatest command in the entire Bible was. When she said she did not know, I asked her if she would like to hear Jesus' opinion about what is most important. Of course, she wanted to know. So I read to her what Jesus revealed to be most important:

> "YOU SHALL LOVE THE LORD YOUR GOD WITH ALL YOUR HEART, AND WITH ALL YOUR SOUL, AND WITH ALL YOUR MIND." This is the great and foremost commandment. The second is like it, "YOU SHALL LOVE YOUR NEIGHBOR AS YOURSELF." On these two commandments depend the whole Law and the Prophets.
>
> —MATTHEW 22:37–40

Love God and love others. Pretty simple! I told my daughter I was thankful that Jesus made the most important command in the Bible so easy to remember. She agreed, quite satisfied with Jesus' answer until I asked the following question: "Kitten (my pet name for her), if this is really the most important thing, then how do we do this? We can't even see God. How can we learn to love Him? And, for that matter, just how do we bring ourselves to love others? Where does all this love come from?" A concerned look came over my daughter's pretty face, and she said, "I don't know, Dad." I then had the joy of turning to 1 John chapter 4 with her, to read from these verses:

> Beloved, let us love one another, for love is from God....In this is love, not that we loved God, but that He loved us and sent His Son to be the propitiation [payment] for our sins. Beloved, if God so loved us, we also ought to love one another.
>
> —1 JOHN 4:7, 10–11

> We love, because He first loved us.
>
> —1 JOHN 4:19

My daughter's eyes opened wide as I taught her that all love is from God, not from our own ability to somehow learn how to love on our own. I told her if we really want to love God and love others as Jesus commanded, then we need to first receive love from Him. Simply put, we can't give out what we haven't first received.

I also told her that there's no way God chose to love us first because we were so lovable in our sinful state. God loved us first because it is the very nature of God to love (v. 8). Finally, I told her that if we want to learn to love God a whole lot, and to love others a whole lot, then we need to keep letting God love us a lot.

That's pretty much it. Like I said, it's simple. If only we big girls and boys would be content with simplicity.

God's love isn't just another doctrine to be tossed into our bag of theology, a childish truth to make us feel warm and fuzzy until we grow up to learn "higher" truths. God's love is the highest truth. God created us with a deep void that can be filled only by Himself. Since God is love, to be filled with God is to be filled with His love. Without a solid, growing sense of God's perfect love for us, we have no other option but to live as pretenders and grabbers in this battleground world, endlessly dreaming dreams that couldn't fill the God-sized void in our hearts even if we achieved every last dream.

"What's in it for me?" I once wanted to know. Perhaps the question is arrogant. Perhaps it is just human nature to want to know. Either way, our Father doesn't begrudge the asking of it. Astonishingly, the Almighty stoops to answer us, bowing lower than we could have conceived in our wildest imaginations. He shocks history, stooping as low as a Roman cross, spilling out the blood of His Son. What's in it for me? What's in it for you? Everything! Everything we were born for! King Jesus now resides within us!

No wonder the enemy strives so fervently to keep our eyes shut. He understands the power we possess in Christ, even when we don't. Once we are saved he knows he has lost our souls, yet he resolves to do all he can to prevent Christ's love from flowing out of our hearts to others. His mission is now damage control; and as always, his weapons are lies and deception. But with so great an adversary, how can we possibly keep from being deceived? How do we keep our eyes open?

God's love for us, manifested in the grace of Christ, got the ball rolling. But we must never stop there. It is His unshakable love and grace that keeps the ball rolling. We must go to Him a lot and let Him love us a lot, even when we have failed a lot. I know it sounds too simple, and too good to be true. But our acceptance by God through the grace of Christ is our anchor and our core identity in this battleground world; and beholding God's loving grace toward us, in Christ, is the reason we've been given eyes to see.

> See how great a love the Father has bestowed upon us, that we would be called the children of God; and such we are.
>
> —1 JOHN 3:1

> Keep yourselves in the love of God, waiting anxiously for the mercy of our Lord Jesus Christ to eternal life.
>
> —JUDE 1:21

> Do not be carried away by varied and strange teachings; for it is good for the heart to be strengthened by grace.
>
> —HEBREWS 13:9

> You therefore, my son, be strong in the grace that is in Christ Jesus.
>
> —2 TIMOTHY 2:1

Our enemy will do everything in his power to keep our eyes from fully opening to such a great love. One of his favorite deceptions is to cause us to focus on our service for Him, instead of on Christ. This is a crafty deception, because it gains us the applause of men. But even as our Lord rebuked Martha (Luke 10:41), Mary's choice is always "the good part" (v. 42). Sitting at His feet drinking in His love seems a waste of time. But abiding in His love never proves vain (John 15:5). We find ourselves laboring even more than all the rest of men and women, and for the right reason (1 Cor. 15:10).

The Father does not need dutiful service from mercenary soldiers in this battleground world. Frankly, God has no needs. But He does have desires. He has always desired to have children to bestow His love upon, children who would love Him in return. In His wisdom the Father knows that children inspired and controlled by His love will carry out the family business of love in this world in a way that pleases Him, and they make better soldiers than a militia motivated through remuneration or fear (2 Cor. 5:14; 1 John 4:18).

The Father's plan for His children often involves pain and sorrow here. His Word is very clear about this. For some, the pain will arrive early and stay late, a dreaded visitor that never seems to leave. At times the suffering will be so intense and so bewildering that our eyes will be blinded, at least for a while. But even when we can't tell which way is up anymore, the Father is aware of every detail, and He remains in control of every tsunami that ever slams into the shores of our lives. He wastes nothing!

The man or woman who has had their eyes enlightened to the love of God and to the vast riches of Christ within them cannot be held back by any power on earth, or from hell. They keep getting filled up with His love, and then they relentlessly carry Christ's love back out into the world. This is the enemy's worst-case scenario, since God's love is a power he simply cannot repel. How marvelous in the eyes of heaven is the sight of a wounded warrior carrying Christ's love from a bleeding heart to other desperately hurting souls, so that their own void of darkness and pain may be filled. When the enemy sees this, he shudders, and the gates of hell are moved.

As the date for Bryson's eye surgery drew near, there was never a day when I did not observe my son's pain, his anguish, and on some days even his torture. As I looked toward his future, I knew a tsunami was rolling out there, somewhere, and I feared the day it would hit. I didn't understand as much then about the importance of our spiritual eyes. I have since become convinced that there's only one way to weather the tsunamis of life. We must have eyes that have been enlightened to the deep love of God for us.

When we are stunned by pain, when our minds are confused and our vision is blinded, when we can't even tell which way is up or down anymore, when we are tempted to turn back in defeat or to just lay down and die, if we are to have any chance whatsoever at renewing our hope and pursuing victory, we must recall to our minds the simplest, most powerful truth in our Father's kingdom:

> This I recall to my mind, Therefore I have hope. The LORD's lovingkindnesses indeed never cease, For His compassions never fail. They are new every morning; Great is Your faithfulness.
>
> —LAMENTATIONS 3:21–23

THE BIG DAY ARRIVES

The day for Bryson's surgery finally came. We had to leave the house at 6:00 a.m. to arrive on time at the medical complex in Roseland, New Jersey. My wife's mom had slept over to care for Janelle and Tim for the day. My wife and I were nervous, and we clashed with each other pretty intensely en route, arguing about everything from the speed of my driving to the quality of her directions.

Dr. Wagner and his staff were wonderful. The anesthesiologist explained all the precautions that would be taken. Then after having him drink some "funny apple juice" to relax him, Bryson began talking up a storm, as if he were drunk (which I suppose he was, practically speaking). He was completely at ease as they carted him into the operating room. "Ease" was not a description I would use for us. My wife and I silently prayed and read books and magazines for the next few hours, and waited (and no, I didn't sneak a swig of the funny apple juice, though I wanted to).

Finally, Dr. Wagner called us in to be with Bryson in the recovery area, prior to his waking. This wonderful, humble surgeon had done a *magnificent* job. But we nervously awaited his waking, to determine if there were any negative neurological effects from the anesthesia. In the days to come we would learn that Bryson was completely fine.

Dr. Wagner told us that Bryson would be dizzy and nauseous for the next twenty-four hours. In fact Bryson was quite ill. From the time we brought him home until I gently placed him into his bed that night he couldn't bear to open his aching eyes and he was so sick he could barely move. His system had been badly shaken. To cheer him we gently played a cassette tape that Mrs. Schlegel had his kindergarten classmates prepare for him. She explained that one of Bryson's worried classmates had come up with the idea that while Bryson was away (he was expected to miss school for a week) he could listen to each of them individually saying, "Hello Bryson," to him on tape.

Bryson silently listened, very pleased to hear the voices of his little friends. But he was not even able to generate a smile due to his nausea and pain. He just lay there, as we kept the lights off. He couldn't misbehave, nor request endless cups of water, nor struggle to get away from us, nor prolong the bedtime routine in any way. Oh, I yearned for him to be able to "annoy" me on this night, but my son was far too ill, far too hurt.

In times like these I wished I could reach down and take his suffering into my own body, so that he could be free. But he neither whimpered nor complained. He just lay there accepting his suffering, like the champion he had repeatedly proven himself to be. He did not itch or rub his sore eyes, as the doctor had warned him against. Once again, my son had risen to the occasion. Once again, I was so proud of him I could scream.

After the tape finished playing, Bryson remained completely still, and we quietly turned to leave the room, thinking he was asleep. But without opening his sore eyes, he turned to me in the dark, and weakly said: "Daddy?" He needed something. I came closer. Very faintly, his nearly inaudible request came in a whisper: "Kiss daddy's eyes?" Believe me, he didn't need to ask me twice. In so many ways, I was being overwhelmed by the tremendous importance of the eyes. I knelt down and came close enough for him to kiss each one of my eyes. Then he was content, and almost as if someone flipped a switch, our little champion dropped peacefully off to sleep.

> In peace I will both lie down and sleep, For You alone, O Lord, make me to dwell in safety.
>
> —Psalm 4:8

A good story to end a long day

Chapter 20

NEXT YEAR IN JERUSALEM

You will no longer see... A people of unintelligible speech which no one comprehends, Of a stammering tongue no one understands.... Your eyes will see Jerusalem.

Isaiah 33:19–20

When he suffered his devastating brain injury as a baby, my son was considered permanently crippled, essentially uneducable and expected never to speak intelligibly. He was nearing eight years old as he entered first grade in September 1993. Bryson's Army had battled for five years, and we all marveled at his progress. But the road was still *so* long and it remained excruciatingly hard to gain even the tiniest increments of progress.

Deep weariness was a given now, but I must tell you how sick I am of referring to how tired I was. Yet it bears repeating since there will be some reading this book suffering from wearying battles that will never cease in this world. You need to be reminded that you are not alone in your exhaustion, or in the depression and anger that sometimes tag along with it. Some of you have had friends who have grown weary of standing with you. They've concluded that your problems should, somehow, have been resolved by now. Instead of supporting and loving you, they've evaluated you and wrapped you into a neat package with their psychobabble label du jour. The friends of Job were quick to blame him for problems he didn't cause and couldn't change, suspecting him of inner, hidden sin. A little knowledge is a dangerous thing, isn't it?

I used to think that Paul prayed three quick prayers for relief from his thorn. I now believe he engaged in three long, gut-wrenching *seasons* of prayer. But the Lord had a higher purpose in mind for that thorn. His unchanging, incurable circumstance was going to teach him how to depend more deeply upon the grace of Jesus Christ, so His power would be perfected in Paul's weakness (2 Cor. 12:7–9). I've sometimes wondered if Paul had any suspicious, fair weather friends as he suffered with his unending, life altering problem.

Sometimes well-intended friends go to the opposite extreme. Instead of condemnation, they comfort us to the point of harm. They can cause us to feel sorry for ourselves, treating us as helpless victims. Such comfort is poison. God doesn't have victims. He has children. A victim mentality engendered through ill-timed, excessive sympathy can kill a struggling person. Irrespective of how cruel our circumstances have been, we remain *personally* responsible to make choices that are obedient to God's Word.

Your circumstances may have crushed you so badly that you can't see straight, but you *can* make a choice. When our strength is gone, we can still choose to keep pressing on in His strength, not with our eyes fixed on the length of our journey nor on those who have loved us poorly, but on the One who daily invites us to come to Him.

> Come to Me, all who are weary and heavy-laden, and I will give you rest. Take My yoke upon you, and learn from Me, for I am gentle and humble in heart; and YOU WILL FIND REST FOR YOUR SOULS. For My yoke is easy and My burden is light.
>
> —MATTHEW 11:28–30

The Lord is indeed gentle and humble, yet He loves us enough to hold us responsible to make obedient choices. When all is black and our resources are gone, when our circumstances seem impossible, even absurd and laughable, we can still *choose* to walk toward Him through the blackness, by *faith*. Though we can't see through the tears, particularly when all is dark, He is near to the brokenhearted and He saves those who are crushed in spirit. Our part is to trust and obey.

> The LORD is near to the brokenhearted And saves those who are crushed in spirit.
>
> —PSALM 34:18

> He Himself has said, "I WILL NEVER DESERT YOU, NOR WILL I EVER FORSAKE YOU," so that we may confidently say, "THE LORD IS MY HELPER, I WILL NOT BE AFRAID."
>
> —HEBREWS 13:5–6

One night my wife and I sat discouraged and exhausted after getting the kids to bed following a particularly hard day. Bryson's program had gone *terribly* that day. I turned to her suddenly and said, "Next year in Jerusalem!" She looked at me like I was nuts (imagine *that*!). To this day it drives each member of my family crazy when I incorporate lines from random movies into our conversations. I find it best to do this without warning, and then act as if I hadn't said something odd or out of context. My kids would argue that I am not only out of context, but out of my mind. But *I* know the context, and it gives me some sort of twisted satisfaction when it takes them a few minutes to catch on that our conversation has taken a hard left turn toward Hollywood.

As for that evening with my wife, I reminded her that this was Tevye's favorite saying in *Fiddler on the Roof* (a phrase of hope that Jews around the world speak out at the conclusion of the Passover Seder and also Yom Kippur). She finally realized I was attempting to inject a trace of humor into our situation (okay, maybe a *small* trace) with a bit of hopeful truth. This saying "stuck" between my wife and me, and we began trading it back and forth as an inside joke on particularly difficult days, glancing at each other and lamenting: "Next year in Jerusalem!" Next year just might bring the fulfillment of all of our long cherished dreams! Maybe our son will walk next year! Who knows, already? We might even reach the "promised land" of stress-free, problem-free living. Next year in Jerusalem!

Not that I really thought we'd ever reach a problem-free "Jerusalem" in this world. A smooth journey would be abnormal here, not a difficult one. As noted in earlier chapters, we live on a battleground, not a playground. Many Christians falsely believe that life is *supposed* to get easier as we trust and surrender to the Lord. Our obedience should result in fewer problems, less hassles, more comfort, more blessing, and more success (as the world defines success, of course). There *should* be a payoff for us here. There should be a Jerusalem! *Oy vey!* If we only knew our Bibles better!

> For to you it has been granted for Christ's sake, not only to believe in Him, but also to suffer for His sake.
>
> —PHILIPPIANS 1:29

> Through many tribulations we must enter the kingdom of God.
>
> —ACTS 14:22

> In the world you have tribulation, but take courage; I have overcome the world.
>
> —JOHN 16:33

> Many are the afflictions of the righteous, But the LORD delivers him out of them all.
>
> —PSALM 34:19

Throughout this book I've attempted to emphasize God's foolish plan of depending upon Him more and on ourselves less. It may now seem to be a contradiction to accentuate our need to take personal responsibility as we walk through our difficulties and sorrows. But once we understand the biblical order of *first* trusting God, we do not then sit back passively and do nothing. Dr. Robert A. Cook used to say, "Faith trusts God then does what it can in the face of impossibility."[1]

Doing what we can as we fight our assigned battles involves choices of our will. One of the most critical choices is to refuse to give up when things get tough, but to keep obeying God and His Word. There are times when pursuing God in obedience may require limping, even crawling toward Him through the blackness of a seemingly endless tunnel, as tears flow. An inch in the right direction today is better than turning back.

The enemy will urge you to take *any* road but the narrow road of enduring the cross assigned to you by God. Your sinful flesh will plead for relief, imploring you to yield, yet again, to your addiction of choice rather than to press ahead. Worldly-wise friends, sometimes even Christian friends, will advise you to escape from your problems as quickly as you can, irrespective of what God's Word teaches.

"Trust your feelings! Use common sense! Improve your situation *any* way you can! God just wants you happy! Go ahead! Leave that marriage. Take those popular prescription drugs to ease your depression, and your conscience. Go to a counselor who will tell you that you *deserve* to be angry. You do not have to forgive, nor do you need to repent for your own sin. To salve your guilty conscience you can simply forgive *yourself.* Come on! Don't be the oddball. The whole world is taking this road toward Jerusalem!"

Seeking worldly comfort and relief appears wiser and frankly, it often feels better than the narrow road of obedience. Knowing Christ in the power of His resurrection? Fine! Bring it on! But in the fellowship of His sufferings, being conformed to His death (Phil. 3:10)? I think I'd rather not. The road of endurance, of waiting and praying, of remaining *in* our problems rather than escaping them, seems irrelevant if not absurd. But this is one of the most critical forks in the road we will ever come to as we suffer. If we are going to follow Christ, we *must* take the path of foolishness (1 Cor. 3:18; Isa. 55:8–9).

It comes down to this. We must choose this day whom we will serve (Josh. 24:15). Will we choose the path offered to us by our enemy, or by a Friend? (John 15:15). The Lord has set before us the road of life and of death, of blessing or a curse. For God's sake, and for ours, we *must* choose life (Deut. 30:19)! Larry Crabb gives some powerful imagery to the choice required of each of us:

> The wind of the Spirit is blowing. But it isn't moving our ship toward the smooth seas of a more pleasant life. It's rather carrying us into the eye of the storm, into the presence of God.... We must adjust our sails accordingly. If we aim for calm waters, we go alone. We resist the wind of the Spirit.... When everything goes against you, the Lamb of the Cross is the Lion of Heaven moving toward His sure purpose. And it's a good one. Hang on![2]
>
> —Larry Crabb

Whether we are able to run a mile today, or just hold our ground, we must be determined to do so in obedience to what God's Word actually says, not what we want it to say. The Lord is just *itching* to step in and do His greater part in our battles. But a life of compromise, of keeping one foot planted firmly in the world, keeps Him from stepping in. If *anything* is clear in Scripture, it is clear that God will not bless lukewarm duplicity.

Only when we stop pursuing the cotton candy this world offers us can we take our seat at the Lord's banquet table. The more we fellowship with the King, the more we realize how truly foolish it is to reach for the idols of this world. We are already wealthy beyond our imaginations in the grace and love of Christ. When our eyes are enlightened, our desire is no longer to grasp, but to *give* from the abundance we have received. Our highest goal is transformed to have the Spirit flow through us for the benefit of others.

> Our Lord's teaching is always anti-self-realization.... His purpose is to make a man exactly like Himself, and the characteristic of the Son of God is self-expenditure. If we believe in Jesus, it is not what we gain, but what He pours through us that counts. It is not that God makes us beautifully

rounded grapes, but that He squeezes the sweetness out of us. Spiritually, we cannot measure our life by success, but only by what God pours through us, and we cannot measure that at all.[3]

—Oswald Chambers

Some of you reading this book are grieving losses so deep that you couldn't describe your pain if you tried. But I have a question to ask you. The question may seem callous, as if I don't care about your pain. But it's a question I believe we all need to consider daily. Here is the question: How badly do you want the life God has destined for you? The flip side of this question is: How badly do you want *Him*?

As we set our sails toward full maturity in Christ, toward our true Jerusalem, if you will, we must understand that a ship *cannot* have two captains. Either Christ is all, or we remain all, simply using Jesus among our panoply of props and idols, all designed to make our lives more comfortable as *we* remain in control. Jesus will not forcefully impose His authority as Captain. It's not His style, nor His plan. But He *never* compromises, and He will *not* be used as a prop. He is a consuming fire or He is nothing (Heb. 12:29). On a practical level, He remains useless to us unless we fully enthrone Him.

Alan Redpath chronicled the battles of Joshua to conquer and possess the land of Canaan, noting that Joshua's battles foreshadowed the battles required of us as we seek to enter the land of full maturity and blessing in Christ. He laments that few Christians seem to understand, or even care about, the nature of the battle to which we've been called. Written in the 1950s, I believe the sad state of lukewarmness Redpath lamented is even more prevalent today. He asks the question I've asked above a bit differently. Instead of, "How badly do you want Him?" Redpath asks, "How hungry are you for Him?"

> Full blessing in the Christian life is not bestowed except to eager, hungry people who press in to receive it.... God does not pour out of His fullness on a plate, as it were, and invite us to help ourselves at a low level of expectancy. He desires every one of His children to press in against all the assaults of the enemy, that we may lay hold of that which is our inheritance in the Lord Jesus Christ, knowing that every foe we shall ever meet in that battle has been met and conquered by our Joshua.[4]

Just as Joshua pressed in to the land of Canaan amidst intense battles, God's Word is clear that we must press in to the land of full blessing in Christ amidst intense opposition. So again, how badly do you want God's best for your life? How hungry are you? How badly do you desire Him? Christ certainly wanted *us* very badly. He bled to death on a cross for us. What is our response? Do we want our full inheritance in Him badly enough to pick up our cross and fight our God-given battles for His sake, and for the sake of others? When we are ready to fully surrender to Him, to forsake every aspect of our self-centeredness, *then* we are ready to fight our battles in the strength of the Lord.

Don't fret if you suspect that the Lord needs to reveal more to you about your duplicity. Of *course* there is more. *None* of us is ever finished with the process of laying aside the deceitful, evil, self-centered flesh that seeks to control us. Far better than thinking we have arrived is the humble awareness of just how far we still need to go. The Lord is not put off by our neediness, nor by our continued stumbles and failures. He remains mindful that we are but dust (Ps. 103:14). But He *is* put off by our arrogance, thinking that we can fight our battles on our own terms, without the grace of Christ.

Do we love and trust God enough to forsake every idol, every false path the enemy offers us? Are we willing to pick up our cross and follow Jesus on His narrow path, even when sorrow, loneliness, and pain are required? The Lord knows when we are pretending and He knows when we are ready. He is watching and waiting. He is just *itching* to step in. What freedom, joy, and power He desires to bestow upon us. *Nothing* can compare with having His wind against our sails as He blows us toward the "Jerusalem" of our full maturity in Christ. He has proven His desire for us. How badly do we desire Him?

> For the eyes of the LORD move to and fro throughout the earth that He may strongly support those whose heart is completely His.
>
> —2 CHRONICLES 16:9

IT SURE DOESN'T FEEL LIKE JERUSALEM

As Bryson entered first grade, he was now in a full day school program, and I was no longer able to perform his NACD program with him in the morning. I didn't mind rising at 4:30 a.m., once again, so that I could return from Manhattan at 2:30 p.m. for his three-hour program. But this presented some difficult challenges for Bryson.

What young child would want to work *so* hard after coming home from a full day at school? Understandably, he continued to exercise his strong will against the required regimen. We continued to motivate him with prizes and treats, with silly fun from teenaged volunteers, and a smattering of dad's firm hand of discipline. Each day's program was an emotional and physical battle which was never easily won. Often, it was hell.

But those daily battles propelled him to a new personal record of forty steps in his "assisted walking." We were grateful for each record, yet we were still mindful that this could only be accomplished with me (or a volunteer) hovering over him to catch him as he fell. He was able to reach ten steps only *once* in every fifteen to twenty attempts. Imagine, if you can, how frustrating *this* much failure was for Bryson. He still stumbled and fell into our arms *fourteen* out of *every fifteen* attempts after merely a *few* steps. Some days he had no successes *at all.* As always, we tried hard to praise and urge him forward. Yet endless doses of daily failure continued to wear on him. It wore on all of us.

I've just described his assisted walking *inside*, on a flat, carpeted surface. Bob

Doman of the NACD pushed us to have him do his assisted walking *outside* on uneven surfaces that would increase the difficulty. We kept our hands on his shoulders from behind and then let him go for as many steps as he could take, grabbing him immediately as he began to fall. His *best* attempt outside was still only a few steps. Tevye might have said, *"Fachadick!"* But making it easy on Bryson wasn't the NACD agenda. God was reminding me daily that "easy" never quite gets any broken child to Jerusalem.

Yet even after all I've said about embracing our difficulties and not escaping them, about crawling in the right direction an inch at a time through the blackness and all the rest of those lofty exhortations, we had finally reached a point in our journey that I didn't want to acknowledge or admit, not even to myself. We simply weren't seeing the progress we needed to see for an individual who aspired to be an independent walker one day.

Due to his full day of school, plus the exhaustive NACD work, we had eliminated most of Bryson's outpatient therapy sessions. Our speech and occupational therapists were excellent, but these therapies were now provided at school. We continued to have our physical therapist visit Bryson once per week. Though I trusted the NACD, I didn't want to let go of her professional opinion. One night after her session with our son, I looked her in the eyes and asked if she believed our son would ever walk independently. She hesitated, knowing how deeply painful this subject was for my wife and me.

She gently advised us that, since Bryson was nearing eight, his pattern of development was fundamentally set. In her opinion, his system had *not* progressed far enough. She complimented us on all the hard work we had done. But this only confirmed her opinion. All the thousands of hours of work performed through the years had not caused him to reach the goal. It was obvious to her that independent walking was *not* a realistic goal for our son. We might break new "records" under closely supervised conditions, but there was only so far his severely damaged brain could take him at this point. No, Bryson would never walk independently.

I stood there blinking, trying to digest her words, trying not to cry. I felt like I had just been hit in the stomach by Muhammad Ali. I was...numb...devastated. Beyond that, I have no idea how to describe my feelings. I felt like digging a hole and crawling into it.

One night soon after this, she brought a walker to our house for Bryson to try. We thought this would be safe, since he was outside on soft grass. But one of his hands quickly lost control and spastically slipped off the handlebar. His head hit the metal crossbar on the way to the ground. He wore a deep bruise for days.

As much as I respected this professional, I realized that the direction she advised was tantamount to giving up on our son. It seemed no different than the recommendation made years earlier to provide him with an electronic device to speak for him. If our highest goal was lowered to the hope of using a walker one day, then this would become a self-fulfilling prophecy. He had worked *so* hard.

Letting go of the dream of seeing him walk on his own was like letting go of breathing. I was determined not to let go.

I suppose my personal resolve, as I describe it to you now, seems hope filled and courageous. The truth is, while I tried never to lack outward confidence in front of the volunteers or my wife, I was *terrified*. Salmon swim upstream, persevering until they reach their destination. But what can they do when the Hoover Dam stands in their way? I was often frustrated to tears after yet *another* demoralizing daily session with my son.

And yes, I was still haunted by that hideous rhyme: All the king's horses and all the king's men couldn't put Humpty together again. During the lowest moments, the taunting of that cursed rhyme was unbearable.

It's Not a Deal Until You Shake on It

When we started with NACD, Bob Doman had not committed himself regarding whether Bryson could ever walk. He simply told us that the brain is the most resilient organ in the body, and he would not rule out walking as all the others had. We were grateful to him for all the progress he had helped us to achieve in so many areas of development. But we were now *five years* into this exasperating program, and our son *still* crawled around the house and across backyards and playgrounds. In my frustration, I was now determined to go to him with the same question I had just asked our physical therapist.

If we were going to continue to be stressed and exhausted getting my son's regimen done every day, if I was going to risk my career falling apart, if our emotions were going to continue to bounce up and down like a yo-yo along with Bryson's regressions, I had to at least know the endgame of all our outrageous, debilitating effort. I didn't want to speak to Bob on the phone. I needed to look him in the eyes. My strength in business was reading people. If he equivocated, I'd know it. And I didn't want to hear any hedging. Bob *knew* how hard we had worked. Our next quarterly reevaluation was in January 1994. I wasn't going to leave that meeting without getting an answer.

The day came, and I tried to appear cordial and nonchalant as I sat across from Bob, even as my emotions were churning. As cool as I had prepared myself to be, I heard myself interrupting Bob as he was speaking and blurting out my question. "Bob, will our son ever walk independently, or not?" Bob paused and sat back in his chair. There was complete silence in the room. His pause wasn't one of equivocation. It was appropriate in view of the magnitude of the question, and the depth of my emotion. I watched him like a hawk, waiting impatiently for his response. Staring back into my eyes, he spoke slowly, and confidently, and I can assure you that I will not forget his words if I live to be 100. He said just four words: "We'll *make* it happen!"

I sprang up from my chair, feeling a bit like Scrooge jumping up and down on his bed when he realized he was still alive on Christmas morning. I don't think I could've been *tied* to that chair! I was exhilarated! I grabbed hold of Bob's hand

and shook it, almost as if I was cementing a real estate deal. It was an awkward moment to be sure. Nonetheless, I continued standing there, staring into Bob's confident eyes, even as tears were forming in mine. Still standing, I listened to the rest of what Bob had to say.

He reminded us that Bryson's muscles and bones were perfectly fine, just as they always had been. *All* his physical problems, even his hypotonia (low muscle tone) resulted from his brain's lack of ability to properly receive and send messages to and from those muscles. Continuing to provide his brain with enormous quantities of *input* with extreme *intensity* and exhaustive *repetition* over an extended period of *time* was still the *only* way our son would one day walk. This was no different than what Bob's guidance had always been. But he had now seen enough of Bryson's progress through the years to know that it would happen, we would *make it happen*, as we pressed on toward "Jerusalem."

If we chose to provide Bryson with temporary "fixes," such as surgeries and hard braces, then immediate benefit may come, but something more important would be taken away. His legs would rely on the strength of those braces, and his muscles and joints would begin to atrophy. Then, much of the hard fought gain that had been achieved toward cross pattern walking would gradually be lost. Bob mentioned quite a bit more about his entire regimen. To be honest, I didn't really need to hear the rest of what he had to say. I had already *seen* what I had come to see. I saw the confidence in his eyes when he said, "*We'll make it happen!*" In my mind, the matter was settled.

Nothing concrete had changed as we walked out of that room. At the same time, *everything* had changed. Bob still refused to give us a timetable, but I trusted him. I left there ready to do battle with renewed hope and confidence. As I strapped Bryson in the car, I could have flown home. That night I called our physical therapist, thanked her for all her love and hard work. We have never been to another professional therapy session. No longer would we have our feet in two camps, nor would we again doubt the road we had taken with our crippled son. One day we were going to arrive at our long sought promised land of seeing our son walk on his own!

There must be no low level of expectancy. Every broken child must press on against the backdrop of pain and endless battles as we seek to lay hold of our inheritance in Jesus Christ. Faith draws a line in the sand. It does not turn back.

> Faith is the assurance of things hoped for, the conviction of things not seen.
>
> —HEBREWS 11:1

> Therefore, do not throw away your confidence, which has a great reward. For you have need of endurance, so that when you have done the will of God, you may receive what was promised. "FOR YET IN A VERY LITTLE WHILE, HE WHO IS COMING WILL COME, AND WILL NOT DELAY. BUT MY RIGHTEOUS ONE SHALL LIVE BY FAITH; AND IF HE SHRINKS BACK, MY

> SOUL HAS NO PLEASURE IN HIM." But we are not of those who shrink back to destruction, but of those who have faith to the preserving of the soul.
>
> —HEBREWS 10:35–39

GOING WITH HIS PASSION

Bryson began doing "quad squats," sinking slowly down with his back against the wall until he reached a "seated" position (with no chair underneath him). His quads (the front of the thigh) became rock hard to the touch as the number of repetitions increased. His calf muscles continued getting stronger through endless toe raising exercises and walking across the room (hands clasped in ours overhead) on his toes with his shoes off. We added a "stepping path" underneath his overhead ladder. It was made out of two-by-fours by my selfless brother-in-law, Jim Schwarz. Bryson had to step into each small rectangle in the stepping path as he grabbed the next rung of his overhead ladder.

He stepped up onto boards made of plywood that we had cut for him at the local mill. Although these platforms were only one-half inch high, this was a *very* high step for Bryson to take. While stepping up onto the platform was extremely difficult, it was even harder for him to step *off* of those boards without falling to the floor. His success ratio, in terms of being able to remain standing as he stepped off the platform, was only once in five tries, even after a full *year* of working hard at this.

He began walking up "mountains" (actually a small hill in front of our house), leaning forward and straining with each step to conquer the "mountain," as we held his shoulders from behind. We did many other new exercises, too numerous to list, six days per week, three hours per day. The regimen worked *all* the vital areas of his body, his brain and his entire neurological system. But the key to our success that year, and every year, came not just from the work, but from a place deep inside my son's heart. If he didn't have a passion for more, then all of our efforts would have been in vain.

Each member of his Army continued to join him as his teammates on the Mighty Ducks, as he scored the winning goal, over and over again. They watched him win countless skateboard competitions. They were members of Captain Hook's crew, walking endless planks into the cold depths. They explored hidden treasures at the top of mountains (stairwells), delivered thousands of pizzas to closets, killed countless bad guys with guns, served as Santa's elves as Santa (Bryson) delivered presents from his magic pillow case, all over the world of our house. They did anything and everything they could think of to keep him walking without knowing he was really exercising.

He became my little buddy as we watched baseball, basketball, football, and hockey on TV. He was becoming even more excited and animated in his sports watching than I was, and that's pretty animated. Janelle, Bryson, and Tim had all spent countless hours in my arms as babies, receiving a bottle or taking a nap, as I watched sports on TV. And they will probably all wind up in therapy one

When we found out that the program wasn't being carried out, we approached the administrator we knew had set the roadblock. We were stunned when she told us that the NACD methods were not *"permissible"* in a public school. Her position, as usual, was rigid, and a stalemate quickly developed. We decided to hold Bryson out of school until the situation was resolved. A meeting was quickly scheduled with the Child Study Team for the next day; and this administrator informed us that if we kept Bryson out of school even *one* more day, she would be forced to *"cancel and reevaluate"* all the services the district had agreed to provide our son, including his full-time aide.

We took this as a threat against our son, and made an appointment to see the district superintendent. In the presence of the superintendent, the administrator denied that she had made her threat, and proceeded to convince him that "state law" would not permit her to utilize materials from the NACD. We knew this was ridiculous, and we apprised the superintendent that numerous districts throughout New Jersey had welcomed the NACD's materials and methods in educating brain-injured children. We expected more backbone from this superintendent, but he quickly decided to back his administrator.

I recount this event not just because it was an important milestone in my son's story, but because most people with healthy children have little idea what families with autistic and brain-injured children are forced to endure as they attempt to educate their children. Situations like these are inevitable in advocating for a handicapped child. I've learned that no matter what your intentions are, others are going to fault you, misunderstand you, and some may even hate you for doing what you *need* to do to protect your child. To state the obvious, the choice to help and protect your child is more important than being liked. Suffice it to say I wasn't very liked in this district.

I don't want to make it sound as if all school districts are obstinate. In the next chapter you will learn that this is not the case. But I've heard *many* horror stories, and I've met many families who were bullied *far* worse in their own districts than we were. If you've ever wondered why there are so many advocacy groups helping families with special needs children, *this* is the reason. And this is why laws that provide protection to handicapped children (and adults) need to be so detailed and rigorous.

But let me conclude this section quite a bit more upbeat. I thank God for federal legislation like the Americans with Disabilities Act. Without it, our son may never have had the opportunity to be included in any of our local schools. And a time was soon coming when we would be thanking God for a courageous, compassionate group of school administrators and teachers in another town, to which we had decided to move.

NEXT YEAR IN JERUSALEM...MAKE THAT KINNELON

We came to believe that our district in Glen Rock would never appropriately meet the needs of our son, and we grew tired of fighting an uphill battle. We became encouraged by the positive meetings we were having with the school system in Kinnelon, New Jersey, and also about our plans to build a new house there. While Bryson's education was the most important factor in moving, we felt that it was time for a new beginning for a variety of reasons. Who knows, already? Kinnelon just might be our "Jerusalem."

Glen Rock was a wonderful town, with two train stations to choose from to commute to Downtown New York. But we had prayed quite a bit about my getting out of Manhattan. I had commuted for eighteen years, and I was tired from rushing in and out of the City to participate in Bryson's demanding program. As we searched for a new home, Ed Gordon agreed it was a good idea for me to transfer to ESG's fast-growing New Jersey Office. I'd become a managing director there, as I had been in our Wall Street office.

Working in New Jersey would help me to have more time with each of our wonderful children. Janelle was now in fourth grade, and believe it or not, I had become a coach on her softball team in Glen Rock (in my spare time). I was excited that in the years ahead I would be able to coach other teams, and attend school band concerts and other important activities. Commuting to Manhattan doesn't lend itself to such things.

As far as the idea to build a new house, I came to agree with this "kicking and screaming." My wife *loved* the idea since it got her creative juices flowing. She was an incredibly talented artist, designer, and decorator. She drew all the details of our Tudor style home on a piece of tracing paper, and brought it to an architect to work out the details. I would have preferred to buy a house that actually existed, one I could *touch*. It's less hassle, and I like to know precisely what the final cost will be. And as tired as I was at this point, I had a tremendous desire for simplicity. But you know who got the better of this discussion, since I've already told you that we were building a house.

One of our friends suggested that we take pictures of each phase of the construction as it progressed, from the raw land, to the completed foundation, to the framing, etc., all the way to the finished product, to be kept in a scrapbook. I should have taken a picture of the original construction estimate…and then *the final bill*! (Okay, I said I wanted to end this chapter "upbeat." I'll stop grumbling.) We never expected Kinnelon to be a stress-free, problem-free "Jerusalem." But the closer our move came, the more we looked forward to our new home and community with high hopes for a brighter future.

As our move approached, my wife mentioned she wanted us to host a "walking celebration" for Bryson's eighth birthday in May. I opposed the idea in view of all that we were juggling, including the building of a house. But I later came to agree with it as I considered all the members of Bryson's Army. These soldiers had come to us when we were desperate. They had helped us to "awaken" our son from his horrible slumber, and they had remained dedicated at this task for five *years*. Bryson was functioning at levels *far* higher than we once dared to hope. We couldn't leave town without thanking them appropriately. Besides, it was time to do this for Bryson. He deserved to be celebrated.

At first, I was hesitant to call his birthday party a "Walking Celebration." Bryson wasn't actually walking yet, not independently. But we had already decided that we weren't giving up, we were going to *make it happen*. In view of that decision, it didn't really matter how much longer it took. The bottom line was that either we believed in our son, or we didn't. The fact that our courageous son could take *any* independent steps at all proved what a champion he already was. We believed! It was time to celebrate!

Quite simply, I'll remember May 8, 1994, as one of the greatest days of my life. The soldiers from Bryson's army, family members, cherished friends, prayer warriors from our church, and numerous others who provided rides and so many other acts of kindness through the years all joined us for the Walking Celebration. Some of Bryson's wonderful professional therapists came too. In all, eighty warriors gathered in our backyard to celebrate with us on that magnificent spring day. Pete Ackerman, our friend and president of Ridgewood Awning Company, set up a large, open-sided tent in our backyard. On this beautiful day, it provided us with shade.

It was an *awesome* party. We were able to officially say "thank you" and "good-bye" to the warriors who had literally saved our son's life. We would no longer rub shoulders with them daily, as we had done for years. The NACD was transitioning Bryson's regimen to gym-like programs. I'd be performing them alone with Bryson in gyms or at athletic fields. We still had a *long* way to go in every area of his development, including our long sought "Jerusalem" of truly independent walking. But his warriors had mightily accomplished *their* task. It was a day to celebrate their efforts, and those of our son.

Bryson was having a great time at his party. We had just purchased the coolest looking vehicle for him. It was kind of a cross between a bicycle and a walker. It was bright blue, with black rubber wheels, and a Ninja Turtles basket on the front. This bike/walker was perfect for occasions like this. He was learning to push it around safely, and on this day it kept him from having to crawl across the yard after his siblings and cousins.

I had spoken to Bryson about the significance of his Walking Celebration, telling him how proud of him we all were, because he was a very special champion, greater than his heroes, Michael Jordan, Deion Sanders, and all the rest. He had worked harder and overcome higher obstacles than *any* of them, and I wanted him to know we were having this party because we knew he was going to accomplish even greater things in the future.

Bryson's response to all this, as usual, was to say very little. He still spoke very slowly, and his sentences remained fraught with omitted words. Yet we knew from experience that words of encouragement and praise made a significant impact on him, sinking much deeper than what was apparent. More powerful than words, the greatest impact on this day came from the fact that all his favorite people in the world had come to celebrate his accomplishments and his eighth birthday. Still, even considering the powerful influence of all these factors, we were about to be shocked by what occurred that afternoon.

My wife sang a beautiful song, using the sound system we had set up. After that, I got up to say a few words and read some Scripture. I told our soldiers how grateful we were for all they had done for our son. After I finished my talk and prayed, our guests went back to chatting among themselves, and all eighty of us were still closely grouped together around the little podium we had set up. And then...it happened.

Maybe it happened because there was such a large group of people in his way. Perhaps it was due to all the pent up excitement and the tremendous pride inside our little champion. He knew that this huge tent and all the fuss were centered on his great accomplishments. Then again, maybe it was simply the movement of the Spirit of God, giving Bryson's disbanding "Army" a gift as they gathered together one last time. Whatever caused what I am about to tell you, I will cherish the moment forever.

The kids had been quiet during our brief program. But now, Bryson's brother, sister, and cousins began chasing each other through the crowd, rushing past us like a wave of water, as if we weren't even there. Bryson wasn't able to maneuver his Ninja Turtle walker through this large group of bodies to keep up with them. When I saw him coming out of the corner of my eye, I immediately stopped talking to the circle of friends in front of me, turning to see if I was really seeing what I *thought* I was seeing. There Bryson was, motoring through the crowd, and his Ninja vehicle was *not* with him. He was walking quickly, almost *running* after his cousins. My jaw dropped. The crowd went still.

We all remained silent, staring at him, then at each other. Suddenly, spontaneous applause and shouting erupted through the yard, springing from incredulous, grateful people who couldn't have held themselves back if they tried. As for me, though in shock, I could've leaped to the clouds. My son had just run *thirty feet* to the back of the yard over very difficult to navigate, *uneven grass*. *None* of us could explain what we had just seen. I can't explain it to you now. He had never come anywhere *near* such an exploit. Even the NACD wouldn't have asked us to attempt it.

I remembered a dream I had, years before. It was a joy-filled dream with Bryson running freely with other children in the park. It was a beautiful sunny day, just like this one. I couldn't hold onto that dream. This time, it seemed my son just might keep on running forever. But he couldn't sustain his run, finally falling face first onto the grass at the back of the yard. Someone ran to help pick him up off the ground. Someone else quickly wheeled his Ninja walker over for him to resume using. It was all over in a matter of ten seconds, I suppose.

Though he had fallen, there wasn't *anything* negative about our champion's amazing feat on this day. This was an *incredible* way to end such an awesome day, such a beautiful era, with Bryson's entire Army there to see it! Untrained? Clearly they were! But there's not a chance you will *ever* meet more dedicated, exceptional warriors. They had fought the good fight, they had finished their part in our son's race, and they had kept their faith, powerfully helping us to keep ours as well. To this day I am convinced Bryson's run at his Walking Celebration was a gift to them, to all of us, from the mighty hand of God.

My wife and I were drained in the aftermath of the party. This was a day never to be forgotten, and we were overjoyed and *awed* at what the Lord had done, encouraged by *so many* blessings showering down on us now. And as sad as it was to say good-bye to all Bryson's wonderful soldiers, we looked to the future with hopes that were sky-high. I could hardly *wait* for all the exciting possibilities ahead.

It sometimes seemed my son's childish fantasies were the only things keeping him going. I guess I'm more like my son than I realized. I've learned there's nothing wrong, better said, there's everything right, with having dreams. But we must hold our dreams loosely, remaining ready to surrender them into the hands of a King who may choose to alter them, delay them, or remove them for His glory.

Hold your dreams loosely. So easy to say! I clung to my long cherished dream of a sunny day when my son would keep on running forever. We'd soon be back to the grind, resuming endless days of perseverance, failure, repetition, and resolve. I didn't know it on that day when I could've leaped to the clouds, but storms were brewing just beyond the horizon, tempests that would blow even fiercer winds against our son, casting serious doubts that he would sustain a feat like that run, ever again.

Jerusalem, oh Jerusalem! Why are you so *hard* to find? Maybe next year our eyes will *finally* see Jerusalem! Oy! Make that Kinnelon!

> Behold Zion, the city of our appointed feasts! Your eyes will see Jerusalem, an untroubled habitation, an immovable tent... But there the LORD in majesty will be for us a place of broad rivers and streams.... The LORD is our King; he will save us.
>
> —ISAIAH 33:20–22, ESV

Chapter 21
FIELD OF DREAMS

I'm fearful of even more shattered dreams, but now I know there's a better way, a better relationship than any flawed one in this world, a higher dream, a more perfect love than I can ask for or imagine, in the person of my Lord Jesus.[1]

Larry Crabb

In the feature film *Field of Dreams*, Ray Kinsella (played by Kevin Costner) was prompted by a mystical voice to build a baseball stadium in the midst of his Iowa cornfield. One day the spirit of Shoeless Joe Jackson of the famous 1919 Black Sox scandal appeared on the field along with numerous legendary ballplayers. One of the last players to appear was Ray's long-deceased father, John Kinsella. Deeply puzzled about his new surroundings, John engaged his son in conversation:

John: "Can I ask you something?...Is this heaven?"

Ray: "No, it's Iowa."

John: "Iowa? I could've sworn it was heaven."

Ray: "Is there a heaven?"

John: "Oh yeah! It's the place where dreams come true."[2]

As we packed up and moved from Glen Rock, I had no illusions about Kinnelon being heaven, but I sure hoped it would be closer to heaven than *Iowa* (sorry Hawkeye and Cyclones fans—that was a cheap shot. And I hope Dan Gable doesn't come looking for me). But I did think the worst of our sorrows were behind us and anticipated that Kinnelon was the place many of our long cherished dreams would come true.

A move to a new community, a new home, or a new job can be just what the doctor ordered to lift us from the inevitable ruts of life. We often see this when a professional ballplayer's career is rejuvenated by putting on a different uniform in a new city. But unless something more significant replaces the adrenaline rush of even our most carefully orchestrated fresh starts, the ruts inexorably return.

Our search for heaven in this world, in one way or another, eventually breaks down. Expectations of reaching a plateau of blessing and comfort can evolve into a deceived sense of entitlement, resulting in bitterness or despondency as our demands for blessings are rebuffed. Worse yet, we might actually gain our coveted blessings and become further deceived that our "faith" is working. Larry Crabb describes this widespread deception:

> We're never more deceived than when we think we're living for God but in fact are living for His blessings. When we persuade ourselves that our job is to pray properly, live morally, and love meaningfully, and that it is God's job to reward us with greater blessings we most want, we're deceived. We have a fleshly view of the Christian life…Christians come in two varieties: those who trust Jesus to get them to heaven while trusting Him now to provide a good life of blessings till they get there, and those who trust Jesus to get them to heaven and discover that what they really want even now is to see and savor Jesus Christ. They're actually willing to lose every blessing and suffer any indignity if it will bring them into deeper relationship with Jesus.[3]

The Lord's way of transforming us into that latter "variety" often involves thwarting our dreams, and sometimes even breaking our hearts. He does this with kind intention, even as a surgeon wounds his patient to remove a cancerous tumor that will destroy him. The Lord's scalpel is perplexing and the process is often replete with anguish and grief. Health fails, even in our children. Finances are ravaged. Relationships painfully crumble, as trusted friends and even spouses betray. The list of life's sorrows is long. A false expectation that we, as Christians, are *entitled* to avoid these sorrows should never be blamed on false advertising from God's Word. The Bible is plainspoken and clear.

Jesus was a man of sorrows, acquainted with grief (Isa. 53:3). It's hard for me to imagine Him seeking His best life *now* after He taught us to seek *first* His kingdom and His righteousness (Matt. 6:33). Our Savior endured the cross, despising its shame so that He could enter into His best life *later* (Heb. 12:2).

Nearly every Christian can quote Romans 8:28:"And we know that God causes all things to work together for good." But to avoid using this as a cliché, we need to understand God's endgame. The "good" that "all things" are working toward has precious little to do with material or temporal blessings. Paul lays out God's endgame in the very next verse:

> For those whom He foreknew, He also predestined to become conformed to the image of His Son, so that He would be the firstborn among many brethren.
>
> —Romans 8:29

I love the idea of being conformed to Jesus' image, of following in the steps of this great King. But how easily I forget the suffering required of my elder Brother. Jesus learned obedience through the things which He suffered (Heb. 5:8). If Jesus Himself needed to suffer, how much more do we require the process of suffering as God molds us toward fullness in Christ? Peter warns us not to be surprised by the "fiery ordeal" which comes upon us for our testing, as though some strange thing were happening to us (1 Pet. 4:12).

I am far too easily caught off guard by the fiery ordeals God sends my way, treating them as strange indeed. I fight against them as things that *shouldn't* be happening, things that God has mistakenly allowed to intrude upon my life. I keep drifting toward that fleshly expectation of arrival on the shores of lasting comfort and blessing in *this* world. But neither you nor I will find it here, no matter how many fresh starts we make, no matter how many times we change jobs, change spouses, and leap over all the other fences toward enticing greener pastures.

The trials and suffering Paul chronicled in his second letter to the Corinthians would seem more fitting for God's enemies, but certainly not for His faithful servants. But Paul wanted to make sure that the Corinthian believers (and we twenty-first century believers) didn't remain "unaware" of his *overwhelmingly* difficult burdens. He specifically wanted us to know that his circumstances were *so* hard he thought he just might die:

> For we do not want you to be unaware, brethren, of our affliction which came to us in Asia, that *we were burdened excessively, beyond our strength, so that we despaired even of life*; indeed, we had the sentence of death within ourselves *so that we would not trust in ourselves, but in* God who raises the dead; who delivered us from so great a peril of death, and will deliver us, He on whom we have set our hope. And He will yet deliver us.
>
> —2 Corinthians 1:8–10, emphasis added

God's purpose in sending "excessive" burdens into Paul's life, *and* into our lives, is to put us so far under the waterline that we will have no other alternative but to recognize that our only hope is to *trust in God and not in ourselves.* Learning this lesson at the deepest levels of our souls never comes from a quick encounter with manageable problems. Our need to trust deeply in God is a lifelong test of endurance, and as one might expect, some of the most advanced and rigorous courses typically come later. Some of Paul's advanced degree tribulations made him "despair even of life." And in chapter 4, Paul reveals the unrelenting nature of the course material:

> We are afflicted in every way, but not crushed; perplexed, but not despairing; persecuted, but not forsaken; struck down, but not destroyed; *always* carrying about in the body the dying of Jesus so that the life of Jesus also may be manifested in our body. For we who live are *constantly* being delivered over to death for Jesus' sake, so that the life of Jesus also may be manifested in our mortal flesh.
>
> —2 Corinthians 4:8–11, emphasis added

Consider the implications of the words *always* and *constantly.* Throughout his letter, Paul details a litany of *relentless* trials and suffering that came his way, including a wide variety of life threatening circumstances. Was God allowing these trials because Paul was slacking off, backsliding, maybe even compromising with sin? Hardly! God was allowing them as Paul was "giving no cause for offense in anything," as he was "making many rich" in Christ. Yet take another look at how the Lord "repaid" him in chapters 6 and 11:

> Giving no cause for offense in anything...in everything commending ourselves as servants of God, in much endurance, in afflictions, in hardships, in distresses, in beatings, in imprisonments, in tumults, in labors, in sleeplessness, in hunger...regarded as deceivers...as punished yet not put to death, as sorrowful yet always rejoicing, as poor yet making many rich.
>
> —2 CORINTHIANS 6:3–5, 8–10

> ...in far more labors, in far more imprisonments, beaten times without number, often in danger of death. Five times I received from the Jews thirty-nine lashes, Three times I was beaten with rods, once I was stoned, three times I was shipwrecked, a night and a day I have spent in the deep...in dangers from rivers, dangers from robbers, dangers from my countrymen, dangers from the Gentiles, dangers in the city, dangers in the wilderness, dangers on the sea, dangers among false brethren; I have been in labor and hardship, through many sleepless nights, in hunger and thirst, often without food, in cold and exposure.
>
> —2 CORINTHIANS 11:23–27

This litany of hardships and injustices actually includes *beatings times without number*! I don't know about you, but if I were beaten *once* I'd complain about it for a lifetime. Imprison me falsely just *one* time and I'd get the best lawyer I could find and make you pay, no matter how long it might take. Yet *all* this suffering (and much more) is detailed almost matter-of-factly by Paul after he has *already* catalogued many other tribulations in his first letter to the Corinthians. As Paul goes on and on, speaking of *constantly* being delivered over to death (chapter 4), of being stoned, shipwrecked, and *all* the rest of it, I want to say, "Enough already, Paul! *You can stop now!* I get it!"

But Paul wasn't seeking to preserve the accuracy of his biographical memoirs, nor was he reaching for sympathy. Paul's purpose is clear, even as I pray my purpose is clear in detailing some of my sorrows in this book. He wants his fellow believers (us) to be *aware* of the way God works so that they will not be unprepared when they are called upon to face similar trials. In his first letter, after he spoke of being hungry, thirsty, slandered, homeless, poorly clothed, treated like the dregs of all things (1 Cor. 4:11–13), he followed up with an outlandish exhortation: "I exhort you, be imitators of me" (v. 16).

My gut response to his invitation is, "I don't think so, Paul, but thank you for asking. Next time I'm in Rome I'll look you up. But don't call me! I'll call you!" But as we consider his exhortation, we are left with only two choices. Either Paul was completely nuts, or he was spot on, and he knew that the treatment God allowed in his life would, on one level or another, come to us also. Paul loved his brethren (us) enough to warn us. He didn't want us to be sitting ducks, unprepared and ignorant, as severe hardship also sweeps into our lives. He wanted to persuade us that our calling in Christ is worth following to the full, without shrinking back, no matter *what* the cost turns out to be.

Paul is not saying all believers in Christ will suffer in the same way he suffered. But we should be aware that Paul's kind of martyrdom is *still* happening to followers of Christ in the twenty-first century. And let's not kid ourselves; this could happen in America sooner than we think as the "religion" of tolerance becomes more and more revered, and as hatred toward the gospel of Jesus Christ continues to increase. And lest we think that the sufferings of Christ are reserved only for those serving in full-time ministry in remote regions, Paul clarified the issue when he taught Timothy: "*All* who desire to live godly in Christ Jesus will be persecuted" (2 Tim. 3:12, emphasis added). God's Word leaves no room for doubt that we will *all* be called upon to suffer as we seek to follow and serve Christ.

But to be honest, persecution and suffering was the *furthest* thing from my mind as we entered our brand-new home in Kinnelon. I had no illusions about Kinnelon being heaven. Still, I sensed this was the place that many of our long cherished and ached for dreams, including the dream of seeing our son walk independently, would come true.

Hmm!...Maybe This Is Heaven?

As we met with school administrators and teachers in Kinnelon, we were beginning to think that, just maybe, we *had* drawn a bit closer to heaven. Dr. Valerie Mosca, the Director of Special Services, wasn't threatened in the least (as our former district had been) that the NACD had developed a program for our son's development. She was *delighted* that help was available to assist them in meeting our son's challenges. What a *refreshing* change! She invited Barbara Frey of the NACD to meet with his teachers to train them regarding how to deliver his demanding academic regimen each day.

There was a "can do" attitude in this district. It seemed everyone understood that the rules and regulations were intended to meet the needs of a hurting child, not for the self-preservation of the "system." Peggy Callahan, Bryson's case manager, quickly proved she knew how to maneuver around endless regulations to provide our son with the assistance he desperately needed. We were all on the same team, working toward the same goal. What a blessing!

Although Bryson was eight and one-half years old, it was determined that he should repeat first grade. Years of developmental function had been lost due to his brain injury. Chasing chronologically aged peers was not important. Providing him with an opportunity to fit in with a comfortable peer group as he moved forward at his own pace was the priority.

The Lord provided a wonderfully competent, kind principal in Marita Dowell. Respected by all in the community, Marita was a solid believer in Jesus Christ. Her lovingly wise methods were about to prove particularly valuable for Bryson as she thought through many potential difficulties and dangers that could be avoided through prudent planning. And blessing upon blessing, Marita selected the *perfect* first grade teacher for our son.

Maybe Kinnelon wasn't heaven, but it sure did seem as if Bette Esposito had descended from there. I'm not referring to her dedication, her kind disposition toward the children, or even to her proven methods of teaching. Bette had taught first grade for decades, and everyone in town knew she was a "10" in each of those categories. But she also possessed a quality that can't be taught at even the finest institutions that train teachers to do what they do. Bette had the gift of a compassionate heart.

Naturally, she was a bit nervous regarding how she could provide for the needs of such a profoundly brain-injured child. Marita arranged to have Bette meet Bryson during a summer barbecue hosted for us by one of our new neighbors. Once Bette saw who Bryson was, the task no longer intimidated her. Her heart simply took over. Love always finds a way to accomplish even the most difficult tasks in life.

Bette was determined to treat Bryson as an individual, as she had always done for all her students. She understood that having him in her classroom would be a tremendous benefit for the other children, helping them learn that every human being has extreme value. One of the first days of school, while Bryson was out of the classroom, Bette used Bryson's example to illustrate that each one of them had unique differences, and that every human being is worthy of respect. Bryson's differences were obvious. He still spoke with difficulty, and he needed an aide to assist him in getting around the classroom.

Speaking of heaven, Bryson's aide, Sharon Klien, was *miles* above Iowa (Dan Gable is going to kick my butt!). We couldn't *believe* it when we met her. In a word, she was awesome! She had a heart to match Bette's, and an incredibly bubbly personality. She loved Bryson to pieces, and her contagious excitement caused Bryson to become enthusiastic about his new school. She cared for our son like a mother hen, and applied her marvelous enthusiasm toward motivating him to accomplish the maximum gains possible in the repetitious academic regimen developed by the NACD.

Maybe it wasn't heaven, but there wasn't a doubt we had made the right choice in moving to this town. The dedication of all his teachers and aides (I wish I could mention them all) in each successive grade propelled him forward, and the fact that such wonderful effort was being expended toward his advancement renewed our hope.

"KINNELON *NOT* HEAVEN! GOT IT! BUT YOU'RE *JOKING? RIGHT, LORD?*"

No, the Lord wasn't joking, and neither was the doctor. Bryson had been getting fevers once a month or so during our first year in Kinnelon. One of our lead doctors at this time was a world renowned researcher in the field of autism. We visited him about twice per year at his office up in central Connecticut. Years before he had theorized that our son's brain injury occurred from an autoimmune response after one of his vaccinations, causing his own immune system to attack his central nervous system. He had also informed us that Bryson's immune system had been permanently compromised.

We thought that the past year's fevers and illnesses had simply been due to his diminished immune system. But in the summer of 1995, a local doctor informed us that Bryson tested positive for Lyme disease. Now we were unsure if all of this year's fevers had been due to his weakened immune system or to the Lyme disease. But irrespective of how long he had been infected with Lyme, the fact that he had contracted this disease was devastating news in light of his severely suppressed immune system.

The Lyme disease presented itself with fevers and flu-like symptoms. Our son's ankle, knee, and shoulder joints were severely in pain, an indication that we had not caught the disease in its early stages. Once the insidious organisms, known as spirochetes, active in the disease reach all the way into the joints, it is far more difficult to treat. The agonizing pain in his joints was exacerbated by the pressure and strain he continued to exert on his skeletal system to compensate for his lack of balance, as he sought to stand and walk.

The *last* thing we needed was a new medical problem. Bryson's damaged motor skills still didn't allow him to brush his teeth, dress himself, or for self-care in toileting. Sudden waves of imbalance still swept him off his feet without warning, and he still suffered painful crashes *daily*, including some that were bloody and excruciating. The scenes remained as brutal as ever, as screams and tears (his and ours) daily echoed through our home. One night we thought he actually lost one of his eyes as he crashed face first onto the sharp corner of an open dresser drawer. "Don't we *ever* get a rest, Lord?"

Based on the severity of his symptoms, it was theorized he had contracted Lyme disease the previous fall. Kinnelon is a community full of deer and wildlife. Since he could crawl much more quickly than he could maneuver his walker across the lawn on our large new property, he often crawled across the yard. But I gave him a bath *every* night and always checked him. I never saw evidence of a tick bite. I was so frustrated I could spit.

There's an old adage: you're moving backward unless you're moving forward. This is true in an amplified sense in brain-injured children. Bob Doman cautioned us that months of passivity would be devastating to our goal of seeing our son walk independently. Our doctor advised us we could perform Bryson's physical regimen in a modified way, and only when the disease was not active (when the spirochetes were dormant). Spirochetes become active approximately every twenty-eight to thirty-two days and wreak havoc for about seven to ten days. Bryson's fevers returned like clockwork, and he needed complete rest when he was sick.

Bryson began missing lots of school time, particularly in second grade. As the disease became progressively worse, the doctor administered more aggressive doses of antibiotics. Month after month we tested him, and he continued testing positive for Lyme. We were advised he'd need to be hospitalized unless he responded to the treatments.

Oh yes, we still had many reasons to rejoice in our new town, but I became extremely discouraged now. I had been so *sure* that Kinnelon was going to be the place our son would finally break free. We left Glen Rock just after the joyous occasion when he had walked, almost run through the crowd at his Walking Celebration. It might've killed me on that day had I known he would not replicate that feat for nearly *two* more years.

I could only sit back and watch helplessly now as my son began regressing. He became frighteningly weak when the fevers came. Sometimes he had to be carried from the couch where he had been watching a Yankee game or one of his videos, to his bed; and he was often in excruciating pain. I was beginning to wonder why the Lord didn't just step in and give him a break. Maybe He could give us all a break while He was at it!

"Don't We Even Get a Slice of Heaven in Macedonia, Lord?...I Mean Kinnelon?"

> I am filled with comfort; I am overflowing with joy in all our affliction. For even when we came into Macedonia our flesh had no rest, but we were afflicted on every side: conflicts without, fears within. But God, who comforts the depressed, comforted us.
>
> —2 Corinthians 7:4–6

I sometimes wondered if Paul ever got discouraged, if he yearned for his suffering to finally come to an end. It almost seems as if he anticipated that his trials would ease up, at least a bit, as he arrived in Macedonia. But he makes it crystal clear that this did not occur. And it's not as if he found a little bit of rest: Even when we came into Macedonia, our flesh had *no* rest. On the contrary, he was afflicted on every side, having conflicts without and suffering fears within.

And yes, Paul struggled with depression as he came into Macedonia. I've heard such nonsense postulated about this. Let's take what the man actually says about the reality of his depression without trying to couch it with ridiculous explanations that Christians don't ever get depressed. God does not hide the truth in His Word. Nor should we!

But learning of Paul's unending trials is a bit confusing to me, and perhaps to you. In my view, he should have graduated from the need to be afflicted by now. After all, he had endured for such a *long* time, serving the Lord mightily without shrinking back in the face of fierce persecution. At a certain point, I want to say, "My goodness, Lord! Paul has given his all for You. Can't You give the man a break for a while?"

We can't be reminded too often that God's ways are higher than ours (Isa. 55:8–9). Instead of exasperation at the Lord's dealings with Paul, or with us, we need to remember the central purpose laid out in his letter: "We had the sentence of death within ourselves *so that we would not trust in ourselves, but in God* who raises the dead" (2 Cor. 1:9, emphasis added).

Don't hear me saying that God never grants His children comfort and rest. His lovingkindnesses indeed never cease, and His compassions never fail. They are new *every* morning (Lam. 3:22–23). He *constantly* showers us with untold blessings, and He often grants us seasons of relative peace. But when we are thinking biblically, we realize how blessed we are, how *incredibly* privileged to be among His soldiers in this battleground world, the side that is destined to win. Soldiers don't think like civilians, nor do they complain when war gets hard. This is their expectation.

Most of us spend a great deal of time and energy strategizing how to elude suffering in this world. God overrides our evasion tactics and brings on all those advanced degree courses of trial and tribulation. The enemy wishes to confuse us, to cause us to conclude that maybe God isn't as much in control as we had once thought, and perhaps not quite as good. God declared: "My people are destroyed for lack of knowledge" (Hosea 4:6). If we are ignorant of God's endgame, His purpose of conforming us into the image of His Son, we will be vulnerable to the life-destroying suggestions that come from the pit of hell.

With respect to the seeming unfairness of faithfulness leading to further difficulties, we are well served to remember that Jesus taught us that "every branch that bears fruit, He prunes it so that it may bear more fruit" (John 15:2). Scripture also declares that God "disciplines us for our good, so that we may share in His holiness" (Heb. 12:10). God knows what He is aiming to accomplish in and through our lives. It is not our place to understand every move the King makes. Frankly, if you understand every difficult circumstance that the King allows to come into your life, you've got a king who is too small. Our King is high and mighty, and His battle plan is often confusing.

If it were up to me, I'd often short-circuit the work of God. But God does not modify His plan to suit my ignorance. If we are wise, instead of demanding an easier battle plan, we will adjust our expectations. Nearly every biography in Scripture bears out that we should anticipate a very long and difficult road in this world. Oswald Chambers reminds us that throughout history, Christ's followers have attempted to evade the road of suffering, to shorten the process. But God's endgame is good.

> In the history of the Christian Church the tendency has been to evade being identified with the sufferings of Jesus Christ; men have sought to procure the carrying out of God's order by a short cut of their own. God's way is always the way of suffering, the way of the long, long trail. Are we prepared for God to stamp our personal ambitions right out?... We never realize at the time what God is putting us through; then we come to a luminous place, and say: "Why, God has girded me, though I did not know it!"[4]

I've grown tired of health and wealth preachers with broad, plastered on smiles, haven't you? They lead people astray by misrepresenting a magnificent God whose ways are far higher than ours. Jesus never sugarcoated the difficulties we will face here. There's only *one* dream that satisfies and lasts in this battleground world, and it's the dream conceived for us in heaven. But one of the hardest things we must surrender is our false expectation of what *we* require heaven's dream to be.

> In the world you have tribulation, but take courage; I have overcome the world.
>
> —JOHN 16:33

> If anyone wishes to come after Me, let him deny himself and take up his cross, and follow Me. For whoever wishes to save his life shall lose it; but whoever loses his life for My sake shall find it.
>
> —MATTHEW 16:24–25

A WHOPPER OF A TALE

One night in 1995 as Tim and I watched a Yankee game on TV together with Bryson, we were all chatting about an awesome feat performed by Don Mattingly, one of their heroes. Mattingly was in his last year with the Yanks. I had brought all three of the kids to Yankee Stadium earlier that season, and Bryson had become the most avid fan you could imagine. Ever the dreamer, he *knew* he was going to play for the Yanks one day.

But the Yankees would have to wait for now. On this night my son was extremely weak and sick. After the game I picked him up and carried him up to his room. As I placed him into his bed, I realized he was very hot with fever, and I asked him if his ankles and knees were hurting him again. He acknowledged that they were. Never a complainer, I knew he was hurting more than he would say.

But he suddenly became agitated, and it was clear he was distressed. With his garbled, slow speech he began to reveal the problem. It had occurred to him that the Yankees had just played a game *away* from Yankee Stadium, and that the team goes on road trips to other cities. I chuckled and asked him why that would trouble him. He responded that he couldn't go on those trips, not even for a night, if I didn't come with him.

I chuckled again, telling him he needn't worry about this, since we had many years to figure it all out. His face remained somber. This was no laughing matter, and he was clearly dissatisfied with my answer. Like most mentally impaired children, Bryson is a *now* kind of guy. There wasn't a doubt in his mind he was going to play for the Yankees, so we might as well deal with it. Ever tenacious, he insisted on receiving an answer to this dilemma *this very night.* He finally put the problem in simple terms that even his dim-witted dad could understand (omitted and mispronounced words added): "Dad, [will] you be there [to] see all [my] games when I pway [play] for a [the] Yankees?" Deeply troubled, he then stared into my eyes, awaiting my answer.

I marveled at the simplicity and purity of his ability to believe. Here he was, a multiply handicapped, severely ill child whose battle just to walk had been dealt a major blow this past year. Yet the faith he held for his future hadn't waivered, not even a bit. As I searched my mind for an answer to his question, part of me wanted to respond by telling him a story, a fairy tale, *anything* that would help him maintain his childlike dreams. But as he lay there peering into my eyes, I struggled to come up with such a tale.

I think the biggest part of my struggle was that, deep inside, I no longer believed in the miraculous tale I wanted to tell him. It's almost funny. There was a time I thought God would perform all the miracles I pleaded so hard for. I was convinced that my son would come *all* the way back to us from the nebulous world of brain injury. He was going to be *totally* healthy in mind, body, and soul. I don't remember when my own dreams died, but it seemed like long ago now. Somewhere along the line, I'm not sure when, the day came when I began to feel like a fool for ever having dreamed so high.

More than I can tell you, I *hated* the thought of asking my son to let go of his dreams too. But now I understood that his cruel circumstances weren't ever going to change. Maybe instead of helping him cling to childish fantasies, it was time to begin easing him toward the harsh realities of his life by letting him know how limited his prospects really were in this world. Perhaps this is exactly what he needed to keep him from being crushed even more in the future. As he lay there peering into my eyes awaiting my answer, I groped for something to say, torn between being honest and telling him a whopper of a story.

Oh, how my son loved baseball. If only I could come up with a story that combined dreams coming true with baseball. Movies like *Field of Dreams* are successful because they remind us that dreams can come true. They touch a place deep within our hearts that is dormant, a place that most of us locked safely away behind a double-bolted door long ago. To open that door in real life risks far too much pain. In a world full of brutal realities it seems best just to leave that door locked and retreat to the safety of dreaming vicariously through movie plots, spectator sports, and romance novels.

There was a place in my heart, and no doubt in yours too, dear reader, that once inspired us. That place literally gave us a passion for living. Remember? That place has been all but forgotten by most of us as we live out our mundane lives here. Yet every once in a while something stirs from inside that locked door, and just briefly, a muffled sound can almost be heard. But we're adults with responsibilities now. The mere suggestion that there could be something, *anything* worth exploring deep down in there *must* be dismissed! Yet we could *swear* we heard...felt...something.

Could there yet be a reason to hope for a happy ending to my story, or yours? That our lives can somehow be rescued? O Lord! Who are we trying to kid? We *can't* allow ourselves to be hurt! Not again! Leave well enough alone! If my dreams were ever made into a feature film it would need to be labeled as "fiction." But just like that whopper of a tale I wanted to conjure up for my son, the dreams that once impassioned me would make one heck of a movie plot!

Imagine someone *actually believing* it would be safe to unlock that door. Hah! I suppose they'd also believe that a Hero would meet us on the other side, making it safe to come out. Right! Maybe the Hero would be a Rescuer who knew the most sordid details of our past, and all our miserable failures, who understood *all* our disappointments and dashed dreams, but *still* came knocking on that door, calling, confident that He could bring about the reclamation of our dreams, and of our lives. Talk about a whopper! *Who do they think they're kidding? Only themselves!*

Movie heroes are valiant, even godlike; sometimes daring even to die for the sake of those threatened with death themselves. My Hero would need to be beyond *any* that Hollywood has ever produced. In view of the *years* the locusts have eaten in *my* life, He'd have to hold time *itself* in His hands. He'd have to possess the power of the universe. Talk about far-fetched! He'd need to be the greatest Physician this world has ever seen. Listen, opening *my* door would mean more than just curing an illness. My Hero would have to specialize in *resurrection*. Only then would it *possibly* be safe to risk opening that door. As I said, fiction! No one would make such a movie! Shear fantasy!

Still, the thought of a Hero like that gives me goose bumps. If a Hero like that ever showed up at my door for real, I'd not only open it, I tell you I'd follow Him *anywhere!* Even if He said I had to change *everything,* and do things *His* way from now on. Walking with such a Hero would be worth *any* cost. What would I really be giving up, anyway? I might even put aside my excuses and stop trying to convince people just how unfair my life has been. Yes, I might put aside my victim mentality and just go after Him!

I suppose the Hero might ask me to leave some of my broken dreams behind. But who knows? A Hero *that* powerful and good just might have *another* dream in mind, a better dream! Oh, for Pete's sake, I'm actually getting drawn into this! Enough already! This whopper of a movie plot is getting *downright* silly! Then again, just *imagine* if a Hero like *that* ever showed up at *my* door...at *your* door.

> Behold, I stand at the door and knock; if anyone hears My voice and opens the door, I will come in to him and will dine with him, and he with Me.
>
> —REVELATION 3:20

> I am the resurrection and the life.
>
> —JOHN 11:25

> Then I will make up to you for the years That the swarming locust has eaten.
>
> —JOEL 2:25

THE GREATEST STORY EVER TOLD

Suddenly a voice interrupted my thoughts: "Dad, you be there?...You see *all* games when I pway for a Yankees?"

I shook off that daydream, finally understanding what I needed to tell my son. I didn't need to reveal brutal realities to a struggling child. I had to become child-like *myself*. In view of the Hero who was knocking at my heart's door, I had every reason to join my son in dreams and miracles yet to unfold. Our Hero would bring them about in His good time, in precisely the manner in which *He* chose to define each one. I looked down as he lay there, sick and in pain. The answer I gave him was direct and confident, as I peered back into his eyes: "Don't worry, Bryson. I don't care how far I need to travel to get to your games when you are a Yankee. Your dad will be right there with you."

And in increasing measure of refinement and detail through the years I've had the joy of telling him the greatest story ever told. My son was all boy, yes he was. I knew he'd *love* this story. What boy or girl wouldn't love it? It's a war story and a love story all rolled into one. What a boring tale it would be if there was nothing life threatening ever to overcome, no Hero who came to the rescue. And the best part is that I didn't have to tell a whopper at all! Not now, not ever! The greatest story ever told is completely true!

In the years to come I revealed some death defying chapters to my son, including ones that tell us we must suffer *many* tribulations here (John 16:33; Acts 14:22). But I made it clearly understood that we have *nothing* to fear. Our Hero has *already* overcome every evil in the world (1 John 4:4), and He has also equipped *us* to be more than conquerors as we fight our battles, trusting in the power of His love for us (Rom. 8:31–39).

Many years later, when it was time to reveal difficult truths about the brain injury he had suffered, my son was prepared to understand that *no one's* story ever needs to end in the hopelessness of a wasted life. How could *that* ever be mistaken for the greatest story ever told? His story, and your story as you read these pages, is not over until our Hero says it is over. He intends to write one final breathtaking chapter that will make up for every broken dream ever suffered here. But before I tell you of that final chapter, I will tell you of something the Hero did for my son shortly after I placed him into bed that night.

Field of Dreams

Irrespective of his weakened condition, my irrepressible son began to ask about playing baseball as the next spring approached. He had heard some of his classmates talking about it on one of the days he was well enough to attend school. I needed to call to find out about this, and I began to get anxious about describing his circumstances to the rec officials in our new town. I was fearful that a decision might be made to exclude him on the basis of liability, or in the interests of other kids who aspired to excel in athletics.

Beyond that, how could I *possibly* describe a child who believed with all his heart he would play for the Yankees one day, though he couldn't even walk independently, a child who still didn't even understand he was handicapped? It was with more trepidation than for any business deal that I telephoned George Shafer one evening, the president of the Kinnelon Baseball Association. To my relief, George assured me he would do *everything* possible to see that Bryson would not only be included, but welcomed. He went a step further. He put Bryson on his own team, making me his assistant coach.

Bryson wasn't well enough to participate in every game that season, but I was thankful he was strong enough for opening day. It's hard for me to imagine *anything* keeping him from the field that gorgeous Saturday afternoon. Some of his friends from school were his teammates, and he *gloried* in every aspect of being on that team. He was *so* excited as I helped him put on his uniform, and he couldn't *wait* for the game. We arrived at the field an hour early (I guess I couldn't wait either).

The start of a new baseball season is a field of dreams for everyone, young and old. The noise and banter throughout the field that day was what you might expect on such a joyous occasion. Parents, grandparents, siblings, and many others were there to cheer on these rookies. As for my rookie, he was raring to go; and I can't adequately describe the pride I had in him on this day.

My anxiety became extremely high as Bryson's first time at bat drew near. Those horrible regression patterns had kept him from being as ready as I had hoped. But this was the furthest thing from my son's mind as he waited on deck. Finally his turn came, and with great effort he approached home plate. The noise throughout the ballpark became hushed. It was obvious the player coming to bat was struggling to remain upright.

He had decided he didn't want me helping him to get into the batter's box, nor helping him hit the ball, as we had done countless times in the yard. He was going to do it just like his teammates. But his recent illnesses had taken their toll. Down he went, crashing to the ground before he even reached the plate. The other players and the fans pretended not to notice, but the crowd became quieter still.

With great difficulty he rose, finally taking his stand at home plate. I wasn't surprised. I knew it would take more than a fall to take the heart out of this champion. As always, Bryson copied the behaviors of his peers in vivid detail. As he settled into the batter's box, after struggling to maintain his balance once more, his stance became a beautiful replication of his heroes on TV.

Though Bryson was nine, this was a league where the coaches pitched overhand to the batters, most of whom were seven or eight. George wisely moved closer to the plate to underhand the ball to a place where he hoped Bryson might get his bat on it. Knowing his difficulty with depth perception, George held up the ball and kept it still for a few seconds as Bryson focused his eyes on it. But after numerous swings and misses to each underhand pitch (this was a non-strikeout league), George called me to the mound as the relief pitcher, knowing that I knew best where his swing would be.

You want to talk nervous? As Bryson stood in his perfect stance awaiting my first pitch against the pin drop silence, I felt the pressure of a pitcher in the World Series with the bases loaded. It was *so* hard to get the ball to go where I knew my son's swing would be. Pitch after pitch after pitch was awkwardly missed, as Bryson struggled to maintain his balance. Finally, he went down once again, and his bat went flying as his body sprawled awkwardly into the dirt of the batter's box. My heart leaped to my throat, and I ran in to him, but he quickly made it clear he wanted no help as he struggled to get off the ground.

I pleaded in my mind for him to get up, as one does for a felled boxer as the referee counts. My son slowly pushed himself back up. I retrieved his bat, and handing it to him I whispered in his ear, "You can do this, champ!" The crowd was respectful and silent as he settled back in his stance, but everyone was feeling the anxiety now. I don't advocate praying for outcomes at sporting events, but I don't think I've *ever* prayed harder.

Finally it happened! His bat touched the ball and it went dribbling weakly in front of the plate. Bryson took off toward first, falling down almost immediately after leaving the batter's box. He fell yet again on his way to first, as the players in the field pretended not to be able to field the ball. With great enthusiasm he scrambled up as quickly as he could each time. At long last, he reached the base and the umpire yelled, "*Safe!*" Several players on both teams congratulated him, and he received a warm ovation from the crowd. His tenacity and courage had touched them all deeply.

And so the great Hero gave us yet another chapter to lift up in thanksgiving and praise on that glorious afternoon. He stood on first beaming. Ever the dreamer, in his mind he *knew* he had come through for his team. I swallowed hard, not wanting others to notice my tears. This was Bryson's moment. But no one in that crowd could *possibly* know how hard he had struggled to reach that base. They saw his moments of struggle. As I watched my jubilant son standing on that base, I saw the anguish and pain of a decade.

The rest of Bryson's season went pretty much as I've described. When he was well enough to play, he fell down between each base, but he was one thrilled ballplayer each time he crossed home plate, which he did several times that year. Sadly, his illnesses began forcing him to miss more games toward the end of the season, revealing just how sick he was becoming. He'd have done *anything* to be at those games.

I was beginning to understand how Paul could say he was filled with comfort and overflowing with joy, and in the *very* next sentence say that he was afflicted on every side, having conflicts without and fears within (2 Cor. 7:4–5). Clearly, the battle never, ever ends in this world. Not until the revelation of one final, breathtaking chapter in the greatest story ever told, which I promised to tell you about.

That chapter makes it clear that, one day, after all our struggles are over here, our Hero will return. This time He is coming not to suffer and die for our sin and shame. This time He is coming as an invincible King, who will bind up our wounds, and carry us home. He will wipe away every tear from our eyes on that great day; and every grief, every loss we've ever suffered in this world will be remembered no more.

John Kinsella got it right. Heaven *is* the place where dreams, the dreams that *really* matter, will finally come true. It will all happen in a twinkling, in the blink of an eye. Oh yes, our Hero is coming back one day. Be of good courage. Take heart! Our salvation is much nearer now, than the day we first believed (Rom. 13:11).

> Now glory to God, who by his mighty power within us is able to do far more than we would ever dare to ask or even dream of—infinitely beyond our highest prayers, desires, thoughts, or hopes.
>
> —EPHESIANS 3:20, TLB

Bryson is as proud as can be after winning the Baseball Championship in Kinnelon.

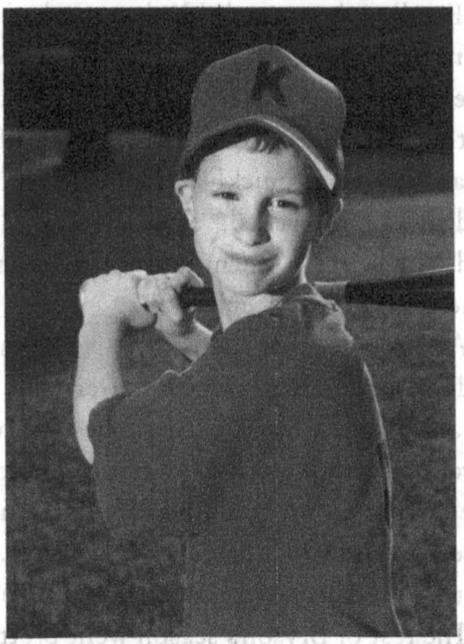

Thrilled to be on the team!

Sometimes he needed a little help.

Chapter 22
BORN TO RUN

I believe God made me for a purpose, but He also made me fast. And when I run I feel His pleasure.[1]

Eric Liddell

LIKE ANY CHILD, my son was born to run. But trying to revive dead brain tissue riddled with lesions of damage would *never* have set him free. We had to continue to train him by stimulating the good tissue that remained inside his injured brain. I *hated* to drive him so relentlessly in his program of development. But recircuiting a brain with exhaustive, repetitious input is a protracted process fraught with difficulty and regression. If he was ever going to get to the place where he could walk, and maybe even run, we had to keep pressing hard toward higher levels of function. Tom Landry depicted the goal of a coach as follows:

> Coaching is making men do what they don't want, so that they can become what they want to be.[2]

It had always seemed unreasonable to some professionals for us to keep driving him so hard, and some even thought us cruel for doing so. They wondered why we simply didn't accept that he was a crippled child. The answer in my mind was simple: because he was born to run, *that's* why! All his life he'd been stuck in a brain-injured prison, and I'd have done *anything* to see him set free. I had no guarantee he'd ever walk, no less run, but I knew he'd do neither if we didn't keep trying. As my old radio friend and chancellor of the King's College, Bob Cook, used to say: "Faith trusts in God, and then does what it can in the face of impossibility."[3] I was determined to press on, precisely in that order.

Not unlike my son's development, our growth in Christ seems unreasonably long and difficult. Many of our Christian friends seem to be following an easier path. They seem satisfied with the toys and comforts of this world. Why not us? Because we were born to run, *that's* why! Yes, the race is hard. It's often *excruciatingly* hard. When the pain and disappointment of life isn't knocking us down, the drudgery of life seems to be wearing us down. But there's not a person alive who knows how long they've been granted to run for Christ's glory here before our race on earth is done. And ours is no perishable prize in the end (1 Cor. 9:24).

I can endure a lot of hardship in my race, and so can you, *if* we can believe there's a purpose. As our Father "coaches" us away from this world's shallow values toward what we've always wanted to be in Christ, our main battle is to keep believing and acting upon the truth. One of the hardest things to endure in this world is Satan's lie that our hardships and disappointments are meaningless. Shakespeare's Macbeth said, "Life is a tale told by an idiot…signifying nothing."[4] If there was simply a Big Bang and we subsequently evolved from primordial soup eons ago, Macbeth would be spot on. Nothing would be worth persevering toward in this world, and all our "get yourself back up, go get 'em" pep talks would be bankrupt and pointless.

Unless God created us for a purpose, we are all just dying individuals on a random, meaningless planet. That's sad. What's even sadder is when Christians born again by the blood of Christ live as if *we* have no meaning. When we believe that random events are ruling our lives, we are deceived and living practically as unbelievers. There is no such thing as a random circumstance. There *is* a purpose, and there *is* a plan. God is still in control, even when our circumstances are so absurd that the notion of His providence appears spurious. Jesus persevered through torture to fulfill His Father's will, and Scripture is replete with reminders that the process of following Him in this world includes the privilege and responsibility of sharing in His sufferings.

> To you it has been granted for Christ's sake, not only to believe in Him, but also to suffer for His sake.
>
> —PHILIPPIANS 1:29

> That I may know Him and the power of His resurrection *and* the fellowship of His sufferings, being conformed to His death.
>
> —PHILIPPIANS 3:10, EMPHASIS ADDED

> For you have been called for this purpose, since Christ also suffered for you, leaving an example for you to follow in His steps.
>
> —1 PETER 2:21

God will test our commitment to follow Him under fire. The refining pot is for silver, and the furnace is for gold, but the Lord tests hearts (Prov. 17:3). It's not for us to complain when the testing gets hard. There's a much better choice than complaint when we are discouraged. You really want to run? Choose gratitude! There's no greater time to glorify God with praise than when life has been unfair, *especially* when we are being pummeled from every side. Wasn't Jesus pummeled to provide us with the grace in which we now stand? We have only a brief time to run our race for Him here. Praise Him now amidst your sorrow and suffering!

We'd all do well to consider Jeremiah's simple question: "Why should any living mortal, or any man, Offer complaint in view of his own sins?" (Lam. 3:39). Isaiah references the futility involved in quarreling with our Maker: "Woe to the one who quarrels with his Maker.... Will the clay say to the potter, 'What are you doing?' Or the thing you are making say, 'He has no hands?'" (Isa. 45:9). The depiction is not only that of a painful process, but a protracted one. Imagine the absurdity of a block of granite complaining as Michelangelo performed his work upon it, because of the time required to complete it. Greg Laurie gives helpful imagery to this.

> Michelangelo was once asked what he was trying to create as he chipped away at a shapeless rock. He replied, "I am liberating an angel from this

stone."...Maybe you are facing a setback...it seems nothing is ever going to change....Be patient...it will take all of your life on this earth and won't be completely finished until you get to heaven. Then you will see that you are God's masterpiece.[5]

The Death Trap

If anyone was born to run, it was Adam and Eve. God created them as the finest human specimens imaginable. But choosing to eat forbidden fruit that was a "delight to the eyes" (Gen. 3:6) never caused them to run at the higher levels of power and freedom promised by the serpent. Satan's insidious lie simply robbed them of the freedom they *already* had to run for God's glory here. Their choice to reach for more outside the will of God sentenced them, and every descendant of Adam since, to live out our lives in a death trap. Jesus Christ blew the hinges off our prison door at the cross, and in Him we can now be reborn to run in freedom once again.

> I will appoint You as a covenant to the people, As a light to the nations, To open blind eyes, To bring out prisoners from the dungeon And those who dwell in darkness from the prison. I am the Lord, that is My name; I will not give My glory to another.
>
> —Isaiah 42:6–8

How foolish and futile it is when men and women sitting on death row keep attempting to free themselves through all the religions and philosophies of this world that exclude Christ. Yet it is understandable when blind people fail to see the Deliverer. After all, they're blind. How much more tragic when believers in Christ lack the discernment to reject Satan's lies, and wind up limping back into prison. Christ made us free, but it is now *our* responsibility to *see to it* that we are not taken captive once again by the principles of the world.

> Therefore as you have received Christ Jesus the Lord, so walk in Him, having been firmly rooted and now being built up in Him and established in your faith, just as you were instructed....*See to it* that no one takes you captive through philosophy and empty deception, according to the tradition of men, according to the elementary principles of the world, rather than according to Christ.
>
> —Colossians 2:6–8, emphasis added

Praise God, we who have been saved by the blood of Christ have been set free from a hopeless death trap. But those who refuse to learn from history are destined to repeat it. If we become tantalized by fruit that promises higher levels of freedom, we in the church can become as deceived as Adam and Eve in that Garden. The choice to pursue "freedom" apart from Christ is a choice to embrace the serpent's lies all over again, and the result is always the same: prison.

All power and glory resides in and proceeds from the Lord Jesus Christ, and God will *never* give His glory to another. Christ is the power of God and the wisdom of God (1 Cor. 1:24). The foolishness of God, in Christ, is wiser than men, and the weakness of God is stronger than men (v. 25). Jesus is the author and perfecter of our faith (Heb. 12:2). He is the Alpha and the Omega (Rev. 22:13). All things were created by Him and for Him. He is before all things, and in Him all things hold together (Col. 1:16–17). *Only* in Christ can sinners like us be reborn; and by the power of His Spirit we have been reborn to run like the wind!

But we're being honest with each other in this book, right? Even as I write a chapter entitled *Born to Run*, there are days I just don't *feel* like I'm running all that well. There are too many days, frankly, when I feel like I'm crawling. I've been following the Lord a long time now, and those days *still* hit me blindsided. For the life of me, I just don't see them coming. Born to run? Limping ahead would seem a triumph on those days. There are times when I feel like slinking into a corner to hide for awhile. Greg Laurie reminds us that we must abide in Christ even when life doesn't feel good, and when it isn't easy.

> To abide means that we are sinking our roots deep into a love relationship with Jesus. It is not simply walking with and serving Him when it is easy, convenient or popular. When we abide in Christ, we remain in fellowship with Him daily, regardless of outward circumstances or inner emotions.... Real spiritual growth comes only through discipline and perseverance.[6]

It is a humbling realization that, no matter what we do, we can't save ourselves. It is *just* as humbling to know that we can't improve ourselves, or grow even an inch, apart from Christ. Our entrance into Christ's life of freedom was based on *His* performance, not ours. Our ability to run our race successfully is based on what Christ *alone* has done, and on what He can *continue* to do in us and through us. The truth is that on our best day we couldn't find our way into the stadium, no less to the starting blocks to run our race, without depending completely upon Christ.

Are you feeling good today? I'm glad. But you and I can never count on how we will *feel* tomorrow. God calls us to walk by faith, not by sight (2 Cor. 5:7), and not by how we feel. When we don't *feel* victorious, when we are battle weary, the enemy is always *right* there to tempt us with tantalizing fruit. He deceitfully aims to slow us down by entrapping us into all manner of sinful idolatry. But the devil will use *anything* that leads us away from reliance upon Jesus Christ, and back into prison. Some of his favorite fruit that is delighting the eyes of countless Christians today can be found in the self-help section of the Christian bookstore.

Even as it would have been futile to attempt to revive dead brain tissue in my son, we underestimate the utter impossibility of attempting to reform sin-riddled flesh. Even God didn't try it. If the truth be fully known, our flesh is *still* stuck in a permanent death trap, still in the process of being corrupted (Eph. 4:22). Our natural sin patterns are so deeply ingrained that we don't have the slightest chance of delivering ourselves from sin's grip. David Roper pictured our propensity to regress toward our natural, fleshly bent:

> We are thrown into this world like a baseball with a spin on it; in time we break and the curve is always down and away.[7]

We could have sworn we had dealt with that bad temper, that impatient spirit, that sudden propensity to lust. Then, *bam*! There we go again, right out of the strike zone. How exasperating! What's the use? But what's the alternative? Do we just give up? No, we are not among those who shrink back to destruction, but of those who have faith to the preserving of the soul (Heb. 10:39). We honor our Savior by getting up again and again by the grace of Christ, trusting in *His* life within us, not in our next attempt to do better in the flesh. We humbly repent of each sin. We ask the Lord to cleanse us, and then we move on in the power of His Spirit. Honestly, isn't this the only way we've ever made any true progress at all?

Don't hear me suggesting that God winks at sin. Sin makes God furious, but not because His rules have been broken. Sin makes God furious because His precious children are being broken as we engage in it. You want to see how furious sin causes God to be? Look at the Cross and see what He did to His Son to satisfy His wrath against our sin. Yet, even when you've failed disastrously, don't ever believe you are beyond the reach of His love or His grace. Our Father will *never* give up on us anymore than I would give up on my brain-injured son. Still, it would be foolish to think He is satisfied leaving us at our current level of practical righteousness and maturity. God will do everything at His disposal to discipline us toward obedience and freedom, including allowing us to reap consequences for what we've sown.

No, God doesn't wink at sin; and we must walk with fear and trembling regarding the damage we can do in an *instant*, both to ourselves and to others, by our sin. Yet, just as my son needed a better plan than to try to revive dead brain tissue (again, we had to stimulate the good tissue), God had a better plan than to revive what was dead in us. He gave us a brand-new life in Christ, so that we can now run our race in freedom once again. Still, we need to understand that the race we've been reborn to run is hardly a sprint. It is a marathon of endurance, and it often takes twists and turns making us feel as if we are moving in the *wrong* direction.

Runners Take Your Mark...Get Set...Backwards

Bryson's race was like that of a mountain climber staggering toward a summit peak in a blizzard. Each time he reached a new milestone of development, it was only by persevering up slopes of torment, amidst many demoralizing slides down the mountain. There was little time for celebration at any plateau, as gale-force winds kept right on blowing and as tentacles from his brain injury latched onto one of his limbs to yank him right back down the slope. Much like your own journey, dear reader, when my son *finally* made it to a hard-earned peak, there was always that *next* mountain to climb, replete with storm systems and demons of its own.

For years, the mountaintop of independent walking kept coming into view, then fading. It was sometimes so close we could taste it. He needed another setback now as much as a mountain climber needs an avalanche. He responded to heavy doses of tetracycline, and blood tests in late 1995 revealed that his Lyme disease had *finally* been eradicated. But the next spring, his debilitating illnesses returned, and he began getting even *sicker* than before. He was spiking high fevers and his skin turned grayish. His doctor was as perplexed as we were.

We returned to the neuroimmunologist in central Connecticut who was internationally respected in the field of autism and brain injury. This was the same doctor who had theorized that an autoimmune response had damaged our son's brain after both of his oral polio vaccinations. He had also informed us that his immune system had been permanently compromised by those autoimmune assaults against his body. He now told us that in the aftermath of the Lyme disease, Bryson's immune system was weakened even more, becoming unable to fight off viral complexes that existed perpetually in his body. He placed Bryson on an expensive new antiviral medication which seemed to help. But new infections continued to set our son back, and regression remained an exasperating reality in his life, and ours, for several more *years*.

I still performed his physical regimen with him when he was well enough, but the frequent illnesses were taking a major toll now. The Kinnelon school system continued doing his academic regimen, but he missed much of his second grade year (1995–1996), and his illnesses caused him to miss about fifty days of *each* subsequent academic year as he grew older. Since there are 180 school days, he missed almost one third of the days each year.

Some of his regression was understandable. But at nearly eleven years old, my son still couldn't brush his own teeth or dress himself. It had been nearly *three* years since his "Walking Celebration," and he still cruised through the house latching onto furniture, and he still crawled across yards and fields, using his bicycle style walker to move about when surfaces allowed it.

"A Three Boys"

We had joined a church near our new home in Kinnelon. Elber Stearns, a dearly loved associate pastor, gave me a key to the church gym so I could perform Bryson's NACD regimen there after school each day. When he was well enough, I came home from work to get Bryson to that gym by 3:00 p.m. every weekday, and we also spent our Saturday mornings there. Janelle was busy with junior high activities now, but Tim always came with us. Bryson was glad for his brother's companionship, and it was good for all three of us to spend time with each other.

Things were different without Bryson's Army. But the three of us became a little regiment all by ourselves. Our tight-knit triumvirate adopted the title: "The Three Boys." Bryson still spoke with great difficulty and he confused the articles "the" and "a." He referred to our brigade as "A Three Boys." Whatever our title, my sons were learning something important about the deep, unspoken bond that develops uniquely among men, and we felt good about our masculine bond.

We live in a day when many would scoff at what I just said about feeling good in our masculinity. Have you noticed in our gender-confused culture that there's a backdrop of anger, almost disgust, against men? There's a steady flow of cultural, media, and educational influences that treat males, and normal male behavior, with contempt. Some school districts have reached the absurdity of not allowing children to run out on the *playground*. Dodgeball? Forget it! Children shouldn't engage in such barbaric games. No one should be hit by a ball and eliminated. Too cruel and barbaric! Too male! Everyone should be a winner, every time.

I wish I was joking in noting that men are viewed by some almost as if we are defective females who need to be healed from the disease of being born male. At the least, many believe that we should be refined to become more "female." At the same time, females are under pressure to become more "male." In our gender confused culture, many school districts no longer consider gender a legitimate factor in the makeup of their classrooms. Why put twelve kindergarten boys with twelve girls? After all, some of the boys might one day decide they want to become girls, and vice-versa. Who's to say? Oh, we've become so enlightened, so clever.

Actually, God is to say. It should surprise no one that our nation is now reaping the consequences for our "clever" perspective. Isaiah spoke of our woeful days when he declared:

> Woe to those who call evil good, and good evil; Who substitute darkness for light and light for darkness; Who substitute bitter for sweet and sweet for bitter! Woe to those who are wise in their own eyes And clever in their own sight!
>
> —Isaiah 5:20–21

God created men and women as equals in His awesome, wondrous image. He created us equal in value, and equal in human dignity. But God did *not* create us the same. He created us with wonderful and distinct differences, as it pleased Him to do so, and not just anatomical differences. Our enlightened culture has displeased God by rejecting His Word and by doing all we can to eliminate the differences in His grand design for men and women. We've rebelled against God by insisting that men and women are the same, though His Word declares: different.

Sadly, instead of lighting the way out of the darkness, many of our churches have acquiesced to our culture's politically correct demands to alter God's perfect design. We've mirrored our culture's agenda in attempting to eliminate biblical roles for men and women within the home and within the church. Our appeasement of the demands being made by our culture has placed many of our churches, and the families within them, in peril of crumbling. The decimation is occurring right before our eyes, yet we've been very slow even to understand the carnage. Mary Kassian put her finger squarely on what has occurred in recent decades.

> The philosophy of feminism is part of the seismic postmodern earthquake.... The cataclysmic consequences will continue to crash on culture's shores like a tsunami throughout the opening decades of the new millennium.... The first version of this book, published in 1992... examined the

> cutting edge of feminist theory and theology.... Readers then understood the inevitable repercussions of such a radical paradigm shift. Now, more than ten years later, the book is gaining an audience among those observing the destruction and seeking to understand its cause—men and women who have been blindsided by the cultural onslaught and are asking "Where did these waves come from?" ... The philosophy of feminism has been thoroughly incorporated into our collective societal psyche. The radical has become commonplace.... Virtually all of us—to one degree or another—have become feminists.[8]

The divorce rate in our society has nearly doubled since 1960.[9] Sadly, it seems that marriages within the Christian community have suffered a fate just as severe, with wives filing for divorce nearly twice as often as husbands.[10] No one should be surprised at these statistics. Marriage is an institution designed by God to increase the glory that is due to Jesus Christ, in that it is a portrayal of Christ and His bride, the church (see Ephesian 5:22–32). Satan hates God and *loves* to dishonor Him by ripping apart Christian marriages. The serpent's enticements haven't changed since he first offered the pleasing fruit of independence and self-sufficiency to Eve in the Garden, as Adam stood weakly and passively at her side.

Don't hear me saying that feminist pressure and confusion about gender roles is the sole reason Christian marriages are dropping like flies. But anyone who fails to see this as a *significant* cause has their head in the sand, in cowardice, or in outright rebellion. We have rebelled against God by following our bankrupt culture in its reckless determination to live out our lives on our own independent terms. As in Jeremiah's day, we have committed two evils.

> My people have changed their glory For that which does not profit. Be appalled, O heavens, at this, And shudder, be very desolate.... For My people have committed two evils: They have forsaken Me, The fountain of living waters, To hew for themselves cisterns, Broken cisterns That can hold no water.
>
> —JEREMIAH 2:11–13

The enemy has made deep inroads against marriage in the Christian community by deceiving many into joining in with our culture's disdain for God's different, complimentary design for men and women. Many churches have blatantly rejected God's design in their official doctrines. Far more churches have conveniently neglected to teach God's standards, lacking both the conviction and the courage to do so in our politically correct day. As a result, young Christian couples are entering marriage without even a rudimentary understanding of biblically designed marital roles, nor an understanding of what it means to be a man or a woman in biblical terms. Without a sound biblical identity, why would anyone be surprised that husbands and wives fail to relate to each other in a biblical way as they attempt to sustain those marriages?

I've touched on this issue a few times in this book because families with autistic, brain-injured, or chronically ill children far exceed every category of statistics in terms of marital failure. If we hope to offer any meaningful help to these vulnerable families, or to *any* Christian family, I am convinced that we need to repent of our ignorance and rebellion. The Lord declared: "My people are destroyed for lack of knowledge" (Hosea 4:6). If our churches truly desire to address the problem that is wreaking havoc in our homes, we cannot continue to offer the same misguided, cowardly, politically correct compromises on manhood and womanhood that are being dispensed by our culture. This is tantamount to dousing a fire with gasoline.

Predictably, the problem is growing steadily worse. Our attempt to eliminate gender differences has not only led to the downfall of marriages, it has also led to cataclysmic transgender issues that are further destroying lives and families, and to the pitiful demands that men should be free to marry men and women to marry women. Instead of repenting of this rebellion, our culture has made it a proud emphasis, as evil judges rule and spineless politicians cower at the word "tolerance." But I don't believe the Lord is as grieved by our culture's brazenness against His design as He is by the lukewarm, cowardly response in our churches. Community-wide repentance needs to occur in the body of Christ far more than in our culture.

Men need to lead the way in this repentance for our failure to lead, and for our failure to remain alert and strong in our sacrificial service to our wives, our families, and our churches. We must make sure that all that we do is done in love, as unto the Lord. A good start to our repentance, men, would simply be for us to stop apologizing for being men. Be proud that God made you a man.

> Be on the alert, stand firm in the faith, act like men, be strong. Let all that you do be done in love.
>
> —1 Corinthians 16:13–14

We must stop being afraid of the politically correct, feminist thinkers of our culture. We should be far more afraid of dishonoring and disobeying the Lord. We need to hear the exhortation of Nehemiah: "Do not be afraid of them. Remember the Lord who is great and awesome, and fight for your brothers, your sons, your daughters, your wives and your houses" (Neh. 4:14). Fulfill your role as a man by giving your life away in service to your wife and family, even as Jesus gave His life away for us. We need to become like the sons of Issachar, "men who understood the times, with knowledge of what Israel had to do" (1 Chron. 12:32).

Godly women, I'm sure this won't be a newsflash to you, but we men cannot do what we've been called upon by God to do without your help. You've been created by God to compliment us as we seek *together* to fulfill the Lord's great commission, and you have greater power than you may realize not only to energize the men in your life but also to turn our dark culture, and the church, toward the light of God's way. God's way is never for women to be disregarded or trampled by men. Jesus is the most authentic Man who ever lived; and He elevated women to heights far above what the culture of His day, or of our day, ever would do.

Men who believe they are entitled to harshly rule over women for their own selfish ends are deceived. They are not followers of God, nor of His Word, and they are not your concern. God will deal with them.

The word *strong* is ill defined in our culture, but it is befitting of countless great women in history; and Scripture lifts up a myriad of women who served God in equal measure as any man. Sarah is but one example of a *truly* strong woman. She did not assert or demand her rights, as "strong" women are coerced to do by feminist forces today. Nor did Sarah acquiesce to her natural fears. Frankly, Sarah had a pretty good reason to fear. She had a fearful, bumbling husband. Abraham was initially so cowardly that he endangered her not once, but shamefully twice, right to the bedroom doorway of lustful, evil kings. God stepped in to save her.

Sarah obeyed God by following her sinful, cowardly husband's leadership, even as she entrusted her well-being into God's hands (see 1 Peter 3:1–6). When you think it through, what woman wouldn't prefer God standing up for her with all His might, instead of standing up for herself? God loves to stand up for those who obey and trust Him above all, but a choice must be made. Jesus didn't concern Himself with His temporal rights. Obeying His Father was His sole concern. In this regard, Sarah's walk with God was in perfect step with that of King Jesus.

Jesus knew He was an *equal* member of the triune Godhead. Clear in His identity, He embraced His role within the holy Trinity, having no need to grasp for the role of the Father or of the Spirit. The Father did not fulfill the Son's role or Spirit's role either. Our God is a God of order. Each member of the Trinity accepted the role They had designed for Themselves. Both men and women in our day need to understand that our efforts to assert our rights or exchange our roles lead us far from obedience, and far from the attitude of the One we have been called to follow:

> Have this attitude in yourselves which was also in Christ Jesus, who, although He existed in the form of God, did not regard equality with God a thing to be grasped, but emptied Himself, taking the form of a bond-servant...He humbled Himself by becoming obedient to the point of death, even death on a cross. *For this reason*...God highly exalted Him.
>
> —PHILIPPIANS 2:5–9, EMPHASIS ADDED

By the way, Abraham did go on to become the man most of us know as the father of faith. Do you think he would have garnered this reputation were it not for Sarah's strength? Not a chance! Oh, that men and women would follow God's Word and not our foolish culture in our day. Talk about a death trap! As marriages and families continue to crumble, the following question must be answered, not by our culture, but by we who bear Christ's name:

> O sons of men, how long will my honor become a reproach? How long will you love what is worthless and aim at deception?
>
> —PSALM 4:2

I call upon every godly man and every godly woman to stop aiming at the deceptions of our culture. Many believe that we are approaching the last days before Christ's return. This is no time for the sons and daughters of God to be limping back into prison over this age-old deception. God's ways are counterintuitive and foolish, and they will never make sense to our natural way of thinking, and far less to our culture. But if we want to prevent subsequent American generations from becoming practically Christ-less, then godly men and women need to immediately bow down together in desperate fear of the Lord and in repentance, praying that God might have mercy on us. Only then can we hope that the Lord will turn back the dismal tide we've allowed to roll right into our churches and homes.

"A Three Boys" Shed A Few Tears

Most of Bryson's exercises in that little church gym revolved around sports. I placed balls on the floor in front of him, ten feet apart, *all* the way across the gym. Wiffle balls, tennis balls, soccer balls, footballs—variety kept it interesting. He performed a "slow walking" routine toward each ball, with me behind him ready to reach out and grab him as he fell. He was required to take one extremely s-l-o-w step at a time on my command. The commands were given several seconds apart, as he strained to remain upright. It was sort of like the steps a bridal party takes down the aisle, only much s–l–o–w–e–r. Bryson came to a complete halt at each ball, slowly bending to pick it up. This routine was geared to increase his ability to stop, and improve his spatial awareness and depth perception as he proceeded toward each focal point: the next ball.

I allowed him to throw each one as he reached it. Balls began flying all over the gym, and Tim and I had to duck for cover. He began having *so* much fun throwing them that he started diving to the ground to get each ball sooner. To motivate him to perform the routine properly, each time he stopped and picked up a ball without needing to be held, and without diving at it, he gained points toward a prize. This routine was excruciatingly hard for him, taking *months* before he made the slightest progress in his ability to stop.

He still often fell suddenly from a standing position, for no apparent reason. We used his trusty skateboard to help him with this. I firmly held onto his shoulders as he stepped up onto it, slowly moving my hands away, before needing to grab him and hold him up. And yes, by design, this exercise was intended to be hard to the point of frustration The skateboard tipped back and forth, challenging him to toughen his balance. He stared at my watch's second hand as I held it in front of his face. Similar to the early days of learning to stand leaning against a wall, our progress came over a period of months and years, one precious second at a time. After one full year of performing this routine, his "record" standing time increased to more than one minute.

He did toe raisers to strengthen his calves, and quad squats to strengthen his upper legs. His "board walking" became more intricate now. He was not only required to step onto each one-inch high, twelve-inch wide, eight-foot long board, but now he was required to "walk the plank." He walked on those boards *endlessly* through the years. After a year, I arranged the boards into various shapes, such as in an "L" or a "V" to practice his ability to turn. In future years, he was required to walk those planks backwards and sideways to increase his agility. He continued stepping high through his walking path (made of two-by-fours), making sure he placed one foot inside each rectangle. During all of these exercises I stood close by and caught him each time he stumbled, which was often. These routines increased in intensity after each quarterly NACD meeting.

The prizes (he still called them "pwizes") Bryson worked toward were no longer earned daily, but weekly. His new passion was his growing hat collection. Each week, after working much harder than I could adequately describe in this book, he received a new hat from his growing list of "favorite" professional and college teams. Bryson was the consummate negotiator (I wonder where he got *that* from) and he often wheedled an extra hat from me during the week for breaking a record standing on his skateboard, or for some other special accomplishment.

As an immediate reward after a hard exercise, we often played an inning of baseball. Bryson was always the Yankees, and Tim the opposing team. I was pretty good at aiming for Bryson's bat now, with my underhand pitches. Still, it often took twenty or more pitches before I was able to touch his bat with a single pitch, as his impaired vision and motor coordination caused him to swing wildly. This amounted to a *ton* of frustration building inside Bryson, and tension often rose to a fever pitch for "A Three Boys" inside that little church gym as minutes ticked away in futility.

Tim had wisdom way beyond his years in making Bryson believe he was winning *every* game, but I expected more maturity from him than I should have as he faced his brother's traumas and anger. He was only *six* when we moved to Kinnelon, and he had already spent most of his life serving his needy "older" brother. I grieved the unfairness for him. But it's funny how God works. Though he is too humble to mention it (obviously I'm not), Tim would later become the "Athlete of the Year" at his high school. And talk about being a real man! He spent his spare time throughout his college career, including every Saturday, serving poor families in underprivileged neighborhoods in the Lynchburg, Virginia, area while attending Liberty University. As I said earlier in this book, no father has ever been more proud of a son than I am of my son Tim.

But as much as Tim sacrificed for his brother, it was a very hard dynamic for Bryson to have a fleet-footed, natural athlete for a younger brother. Tim could always smack the ball way across the gym, while Bryson continued to swing and miss endlessly. Bryson not only became traumatized and angry, sometimes he got hurt falling to that hard gym floor. When a mentally and emotionally impaired child is upset and angry, believe me, you know it. The anger and frustration comes flying fast and furious in all directions, as it did toward me and Tim.

Bryson became *so* frustrated when he couldn't make the game turn out the way he had fantasized. He often demanded to start each game over from *scratch*.

Then *I'd* get uptight, knowing we only had a limited amount of time to spend in these games so "A Three Boys" could finish his regimen and get home for dinner with our two precious girls (my wife and daughter). I was trying so hard to make this fun, but we had *so* much work to do. As in any sport, when you add the element of a time clock, things can get tense in a hurry.

It takes the wisdom of Solomon (and then some) to resolve sibling rivalries. Sometimes I relished a good argument between "A Three Boys." Not so much because I'm basically stupid (well, maybe *that* too). But if I live to be 100, I'll *never* forget those depressing years when Bryson could argue with no one, when he couldn't speak at all. I tried my best to get the program back on track by giving both boys some combination of encouraging "pep talks" or appropriate discipline. Bryson's desire to finish his programs to get that week's "pwize" was always a key motivating factor. But the linchpin of any success I ever achieved was to consistently verbalize that I loved and believed in both of my sons. This was easy, since it was true.

Yet, on some days, as Bryson's dreams turned into nightmares and his frustration and jealousy against his little brother reached a peak, a huge torrent of anger was unleashed against both of us. On those occasions it became necessary to discipline him firmly by having him sit on a bench, or even by taking away a coveted "pwize." There were other times when I chose to allow Bryson to vent his anger (especially against me) *without* disciplining him. He had every reason to be frustrated and angry, and he often reached the point of needing to get those frustrations out.

"A Three Boys" suffered through some highly emotionally charged days. I had read several of Dr. Dobson's books, but on some days everything I tried failed. *Everything!* There didn't seem to be answers *anywhere* instructing a dad how to deal with a child whose dreams were so absurdly unreachable, a child who was *so* badly broken that he didn't even understand that he was broken. I was below the waterline, gasping for air, more times than I can convey to you; and tears began to flow from all directions on those days as "A Three Boys" became two unhappy campers and one very discouraged dad. And where was God at such desperate moments? I had no idea! To say I was grieved at the way things had to be for our struggling family is an understatement.

Born to *run?* What a *joke* it all seemed on such days. I thought "A Three Boys" would create memories we'd cherish for a lifetime. I thought we'd look back and realize that, with God's help, Bryson had *finally* conquered that elusive peak of walking independently. Maybe he'd even learn to ride a bike one day, or brush his teeth, or tie his own shoes. Who *knows* what I thought? The only thing I knew for sure on those gut-wrenching days is that I felt like a fool for ever having dreamed so high. After all the *years* of excruciating work! After all the illnesses and regressions! Is *this* what we had come to? Instead of victorious mountain peaks, "A Three Boys" were all at each other's throats. I sometimes stepped outside that little church gym so my sons wouldn't see their dad's anguish, or my bitter tears.

We were born to run, oh yes we were; but our enemy knows just when to show up, doesn't he? Sometimes you can almost hear laughter billowing up like smoke from the pit of hell as the serpent tempts us to give up. But don't believe his vicious lie that your race is hopeless, that you've stumbled too many times to get up again and continue on. If your heart is still beating, if your lungs still have breath, if you're reading these words, it is *not* too late.

Clearly this world is a death trap. Who wouldn't choose to give up and give in to the perversity and idolatry the enemy offers us as an escape hatch, so we can get away from all the senseless pain? But through the years I've become convinced that God is near to the brokenhearted, and that in His good time He will reach out to save those who are crushed in spirit (Ps. 34:18–19). Even a humiliating stumble in the race today or a demoralizing defeat in battle tomorrow never needs to define your race, or mine. God is still on His throne and our race is not over until *He* says it's over, or until we quit.

And even if you have quit, as I'm sorry to say I've done from time to time, our God is so great that He can get us *right* back into the race, as we turn to Him in repentance, surrendering to Him once again. Oh yes, we were born to run, but the Lord never delights in those who believe their own race to be perfect, nor in those who rely on their own natural speed and strength as they run. He favors those who fear Him, and those who understand that *He* is their only hope.

> He does not delight in the strength of the horse; He does not take pleasure in the legs of a man. The LORD favors those who fear Him.
>
> —PSALM 147:10–11

BORN TO RUN

I watched him on the playground at school one day as his classmates took turns kicking the ball for him during a game of kickball. Then they helped him grab onto his bicycle-walker to "run" the bases. Tears welled in my eyes as those sensational kids nearly fought over who'd get the next chance to help my son. Each night after tucking him in, I put the walker in the corner of his room. My heart ached for the day when he might no longer need it.

I still believed my son would walk independently one day, but I'd be lying if I told you my faith didn't waver sometimes. A few years earlier, Bob Doman calmed my fears by saying, "We'll make it happen." After each illness and regression, Bob kept pushing us, again and again, to begin our trek back up that seemingly impossible mountain. Inexplicably, at our next quarterly evaluation, Bob informed us it was time to teach Bryson to *run*. I just smiled and shook my head. This was clearly ridiculous. But Bob was able to see what others couldn't yet see.

He reminded us that walking is the act of "falling forward." Doing so without actually falling down, crashing into a wall, or slamming into other objects is the hard part. Bryson's main challenge now was in learning to stop. Bob reminded us that for the past several quarters, this is *precisely* what we had been working on in that little church gym. He was now convinced that the infrastructure had been sufficiently built within Bryson's brain and body. He was ready not just to walk, but to *run*. This is how we were going to attempt it.

I was to walk backwards, urging Bryson to "run" toward me. I was thankful that in addition to being a quarterback, I had spent years on the football field as a defensive back. I was good at backpedaling while watching the receiver in front of me. But knocking down passes in the secondary was a cakewalk compared to this situation. I kept my eyes peeled on my boy, ready to reach out in a split second to grab him as he stumbled toward that hard gym floor, which he did *repeatedly* during those first weeks, as soon as his legs began to move forward.

Yet, even with all the tension, I absolutely *loved* this! It was exhilarating! These many years later, I can't think of a memory more cherished than the elation on my son's face as he realized what was happening. He was *thrilled* by it! After all the agonizing years of seemingly fruitless, foundational input, my precious boy was beginning to *run!*

And as the months turned into years, my son began to run like the wind. Oh, don't get me wrong, his gait remains wobbly to this day, even as I type these words, and he still sometimes stumbles and falls. But as he ran in that little church gym, I didn't see a boy running toward me who was handicapped. I saw a magnificent champion running a race that was superb, perfect in my eyes; and I wanted him to feel his daddy's pleasure as he ran.

We are all running a race here, dear reader. Honestly, there's been more trouble in my race than I ever dreamed possible when I was a young runner. I'm nearer to the end than the beginning now, and I've learned that our Father knows how to give good "pwizes" to each of His children as we run the course He has laid out for us here. Sometimes, from His storehouse of wisdom and grace, those gifts involve splendid wonders; and it is with reverence I tell you of a miracle that came during those days of anguish and joy in that little church gym. A day finally arrived when I picked up the walker of a child once declared to be permanently crippled, not to place it in the corner for the evening, but in the attic, never to be needed by him again.

How inscrutable and glorious is our great King? When you think of it, each one of the King's children is broken and crippled in our own way. Yet none of His dearly loved children have been born to limp along timidly, to walk hesitantly, or even to jog cautiously toward the goal. We've been born to run and to win the race set before us, knowing that our Father sees the perfection of Jesus Christ in us as we run for His glory.

And a day is coming, not too long from now in the scheme of things, when the race of each child will come to an end. We will see a stadium, a grand coliseum on the horizon, at the entrance of heaven. This is where we will take our final lap in a mortal body. We will hear thunder rumbling up ahead; but as we draw nearer, we will realize that the noise isn't thunder at all. It's the roar rising up from a great cloud of witnesses in that arena, a roar that grows louder with each step we take. The roar will be for King Jesus, to whom *all* glory is due. The roar will also be for you, as you press on for His glory.

Perhaps the most startling thing is that the great King's own race didn't appear victorious here, at least for a while. Frankly, it appeared to be the worst defeat in history, that is, if you looked at His race on Friday. Oh, but His race wasn't over on Friday, was it? As He hung on a cross, tortured and bleeding to death, He had an unseen Father on a throne far away; and events were being orchestrated that would astonish the universe and silence *all* evil. Take another glimpse at our risen Champion on Sunday, and remember His glorious purpose. Now remember yours! Run the race that has been set before you, fixing your eyes on Jesus, the matchless, risen King.

> Therefore, since we have so great a cloud of witnesses surrounding us, let us also lay aside every encumbrance and the sin which so easily entangles us, and let us run with endurance the race that is set before us, fixing our eyes on Jesus, the author and perfecter of faith, who for the joy set before Him endured the cross, despising the shame, and has sat down at the right hand of God.
>
> —HEBREWS 12:1–2

> Now to Him who is able to keep you from stumbling, and to make you stand in the presence of His glory blameless with great joy, to the only God our Savior, through Jesus Christ our Lord, be glory, majesty, dominion and authority, before all time and now and forever.
>
> —JUDE 1:24–25

Balancing act at the Kiel School gym in Kinnelon

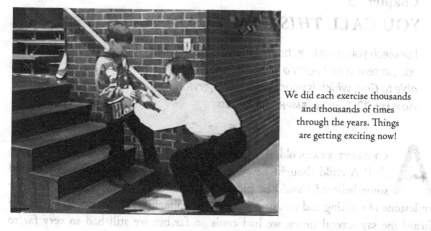

We did each exercise thousands and thousands of times through the years. Things are getting exciting now!

I was often so proud of this kid I could scream.

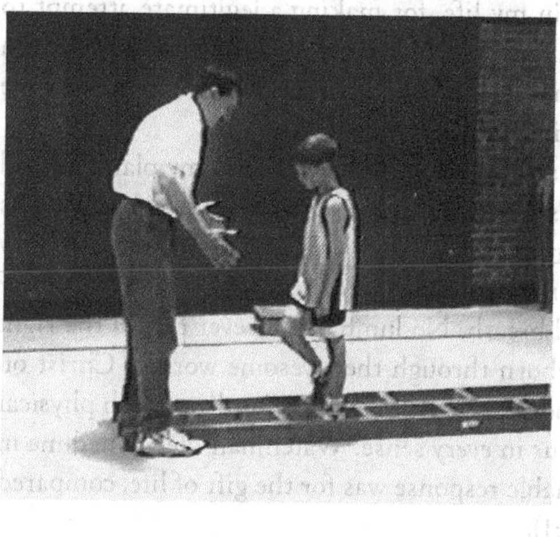

Steppin' up at Stonybrook School in Kinnelon

Chapter 23
YOU CALL *THIS* REASONABLE?

I beseech you therefore, brethren, by the mercies of God, that you present your bodies a living sacrifice, holy, acceptable to God, which is your reasonable *service.*
ROMANS 12:1, NKJV, EMPHASIS ADDED

AT TWELVE YEARS old, Bryson was not only walking, but *running*. Imagine that! A child thought never to walk, never to speak intelligibly, a child some believed should be placed in an institution. The long yearned-for milestone of walking and running represented a *magnificent* victory. Yet, as you've heard me say several times, we had come so far but we still had so very far to go. Isn't this true of your life too, dear reader? While the Lord has done magnificent things, your road remains so long; you still have such fearful questions, such daunting mountains looming ahead. Don't finish this book merely to pick up another in your quest for hope. No book, no renewed personal resolve, no program of improvement can help you until *all* your hope is in Jesus Christ. Then you will realize that being on the path with Him means more than any notion of reaching a destination, more even than conquering all those intimidating mountains.

Bryson wasn't the only one who had come a long way. As a younger Christian, I thought that my faith somehow *entitled* me to experience smooth sailing, calm waters, and success, as the *world* defines success. I couldn't fathom a God who would allow cruel suffering to occur in my life and family without wrapping it all up for good, neat and tidy, according to my timetable and definition of good, of course. I'd never have expressed it this way, but I assumed that God somehow *owed me* for believing in Him, for taking a stand for Him. I should be rewarded for giving Him a significant *part* in my life, for making a legitimate attempt to limit my sinful passions and live above the standards of this world. My, what a grand sacrifice I was making! I just hoped God appreciated it, and blessed me accordingly. How arrogant and blind!

My attitude of entitlement caused me to try to fit God into my plans instead of seeking how I might fit into *His*. Present my *body* as a living sacrifice? What's in *that* for me? How easily we forget that we are living and breathing this very moment, and not a mixture of inanimate clay and dust, because the Creator chose to grant us physical life and breath. No lump of clay ever *earned* the right to be alive. We who have been reborn through the awesome work of Christ on the cross have also received the undeserved spiritual life. Our lives, both physical and spiritual, have been gifted to us in *every* sense. Watchman Nee nailed me in terms of what I *thought* my reasonable response was for the gift of life, compared to what God asks of us (Rom. 12:1).

> The trouble with many Christians today is that they have an insufficient idea of what God is asking of them. How glibly they say: "Lord, I am willing for anything." Do you know that God is asking of you your very life? There are cherished ideals, strong wills, precious relationships, much-loved work, that will have to go; so do not give yourself to God unless you mean it.[1]

How easy it is to overlook scriptures that don't serve my own shallow, selfish ends. As a young believer I somehow missed the fact that God's name is "Jealous" (Exod. 34:14), that He is a "consuming fire" (Heb. 12:29). He will not accept lukewarm duplicity from any child. No one spoke the truth like Jesus, including the truth about what is *reasonable* in our service for Him:

> Which of you, having a slave plowing or tending sheep... will he not say to him, "Prepare something for me to eat, and properly clothe yourself and serve me while I eat and drink."... So you too, when you do all the things which are commanded you, say, "We are unworthy slaves; we have done only that which we ought to have done."
>
> —Luke 17:7–8, 10

Frankly, that Master-slave relationship strikes me as a bit harsh. But is God a harsh, cold Master? The god of this world tries to deceive even followers of Christ into thinking so. But the redemption of our lives at the cross was no cold, backroom business deal from one cruel taskmaster to another to regain captured spoils of war. God didn't send His Son to die merely to enlist us into His service as mercenary soldiers to fight His battles in this world. Oh, how twisted our minds can become when we don't understand the depth of God's love for each one of us!

But what about all this "jealousy" and "consuming fire" stuff? Isn't that a bit over the top? For those of you who are married, I can only hope your spouse is jealous of you in the biblical sense. I hope you are jealous for your children too, the way our Father is jealous of each one of us.

> By "jealous," it doesn't mean that God is one who is controlling and demanding and flies into a rage without the slightest reason or provocation. The jealousy the Bible is speaking of is the jealousy of a loving Father who sees the possibilities and potential of His children and is brokenhearted when those things are not realized, or worse, are wasted and squandered.[2]
>
> —Greg Laurie

Oh, how our Father loved us to pay such an enormous price to redeem us through the murder of His Son at the hands of evil men! Oh, how our Savior suffered for us, holding *nothing* back as He bled to death! My *great sacrifice* for Him? How backwards! I had no idea, on a brass tacks basis, who I was dealing with. My shallow view of God's sacrifice for me on the cross carried over to an equally shallow view of my reasonable response to Him for such love. It is arrogance to think God owes us *anything*, including an explanation for the suffering He allows to occur in our lives.

Our sense of entitlement is an age-old temptation that stems from the pit of hell. Don't buy it! God is our Master and He is our Father, more loving than we will ever comprehend. Our part, our response, being recipients of His incomprehensibly grand gift in Christ, is to please Him in gratitude by obeying Him, by seeking His glory, and yes, by presenting our bodies as living sacrifices to Him. *This*, and nothing less than this, is our *reasonable* service, whether we understand what He allows to occur in our lives or not. *Especially* when we don't understand!

WHAT'S *REASONABLE* ABOUT CHISELS AND KNIVES?

> Am I prepared to let God grip me by His power and do a work in me that is worthy of Himself? Sanctification is not my idea of what I want God to do for me; sanctification is God's idea of what He wants to do for me, and He has to get me into the attitude of mind and spirit where at any cost I will let Him sanctify me wholly.[3]
>
> —OSWALD CHAMBERS

For many of us, there's a vigorous push and pull, sometimes even a knock-down, drag out battle within us to come to grips with what the Lord considers "reasonable." Have you been disappointed that your suffering did not end, and perhaps got worse, after you received Christ Jesus as Lord? Have you fallen for the serpent's deception that the cross of Christ is the *ending* point of faith, and not merely the beginning? How foolish to think that the birth of a baby is the end of that child's growth in this world. Growing up is hard, and we all have such a *long* road to travel toward the image of Christ. We become bewildered when we don't remember that our walk with the King is a long, long road fraught with *many seasons* of tribulation and sorrow.

Jesus made it clear that in this world we *will* (not might) have tribulation (John 16:33). The first message Jesus gave regarding Paul as a new believer was, "I will show him how much he must suffer for My name's sake" (Acts 9:16). How's that for a welcome to the family? Later, after being *stoned*, Paul got up and encouraged the souls of the disciples. But do you remember how? Was it through some pie in the sky exhortation predicting ease and comfort? Hello! The man had just been *stoned and left for dead*! He forewarned them, "...strengthening the souls of the disciples, encouraging them to continue in the faith, and saying, 'Through *many* tribulations we must enter the kingdom of God'" (Acts 14:22, emphasis added). Paul even declared that God had made it clear to him that imprisonment and affliction awaited him in *every* city (20:23).

It sounds so nice and comfortable in Sunday school class to remind each other that our faith must be tested to grow. Testing is such a bland term. If we don't want to be disillusioned, we must remember that testing invariably involves suffering. The next time you drive over the Golden Gate or George Washington Bridge, you had better hope the steel has been tested. Your life is far more precious than a piece of steel in your Father's hands. He is not merely interested in your utility. The Father is preparing to bring you higher as a much loved son, a much loved daughter. And lest we think that our obedience spares us all further suffering, Jesus reminds us that when we bear fruit in obedience, we are not spared the pruning knife. We invite it!

> Every branch that beareth fruit, he purgeth it, that it may bring forth more fruit.
>
> —John 15:2, KJV

Jesus is teaching His disciples about the concept of being purged (or pruned) by our great Father-Gardener. Maybe it's just me, but frankly, even after I come to understand my need to be tested and tried, I *still* don't like imagery that depicts knives hacking away at me. Not only am I uncomfortable by the notion of such "purging" (ouch!), but as I look through Scripture there doesn't seem to be any end to it in this world. Sometimes I feel like screaming, "Lord, don't we ever graduate from the need to be 'purged'?"

I'd like to think I've become so mature in my walk with the Lord that I'd never again cast Him aside and begin relying on myself. But Scripture continually reminds us that we *all* need *continual* pruning, suffering and even long-term thorns to keep us dependent upon God. Andrew Murray provides some clarity regarding our nature, and the necessary process that must ensue.

> In the whole plant world there is not a tree to be found so specially suited to the image of man in his relation to God as is the vine. There is none of which the natural tendency is so entirely evil—none where the growth is so ready to run into wood that is utterly worthless except for the fire. Of all plants, not one needs the pruning knife so unsparingly and so unceasingly.[4]

As all parents know, it's one thing to trust God and rely upon the sufficiency of His grace for our own suffering and pain. It's even harder to trust Him when our children suffer. It often seems that there's no rhyme or reason to the trials God sends our way, but His choice of the sufferings that each one of us must endure is not ours to question. Some of God's children will be tested more severely than others, so that they will grow mightily in grace and be of highest use to the Master. As a soldier of Christ, Paul expected hardship and suffering as necessary elements in the process of being conformed to Christ's image. What about you, fellow sojourner? What were you expecting?

Our plans are so dear to us. God often uses His prerogative to disrupt those plans. We can't control the circumstances that arise, but we can control how we will respond. We can become angry, disgusted, and bitter, fighting against God's disruptions; or we can entrust ourselves into His good hands. Have you noticed that sooner or later God always wins? Our best move when times of testing come is to surrender fully and immediately, eagerly desiring His will to be accomplished in and through our lives. Gethsemane is always a time of decision. My will, or His? Our Father will draw each season of suffering to an end when it has achieved His purpose.

> All discipline, for the moment seems not to be joyful, but sorrowful; yet to those who have been trained by it, afterwards it yields the peaceful fruit of righteousness.
>
> —HEBREWS 12:11

> After you have suffered for a little while, the God of all grace, who called you to eternal glory in Christ, will Himself perfect, confirm, strengthen and establish you.
>
> —1 PETER 5:10

Is it reasonable for God to expect us to present our lives, even our bodies to Him? In view of God's endless mercies toward us, in view of the desperation of those all around us for whom we possess the *only* remedy and hope, in Christ, is there anything in this world more reasonable? God *is* a consuming fire and He will *never* be satisfied with a partial, lukewarm commitment to Him. But don't make your commitment lightly, for all hell is going to break loose against it.

When things get hard, when we are called upon to suffer for a season, even a long, perplexing season that we simply don't understand, what will our response be? Will we press on toward the prize of the upward call of God in Christ? Will we humbly thank Him for the privilege He has granted us to suffer for Him, even as He suffered for us? Or will we turn back in defeat?

> Every time my theology becomes clear to my own mind, I encounter something that contradicts it. As soon as I say, "I believe God shall supply all my need," the testing of my faith begins. When my strength runs dry and my vision is blinded, will I endure this trial of my faith victoriously or will I turn back in defeat?[5]
>
> —OSWALD CHAMBERS

TSUNAMI!

Praise God, Bryson was running! Yet he still fell without warning, abruptly losing his balance as if a giant wave knocked him off his feet. After all these years, his crashes were still bloody and excruciating, as his body hit various hard, sharp objects on the way down to the floor. After *all* these years, the stress in our home remained intense. Bombs went off daily, sometimes several times a day, as his growing body went down. And yes, after all these years, the scene remained so similar, and I mean brutal, with screams and tears (his and ours) echoing through our home.

One Saturday morning in February 1997 I was reading in my home office when I heard a loud crash just outside my door. I called to him to see if he was all right. I had learned that receiving no answer was not a good sign, usually indicating he was too injured or hurt to answer, that the pain had taken his breath away. I leaped up and ran toward the door. There he was, crumpled in a fetal position in the miniature alcove between the dog's bed and a section of drywall which forms the alcove, just outside my door. The pain was too intense for him to speak, like when your toddler gets hurt and his breath gets sucked out of him for a moment before the wailing begins. He was literally shaking, pointing to his ear, indicating that he was in horrible pain.

As I picked him up, the screams finally came along with tears streaming down his face. He was grabbing at his ear. Between sobs he blurted, "Ear hurts, Dad." His ear was bleeding. His head had hit the sharp corner of the wall full force. Due to his motor damage he still didn't possess the reflexes to reach out to prevent his head from making a direct hit on this sharp corner. Nor could he keep himself from sliding slowly and excruciatingly down, with the full weight of his body pinning his head and ear to that sharp corner, all the way to the floor. The side of his head was bruised, and the skin on his ear was scraped off, from his helpless agonizing descent.

He wept for a long time as I held him. This was unusual for Bryson. He was still such a tender child, yet he rarely cried anymore. It was as if he'd developed a hard emotional shell to enable himself to cope with the sheer quantity of his painful accidents. He had already fallen painfully in the bathroom that *very* morning. He was wearing bandages from this week's falls alone, and he had a deep bruise on his shoulder from a crash just *yesterday*. This time, as was the case with many of the worst accidents (smashed out teeth, badly injured muscles and bones, the time he nearly lost an eye...etc, etc.) he quivered in my arms for a very long time.

Oh yes, we still praised God for the progress, and He was worthy of every bit of that praise. But there's something enigmatic and indescribable about balancing hope and progress with crushing pain and sorrow in a long-term situation that never, ever really changes. There's a desperation that either causes you to become embittered, or keeps you close to the throne of mercy and grace, giving you the wisdom that you had better not stray far from it. This day was no different than so many others, year after pain-filled year. Our gorgeous son continued being gradually and methodically maimed and scarred. This is why I will not offer easy answers or success formulas in this book. What formula would you give me at a moment like this? What cliché? What pious platitude?

This book is not about a success formula. It is a about a Person, a mighty King who stoops low enough to walk with us as we face life's horrors and fiascos during our long journey in this world. Don't pity the person caught in an unending, nightmarish dilemma who is learning to walk with the King. That person's pain will one day end, and the reward for his endurance will be high. Pity the person who thinks that their pious platitudes and formulas are sufficient for them, that they can manage their lives without surrendering fully to this magnificent King.

As he began to calm down, still sniveling, Bryson looked up and asked me something in his broken speech that he rarely wanted to talk about: "Dad, why I hurt myself so much?" I was panicked, realizing that I had no good answer for him at this moment. In view of his mental and emotional limitations, how could I truthfully explain his brokenness? How do you tell a tender soul that he must face torture throughout his lifetime because his brain was injured when he was an innocent baby? I just stood there, holding my growing, adolescent boy tight for a very long time, patting and rubbing his back as if he were a toddler, telling him it was going to be okay.

Later that same morning, Bryson became wild and uncontrollable. His screaming tantrum ended with me trying to persuade him to come out of a dark closet in his room. If I live to be a hundred, I'll never forget his words as I stood helplessly outside that door. He screamed, over and over, that he hated me, that he hated himself. With garbled, impaired speech He just kept screaming in a shrill voice I'd never heard before, *"I dumb and ugly*! No one likes me! I wish you had different son who wasn't ugly! I don't like myself! I dumb and ugly!" He kept screaming it over and over as I stood at the door pleading for him to come out, but to no avail.

On my hands and knees now I pleaded, telling him how much I loved him, how much *everyone* loved him, telling him how terrific he was, but his screams drowned me out. I felt sick to my stomach. I was praying silently, but very hard now. The only thing I could think to pray was: "God, help us! Please, God, help us!" As my son kept screaming, tears filled my eyes, as they do now as I write these words many years later. My thoughts flew fast and furious: "Not this, Lord! Not after all he's been through. Stop it now! This nightmare is more than I can bear!"

That very *same* week in February 1997 he suffered another bad accident. I included this following entry in my journal:

> A panicked call from my wife! "Barry, come quick! He's really hurt!" I raced up the steps to the upstairs bathroom to find my son shaking in pain. With a quivering voice he said, "It hurts, Dad." He had fallen hard into the corner of the doorway, and bounced directly to the hard bathroom tile floor. Again, his reflexes didn't allow him to cushion the fall… "I wish I didn't fell, Dad" (Bryson still uses the wrong tenses of words). It is breaking my heart to see this tender boy continue to suffer such intense pain.[6]

And finally, from that very *same* week, one final journal entry:

> I told God about my anger in no uncertain terms. The conversation was not for the faint of heart. I later apologized for the language I used. I was thankful for His reminder that as my Father He responds to my anger wisely and compassionately, even as I try to do when Bryson unleashes one of his rage-filled, screaming tirades against me and against himself from the closet. During those moments of anguished, screaming pain, I am all my son really has. During my weakest moments of screaming, anguished pain, my Father is all I really have. If He ever leaves, if His grace ceases to be sufficient when my anguish and even my anger lets loose in His direction, I'm finished![7]

I could only hope that this episode of tortured, mentally impaired, self-hatred from the closet would prove to be an isolated incident. But this was just an early wave of the tsunami that had been rolling in his mind for many years now, as he neared twelve years old. Bryson is a young man in his mid twenties as I write this book, and waves keep crashing onto his shores at various intervals to this day. After all these years I remain just as desperately in need of the mercy and grace of God as I help him to deal with them. After all these years sometimes the best prayer I can come up with is still: "Help us, Lord! Please, God, help us!"And after all these years the Lord has never left us, never forsaken us (Deut. 31:6; Heb. 13:5). The King walks with us through every trial and every sorrow, and His grace remains sufficient. If not, then frankly, I'd truly be finished.

The Steps up the Mountain

Debilitating infections from his suppressed immune system continued setting Bryson back, but every week that he was healthy we pressed on with his physical regimen. "A Three Boys" no longer worked together in that little church gym. The workouts were now just between Bryson and me in the gymnasiums at Stonybrook School in Kinnelon. Our old friend, Bette Esposito (Bryson's wonderful first grade teacher), had become the principal of Stonybrook, and she made sure the gym was available for our use each morning from 7:00 a.m. to 9:15 a.m., when the bell sounded for his fourth grade class to begin. We still performed many activities described in earlier chapters, along with many new ones. The NACD, ever asking us to do the "impossible," informed us it was time to teach him to climb up and down a flight of stairs.

We had begun preparing him for this task two years earlier at the Kiel School, where Principal Marita Dowell had allowed us to use the gym whenever we needed it. The Kiel gym was actually an all purpose room, having two steps rising to a stage. That stage may as well have been Mount Everest to Bryson. Like a fierce dragon, he blew fear-stoked fire to dissuade me from bringing him anywhere *near* those stairs. This was no different from his terror of taking his first step onto soft foam padding in our family room years before. But I was now an old pro at breaking his goals down into the tiniest micro-accomplishments. When I finally persuaded him to come to the base of that "mountain," I held his shoulders firmly from behind and implored him simply to lift one foot and gently place it on the first stair, then put it back down to the floor.

The initial goal was not to actually climb the stairs, just to get him used to the feel of lifting his foot up to the lowest step as he remained safe in my grasp. I didn't ask him to put any weight on that stair. Just lift his foot up to it, then put it back down. It took several weeks for my terrified son to put his foot up there without an intense argument. In the months ahead we progressed *very* slowly toward simply leaning forward, and then putting a *tiny* bit of weight on that foot. By the time he entered fourth grade, it had been two full years since placing his foot up on that first step at Kiel School, and we now began working toward conquering all six steps to the higher stage at Stonybrook. I still stood right behind him, instantly grabbing his shoulders each time he faltered.

My little negotiator had not only graduated toward higher goals but higher "pwizes" too. He now received a professional sports cap once per week, plus an authentic sports Jersey once per month. We also set goals for him to receive additional prizes for the special challenges we agreed on, and for breaking new records. He now owned the greatest hat collection you ever saw, along with a closet full of Jerseys from his favorite football, basketball, and baseball teams.

It's easy to think that these "pwizes" were excessive, and perhaps they were. But it's impossible to convey how hard it was to motivate a mentally impaired twelve-year-old to do such excruciatingly difficult work each and every morning. With the clock ticking against childhood, along with serious illnesses, painful injuries, and traumatic emotional tsunamis, the pressure to overcome his resistance against the work and press on toward higher freedom for him was as intense as ever.

Learning to come down a flight of stairs is a *whole* different ballgame than climbing up, and he was now hard at work attempting this. I stood just below him on the stairs, with one hand in ready position a few inches from his chest, ready to catch him as he fell. He couldn't climb down like you and I do, placing one foot down on a step, then passing that step by in order to get to the step beneath it with the opposite foot. It would be another full year before we could even *begin* tackling that accomplishment. First, we had to work slowly, v-e-r-y s-l-o-w-l-y, on coming down with each foot to the *same* step. If he was successful in placing his left foot down to a step, he would then work hard toward bringing his right foot down to that very same step.

I would tap each wooden step very loudly several times with my free hand so that Bryson would hear the noise and then focus his eyes onto the "target" step, then verbally coach him:

"Slow, slow, slow, Bryce… You can do it, man… Don't plop down… Slowly now, just sink s-l-o-w-l-y down like you have a parachute up above you… Strengthen the strong muscle in your other leg and sink s-l-o-w-l-y down until the stair stops your foot… That's it.… You're doing it, champ!… Slow now. Fantastic! You made it, Bryson! You are so great! What a champion you are!

"Now, let's bring down that other leg, big guy. If you can make one foot come down, you can do it with the other. Daddy won't let you fall. You can do it! Let's go, champ! Strengthen the strong muscle in your leg, and let's go! I'm so proud of you! You are the greatest champion I've ever seen. Come on! Let's bring that other foot down where Daddy is tapping on the stair. Slow, slow, slow, like you have a parachute; just sink down and let the stair stop your foot."

Bryson succeeded about one time out of every ten attempts at getting both feet to that next lower step without needing to be held. As always, his frustration from failure defies description. He needed exhaustive verbal praise and affirmation *just* for trying. Each time he faltered, I merely set him back up for another try. As always, days turned into months, and months into years. Bryson's ability to do perfect ascents and descents on that "mountain" kept right on increasing.

His other activities also became more challenging. He still proceeded through his two-by-four walking path, only now he needed to "run" through, like football players run through tires or ropes. He often tripped on the two-by-fours, but I never let him hit the ground. He walked frontward, backward, and sideways on his twelve-foot planks now, as I moved them into differing angles. He jumped between them as I kept separating them for longer and longer leaps. We still used his cherished skateboard. Only now, it had a rope attached to it, and I would slowly pull him all around the gym as he maintained his balance on it, like a *real* skateboarder. The rope was only two feet long so that I could reach out and grab his arm each time he faltered off the board.

We did a "football" drill in which Bryson was required to close his eyes and pretend he was a running back as I jolted his upper body and shoulders (sort of like a tackle) from all sides. Since his eyes were closed, he never knew where the next "tackle" would come from. Like his hero Emmet Smith, he tried *so* hard to stay up; but I always grabbed him when he was heading down.

He was a huge Michael Jordan fan. As a reward for successfully completing a difficult activity, I would allow him to shoot a basketball toward the eight-foot baskets in the Stonybrook gym. Stonybrook's beloved gym teacher, Mr. Cutney, gave us a basketball to use. There was just one problem. Bryson couldn't get the ball more than a few inches away from his body. Sometimes his arms shot spastically upward, as the ball merely dropped to the ground. He'd get *very* upset at this, not understanding why he couldn't do what his heroes on TV could do, nor even what his little brother could do. I consulted with Bob Doman about this. As usual, he had the answer.

Bryson didn't like it when we brought a twelve-pound medicine ball to the gym. He liked it even less when I asked him to heave it up toward the basket. This didn't make any sense to him. I'll spare you most of the heated words we exchanged, but I think he nailed me on the "moron" thing. Anyway, when he began to understand that this would ultimately help him to reach the basket with a real basketball, he started trying *real* hard to heave up that black medicine ball. What experience and knowledge I gained from Bob Doman! It wasn't that Bryson lacked the *strength* to reach that basket. But Bob knew that shooting a basketball required the coordinated movement of the entire body. The shooter's body, legs, and arms all need to cooperate together.

As he bent down into a squat with that heavy ball, either his body would work in concert to push it up toward the basket, or he'd quickly be on the ground with a big, black ball on top of him. This did happen several times (I'll spare you the invectives). But amidst angry insults hurled in my direction, my courageous kid started pushing and pushing. I mean hard. *Real* hard! In typical Bryson fashion, when he decided he wanted something badly enough he was a pit bull. After each five-minute session with the medicine ball, I'd hand him a basketball. He *still* couldn't reach the eight-foot basket. But day after day, month after month his coördination began to improve.

Once again, my son amazed me. As I handed him the rebound from each "air-ball," he seemed unaware that I was even in the room. As he set himself for each shot, I realized He was very far away. He was Michael Jordan in the NBA finals, as the clock ticked down with the game on the line. For most of his fourth grade year, he never did reach that eight-foot basket. But he kept relentlessly trying, time after time, shot after shot, with no realization of the time that was passing by. Eventually, I'd have to insist that we move on to another activity. We had about twenty exercises and drills to complete during that two-hour session. But it won't shock you by now to learn that my little champion eventually did score a basket toward the end of that year, just about the time he turned twelve years old in May 1998. It then took another *year* to successfully reach the ten-foot basket. But nothing could ever hold him back when the fire of passion was lit inside.

This particular morning he was having a great time shooting at the eight-foot basket, and he was very proud. Just that week he had received his much-anticipated Pittsburgh Steelers hat for his "pwize." The hat was black, with the Steelers insignia on the front; and Bryson thought it was the coolest in his collection yet. We always finished our morning workout in the nurses office to do Bryson's spinning regimen in her swivel chair to stimulate his vestibular region (the inner ear), and to do his eye exercises. As always, Bryson held his new hat behind his back for Nancy Petronino, the nurse, to guess what his latest prize was. Nancy could never guess the "pwize" correctly; and, after a few guesses, Bryson proudly pulled out the Steeler hat for her to see.

When the bell rang at 9:15 a.m., I always gave Bryson a big hug, then watched nervously as he ambled down the crowded hallway toward his classroom, which was about fifty feet from the nurse's office. This was a special morning, as he proudly wore his Steelers cap. But before he went, he had an important question he wanted to get settled. I could tell that whatever was on his mind was serious, so I knelt down beside him and looked him in the eye. I'll add in the words he omitted: "Dad, [will] you [come] see me pway in a [the] NFL when I [I'm] a quarterback someday." You already know my answer: "Bryson, I wouldn't miss it for the world."

I strained to watch him walk through the crowd, hoping he would make it to his class without falling. He suddenly turned around, straining to see me. I held up my arm so he could see me above the mob of kids. When he saw me, he yelled, "I wuv you, Dad." As he stood watching me wave, he slowly began losing his balance as the weight of his backpack pulled him toward the wall. The other kids marched around him, pretending not to notice as his body fell to the bulletin board. He fought for his balance, pushing himself back to a standing position. With the wipeout averted, and my heart coming back down from my throat, I called, "I love you too, Bryce," and gave him the "thumbs up" sign. He returned the "thumbs up," and happily wobbled down the hall to his class, excitedly showing everyone his new Steelers hat as his aide led him inside.

As I drove to work that morning, I had a sense of peace and satisfaction. As difficult as those days often were, with injuries and illnesses and even an occasional emotional tsunami hitting our shores, I had a sense that things were turning around for my son now, and for our struggling family. Somehow we were going to make it. The climbing of the stairs, the scoring of baskets, the joy on his face as he showed off his new Steelers hat; well, let's just say those impossible mountains looming ahead were starting to look just a bit less intimidating.

Calling Down Fire

> "Lord, do You want us to command fire to come down from heaven and consume them?" But He turned and rebuked them, (and said, "You do not know what kind of spirit you are of; for the Son of Man did not come to destroy men's lives, but to save them.") And they went on.
>
> —Luke 9:54–56

Watch out when you sense that your mountain trail has, at long last, become smooth. God still has the prerogative to disrupt our plans as He weaves His higher purposes into our lives. Still, this was the *last* thing I *ever* anticipated God would allow. We knew those kids on the bus, and we knew their families. Some of them had been friends with Bryson for a few years now. He had begun the year so excited that he could finally come home on the bus with them. I always drove him to school in the morning, so we could do his early gym program. The bus ride home was only a *five*-minute trip. We thought it was safe, that it would be a growing experience.

Bryson's aide always got him onto the bus, and made sure his seat belt was secure. As the bus arrived on our block, my wife helped Bryson out of his seat belt and down the stairs. Bryson came off the bus that day *without* his prized Steelers hat, and my wife called me at work to let me know that Bryson was shaken and upset. By the time I got home from work, the mystery wasn't solved regarding what had upset him, nor was the whereabouts of the Steelers hat known. I questioned him gently, but he was still so traumatized he would say nothing.

Bryson would never have told on those bullies, not only due to fear and intimidation, but because he didn't possess the mental, emotional, or psychological ability to communicate such matters. We might never have known about it, had it not been for a courageous young girl who informed her mother about the cruel harassment that was ongoing, day after day, and also due to the missing Steelers hat. After remaining silent for some weeks, she had mustered the courage to tell her mother on this day, as the situation escalated to new levels. Her mother reported it to her teacher, who immediately informed Bette Esposito, the school principal.

We soon received a call from Bette, and what had happened became clear. Amidst the sad litany of torment throughout my son's life that had caused him to scream from his closet and make him wish he was "somebody else," one more element of his torture was now clear. The fifth grade bullies on that bus had been harassing Bryson (still in fourth grade) for some time now. On this day they had disconnected his seat belt and urged him to get up to kiss his seat, then they compelled him to stumble across the aisle to try to kiss the girls. They also coerced him to do a number of other degrading things, even as they made fun of him for being a "stupid moron."

How vicious and brutal to prey upon a handicapped boy, a child who was barely hanging on to his dignity, not to mention his will to live. He was trying *so* hard to be accepted even by them, his cruel abusers. He was confused about what they were doing, and why. Finally, those malicious punks coaxed and chanted for my son to throw his brand-new Steelers hat out the window. None of those bullies knew, or cared, how he valued that hat. None knew how hard he had worked for it. They cajoled and cheered until he yielded to their harassment. His tormented mind didn't possess the capacity to resist them. He finally relented, and threw his treasure away.

After Bette's phone call I was numb. The reason for my son's traumatized state was clear. These bullies were not only endangering his health, having him stumble through that bus, far worse, they were torturing his soul. And for *what?* For a few laughs, *that's* what! Oh yeah, what had happened was now clear. But that's not all that was clear to me. It immediately became clear how I'd handle this. I was going to call down fire upon those punks. No, I wouldn't touch those kids. I was too smart for that. But having coached in town the last few years, I knew their *fathers*. I'd go *right* to their houses and beat *them* to a pulp, and I'd do it at a time when I could be sure that their punk kids *watched*. As a quarterback in college, I prided myself in being as tough as some of our much bigger linemen, and had bench-pressed more than most of them. In my forties now, I was still in decent shape. But this wasn't a matter of size or of strength (nor obviously of intelligence). It was a matter of rage. I couldn't have been tied at this point.

This wasn't a good moment to ask me if I thought it reasonable to present my body as a living sacrifice to God. How much more was my defenseless *son* supposed to sacrifice? I was absolutely *enraged!* After all he'd been through for *so many* years now! Present my body as a living sacrifice? None of it seemed reasonable at this moment. *None* of it! Somehow, I agreed with Bette to allow her to meet with the boys the next morning before I took any further action. While I relented for the moment on what I was planning, I went out along that bus route searching for my son's hat. I never did find it. Thank God I didn't run into any of those kids.

Casting Mountains into the Sea

Silence filled the room the next morning as Bette began speaking to them. At first, these scared little rats were just afraid of getting into trouble. But under the guidance of this wise principal, the tide had begun to turn, and now the only sound in that office was that of weeping.

Bette had called all four of the offending bullies into her office, without telling them why she had called them in. They were not aware that the brave little girl had informed her mother about what had been going on and, well...you know the rest of it. Without mentioning Bryson's name, Bette had asked the boys if they could tell *her* about something very wrong that was happening on the bus. One by one, the boys confessed that they had been "teasing" Bryson.

Bette then asked them if they had *any* idea who Bryson was as a human being. The silence intensified now, and she began to tell them his story. Having had him in her class for an entire year, and having been our friend for several, she was well qualified to tell it. She informed them that Bryson was once just as sharp-minded, strong, and healthy as any of them. She revealed that something terrible happened to him when he was very young. She told them that he had nearly died, and that when he survived he was left permanently brain injured and crippled.

She informed them how Bryson had battled back, working relentlessly throughout his entire lifetime just to get to the point during the last few years at which he was able to walk, and do some of the simple things that healthy children like them merely take for granted, such as attend Stonybrook School. She told them Bryson had more courage than *anyone* she had ever met in her entire life. She told them that he worked extremely hard every single morning before they were even awake, *right* in the Stonybrook gym, in his courageous effort to recapture fragments of life that his injury had robbed him of. Then Bette sat back and remained silent.

The faces of all four boys turned white now, and the two "toughest" ones were crying. Bette had made her point convincingly. She turned the situation completely around, giving these boys the opportunity to see the seriousness of what they had done, and a chance to grieve their damaging behavior deep down. At the same time, she had revealed to them a glimpse of just how exceptional and courageous a person Bryson really was.

Her point powerfully made, Bette suggested that the boys come to an agreement amongst themselves regarding how they should make amends for the damage they had done. On their own, the boys decided that they would not only apologize to Bryson, they would become his troop of protectors and guardians in school, and especially on the bus. These "tough" guys made a pact that no one would dare to hurt Bryson's feelings, ever again, or they would have to answer to them. Oh, I know what you're thinking. I thought the same thing when Bette first told me about this. But in the years to come, those boys made good on that pact.

I hung up the phone later that morning after Bette finished informing me of this resolve to the situation. Now it wasn't only those boys who were in tears on that day. I was amazed. Make that stunned! I was also ashamed and more than a little afraid at what I knew I was capable of, and how little I had trusted God to resolve this situation in His own way. God only knows how His Spirit gave me restraint. I don't remember praying for it. I didn't even want it! Nor did I want to talk to God that previous night. I just wanted revenge!

I have no doubt there are many sitting in jails right now who were equally convinced they needed to take matters into their own hands. Praise God that He provides a way of escape, if we will take it (1 Cor. 10:13). But don't ever try to limit how our King might choose to deliver us from temptation. All I can tell you is that, on this occasion, He delivered me from doing harm in *spite* of myself, not due to any righteousness or maturity on my part. I didn't even have the presence of mind to know *how* to pray in this situation. I guess God had that base covered too (Rom. 8:26). Praise Him that He remembers the frailty of our flesh, and provides for our lack by His Spirit. Praise Him that He uses even our shameful moments to teach us, again and again, that *He* is our only true hope for change. Clearly, if His lovingkindnesses or compassions *ever* cease, we are all finished! But, praise God, His mercies endure forever (Ps. 136, NKJV).

It's funny. I once thought all the mountains needing to be conquered in my life were out there in front of me. Through the years I've realized, often to my shame, that some of the most dangerous mountain peaks that ever need to be conquered, some of the vilest "hell" that can ever break loose against my commitment to Christ, isn't "out there" at all. Those dangerous peaks are more like volcanoes than mere mountains, and they exist inside my own fearful, fleshly soul.

King of the Mountains

While tucking Bryson into bed that evening, I gently questioned him about what had happened the previous day on the bus ride home. Knowing how confusing and threatening this situation had been for him, I tried to be nonchalant, mixing in some discussion about the week's upcoming NFL match-ups. My son possessed neither the intellectual skill nor the emotional capacity to say much about what he was feeling deep inside. But finally, he began to open up a bit. As always, I'll add in his omitted words.

"A [the] boys like me again. They said they [were] sorry." A vestige of tears formed in his tender eyes. They were tears of relief, I think, now that the cruelty and oppression were over. I waited, hoping the tears might begin to flow more freely. He needed them to. He needed to allow some of his grief and anguish to flow out along with those tears. But as mentioned, my little tough guy had developed a pretty hard shell around his fragile soul. His eyes just remained slightly wet, and that was all, at least for now. I took one more stab at pursuing this deeper, asking him if it had made him sad when the boys were being mean to him. But seeing the look of concern on my face and noticing the intentional tone in my voice, the mist in his eyes dried up quickly. He abruptly changed the subject, saying, "Smile, Dad. Be happy! They [are] my friends now."

> Bryson, you are a young man in your mid-twenties as I write these words, and you don't even remember this incident, do you? Nor does your injured

mind have the capacity even now to understand many of the sad and difficult things I've written in this book, things that have drastically altered the course of your life. But I will never forget these events, my son; and I also remember the request you made of me on that day, long ago. I will be happy, not only because I know what is going to happen for you one day, but for me too, and for all who long for the great King's appearing. And you want to hear something funny, my boy, something I never learned until I was far older than you? As I gaze back on all the mountains we've already climbed together, you and me, I finally realized it was never our task to conquer those mountains at all.

Jesus is King of every mountain, my son, and He has already conquered them all. Nothing *ever* challenges His power. Of course, we have our part in climbing them, but our part is often very different than what we think it is. Our part is to make right choices as we walk with the King, day by day. The King has so much yet to teach us. We are to listen to Him, to obey Him, and to repent of our sinful choices and actions when we have failed to obey.

But do you want to hear one of the strangest tasks the King has given us to do, my son? We are to surrender our lives and *even* our bodies fully into His good hands, even as the great King surrendered His body for us on a cross long ago. You asked me to be happy, my son. *This* is the way to be content and happy in this world. It is the King's way; and as strange as it sounds, it is the *only* reasonable way to live.

And though you still don't like to talk about your anguish and your pain, the King remembers all the crushing blows that have ever injured your body, and He has never forgotten a single detail of all those tsunamis that have crashed upon your shores. He knows that the repair of your tormented mind and tortured soul is one of the highest mountains you still need to climb in this world. But did you know that there are many tortured regions in my own soul still badly in need of repair? Yes, this is true of your dad, and the same is true of the soul of every person reading your story in this book right now. We've all suffered indescribable pain in this world, and we all need to climb that very same mountain with the King so that we can be healed too.

But the end of the story is the best part, my son. All those who belong to the King and who have worshiped Him in this world will see Him face-to-face one day. There will be no more mountains to climb then, since His work in us will finally be done. When we see Him, we will be like Him, changed in an instant. Then Jesus, the great King of the mountains will bring us all home. There will be no more pain, no more sorrow on that day, nor will there ever be again. That will be a great day, my son; and I will be happy. Yes, my boy, that's going to be a great day.

Beloved, now we are children of God, and it has not appeared as yet what we shall be. We know that, when He appears, we shall be like Him, because we shall see Him just as He is.

—1 John 3:2

Chapter 24
THE TIMES THEY ARE A-CHANGIN'

Come gather 'round people Wherever you roam And admit that the waters Around you have grown And accept it that soon You'll be drenched to the bone.... For the times they are a-changin'.[1]

Bob Dylan

Some of you reading this book are grateful that God has enabled you to overcome some steep obstacles in life. You've seen, again and again, that the Lord never leaves, never forsakes, that He's always good to His Word. No doubt, you've got a few scars from past battles. Who doesn't? But those battles have seasoned you, somehow they've strengthened you. Now, at long last, you can *finally* catch your breath. Your confidence is returning and you almost feel ready to take on new mountains, to strive toward new opportunities with a sense of freedom and purpose. You're ready to live your best life now! Then it happens. Another earthquake! The landscape begins moving violently and your future, once again, becomes a frightening, moving target.

You thought you had that disease beaten. A new medical report now indicates there's another problem. A phone call informs you there's been an accident. Someone you love is gone. You didn't even have the chance to say "good-bye." You find a stash of drugs in your son's drawer. You knew he was hanging with the wrong crowd, but you never suspected *this*! Your teen daughter tearfully confesses she is pregnant. You prayed *so* hard for her to turn from her rebellion. Your husband stuns you by announcing he's leaving you for a younger woman. How could he betray the family like this? Your wife coldly informs you she is filing for divorce. Our culture and her friends, even at church, have convinced her that she deserves to be happy. A business partner swindles you out of the fortune that took *decades* of sweat and blood to build. All hopes of retiring to that golf community, or even with a shred of dignity, now have vanished.

Freedom? Purpose? Forget it! Life has once again been flipped like a pancake, and the future that looked so stable and promising a moment ago has turned into MacArthur's Park.

There are seasons in life when the seas are calm and the sailing is smooth. Praise God for those. But when we convince ourselves that all the storms and sorrows of life are behind us, get ready for a reality check. The times are *always* a changin.' Sometimes the changes are for the good, but sometimes they slam us back down to the turf, knocking the wind and even our desire to live right out of us. In the blink of an eye we can find ourselves in a valley that is deeper and darker than we've ever known. Only this time, the supports we've been able to stand on in the past may have turned to quicksand. We're not as young as we once were and our health is faltering, the relationships we've always counted on have crumbled, the financial portfolio once capable of cushioning our fall isn't quite as stellar. We're quickly overmatched, and we know it.

Often, the changes that bring discouragement are less dramatic, just the natural consequences of life moving on. One wouldn't expect them to be traumatic. Yet change is always hard, even the normal, anticipated changes of life. Your last baby leaves for college or gets married and your nest is now "suddenly" empty. You knew this day would come and you thought you'd be ready. But it's *crushing* you. You'd always been so close with your kids. They were your best friends. Now they're gone, and a hole the size of the Grand Canyon is left behind, in your home and in your heart. Some of you could only wish for such pain. You were never as close with your children as you dreamed when they were born. Anger, rebellion, and screaming matches marked their adolescent years. The wars left you battle weary and broken. Now that they're gone, your empty nest stands as just another monument to a life fraught with failed, pain-filled relationships.

For many, retirement ushers in change, but hardly the leisure and adventure you dreamed of. Instead, there's month after month of boredom, loneliness, and health challenges. Plans for that second career never quite took root, and your kids and grandkids never seem to have enough time to enjoy all the ball games and fishing trips you envisioned. All those Viagra commercials seem just a cruel joke. Your bitter relationship with your spouse makes you fantasize of painting water colors on the beach in Tahiti, alone. In your quiet moments, you wonder what all the years of hard work have really been for, who in the world you are.

I don't mean to present a jaded view; and frankly, I don't think I've done that. Pleasant surprises and blessings often come to our lives during times of transition. But one thing is certain in a world fraught with change: we all need something to hold onto. Times of change are times of vulnerability, sometimes causing us to feel numb and out of control. It should come as no surprise that a serpent shows up during these times, to offer us some of his age-old "wisdom."

He has no lack of gurus numbered among his troops, just ready and willing to offer us safe passage through the minefields of change. Their methods can seem novel, but there's nothing new under the sun. Satan is the consummate master marketer. To every generation he recycles and repackages the *same* deceptive wares he has been selling the human race since the dawn of time. His theme of deception was first revealed in the Garden of Eden, and it was designed to convince Adam and Eve that they could handle the challenges of life without God. David Tripp illustrates this in his excellent book *Instruments in the Redeemer's Hands.*

> Satan was offering a different path to wisdom.... His words suggest that however beautiful God's revelation, it is not really necessary. Satan's wisdom places people's lives in their own hands, so that they rely on their own ability to think, interpret, understand, and apply. The Serpent is selling Eve the most attractive and cruelest of lies, the lie of autonomy and

> self-sufficiency. He offers her wisdom that does not need to bow the knee to God.... Adam and Eve must listen to one voice or the other, and their decision, like ours, has lasting implications.[2]

We must be careful who we listen to as the tides of change roll into our lives. Irrespective of whether we've been tossed into a deep, dark valley or find ourselves facing a relatively painless transition, we are susceptible targets. If the serpent had horns and a tail, we'd spot him coming a country mile away. But when he shows up as an angel of light (2 Cor. 11:14) offering efficacious wisdom sugarcoated with a few Bible verses, discernment becomes far more difficult. To avoid being deceived during seasons of change, we need something solid to hold onto, something that never changes, something that will prove worthy as an anchor for our souls.

> Jesus Christ is the same yesterday and today and forever. Do not be carried away by varied and strange teachings; for it is good for the heart to be strengthened by grace.
>
> —HEBREWS 13:8–9

> God is our refuge and strength, a very present help in trouble. Therefore we will not fear, though the earth should change and though the mountains slip into the heart of the sea.
>
> —PSALM 46:1–2

GINGERSNAP

The times were indeed a changin' in our struggling family, and so was Bryson's body. He faced the bizarre world of middle school with the mind of a tender young child inside the rapidly changing body of an adolescent. The middle years are difficult times of change for every child. For Bryson, they represented just one more mountain of absurd impossibility. His severe lack of balance and primitive motor skills still didn't afford him the ability to bathe, dress, or toilet himself; and it was becoming clear that goals such as riding a bike, hiking a mountain trail, or even tying his own shoes would probably never occur.

His physical limitations, while exhausting, continued to be relatively easy to deal with as compared to his mental impairments. Angry traumas erupted daily within his soul, as sparks of frustration lit emotional brush fires without warning. Those brush fires had to be quickly and shrewdly dealt with to keep the entire forest of his mind from being set ablaze. Parents of a brain-injured child must always be on their toes, *especially* during the middle school years.

I felt the need to be more in prayer than ever during this difficult season of his life. I knew what Paul had taught about praying without ceasing (1 Thess. 5:17); and this seemed wise, even vital. But frankly, this instruction never seemed all that practical in a world that required such intense effort and focus just to make it through another day. How does one pray continually while at the same time sweating bullets to get all the necessary daily tasks done? Praying without ceasing is a pleasant notion to talk about in Sunday school, but honestly, not very realistic. If the Lord wanted me to obey this command, then He was going to have to enlighten me.

As inept as I was in praying without ceasing for my son, there was one thing I knew Bryson could *always* count on, namely, his yellow lab, Gingersnap. Ginger had become an illustrious member of the Milazzo household several years back, when Bryson was eight. Ironically, we originally planned for her to become a walk dog for our son. But when Bob Doman declared, "We'll make it happen," and we determined once and for all to set our sights solely toward independent walking, Gingersnap's role was refocused merely as the family pet. But don't hear me saying Gingersnap was ordinary. I told you way back in the introduction to this book I'd be brutally honest with you. The truth is that *your* dog is ordinary, not Gingersnap.

Now, don't get huffy with me. I'm sure your dog is fine. But how can I describe Gingersnap? I'll stop just short of describing her as a superhero. But in Bryson's eyes she was as supernatural as a dog could be. Her nose got into just about *everything* in the Milazzo home, including Bryson's bath routine. You didn't need to tell her it was bath time. The three of us all nearly killed each other eagerly attempting to get through the bathroom door simultaneously. Well, at least two of us were eager. The third was a weary, if not wickedly handsome dad (so much for honesty). But regarding the bath, darned if that crazy dog didn't *love* the taste of shampoo!

She'd go bananas as I lathered Bryson's hair, just waiting for cups of warm water to be poured over his head. Bryson giggled up a storm as Gingersnap lapped at his shoulders as the shampoo cascaded down. He thought it was absolutely hilarious that her snout and his dad's shirt were both thoroughly soaked at the end of bath time each night.

After getting him clean I'd let my son play in the water a while, as Gingersnap and I sat on the bathroom floor and waited. I'd say we waited patiently, but I'm trying hard to be honest (and handsome) in this book, remember? As always, I had *so* many loose ends hanging in my work and in my life. Patience wasn't my highest virtue, not by a long shot. Too much on my mind! As always, Bryson drifted into a fantasy world as he played. But as I sat there, waterlogged, something noteworthy *always* occurred, not just once, but several times during each bath. Bryson would suddenly turn to me and greet me as if I'd just walked into the room. I hadn't gone anywhere, yet he'd turn and enthusiastically exclaim, "Hi, Dad!" And a few moments later as he played on, he'd do this again, "Hi, Dad!" then again, and again, every few minutes.

This greeting would also continuously occur as we sat at the dinner table, watched the Yankees on TV, or drove in the car. In fact, it was typical for him to render a periodic, "Hi Dad!" *whenever* we were together. Each time my presence came back into his conscious awareness, he'd greet me with an enthusiastic, "Hi, Dad!" as if he hadn't seen me in a week. It didn't matter where we were, or who was there to overhear him. And each time he greeted me I simply responded, "Hi, Bryce," no matter where we were, no matter whom else heard our interaction. Therapists have advised me that this is a phenomenon called "perseveration." Through the years I've come to believe that this aspect of childlike behavior ought not to be diminished by a clinical label. In fact, I've come to believe we must *all* become childlike.

> Truly I say to you, whoever does not receive the kingdom of God like a child will not enter it at all.
>
> —Luke 18:17

Paul's exhortation to pray without ceasing isn't a suggestion, it's a command (1 Thess. 5:17). But if we ever hope to obey this command, we had better figure out how to become childlike. One of the hardest things for mature adults to admit is that we don't really have a clue how to pray (Rom. 8:26). With all our sophisticated knowledge, it's so easy to miss the simplicity of our need to cry out to our Abba or Daddy (v. 15). "Please forgive us, Daddy, for our 'maturity.'" Oswald Chambers drew a picture of the "nowness" of prayer.

> We make prayer the preparation for work, it is never that in the Bible.... Don't say—I will endure this until I can get away and pray. Pray now; draw on the grace of God in the moment of need.... Keep drawing on the grace of God in every conceivable condition you may be in.[3]

For years I was utterly confused by the concept of "practicing the presence of God." Was this "practice" just for monks like Brother Lawrence? Was it like practicing piano? Maybe it was more like taking batting practice. Don't smirk out there! Most of you are just as "mature" and lost about this as I am. You've tried just about *everything* to pray without ceasing, to practice the presence of God, haven't you? When I realized my need to become childlike, I finally started getting somewhere. When I began laying a, "Hi, Dad," on my Daddy each time I consciously remembered He was with me throughout the day, what a difference this began to make! This will make a difference for you too. Give it a shot and see what happens.

Start saying, "Hi, Dad!" to your Abba Father *each* and *every* time you remember His presence throughout the day. Don't think this represents a flippant attitude. The fear of God is the beginning of wisdom (Prov. 9:10). But once we've begun in wisdom and committed our lives to Daddy, we've received a spirit of adoption as sons by which we can (and must) cry out to Him (Rom. 8:14–15). God *is* with us. Accept this in simplicity without trying to connect all sorts of lofty theology to it. If we start trying to put the reality of Daddy's presence into a doctrinal test tube to analyze it, we'll wreck it. We walk by faith in God's Word. Accept it. More importantly, *say* it!

Don't think I'm asking you to pretend or to play a game of make-believe. Bryson wasn't pretending. He was simply *remembering* that his daddy was with him, and so must we. When you think this through, there's no pretending involved. We're merely acting upon reality. In his outstanding book *The Red Sea Rules*, Robert Morgan revealed how he speaks to God directly and simply, visualizing God actually being in the room with him.

> I speak to Him naturally as to a friend. It isn't a matter of projecting an imaginary image of God and pretending He's there. It's a matter of recognizing the presence of God who really is there.[4]

Say, "Hi, Dad," out loud when you're alone driving in your car. Say, "Hi, Friend" (John 15:15), when you're out for a walk. Whisper a quick, "Lord, I need You now," when you're in a tight spot and need some wisdom fast. Say, "Dad, your boy is in trouble," when you're tempted to dwell on that lustful image. "Hi, Jesus, your girl needs help," when you're just dying to add to that gossip. It will be twice as hard to act upon that lust or participate in that gossip when you remember Daddy is with you. When a testy situation develops, say, "Hi, Jesus, this situation is all wrong and I'm getting way too angry. I need You right now, or I'll say something I'll really regret!" Say, "Hi, Dad," when you're afraid. Hear Him remind you to trust (Ps. 56:3–4). When you're doing the best you can at work, yet the wheels still keep flying off, whisper, "Hey, Dad. You know I'm really struggling here. Thanks for being with me so I don't have to struggle alone."

If we will reach out in a simple, "Hi, Dad!" way each time we remember His presence, several things are bound to happen. First, we'll delight our Daddy's heart, even as Bryson always delighted me, and still does to this day in his mid twenties (yes, he still says, "Hi, Dad!"). But with Daddy, what we give is always far exceeded by what we receive back. Daddy will encourage our hearts, reminding us that He will *never* leave, *never* forsake us (Heb. 13:5), that He has *no* condemnation for us (Rom. 8:1), that He remains solidly *for* us as His precious sons, His precious daughters (v. 31). And when the next tsunami of devastating change slams across our shores, we'll be in the practice of the presence of our King, our Shepherd, our Savior, our Priest, our Teacher, our Friend, and, of course, our Daddy. His presence will give us the peace to survive, and the joy and confidence we need to thrive in the midst of every sorrow.

Daddy has made us vastly wealthy, but it is our choice whether that wealth will provide us with any practical benefit when unwanted changes come flooding into our lives. The King's kids don't honor Daddy by cringing in fear. We honor Daddy by trusting that He holds eternity in His hands, and by believing that we are *never* victims of chance. We honor Daddy by moving into the stream of His presence and power, as Amy Carmichael so eloquently taught.

> From hour to hour, He can and will lead us on to triumph—if we look to Him.…Over and over again I have seen the Lord do "impossible" things. I think He delights to do the impossible! And He delights to meet the faith of one who looks up to Him and says, "Lord, you know that I cannot do this—but I believe that you can!"…All the tremendous forces of nature—weather and politics and human nature too—are all at the beck and call of our God.…How utterly foolish it is to plead weakness when we—even you and I—may move into the stream of that power. If only we will.[5]

It takes a child to believe that Daddy is in control of the forces of nature, weather, politics, and human nature too. Are we willing to trust with childlike faith, or are we merely content to *say* we believe as we practically rely on our woefully inadequate, "adult" resources? We have been invited by Daddy to move into the stream of His power. Don't be too sophisticated for your own good. Don't wait until new waves of sorrow and change arrive at your shores. Live as a child. Practice His presence *now*. Look up with childlike faith and say it! "Hi, Dad!"

> For you have not received a spirit of slavery leading to fear again, but you have received a spirit of adoption as sons by which we cry out, "[Hi, Dad!] Abba! Father!"
>
> —Romans 8:15

You Call This Vacation?

Bryson had always been a square peg in a world of round holes. During the middle school years the holes seemed to be getting smaller, even as his body was getting larger. We tried to battle back against the stressful tides of change by getting away for day trips. What bittersweet family times these were. I remember going to amusement parks such as the Land of Make Believe in Hope, New Jersey. Tim and Janelle raced right over to the roller coaster and other rides geared for healthy, older children, as I strapped Bryson into the cockpit of a kiddie airplane ride.

The ride lifted him up off the ground, maybe ten feet, then circled gently up and down, round and round. I prayed silently that he might not notice that all the other kids were half his age, and that his siblings were enjoying rides and amusements that he couldn't participate in. He seemed to be having fun; but at the same time I had the strong impression he was sad, that deep inside he knew he was out of place on that ride, and in this world. I couldn't help thinking that his feelings must be a cauldron of confusion, even as mine were, as he kept circling round and round gripping his steering wheel, and as the other parents tried not to stare.

The scene was similar when we took him for pony rides at the local zoo. Other parents snapped away with their cameras as their young children waived and held onto the horn of the saddle with one hand. Bryson clung to that saddle horn with both hands, and I clung to him with both hands right next to that pony as we circled around, to keep him from falling off. We were both clinging to the past, I suppose, both terrified to let go. Oh, but, ready or not, the tides of change had come. My son was too big to be inconspicuous, and despite his mental challenges, he was too smart not to notice that he didn't fit in. It was beginning to seem impossible to fit him in *anywhere*.

I've mentioned a few times in this book that I heard a clock in the background, ticking away against my son's childhood. The waves of change relentlessly swept in during those awkward middle school years, and that cursed clock was deafening, *taunting* me that no matter what we might choose to do for him now, it was too late. We had fought the good fight. We had given it our very best shot. We had failed!

"Oh, Daddy! Won't it *ever* get easier? Will my son *always* be faced with such hell in this world?" *Every* phase of his life had been a knockdown, drag out battle. It had been a war to wake him from his slumber in the years following his brain injury. It had been a war to get him talking and walking. It had been a war to get him into school with normal peers. It had been a war to battle for his health against infections and diseases that nearly killed him. With adolescence now upon us, I wasn't even sure where the field of battle was anymore. Bryson was making his desire for more in life stridently known through continual episodes of anger and frustration. Not knowing how to comfort him, there were days when I felt like throwing up the white flag.

We tried each summer to bring a modicum of rest to our struggling family by taking our show on the road. Our custom was to vacation at Camp of the Woods, a Christian resort in the Adirondack Mountains of New York. There were uplifting spiritual opportunities and lots of fun, healthy activities for the entire family. But as all families with special-needs children know, the word "vacation" is a misnomer. In many respects, vacation is harder than just staying home.

Camp of the Woods is nestled around a gorgeous Adirondack lake, with natural terrain that was too rugged for Bryson to walk independently on. I carried him on my back or on my shoulders for most of the week as we took hikes and traveled from one activity to another. This made me determined to continue working out to remain strong enough to carry him. He wasn't getting any smaller, and I wasn't getting any younger—although arguably I *was* getting better looking. Oh, why did I promise to be honest in this book! The truth is, I was the only one arguing this.

As usual, Bryson wanted to participate in everything, but modifying the activities to meet his needs was an exasperating chore. The mini-golf course had natural and manmade "hazards," which were beautifully designed. But few things in life are more hazardous to a child with cerebral palsy than the fun stuff. I carefully carried him to each hole, placing him down in front of the ball, and tried to keep him balanced as he took his swing. He'd get *so* frustrated when his uncoordinated hands couldn't hold the club straight. I needed to position his club so that it faced the ball, and then gently move his hands and club toward the ball. He'd sometimes angrily whip the club out of my hands, and take a wild swing. I got clonked on the shins (and on other body parts that shall remain nameless) more times than I can remember. I recall my back aching, and my emotions hurting far worse as I tried to calm my son's frustrations in the summertime heat.

For several years we rented a cabin owned by friends, Manny and Arlene Laidig. When not at the resort, Bryson wanted to spend every waking moment playing Wiffle Ball on Manny's front lawn, with the Jacobsen kids from next door. I was always the pitcher, placing the ball where Bryson could hit home runs with his plastic "Monster Bat." Bryson was in his glory, fantasizing that he was hitting 'em out of Yankee Stadium. "A three boys" often went onto Manny's spacious front lawn by the lake, and I hit hard baseballs to them. Tim would get high pops, and I'd hit very slow grounders to Bryson. His deficient eye-hand coordination most often prevented him from getting the ball into his glove, but sometimes he was able to knock it down. Then he'd nab it, and throw it, usually wild, somewhere. Much patience was required by Tim as Bryson demanded endless do-overs before Tim's next turn.

Playing basketball was a bit more challenging. Bryson couldn't dribble the ball, nor could he reach the ten-foot basket consistently. So I became his basket, making a hoop with my arms. My chest was the backboard. He juked around the court without even trying to dribble, clasping the ball with both hands, fighting to maintain his balance. Finally, he'd make his big move and shoot or dunk the ball through my arms. You name it; he tried *everything*, from ping-pong as we held the paddle in his hands, to floating in a tube in the lake, to riding on the back of my bike, an adolescent boy on a special trailer made for younger children.

The emotional and physical energy required *every* hour by special needs families fighting to fit their square pegs into this world's round holes is beyond words. These families are often exhausted and demoralized, though they may not show it. Their stress *never* ends, whether on vacation or at home. If you happen to notice such a family on vacation, encourage and help them in some small way. No, you can't solve all their problems. Then again, little acts of kindness are never really all that little, are they? Open your eyes and be bold in God's love (Eph. 2:10).

Toy Helmets and Wake-up Calls

Sunday afternoons in the fall meant watching football, and going out to our front yard at halftime so Bryson could play in his toy helmet. I'd throw long passes to Tim, and at ten years old he was already catching them with one hand. As I've already mentioned in another chapter, Tim would one day become the Athlete of the Year at his high school. Yet right from birth, it was never easy to be a brother to Bryson. You want to know a good definition of the word *champion?* A champion is someone who does what is necessary in life without complaint, even when it's hard. The thing that made me proudest of Tim is that he *never* complained. He had a servant's heart, always helping to fit his square peg brother into all those holes, even on those toy-helmet days.

Bryson proudly wore his toy Cowboys helmet as he huddled us up and called some of the zaniest triple reverse pass plays you ever saw. He seemed oblivious to the passing of time, and much patience was needed by Tim and me. Bryson always wound up running for a touchdown on his turn, at least on the plays he could stay up. If he fell or threw a wild pass, he'd insist on a do-over. Ever the obsessive perfectionist, those plays were run over and over. He had the perfect ending in mind for every play and every game. Sometimes, "perfect" takes forever and a day.

This particular Sunday afternoon I took Bryson to the junior football field in Kinnelon, which was set up with real yard lines and end zones. I didn't know the Kinnelon Colts team was having a real game against a rival town on this day, but it didn't bother Bryson that we couldn't play on the official field. The referee's whistles and the noise of the crowd only added to his excitement as we played on the practice field off to the side. Though Bryson still struggled to walk without falling, he somehow remained confident he'd play in the NFL one day, like his heroes Troy Aikman, Emmet Smith, Deion Sanders, and Brett Favre.

Tim had stayed home on this day, so it was just me and Bryson. He'd let my kickoff roll to a stop, then he'd scoop up the ball and begin running. I'd dive on the ground just past him as he eluded my "tackles." Sometimes he lost his balance and fell, pretending to be tackled; sometimes he made it all the way to the end zone. No doubt, my son was having a blast, but moments like these were bittersweet. My son still seemed to have no idea he wasn't really breaking tackles, or that his toy helmet wasn't like the real ones worn by his peers on the field *right* next to us.

After their game was over, Bryson saw some of his classmates in their Kinnelon Colts uniforms walking by. Never one to be shy, he called for them to come and join us in our game. There's *nothing* he enjoyed more than playing a "real" game with friends. A few answered that they couldn't. No problem! Bryson simply began calling out to the others. Some of the players had taken off their shoulder pads and were hanging out with cheerleaders by the snack barn. Others were on their way to the parking lot with parents, ready to go home. None were willing to join Bryson in our game on this day. So we decided to keep on playing ourselves.

I kicked off to him again and chased after him. I dove on the ground next to him, as he juked past me on his way to another touchdown. I knew he was trying *so* hard to stay up and run for long touchdowns, to impress his friends nearby. He fell several times during our game, but he was savvy enough to make his falls appear to simulate being tackled to the ground. After about thirty minutes more of play, with his knees scraped and dirty, Bryson decided that his Cowboys had defeated my team, the Jets, 52–7.

He looked across the field to see several of the kids who said they couldn't play with us now playing a pick-up game of their own. This seemed to hurt my son, since this is exactly what he had wanted them to do with us. I couldn't blame those kids. I knew how difficult it was to include Bryson. On other days some of those same great kids would've gone out of their way to include him. But sometimes it just didn't happen. Today was one of those discouraging days. My son said nothing, yet I could tell he was taking the rejection hard.

Noticing the hurt in his eyes, I immediately suggested that we go for ice cream. He refused. He had just been through a tough bout with a debilitating illness, and Monday would be his first day back in school in *two* weeks. Maybe we had overdone it. Maybe he was just exhausted. Taking one more shot, I again suggested that we go for ice cream. But keeping his head and eyes down he softly said, "Let go home, Dad" (he still couldn't say "let's"). I'd rarely seen my son this dejected. I felt helpless, impotent. Not knowing what else to say or do, I just picked him up and carried him up the steep hill that led to the parking lot.

Bryson still liked to sit in the back seat, like a young child. I buckled his adolescent body in, and we began our drive home, in silence. Usually my son was full of chatter after a good game on a Sunday afternoon. Clearly he was hurting now, and I began to think about what might cheer him up at home. My thoughts began to wander to what might have been had he not sustained his tragic brain injury. Instead of being avoided by other kids, would they be arguing over who could have him on their team as they chose sides? Would he be the star athlete that his little brother was becoming, and the star of that Kinnelon Colts team? One thing's certain, there's *no way* he'd be off to the side in a toy helmet, trying to stem the tide of his loneliness with his dad. As my mind filled with all these thoughts, bittersweet took a hard left turn toward bitter.

I was deep in thought now. Yes, we'd come a long way. No one will ever convince me we hadn't received mighty miracles from the hand of God. But why hadn't God *finished* those miracles? Why didn't He heal him *completely?* I looked at my discouraged son in the rearview mirror. I remembered how sad he looked in his child seat many years before as I drove him home from a Manhattan hospital, after the gravity of his brain injury was confirmed. That picture will be etched in my mind forever, and I'll *never* forget that dreadful nursery rhyme springing to my mind for the first time, "All the king's horses and all the king's men couldn't put Humpty Dumpty together again." Now, *all* these years later, here my son was, *still* in the back seat, *still* broken, *still* so sad. *O God!* Won't this nightmare *ever* end?

My son's body was growing toward manhood. His mind was not. How long can these toy-helmet days last? What if he always remains so childlike, so vulnerable? How can he ever understand, no less accept his challenges as a square peg in this round-hole world? What will happen when I'm no longer here to bathe him and tie his shoes? After all he had lost, all he had suffered through the years, I could tolerate just about *anything* but the thought of my son winding up dejected and hopeless, hating his life. If *that* was the result, what had all the excruciating work, all the progress, all the miracles been for? What if the critics were right all along? They had warned us we were just building up false hopes, both for ourselves and for our son. And what if…? Suddenly my thoughts were interrupted—make that jolted back to reality—from the back seat: "Hi, Dad!"

Bryson had suddenly remembered that his daddy was with him in the car; so as always, he greeted me. His tone wasn't as enthusiastic as usual, and his subdued greeting seemed more of a question this time. Still, his voice rang in my ears like an alarm bell, a loud wake-up call. I suddenly realized that this was no time to try to answer all these questions floating in my head. And it certainly wasn't the time to accept the fear being offered up on a silver platter from the pit of hell. I shook off those faithless thoughts and tried to refocus.

My vulnerable son didn't need my fear added to his discouragement. It was time to answer his greeting, his question, with *confidence.* Somehow I had to help him understand that everything was going to be okay. But how? My brain-injured son still couldn't comprehend all that much about the great King of the universe, the only One who could possibly make everything "okay." Then it struck me. Neither did I! No, Bryson couldn't grasp complex theological concepts about his Creator. But he *did* have a daddy, one who was very near. I had better stop pitying myself and begin looking at things a little more simply, just like my son.

None of us understands all that much about Daddy, do we? The sum total of all our erudite sophistication is mere sandbox play in terms of truly understanding. Wise men and women realize that there's a higher question, one that is more important than all our lofty theological debates. Whose daddy are you, dear reader? *That* is the question. To give up and give in to our personal fears and languish in despair is to forfeit the opportunity to love those who desperately need us in this world, and to fail to be someone's daddy, mommy, brother, or sister.

Clearly, I didn't have all the answers for my son's future, or for my own in those days. I still don't possess those answers as I write these pages, these many years later. Honestly, the future still seems so impossible sometimes. But I praise God that Jesus, the One who exhorted us to become as a little child, has explained all that I really need to know. He is the radiance of God's glory, the exact representation of His nature. I had better keep looking to *Him* if I hope to gain *any* insight at all.

The times are always a changin', and there's no way to stop them from relentlessly moving on. So let 'em change! Bryson's childlike greeting from the backseat reminded me there *is* a Daddy-King. Instead of demanding answers, perhaps we can all become like my son and simply trust that since Daddy is near, everything is going to be okay. As I continued driving I realized this was the only answer I needed at this moment, the only answer I'd ever need for any other moment. I blinked away the tears, cleared my throat, and answered him with the confidence he deserved and needed to hear from his daddy: *"Hi, Bryce!"* Daddy is near to the brokenhearted and saves those who are crushed in spirit (Ps. 34:18).

The Loser Now Will Be Later to Win

> Come writers and critics who prophesize with your pen…keep your eyes wide, the chance won't come again…the loser now will be later to win, for the times they are a changin'.[6]
>
> —Bob Dylan

When I played interscholastic sports in high school and college, my definition of *winner* and *champion* was cut and dried, designated solely to those who came out victorious on the scoreboard. If you challenged me on that meaning, I'd have defended my definition with vigor, thinking that only losers might suggest otherwise. Don't tell me that you're one of *those* who think that playing a good game has as much value as actually winning? Give me a *break!* What was it that one of my childhood heroes said? Oh yes, Vince Lombardi said, "Winning isn't everything, it's the only thing."[7] Take *that, loser!* Case closed! Or is it?

Yes, the times, they were a changin' during Bryson's middle school years.

And with all due respect to Vince, my definition of the word *champion* was also changing. Maybe my square peg son couldn't participate in organized football, but he strove to participate in as many recreation league sports as he could during adolescence. He went after this with more passion and heart than I can convey here. He absolutely *loved* it all!

Of course, I coached all those teams too. Once you sign up to coach one team in a little town like Kinnelon, it is simply assumed you'll be coaching the next sport, and then the next. It's kind of like a contract—signed in blood. But I loved it too. I've always loved helping kids reach for higher goals. No doubt I loved being out there with my own sons. This also gave me the opportunity to keep a close eye on Bryson as he struggled to fit in to all those round holes. The other coaches and parents in Kinnelon were gracious, make that *sensational,* in modifying whatever needed to be done to help fulfill Bryson's passions and fit him in.

Sometimes their kindness went above and beyond, as it did during his first basketball season. Just before the first game, league commissioner Mike Marroccoli approached me together with a few coaches and asked me to play six players on my team (instead of five) when Bryson was on the court. They reasoned that since Bryson couldn't dribble or pass the ball, our team would be at a serious disadvantage unless we did this. I declined their offer. It was sort of, you know, real men don't eat quiche and real champions don't take charity and all that. But they approached me again and this time they insisted, saying this would give Bryson more playing time. I relented, and I think those coaches got a bit more than they bargained for. The ever tenacious Bryson flew around that court with his hands up defending our basket as if he was defending the Hope Diamond. He gained the respect of everyone. He already had mine.

Apparently he also impressed the referees, including Fred Wolke. Fred was a dignified man who worked for Kraft Foods during the day and gave joy to the kids at night. He passed out candy from a brown bag after each hotly contested game. As Fred observed Bryson's limited abilities, it was not uncommon to hear his whistle stop play to put him on the foul line. Somehow he knew what a thrill this would give him, and he moved him up closer to the basket, from where he had a chance. And when one of his teammates handed Bryson the ball during play, he'd walk up to the basket to shoot, bend down in the deep knee bend technique he had learned with his medicine ball and heave up a shot. Some of his shots actually went in! Although the games were competitive, players on the opposing teams always allowed him to get off his shot.

On Saturday afternoons Bryson played roller hockey, in sneakers instead of skates, at the local Boys and Girls Club. He played his heart out, bouncing right up each time he fell to the parking lot pavement we played on. Program director Jen Pandolfo and numerous others at the club were more than kind. They placed Bryson (and Tim) in the league's all-star game. Bryson's photo was put in a local paper, and he was given complimentary tickets to see a New Jersey Devils hockey game. He was thrilled that all the Devils signed a stick for him. Executives at the Boys and Girls Club refused to accept *my* thanks, insisting they should be thanking me for giving them the privilege of having my son in their program. I was overwhelmed.

Bryson's love of baseball exceeded just about everything. He was *certain* he was the best player out there, which posed no small dilemma for me as coach. How many kids can play shortstop, as Bryson believed was his birthright? Somehow I got him to buy into the concept that Paul O'Neil was just as valuable to the Bronx Bombers as Jeter, and that we really needed him in right. This was *much* safer than infield. Those kids could hit rockets with their aluminum bats, and there was no way Bryson could have moved his body out of the way. Still, the outfield/infield issue wasn't the last of the positional controversies on Bryson's mind. Far from it! He had decided he was our team's best pitcher. Since I was the coach, I could put him in. Case closed in his mind!

If you ever need to negotiate something, I'll let you borrow Bryson (for a small fee). To this day, he is your prototypical pit bull. When he wants something badly enough, he becomes the immovable object *and* the irresistible force, all rolled into one. Since the early days of his brain injury it had been clear that God had left tenacity behind for him as a gift, though much had been taken away. Without this gift of grace, I doubt he'd ever have walked, spoken, or gained back so many seemingly unattainable functions. But during adolescence, his deep-rooted spirit of tenacity often manifested itself as relentless, hard-headed obstinacy.

He was like a heat seeking missile targeted squarely on his dad. He seemed to take it for granted that I could fix everything, and that I should somehow be able to make all his impossible dreams fall into place. How did this play out when I couldn't do that? Let's just say everything wasn't always sugar, spice, "Hi, Dad," and everything nice. Have you ever been told that you are ugly and that your mother dresses you funny? Have you been angrily informed your breath is bad and that you happen to be a moron? He didn't hesitate to offer these kinds of opinions, and some nastier ones too. I may be a moron, but I'm not stupid enough to share those opinions in this book.

But I can tell you that I vividly remembered those unbearable years when it was predicted he would never speak at all, and I clearly understood now that I was dealing with a young man without the emotional capacity to cope with his exasperating limitations. And if you think I was mature enough to bat 1,000 as I tried to handle each angry, mentally impaired, adolescent trauma, including this pitching issue, you're viewing this from the nosebleed section of the upper deck.

Bryson began to make my life *miserable* when I didn't use him as one of our pitchers, and I didn't have the slightest *idea* what to do. I sought the counsel of the other teams' coaches. Once again I was overwhelmed with their understanding and compassion. This is what we came up with. Once per week, we *added* an exhibition half-inning to the *start* of a game. We'd be out in the field as the home team, and Bryson would be our starting pitcher. He was the only player (on both teams) who didn't know that his half-inning didn't count. Even the umpires were in on the situation. I told Bryson that since he was one of the older kids in the league (actually the oldest) he could only pitch for one inning. He (unhappily) accepted this condition.

But what joy he had pitching. Ever the great copycat, Bryson's form from watching his heroes on TV was *amazing*. He threw that ball for all he was worth, and amidst countless pitches that went all over creation (and over the backstop), darned if he didn't smoke a few right down the pipe! The catcher threw the ball back to our first baseman each time, who handed it to Bryson for the next pitch. Whenever a pitch got close enough for the batter to swing, he'd miss (on purpose), or take the pitch and umpire Bill Holbeck would bellow "Steee-riiike."

Surprise, surprise, Bryson struck out just about everyone that year. To speed things up, since it was often very hard for him to get three pitches near the strike zone for each batter, sometimes the batter bunted, making sure our fielders threw him out, or the ump would allow some batters to walk. Then, they'd try to steal second on the next pitch, and our catcher always threw them out. Bryson's ERA was a sterling 0.00 that year. He still talks about his pitching prowess to this day, comparing himself to Mariano Rivera.

But not all his baseball playing was fantasy. Far from it! During the regulation innings he was cut no slack. He struck out numerous times those years and also drew many walks (legitimately). He *loved* running the bases. Our team got to the championship game one season, which was a big deal in our town. All the kids wanted that championship trophy so badly. I was never half as nervous in my playing days as I was prior to that championship game. Wayne Schonland, our assistant coach whose son Todd was our star pitcher, felt the same way. We both had butterflies.

Well, you couldn't have scripted it better. We were down 4–3 with two outs in the fifth inning of a six inning game. Runners were on first and second as Bryson strode to the plate. Our bench and the crowd went crazy as he worked out a walk, loading the bases for his brother, Tim. On the first pitch, Tim slammed a line drive into the gap in right field. *Yes*, this could be it! *Just* the blast we needed! This would clear the bases and lead us to the championship! The crowd was going nuts! From my third base coach's box I waved the first two runners home, not noticing what was happening on the other side of the infield. I was probably the last person to realize that Bryson had *fallen* between first and second. He was just laying there. This was a *disaster*!

Pandemonium was breaking out, and everyone was now screaming for Bryson to get up, including Tim who had already caught up to him on the base path. Bryson was trying his best, but in his excitement he had fallen hard, and his legs had gotten all tangled underneath him. The right fielder finally caught up to Tim's drive deep in right center. If he could relay it to second before Bryson reached the base, his force out would be out number three, and the two runs that we thought we had just scored would be erased. He threw it to the relay man with Bryson still down. My heart sunk. As nervous as I had been up until then, I hadn't yet stooped to pray for the outcome of a kids' game. But I was praying very hard now! "Don't let this happen, Lord! If we're going to lose, then let us lose. But not this way! Not in a way that will crush my son and scar him in a way he'll never forget! Anything but that! Please, Daddy!"

Finally he rose, and began heading toward second. The fielder's throw was strong and seemed on line. The play was going to be close. As he neared the base, Bryson did something I had never seen him do before, something I had no idea he was capable of doing. With a full head of steam, he leaped through the air, diving headfirst toward the bag. With outstretched arms he went sprawling into that base like Jeter, *just* as the ball arrived. From where I was standing, I had no idea whether he was safe or out. The only thing I was certain of is that I wasn't breathing. Every eye on that field moved to the second base ump. "*Safe!*" he cried.

I was shaking like a leaf, and tears of relief filled my eyes. But no one could have noticed, not with the bedlam that was going on. Tim was clapping on first and our players were jumping up and down on the bench. An ovation erupted throughout that field. Even the opposing coaches, players, and their parents were clapping for my son. And Bryson? He tried to act like it was no big deal. He had merely come through for his team. What did everyone expect, anyway? As his daddy, I knew better. I knew he was thrilled right down to the core of his soul. I looked for his broad smile; and finally, out it came, as he stood on second. He couldn't contain it. We went on to win the championship that night. It was a game that "A three boys" will remember forever.

Our toy-helmet football games continued to be played on our front lawn that coming year. Only now, they were played with the knowledge that Bryson had proven his mettle out on the real ball fields of our town. It's funny. I thought that cursed clock had already struck midnight. I had resigned myself that his brain injury had robbed him permanently from all the activities that would thrill his soul during that very difficult period of change. I was learning that Daddy holds time in His powerful hands, and He can reset any clock. My son was a square peg in a world of round holes; yes, that was true. But Daddy can be very creative in fitting His square peg children into holes in this world. Sometimes He even uses colts and locusts. Don't ask; just read on.

The Ultimate Champion

Then I will make up to you for the years That the swarming locust has eaten.

—Joel 2:25

Thanksgiving is my most enjoyable time of year, signaling the start of the holiday season. As I stood in line at Famularo's Deli that Thanksgiving weekend, a man tapped me on the shoulder, proceeding to introduce himself. Ross Cappuzzo indicated he had seen Bryson on the Kinnelon ball fields, and that he was inspired by his courage. We chatted a few minutes, and then he asked me a question that nearly floored me. He said he was the head coach for the Kinnelon Colts football program, and he wondered if Bryson might enjoy playing on the team.

Ross had no idea that Bryson played countless fantasy games in his toy helmet, right alongside his team. Nor could he have realized by my measured response that I was leaping inside. As I drove home, my enthusiasm began to wane. What was I *thinking*? He had lost so much already due to his brain injury. Football is not exactly a sport in which contact with your head can be avoided. In fact, hard hits are a huge part of the game. But in a subsequent meeting with Ross, he assured my wife and me that we could keep Bryson safe. Ross and I laughed that it wouldn't matter if he fell down on each play, since most of the players wind up on the ground anyway.

We petitioned the league for a waiver for him to play with the younger kids on Tim's team, which Ross would be coaching. Those kids would be smaller and less able to hit as hard. We'd also make certain that Bryson was only placed into games under the close supervision of our coaches, and the referees, who'd be informed of his presence on the field. He'd play primarily in the league's "B" team games, in which coaches were allowed on the field. The coaches on the opposing side would also be made aware of his presence. The league office answered our letter, graciously allowing all of this, and I became one of the Colts assistant coaches.

The night of the first practice I realized how far over our heads we really were. As always, Bryson was a great copycat; but try as hard as he might, he had no shot at the calisthenics. He only flapped his arms up and down during jumping jacks. He couldn't jump or move his feet at all. Along came Coach Phil Gatti, a powerfully built man. Phil did not know me, nor of Bryson's circumstances. But sometimes the most powerful men have the tenderest hearts. He knelt beside Bryson, patiently teaching him to perform sit-ups and push-ups. My mind drifted to another scene, as Jesus knelt beside a basin of water to wash the disciples' feet. This great man had a son, Chris, who was one of our strongest, best players. Like his dad, his heart had a tint of gold.

Along came Steve Poznak, another imposing coach, teaching Bryson to stretch. Both men exhorted and congratulated Bryson for his effort, making him feel like a million dollars and making me feel like more. As I considered all these wonderful men on the field with us, I continued getting glimpses of Daddy's definition of the term *champion*. I said earlier that a champion is someone who does what is necessary in life without complaint, even when it's hard. These men were teaching me a bit more. Champions also have eyes that can see, and hearts willing to respond to what is seen. To this day I remain in awe of these men, and of all the coaches who sacrificed for Bryson during that unforgettable season, and all through the years.

Bryson did a great job in our "B" games under the guidance of Coach Ed Kriskewic. You want to talk champion? This humble man had just lost his wife in a tragic auto accident one month prior to that season. Incredibly, he kept his family going while serving all our players out on that field, including his own two grieving, now motherless sons. Ed, who had also become the single dad for a five-year-old daughter, made sure Bryson was in the right spot, at the end of the offensive line or at safety on defense. I was astonished as I considered this man's courage and integrity.

Bryson got more involved in the action that season than any of us anticipated. It was impossible to hold him back. One of our main challenges was dealing with his relentless negotiating tactics to get more playing time in our "A" games. Though most of the kids in the league were three years younger, you'd be surprised how hard ten-year-olds can hit.

One Saturday morning during an important "A" game against Pequannock, Jim Deveau, our most enthusiastic coach, saw an opportunity. We were leading by a couple of touchdowns late in the fourth quarter on our home field, and our defense had our opponent backed up on their two-yard line. Jim, our defensive coordinator, called for time-out and for Bryson. He took Bryson with him onto the field and into the huddle. He looked into Chris Gatti's eyes and let him know Bryson was going to line up as the "nose tackle," directly opposite Pequannock's center. Chris understood that the opposing team's center was not to lay a *finger* on Bryson. Jim knew Chris could handle this. He was one of the strongest, toughest players in the league.

To be perfectly honest, I wondered what had possessed Jim as he trotted off the field, especially when I saw where Bryson was lining up. What was my son *doing* in the *middle* of the line right next to the ball? Hello? My heart was beating fast as Pequannock broke its huddle. Two of our linebackers lined up on either side of Chris and Bryson, who were both in the down position. As the quarterback began barking his signals, I felt like bolting out there; but Jim held out his hand to my chest and said, "Just wait." After an eternity, the ball was snapped, and much of what occurred during those next five seconds remains a blur in my mind to this day.

There was a crash of bodies at the line, and then several green jerseys converging toward the quarterback who was back to pass in the end zone. Finally, the quarterback went down underneath several bodies, *including* Bryson's. Chris had pushed and nearly carried my son back there, and together they had tackled him for a safety! Everyone was going insane, leaping up and down, but no one more than Jim Deveau, who nearly leaped to the clouds. As mentioned, Bryson is in his twenties now, and his mind still reaches the clouds as he talks about that play. And to this day he still reverently refers to Coach Cappuzzo and all these other great men as "Coach."

The rest of that season had its highs and its lows. Tim performed extremely well. Both boys experienced their share of bumps and bruises. As Ross Cappuzzo pointed out, Bryson *never* told us when he was hurting, which scared us half to death. But this didn't surprise me at all, since he had grown up experiencing intense pain. To Bryson, bearing up was akin to breathing. He was forced to miss some games toward the end of that season, due to his disturbing pattern of illnesses. But when he was healthy enough to participate, he had the time of his life.

The times were indeed a changin' in Bryson's life, as they constantly do in every life. Sometimes the changes bring joy and comfort, as that wondrous football season did for my son. Sometimes they decimate us, and we fail to understand why the Lord has allowed us to come upon such a grievous, humiliating place. When the tides of change bring us so low it's nearly impossible to believe we could ever rise again, when loss and catastrophe slam us so hard we can't even move a muscle, when it hurts so bad we're not even sure anymore that we want to go on, there is one thing, at all cost, we *must* hold onto.

There is a Champion whose sees all our pain, and whose heart is willing to respond to what He sees. We must hold onto the Truth, Jesus Christ, who created the universe and rules every *inch* of it. Our rules don't bind Him. Even death couldn't hold Him. He is the Alpha and the Omega, the beginning and the end, the ultimate Champion. He holds time itself in His mighty hands, and He even makes up for the years that the locust has eaten, in His way, in His time.

The only fear that any child of His could ever have is the fear that somehow our Champion might one day be defeated and His love for us extinguished. But in Him there is no change, nor shifting shadow. He is the same yesterday, today, and forever (Heb. 13:8). In other words, in this world of tribulation and sorrow we have *nothing* to fear. And that, dear reader, will *never* change.

> For the mountains may be removed and the hills may shake, but My lovingkindness will Not be removed from you, and My covenant of peace will not be shaken.
>
> —ISAIAH 54:10

> For I am convinced that neither death, nor life, nor angels, nor principalities, nor things present, nor things to come, nor powers, nor height, nor depth, nor any other created thing, will be able to separate us from the love of God, which is in Christ Jesus our Lord.
>
> —ROMANS 8:38–39

This chapter is dedicated to the memory of Ryan Cappuzzo, Bryson's dear friend and teammate from the Kinnelon Colts football team, and to his father Ross Cappuzzo, a man who has taught many people in this world the true meaning of the word *champion*.

Chapter 25

THE PROVING

You have been distressed by various trials, so that the proof of your faith, being more precious than gold which is perishable, even though tested by fire, may result in praise and glory and honor at the revelation of Jesus Christ.

1 Peter 1:6–7

And do not be conformed to this world, but be transformed by the renewing of your mind, so that you may prove what the will of God is, that which is good and acceptable, and perfect.

Romans 12:2

This book is my family story. Your family story differs only in detail, *not* in geography. I've mentioned a few times that we've been born onto a battleground, not a playground. Only those who wish to remain asleep will consider this admonition to be paranoid. Jesus plainly told us that the thief comes to steal and kill and destroy (John 10:10). Peter warned us that our adversary, the devil, prowls around like a roaring lion, seeking someone to devour (1 Pet. 5:8). Paul taught us that our struggle is not against flesh and blood, but against the rulers, against the powers, against the world forces of this darkness, against the spiritual forces of wickedness (Eph. 6:12). We have no reason to fear, for greater is He who is in us than he who is in the world (1 John 4:4). But vicious attacks *will* come against us, whether we realize we live in a war zone or not.

Pity the unsaved civilians who remain naïve to the bullets flying all around them. Shame on the "loyal" soldiers for Christ who believe they can live exactly as the world lives, who rationalize that they can offer Him a half-hearted commitment in return for His blood. Yet we need to be *very* careful before we condemn the latter. There's not a soul in this world, least of all this author, who's made so fervent a commitment to Christ that we can afford to lay down vigilance to pick up arrogance. Yes, we're at war. But when we want to see one of our greatest enemies, we need only to look in the mirror! Sin is ever crouching at the door for each soldier of Christ (Gen. 4:7). Too often in my life I've *deliberately* left that door unlocked, even ajar. No, there's far too much duplicity in my own heart to justify pointing a finger at the "lukewarm."

When all is said and done, what will my personal story prove in this battleground world? What will yours prove? Peter told us that our faith must be *proven* through various trials, being more precious than gold (1 Pet. 1:6–7). It seems, then, that faith is of extreme value in the proving out of our personal stories. But when we are honest with each other, we will agree that if our stories have proven *anything*, they've proven how desperately we need Christ to cleanse and revive us every day as we continue to walk, and sometimes to stumble, in this world.

In that same chapter, Peter made it clear that we must fix our hope *completely* on the grace to be brought to us at the revelation of Jesus Christ (v. 13). Peter was no stranger to personal failure, and he knew that Christ's story *alone* is a proven quantity. It was proven on a cross stained with sacred blood. In the end, it won't be my personal story of faith, or yours, that will be exalted. Only Christ's story of love, grace, and faithfulness to us will be worthy of exaltation.

After so many years crawling through the playgrounds of his life, God chose some very creative ways to make up for the years the locust had eaten in Bryson's life, and he took such joy in staking his claim to fame on the athletic fields of our town. Those joyous days quenched his thirst for life a bit, even as they did mine, and those memories will be forever cherished in my heart. Yet the pages of every family story relentlessly turn, and even our most treasured, "proven" victories ebb away. Our call is to let go of the past in order to pursue the future with and for Christ. Paul said: "One thing I do: forgetting what lies behind and reaching forward to what lies ahead, I press on toward the goal for the prize of the upward call of God in Christ Jesus" (Phil. 3:13–14).

I'd love to tell you that I "pressed on toward the goal" seamlessly during Bryson's middle years, but this story would be less than honest if I withheld some of the hellish episodes of trauma and fear that sprang from my son's fragile soul, and from mine too, as we pressed on. I remained grateful for his amazing progress, but as his peers set their sights on drivers' licenses and dating, it was becoming clear that Bryson might never cut his own food or tie his own shoes. His physical limitations, while exasperating, were relatively easy to deal with as compared to his mental and emotional impairments. The floodgates to the future were opening wide, and some of the waves that swept in during those years were so fierce it seemed his will to live might be swept away, right along with all our cherished memories and "proven" victories.

Bryson had come a long way since the early days when it was predicted he'd never walk or speak intelligibly, that he'd be better off living in an institution; and I was more grateful for his progress than I can tell you. But fresh installments of sorrow arrive during each new season in the life of a brain-injured child, and I couldn't keep from grieving all that was lacking in him still. Immense confusion arose in his mind as he began to realize that his beloved recreation league sports could no longer be modified for him at the interscholastic level. My childlike son was not ready to accept that he wasn't the greatest athlete in town. I continued to plead that the Lord would heal him completely. Yet it was not for me, as a lump of clay, to understand the ways of the Potter. It was mine to surrender to the work of His hands (Jer. 18:6).

Ah yes, the ways of the Potter, and my *glorious* surrender to Him. Such eloquent words! I almost feel like deleting them, being painfully aware of *so* much that is lacking in me still. It is *solely* due to undeserved grace that I have *ever* come to love God, or surrender *anything* to Him. My road to surrender has often involved erratic, fist in the air *refusals* to submit to Him. The Lord has overcome these with His love and with His discipline (which again, *is* His love). Even now as a "vigilant soldier" sharing this story with you many years later, my lack often springs out and haunts me, even as my son's brain-injured lack continues to haunt him. I sometimes feel like giving up altogether as I stumble, yet *again*, at the most inopportune times. How about you? Every honest soul must come to an awareness of our own lack as we press on.

Some of you reading this book have traveled a long road fraught with difficulty and pain. Again, your family story differs from mine, but only in detail, *not* in geography. The notion that we live on a playground, not a battleground, seems absurd to you now. Just like me, you've experienced God's deliverance, many times in fact; and you've been grateful. Yet now, after *all* these years, you've *again* been slammed to the mat. You didn't see it coming. You thought you'd learned every lesson God could *possibly* want to teach you. You *never* expected that the Lord would allow you to be brought so low *again* in this world! But new waves of sorrow have swept in from your blind side, threatening to plunge you beneath the waterline, once and for all.

Sometimes I just feel like screaming:

> *I get it, Lord! I know that my faith is more precious than gold. I know that I must go through various trials, tested by fire, so that the result will be praise and glory and honor at the revelation of Jesus Christ. I know that You want to polish Christ's image in me, to prove out the will of God in my life* (Rom. 12:2). *But I don't think I can take anymore! It's not that I don't care about proving out Your will. But I'm battle weary! Don't You see that, Lord? Can't You just let me rest a while? Is that too much to ask, Lord?*

In reality, I don't believe the above rant is too much to ask of our compassionate Savior. Nor do I think that He tires of hearing our anguished cries and frustrated pleas. Yet I've come to believe that Jesus will often choose to interrupt our rants and our questions with a question of His own: "When the Son of Man comes, will He find faith on the earth?" (Luke 18:8).

> *Um…, Jesus, You certainly need no permission to interrupt me as I'm writing this chapter. After all, You're King of the universe. But if You don't mind my saying so, I'm trying to convey something important to the readers about our mutual lack as we press on toward the goal. Now here You come, breaking right into this chapter asking a question about finding faith? I don't follow, Lord. And to be honest, I don't think Your interruption is helping! Your question seems a bit out of context, don't You think? And at the risk of being a little dense, Lord, could You be more specific*

with Your question? Faith in what exactly? Faith in my ability to make up for my own lack? Faith in my resolve to press on for Your glory? Help me out here, Lord! I don't get it!

When the Son of Man comes will He find faith on the earth? His question does seem a bit out of context. If He'd just give us what we need, what we are crying out for, then we'd gladly exhibit the "faith" He is looking for. But since Jesus is taking the time to ask us a question, it seems wise to lay aside our questions and consider how we will answer His. As we grope for an answer, we might let Oswald Chambers help us to consider our sometimes wimpy definition of faith:

> A saint's life is in the hands of God like a bow and arrow in the hands of an archer. God is aiming at something the saint cannot see, and He stretches and strains, and every now and again the saint says—"I cannot stand any more." God does not heed, He goes on stretching till His purpose is in sight, then He lets fly. Trust yourself in God's hands.... Though He slay me, yet will I wait for Him.' Faith is not a pathetic sentiment, but robust vigorous confidence built on the fact that God is holy love. You cannot see Him just now, you cannot understand what He is doing, but you know Him.... Faith is the heroic effort of your life, (in which) you fling yourself in reckless confidence on God.[1]

Though we are often blind to God's goal for us, we can take comfort in the reality that *He* knows what He is aiming at, and that *He* knows what He's seeking to accomplish in and through our lives. There are times when He will ask us to stand firm in our faith against tsunamis that have the power to wipe us, our "proven" victories, and even our cherished memories clear off the map. As He goes on stretching and performing His unseen work within us, let's continue to be honest with each other. We're *all* lacking as we seek to stand at these times, and not just a little.

Just when we think we're mature, sanctified soldiers, that we're no longer quite so desperate for grace, that we're ready to do great things for God out of our experience, we can find ourselves squarely off the path. When we even *begin* to think we can prove *anything* in our lives without setting our hope *completely* on the grace to be brought to us at the revelation of Jesus Christ, we are deceived. We will never get to a place of self-sufficiency. Oswald Chambers warns us:

> It is a bad thing to be satisfied spiritually. "What shall I render unto the Lord?" said the Psalmist. "I will take the cup of salvation." We are apt to look for satisfaction in ourselves—"Now I have got the thing; now I am entirely sanctified; now I can endure." Instantly we are on the road to ruin.[2]

As fierce waves threaten to destroy us, God is giving us a unique opportunity to prove to the world that *He* has the power to deliver any person from any storm. In the midst of such tempests, what can any of us *possibly* render unto the Lord but the cup of salvation? *Only* His grace in providing for our every need is worthy of lifting up. And the only thing worth offering to any other hurting soul in this battleground world is the same stuff from that cup we so desperately need daily ourselves: the forgiveness, mercy, grace, and power of the Lord Jesus Christ. In the end, if our personal stories are going to prove *anything*, they must magnify the Lord.

Our lives can prove that victory, as *He* defines victory, is not only possible for people who lack, but certain *if* we will trust in Him *alone*. My son's lack of development as a brain-injured person was obvious. But is our own lack any less obvious when compared to the holiness of God? Let's face it. Our performance won't ever shine flawlessly for Christ, nor, dare I say it, does He want it to. Even on our best day on earth we are still *far* too lacking to represent His perfection. When Jesus asks if He will find faith on the earth, don't miss His point! The victory that overcomes the world is our faith in *Him* (1 John 5:4), not any deceived notion of faith we can place in ourselves.

And in terms of proving something, let's be clear that God has absolutely *nothing* to prove. His love for us was proven beyond question by Christ's blood shed on the cross. I've been walking with the King a long time now, and I'm convinced *everything* He allows to occur in our lives is intended for our good. I had a son born completely healthy. His brain was profoundly injured. In many respects his life was ruined before he even had his fair shot at living in this world.

Then came all those excruciating years of fighting his way back, all the impossible battles, the exhilarating victories, the demoralizing defeats, the suffering, the anguish, the cruelty, the pain. Wait a minute...Did I say for our good? I almost wanted to *die* much of the time! But through it all, God gave me a front row seat as He kept working things out in His own mysterious way.

As Bryson reached adolescence, I had now worked only half days for a dozen years. This was not only to rehabilitate my son, but to try to hold my hurting family together in light of his relentless needs. I reserved "date night" for my wife, though it was getting harder to find babysitters who could handle Bryson. I dedicated afternoons for Tim to decide whatever *he* wanted to do alone with his dad. We literally had to sneak out so Bryson wouldn't insist on coming. Sometimes we shot baskets or hit fly balls. Sometimes we went for ice cream. I carved out time for breakfasts and dates with my beautiful daughter, Janelle. I don't regret any of the time or sacrifice. My only regret as I look back is that I didn't give my family much more.

Through all those years of working half days, God blessed us beyond what I ever dreamed. We had a gorgeous home in an affluent community, a vacation home on a scenic lake, and a net worth that could sustain us for the rest of our lives. I hesitate to say this because there will be many reading this just as dedicated to their families and fervently committed to Christ, yet financial reward has not been realized. Despite what health and wealth preachers proclaim with their phony smiles, there's *no* biblical formula for material success in this world. The foxes have holes and the birds of the air have nests, but the Son of Man had nowhere to lay His head (Matt. 8:20). He was dirt poor in this world. A servant is not above his Master (10:24), and Jesus didn't suffer on a cross to leave us a success manual. He died to give us eternal life in Himself.

God was *just* as faithful to me in the coming years when financial upheaval came, and I lost *everything*. I'm not referring to something that occurred in the distant past, something I can proclaim "victory" to you about. As I write this book I am battling financial peril that is more devastating than I *ever* expected the Lord would allow. I'll tell you more about this in the concluding chapters. Yet during Bryson's middle years God provided us with great material affluence, and He provided me with a platform from which to serve broken people.

I began accepting speaking engagements to reveal God's power to sustain hurting souls from any "hopeless" situation. I was teaching adult classes in my church. I began a men's ministry in my home that was impacting lives in our community. I left the corporate world and opened a small commercial real estate company. It was my desire to follow the example of Paul, who remained a tentmaker as he served Christ. Things were far from easy as emotional tsunamis kept hitting Bryson's shores. But by this time I was well experienced in God's ways. I'd go as far as to say that His plan had been proven in my life. Clearly, my family story was a success story.

The mistrust and anger that once rose up against God from my lacking soul was a thing of the past. The distant past! Never again could I conceive of fostering a doubt in my heart. God had indeed given me a front row seat as He kept working out His mysterious plan in my life, and if *anyone* was qualified, *I* was well qualified to serve Him now. I hope that doesn't sound overconfident, even arrogant. I'm just saying that God and I were on the same page now. I had gotten with the program. I was fully on board. How else can I put it? I was God's committed soldier. Are you getting this out there? There was no need to debate this. Or was there?

DEBATING HORATIUS

> Put Me in remembrance, let us argue our case together. State your cause, that you may be proved right.
>
> —ISAIAH 43:26

Ah, good old Horatius Bonar, famed Scottish author and hymn-writer from the 1800s. If you look through some old hymn books, you'll come across his name. Some of his teachings and admonitions are difficult for modern ears to hear. I came to agree with him only after wrestling with his positions and, as you will see, grappling a bit with Dr. Bonar too. In fact, as I struggled with this man, there came a time when I decided to host a full-fledged debate against him.

I realize that hosting such an event is controversial; and, to be honest, I've never been sure of the correct protocol for debating someone dead as long as he. Granted, some find the practice distasteful altogether. I understand their sensitivity. After all, why not just leave the poor man alone, you know, since he's dead and all. But somehow I don't think my old friend Horatius will mind if you listen in on one of our contentious debates.

His words are foreboding concerning what lay ahead for some, I daresay most of us, in our walk toward maturity in Christ. His notion about *proving* something was particularly hard for me to understand during Bryson's middle years, when I thought I was so qualified to serve the Lord. I ask you to listen in now to my debate with Horatius (H). As you do, pay close attention to some vital truths that Dr. Bonar claims must be proven out in the hearts and lives of every believer.

> **H:** "There are no beings about whom we make so many mistakes as our own selves. 'The heart is deceitful above all things,' and besides this, the 'deceitfulness of sin' is unsearchable. So that when the deceitfulness of our hearts and the deceitfulness of sin come together, we need not wonder that the effect should be ignorance of ourselves."[3]
>
> **Me:** "Now, hold on there just on a minute Horatius! Be careful who you're calling ignorant! There was a time in my walk with the Lord when I *was* self-centered. I said so right in this book! I know there are many uncommitted, lukewarm Christians out there; but I'm *not* one of them. The Lord gave me a new heart. I'm good H. Got it covered man!"
>
> **H:** "We shrink from the exposure such a scrutiny would make…the search is a painful one, and we would rather postpone it. It might bring many things to light which would shock and humble us. It might alarm us with the extent of the evil which still remains in us.…Hence we are slow to learn, or even to inquire into, the evil that cleaves to us still.…We do not know ourselves. Our convictions of sin have been but shallow, and we are beginning to imagine the conflict between the flesh and the spirit is not so very fierce and deadly as we had conceived it to be. We think that we have rid ourselves of many of our sins entirely, and are in a fair way speedily getting rid of all the rest. The depths of sin in us we have never sounded; the number of our abominations we have never thought of marking."[4]
>
> **Me:** "There you go again, Horatius! I Googled you and saw your portrait. I'm trying hard not to judge a book by its cover, but I *thought* you might be one of *those!* If you don't mind my saying so, you're a bit…*creepy looking.* No, I don't want to go there. I apologize, brother. Poking fun at your appearance is low drawer. Let's keep this debate amicable, okay? It's just that what you're saying rubs me the wrong way! I've made *tons* of progress in my spiritual walk, and I'd appreciate some props for that. How about it?"

H: "We thought...we have overcome many of our corruptions. The old man was crucified. It seemed dead, or at least feigned itself to be so in order to deceive us. Our lusts had abated. Our tempers had improved. Our souls were calm and equable. Our mountain stood strong, and we were saying, 'We shall not be moved.' The victory over self and sin seemed in some measure won. Alas, we were blind! We were profoundly ignorant of our hearts."[5]

Me: "Now look here, Dr. Bonar! Now I'm not sorry for what I said about your looks! I'm on my best behavior here trying to keep this debate cordial, and you keep calling me 'ignorant!' You look like a shriveled up prune, pal! How do you like that? Look man, I know I'm not perfect, but get off this jazz about 'evil' and the 'depths of sin.' I've suffered through many hardships in life that you know nothing about! Adversity I never bargained for! I don't know about you, Horatius, but I've walked victoriously through it all. Didn't they teach you old-timers about the transforming power of the grace of God in your day?"

H: "Well the trial came. It swept over us like a cloud of the night, or rather through us like an icy blast, piercing and chilling us to the vitals. Then the old man within us awoke, and, as if in response to the uproar without, a fiercer tempest broke loose within. We felt as if the four winds of heaven had been let loose to strive together upon the great deep within us. Unbelief arose in its former strength. Rebelliousness raged in every region of our soul. Unsubdued passions resumed their strength. We were utterly dismayed at the fearful scene. But yesterday, and this seemed impossible. Alas, we knew not the strength of sin nor the evil of our hearts till God thus allowed them to break loose."[6]

Me: "Your judgmental characterizations are getting old and you're *really* getting on my nerves now! Frankly, I'm feeling disrespected. Look, you don't know me man! I don't just talk the talk like some of you nineteenth century holy rollers. I've walked the walk! Rebelliousness in *every* region of *my* soul? Maybe *you* had *unsubdued passions* till the day you died, old man, but don't go projecting *your* stuff onto *me*! Deal with your own fierce tempests!"

H: "It was thus He dealt with Israel; and...led them into the desert...'to humble thee, and to prove thee, to know what was in thine heart' (Deut. 8:2). Their desert trials put them to the proof. And when thus proved, what iniquity was found in them! What sin came out which had lain hidden and unknown before! The trial did not create the evil: it merely brought out what was there already, unnoticed and unfelt, like a torpid adder. Then the heart's deep fountains were broken up, and streams of pollution came rushing out, black as hell. Rebellion, unbelief, fretfulness, atheism, idolatry, self-will, self-confidence, self-pleasing—all burst out when the blast of the desert met them in the face.... Thus they were proved."[7]

Me: "You don't impress me with your poetic narrative, and you're not scaring me either. Look, I don't mean to be insulting, H, but you've been dead a long time. I'm giving you a golden opportunity to have some relevance in the twenty-first century, and you're blowing it! You're embarrassing yourself! I ask you about grace, and you go right back to the Old Testament. Don't get me wrong, it's a good story and all. But that was another age and time. We have the Spirit of God living in us now. We've reached new heights. At least I have!"

H: "Even so it is with the saints still. God chastens them that He may draw forth the evil that is lying concealed and unsuspected within. The rod smites us on the tenderest part, and we start up in a moment as if in arms against God. The flesh, the old man, is cut to the quick, and forthwith arouses itself.... When it was asleep we did not know its power, but now that it has been awakened, its remains of strength appall us.... When calamity breaks over them like a tempest, then the hidden evils of their hearts awake. Sins scarcely known before display themselves. The heart pours out its wickedness. Hard thoughts of God arise. Atheistical murmurings break out and refuse to be restrained. Questionings both of His wisdom and of His love are muttered; yea, how often do they assume a more explicit form, and we ask, 'If God be so loving and wise, why is it thus?'"[8]

Me: "You're incredibly persistent! I admire that in a man. But you're a broken record, H! You remind me of a pit bull, and I don't just mean your portrait; although...No, I promised not to go there again. My point is there's no reasoning with you, H! Torpid adder? Black as hell? Atheistical murmurings? And you're trying to teach me? What is it? Do you have unresolved childhood issues, some kind of weird hang-up? Maybe you're ticked at your parents for naming you Horatius. I'll bet the kids on the playground creamed you for that one. Get over it, man! By the way, I often find myself asking God, 'Why is it thus?' Oh no! Now you've got me talking in that stuffy old English! Argh!"

H: "Lord, what is man! And what is a human heart—the heart even of thy saints—when proved and held up to view?...'O heart, heart,' said John Berridge of himself, 'what art thou? A mass of fooleries and absurdities, the vainest, craftiest, wickedest, foolishest thing in nature.' What deep hidden evil, what selfishness, what pride, what harsh tempers, what worldliness, come out in a moment, when the stroke goes deep into the soul!"[9]

Me: "Debating you is like talking to a wall, Horatius! Look, I've been honest throughout this book about some incredibly deep sorrows in my life. I think I've been a model of restraint. For goodness sake, you're exasperating! The foolishest thing in nature? In my view, the only one proving himself to be foolish in this debate is you! Yeah, that's right, H.B. I'm sorry, but someone has to say it!"

H: "How long Job remained steadfast, holding fast his integrity and confidence in God! Stroke after stroke laid him prostrate, yet he gave glory to God in the midst of desolation and sorrow. The inner circle of self had not been reached. But when a loathsome disease drove him to the dunghill, and his friends rose up against him...then his faith and patience gave way. The very center of his being had been reached and probed; and forth came the stream of impatience and unbelief. It takes a sharp arrow and a strong drawn bow to pierce into the inmost circle; yet God in kindness spares not. The seat of the disease must be reached, and its real nature brought out to the light."[10]

Me: "Okay, okay! I got a little steamed for a minute and got off topic. Not good for a debater. Look, I'm not about to challenge the story of Job. But that was him, not me. And Job didn't have the New Testament, did he? You're a Christian preacher! You should know better than to dwell only in the Old Testament. You know I've got you there H! And don't give me this 'I've been dead for 150 years' jazz. I know you're hearing me!"

H: "Of all the evils which are thus drawn forth from the heart of the saint, the worst, and yet the commonest, are hard thoughts of God. Yet who would have expected this? Once, indeed, in our unbelieving days our souls were full of these. Our thoughts of God were all evil together. When the Holy Spirit wrought in our hearts the mighty change, the special thing which He accomplished was teaching us to think well of God, showing us how little He had deserved these hard thoughts from us, how much He had deserved the opposite. The wondrous story of manifold

> love, which the gospel brought to us, won our hearts and made us ashamed of our distrust. We said then, Surely we shall never think ill of God again. 'Though he slay me, yet will I trust in Him.' We thought the affliction would only make us cleave to Him the more. Yet scarcely does He begin to smite us than our former thoughts return. We wonder why He should treat us thus. We suspect His love and faithfulness. Our hold of His grace seems to loosen, as if at times it would wholly give way."[11]

> **Me:** "My dear, Dr. Bonar! I'm standing right in front of you! Where are all these hard thoughts of God you say are the worst, yet the commonest of evils? You have no answer, do you? I'm not surprised! Look, there's no way I'd suspect God's love and faithfulness ever again! I understand God's ways now! My grip of His grace won't loosen; even though apparently, yours did! And at the risk of sounding smug, let me just say I'm quite confident my 'former thoughts' won't return, no matter how much God decides to 'smite' me.
>
> "But I invited you to the twenty-first century as my guest. Let's end on a positive note. I've gotta hand it to you, H. You're as erudite as they come, and one heck of a debater! Let's agree to disagree on this 'heart of the saints' issue, okay? And don't worry; I won't embarrass you by declaring a winner to our debate. Thank you very much for coming, Dr. Bonar."

Thank you too, dear reader, for listening in on this debate. It seems old H.B. knew the subject of the heart quite well, didn't he? He also knew that the ice becomes dangerously thin when we conclude that we've reached a precipice of maturity and mastery over sin, anger, and temptation. Self-confidence is never Christ confidence. It is always false confidence (Phil. 3:3; Gal. 3:3).

Of all people, I should have been wary about unanticipated regressions. They are an inescapable part of the development of every brain-injured child. I've come to believe they are also an inescapable part of the walk of every child of God. It was almost as if Dr. Bonar was my personal prophet. I was about to learn, once again, how fragile and desperately needy I was, how needy I still am to this day. Despite our proclamations of loyalty and commitment to Christ, replete with the bows we dare to take in front of one another for it, there's only one honest story that has ever been entirely proven. It is the story of Christ's love, loyalty, and commitment to us.

Landmines and Missiles

Childlikeness is a gift retained by special, brain-injured children of all ages. To this day in his mid twenties, Bryson retains a childlike innocence that brings a quick smile to your face and, sometimes, a tear to your eye. With this gift comes great vulnerability, the defenselessness of a child that you hope and pray no one ever tramples upon. I said earlier that God has nothing to prove, and I still believe that's true. But my hope for God's protection for my vulnerable son was about to be severely disappointed and my faith harshly tested during Bryson's middle years.

Gale force winds blasted him in the face daily as he attempted to cross the bizarre terrain known as middle school. As the gap between his abilities and those of his peers widened, his childlike mind prevented him from fully understanding he was different, and why. Debilitating illnesses still set him back, and he continued to be plagued with painful accidents. And yes, tsunamis of self hatred kept arriving, like those described earlier as he screamed from his closet, "I dumb and ugly!...No one likes me!...I wish you had different son!...I don't like myself!"

I knew middle school would be a severe testing ground, but some of the landmines took me *completely* off guard. Bullying has always been a prevalent problem in our nation's schools. If you can believe it, during those middle years two different bullies actually beat my son, a helpless child with cerebral palsy! One of those bullies actually tackled him to the locker room floor! After having such a wise and strong principal in Bette Esposito in elementary school, I quickly became disappointed in our middle school administrators. It became clear in the aftermath of those beating incidents that leadership in that school was a "no-show."

Out of options, I discussed this situation with the chief of police in our town. He was dumbfounded regarding why the school was unable to properly discipline these offenders. After the school officials found out about my visit to the police, promises of protection were made; but sadly, these promises amounted to little more than lip service, and things didn't get much better.

In the absence of appropriate action by those school officials, it turned out that one of those bullies was later beaten up in the bathroom by a few of Bryson's protectors. This incident in the bathroom was done unbeknownst to me, though I wouldn't have opposed it if I had known about it. It was later revealed to me by a father of one of Bryson's protectors, who ironically, was on our town's school board. And yes, in case you're wondering, one of those protectors was among the self-proclaimed guardians who had vowed to protect my son after the bus incident described in an earlier chapter. That particular bully never tried to harm my son again.

Most of Bryson's peers were as kind and compassionate as they had always been since we moved to Kinnelon. Ray Sikora, his teacher in the self-contained special education class for all three of his middle school years, was outstanding. But again, middle school is bizarre territory, with hormones flowing and pecking orders being constantly tested. With a very muddled self-concept, Bryson kept trying *so* hard to fit in to this wacky world; and as he courageously crossed that terrain, some brutal attacks continued. I have no better explanation for the vicious attack I'm about to describe other than to say that evil waits, evil lurks, and evil seeks opportunities to attack those who are vulnerable, for evil's own perverse ends.

The moment I saw him that Friday afternoon I knew something was terribly wrong. He had just been driven home from the bus stop by my wife. I came to give him a hug in our foyer, but he refused it. He was so distressed he couldn't speak. When I asked him what was wrong, he lunged at me and sunk his teeth deep into my forearm—I mean hard! I was wearing a suede leather jacket, and his jaw locked on me *so* hard I couldn't get him loose for several seconds. He then ran off toward his room, falling on the stairs a few times as he sped up them, going straight to his closet, slamming the door. I removed my coat and ran after him, praying as I followed. His teeth had left deep red marks on my arm, amazingly right through my coat.

It took some time to get him to come out of the closet and sit on his bed, but it was fruitless trying to get him to talk. He didn't seem physically hurt. I asked him if someone had done something mean to him. He wouldn't answer. The more I asked, the more upset he became. As I persisted in questioning him, a look of terror came to his face that I hadn't seen in my son before. It was obvious that he was confused and horrified, but he would say nothing.

I received a call from his aide, a wonderful woman who had her own daughter in the school. As always, Bryson had been with his aide the entire day *except* in the gym, the cafeteria, and on the way back from the cafeteria to return to his special class after lunch. Allowing him to be unattended during that time was a planned idea, one that my wife and I had agreed to. The idea seemed viable, in order to give him more independence as he reached higher grade levels. But none of us envisioned how opportunistic evil could turn out to be. On this day, it took aim at my son's soul like a rifle shot.

Their plan was as sadistic as sending a puppy, wagging its tail, out onto a busy freeway after a favorite toy. They cornered my son in the hallway and convinced him that he had to do *exactly* as they instructed if he wanted the girls to "like him." They sent him out as a guided missile, stumbling across that hall, trying to keep his balance. One female target after another they sent him toward, as they hid in the shadows. They made sure he knew his mission would only be successful if he put his hands directly on their breasts. They reminded him that this would prove him to be cool, and that the girls would indeed like him for it and want to be his friends.

As their missile began to hit the target and those girls began to shriek, those punks began to roar with laughter. It didn't matter to them that his mind was being twisted and mangled, that part of his soul was being destroyed, along with his reputation. In their minds, the splatter of road kill was just a part of the show. They needed an animal for their circus, and in my vulnerable son they had the headline act for the center ring. Oh yes, this was the greatest show on earth, and these malicious punks were the ring masters.

After I hung up the phone I wanted to vomit. I wondered why the school officials hadn't called. I called them. It was a Friday afternoon, and a few officials were still there. They said they had heard something about it, but were unsure of the details. They'd need to explore it Monday. It seemed to me they had little concern that a vulnerable child was being preyed upon right under their noses. I guess the situation was inconvenient for them, occurring just before the weekend and all. And I suspected they knew more than they were telling me, that they didn't want to reveal names, hoping to hand out just another slap on the wrist when this all blew over.

I got on the phone and called a few fathers of some of the boys I had coached. They promised to speak with their sons and get back to me. They called back that evening and told me they couldn't be certain, since their sons didn't see it, but suggested a few names I should follow up on. I wondered what to do. I had tried the police before, and this seemed a possibility. But I didn't have solid evidence of those who were involved. I was in a quandary, feeling my lack *big time.* But with my son's fragile mind being destroyed, I knew that action of some kind *had* to be taken. The rest of that night I kept Bryson close to me and comforted him, while praying hard that I wouldn't mess things up too terribly the following day, as I sought to protect him.

The next morning, Saturday, I was on the doorstep of one of Bryson's classmates at 9:00 a.m., telling his father we needed to discuss something very serious. The father invited me in, saying he would go up and wake his son. The boy came down a few moments later. He was still groggy from being awakened. I laid out the situation, informing both of them what I had heard about his participation in my son's harassment. The boy vehemently denied being involved. The truth is, based on the information I had I wasn't certain about his involvement myself. I was careful not to directly accuse, but before I left I issued a warning. At the risk of sounding like Arnold Schwarzenegger in *The Terminator,* I told them if *anything* like this ever happened again I'd be back, and my visit would be *far* less pleasant than this one. I didn't say whether I'd bring the police or just show up myself. My point was clear enough.

As mentioned earlier, I'd love to tell you that I "pressed on toward the goal" seamlessly during Bryson's middle years, and that the waters were calm. But if I withheld some of the hellish episodes of trauma and fear that sprang from my son's fragile soul, and from mine too, as we pressed on, you'd be reading a fictional version of my family story, not an honest one.

Some people in that little town thought I was a complete maniac. Others thought I should be nominated for sainthood. Yet I've learned that peace never comes from the appeasement of evil, and doing what is necessary won't always win the approval of others. Nor does it have to! Far more important than the opinions of others is our responsibility to protect those who are vulnerable in this world, irrespective of whether they are family members, or others who are weak. In this case, the word got around to all those malicious punks that they had better not come near Bryson again. That was worth more to me than anyone's opinion, or of my reputation.

I'm not really sure what the long-term emotional impact of this incident was on my son's soul, nor the impact of so many of the landmines that exploded in those days. But of some things I have become sure. There's only so much that a parent can endure when your child is being harmed, and these ongoing conflicts can leave you battle weary and despondent. Personally, my hope and trust in the Lord for His protection for my vulnerable son had taken a serious hit.

When the Son of Man comes, will He find faith on the earth?

—Luke 18:8

You gotta be kidding, Lord? That's the last thing I want to hear right now! What in the world does faith have to do with battles like these? And to the extent that this chapter is about proving something, I'd like something proven to me right about now! It's no shocker to find teenaged punks in this dark world who prey on those who are vulnerable. Nor is it a surprise to learn of gutless school officials and other inept authorities who fail to protect the weak. But I'm beginning to wonder what heaven's excuse might be for failing to protect my son! Yeah, I said it, Lord, and I'm glad I said it! I'm beginning to wonder if belonging to You, Jesus, really matters on a practical level in this battleground world! And I'll tell You something else, Lord. I wouldn't be surprised if some of my appalled readers are wondering the exact same thing!

Jesus Throws a Party

All in all, it seems Dr. Bonar was spot on. God knows our frame, and He remembers that we are but dust (Ps. 103:14). Sometimes it's good for us to remember the same. Paul called himself *chief of sinners* and declared, "Wretched man that I am" (Rom. 7:24). When all was said and done, he boasted not of his accomplishments but of his weaknesses (2 Cor. 12:9). Yes, it's good for us to remember that we are flesh and blood. Perhaps it's even good, dare I say it, for nonbelievers in this dark world to see some of our flaws too. It's hopeful for them to see that we bleed just as they do, and that the treasure we're attempting to share with them is Jesus' treasure, *not* our own.

Many of you reading this book are experienced war veterans. You've lived long enough, and you've failed big enough, to understand that no matter how mature we begin to *think* we are, vicious battles can suddenly arise that bring us right back down to our knees, and back to reality. And since this chapter is about proving something, I must honestly tell you that there have been times when I've come to the point of not caring if my life proved a blessed thing to *anyone*, not even to God. I've sometimes been so exasperated and weary amidst the unending attacks, afflictions, and landmines detonating all around me, that I've considered quitting altogether.

But no matter how exasperating or hard life ever gets, Jesus will not allow us to shirk off His seemingly out of context question. When the Son of Man comes, will He find faith on the earth? What is my answer? What is yours? What are we *really* proving with our lives? Attaining the kind of faith Jesus seeks to instill in our hearts requires *brutal* honesty—with ourselves and also with Him. Just when we begin to see ourselves as mature, sanctified soldiers, no longer quite so desperate for grace, ready to do great things for God, get ready for a fall. The truth is that we're *all* lacking big-time as we seek to stand against the tsunamis of this world.

When we're battle weary and tempted to throw in the towel, where can we go to find renewed hope? During times like these I've needed to attend one of Jesus' parties. What's that you say? You didn't know that Jesus hosts parties? I certainly hope that you do know this, and that you've attended a few. Surely, you're on His invitation list. He asked *all* who are weary and heavy laden to come (Matt. 11:28). But you must understand before you RSVP that Jesus' party is not a formal function where you will be expected to put on your best suit and pretend everything is fine as you politely engage in small talk. His is a far more peculiar bash.

Where else will you ever be invited where the host allows you to bring the foul sack of trash you've been lugging around? Don't ever believe that the rubbish you're laden with must be dumped elsewhere before you'll be presentable enough to attend. If sorrow or anger or fear is all you have to offer Him as a housewarming gift, by all means bring it! Don't stay away. He wants you to come to His party, no matter how twisted your battles have caused your soul to become.

Even so, there have been times when my parties with Jesus have been pretty rough. I'll tell you about one of them that occurred right around the time Bryson suffered the abuse I've described to you in middle school, resulting in him biting my arm. I'll tell you about this party in the first person as if it's happening now, so you can attend it with me in my memory.

The Night of the Party

I don't really want to be here, but I've got *nowhere* else to turn. I straggle up to the entrance, and the door opens even before I knock. Jesus greets me with a warm smile. I think I'll hold back a bit, and exchange a few pleasantries, "Praise You, Lord, for this and that." It seems the right thing to do. But despite my intentions, angry words come blurting out of my mouth, right here on His doorstep: "I've tried to be a good Christian, Jesus! Look how You've repaid me!"

I am suddenly aware that He has the power to strike me down for my challenge. But He calmly says, "Come in, child." I am surprised to find this almighty Rock of my salvation to be different than I expected. The Rock isn't hard at all, but…gentle, humble. I am momentarily disarmed. With mixed emotions I begin to feel safe enough to dare to ask what I've come to His party to ask. It's a question that has often tormented me, haunted me for many years in fact. It seems now or never. As I look around I realize I am the only one at His party tonight. There's no rush, I suppose. I'd better take a few moments to think through what I've come to His party to say.

As I do, a tinge of anger arises. I think to myself, "If this gentle One is so loving and kind, then why didn't He simply prevent the tragedy that so devastated the life of my once healthy son? He's *supposed* to be in control of all things. If *that's* true, then I've got to wonder how good He really is after all! An innocent baby? His brain profoundly damaged? His *whole* life destroyed in such a *senseless* way before he even had his fair shot at living in this world? He's gotta be *kidding*! At the very least, He *owes* me an explanation!" Then I smirk and think, "He'll *need* to be God if He's going to talk His way around *this* one."

My mind revisits some of the details of my son's life of pain. I see the other kids laughing and calling him a "dog" because he needs to crawl on the beach as a six-year-old. A few years later, I see the degrading things he is forced to do on the school bus. I remember age nine. He isn't even walking independently, yet he proudly staggers up to the plate. I stand there praying for him to hit the ball, "Just this one time, Lord!" Pin-drop silence spreads across the field as the crowd notices his struggle to remain standing. He still thinks he'll play for the Yankees one day. His injured mind robbed him long ago of the ability to understand that he is permanently handicapped. Pitch after pitch after pitch is awkwardly missed, as the coach gently underhands each one. Finally, as if to *mock* my prayers, this determined little boy who's trying so *excruciatingly* hard to maintain his dignity, falls *flat* on his face in the batter's box! The crowd grows quieter still. It seems an eternity before he is able to rise to his feet, to try again once more.

My mind is moving quickly now, and my anger is reaching a peak. I recall his torture from *endless* accidents and falls. There was never any stopping this irrepressible child from attempting to stand and walk, though his injured brain wouldn't allow it. Day after day, year after year, he crashed hard to the ground, not possessing the reflexes even to reach out and cushion his falls. Times without number I held his breathless body in my arms, literally shaking with excruciating pain. I remember the bashed out teeth and the blood, and the time he nearly lost his eye. Worst of all was the horrified look on his tear covered face, as if to say: "*Why, Dad? Why can't you stop this from happening to me? You're my dad!*" I remember the demoralizing impotence, powerlessness, not even knowing how to *begin* to help my boy. And I remember the scars *all* over his once perfect body. God only knows the scars in his tormented mind!

My mind is reaching the point of frenzy now, just thinking about those scars, including the ones inflicted on his soul by those heartless punks. Ready to burst from keeping all these thoughts inside, I can stand it no longer, and with *rage* I scream out in the direction of my Host: ***"What about the scars, Jesus? What do you have to say for Yourself about my son's scars?"***

As soon as the words leave my mouth, I begin to notice something I think I once knew. With my defiant question still echoing across the room, I see, incredibly, that Jesus also has scars. How could I have failed to remember? Perhaps I chose to forget. Either way, I haven't noticed them recently. I've been too busy considering my own pain. Ashamed, I try to look away, but He catches me in His gaze.

I am frozen, wondering what He will do now. Astonishingly, I feel no reprisal for my arrogance, only pure compassion. I dare to move closer, seeing something more amazing still. There are tears in Jesus' own eyes. It seems as if *He* is in pain now. I don't understand. Why is He *still* crying over the scars He suffered so long ago?

Then I start to tremble, falling to my knees as the truth slowly begins to dawn. Without His speaking a word, I finally begin to remember the only answer to my question I really need to know. His tears are not for *Himself*. His tears are for my precious, broken son. And amazingly, His tears are for me, and they are for you.

His tears are for every scar that has ever maimed and disfigured our bodies, every act of cruelty that has ever twisted our souls, every moment of anguish and pain we have suffered in this battleground world. He knows we've all been broken due to the sin and abuse perpetrated against us by others, which is so easy for us to see. He also knows of the sin lurking hidden within each one of us, sin to which we often choose to remain blind, sin which causes us to abuse others even as it rots us from within. He knows we are worthy of death for our rebellion against Him, and for the harm we have done in this world through our own foolishness and selfish sin. Despite all this, His mercy endures forever (Ps. 136, NKJV), and our healing is as near as His outstretched arms.

Jesus' own scars were inflicted because He loved us more than *anything* in His lavish kingdom; He loved us so much that He was willing to pay a price for us that shocked the universe. The almighty King, the Creator Himself, stepped down from His throne as the Son, allowing His body to be beaten and broken by the very ones He had created. Because He paid such an astonishing price, a day is now coming when there will be no more suffering, no more pain for all who belong to Him. On that day He will carry every broken child home to be with Him forever, and we will finally be made completely whole. He will wipe every tear from our eyes on that great day, and the sorrows of this world will be remembered no more.

Still trembling and bowed now, with eyes that have been opened to such wondrous things, I realize how unworthy I am to be in this King's presence. It seems best just to slip out of His party quietly, but I find myself still frozen, unable to rise from my knees. His loving gaze makes it clear that His mercy and grace are more powerful than my sin and shame. Not another word is necessary. I rise to my feet as His arms open wide to embrace me.

FOREVER PROVEN

What are you attempting to prove with your life? What am I attempting to prove with mine? When the Son of Man comes, will He find faith on the earth, or will He find us still bitterly blaming Him for the attacks that came against us not from heaven, but ultimately, from the pit of hell? We have a brief time in this world. What will it take for us to finally understand?

Because we were dead in our sin and without hope in the world, He gave up *everything*, even His own life, spilling His sacred blood to win a war for us that we could *never* win for ourselves. Only *one* story will prove worthy on that great day of His return. It won't be the story of our mighty achievements for Him. It will be the story of the undeserved love, mercy, and grace that He lavished upon us. His arms remain open wide for us now. Will we come to Him and allow Him to embrace us, surrendering to Him fully, so that He can prove *His* life through us?

> My Father, this is my prayer of commitment...and I pray this, trusting You to be faithful to all I commit:
>
> Prove Yourself through all that I am, all that I have, all that I do...my goals, my work, my possessions....All of it is empty apart from You.
>
> Fill me, and continue to fill me, so that the sum of my days here on earth is not vanity.
>
> Keep close to me...nudge me back into this path of Life when I begin to wander.[12]

God always proves faithful

Chapter 26

DEATH IN THE POT

When Elisha returned to Gilgal, there was a famine in the land. As the sons of the prophets were sitting before him, he said to his servant, "Put on the large pot and boil stew for the sons of the prophets." Then one went out into the field to gather herbs, and found a wild vine and gathered from it his lap full of wild gourds, and came and sliced them into the stew, for they did not know what they were. So they poured it out for the men to eat. And as they were eating of the stew, they cried out and said, "O man of God, there is death in the pot."... But he said, "Now bring meal." He threw it into the pot.... Then there was no harm in the pot.

2 Kings 4:38–41

On September 11, 2001, an attack came against our country that woke us brutally from our slumber. We shouldn't have been sleeping, since that same enemy tried to take down the Twin Towers of World Trade Center in 1993 via a sophisticated 1,500 pound bomb detonated in the subbasement parking area. The intention was to knock the North Tower (Tower One) into the South Tower (Tower Two), bringing both towers down. It failed to do so, but it injured more than 1,000 people and killed six. Still, we failed to understand that evil never stops until it is determinately stopped, and in horror we watched those towers sink to rubble on 9/11. Stunned with indescribable torment, thousands of families were brutally and forever changed, and our country wrestled with the perplexity of responding to such an insidious, hidden enemy. Amidst our bewilderment one thing was crystal clear. Life as we knew it would never again be the same.

Later that same month, an event just as devastating occurred in my life. This event and its aftermath tested my faith, my strength, my courage, even my will to live, beyond any sorrow described in this book. I prayed, pleaded, and begged God for a different conclusion, but like those towers, much of what I held dear in life was reduced to wreckage before my eyes. My wife's decision to end our nineteen-year marriage evolved into a protracted separation, then a divorce. It seemed my embattled family had finally suffered a mortal wound. I was stunned and bewildered regarding how to move forward in life, and again, whether I wanted to.

I was ready to leave the business world behind, confident that the Lord would open new doors of opportunity through which Jesus Christ would be lifted up and embraced by suffering, dying people in this world. I thought He was going to prove Himself through my life, through our lives *together* as a married team. All this seemed a bitter joke now, as smoke and debris flew from that wreckage in every direction. Deep depression and fear pervaded my life along with that smoke, and I was sorely tempted to give up for good, to pray Elijah's prayer: "It is enough; now, O LORD, take my life" (1 Kings 19:4). Yet children were involved, innocent ones who were now very vulnerable. Despite my exasperation with life and with God, He remained faithful, assembling wise counselors and loyal friends without whom I couldn't even have stood. I was near blind, but one thing was crystal clear. Life as we knew it would never again be the same.

More than a decade has unfolded since the events of this chapter, and they led to a long desert season in my life as a single father that has been sorrowful and debilitating. I'd *never* have chosen this wilderness, nor the gall and bitterness that came with it, especially the sorrows that came to my children. Yet it was in this desert that the Lord burned many of the lessons recorded in this book deep into my soul. I've learned that our King wastes nothing, and that He sometimes chooses to accomplish work within us that can only be performed in the dead of winter. Some of you are in a devastating wilderness season as you read these words. It's cold and you're weary, ready to give up the fight, even as I was sorely tempted to do many times during these years.

I've been careful in this book to offer no pious sounding platitudes or easy-to-follow formulas. My pain has been far too real for cotton candy formulas, as has yours. Because of His deep love for us, God delivered up not a formula, but a Son. His Spirit lives inside us to instruct and empower us to meet every challenge we will ever face here, and each brutal winter season. But *why* has God given us a Person and not a method or formula? Because He knows our stubborn, independent bent, and He knows we'd attempt to live out our precious formulas in the flesh, without Him. The flesh *always* meets its match in our personal frailty and sinfulness, in the sinfulness of others, and in the unceasing battles of life. If Jesus Christ didn't prove Himself to be all God's Word promised, I'd never have survived my brutal winter season, or the divorce.

Statistics indicate that more than 80 percent of marriages in which there is an autistic or handicapped child end in divorce.[1] I can neither verify nor dismiss such statistics. Stress is a killer. We all know that. Long-term suffering in a family, particularly when caused by the agony of a child, can cause any marriage to become fragile. But every marriage is fragile in its own way, and I never attributed our marital problems to Bryson's condition. Things were difficult in our marriage from the start, just as marriage has been for many of you. But I always thought we were going to make it. The way I saw it, there was no other alternative. And I truly thought the worst was behind us, that we were making progress. Like that attack on the World Trade Towers, I just didn't see it coming. I'm not saying I shouldn't have seen it. I'm saying I never *dreamed* that the enemy could enter the gates of my home and take my marriage down. I hope every married person takes note of what I just said.

> The kings of the earth did not believe, Nor did any of the inhabitants of the world, That the adversary and the enemy Could enter the gates of Jerusalem.
>
> —LAMENTATIONS 4:12

No one should hear me attempting to vindicate myself in saying I didn't see it coming. This is more of an indictment than a vindication. Did Adam have a valid excuse in not dealing decisively with what he should have seen and dealt with in the Garden of Eden? It's worth noting that God came looking specifically for Adam (and not Eve) after they both sinned. As the head of my home; as the leader, protector, and provider; God appointed me to be as the husband. I offer no excuses, but accept my God-given responsibility for my tragic marital failure.

And in referencing that an enemy entered our gates, no one should infer that either I or my former wife was the attacker. I'm not saying that at all. There's another attacker who knows how to come into a home to divide and conquer, even as he came into the Garden of Eden to conquer the very first couple. Did you ever stop to think about what Paul taught about our "struggle" in this world? "Our struggle is not against flesh and blood, but against rulers, against the powers, against the world forces of this darkness, against spiritual forces of wickedness in the heavenly places" (Eph. 6:12). I'm not asking you to understand all of that. I don't understand it clearly enough either. But at the very least, every married couple needs a basic understanding that the husband is not the enemy, nor is the wife the enemy. The enemy is the enemy. John Eldredge had this to say about marriage:

> Marriage is a stunning picture of what God offers his people... a living metaphor... a walking parable, a Rembrandt painting of the gospel. The enemy knows this, and he hates it with every ounce of his malicious heart.... Like in the Garden, Satan comes in to divide and conquer.[2]

If Eldredge is right, if the enemy seeks to divide a marriage to conquer it, then a couple must do anything it takes to stick *together.* Simple, right? Never mistake simple for easy! I've mentioned several times in this book that we've been born onto a battleground, not a playground. I'm convinced that God's Word means precisely what it says about the nature of the battles we're called to fight in this world. Many of those battles take place right in our own hearts and minds. If we desire to walk in Christ's victory, we must trust in Him *alone,* referring each thought and feeling back to Him, repenting often. Trusting in our own common sense, in the advice of well-intended friends, and in the wisdom of this world is not *nearly* good enough. We're *far* too prone to deception and Satan is "a liar and the father of lies" (John 8:44). You think you can stand up to him? Think again. Christ alone conquered him. Trust in *Him!*

A good acronym for fear is False Evidence Appearing Real. Satan is a master at stoking fears wrought through misperceptions. He's particularly skilled at distorting the motivations and intentions of words spoken and actions taken between spouses. In her outstanding book *For Women Only,* Shaunti Feldhahn presented the results of her survey of men's thought patterns, revealing that these are dramatically different than the thinking patterns of women. No shock there. With her husband Jeff in *For Men Only,* a survey revealed that women's thought patterns are also stunningly different than men's.[3] Again, no bombshell. But the specifics became intriguing.

Shaunti asked the men what they truly desired most for their wives to understand about their hearts' innermost desires. She was shocked to find that the highest desire of husbands, ahead of sex and all the rest of the issues she expected to be ranked highest, was a desire for their wives to understand how deeply they really did love them. Inherent in this response was a frustration among husbands that no matter how hard they tried to convey their love to their wives, they didn't seem to believe or accept the depth of the love they had for them.[4] This response jumped out at Shaunti not only because it was the number one response of husbands, and totally unexpected, but because it nearly *doubled* the second highest issue on men's minds in the survey.

One of my goals in this family story has been to keep it honest, so it might be helpful to you and your family. I've included a number of humorous anecdotes and warm remembrances that occurred between my wife and me during happier times. Those were real, as was my deep love for her. This chapter deals with divorce, and with matters more distressful than I could adequately describe to you. Prudence dictates that I say only a few things about the sorrowful final years of our marriage, and about the divorce. First about the marriage: There were two sinners in our marriage, just as there are two sinners in your marriage and two sinners in every marriage. Now about the divorce: I didn't initiate it or want it, and there were no biblical grounds for it. My former wife no longer bears my name, and has requested that I not use her name; and this is why I have not done so anywhere in this book. To the extent there were any sins or behaviors that contributed to the divorce, I will speak only of my own.

Please don't hear me suggesting that because we're all sinners we can be cavalier about our sin, sweeping it all under the "Jesus rug" as if it doesn't matter. Don't fool yourself. Our sin wounds others for whom Christ died, and grieves His heart. That "rug" (the cross) is soaked with innocent blood, shed for us. Sin destroys life, and in *His* strength we *must* battle against it, and repent when we've fallen.

But again, being honest, even with a healthy fear of sin and a grateful reverence for the cross of Christ, I'm daily reminded of how far I've yet to travel toward perfect love in my life. I tend to shy away from those with an air of perfection, don't you? Jesus came to heal the sick, not those who are well (Luke 5:31). When we cry out for mercy with humble hearts, He cleanses us, and real confidence returns to our lives as we follow Him. If I thought for a single minute God's mercy didn't endure forever (Ps. 136, NKJV) or the grace of Christ wasn't a valid answer to *every* real-life problem, every sin, and every failure—including marital failure, I'd never have written this book.

In this chapter, I will attempt to answer the following question: If it's through Jesus Christ and the power of the gospel that God reconciled all things to Himself (Col. 1:20), then why are so many Christian husbands and Christian wives not able to reconcile with each other? As you read this chapter and reflect on this question, I pray that many eyes will be opened to see that the answer can actually be found in the question itself.

My reflections on marriage in this chapter will be general and founded on Scripture, not specific to my marriage. As a result of my emphasis on the Bible, I expect I'll be criticized for some things I'll say that contrast with the temporal values embraced by many in the Christian community today. The church is riddled with man pleasers and woman pleasers, as the scourge of divorce is ignored at best. At worst, we are attempting to douse a raging fire with tanks and hoses full of politically correct gasoline. Jesus called us to follow Him on a narrow path, not a popular highway; and I've written this book in order to help men and women whose hearts remain open to His truth, not to avoid criticism. When you've seen the pain in innocent children's eyes, you stop fearing what man might think of you and stand more in reverence of what God requires of you.

Many in the church have forgotten we are the bride of Christ, and that the covenants we make to each other as husband and wife in our earthly marriages depict His eternal covenant with the church, bringing added glory to Him. It is an understatement to say that marriage is a very serious matter to God, and that divorce should be nearly unheard of within the church. But there's a famine in the land in our day. In an attempt to nourish ourselves in the face of this famine, wild gourds of Christ-excluding, humanistic wisdom have been sliced into the stew. There is death in the pot, and we are suffering carnage in our homes and marriages as we continue to consume it.

> When Elisha returned to Gilgal, there was a famine in the land. As the sons of the prophets were sitting before him, he said to his servant, "Put on the large pot and boil stew for the sons of the prophets." Then one went out into the field to gather herbs, and found a wild vine and gathered from it his lap full of wild gourds, and came and sliced them into the stew, for they did not know what they were. So they poured it out for the men to eat. And as they were eating of the stew, they cried out and said, "O man of God, there is death in the pot."...But he said, "Now bring meal." He threw it into the pot....Then there was no harm in the pot.
>
> —2 KINGS 4:38–41

As in the day of Elisha, our *only* hope is repentance, a word rarely spoken in churches today. We must stop consuming the humanistic poison that has been sliced into the stew, and in repentance return to our Husband, Jesus Christ. He alone can provide us with the life-giving meal of truth from His Word, so that there will be no harm in the pot and His Spirit can bring nourishment and revival back to our churches, marriages, and families.

Before we look at some of the "wild gourds" that have been sliced into the stew in our day, I want to speak to you very personally about the pain that divorce brought to me, and especially to my children. These matters are extremely difficult to write about; and frankly, I'd rather do *anything* else. But if describing the agony that came to one family will help just *one* married couple to reject divorce and find hope *together* in Jesus Christ, if it results in the pain of just *one* child's eyes being prevented in this world, I'll be grateful to the Lord.

How Do You Pull It Together after It's Been Pulled Apart?

In the 2007 feature film *The Brave One*, Ericka (played by Jodie Foster) is a New York City radio DJ who is just about to be married. In the opening scene, Ericka's fiancé is brutally beaten to death by Central Park thugs, while Ericka is also beaten and left for dead. After a long hospital stay, she survives. Many months later Detective Mercer (played by Terrence Howard) meets Ericka in a coffee shop and says to her: "You must have loved him very much" (speaking of her murdered fiancé). Foster acknowledges that she did. Detective Mercer then asks: "After something like that, how do you pull it back together?" From bitter, pain-filled eyes Ericka looks across the coffee shop table and stoically answers: "You *don't!*"[5]

I've been dreading writing this chapter, not because I'm afraid of what people will think of me, but because the divorce nearly killed me. The thought of revisiting the horrors by writing about it is repulsive. The depths have been so low, the misery so immense, I've struggled with a "why bother" attitude even in attempting to describe it to you. From early on, well-intended friends have exhorted me to "move on" past my pain. In a sense, they're right. Yet because I love them I pray they'll never need to fully understand. I don't want them to walk through it, which is the only way to truly know the devastation divorce brings to one's family, and to one's soul.

As a Christian man, I'd never say lightly that something challenged my will to live, as I did earlier. Yet the divorce did make me wish I was dead at times. If God's Word didn't prove to be *completely* trustworthy and true, I'm convinced my life would have ended. Even if I survived in terms of lungs breathing and heart beating, I'd have been dead as a doornail emotionally. God's Word alone revived me from the depths again and again. David said essentially the same when he wrote: "If Your law had not been my delight, Then I would have perished in my affliction. I will never forget Your precepts, For by them You have revived me" (Ps. 119:92–93).

If you pull apart a peanut butter and jelly sandwich, where does the jelly begin or the peanut butter end? Oh, I realize the psychobabblers will have a field day with what I just said. It takes two whole people to form a successful marriage. I get it. But God's Word says that those two people become *one* flesh. After all these years I'd still echo Ericka's words. There are some things you just don't get over. I'm not saying there's no healing or hope. I'm saying that the immense, agonizing aftermath of a divorce continues on and on and, in some respects, never ends. At the risk of making it sound like "Hotel California," divorce brings you to a place of brokenness you check into, but from which you don't ever leave. At least part of you doesn't.

I have a widowed friend whose husband died while working out at the gym. He was in his 40s, and the picture of health. The disaster was sudden, and she didn't even have the chance to say good-bye. I can't think of anything more grievous. Yet she told me that my situation was "much" worse than hers. Without any way diminishing the torturous grief suffered by widows and widowers who read this, divorce *is* harder in certain ways. John Piper speaks of this, and David's words from the psalm also shed light on this kind of relational sorrow.

> It is emotionally more heart-wrenching than the death of a spouse. Death is usually clean pain. Divorce is unclean pain. In other words, the enormous loss of a spouse in death is compounded in divorce by the ugliness of sin and moral outrage at being so wronged.[6]

> For it is not an enemy who reproaches me, Then I could bear it; Nor is it one who hates me who has exalted himself against me, Then I could hide myself.... But it is you... my equal, My companion and my familiar friend; We who had sweet fellowship together Walked in the house of God in the throng.
>
> —PSALM 55:12–14

Many books on the market will tell you the grass is greener on the other side of a divorce. "You *must* be true to yourself." "Life is short." "You owe it to yourself." "Kids are resilient." "Go ahead!" "Your children will be better off if you bring your unpleasant marriage to an end." "Johnny now has *two* families." "Julie has new siblings." "Hooray!" "It's *all* good!" Actually, it's humanistic trash, a lie that's been passed on to us from the pit of hell! The liar doesn't want you to know the permanent devastation divorce will bring to you, to your children, to your family legacy, to future generations, to your career, to your finances, to *every* aspect of life near and dear to you. But if you remember only one thing I tell you in this chapter, *please* hear my warning about the anguish that *will* (not *might*) come to your children.

The legal proceedings were costly, protracted, and agonizing. When the nightmare of separation leading to divorce began in my home, Janelle was seventeen, Tim was twelve, and Bryson was, by far, the youngest at fifteen. Despite all his progress, it was now clear he'd always be childlike. I began raising my children alone during that time, and have done so to this day. The court settlement named me sole custodial parent for the boys, and permanent guardian for Bryson, who was ruled incompetent to manage his affairs. My daughter chose her own residence, living with her brothers and me until she was married many years later. Yet that is getting ahead of the story.

This book has revolved around events occurring in the life of a brain-injured child. I'll hold to that format in this chapter, focusing chiefly on how the divorce affected Bryson. But in focusing on him I risk underemphasizing the tremendous harm and crushing pain that came to all three children. To put it bluntly, the divorce tortured them. If you're tempted to believe it will be different for your children, *don't* buy it! You're being deceived. It won't.

A Cocoon and a Tsunami

Throughout his life Bryson had suffered the exasperation of a butterfly trying to break free of a cocoon in which something had gone terribly wrong. I remember the early years like they were yesterday, when it was thought best by some for him to live in an institution. He'd be barely educable, and might never even speak. His injured brain made his cocoon a virtual prison, thwarting his quest toward freedom, again and again. But he'd fought so hard, come so far. There was so much to rejoice in, and praise God for. In so many ways his life was a miracle.

But his awakening from his brain-injured slumber was far from perfect, leaving him overtly flawed mentally and emotionally, with speech patterns that remained arduous; and we now realized he'd suffer from cerebral palsy the rest of his life. The NACD had instructed us to begin phasing out his physical regimen to focus on his academic needs and on his emotional well-being during his middle school years. They warned us of the adolescent storms on the horizon, knowing that hormones would be flowing through him like a raging river as those storms arrived.

Relationships had always been the air supply of Bryson's life, and his fun-loving personality remained one of his greatest strengths. Yet connecting him with friends had always been *so* difficult due to his physical, cognitive, and linguistic limitations. His passion for sports had helped to connect him with peers for a few brief years, but a huge void entered his life as his beloved recreation league sports began aging him out at the *same* time that the social scene, with all the interest in the opposite sex, spiraled beyond his reach.

Adjustments need to be made in the dreams of every child during adolescence, yet for the typical child compensations are far more easily found. When the childhood dreams of mentally impaired and autistic children wither during adolescence, a void the size of the Grand Canyon invades their souls. If you think I've just exaggerated, ask any parent of a dejected, mentally impaired child during the adolescent years. A sense of hopelessness and despondency often runs deep for the caregiving parents, the siblings, and, of course, for the disheartened child, as they face the futility involved of attempting to fill that canyon.

Meeting Bryson's needs was like fighting the law of gravity as middle school drew to a close. All the years of exasperating limitation had pulled his soul toward anger, self-hatred, and despondency. Amidst all the rejection and loneliness, not to mention the torture of those who abused him emotionally, he began exhibiting frightening episodes like those described, in which I begged him to come out of his closet as he screamed: "I wish I not have stupid body!...I hate my body!...I wish you had different son!...I stupid!...I hate myself!"

God sometimes puzzled me by His absence when it seemed clear we needed Him most. Yet despite the way it often looked and felt, the King was far from absent. I'll always be grateful for the support of men He sent, men like Matt DeLorenzo, our *legendary* youth pastor. Yes, I said "legendary." Matt was the wisest man I've ever known in understanding the needs of vulnerable young people, and youth leaders from across our region sought his wisdom. He knew the Christian life was designed by God as a team sport, not a solo event, and that lone sheep often get slaughtered. And oh, does the wolf know when to pounce!

He came to my home on Bryson's fourteenth birthday to bring him out to meet some mentors. Ever fearful of new situations, Bryson refused to go. He simply wouldn't get out of his chair. But similar to Bryson's pit-bull tenacity, Matt was not prone to giving up either. He knew Bryson was terrified. This dear man, who was in his mid 60s, sat on the floor of my family room for *two solid hours* that day, chatting with my son, building up his confidence. Finally, Bryson had the courage to get up off his chair and go with Matt and me to Pizza Man in Pompton Plains. He had a *sensational* time, making friends who'd encourage him now and then during those fearful years.

As I stepped back from being "Dad," I *so* admired my son. He'd broken free of his cocoon, beaten *immense* odds, rising up from the most demoralizing setbacks imaginable. Sometimes I thought there was nothing on earth, or from hell itself, that could keep him from rising back up to his feet. I thought the worst was behind him now, that the seas would remain calm for a season, perhaps even a long season. But the worst wave was rolling just beyond the horizon. All he'd endured his entire life, all the immense frustration and even the cruelty of those punks in middle school, proved to be child's play in the devil's hands compared to that wave, that tsunami named divorce.

I'm convinced that the serpent makes a special note of where the most vulnerable souls live in this world, and he knows the most opportune time to make his return (Luke 4:13). My son was gasping for air during this time, as wave upon wave of fear and loneliness slammed onto his shores. I felt utterly helpless so much of this time, sensing that those adolescent waves would wipe him out. This was no time to let go of him, but it was hard to know how to keep his head above water anymore, or even how to answer his tirades from the closet. Like a one-two punch, the torture he'd endured his whole life had set him up, now he struggled like a boxer on the ropes as the enemy came in for the kill and as the shadow of that tsunami began to block out the sun.

THE SENDING OF TITUS?

It was August 2002, and we were up at our vacation home. Janelle was already off to her freshman year at Wheaton College. My wife and I had been separated for a year, but we were together talking in the backyard, just below his window. I had no idea he was listening from behind the screen, but he'd overheard the entire conversation, during which it became clear to him that reconciliation between mommy and daddy seemed impossible. After his mother left, I looked up and saw the horror on his face, and got a sinking feeling in the pit of my stomach.

I *raced* up the stairs, but he'd locked the door. He was screaming: "You and mom [are] getting [a] divorce." I pleaded with him to open the door. When he finally did, I'll never forget his demeanor. His face was dark, and he removed his North Carolina Tar Heels hat (his favorite team), looked me in the eye, and said (with his typical broken speech pattern): "I going [to] fwip my hat.... If it lands dis [this] side up, [then] I live.... If it lands dis [this] side up, [then] I die.... I wanna die, Dad.... I wanna burn in hell.... I wanna burn in hell wite [right] now!"

I remembered the first sounds coming from his tender lips at nearly three years old, after his therapists warned us he'd never speak intelligibly. Those beautiful sounds seemed to be coming directly from heaven. Now, from those same lips came words that terrified me. He began screaming, over and over, that he wanted to burn in hell. I tried to hug him, but he pushed me away. I felt helpless. I had no choice but to let him scream it all out, trying to comfort him the best I could. After what seemed an eternity, he calmed down. I tried to convince him everything was going to be okay, but he had no interest in what I was trying to tell him.

I put *The Mighty Ducks* movie in the VCR and called Tim to come to watch it with him. I always knew Bryson would be okay if Tim was with him. It hadn't been easy growing up with such a needy "older" brother, and Tim had strength of character far beyond his years. It occurred to me that Bryson wasn't the only one who had been robbed of his childhood. Yet I don't recall Tim *ever* complaining. What I do recall is him rising to the occasion, over and over, in a way that would make any father proud. I am proud of him now, as I write these words.

Bryson's tirade was over, at least for now. Others much worse loomed in his future. I went into a spare bedroom, collapsed to my knees, and just began weeping. The impact of the divorce was destroying so much now. On my knees in that bedroom, I literally begged God to show up, to somehow let me know that my kids would make it through this disaster. Suddenly, as if God were speaking to me, 2 Corinthians 7:5–6 entered my mind, in which Paul said: "We were afflicted on every side: conflicts without, fears within. But God, who comforts the depressed, comforted us by the coming of Titus." Almost as an afterthought, I prayed in response: "Lord, I could definitely use a 'Titus' right now. Please send someone to help us."

I checked the boys, and they were still watching the movie. I put Gingersnap the wonder dog on her leash and started walking down White Rock Trail, the long dirt road from our lakeside home leading to Route 8 in Speculator. After five minutes of walking, just as I approached Route 8, a Jeep literally screeched to a halt on the other side of the road, startling me as it pulled to the shoulder. Two large men jumped out of the vehicle, and started walking right toward me, fast. It was dusk and I had no idea who these men were. I froze. One of them called out, "Are you Barry Milazzo?" I answered that I was. My heart was racing. I thought, "What now, Lord? How much worse can this day possibly get?" Both of them kept coming straight toward me, across Route 8, picking up their pace now. This couldn't be good. I braced myself, doing my best to stand my ground, with Gingersnap looking on. As they arrived, one of them reached for me.

Warren Struz, a tall powerful man, grabbed my hand, taking it in his larger hand, and began shaking it. Big Dave Carlson gave me a bear hug. I still had *no* idea who these men were, but it was sinking in they intended no harm. I stood dumbfounded, and Gingersnap was wagging her tail as Warren began to explain: "We've been out looking for you for the past half hour and were just about to give up. We knew your place was on this side of the lake, but we didn't know where. Your sister Linda is a friend of mine from Hawthorne Gospel Church in New Jersey. She told me you were *really* hurting, and she knew I was coming up to Camp of the Woods this weekend. She asked me to find you and see if I might be able to encourage you. Maybe you can come to my cabin, so that we can talk for a while, and pray."

In an understatement, I was stunned. I told Warren I needed to get back to my boys, but that I might be able to come after their bedtime. Warren responded, "I don't care how late it gets. Here are the directions to my cabin. We'll be waiting for you." With that, those two large men jumped back into Warren's Jeep, and were gone. Overwhelmed, I thought, "Could it be that these guys came in response to my prayer?"

Indeed they had, and I'll tell you about my midnight meeting with them in the next chapter. But first, I will return to the issue of the wild gourds of Christ-excluding, humanistic wisdom that have been sliced into the pot in our day, "wisdom" that has poisoned countless churches and marriages and deeply grieved the heart of our eternal Husband. I ask every married person to pay serious attention to the things the Lord has led me to lay out here, especially those of you who are tempted to believe that divorce is the only answer for your pain-filled marriage.

WORLDLY AND WIMPY

> Wimpy theology is plagued by woman-centeredness and man-centeredness. Wimpy theology doesn't have the granite foundation of God's sovereignty or the solid steel structure of a great God-centered purpose for all things.[7]
>
> —JOHN PIPER

It is an understatement to say many churches are worldly, and wimpy, in our day. Many Christians use the Bible as an à la carte menu, picking and choosing what appeals to them. One of the prized Asherah poles of our day is the worship of "tolerance." If someone *wants* to believe something that pleases and comforts them, something that caters to their selfish desires, we feel compelled to sanction that belief as worthy of acceptance, even applause. God is not applauding.

If the Creator of this universe wrote you a personal letter, wouldn't you just tear open the envelope and read it eagerly? God *has* written a very personal love letter to human beings, particularly to those in the church, His bride. His letter reveals His deep love for us, and His wise guidance to protect us in this battle-ground world. In that love letter, the Bible, we find the God-centered purpose for all things Piper spoke of. The letter begins with the story of Adam and Eve, who had *everything* going for them. Every need was met, every delight and adventure was theirs for the taking. They even had the benefit of God walking lovingly alongside them in that garden of paradise. They had *all* this going for them, yet they *still* rebelled against Him.

Before we look down on that first couple for their senseless rebellion, let's realize that we also have *everything* going for us today, in Christ. Yet, to the grief of our Lover's heart, we've proven, again and again, that we'll choose what *we* want, even when we *know* that what we want is the *opposite* of what God has spoken in His love letter. Like Adam and Eve, we think we can do better for ourselves. As Andrew Murray said, we want just enough of salvation to give us an escape from hell, and provide us with comfort and happiness until we get to heaven:

> In selfishness, we look upon salvation merely as the escape from hell. And in this same selfish way, we want only so much of holiness as is needful to make our personal safety, comfort and happiness secure. Jesus Christ came meaning for us to be restored to the state from which we had fallen. Salvation then, is the state in which the whole inner man—the heart, the will, the life—is given up to the glory and service of God.[8]

"Glorify God with our lives? Listen, Andy, this is the twenty-first century. I'll attend church, sing some praise songs, maybe attend a small group—all that and more. If my life happens to glorify God along the way, then fine! Just don't ask me to do it at the expense of my *happiness*! Let's be real, Andy baby. And don't hit me with that jazz about Jesus not regarding equality with God a thing to be grasped, emptying Himself, humbling Himself, obedient to the point of death (Phil. 2:–8). Listen, I applaud Him for that. Great Savior! Awesome! Precious to me! Did I say great? But have that attitude myself? That would mean I'd need to surrender *everything* to Him, even my marriage. *No way* am I humbling myself *there*! That's a bit extreme, and you *know* it! Even my pastor doesn't hit me with such heavy stuff. Frankly, Andy babes, and I mean this as no insult (I *do* believe in tolerance, even for *you*), my pastor's a whole lot easier to listen to than you are!"

> For the time will come when they will not endure sound doctrine; but wanting to have their ears tickled, they will accumulate for themselves teachers in accordance to their own desires, and will turn away their ears from the truth and will turn aside to myths.
>
> —2 Timothy 4:3–4

One myth that secular society has embraced today is that marriage is a man-made institution. If it's man-made, then *we* have the right to modify it as we please. Instead of standing firm against this grievous error, many equivocating churches have embraced various forms of wimpy theology to appease this worldly perspective. Presumably, these churches have done so in order to remain "relevant" to those who might be more interested in their "wimpiness" than in hearing truth spoken from God's Word. How sad this must make God! When will we ever learn that there's nothing quite as relevant to dying human beings as God's love letter to us?

Marriage was God's idea, His *specific* design. It is *anything* but man-made. He instituted marriage as a covenant between man and woman for the expressed purpose of enhancing the glory that is due to Jesus Christ. Marriage does this by depicting the covenant relationship between Christ and His bride, the church (Gen. 2:24; Eph. 5:32). And He has established defined roles, replete with a line of authority and responsibility within marriage. These roles reflect the order that exists in the triune Godhead, the order that has *always* existed between Father, Son, and Holy Spirit. John Piper describes the purpose and roles of marriage, below:

> The ultimate meaning of marriage is the representation of the covenant-keeping love between Christ and His Church.[9]
>
> Husbands are compared to Christ; wives are compared to the church. Husbands are commanded to love as Christ loved; wives are commanded to submit as the church is to submit to Christ. It is astonishing how many people do not see this when they deal with this passage (Eph. 5:22–25)....I have in mind those who would be called egalitarians—the ones who reject the idea that men are called to be leaders in the home.[10]

Much of what the Bible teaches, including the teaching regarding the purpose of marriage and the roles God has established within marriage, is scoffed at today. My purpose in this chapter is not to debate what God does not debate. His design for marriage is clear and it is wise. But I do want to discuss one of the most ignored biblical truths concerning marriage: God's clear instruction concerning the *permanency* of the marital covenant.

The Bible is clear that we do not have the right to break the marital covenants we've made before God. We do not have the right to break them for the sake of self-realization, nor for personal fulfillment, nor for all the greener pastures that our society reveres. Nor do we have the right to break them to pursue the idol of happiness, an idol that is worshipped far more than God in many churches, and in many of our hearts. We're not even permitted to break our covenants for the reduction of pain. John Piper described the permanency of marriage this way:

> If Christ ever abandons and discards His church, then a man may divorce his wife....If the blood-bought church under the New Covenant ever ceases to be the bride of Christ, then a wife may legitimately divorce her husband....It simply does not lie within man's rights to destroy what God created.[11]
>
> *Covenant breaking is a way of short-term pain reduction. But in the process of reducing our pain we destroy life.* Pain-free relationships are assumed as a right. But God promises His people something better.[12] (emphasis added)

Instead of lighting the way for secular society to come out of the darkness to find the "better" promise of God that Piper spoke of, the Christian community has largely *followed* our culture into the darkness of rampant divorce. Ironically, even secular studies now *consistently* reveal that in most cases, unhappily married couples who reject divorce wind up less depressed and happier in the future compared to those who have bailed out via divorce. A study conducted by the Institute for American Values concludes: "Two out of three unhappily married adults who avoided divorce or separation ended up happily married five years later."[13]

But do we really need the validation of secular studies to guide our choices and behavior as believers? Shamefully, yes! Without getting into a debate over statistics, I'll simply say what every aware Christian already knows: Christian marriages are dropping like flies. The marriages of many Christian leaders are falling too.

We need not scratch our heads, searching for the answer to "Christian" divorce in the latest sociological theorem. We need only to look to God's Word, and remember that His ways are *far* higher than ours (Isa. 55:8–9). The Spirit of God and the spirit of this world are mortal enemies. We need to repent of choosing the world's ways. We also need to understand that a choice to stand in the middle is a choice for the world, a choice to become God's enemy.

> You adulteresses, do you not know that friendship with the world is hostility toward God?...Whoever wishes to be a friend of the world makes himself an enemy of God.
>
> —James 4:4

Don't hear James wrong. God loves His enemies. Indeed He died for them (us), and through His Son's blood He turned them (us) into His sons and daughters (Rom. 5:8–10). Yet love never sits on a fence and God never compromises with His enemies. There are far too many fence sitters in our day making an unholy alliance with the enemies of God in this world. Nancy Leigh DeMoss points out that many "Christian" resources have moved beyond compromise and into rebellion. As in the day of Ezekiel, they are actually strengthening the hands of the wicked by promising life to those who have no intention of repenting and returning from their wicked ways:

> With lies ye have made the heart of the righteous sad, whom I have not made sad; and strengthened the hands of the wicked, that he should not return from his wicked way, by promising him life.
>
> —Ezekiel 13:22–23, kjv

> Walk into a Christian bookstore today and you'll probably find a modern example of a problem Ezekiel addressed. Sadly,...many of today's Christian authors, speakers, and counselors are "strengthening the hands of the wicked" by telling people they don't need to repent for sin...their teachings, for example, justify anger...
>
> "Actually, it's healthy to go ahead and express your feelings." (Nancy: "and selfishness")...
>
> "You've got to put boundaries between you and demanding people" (Nancy: "irresponsibility").

"You have every right to act that way; you've been wounded by others…" (Nancy: "We need to constantly be asking ourselves, 'What's the message here? What does the Bible say?'")[14]

More Christian books have been written about marriage in recent decades than at any time in history, yet divorces keep occurring *unchallenged* in our equivocating, politically correct churches. Many of today's authors, churches, seminaries, and counseling offices are pointing us toward the standards of our culture and the tenets of pop psychology as if they were doctrines from God. Along with DeMoss, we all need to be asking, "What does the Bible say?" Jesus addressed the religious experts of His day the way I believe He'd address many of our "experts."

> Rightly did Isaiah prophesy of you hypocrites, as it is written: "THIS PEOPLE HONORS ME WITH THEIR LIPS, BUT THEIR HEART IS FAR AWAY FROM ME. BUT IN VAIN DO THEY WORSHIP ME, TEACHING AS DOCTRINES THE PRECEPTS OF MEN." Neglecting the commandment of God, you hold to the tradition of men.… You are *experts* at setting aside the commandment of God.
>
> —MARK 7:6–9, EMPHASIS ADDED

Many are experts at setting aside God's commands in our day, particularly the sacred command: "What therefore God has joined together, let no man separate" (Mark 10:9). Separation is often the knee-jerk recommendation when difficult marital issues arise, despite the lasting harm that often results from it, especially for the children. Yet there are far more subtle forms of separation being recommended by today's Christian "experts," and their insidious methods are among the most poisonous "gourds" being sliced into the pot in our day.

As if married couples don't have enough to contend with as they strive to maintain oneness and intimacy amidst the challenges, trials, and losses that come to us all in this battleground world. As if it's not difficult enough to stand against a hidden but very real enemy who seeks to divide and conquer, an enemy who is just itching to enter into any crack or crevice that exists between them, so he can widen it. "Christian experts" today have written endless books addressing the most effective methods for husbands and wives to establish "boundaries" between each other. We may as well encourage couples to establish barricades, or the Berlin Wall, because in my opinion *that* is what their worldly-wise methods most often result in between spouses on a practical level.

These experts are eager to sell you their books, send you their counseling keys, and refer you to affiliated counseling offices. We're talking a full-service salon. Some of their books even diagram pie charts for you, "educating" you regarding just how you're being mistreated in your marriage. Don't be shy, guys and gals. Step *right* up and get your slice of pie. We're here to help you, and we'll make sure you get a juicy slice that will convince you that your "rights" haven't been adequately catered to in your marriage! Sure, it'll make you mad at your spouse, but go ahead. Eat it! After all, you *deserve* to be mad. It is your right! If you doubt this, wives, just check with your girlfriends who are *just* as angry with their husbands as you are. If you doubt this, husbands, check with your angry guy friends, those with wives just as "impossible" as yours. *They'll* let you know the score! Or you can simply check with the psychologists all on those afternoon TV shows. Listen, the whole world is enlightened about victimhood and the need for personal empowerment and about getting our needs met *now*. What are you waiting for? Don't be left behind. Take a bite of that pie, and seize your rights!

In His love letter to us, God offers an embarrassingly unenlightened view. He urges us to bear up under sorrows even when we are called upon to suffer unjustly in marriage. He offers us a path of humility in which we remain mindful that there are *two* sinners in every marriage. Through *mutual* repentance, and the provision of undeserved forgiveness and grace toward each other, even the most difficult marriages can be saved. But don't be fooled, taking the path of Jesus won't result in receiving favor from the experts of this world, and there is no middle road. We must choose the path of Jesus, or the world. Before making your choice, listen carefully to the words of Andrew Murray below, and then to Peter, to understand what the path of Jesus truly is:

> If a terrible, painful injury is done to us, or if we suffer injustice, the first thing we must do is to lay hold of a God-like disposition. This is the only way to keep our spirit from latching on to a sense of wounded honor. If we allow the wound to fester, then we will begin down the wrong spiritual path. We will need to insist on our rights, or we will react by paying back the offender what we think he deserves.... Learn to forgive the way God and Christ forgive—freely, to the extent that blood was shed... forgive each other, just as in Christ God forgave you (Eph. 4:32).[15]
>
> —Andrew Murray

> For this finds favor, if for the sake of conscience toward God a man bears up under sorrows when suffering unjustly. For what credit is there if, when you sin and are harshly treated, you endure it with patience? But if when you do what is right and suffer for it you patiently endure it, this finds favor with God. For you have been called for this purpose, since Christ also suffered for you, leaving you an example for you to follow in His steps, WHO COMMITTED NO SIN, NOR WAS ANY DECEIT FOUND IN HIS MOUTH; and while being reviled, He did not revile in return; while suffering, He uttered no threats, but kept entrusting Himself to Him who judges righteously.
>
> —1 Peter 2:19–23

As you make your choice between finding favor in the eyes of God versus the favor of the world, don't underestimate how *vastly* different the two paths are. Humanistic wisdom knows *nothing* of putting aside our rights and picking up a personal cross to follow a King who surrendered all His rights as He was nailed to His cross. The "wise" of this world focus on temporal things. They have no understanding about the power and wisdom of a Savior who promises to accomplish goals through us that go far beyond what can be seen. They do not believe in a God who is big enough to work all things out in our marriages and families in His way and time. They have no idea that, through our obedience, the King will *always* do a better job of standing up for us than we can do by following the world's self-focused methods of elevating our own rights.

You want to start a war with your spouse? Go ahead and give Jesus Christ lip service while choosing from among the panoply of wise sounding methods of trying to "fix" or change your spouse by declaring boundaries, setting consequences for their transgressions, and by demanding all the rights you're convinced you deserve. When we attempt to change the hearts of our spouses, particularly as we ignore the logs that exist in our own eyes, things get dark and scary in a hurry, and divorce lawyers begin to smile.

Again, God delivered up not a method or a formula, but a Son. He teaches us to bear with one another and forgive each other *just as* He has forgiven us (Col. 3:13). He teaches us to forgive *everything* so we won't be taken advantage of by the devil (2 Cor. 2:10–11). He teaches us to speak truth in love, even when it's hard, to be angry and still not sin, not giving the devil an opportunity (Eph. 4:15; 25–27). He teaches us that love bears all things, believes all things, hopes all things, *endures* all things (1 Cor. 13:7). But the *best* part of all His teachings is that the Son doesn't merely lay out all these hard commands and then leave us alone to, somehow, figure out how to accomplish them. He lives *inside* us to daily empower us as we seek to obey His truth.

Yet, as in all deals that sound too good to be true, there *is* a catch in Jesus' simple way. The "catch" is that this King requires our *full* surrender to Him. Again, Andrew Murray reminds us that there can be no compromise, no standing in the middle between Jesus and the world's ways.

> Make no mistake, the spirit of this world and the Spirit of God are engaged in a life-and-death conflict with each other. That is why God has always called on His people to separate themselves from the world.... Nothing but light can drive out darkness. Nothing but the Spirit from heaven can expel the spirit of this world. When a man or woman does not surrender to God, to be filled with the Spirit of Jesus and the Spirit of heaven, they must remain under the spirit of this world.[16]

Irrespective of whether we are attempting to change our own behavior at the heart level, or we are attempting to change the hearts of our spouses, we are *woefully* inadequate for the task. There's not a soul on earth who has ever saved himself from sin by trying to make changes in his or her life, nor as others made demands upon them to change. Paul tells us: *just as* we received Christ Jesus as Lord, we are to walk in Him (Col. 2:6). Only Jesus Christ can save us, and only His Spirit can affect the continued heart changes *He* wants to bring about in our lives, *and in the lives of our spouses.* Heart change is God's business; and frankly, even the most well-intentioned Christian "experts" are on thin ice in pretending that their humanistic formulas can replace the gospel.

But let's face it. The notion that Jesus Christ is a valid answer for human problems, no less to marital problems, has always been considered foolish by the world. The difference today is that reliance upon Jesus Christ is not only scoffed at by the world. Tragically, Jesus' way is also sneered at within the church itself. Paul feared the serpent's strategy to lead God's people astray from Christ, even as he first deceived Eve in the Garden of Eden:

> But I am afraid that, as the serpent deceived Eve by his craftiness, your minds will be led astray from the simplicity and purity of devotion to Christ.
>
> —2 Corinthians 11:3

Paul's fear has been broadly realized in our day. The scandalous amount of divorce in the church is not the cause of our problems. Divorce is merely a symptom of our core problem. It is the collateral damage of a pervasively deceived and faithless Christian community that has been led astray from the simplicity and purity of devotion to Christ. Our perpetual attempts to seek humanistic resources to resolve life's "real" problems prove just how far we've gone astray. We're quick to outsource our personal problems, including our problem marriages, to the "wise" of this age, in the sanctuary of the psychological counseling office. We've sought this "wisdom," and the humanistic methods that come with it, to the exclusion of Jesus Christ. Naturally, these methods have proved useless, and our faithless rebellion has had a cataclysmic impact upon our homes. Paul reminds us:

> Let no man deceive himself. If any man among you thinks that he is wise in this age, he must become foolish, so that he may become wise. For *the wisdom of the world is foolishness before God*. For it is written, "He is the one who catches the wise in their craftiness"; and again, "The Lord knows the reasonings of the wise, that they are useless."So then let no one boast in men, for *all things belong to you.... All things belong to you*, and you belong to Christ; and Christ belongs to God.
>
> —1 Corinthians 3:18–23, emphasis added

Please don't miss that Paul *repeated*: "all things belong to you." Paul *knew* God provided *everything* we need in Christ. The serpent knows it too, and he seeks to discredit this very fact. Attacking the veracity of God's Word has *always* been his tack in separating man from God, and man from woman. He brings distortions of God's Word, even as he brought them to the first home in the Garden. But don't expect him to show up at your door as a blatantly heretical opponent of Christ. You'd see him coming a mile away. The angel of light incorporates truth from the Bible in his appeal to us, making his "wisdom" nearly irrefutable. Yet, if you listen carefully, there's always a "truthful" variation of the deceitful question he first posed to Eve: "Did God really say?" (Gen. 3:1, niv).

Satan's lies are almost always affirming to our common sense, to the way our flesh is *already* urging us to go. Oswald Chambers said, "Nothing Jesus Christ ever said is common sense, it is revelation sense, and it reaches the shores where common sense fails."[17] Only Truth and Light (Jesus Christ and His Word) can extinguish the lies and deceptions the enemy brings to each life and to each marriage through "common sense," to destroy it.

Ah, Truth and Light! That just wraps it up nice and tidy, doesn't it? We can simply let go and let God extinguish all the lies the enemy brings to our front door to destroy our homes and families. Hooray for Jesus! He's got it covered. Now, we can go back to our comfy homes and live as *we* please. "Jesus is on our side! What's for dinner? Pass me the remote…" Have you ever stopped to consider the cancers of the soul Jesus warned us about?

> The eye is the lamp of the body; so then if your eye is clear, your whole body will be full of light. But if your eye is bad, your whole body will be full of darkness. If then the light that is in you is darkness, how great is the darkness!
>
> —MATTHEW 6:22–23

Whoa! Hold on a minute, Jesus! We just settled the fact that our part is easy. That we can count on You! You proclaimed Yourself to be the way the truth and the life. If that's who You really are, then You should extinguish the lies, the darkness, and all the deceitful traps the enemy brings to our souls to cause our homes to come crashing down. What's all this "If the light that is in you is darkness" stuff?

Don't throw us a curveball now, Jesus! Life is hard enough! We need You helping us, not trying to strike us out! If all that humanistic trash being presented today with the label of "Christian" isn't the answer, then You've got to be the Answer! If You aren't, I'm really going to give up this time. So tell us! Are You the source of Truth and Light we can count on to protect our lives and marriages from the evil one or aren't You?

Indeed, Jesus will extinguish all the darkness the enemy can bring to our minds to destroy our homes. But we must respond by *knowing* and *obeying* His Word. Jesus used *one* line of defense against Satan in the wilderness: "It is written.…It is written.…It is written" (Matt. 4:4, 7, 10). If King Jesus needed to rely upon Scripture, then how much more do we need to know what His Word says, and obey it?

> Why do you call Me, "Lord, Lord," and do not do what I say? Everyone who comes to Me and hears My words and acts on them, I will show you whom he is like: he is like a man building a house, who dug deep and laid a foundation on the rock; and when a flood occurred, the torrent burst against that house and could not shake it, because it had been well built. But the one who has heard and has not acted accordingly, is like a man who built a

> house on the ground without any foundation; and the torrent burst against it and immediately it collapsed, and the ruin of that house was great.
>
> —Luke 6:46–49

It's hardly coincidental that Jesus posed His pathetic question: "Why do you call me 'Lord, Lord,' and do not do what I say?" *immediately* prior to His teaching on the house (marriage) that stood versus the house (marriage) that collapsed. Pay *very* close attention to how Jesus lays this out. He said *"when"* the floods come, not *"if."* Floods *are* coming against our homes, dear reader. Make no mistake about that! A torrent will come against *every* house. The only question will be: have we built our homes on a solid foundation? Obedience matters.

And we dare not become lax because we've been obedient in the past. Even when Jesus defeated Satan with Scripture, he didn't disappear for good, did he? He simply left until a more "opportune time" (Luke 4:13). There is no season to be careless. Most of us can call to mind a couple who got divorced after *decades* of marriage. I'm speaking of solid Christian couples. Perhaps they were in ministry together and you were *shocked* to hear of their divorce. In order to keep our eye clear, we must obey God's Word throughout a lifetime, humbly repenting each time we fail. Paul told us we must take "every thought captive to the obedience of Christ" (2 Cor. 10:5). Does that sound too hard? There's an enemy lurking at your family gates who would love *nothing* better than to dishonor God by taking down your marriage. If the serpent gets what he wants, *then* you'll begin to understand "hard."

From start to finish, we're dealing with ingenious deceptions cultivated by a brilliant adversary seasoned in his craft and timing. He lays landmines for us to step on *years* in the future. Those landmines are often buried with abuses we've suffered in our past, pain and shame we've long since forgotten. Satan remembers those wounds, particularly the ones that have caused us to erect hard shell attitudes of "I'll make sure no one hurts me like that ever again!" When these fearful, self-reliant attitudes are not repented of, and those landmines of past abuse are not diffused by covering them in forgiveness, they cause us to choose fear instead of trust, bitterness and hardness of heart instead of *mutual* repentance with our spouses. Those landmines almost always detonate at the worst *possible* time, when there's already a confluence of stressful trials pressing in on seemingly every side, and during vulnerable times of mid-life physiological change. All hell breaks loose when they explode, and we become prone to believe that our spouse is the enemy, the cause of *all* our sorrow and pain, as the serpent remains hidden.

Oh, what's the use! How can we *possibly* defeat so savvy a serpent? Indeed, we are sorely overmatched. Yet, if we will repent of our alliance with the world and its ways, we'll realize that our Champion has *already* defeated Satan *resoundingly* (1 John 4:4). Confidence is our birthright as followers of Jesus Christ. But again, we play a *vital* role, a role that brings us right back to obedience. We render God's Spirit practically useless in our lives when we deliberately disobey and as we straddle the fence between the Word of God and the worldly experts who seek to distort it. Yes, the weapons of our warfare are divinely powerful (2 Cor. 10:4). But the ignition switch to our weaponry is not found in worldly-wise methods or in psychobabble. The key that unleashes the power of His Spirit into our lives is obedience to the Scriptures. Jesus said:

> Is this not the reason you are mistaken, that you do not understand the Scriptures or the power of God?
>
> —MARK 12:24

Against the backdrop of a shameful epidemic of divorce in the church today, is this not *precisely* the reason *we* are mistaken? The smug religious leaders that Jesus battled against didn't have ears to hear. But do *we* understand the Scriptures? Do *we* believe in the power of God? If we did, we wouldn't continue to seek "wisdom" from the darkness of the world. If we truly want to understand why our marriages are falling apart, we need to consider Jesus' statement above in the context of His Father's warning from centuries before: "My people are destroyed for lack of knowledge. Because you have rejected knowledge, I also will reject you" (Hosea 4:6).

Wow, that's heavy! No *wonder* we prefer wimpy theology. "But since our marriages and homes are being destroyed, I'll bite, Lord, but please be clear. This is the longest chapter and my readers must be bleary-eyed. What *is* this great knowledge we've rejected? I'll bet it's fraught with scholarly wonders, lofty theology that's hard to comprehend." Hardly! When we truly want to know God's knowledge, we need to become as a little child. Jesus loves me, this I know, for the Bible tells me so. That nails it! God's wisdom *is Jesus Christ,* and the wondrous, miraculous power of the gospel.

Do we desire peace in our lives and in our marriages? He *Himself* is our peace (Eph. 2:14). Jesus became to us wisdom from God, and righteousness and sanctification and redemption (1 Cor. 1:30). He is the Alpha and the Omega, the beginning and the end (Rev. 22:13). He is the radiance of God's glory (Heb. 1:2–3). Jesus is the Creator of *all* there is. Hello? No truth in Scripture is more replete than the truth that Jesus Christ is the way, the truth and the life (John 14:6). There *never* has been another way, and there never will be another way. Jesus is heaven's provision not only for eternal life, but for every challenge or problem we will ever face in this world, including our marital problems.

We've been created by Him (Jesus) and for Him. He is before *all things,* and in Him *all things* hold together (Col. 1:16–17). We are very tragically mistaken in this day of rampant divorce in the church because we've missed the most obvious, simple truth. God *always* means what He says. When He said "all things" hold together in Christ, He really did mean *all* things, *including* our marriages. The power of God, in the Person of Jesus Christ, is the only way Christian marriages can possibly hold together in this battleground world. So why isn't it happening?

There's a famine in our land. Our famine isn't for want of food, but of obedience to the truth. Our compromised view of Scripture has given us what our itching ears have longed to hear, but left us with hearts that are starving and homes that are falling apart. We've rejected God's knowledge, Jesus Christ, and we are indeed perishing (Hosea 4:6). Instead of repenting and turning back to God's Word, we've redoubled our efforts to seek wild gourds of Christ-excluding, humanistic thought. Oh yes, there's death in the pot in our day, and its poisonous content is being brazenly dispensed from errant seminaries, churches, books, and counseling offices.

On September 10, 2001, no one dreamed that an enemy of the world's mightiest nation could strike a blow deep within our borders, right into the World Trade Towers *and* the Pentagon. The next day we came to understand that evil never stops until it is determinately stopped. Satan has struck a blow *just* as deep into the hearts of our churches and homes in our day. With such a *huge* success rate, don't expect our enemy to change his strategy. Legendary coach Vince Lombardi never stopped running his famed Green Bay Packer sweep down the throat of an opposing defense until they *proved* they could stop it. Obviously, something far more critical than touchdowns is at stake in the battle we face in the church, in our marriages, and in our families.

Just as our nation was confused regarding how to fight back against such an insidious, hidden enemy, the church is floundering in our day, seeking solutions from the darkness of human wisdom. Remember, Jesus said: "If then the light that is in you is darkness, how great is the darkness!" (Matt. 6:23). Clearly, we need to turn on the light once again. But amidst such darkness, where can light be found? The prophet foretold: "The people who walk in darkness Will see a great light; Those who live in a dark land, The light will shine on them" (Isa. 9:2). The promised One said: "I am the Light of the world; he who follows Me will not walk in the darkness, but will have the Light of life" (John 8:12). If the church no longer believes that Jesus Christ is the Light who is able to brighten the life of every person, and the marriage in every home, than what do we believe?

The sons of the prophets cried out, "Oh man of God, there is death in the pot." Elisha called for wholesome meal to be thrown into the stew, saving them from certain death. The question for us in this day of great darkness and rampant divorce is: Will *we* cry out to the King of kings, of whom Elisha and all the prophets foretold? Truth from His Word must be thrown back into the pot if our churches and homes are to be saved. Our Bridegroom stands at the door knocking (Rev. 3:20). Will His bride, the church, open the door?

A Titus

> We were afflicted on every side: conflicts without, fears within. But God, who comforts the depressed, comforted us by the coming of Titus.
>
> —2 Corinthians 7:5–6

I stood on the corner of Route 8 amazed as Warren's Jeep sped away. Then I turned and began walking back to our vacation home, with Gingersnap alongside. The weight of the world was still heavy on my shoulders, but it seemed to be easing now, if only a bit. I wondered about what had just happened. Was it a coincidence, or was it actually possible that God had just stepped in as He sometimes does in this world, in ways that seem to be a fluke? It had already occurred to me that if I hadn't arrived at Route 8 at the end of White Rock Trail at the *exact* second Warren was driving past, I wouldn't have met him at all that desperate night.

It took until 11:30 p.m. to get the boys to bed. Bryson was still upset, but during bath time I heard a giggle or two as faithful Gingersnap lapped at the shampoo cascading down his shoulders. Along with those giggles, the weight on my own shoulders eased just a bit more. When I was certain both boys were asleep, I set out to find Warren's place in Piseco, the next town over, arriving around midnight. Warren met me at the door with a big smile. After serving me iced tea, he began sharing his story, and there was no longer a doubt that God had sent me a "Titus." I was reminded that night that no matter how hard things ever got, God would still be on His throne, and He'd still have a plan. With nowhere else to turn in this dark world, I was counting on it.

Bryson with Gingersnap, the love of his life

Hikes were best taken on Dad's shoulders. "Keep me strong, Lord, he's getting bigger."

Near our vacation home in Speculator, New York, with faithful Gingersnap

Chapter 27
WORTH FIGHTING FOR

Thank God that in the moment when someone has been crushed seemingly beyond help, when the things that he has cherished most in life have crashed around him, and he is left in the shattered wreck of what once he thought was a home, the Lord Jesus holds out His hand to aid. Thank God, he takes the clay that has been marred, the precious, soiled, broken life, and molds it again.[1]

ALAN REDPATH

I SETTLED INTO A comfortable chair in the living room of Warren's cabin at midnight, still wondering if he was the answer to the prayer I prayed earlier that evening. If I ever needed a "Titus" it was now. I had just observed my brain-injured son acting out in a terrifying, suicidal meltdown. I could hardly believe the words proceeding from the mouth of this child who was once thought never to speak at all. I was shocked, depressed, and honestly, I was scared to death. I couldn't have tolerated shallow advice or simplistic platitudes on this night. Thankfully, Warren offered none. He simply reminded me God was still in control.

I was surprised to learn that the previous year Warren's wife of more than twenty years had filed to divorce him. The circumstances of his situation were different than mine, and his children were grown. Yet, similar to my situation, his divorce was unwanted by him, and it had shocked all who had known them for many years, particularly at their church. I was encouraged to hear that the leadership of Warren's church had stood courageously and firmly against the divorce, supporting him through the ordeal in view of the fact that there were no biblical grounds for it.

Warren was an earthy man, the proprietor of an auto body shop; and I respected him immediately for his lack of pretension. Either of us would have laughed at the prospect of defending ourselves as "good" men, or as having arrived at being all that God called us to be. We both knew we had many flaws, and far to travel in fully manifesting the love of Christ in our hearts (Eph. 5:28; 2 Cor. 5:14). Men who get just a glimpse of their own selfishness and sinfulness, and of course this goes for women too, understand that the challenge to maintain loving relationships at home is a laughably unwinnable battle, unless that battle is entrusted to the grace of God.

If it's through Jesus Christ that God reconciled all things to Himself (Col. 1:20), then we wondered, why are so *many* Christian husbands and wives not able to reconcile with each other? As we spoke about the astonishing rate of divorce within the Christian community, Warren indicated that many middle-aged men continue to betray their families by abandoning their wives for "greener" pastures.

By greener pastures, these selfish men typically mean that they intend to pursue younger, sexier versions of what their wives once were, shamelessly trading in the mothers of their children as if they were a used automobile. There's hardly a church that doesn't have at least one single mother who has been left behind to suffer and struggle to raise her children alone under similar circumstances.

Yet Warren also noted a paradigm shift within our culture, and within the church, in which middle-aged women are now filing for divorce in greater numbers than the traditional pattern of men who divorce their wives. Many in our culture have applauded this shift, considering it a sign of equality and progress for women. This twisted response should surprise no one, in view of the darkness of our culture. What is surprising, and disheartening, is that many churches have joined hands with our culture by ignoring the latter pattern, by excusing it, or by embracing humanistic solutions for the healing of those troubled marriages. In this chapter I will not recap the wild gourds of humanistic thought and method that have been sliced into the "Christian stew" other than to say that, for those with eyes to see, such "solutions" represent a clear and proven legacy of failure, leaving struggling families with seemingly nowhere good to turn.

Warren and I talked and prayed for an hour that night, and before I left he provided me with a very good place to turn. He gave me the number of a biblical counselor who had helped him through the very painful time of his divorce. I resisted this at first, telling him that in the past I had sought help from several "Christian" counselors who never opened the pages of a Bible, and never suggested that obedience to God's Word was in any way relevant to the difficulties in my home. Sensing my resistance, Warren informed me that this counselor, Dave Wanner, had been delivered from a degrading life of bondage to sin through the power of Christ, and his ministry was founded upon the truth that Jesus Christ and His Word, the Bible, is God's answer for every "impossible" situation in life. That, indeed, sounded different.

I called Dave later that week, and this proved to be one of the wisest decisions I've ever made. I thought that Warren was the "Titus" (2 Cor. 7:6) God sent into my life out on Route 8 that night. In the coming months I realized that Warren was merely God's obedient servant to direct me to Dave Wanner. Dave would prove to be a very faithful "Titus," and he was going to teach me how to take refuge in the shadow of God's wings until destruction passed me by. Those wings were desperately needed by my children too, particularly my very vulnerable son, whose life was now in more peril than I knew.

> Be gracious to me, O God, be gracious to me, For my soul takes refuge in You; And in the shadow of Your wings I will take refuge Until destruction passes by.
>
> —PSALM 57:1

Battle Weary

I was still a bit skeptical as I entered Dave's modest apartment in Hoboken, New Jersey; but I soon found Dave to be one of the most loving and compassionate men I'd ever met. To call a man "loving" sounds weak, as many mistake Jesus for being weak. Yet Dave was down to earth, gritty, and bold in his love. Bold enough to take me to task and confront me concerning many of my own fearful, sinful attitudes. He helped me to choose trust instead of fear, forgiveness instead of bitterness, and he opened my eyes wider to the wondrous love, power, and utter dependability of God. If I ever needed God to be loving, powerful, and dependable, it was now.

I had read somewhere that suffering a cataclysmic event, such as the death of a family member, a bankruptcy, or a divorce, can diminish a person's physiological functioning to 15 percent of the normal capacity, as 85 percent of their energy is drained off simply in attempting to deal with the stress and the grief. I can't vouch for that statistic, but I can tell you that there were days when I was so depressed it felt as if the gravity of the earth had tripled. It was often a significant effort just to summon the energy to get up and walk across the room. It seemed as if the enemy had not only dragged my soul to the bottom of a dark valley, but that he had dug a hole and buried me there. I felt not only as if I were trapped at the bottom of the deepest ocean, but that a heavy chain bound me down there. You get the idea. I was a desperately demoralized and weary man; and I saw no way, no hope whatsoever to fight the battles looming ahead.

Some of you reading these words know precisely where I was. You've experienced your own tragic events in life, many of them coming quickly in succession. Wave after wave has knocked you down, and all you can see now is an even bigger wave barreling directly toward you as you try to regain your footing. The notion that God loves you is nice; but frankly, how is that even relevant when you are gasping for air? You're fearful of that next wave; and you can hardly *believe* that God has allowed you to be slammed so many times. Perhaps this is your deepest pain, the fact that you don't understand why God hasn't stepped in to prevent all the carnage, why He isn't stepping in even now to come to your rescue, as your circumstances grow darker.

Like Frodo in the feature film *The Two Towers*, you can get to the point of being so battle weary it hardly seems to matter anymore. So many bad things have happened, so much has already been destroyed in your life, and in the lives of those near and dear, that can never be made right again. Honestly, you don't really care anymore about the battles that may be looming ahead. You know you don't have what it takes to get up again and fight; and in your honest moments, you're not even sure there's anything left that's worth fighting for anyway.

When life brings you to this low point, you need a *whole* lot more than a "go gettum, you can do it, you're gonna land on your feet" kind of pep talk. You need compassion to be sure, but you also need truth, the kind of truth that will train your hands, once again, for battle (Ps. 18:34). Frodo needed his loyal friend Sam to remind him there was still something worth fighting for.

> **Sam:** "I know. It's all wrong. By rights we shouldn't even be here. But we are. It's like in the great stories, Mr. Frodo. The ones that really mattered. Full of darkness and danger they were. And sometimes you didn't want to know the end. Because how could the end be happy? How could the world go back to the way it was when so much bad had happened? But in the end, it's only a passing thing, this shadow. Even darkness must pass. A new day will come. And when the sun shines it will shine out the clearer. Those were the stories that stayed with you. That meant something. Even if you were too small to understand why. But I think, Mr. Frodo, I do understand why. I know now. Folk in those stories had lots of chances of turning back, only they didn't, because they were holding onto something."
>
> **Frodo:** "What are we holding onto, Sam?"
>
> **Sam:** "That there's some good in this world, Mr. Frodo. And it's worth fighting for."[2]

In God's sovereignty, Dave Wanner came alongside to remind me there were still things in this world that mattered, that were worth fighting for, including my desperately hurting children. He knew that the battles of life had worn me down, and that I had many fears and concerns about the future that were far too big for me. He pointed me to God's promises, including the awesome promise that He would accomplish what concerned me as I sought refuge in Him.

> Be gracious to me, O God, be gracious to me, For my soul takes refuge in You; And in the shadow of Your wings I will take refuge Until destruction passes by. I will cry out to God Most High, *To God who accomplishes all things for me.*
>
> —PSALM 57:1–2, EMPHASIS ADDED

> Though I walk in the midst of trouble, You will revive me; You will stretch forth Your hand against the wrath of my enemies, And Your right hand will save me. *The LORD will accomplish what concerns me*; Your lovingkindness, O LORD, is everlasting; Do not forsake the works of Your hands.
>
> —PSALM 138:7–8, EMPHASIS ADDED

In his Sam-to-Frodo kind of love for me, Dave provided me with two things that are essential in helping any person to move forward from the dark valleys of life. He showered me with grace *and* truth. He knew that compassion can help a person regain equilibrium, but if truth is lacking, compassion can ultimately prove irrelevant. He also knew that hammering a person with truth, in the absence of mercy and grace, can be brutal. Most of all, he knew that *all* that is ever necessary to undergird a discouraged person resides in perfect proportion in Jesus Christ, who is *full* of grace and truth. He brought me to meet with Jesus, again and again, in His written Word.

> All the paths of the LORD are lovingkindness and truth.
>
> —PSALM 25:10

> Your lovingkindness and Your truth will continually preserve me.
>
> —PSALM 40:11

> And the Word became flesh, and dwelt among us, and we saw His glory, glory as of the only begotten from the Father, full of grace and truth.
>
> —JOHN 1:14

I'm resolved, until the final page of this book, to lift up Jesus Christ as the *only* valid answer to your impossible problems, even as He remains the only true hope for mine. Don't hear me telling you that Jesus *has* your answer. Hear me boldly proclaiming that He *is* your answer, irrespective of what you believe your biggest problems are in this world right now. If my problems, or yours, are too big for King Jesus, then frankly, we are in far bigger trouble than we know. But Jesus conquered even death, and He holds eternity in His hands. He can certainly handle our problems. He will do so in His way, and in His time, as we entrust ourselves to Him *alone*.

Yet, even as I proclaim Jesus to be the answer, it must be understood that Jesus Christ has a body in this world, a body of believers known as His church. King Jesus will often act miraculously and directly on our behalf through His Spirit, and He does so many more times than our faithless eyes are able to perceive. Yet He will most often utilize the services of people, especially the members of His body, even as He sent Titus to Paul in his time of need (2 Cor. 7:6), and Dave Wanner to me, or when He assembled Bryson's Army to battle for his ability to function in this world. But are these human connections also to be considered miracles? You bet they are! Again, it takes eyes that can see, but God's miraculous touch often comes to us in human form.

And just as it is important to keep our eyes open to see how He may provide for us through the touch of others, let us also remain alert to see those people whom He places in our path each day, so that He can extend His miraculous touch through us to them. Joni Eareckson Tada speaks of the nobility of the cause we have been called to as God's hands and feet in this world. Being a member of Christ's body is serious business; and we can never predict when the Lord will lead us to do or say something that will turn a person's day around, or perhaps, even save their life.

> God's heart intent is to alleviate suffering and he is bending over backward to do it. He is moving heaven and earth to dry the tear, lighten the load, ease the burden, mend the marriage, give to the poor, care for the widow, stamp out crime, help the elderly, uphold justice, bandage the battered, and

> much more. God rallies us to his noble cause, but we often fall behind. God longs to push back the pain through those who serve as his body, his hands and feet on earth.[3]

I'm convinced that we'll never understand the impact of the "little" things God has prepared in advance for us to do for others each day until we see Him face-to-face (Eph. 2:10; Phil. 2:12–13). And the fact that you've been wounded in battle by no means disqualifies you from vital service as a member of His body. On the contrary, those wounds have been designed to prepare you for even greater service. In the feature film *Black Hawk Down,* after his squadron came under heavy enemy fire, Colonel McKnight ordered a soldier to drive the truck they were holed up in so they could escape peril. The soldier, realizing he'd been hit, responded, "But I'm shot, Colonel." McKnight barked back at the soldier, "Everybody's shot.…Get up there and drive."[4]

Yes, we've all been shot, and most of us have experienced disastrously broken dreams. But throughout history the Lord has performed some of His greatest miracles through soldiers who have been wounded the most severely, including those who have failed the most disgracefully. Don't *ever* believe you've failed too much, or too often, to be used by God. Jesus said that a man or woman who has been forgiven much, loves much (Luke 7:47). Unless a grain of wheat falls to the earth and dies it cannot bear fruit (John 12:24). Resurrection life is Jesus' way. He delights even in making dead bones get up and live again (Ezek. 37:3), and He can also make up for the years that the locusts have eaten (Joel 2:25).

During a full year of meeting together, Dave Wanner and I continued to pray that my wife might become willing to join us in our counseling, in the hope that the miracle of reconciliation might take place through the power of Jesus Christ. Sadly, this never occurred, and my heart was broken beyond my ability to describe, particularly in a book.

I had little time to grieve. I had become the single parent of a struggling, hurting family with the high maintenance needs of a brain-injured, multiply handicapped child. If I had *any* chance of leading this war-torn group to the brighter day that Sam spoke of, I needed to fix my eyes on a King who has promised our safe arrival there. Dave prepared me for the difficult battles looming ahead by bringing me to the truth of His Word in the midst of hardship, again and again.

> We count those blessed who endured. You have heard of the endurance of Job and have seen the outcome of the Lord's dealings, that the Lord is full of compassion and is merciful.
>
> —JAMES 5:11

> After you have suffered for a little while, the God of all grace, who called you to His eternal glory in Christ, will Himself perfect, confirm, strengthen and establish you.
>
> —1 PETER 5:10

"I . . . Go to a Drawer Get Knife"

I was laughably ill equipped to become a homemaker; but as I found myself in the deep end of the pool with children who were depending on me to keep their heads above water, following Jesus became a simple matter, albeit not an easy one. Jesus said: "Greater love has no one than this, that one lay down his life for his friends" (John 15:13). So much for "easy."

By the fall of 2003, I had been separated from my wife for two years and parenting my sons alone for more than a year. My daughter was away at college for most of the year, while Bryson and Tim were entering high school and junior high respectively. The enemy, who always seeks an opportune time, bore down on my mentally impaired child once again to destroy him.

If there was one thing that had always propelled my son beyond the meager expectations of medical experts who simply couldn't believe in miracles, it was his ability to dream. Naturally, this is exactly how the enemy came at him. So many dreams were being wrenched from his hands as an adolescent. He was gasping for air emotionally, battling to hold onto an identity that had been founded upon a family that loved and believed in him, whose members had always loved and believed in each other, no matter what. As the family structure he had always counted upon was being dismantled, it was as if a piece of his soul was being destroyed along with it. He simply didn't have the capacity to process the devastation, or to bear it.

Jesus described the enemy as a villain who seeks to steal and kill and destroy (John 10:10). I've come to understand that he is relentless toward those goals. Since that frightening scene the previous summer when Bryson uttered threats against himself, I had done some research about mentally impaired children who commit suicide. I was resolved that the enemy simply could not have my son, and I was prepared to do *anything* to provide for his safety. I'd love to portray myself as heroic, but the truth is that my resolve would have been tantamount to an ant defying a roaring lion unless a great King stood with me. I was scared to death, needing to cast my desperate fears onto Him again and again (Ps. 56:3–4; 1 Pet. 5:7). The King provided me with a sense of peace that surpassed comprehension (Phil. 4:7), but that peace was about to be tested severely as another life threatening situation arose for Bryson in early September 2003.

It was a Saturday night, and my boys and I were watching a Miami Hurricanes versus Florida Gators football game, the first big game of the year. Midway through the first quarter, my wife entered the room to discuss something with me. We had been unofficially separated for nearly two years, but we remained in the tense and unhealthy situation of both still residing in separate quarters of our large family home. The divorce would not be finalized until 2004, at which time my former wife relocated elsewhere, and my three children and I remained in that home. On this particular evening, the communication between us became extremely strained and difficult.

No one should hear me placing blame on my former wife, not when my own sins required as much of our Savior's blood to cover them as for any sinner on this planet. The point that needs to be reiterated here is that children are *always* deeply affected by divorce, and by the conflicts that typically accompany it. My mentally impaired son was already struggling badly during this sorrowful time of change, and the enemy is dreadfully savvy in seizing opportunities in the lives of those who are most vulnerable.

After my wife had left for the evening, both boys remained extremely upset at our interaction. I turned off the TV and asked if they were okay. They didn't say much. We prayed together for a few minutes, after which I asked them if they felt the need to talk about the situation further. Tim said nothing, but Bryson looked up at me with a very troubled, eerie look on his face and spoke the following, chilling words. As always, I'll fill in his omitted, missing or incorrectly spoken words from his garbled speech in brackets: "When you go [to] bed, I [will] come back down and go to a [the] drawer [to] get [a] knife and kill myself."

I was stunned, and remained silent for a moment. I groped for something to say, but nothing came. I tried to act composed as I stalled, but I was feeling sheer panic now. I turned the TV back on, hoping to distract Bryson's mind toward the game as I thought and prayed silently. Once he seemed settled and into the game once again, I asked him if he would excuse me and Tim for a minute (which is all I dared to leave him), and I asked Tim to join me in my home office, which was directly next to the family room.

"A friend loves at all times, And a brother is born for adversity" (Prov. 17:17). It's hard to imagine any brother fulfilling this Scripture more completely and consistently than Tim had done since he was little. He didn't really need that brief meeting. He was far ahead of his age in terms of maturity and responsibility, and I could always count on the fact that Bryson was safe when Tim was around. But I told him to keep a close eye on his brother as I made some phone calls, and to summon me immediately if anything further occurred in his behavior that was troubling, or if he issued any additional threats. He nodded. Enough said. I was *that* confident in him.

The first call I made was to Dave Wanner, and I was extremely distressed when he didn't answer. I left an urgent message, asking him to call as soon as possible. I then called Phil Mandato, my best friend and college teammate. He listened as I told him what happened, and as I cried. I don't remember what he said in response, but I do remember that there hasn't been a time in life when Phil has failed to be there when I needed him. Yes, a brother is born for adversity, and having just one friend like him makes a man wealthy. As always, Phil reminded me that the Lord would work things out. After that conversation I went back to join the boys. Tim was doing his best to develop some chatter with his brother, but the mood remained somber.

At halftime I suggested to Bryson that we should do his evening bath right then, and then come back down to see the second half of the game. Bryson agreed to this, and we went upstairs with faithful Gingersnap for a warm bath, which I hoped might calm and comfort him. I tried to say something wise. "Don't worry, Bryson. Everything's going to be okay." I was stumbling badly over my words, realizing they were as empty as they sounded. I tried again, saying something equally shallow. I was praying hard now, and the Lord finally gave me the thought to simply tell him that I loved him very much. He responded angrily to this, and I became even more alarmed as he shut down completely, becoming deadpan. Even the lavish licks on his shoulders from the large tongue of Gingersnap as I washed his hair failed to brighten his darkness.

After I got him dressed again, I picked him up and carried him down the stairs (the easiest way on this volatile night) and brought him into the family room, placing him into his favorite chair in front of the game. The Miami Hurricanes were getting shellacked by the Florida Gators, which isn't exactly what the doctor ordered. Bryson was a huge Hurricanes fan. It would be several more years until he'd become a Gator fan, when Tim Tebow ruled the land.

If you've learned anything about Bryson throughout this family story, you know he is *all* about his dreams and his heroes, and he is always *all* about the game he is watching at the moment. I mean he gets personally invested, totally immersed in it. On this night, when so much was troubling him, this wasn't a good thing at all. The Gators scored yet *another* touchdown midway through the third quarter to go up 33–10 versus Bryson's hapless Canes.

I've never been a believer that God determines the outcomes of sporting events, and I don't believe He did so on this night. Yet there's something strangely fascinating about so many events in this world that seem to be mysteriously stirring in a great pot in heaven. Something began happening in that game which was remarkable, as quarterback Brock Berlin began leading his Hurricanes back. They scored a few touchdowns, and even a two point conversion *before* the end of the third quarter, pulling to within 33–25 entering the fourth quarter. I was relieved for the moment as I observed Bryson being drawn in, *really* starting to get into it.

Well, you couldn't have written the script any better for Bryson. Berlin led his team all the way back and the Canes won it on a Frank Gore TD with just over a minute to go, making it 38–33, which is the way it ended. Bryson was very excited and animated now, which was a *huge* relief; and he became even more excited when he heard Brock Berlin give his Christian testimony right on the field after the game, glorifying Jesus Christ.

The tension had eased, but I was by no means less alarmed than before that thrilling fourth quarter. In fact, since Bryson's words of self-harm were so specific in terms of what he intended to do after I was asleep, I was afraid to go to bed. So we all stayed up watching ESPN Sports Center. Finally the phone rang at about midnight and I ran to get it, taking Dave Wanner's call behind closed doors. He apologized for calling so late, saying he had been ministering to a group at his church, Redeemer Church in Manhattan. I cut him off in mid-sentence, blurting out all that had occurred that evening, specifically repeating everything Bryson had said.

After he understood the situation, I asked him, "Dave, how can I be sure it's safe to go to sleep tonight after Bryson was so specific in saying that he intends to use a knife to kill himself?" Dave asked if he could speak with Bryson on the phone. Tim helped me to coax Bryson to come in to my office, but he refused to get on the phone, and would not even sit in the chair in front of my desk. He remained standing near the doorway with the door open. Each time I asked him to come over and get on the phone to speak with Dave, he fearfully refused. The memory of that football game had faded completely now, and his visage was fraught with distress. It was clear that he remembered what he had said earlier that evening, and he obviously didn't want to talk about it. He wouldn't even allow me to place the call on speaker, so that Dave and I could both speak with him together. He was petrified.

Dave told me to stop insisting that Bryson get on the phone, and he instructed me to simply ask Bryson a few questions as he relayed them through me. The first question was peculiar. Dave wanted me to ask Bryson if he had heard a voice telling him to get a knife and harm himself with it. Before relaying this startling question, I asked Dave if he was certain it was wise to ask him this, since it might frighten and confuse my son further. Dave told me to make sure Bryson knew I wasn't referring to an audible voice he could hear with his ears, but a thought in his head that seemed as clear and real as a voice speaking to him. I was still uneasy, but I trusted Dave. I gently said, "Bryson, when you were saying those things about getting a knife to kill yourself, did you hear a voice, a thought in your head urging you to do that?"

Immediately, as if rays of sunshine had filled the room, a relieved look spread over Bryson's troubled face. He answered (as usual, I will fill in his omitted words), "Yeah dad, I heard [a] voice." Shocked, I relayed his response to Dave, who told me that this is what he suspected. He told me that Bryson had been just as petrified by that seemingly authoritative voice in his head as I was at hearing Bryson speak his threat of self-harm. He had been afraid to tell me about the voice, not only because he was frightened and confused by it, but because he thought I'd never believe that a voice had instructed him in this manner. He was now relieved because it was out in the open, and he knew that his dad understood what had happened.

Then Dave asked me to be *very* clear in telling Bryson that he did not have to obey that voice. I looked Bryson in the eyes and told him that this voice was not from Jesus, that it was from the mouth of a liar, and he did not have to obey that voice or pay any further attention to it. As I gave Bryson these instructions, his shoulders relaxed completely, and amazingly, his visage transformed even further to reflect a spirit of tranquility. I was absolutely stunned.

In the years following that night, I learned quite a bit more about the nature of spiritual warfare, including the vicious lies that can infiltrate our minds if we allow it. None of us can afford to passively believe all that enters into our minds. Such passivity can leave our souls open to fear, condemnation, and even to deadly and dangerous suggestions sent from the pit of hell. Christian leaders throughout the centuries have understood the nature of the attack that can come against us from the father of lies:

> Do not easily suppose dreams, voices, impressions, visions or revelations to be from God. They may be from Him. They may be from nature. They may be from the devil. Therefore, do not believe every spirit, but try the spirits, whether they be from God.[5] (John Wesley)

> What are the "fiery darts" that Satan shoots at us?... They are thoughts of one kind or another.... I have sometimes been prayerfully meditating on the Word when suddenly a terrible thought would invade my mind.... Satan wants us to think that we are to blame, because this kind of thinking would make us discouraged.... But he is to blame!... The important thing is to quench that dart immediately. Instantly look to Christ by faith. Recall some promise of the Word, and believe it. Otherwise the fire will spread, and... get beyond your control.[6] (Warren Wiersbe)

> In a survey of 1700 professing Christian teenagers, 70 percent admitted to hearing voices, like there was a subconscious self talking to them. I don't believe they are psychotic or paranoid schizophrenic. There is a battle going on for their minds. I have shared with many tormented people that they aren't going crazy but are under spiritual attack. They usually respond, "Praise the Lord, someone understands." It's freeing to know this truth, because if there is a battle going on for our minds, we can win that war.[7] (Neil Anderson)

Teens are a particularly susceptible group, but I agree with Anderson. Christ is greater than the liar, and therefore we *can* win that war (1 John 4:4). We win it by coming to know our Savior's voice as intimately as though we were hearing our best friend. King David knew he'd have been dead many times if God's voice, His Word, had not become his delight (Ps. 119:92). We must all get to the point at which God's Word is *that* precious to us. As we read it, meditate on it, and think it through with a determination to obey it, the serpent's fiery arrows become just a flickering flame of powerless lies against the rushing waterfall of God's Spirit of Truth.

Since Bryson would never progress to the point of being able to open his Bible to find and read a passage of Scripture on his own, those who loved him needed to take up the slack by literally becoming his Bible, quoting and teaching it to him in small, bite-sized pieces. Praise God that His Word is not hard to understand. Praise Him that He has given it to little children who can receive and obey the simplicity of it, not to the wise and learned in this world who would obfuscate it in order to justify their refusal to believe (Matt. 11:25).

As I prepared Bryson for bed, I gently reminded him that he could always let his dad know when frightening or confusing thoughts came into his mind. I also told him the only voice he ever needed to obey was the voice of King Jesus, the Savior who would never, ever stop loving him, and who would never leave him. After I prayed with both boys, I tucked Bryson into bed, and then Tim went into his room.

I stood in the hallway peering through a crack in Bryson's bedroom door for a long time that night, just to be sure the storm had indeed passed. It was clear to me now that some things in this world were very much worth fighting for. A pang of fear entered my heart just then, together with thoughts of my frailty and impotence to fight the battles looming ahead. But a friendlier voice entered my mind, asking a question: "If God is for us, who can be against us?" (Rom. 8:31, NIV). God's voice reminded me that the war had already been won on a bloodstained cross long ago. My main battle now was to believe in the One who had trampled all His adversaries, and the enemies of all who belong to Him (1 John 5:4; Col. 2:15).

I looked back into Bryson's room, noticing that he slept peacefully now. I realized I was just like my brain-injured boy. I needed a Hero, a Champion in this world every bit as much as he did. The evil voice came, yet again, and tried to invade my thoughts. Somehow I knew I should agree with that dark voice this time, while no longer feeling threatened by his accusations.

I was indeed pathetically weak and inept, yes; in this he was quite right. "But sleep on, my hurting, troubled little boy, sleep on." Heaven has indeed provided a Champion for us, a Savior who has determined that we are very much worth fighting for. He has promised to do so always, as we continue to trust in Him.

> For they will cry to the LORD because of oppressors, and He will send them a Savior and a Champion, and He will deliver them. Thus the LORD will make Himself known.
>
> —ISAIAH 19:20–21

> Who will separate us from the love of Christ? Will tribulation, or distress, or persecution, or famine, or nakedness, or peril, or sword? Just as it is written, "FOR YOUR SAKE WE ARE BEING PUT TO DEATH ALL DAY LONG; WE WERE CONSIDERED AS SHEEP TO BE SLAUGHTERED." But in all these things we overwhelmingly conquer through Him who loved us. For I am convinced that neither death, nor life, nor angels, nor principalities, nor things present, nor things to come, nor powers, nor height nor depth, nor any other created thing, will be able to separate us from the love of God, which is in Christ Jesus our Lord.
>
> —ROMANS 8:35–39

Chapter 28

WHATEVER KILLS YOU MAKES YOU STRONGER

John at the bar is a friend of mine, he gets me my drinks for free. And he's quick with a joke, or to light up your smoke, But there's somewhere that he'd rather be. He says, "Bill I believe this is killing me," as the smile ran away from his face, "Well, I'm sure that I could be a movie star, if I could get out of this place."[1]

Billy Joel

I was now a single father. That thought still kills me, more than a decade later. But my hurting sons needed me to step up to raise them, and my college-aged daughter, hurting just as badly, needed a family home to return to. If I ever needed God's wisdom, it was now.

As I've emphasized throughout this book, God's ways are *far* higher than our ways, His wisdom *far* different than ours. It's not even a close call, which is why the prophet depicts the chasm between God's thoughts and our human thoughts as the distance between the heavens and the earth (Isa. 55:8–9). If we ever hope to bridge that enormous gap, we *must* reject the wisdom of this age and choose God's foolishness (1 Cor. 3:18–19).

Humanistic wisdom and shallow "Christian" teachings both focus on seeking happiness in this world, right *now*. According to God's foolish ways, life emerges from death, not from the evasion of suffering, and certainly not from the direct or immediate pursuit of comfort and happiness. The concept of delayed gratification is ridiculous to modern ears. And those ears certainly cannot hear the words of a King who uttered the outrageous statement: "Whoever wishes to save his life will lose it; but whoever loses his life for My sake will find it" (Matt. 16:25).

Secular wisdom also tells us that whatever *doesn't* kill us makes us stronger, in ourselves. The Bible flips this popular sentiment over, revealing it's the things that actually *do* kill us that make us stronger, in Christ. Don't think that the difference here is merely a matter of semantics. At this painful juncture of my life, with so much that was *just killing* me, I needed to operate by God's truth. You'll need to do the same, dear reader, if you want to not only survive, but benefit from those painful events in your life that threaten to kill you.

Sooner or later, God sees to it that we all find ourselves mired in holes so deep and treacherous we wouldn't have the slightest hope, not even a prayer of clawing our way out of them. It's not a matter of *if*, but *when* this will happen. Even the mighty apostle declared this to be the case regarding the affliction that came to him in Asia.

> For we do not want you to be unaware, brethren, of our affliction which came to us in Asia, that we were burdened excessively, beyond our strength, so that we despaired even of life.
>
> —2 CORINTHIANS 1:8

Don't think that the afflictions that made Paul think he might just die were a fluke. These were a part of God's plan for him from the beginning. Shortly after Jesus struck Paul with blindness on the road to Damascus, He told Ananias: "I will show him how much he must suffer for My name's sake" (Acts 9:16). Paul, having gotten with the program, later taught it to others: "Through many tribulations we must enter the kingdom of God" (14:22). Why would the Bible make such disturbing declarations concerning Paul's life, and ours? If God is as loving as Scripture declares, He must have a purpose in allowing circumstances in our lives that are *just killing us.*

Our enemy wants us to miss that purpose, and conclude that God is indifferent to our pain. Ultimately, he wants us to "curse God and die," as Job's wife urged him to do (Job 2:9). Paul wanted to make certain we didn't remain unaware of God's grand purpose for allowing such "deathly" circumstances.

> For we do not want you to be unaware, brethren, of our affliction which came to us in Asia, that we were burdened excessively, beyond our strength, so that we despaired even of life; indeed, we had the sentence of death within ourselves, *so that we would not trust in ourselves, but in God* who raises the dead; who delivered us from so great a peril of death, and will deliver us, He on whom we have set our hope. And He will yet deliver us.
>
> —2 CORINTHIANS 1:8–10, EMPHASIS ADDED

Let's be honest. God's method of placing us into situations that are *just killing us* so we will rely on Him, and not on ourselves, doesn't appear to be all that loving, does it? Frankly, it seems a bit manipulative, perhaps even cruel. But the kindest thing God could ever do for sons and daughters whom He loves is to kill off our reliance upon *any* resource that is not truly reliable. The truth is that *we* are the most unreliable resource imaginable. In our natural minds we remain stubbornly blind to this truth, clinging to the myth of our own self-sufficiency. But any goodness we've attained is not from achieving it ourselves, and we are *anything* but self-sufficient.

God created us in His own image, making us capable of accomplishing marvelous achievements in this world. The Bible even says of us: "You are gods, And all of you are sons of the Most High" (Ps. 82:6). But as C. S. Lewis said, we can become like the fragrance of a flower that concludes it is so wonderful it no longer needs the flower to sustain it.[2] The truth is, we couldn't draw our next breath if God didn't grant it to us. We've got one shot, one hope to live the lives God created us to live. Jesus Christ is that hope, and His grace *alone* is our sufficiency.

Naturally, we would all settle for a religion that would make us stronger and more capable in ourselves. It would suit us just fine to become merely a new and improved version of ourselves, a makeover of what we have always been, with us retaining full control of our lives, of course. We must remember the enormity of our need before God, in view of our sin. Jesus didn't come to heal sick men and women. He came to *resurrect* dead men and women. Our only hope is to be born again as a new creation in Christ (John 3:3; 2 Cor. 5:17). Christ died to pay the penalty for our sins; and praise God, His sacrifice on the cross has sufficiently completed all the dying that will ever be necessary for us to *become* new creatures in Him (to be born again). Yet death is also a key player in God's plan for our sanctification, the process by which we grow to become increasingly like Christ.

Although it doesn't preach well in our selfish day of demanding happiness on our own terms right now, Scripture is clear there is a process of death that *must* play out in our lives. In the same letter which began with Paul's honest declaration that he despaired of life so that he might learn reliance upon God, he later reinforces his emphasis about this continuing process of death. This process is geared not only to strengthen our reliance upon Christ, but also to make it perfectly clear to others that Christ is our *only* hope, even as He is their only hope.

> For we do not preach ourselves but Jesus Christ as Lord....But we have this treasure in earthen vessels, so that the surpassing greatness of the power will be of God and not from ourselves; we are afflicted in every way, but not crushed; perplexed, but not despairing; persecuted, but not forsaken; struck down, but not destroyed; *always* carrying about in the body the *dying* of Jesus, so that the life of Jesus also may be manifested in our body. For we who live are *constantly* being *delivered over to death* for Jesus' sake, so that the life of Jesus also may be manifested in our mortal flesh. So *death works* in us, but life in you.
>
> —2 Corinthians 4:5–12, emphasis added

Paul's use of the words *always* and *constantly* is daunting, particularly since the subject matter is my personal death, and yours. Honestly, sometimes I feel like screaming toward heaven:

> *Lord, I understand what You are trying to do. I mean, I get it already! But the afflictions and painful trials You are allowing, and the length of time You're allowing them to go on and on without relief, well, it's just killing me, Lord! Does life have to be this hard forever? Is there an endgame to all this death and dying? If so, what is it? I can't take much more!*

There is an endgame; but again, it doesn't preach well in our self-focused day. Jesus wasn't tortured to death so we can now continue to live for our own purposes, compartmentalizing Him into a neat little corner of our lives. We need to understand the serious nature of the family business into which we've been born, and we dare not overlook scriptures that describe God as a consuming fire (Heb. 12:29). I'm no fireman, but I get the idea that this kind of fire won't ever stop burning until its objective is *fully* accomplished. God is determined to fill us completely with His Spirit, to consume us so fully with His intense fire of love for us that it will spill over like a flood to others who need His grace and love as desperately as we do in this cold, dark world.

Before our minds drift toward a dreamy definition of that love spilling over, let's remember that Jesus taught us that in order to bear fruit, a kernel of wheat must fall to the ground and die (John 12:24). Again, He was clear about the involvement of death in His purpose *and* in our purpose in saying: "Greater love has no man than this, that one lay down His life for His friends" (15:13). Paul went right to the point in revealing that "death works in us, but life in you" (2 Cor. 4:12). Scripture is consistent and clear about God's endgame being one of sacrificial love pouring out from our lives so that death will produce life. Even so, the path of sacrifice that Jesus lays out for us will often be perceived of as foolish by others, and even ridiculed by them. Be ready for this.

Not many of my friends understood the choices the Lord led me to make to hold my family together and protect my children during this time. They knew I had suffered a devastating financial settlement during the divorce, and that my expenses in providing for a family with a chronically ill, multiply handicapped child were enormous. To them, common sense dictated my return to commercial real estate, hiring a full-time homemaker to care for my kids. Only a few of my closest friends knew that Bryson had already displayed a propensity toward suicide, and most had no concept of the daily responsibilities and complexities involved in caring for a brain-injured child.

When the Lord asks us to pick up our cross and follow Him (Matt. 16:24; Mark 8:34; Luke 9:23), we should not expect a path that meets with the approval of others, or a plan that satisfies even our own common sense. The Lord had already made it clear that my children were worth fighting for. He now required me to lay down my life for them in a very specific and peculiar way. These children were crushed, and I needed to obey the Lord in providing for their long-term well-being, both spiritually and emotionally, at the cost of my financial prosperity.

> It is easier to serve God without a vision, easier to work for God without a call, because then you are not bothered by what God requires; common sense is your guide, veneered over with Christian sentiment. You will be more prosperous and successful, more leisure-hearted, if you never realize the call of God. But if once you receive a commission from Jesus Christ, the memory of what God wants will always come like a goad; you will no longer be able to work for Him on the common-sense basis.[3]
>
> —OSWALD CHAMBERS

ROADWAY IN THE WILDERNESS

> Do not call to mind the former things, Or ponder things of the past. Behold, I will do something new, Now it will spring forth; Will you not be aware of it? I will even make a roadway in the wilderness.
>
> —ISAIAH 43:18–19

The Lord will not ask us to move backwards in life after He brings us into a wilderness place that is *just killing us.* In His time, a new roadway will spring forth. But without the eyes of faith, the Lord could build an eight-lane freeway for us and we'd miss it, which is why the Lord asked: "Will you not be aware of it?" The Lord does not require us to possess faith that can see miles into the distance. All we need is the faith to move forward on His roadway one step, one day, one decision at a time, with our eyes on Him.

The church we had attended for years had played a wonderful role helping my family in many ways, including the countless hours "A Three Boys" had spent in the church gym teaching my brain-injured son to walk, and to run. The great majority of believers in that church were humble, godly people who understood the sanctity of the marital covenant. Sadly, some strategic members of that community gave tacit approval to the divorce by refusing to oppose it, and by choosing instead to take sides between my wife and me. I nearly begged certain individuals to stop choosing sides, even if they indicated they were taking "my" side.

There are two sinners in every marriage, and those who choose the side of one sinner against the other as a marriage spirals toward divorce become tools in the enemy's hands to break apart the only "side" that matters, the side of a God-ordained marriage and family. I was deeply saddened as some took aim at me with a readiness to condemn, without any knowledge of who I was as a man, a husband, and a father.

Please don't hear me defending myself as "good" or this book will become a joke book. Those who took my side missed the point just as badly. The truth back then, and still today as I write these words, is that I am worse in my flesh than they would have even thought to accuse me of being. As mentioned in an earlier chapter, if we were all forced to carry a sign listing our top ten greatest failures and sins, no one would know about my worst sins, or yours. We'd all be too busy trying to cover up our own sign. As Steve Brown says, "There is nothing you can say about me that isn't either true or potentially true."[4] It took the lifeblood spilling out of the only Man who was ever truly good in this world to save me from my sin, and you from yours.

Paul spoke of how unqualified we are to judge the *motives* of others as we try to evaluate their lives, and he used the example of himself and Apollos to warn others in the church against the arrogance of favoring one imperfect human being versus another:

> But to me it is a very small thing that I should be examined by you, or by any human court; in fact, I do not even examine myself. For I am conscious of nothing against myself, yet I am not by this acquitted; but the one who examines me is the Lord. Therefore, do not go on passing judgment before the time, but wait until the Lord comes who will both bring to light the things hidden in the darkness and disclose the motives of men's hearts; and then each man's praise will come to him from God. Now these things,

> brethren, I have figuratively applied to myself and Apollos for your sakes, so that in us you might learn not to exceed what is written, so that no one of you will become arrogant in behalf of one against the other.
>
> —1 Corinthians 4:3–6

By the fall of 2003 I had been parenting my children alone for nearly two years, and Bryson had just threatened to take his own life for the second time. It became clear that it was best not to expose my children to an environment where there was misinformation and gossip circulating about our family, and where some were arrogant enough to choose sides. The Lord led me to a church that would help me protect my children during this frightening time, and raise them in a place where we could make progress on that roadway in the wilderness.

I don't lightly say that the reason I'm still standing today, no less writing a book, is largely attributable to the love that enveloped us at that little church. Pastor Bruce Ebersole of Christ the King Church in Denville, New Jersey, is one of the most boldly loving men I've ever met, a true shepherd in the way Peter exhorted pastors to be (1 Pet. 5:2–3). In our equivocating, politically correct day, I came to appreciate him for his courage not only to speak out the truth, but to live it out. Edmund Burke said, "All that is necessary for the triumph of evil is that good men do nothing."[5] Sir Winston Churchill said, "Without courage all other virtues lose their meaning."[6] There wasn't a whole lot of lost meaning in Bruce's ministry, or in this Spirit-filled church.

Yet before officially joining Christ the King as a member, I needed confirmation that this was truly the right fit for my hurting sons. Bryson was now in high school, and Tim was also now entering high school as a freshman. I was very anxious as I drove my sons to the home of David and Dorothy Kolk, the youth group leaders who were hosting a bonfire in their backyard for the kickoff meeting on a Friday evening in September 2003. I had spoken with Dorothy on the phone earlier that week, and was encouraged by her compassionate response as I stuttered to explain my brain-injured son's physical and mental profile. I was even more encouraged as a group of kids rose from their chairs and warmly greeted my boys in her backyard that night.

My anxiety got the best of me as I drove back toward Kinnelon after dropping them off. I was nearly in tears as I called my sister from the car, saying, "Linda, this *has* to work! It just *has* to! Those boys are hurting so *badly!*" My dear sister prayed as only a godly woman like her can pray. And after picking my boys up at 10:30 that night, I was nearly in tears again, but not because those prayers were unanswered. Now, I held back my tears because God had answered them so magnificently! The friends my boys met that night would soon become family, and Dorothy and Dave quickly became Aunt Dorothy and Uncle Dave. There was *no way* I could parent these kids alone, and the Lord was bringing in reinforcements.

I praise God for providing a roadway in that desert. But please note that He never promised an escape *from* the desert. He merely promised to provide a way

> I'm so tired of hearing about the victorious Christian life I think I will die. Do you know what the victorious Christian life is? It is keeping on trucking for another day. It is being faithful—just barely. It is keeping from messing it up too terribly.... Who is a true victorious Christian? It is someone who has his or her nose above water...someone who's afraid of drowning, but who knows God's faithfulness in the past...someone who has been tempted and maybe failed, yet who keeps crawling, wounded, back to the throne, because of God's grace. It is someone who's not sure about tomorrow, but who has no other place to turn but to God, because He is Life.[8]

I began writing this book many years ago, thinking that my son's courageous journey to conquer his brain injury would inspire people. I put the book down over a decade ago, after realizing my divorce was unavoidable. During these long years of wilderness travel, I've been far too busy, and frankly, too exhausted to pick it up again. In 2009 the Lord nudged me (more like clobbered me) to rewrite this book from scratch. After five years of attempting to complete it, I realize that far less is clear to me now than when I first thought to write it years ago.

But even though much is still unclear, and life is still killing me in many respects as I write these words, I've learned that as we trust Him day by day and step by step, King Jesus will not only provide a roadway through the wilderness, but that He also graciously provides rivers of refreshment for us as we travel through the desert.

Rivers in the Desert

> I will even make a roadway in the wilderness, Rivers in the desert.
>
> —Isaiah 43:19

No doubt, Jesus often seems to be late in coming to our rescue; but as mentioned several times in this family story, He often provides for our needs through the "little" things He prompts others to do to help us.

Steve Woodruff and his wife Sandra from Christ the King Church were the first to invite my family for dinner. After a wonderful meal, my boys disappeared with the Woodruff boys to their basement, and Steve and Sandy compassionately listened as I poured out our family story. Nathan and David were roughly the same age as Bryson and Tim, and they immediately became tight friends. Sandy was an awesome cook, and they never needed to twist my arm as they often invited us for Sunday dinners after church. Even with five sons of her own, I can't tell you how many times Sandra found the time to do motherly things I simply couldn't do, including sewing Bryson's favorite shirts or shorts, and repairing his treasures, including the necklaces and bracelets he obsessively wore.

One day Steve was at my house with his boys and he noticed I was so weary I looked like I could drop. He insisted that he watch over Bryson and hang with the boys as I went upstairs for a nap. Later, when I came back down, Steve had cleaned up all the chaos in the kitchen that had gotten ahead of me for about a week. Sure, that was just a little thing, but I was literally *surviving* on little things now. They were rivers in the desert.

Pastor Bruce and his wife, Sharon, another amazing cook, also invited us often for dinners. After eating my cooking daily, I don't remember many complaints from my boys (make that zero) when we were invited to these wonderful homes. To this day, Bryson calls Pastor Bruce "Uncle Bruce," and what a great uncle he has been.

Amidst this time of turbulent change, rivers kept flowing from the Kinnelon schools. Dr. Valerie Mosca, director of special services, had served us faithfully since Bryson was in first grade. As he entered high school, Chris Hartmann became Bryson's special education teacher and Valerie selected another sensational aide, Nikki Perinotti. Nikki was a mother of three children, and she nurtured and protected Bryson like a mother hen.

Speaking of mother hens, Sharon Toriello, who was honored as principal of the year in the State of New Jersey in 2004, restored my faith in the ability of school administrators to respond courageously to bullying (you'll recall my disappointment in our middle school administrators). Sharon called me regularly, and her door was *always* open when I had a concern. With a serpent from hell always lurking, those concerns *never* ended.

One day Sharon called me with shocking news. Another student, in shop class, had threatened to slit Bryson's throat. One of Bryson's classmates overheard this threat and reported it to the teacher. Sharon sprang into action, and by the time I heard about it, the boy who had made the threat was being positioned to be expelled. But Sharon wisely arranged a meeting between me, this boy, and his father. During that meeting I became convinced that this boy's threat was empty bluster, made to get a laugh.

Although I knew that Bryson had been truly frightened in view of his vulnerable, childlike mind, Sharon and I agreed that mercy was called for. I looked this boy in the eye across the table and told him that I had personally made more dumb mistakes in my life than I could remember, and I was grateful when people gave me a second (or third) chance. The boy was remorseful, and he cried right there in that meeting. He returned to school the next day, and Bryson not only gained another friend, but also another pair of watchful eyes to look after his safety.

Speaking of rivers, the wheels were always turning in Chris Hartmann's head, and he called me one day with a "brainstorm." He knew that sports made Bryson "tick," and he had come up with the idea of making Bryson the sports reporter for the five minute student program that was telecast into each homeroom and throughout the Borough of Kinnelon each morning on the local cable network. When Chris asked what I thought, the only thing he heard was my gulp on the other end of the phone. Bryson was still having trouble speaking in full sentences, and he couldn't read beyond a rudimentary level. It was a stretch to think that he could read a sports report off of cue cards with the pressure of a camera lens focused on him.

Bryson's job as the sportscaster was to report the professional sports scores from the most recent Yankees, Mets, Rangers, Devils, Knicks, Nets, Giants, and Jets games, depending on the season. Since the games he would report were from the previous evening, he didn't have much time prior to each broadcast to memorize those scores, and he was extremely nervous prior to his first broadcast. But, as always, Bryson rose to the occasion, bringing tears to my eyes; and from the feedback I got, bringing tears to the eyes of many others in our town.

So many rivers were flowing now. It was a Friday morning when I got a call from Bryson's gym teacher, Nino Capra, telling me that something important had happened, and he wanted me to come down to the school right away to talk about it. To be honest, I was busier than a one-armed paper hanger that day, and I nearly pleaded with Mr. Capra just to tell me on the phone what had happened. But he *insisted* I come down, and that afternoon I found myself staring up at the ceiling of the Kinnelon High School gym with him.

All year, Nino had been disturbed by Bryson's lack of balance and motor skill, but he had been impressed with his tenacity (what a surprise). One of the school's football coaches, Nino was tough as nails, but tender inside. He couldn't be satisfied with having Bryson sit on the sidelines of *any* activity, and he had invented a seated contraption (buying parts from funds out of his own pocket) to attach to the gym's rope system. Long story short, my courageous son had pulled himself all the way up in that contraption and touched the ceiling of that gym.

Like me, Capra is an emotional Italian, and he was waving his arms as he spoke saying, "He touched the *ceiling* Mr. Milazzo! *He touched the ceiling!*" You won't find it surprising that as this river flowed, so did the tears of two Italian men that afternoon, as we stood there, staring up at that gym ceiling.

And the wheels kept turning in Mr. Hartmann's head. He argued before the school's National Honor Society committee that irrespective of his lack of academic acumen, in view of his challenges, Bryson should be elected to the National Honor Society. He got a few other teachers to join him in nominating Bryson, and at the risk of sounding like an utter crybaby, the tears come even now as I type these words, thinking back on that great night in the Kinnelon High School auditorium. Here was a boy, once thought to be so uneducable it would be best for him to be raised in an institution, now being inducted into the National Honor Society! And as Sharon Toriello announced Bryson's name, and Nikki Perinotti helped him up onto that stage, there were two *full* rows of Christ the King Church members who shared my tears, and my pride in my son.

Rivers were flowing in Tim's life too. Tim was now on the Kinnelon High baseball squad, pitching and playing center field, mostly for the junior varsity. He was a string bean, weighing all of 135 pounds soaking wet. Late in the season the arms of the varsity pitchers were getting worn and sore, and Kinnelon had a few doubleheaders coming up. Tim was called upon to pitch for the varsity, and I could hardly believe it as he had a *no-hitter* going into the last inning. He subsequently gave up a hit, but his complete game shutout victory helped to solidify a slot for Kinnelon in the upcoming county tournament. Tim was awarded a varsity letter, as just a freshman!

Dried Up Rivers, Emotional Swings, and Getting Stoned

And the waitress is practicing politics, As the businessmen slowly get stoned.[7]

There was so much to be thankful for now, as all these rivers flowed. But rivers have a way of drying up in the desert. As they do, we can quickly become grumblers, even as the Israelites grumbled against Moses, and were ready to stone him when they could no longer find water in the wilderness (Exod. 17:3–4).

Don't hear me telling you I was ready to stone anyone, nor that I was spending time in bars getting stoned. But grumbling was a sore temptation now, as a very painful reality loomed over my struggling family like the Sword of Damocles, a peril that I feared might just kill us all.

Pursuant to the terms of my divorce settlement, I was required to sell our family home no later than the summer of 2005 to pay off the balance of the settlement. I *desperately* tried to figure out a way remain in that home to keep my sons in a stable environment, but in view of the overall settlement I could no longer afford to buy out my former spouse's share. Bryson was extremely upset when he realized we needed to move, and even more upset when he realized he would no longer be returning to Kinnelon High, a place where he had many friends, and where he had become a celebrity. But the sale of our home was finalized that summer, and we were on our way to make a new life for ourselves in a rented home in Oakland, a more affordable community nearby.

Bryson was a creature of habit to an obsessive extreme. His room in Kinnelon was set up with exactitude, with all his heroes' posters on the walls, and a collection of *hundreds* of hats arranged just so. He had collections of necklaces and sneakers and favorite rubber bands (*thousands* of them, arranged by color) and *dozens* of cans of colognes on his dresser, (just the right scent for each occasion). When he began obsessively spraying those colognes on his body, the "smoke" rising up in the air nearly blocked out the sun.

I experienced powerful emotional swings as I began packing up two decades of family memories; and I was desperately fighting anxiety and depression as I met with Gordon Dahl, an elder from Christ the King Church, along with his wife, Sharon. The Dahls are the most selfless servants *anyone* has ever met. I told them I didn't see how I could *possibly* get this move done, since I was so very weary. They prayed with me, encouraging me that this task could not only be done, but that the church was going to see to it that more rivers would flow to help us.

They put a team, more like an *army*, of men and women together to prepare everything for the July 2005 day when the moving van would arrive. Understanding

Bryson's extremely obsessive nature, Sandy Woodruff took it upon herself to make a sketch of the *precise* setup in Bryson's room in Kinnelon, and she took that sketch down to our rented home in Oakland along with all his posters, photos, hats, and his endless collections and treasures, and replicated them in his room there. Only a mother's wise and loving heart could think of such a thing.

Steve Horvath came and helped Tim pack up his room. Sandra Stahr and several other women from the church packed and moved my kitchen. John Linson organized and moved my tools, and he also moved the boys' trampoline, rebuilding it from scratch in our new yard. Danny Salvatore and Bill LaFlesh performed the punch list for my Kinnelon home to get it ready for the closing. Josh Kitchen, one of our youth leaders who had been spending a lot of time with both my sons, installed the coolest basketball court you ever saw in our new basement, with a hoop at just the right height for Bryson to be able to dunk. What a thrill this was for Bryson.

Chris Luski, one of our youth leaders, and a young married man in our church, visited Bryson often during this time, sitting and chatting with him as they played video games. Gene Angelo, a powerful man with a tender heart, did the same, as did Jim MacLean, one of the other great young men from the church. What a relief to know that so many were coming alongside to speak words of truth and comfort to both my sons during this turbulent time.

Yet there was something troubling me as the move drew near, and it struck me deeply during a late night conversation with my daughter from Chiang Mai, Thailand. Janelle was in Thailand for five months under a Wheaton College program known as HNGR (Human Needs Global Resources), serving in an aftercare program for women who had been rescued from the rampant sexual trade there. Those rescued slaves were brought to the New Life Center in Chiang Mai, where my daughter was helping them to rebuild their lives. I was often on the phone praying and encouraging her in this extremely difficult work. The young women she was attempting to help had been crushed, and my daughter was so sensitive that her own health was affected at times.

Late one night (due to the time difference), Janelle shared another deep concern. "Dad, it's kind of weird. Here I am in Thailand, thinking about coming home, but I don't even know where 'home' is. I won't be moving back into my old room, and we won't even be living in the same town. It's gonna be kind of strange."

As I hung up the phone I became sad for her. She had been away at school, and now in Thailand, for the past few years. Her own suffering had occurred mostly in isolation, without direct support from us as her family. Now the home she had known since she was a little girl would be gone without her even being able to say good-bye.

A few ladies at the church wept when they heard this. Sandra Berg stepped forward and carefully packed up everything in Janelle's room. Then my dear sister Linda and her servant-leader husband, Jim, replicated Janelle's room in our new home in the same manner that Sandy Woodruff had done for Bryson. If I told you that these servants did a sensational job it would be an understatement. Janelle was an artist, and she had loved Asian things since she was a little girl. She actually had a Japanese gong in her room. When she came home from Thailand, and entered her new room, it was filled with her own artwork and her cherished Asian artifacts.

I could go on and on, but there's no way I could adequately convey what all these rivers truly meant except to say that they saved my life, and the lives of my children. If I live to be 100, I will be thanking King Jesus for those refreshing rivers, and for the wonderful individuals through whom they flowed.

Whatever Kills You Makes You Stronger

Well the dreaded day came, and the moving van did too. Janelle was still in Thailand, so it was just "A Three Boys" saying good-bye to our home in Kinnelon that day. I knew things would get chaotic, and that Bryson shouldn't be present to see his home being dismantled; so early that morning I brought him to stay with his Aunt Linda and her children, his cousins. They lived in Oakland, the same town to which we were moving.

That afternoon, in the midst of the chaos, as I was scurrying around answering questions of the movers, I noticed that Tim was out on the deck, just leaning against the rail with his hands in his pockets. My heart stirred, and I realized the Lord was prompting me to go outside and lean on that rail with him. Tim had grown to be a strong young man, and as I've said numerous times in this book, there has never been a father more proud of his son than I am of Tim. But I sometimes needed to stop and realize he had grown up too fast, and too hard. Since the day he was born, there had always been so much trouble in his brother's life; and now he had seen evil wreak havoc and destruction against his own home.

To know Tim was to know he'd never hesitate to step up to the plate and act courageously, particularly when the well-being of others was being threatened. To truly know him was to realize he was a private person, and a man of few words. In his silence that afternoon I knew something was troubling his soul. As we continued leaning on that rail, and as the movers kept shuffling in and out with all our stuff, he quietly said, "It's sad, isn't it, Dad?" This was a mouthful for my son, tantamount to opening up and saying, "This is just killing me, Dad!"

This was one of those moments when, in a perfect world, I'd have rendered a memorable response. I mean, I would've totally nailed it, saying something wise and fatherly, perhaps even something melodious like, "Son, let me play you a memory, I'm not really sure how it goes. But it's sad and it's sweet, and I knew it complete when I wore a younger man's clothes."[9]

But I just groped for something meaningful to say, remaining silent as we continued leaning against that rail. The thought entered my mind to tell him that when I built this house many years before, I dreamed of growing old in it with his mother, of having our grandchildren, *his* children, come to visit us one day here. But clearly my son didn't need to hear about my broken dreams now, not when he was struggling to deal with his own.

After a long pause, with both of us still staring straight ahead, I answered my son's question as gently and quietly as he had asked it: "Yeah, Tim, it's sad."

In the many years since, the Lord has been teaching me something we all need to know, and cling to for dear life at times, especially when tribulations bring us so low we think we might just die. There's an almighty King who rules every inch of the universe, One who sees all our pain. The King loved us so dearly that He stepped down from His throne to suffer a brutal death for our sakes on a cross. This event shocked all creation, including legions of angels. But the wise King knew something that no human or angelic eyes could yet see.

The King's ways remain foolish to the wise in this world. But those who know Him and love Him ultimately learn a great secret, and their eyes are opened. Death must always occur before there can be new life. The trials and afflictions that are *just killing us* here, even those tribulations that cause us to become weaker and weaker in ourselves, ultimately make us stronger and more useful in the hands of the great King, as we trust in Him alone.

> But we do see Him who was made for a little while lower than the angels, namely, Jesus, because of the suffering of death crowned with glory and honor, so that by the grace of God He might taste death for everyone.
>
> —Hebrews 2:9

> Precious in the sight of the Lord Is the death of His godly ones.
>
> —Psalm 116:15

> For to me, to live is Christ and to die is gain.
>
> —Philippians 1:21

> So death works in us, but life in you.
>
> —2 Corinthians 4:12

Chapter 29
THE EXPECTED ONE

Now when John, while imprisoned, heard of the works of Christ, he sent word by his disciples and said to Him, "Are You the Expected One, or shall we look for someone else?"
MATTHEW 11:2–3

A MIDDLE-AGED MAN WAS passed over, yet again, for the promotion he had coveted for years, and it began to sink in that he was dead-ended in his career. His wife hassled him endlessly, his teenaged kids were rude and rebellious, and the bulge in his midsection made a comeback at the gym seem laughable. *Nothing* had gone as expected in his life, and he became deeply depressed, wondering whether he should even go on living. His friends urged him to see a psychiatrist; and for a full hour the man sat on the psychiatrist's couch, pouring out his regrets, his frustrations and his anger, as the doctor silently made notes on his pad. Finally the psychiatrist put down his pad, looked at the man somberly, and said, "You are manic depressive and borderline psychotic! You need to be admitted to the hospital *immediately*!" The man was stunned, and sat quietly for a moment, staring in shock. Finally he said, "Well, I'm going to want a second opinion." "Okay," the psychiatrist said, "you're ugly too!"

That's an old joke, and to the extent it gave anyone a chuckle, it's because no one would expect a psychiatrist to say something so outrageous and unprofessional. But have you ever stopped to consider how outrageous it was for John the Baptist, of *all* people, to begin to doubt if Jesus really was the Expected One? John was Jesus' cousin, and he had known Him *all* his life, from *before* birth in fact. Their mothers were pregnant at the same time; and as just a fetus, John had literally leaped inside Elizabeth's womb when he heard Aunt Mary's voice, the blessed woman who carried the Expected One inside her (Luke 1:41).

Throughout Elizabeth's pregnancy, John's father, Zacharias, was stricken with silence for disbelieving the angel's message about his son's mission. His speech was restored only after John was born; and there's not a doubt but that Zacharias zealously taught John that his mission in life was to be the forerunner of the Messiah, *just* as the angel foretold. John couldn't have been any clearer than in his own proclamation that Jesus was the Expected One when he said, "I myself have seen, and have testified that this is the Son of God" (John 1:34). He also proclaimed that he was unworthy even to stoop down to untie the thong of Jesus' sandal (Mark 1:7). And to the extent that there was *any* doubt remaining in John's heart, the Father's voice bellowed from heaven as Jesus rose up from the water after John baptized him, saying, "This is My beloved Son in whom I am well-pleased," as the Holy Spirit descended upon Jesus as a dove (Matt. 3:16–17).

It was *inconceivable* now that John could *ever* be tempted to doubt that Jesus was the Expected One, the One for whom he had invested his entire life's work, with all the zeal of his passionate heart. Yet, astonishingly, John did begin to doubt: "He sent word by his disciples and said to Him, 'Are You the Expected One, or shall we look for someone else?'" (11:2–3). How in the *world* did John reach this point of equivocation? It just doesn't add up.

I think, as he languished day after day bound in Herod's dungeon, the ever pragmatic John realized he wasn't getting out of there alive. He knew Herod's wife wanted him dead; and, in fact, his murder would soon be carried out as the cowardly, narcissistic Herod served up his head to his wife's daughter on a platter (14:11). This was far from the meritorious ending this gallant man's life deserved, and honestly, not something we'd *expect* God would allow in the life of one of His most faithful servants. But this makes me wonder, what did I expect God would allow in my life? What did you expect He would allow in yours?

You never expected that phone call informing you that the cancer you had beaten has returned. Another miscarriage, after you've waited so *many* years? You are shocked and devastated, not only by your daughter's ugly rebellion but that she left home with such vile accusations on her lips. You couldn't have *imagined* facing bankruptcy, just a few years ago. You were on top of the world! You'd have bet your life that your husband (or wife) would *never* abandon you. Now you face *years* of bitterness, loneliness and hardship. No one anticipates being raped, not even in their worst nightmare. You've been violated right down to the core of your soul. It's hard enough to lose a parent to death, but it's hell to see such a dignified, sharp-minded individual imprisoned in the in-between world of Alzheimer's. No parent expects to *ever* face the horror of burying their own child. The senseless tragedy came so suddenly. You didn't even have the chance to say "good-bye."

Unexpected calamities invade our lives like a flash flood in this world. It is by no means morose, just wise to number our days aright (Ps. 90:12), remaining mindful that none of us are getting off this war-zone planet alive. Oh yes, it's easy to read of the Baptist's equivocation and think we'd be more "faithful," particularly when our seas are calm. Those whose lives and families have been ripped apart by loss and grief know better, don't you? When our cherished hopes and dreams of how life should unfold are blown to smithereens, the most natural thing in the world is the temptation toward doubt, despondency, or bitterness.

No, the Baptist's equivocation doesn't surprise me. What does surprise me is Jesus' compassionate response to his withering faith. One might expect that Jesus would send John's disciples right back down to that dungeon to chastise him, saying: "How dare you, John! And after all we've been through together! You who called others to repentance ought to repent yourself, in shame, because of your unbelief! You were responsible to fulfill only one mission in this world, and now you've blown it! Some forerunner you are!"

But instead of taking umbrage against John, the Expected One simply spoke the truth, telling those disciples to report back to John that "the BLIND RECEIVE SIGHT and the lame walk, the lepers are cleansed and the deaf hear, the dead are raised up, and the POOR HAVE THE GOSPEL PREACHED TO THEM" (Matt. 11:5). He added a gentle, but truthful rebuke: "And blessed is he who does not take offense at Me" (v. 6). He then turned His attention toward the crowds; and instead of publicly criticizing John for his doubts, Jesus chose to praise him for his life of service: "Truly I say to you, among those born of women there has not arisen anyone greater than John the Baptist!" (v. 11). What a merciful and compassionate King!

Yet notice that Jesus didn't explain to John why he needed to remain in that dungeon, nor did He promise that his circumstances would soon get better. In fact, those circumstances were about to become *far* worse. Nor did the Lord explain Himself to Joseph as he languished in prison for years, nor even to the longsuffering Job, in terms of why his life had become so *brutally* hard. Don't expect that He will explain Himself to you either, dear reader. God created the human race from dust and clay, and we live and breathe according to the kindness of His will. When we do not understand the sorrows that pierce our souls like shrapnel, it's up to us to decide whether we will doubt and curse, or wait upon the Expected One, in humility and trust.

In this book I've told you of some unexpected sorrows that made me want to die. There were times when the urge to take offense against God and raise my puny fist against him seemed overwhelming, even righteous. Oh yes, I had come to know the Expected One, certainly I had. But when your cherished hopes and dreams are decimated right before your eyes, pious platitudes and pretentious facades just don't cut it, do they? I've offered no easy answers; and as I conclude these final chapters, I'll not attempt to explain what God refuses to explain. Instead, I will point you back to the Expected One, who possesses the power to give sight to the blind and cause the lame to walk, who raises the dead and preaches the gospel to the poor.

The only explanation God will ever make is the one He has *already* made, when the Expected One allowed Himself to be stretched out on a brutal Roman cross. He suffered the punishment *we* deserved for our sin, even death, so we can walk free from sin and receive life eternal, in Him. It is an understatement to say God's explanation was unexpected. It was shocking to those closest to Jesus, and to the hosts of heaven. We ought never to become too familiar with the wonder of it, neglecting the intensity of His love for us that drove Him to that cross.

> God called Jesus Christ to what seemed unmitigated disaster. Jesus Christ called His disciples to see Him put to death; He led every one of them to the place where their hearts were broken. Jesus Christ's life was an absolute failure from every standpoint but God's. But what seemed a failure from man's standpoint was a tremendous triumph from God's, because God's purpose is never man's purpose.[1]
>
> —OSWALD CHAMBERS

Even as the inscrutable purpose of the Expected One remained completely within His Father's control when all appeared darkest, nothing that happens to us, though it may take an unexpected turn toward sorrow or even toward dread, is *ever* beyond the Father's control to weave into His grand plan for His glory and for our good.

Shallow acceptance of this truth is simple to grasp. Yet, while it is so easy to proclaim that we will pick up our cross and follow Christ no matter what, our expectations can be the bane of our existence as that cross begins to weigh heavy upon our shoulders. We so easily forget that as a kernel of wheat must die before it can bear fruit, so must we die in order to be transformed into Christ's image, ultimately bearing fruit that honors Him. Amy Carmichael offers a reality check, in terms of what we should expect as we choose the way of the cross.

> If I forget that the way of the Cross leads to the Cross and not to a bank of flowers; if I regulate my life on these lines...so that I am surprised when the way is rough and think it strange...then I know nothing of Calvary love.[2]

Wasting Away in Margaritaville[3]... Make That Oakland

> Notice God's unutterable waste of saints....God plants His saints in the most useless places. We say—God intends me to be here because I am so useful....God puts His saints where they will glorify Him and we are no judges at all of where that is.[4]
>
> —Oswald Chambers

My computer has lain fallow for several months as I've groped for a meaningful way to conclude this book. I almost regret my commitment to be honest, because there's *much* I'd rather conceal. The urge I feel to end this very personal story in a manner in which my life can be seen as "victorious" is as strong as an alcoholic's craving for his next drink. But my circumstances are rather humiliating right now; and if I am going to honor my pledge to be truthful I must honestly tell you that my life has turned out to be an utter waste.

My life is a failure by every measure of competence and success this world values; and I've wasted away, reaching levels of debilitation you'd expect to observe in the life of a drunk lying in the gutter. This isn't because I've had too many margaritas (though I'd be lying if I said I wasn't tempted to drink at times). Yet, at about the time I became a single dad, I also became a teetotaler, every bit as much as John the Baptist was a teetotaler.

Oh, I used to enjoy a few cold beers as I watched Yankee games with my sons. But one warm summer night, Bryson turned toward me from his seat (which is always obsessively *right* next to the TV) and asked, "Dad, how [does] that beer taste?" Panic struck me, like a lightning bolt. I had seen his propensity to be dragged toward the intentions of hell, more than once; and I suddenly realized that if he were *ever* to imbibe alcohol when he came of age, he'd literally go insane.

I was one of his heroes and he wanted to be like me. Alarm bells were ringing now. As the sole caregiver of a mentally impaired, handicapped child there's *never* a time when it's safe to be under the influence of *any* spirit other than God's Spirit.

I looked at my little child, now bearing an adolescent's body, and said, "Terrible, Bryson! The beer tastes terrible!" I got up, walked to the kitchen, opened every remaining bottle from the case in the fridge, and poured it down the drain. As I write these words, I haven't had a drink of any alcoholic beverage in a dozen years. So clearly, I haven't wasted away through drunkenness. Then what in the world happened to cause my life to become such a waste? If this was easy to describe, I wouldn't be sitting here struggling to conclude this book.

I trust that the events next revealed to you will not be understood to be a complaint against God. Yet the circumstances that unfolded in the years ahead were *anything* but what I expected, and I believe I know what that Baptist was thinking and feeling as he sat in that dungeon, completely bewildered by what his lifelong Friend, Jesus, had allowed to occur in his life.

EXPECTATION MEETS ENERVATION

> Has the Lord ever asked you—"Wilt thou lay down thy life for My sake?" It is far easier to die than to lay down the life day in and day out with the sense of the high calling.[5]
>
> —OSWALD CHAMBERS

Most parents of young children understand the need to lay down their lives for a while, along with some comforts (like sleep), maybe even some hobbies, to properly care for their children. But there's an expectation, even if you become a single parent, that your children will be emancipated at some point, and that your life will one day get back to "normal" (whatever *that* is).

As Bryson entered adulthood, his childlike needs came tagging right along. He still needed to be daily bathed, shaved, toileted, have his teeth brushed, shoes tied, food cut up, his toenails too. I could go on and on, but you get the idea. And no, you're not experiencing an episode of déjà vu. I said the *exact* same thing in the last chapter, and it bears repeating because every day of my life for an entire decade resembled an absurdly repetitious, real-life version of Bill Murray's *Groundhog Day*.[6]

New Jersey offers schooling until age twenty-one for special-needs students. Bryson attended ECLC, a *wonderful* school nearby to Oakland. His immune system deficiency still made it impossible to fend off the infections he was exposed to at school; and, as had been the case in Kinnelon, this caused him to be home sick much of the school year.

Although he was now an "adult," his emotional needs remained those of a sick toddler. You moms know what this is like. Not a day at the beach! All expectations of accomplishing the things you planned to get done that day must be shelved, as interruptions flow unabated in your direction, and your own limits become strained as you dole out Lipton soup and introduce medications that they *vigorously* fight against receiving, and as you do your best to entertain them.

I had him evaluated at Hackensack University Medical Center, and four tiers of extensive testing were recommended, with an eye toward deriving a treatment plan. The doctor was brilliant, but I declined those evaluations, realizing that we would be chasing the wind. Most of those evaluations had been performed in the past; and honestly, Bryson's emotionality now made it hard even to get him into the car to go to places he *wanted* to go, no less to doctors' offices and hospitals.

Parents of young children expect bathroom mishaps to occur, and the messes are relatively containable. As an "adult," Bryson continued to get himself into *such* fixes. I'll never understand how, in addition to soiling his socks and shoes, excrement also got onto the walls, and occasionally, into his hair. When calamities such as these arose, *all* human activity ceased. Conditions were sometimes *so* bad that baths number two and three for that day were needed, right in a row, followed by hours of clean up in the rooms he'd been in, not to mention the soiled clothes.

These were among the most bizarre moments of my life; and the devil was right there, taunting me about how absurd and pathetic my life had become. I was barraged with feelings of anger, defeat, and loneliness, knowing there was so much else I needed to get done, but feeling powerless, almost numb to the reality that life was passing me by. In the midst of my exasperation, the Lord reminded me that the soul of someone far more vulnerable than mine was at stake. I needed to lay aside my feelings and build up my son, whose self-esteem was being *battered*.

"Don't worry, Bryson. This happens to everyone!" And when he called me in the middle of the night, having wet his bed yet *again*, I simply cleaned him up, put dry clothes on him, turned the mattress over and remade the bed, and tucked him back in, doing my best to make sure that he didn't feel even worse about himself than he already did. "Sorry, Dad," he said dejectedly. "Are you *kidding*, Bryson? I did the *exact* same thing, just last week!" Maybe that's a white lie in some people's estimation. As the caregiver of a mentally impaired "child," you cannot worry about "people's" estimation.

But I'm sure I was quite a sight carrying his mattress out to the backyard the next day, to lay it in the sun. I already felt a bit conspicuous being the only renter in a nice neighborhood of homeowners, and the single father of three. Talk about a square peg amidst round holes. Everyone was cordial, and some Christian neighbors were friendly and kind; but everyone was frightfully busy, and no one had the time even to *begin* to understand what was happening in my home. Behind closed doors, I was gasping for air, burning out, and I mean like toast.

Toasted or not, there was *no* time for rest. My son's adult-sized body kept crashing unmercifully to the ground, due to his cerebral palsy (poor balance). As I write these words, I am bleary eyed in the aftermath of my son crashing to the ground at 4:00 a.m. *just* this morning, as he was coming back to his room from the bathroom. The crash literally rattled the house, and I raced to his room to pick him up and help him back into bed. Thankfully, he only suffered bruises this time. But at the risk of giving you another episode déjà vu, these past few years as I conclude this book he has broken one tooth and he has cracked another tooth, he has injured his wrist and he has broken his ribs, he has seriously injured his knee, he has broken his leg, and the beat goes on.

Rodney Dangerfield, the comedian who endlessly complained but never got any respect, carped in exasperation that his wife was at the beauty parlor for two hours; and that was just for the estimate! Well, that joke doesn't fit into this chapter, does it? But it *was* unexpected, so perhaps it does. Either way, I'm beginning to feel like a complainer. But I can assure you, the injuries I've described in this book are *just* the estimate.

Our compassionate physical therapist, Lynda Eisen, and skilled dentist, Joe Sluka, comforted Bryson *and* me more than they could possibly have known, as Bryson recovered from his injuries, and broken teeth were replaced. Dr. Hervey Sicherman, our wise orthopedic surgeon, made the right call again and again, guiding us toward healing and helping me to keep a lid on my emotions. I'll never forget him saying, "Hang in there, Dad, you're doing a *great* job!" as I turned to leave his office after treating one of his many injuries.

I'll also never forget the "little" blessings God sent after Bryson broke his leg. A group was organized by nearby Hawthorne Gospel Church, and George and Jeanette Venarchik, Joe and Bethanne Pellegrino, and many others provided us with meals. In terms of the unexpected, Martha Quijano was one of the first to show up with a meal. Martha is a single mom in the midst of an intense personal battle against a brain tumor and seizures. She has waged her courageous battle with dignity and grace, and praise on her lips toward God, even as she has raised her daughter alone. To say that I was humbled when she showed up at my door would be an understatement.

And I won't forget Mike Marroccoli taking off from work to help carry my son back to Dr. Sicherman's office in a snowstorm, nor how deflated I was as the doctor looked at the X-rays, month after month and exclaimed "nothing has changed," as that leg stubbornly refused to heal. Nor will I forget the nerve-wracking, back-breaking baths I gave my son daily, doing my best to keep his cast dry with a plastic sleeve, lifting his large frame from the tub to get him dressed. And I certainly won't forget that my son, who had been trying *so* hard to become independent in his toileting, went *all* the way back to square zero in this quest during those *long* months of recovery.

That broken leg occurred in 2010 (Bryson was twenty-three), and I can tell you this was a time when I sometimes looked toward heaven with utter bewilderment. It had taken many *years* of excruciating effort for my son to prove the experts wrong and *finally* begin to walk independently. When he broke his leg it was almost as if God had *invited* the enemy to level us, yet again. I envisioned

Satan standing over us, taunting us, daring us not even to *try* to get up again, lest his wrecking ball swing back and level us once more.

I had begun working from home nearly a decade prior to that broken leg, when it became clear that it was neither physically nor emotionally safe for my son to be left alone. Bryson wasn't a candidate for a babysitter, or to shoehorn him into a day care facility that would cause him to consider suicide again. My divided focus as a commercial real estate broker and caregiver for a multiply handicapped child was laughable as a business model.

Bryson's expenses were great, and the costs of running a home and putting my other children through college were high. With my feet planted in quicksand and my cash flow gushing toward a sea of red, my life's savings were decimated. After working *so* hard for decades and becoming a multimillionaire in my early forties, it was a tremendous affront to my pride when bankruptcy became a legitimate concern, and as it became likely that I'd never be able to buy a home again.

Since a man's identity is inextricably linked with the work he does as the provider for his family, I *pleaded* with the Lord to set me free to live a "normal" life. Many times I got so fed up that I looked up and said, "I've had it, Lord! I'm going back into business!"

The Lord gently reminded me that Peter also declared his intention to return to a vocation known to him in saying: "I am going fishing" (John 21:3). Jesus rebuked Peter by inquiring if he really loved Him at all. If he did love Him, it was time for Peter to prove it by choosing to *truly* follow Jesus, not by going back to what was comfortable and "normal." The real question for Peter, for me, and for all of us, *always* is: Will we tend His lambs? (v. 17).

The Holy Spirit was unmistakable. He was providing me with the *one* shot I'd *ever* have to provide for the emotional and spiritual needs of three lambs, including a deeply injured lamb who'd have been torn to shreds by wolves had I failed to obey. Yes, I was going to be poor, but He was going to make me wealthy in the lives of children who would one day go out into the world to do greater things. Even so, I received no promise that my personal circumstances would improve if I obeyed. On the contrary, I was about to learn what it means to become utterly wasted.

I burned the candle on both ends, as Bryson ate, drank, and breathed his beloved sports, often staying up late to watch them. With so little in his life he could control, my twenty-something son wasn't about to be told to go to bed until those games were over. And while most aging parents wouldn't think to stay up and watch them with their young adult children, there was no way I could go to bed before him, since he couldn't untie his shoes or get safely into bed.

An hour with coffee and God's Word early each morning was *indispensible* before facing Bryson's blizzard of needs, far more important than an additional hour of sleep. But, of course, this was the flame at the other end of the candle. I was also getting up several times during the night, due to middle-aged male problems. My urologist told me that my prostate was the size of a grapefruit (how comforting). More serious health issues were also involved which had not yet been discovered. There's nothing more boring than people talking about their health problems, and I won't dwell on mine, other than to provide a snapshot or two in the concluding chapters.

But you've been reading a book written by the most sleep-deprived author in history. If I sat on a psychiatrist's couch, I doubt he'd have called me "ugly," but there's a chance he'd have diagnosed me as catatonic, particularly if he failed to realize I was actually sleeping on that couch. I began doing *ridiculous* things, like turning on the coffee pot with no coffee *or* water in it, bumping into furniture and knocking over beverages due to lack of coordination, turning on the water in the tub and forgetting about it, standing in a room while having *no* idea why I was even in that room.

There were more dangerous faux pas, such as leaving the car in drive while getting *out* of it. Maybe I wasn't drinking myself toward Margaritaville, but when you're continually stressed, physically exhausted, and emotionally drained, there's precious little difference.

Wasted or not, it was never far from my sleep-deprived mind how suddenly my son's demeanor could turn dark. Henri Nouwen lived among mentally impaired adults in France, observing that one moment they can love you like no one else on earth can love you. The *next* moment, like flipping a switch, their love can turn to fear, anger, and to a suspicious "what have you done for me lately" attitude.

Does Bryson still love me when he's upset and angry, when he tells me he hates me and wishes I was dead? Does he still love Jesus during those moments when he declares he wants to burn in hell? Yes, he loves us. But I can never forget, and the Expected One *certainly* knows, he is a scared little boy inside. Without sheer tenacity, he'd never have walked, nor achieved many other praiseworthy accomplishments. Somewhere along the way his relentless nature became a double-edged sword.

William Congreve wrote a play in the seventeenth century in which it was said (paraphrased), "Hell hath no fury like a woman scorned."[7] As the lights came on that he wouldn't play for the Yankees or the Dallas Cowboys, and that he'd never drive a car or tie his own shoes, hell issued forth a fury from my son's soul that might best be depicted as that mythically scorned woman on steroids.

Parents of toddlers expect occasional tantrums and whining for candy at the check-out counter. The wheedling of a mentally impaired adult, buttressed with fear-driven anger, is a *whole* different ballgame. He was a pit bull of a negotiator and a fierce manipulator. As I tried to reason with him, my obsessive-compulsive son routinely chewed me up and spit me out. When his obsessively tenacious nature merged with his unrelenting desire for more in life, and his long held dreams kept crashing onto the jagged rocks of his vexing limitations, he simply couldn't cope. As the astronauts of Apollo 13 declared: "Houston, we have a problem!" the only thing I could often think to pray now was: "Oh, Daddy! We've got a problem!"

His foghorn voice often startled me from my dazed stupor as his nonstop demands bellowed across the house. Changing a video game, getting him a snack, telling him for the eighteenth time what dinner was going to be that night (and hearing him respond: "I'm not eating that!"), helping him change into new outfits umpteen times each day (Syracuse, Kentucky, or Duke shorts, and a myriad of other teams), helping him sort through *thousands* of silly bands until he found *just* the right one, helping him with toileting, responding to frantic calls to watch a replay on ESPN, or to kill a fly buzzing in the room (all human activity *must* cease until *any* insect in our home went "the way of all flesh"), or to watch a Christmas movie for the eightieth time in *September*, or to give him a second bath, or to put medicine on an "urgent" pimple or bandages not only on real injuries, but also on his growing list of imaginary ones (if Kobe Bryant had tape on his fingers, Bryson "needed" tape on his too). My obsessive son *needed* everything that his simple, overly-active mind could think of, and he "needed" it all *now, now, now!*

Bryson had *immense* staying power, and there was almost always an underlying urgency in his spirit. He just kept coming at me with the force of a steamroller, *pleading* for me to fulfill requests I no longer had the energy or the financial resources to provide. When he perceived that the next hat, bracelet, necklace, Hollister shirt, pair of basketball shoes, the next *"candy"* of *whatever* sort would fill his void, he *never* let go of it, nor of me. He was a heat-seeking missile locked onto Dad.

Of course, there was a thief involved (John 10:10), a liar who knew *exactly* when to push his buttons of inadequacy and fear. The medical explanation for those "buttons" is complex. He had sustained extensive damage to his frontal lobe when he suffered his global brain injury. The frontal lobe is the seat of human emotions, and instrumental in one's ability to reason. My son had no concept of such things. He just kept thinking that Daddy could always make everything work out okay.

Neither of us realized how dangerously weary Daddy had become now, both physically and mentally. Living in close quarters with an often angry and frustrated, mentally impaired person can cause the caregiver to become mentally impaired too, particularly if he can't get away to regain some perspective. I'd like to tell you that as a believer in Christ I flawlessly rose above the strain. Yet even a tiny bit of self-awareness made me realize I was on thin ice now, like a rubber band ready to snap. The truth is, I was already crashing through that ice, as installment payments on long-term debts of stress and sleep deprivation began coming due.

It didn't take much to cause an occasional outburst of anger from me. Perhaps from burning my hand while getting dinner out of the oven, or having it drop on the floor and seeing the dog pounce on it. Maybe from realizing I had forgotten my phone while halfway to an appointment as I tried to keep my failing business alive.

I was burned out, oh yes, and wasted big time! But had I also become mentally ill? Who in the world knows? Yet I can tell you that my reclusiveness and isolation was becoming harder to fight.

As my groundhog days continued, month after month and year after year, I was grateful for the few loyal friends who stood with me, without yielding to the propensity to evaluate my life. Based on the tidy judgments of some who had little idea of the daily battles in my home, I was regarded as if I was a drunk in the gutter for suffering financial difficulties. I came to cherish quotes from bold men like Theodore Roosevelt:

> It is not the critic who counts; not the man who points out how the strong man stumbles, or where the doer of deeds could have done them better. The credit belongs to the man who is actually in the arena, whose face is marred by dust and sweat and blood; who strives valiantly, who errs, who comes up short again and again, because there is no effort without error and shortcoming; but who does actually strive to do the deeds; who knows great enthusiasms, the great devotions; who spends himself in a worthy cause; who at the best knows in the end the triumph of high achievement, and who at the worst, if he fails, at least he fails while daring greatly, so that his place shall never be with those cold and timid souls who neither knew victory nor defeat.[8]

But even as the opinions of others became less important to me, Bryson was becoming obsessively concerned about his own appearance, particularly about his hair. Since getting him out of the house was tantamount to pulling a tooth, I became his barber. He'd decide suddenly that he *needed* a certain style, and that heat-seeking missile followed me around the house, even pounding on locked doors as I tried to sneak a brief nap, until I agreed to provide the requested hairdo.

Trusty clippers in hand, I gave him Mohawks, reverse Mohawks, Marine cuts, spiked hair, shaved heads—any style was available at Dad's salon. I'll never forget the looks I got while asking random ladies for advice at Walgreens, regarding the best method of bleaching one's hair platinum blonde (not the wisest question to ask, particularly if the woman is blonde; but I digress).

I'll also never forget the day my son began screaming as I poured water over him in the tub after I shaved his head completely. A peculiar conversation ensued, and I finally realized he was *so* pleased with the absence of hair on his cue-balled head, and he thought his hair would grow like grass if his head was "watered." I laughed, and spent the next few moments explaining that hair doesn't grow the same way as grass. He listened carefully, nodding in agreement, apparently grasping the concept. Yet, when I began pouring water on him again, he just renewed his screaming.

My sleep deprived mind was a little slow on the uptake, but you're catching on, aren't you? I was attempting to reason with a very conceptually wounded "child." In some ways his mind was *perfectly* normal, even brilliant. In others, there was a total disconnect from reality.

In my mental weariness, I missed a few of those "disconnects," such as the time I learned that the athletic tape he constantly wrapped the imaginary injuries on his wrists with (to look like Kobe Bryant) needed to be removed occasionally, especially during bath time, so that the dampness wouldn't cause his skin to rot. When I finally saw the skin ulcers, I nearly gagged.

He went from one odd obsession to another. After I taught him to shave with an electric razor, he began shaving for several *hours* each day. When he complained that the razor I purchased for him wasn't adequate, I purchased several more shavers and groomers he had seen on TV. I didn't try to intervene in this obsession, since he complained that the hair on his body felt like ants crawling on him. I reasoned that he was relatively safe sitting on his bed as I heard those groomers and shavers humming, much safer than when he had stolen my sharp razor and cut himself with it. But he just kept shaving more and more, until he was shaving every bit of hair off of his body, *including* his eyebrows, fingers and toes. In my weariness I conveniently overlooked that he was sometimes bleeding now, as he obsessively shaved his skin raw.

One day he saw an advertisement for Nair. I denied his request to buy this for weeks. But he wore me down like Chinese water torture; and well, you've probably already guessed that I gave in. I cautiously followed the instructions by rinsing off the cream after about ten minutes from the areas to which we had applied it. One evening that same week he began to squirm in pain at the dinner table. It finally registered in my sleep-deprived mind that he must've found where I had hidden that Nair! I yanked off his shirt to find *horrible* chemical burns all over his chest and stomach! He had smeared it on in the morning and simply gone about his day! I was on my way to the emergency room with him when Sheryl Fieldhouse (a nurse) returned my SOS call, and guided me through the process of treating those burns at home. Oh why, oh *why* did I buy him that Nair? Honestly, I no longer had any idea how to say "no" to my son.

Vince Lombardi once said, "Fatigue makes cowards of us all."[9] You'd better believe I was afraid. I was dealing with a *very* driven, often angry, mentally impaired "child" who was sucking me dry, and who had threatened suicide more than once. Beyond my fear of what he might do to harm himself, I was also becoming increasingly fearful of reaching my own limits now, due to the unceasing stress. Was it conceivable that I could *ever* physically harm my son, this lamb I so loved, in a fit of personal rage? Honestly, I didn't know, and there's no way I wanted to find out. I often found myself out on the front lawn, counting to ten, crying out to God for mercy and help.

I could hardly *bear* the thought of that next childlike need, that next incredible mess, that next bone-breaking injury, that next debilitating illness, that next volley of *incessant* three-year-old questions, that next refusal to eat what I served for dinner, that next angry trauma, that next insult informing me that my breath was bad or that I was "stupid" as I struggled to untie a knot in his shoe, that next request to cut his toenails or get him a snack at 11:00 p.m. as the game du jour headed into the fourth quarter, that next odd disconnect. Any and *all* of it was *just* around the corner, and the stress in my home was often thick enough to cut with a knife.

I sometimes took quick trips to the store now, not only for groceries, but just to get out of the house to clear my head, to see a few friendly faces, to *finally* converse with an adult, if even at the checkout counter, to talk to *anyone* who'd greet me without *demanding* something from me.

Maybe it was the stress, or the sleeplessness, or the yet undiscovered physical disease. Maybe it was the monotony, or the broken heart from experiencing so much emotional pain and loneliness. Maybe it was the reality that my body sometimes *ached* to hold a woman in my arms once more instead of caring for the *endless* needs of an adult child. Oh, but I'm beginning to sound like Rodney Dangerfield again, and I fear I've just been spinning my wheels attempting to describe how my life became a waste.

Whatever the cause of my "wastedness," somewhere along the way I became like a boxer in the corner getting pummeled with my defenses down, too dazed and confused to realize that the fight was already over, and I was about to fall.

UGLY TOO?

The doctors in the ER at Valley Hospital wanted to know if I had been in a fight, or had perhaps been drinking. I suppose when someone shows up the way I did, with my head wrapped in a towel to stop the bleeding, these are reasonable assumptions. But after a myriad of tests revealed zero alcohol in my body, they realized I was in earnest in telling them I had woken in a pool of blood at 4:00 a.m. on my bathroom floor, with *no* idea why.

They also realized I was serious in telling them I had waited at home until it was time to get my son out of bed at his normal time in order to put him on his ECLC school bus, which picked him up in my driveway at 8:25 a.m., and had then driven myself to the hospital wrapped in that towel.

As mentioned, I won't provide unnecessary details about my medical condition. Yet with all I've written about being wasted, it does not lack irony that doctors ultimately discovered a diseased liver typically indicative of a heavy drinker. Scans performed in the ER on this day also revealed a concussion, and a nose that had been broken in four places. The gashes around my face and nose were so deep that the emergency room doctor wouldn't touch them, and she informed me that a plastic surgeon was on his way to repair these wounds.

My face was a wreck, and no one would have blamed him if he had called me "ugly," but Dr. Sidney Rabinowitz was far more kind. In fact, he was a very compassionate man. I asked him if he could make me look like Richard Gere, and he laughed (a bit too hard for my liking). But I told him I had made several calls, and found no one available to help my handicapped son off the school bus that was scheduled to arrive in my driveway at 3:15 p.m. Therefore, I was going to skip the surgery and leave, since it was already noon. When he understood the situation, this kind doctor promised to complete his work by 2:30 p.m. so that I could make it home in time.

This brilliant surgeon repaired my face, nose, and forehead with precision;

and though I looked more like Frankenstein than Richard Gere, I was soon driving myself home with a concussion. The ER doctor wasn't happy about that. Nor had any of the doctors yet figured out *why* I had passed out. But you know, don't you, dear reader? And as you might've guessed, I was woozy for several days, almost as if I had consumed too many margaritas.

Bryson's emotionality became even more fragile as he observed my wounds, and as his confused, frightened mind grappled with the concept of Daddy's mortality. Tim, still in high school, stepped up as my right arm as always, spending extra time with his brother as I regained my equilibrium. My nose and face gradually healed, and though I tried reaching for compliments, *no* one mistook me for Richard Gere (and I *promise* not to mention it again).

Yet, I will tell you that my next collapse would be far worse, and instead of driving myself to the hospital, I'd be taken from my home in an ambulance. As a result of these incidents, and all that has been involved in their aftermath, it has taken several more years to write this book than I ever expected; and I've often thought the effort to finish it might kill me, to the extent that these collapses failed to do so.

The Expected One has squeezed this story out of a weak and weary soul and onto these pages through feeble hands indeed. This, of course, is *exactly* what He wanted, so it would be written from utter desperation, in total dependence upon Him, which is the theme of this book:

> For we do not want you to be unaware, brethren, of our affliction which came to us in Asia, that we were burdened excessively, beyond our strength, so that we despaired even of life; indeed, we had the sentence of death within ourselves, so that we might not trust in ourselves, but in God who raises the dead; who delivered us from so great a peril of death, and will deliver us, He on whom we have set our hope. And He will yet deliver us.
>
> —2 Corinthians 1:8–10

I have been convicted from the very first page of this work that I am writing to an audience of people who desperately need hope, even as I *still* desperately need hope, and as Paul did too.

But is it correct to say my life became a waste? Did many years as a single dad and sole caregiver to a mentally impaired child cost me my sanity? This is a subjective matter, kind of like being ugly, I suppose, and I cannot give you a clear answer. Yet, I can tell you with certitude that my life turned out to be far from what I expected, and in many respects, far from what I wanted. My guess is that some of you reading this book right now would say the *exact* same about your own broken, wasted lives. But at the risk of appearing to be unfeeling, does it really matter?

In one of the most famous lines in movie history, Rick (Humphrey Bogart) held tightly to his beloved Ilsa (Ingrid Bergman), knowing he'd probably never see her again, and said: "I'm no good at being noble, but it doesn't take much to see that the problems of three little people don't amount to a hill of beans in this crazy world."[10]

I don't mean to be cavalier about your suffering and pain any more than I might appear to be calloused about my own. But as Rick came to understand, there's a higher question, a more important issue than our personal problems in this crazy world. I don't think it's a stretch to think that a Baptist sitting in a dungeon long ago knew *precisely* what that higher question was.

That higher question is not about how we can be rescued from our personal dungeons, nor how our fortunes can be regained, or how our relationships can be rebuilt or even how our health can be restored. Intriguingly, although his head was literally about to roll, the Baptist's question was not about his circumstances at all. The highest question is always and only about the authenticity of a Person: "Are You the Expected One, or should we look for someone else?" (Matt. 11:2–3).

Although He was a King by whose mighty power the universe was created, and for whom it was created and in whom all things within it hold together (Col. 1:16–17), the Expected One humbly answered John's question with words that belie His awesome power: "The BLIND RECEIVE SIGHT and the lame walk, the lepers are cleansed and the deaf hear, the dead are raised up, and the POOR HAVE THE GOSPEL PREACHED TO THEM " (Matt. 11:5–6).

Whole or broken, wasted or sane, the Expected One is invincible in His power to deliver us. More awesome still, is His boundless love and compassion for *every* injured lamb in His fold. He shares your concern for every personal problem you will ever face here, including each sorrow that doesn't amount to a hill of beans in anyone else's eyes. If it cuts you deeply, it draws the rapt attention of the Expected One. This glorious King takes notice even when a tiny sparrow falls to the ground. Surely, He stores your tears in His bottle, recording them all in His book (Ps. 56:8).

It may be that the Expected One will restore all you've ever lost, and every broken dream you've ever suffered here will one day come true, as He ultimately did for Job (James 5:11). Then again, it may be His will to allow your head to roll. Weeping may last for the night, but a shout of joy will come in the morning (Ps. 30:5). When we see Him face-to-face, He will wipe away every tear from our eyes, and every injured lamb, every broken soul will finally be made whole.

I've written this book with the goal of revealing as much as I can about this King's magnificence. I'm nearly finished, and I haven't scratched the surface. In the ages to come we will learn astonishing things about the surpassing riches of His grace in kindness toward us in Christ Jesus (Eph. 2:7). We will praise Him for all eternity for the enormous price He paid for us as His love drove Him to a brutal Roman cross, when He willingly stretched out His arms, shedding His sacred blood for you, and for me.

Amidst all the things worthy of endless praise, I will be praising Him for something I *never* expected, at least for a time here, could ever elicit praise from my weak and weary soul. I will praise Him for granting me the privilege of "wasting" my fault-filled life for a struggling family and an injured little lamb, even as He "wasted" His precious, perfect life for me, and for you.

Greater love has no man than this, that one lay down his life for his friends.
—John 15:13

The Son of Man did not come to be served, but to serve.
—Matthew 20:28

For you have been called for this purpose, since Christ also suffered for you, leaving an example for you to follow in His steps.
—1 Peter 2:21

The National Honor Society induction ceremony. "Lord, You are truly amazing!"

Chapter 30
WHEN FIG TREES DON'T BLOSSOM

Though the fig tree should not blossom, And there be no fruit on the vines, Though the yield of the olive should fail, And the fields produce no food, Though the flock should be cut off from the fold, And there be no cattle in the stalls, Yet I will exult in the LORD, I will rejoice in the God of my salvation. The LORD God is my strength, And He has made my feet like hinds' feet, And makes me walk on my high places.
HABAKKUK 3:17–19

IN THE PREVIOUS chapter I told you of my desire to conclude this family story in happily ever after style, with every loose end tied neatly into a bow. I *yearn* for this, not just to vindicate my life, but to prove myself worthy of praise by all who read this book. Sorry if my vanity disappoints you. But despite my compulsion to appear "victorious," the truth keeps pulling me like the weight of gravity right back down to earth. There are so many frightening loose ends dangling as I seek to complete this book. Instead of tying them into a bow, I fear they might wrap themselves around me and strangle me. I am at the absolute low point of my life in terms of health, energy, finances, and loneliness, with deep anguish and trouble in *so many* vital areas. So much for storybook endings!

It's been six months since I completed the most recent chapter, "The Expected One," and I sit here with my life fraught with circumstances that are the *furthest* thing from what I *ever* expected. I am frustrated, debilitated, and humiliated, groping to find the energy just to *begin* this chapter. I've already been interrupted several times today to bandage my mentally impaired son and clean up his blood. He bleeds every day now from shaving head to toe, including his eyebrows, fingers and toes, compulsively going at it for *hours*. I won't revisit all of his bizarre obsessions and habits as he nears his twenty-eighth birthday, except to note that they are still myriad. Yet none of these, not even his shedding of blood, are among the most frightening loose ends dangling now.

After *years* of struggling, I am still suffering the aftermath of the same perplexing health problems that led to the frightening collapse I told you about in the last chapter. That collapse in 2006 resulted in a severe concussion, a nose broken in four places, plastic surgery, and great bewilderment regarding why no one mistook me for Richard Gere (though I remain shamelessly willing to reach for this phony compliment). But I digress, and I must hasten to add that there was far more bewilderment regarding what had *caused* that collapse.

So many doctors have performed endless tests and scans in the years since, and a piece of one of my diseased organs was sent to a notable institution far across the country for analysis (who says I don't get to travel?). A few diseases with long names were identified for the malfunctioning organs; and I've now heard so many medical opinions, tried so many treatments without *ever* getting any better, at long last I've become tired of it all. After all these years, the medical jargon still falls short of an obvious reality that defies all the doctors' charts.

I just told you matter-of-factly that my son bleeds every day. This is just *one* of the numerous, bizarre, beyond words daily events now considered normal in my home. In the last chapter I openly questioned my sanity. I can't be sure, but I may now be nuttier than a fruit cake. Perhaps I am simply burnt out. Who knows anymore? But I'll tell you something that is *far* from sane. It is literally insane to consider so many of the intensely stressful events I deal with on a daily, weekly, year in and year out basis to be "matter-of-fact" and "normal."

No doubt, your circumstances differ from mine. But if you are subject to excessive, long-term stress, this will manifest itself in your life, probably in a way you cannot predict. Extreme stress isn't graded on a curve like an exam, with the mean average of the class receiving a satisfactory grade. When oppressive circumstances become routine in your experience, don't expect your mind and body to give you a pass just because this has now become your "norm." Intense stress often seems harmless for a while, even as carbon monoxide seems harmless as you first breathe it in. It will catch up with you, twisting your mind, body, even parts of your soul.

As I wrap up this book, I lack answers for *way* too many of my own vexing problems to offer any solutions for yours. But I will remind you that God's ways are far higher and far different than ours (Isa. 55:8–9). The wisdom of the world will tell you to get out of your dreadfully stressful situation *any* way you can. Escape it, run from it, medicate it—*whatever* it takes! Our culture considers our comfort to be *far* more important than the responsibilities God calls upon us to take up, and to endure. Picking up our cross to follow Christ? That sits well in adult Sunday school, with a good cup of coffee, and we nod in agreement. But in *real* life?

> *Come on now, Jesus! If You don't mind my saying so, the notion of bearing up under hellish circumstances is archaic! My friends at church, even some of those who nod in Sunday school, are advising me to love myself more than that! They appreciate what even You don't seem to understand! Everyone knows we only go around once in life, and we've got to make the most of it. There's no way I'm going to let others bog me down! They should learn to fend for themselves! Listen, Jesus, crosses are hard! They involve blood! Why should I follow the treacherous, narrow path You are pointing me toward when the most popular "Christian" self-help books promise to get me to the high places of this world via a far easier road?*

God's ways will never make sense to the wise in this world. But if we wish to follow Jesus, we must be willing to follow Him along a narrow road that is often fraught with difficult, exhausting, and lonely responsibilities that sometimes seem meaningless and absurd, and which may last for years, perhaps even for a lifetime. Yet, if we want our feet to be transformed into hinds' feet with the dexterity and nimbleness that can dare to tread on the *true* high places of life breathing in the rarified air of exulting in a King who grants us His power in our weakness to engage in loving acts of service on earth that will be remembered for all eternity in heaven, then the narrow path of Jesus is the *only* road that the truly wise person can choose.

> If anyone wishes to come after Me, he must deny himself, and take up his cross and follow Me. For whoever wishes to save his life will lose it, but whoever loses his life for My sake and the gospel's will save it. For what does it profit a man to gain the whole world, and forfeit his soul?
>
> —Mark 8:34–36

> So often we murmur at the narrow round of daily duty. So often we think we are worthy of something bigger. Our little sphere of service seems so inadequate and so unworthy.... Every hour of it is essential if God would make you a man (or woman) He can use. We must suffer if we would reign.[1]
>
> —Alan Redpath

After that collapse in 2006, I continued caring for Bryson's "matter-of-fact" needs from an extremely debilitated condition. His immune system deficiency still often caused him to be sick, and he still suffered *brutal* injuries, always without warning. He was a black hole of need, lacking the *slightest* degree of empathy for his dad's newfound frailty. Caring for an often frustrated, angry, mentally impaired young man would have been the greatest challenge of my life even if I had been younger and healthier. Trying to describe what it was like to care for his unending needs while fearing I might collapse again brings me back to the point of being "beyond words."

Instead of attempting to describe the indescribable, I'll show you a few snapshots from our family photo album from the years following my collapse in 2006, up until the present time (2014). You will see a photo or two depicting how Bryson continued adjusting to adulthood, including how he handled the difficult time of "empty nesting" in our home. I will also show you one more photo of that vexing broken leg he suffered in 2010, with a brief snapshot of his painful journey toward walking once again.

If you look closely at these photos you will notice a King in the background, the very same King who evidenced Himself by inscrutable miracles throughout this family story. As in your own photo album, the King's methods and timing often differ from what we would choose; and without the eyes of faith we can be tempted to believe He has never been present at all. King Jesus is ever present, always aware of *everything* that concerns us (Ps. 138:8; Matt. 10:29). Yet His miracles are often misunderstood to be only natural events in this world, especially when He performs them through the loving hands of His other children.

As you will see, the King can just as easily call upon the animals He created for His glory to participate in those miracles too.

Snapshot: Queen of the House

Bath time had always been one of the highlights of Gingersnap's day, and certainly of Bryson's. I carried her up the stairs those last few months, when she could no longer make it on her own. She still lapped at his shoulders as the shampoo cascaded down, causing him to giggle with delight, until the day she died in the spring of 2007. She was queen of our house, no doubt about that, and unquestionably the love of my mentally impaired son's life.

Bryson lacked the ability to reason things out the way you and I do, especially regarding matters of grief. He was shaken to the core; and since Gingersnap had died, it seemed eminently reasonable to him that he should also die. I needed to watch him closely during those terrible days of trauma. Satan *always* lurks (1 Pet. 5:8), and he can strike with a serpent's precision, ripping the heart right out of a vulnerable soul. Even so, we must not give in to our fears, nor attempt to fight against this enemy on our own. When face-to-face with a serpent, we must be as wise as a serpent, keeping our eyes focused upon the King, with our ears attentive to His voice alone.

> Greater is He who is in you than he who is in the world.
>
> —1 John 4:4

> I will stand on my guard post And station myself on the rampart; And I will keep watch to see what He will speak to me.
>
> —Habakkuk 2:1

> Although the Lord has given you bread of privation and water of oppression, He, your Teacher will no longer hide Himself, but your eyes will behold your Teacher. Your ears will hear a word behind you, "This is the way, walk in it," whenever you turn to the right or to the left.
>
> —Isaiah 30:20–21

Gingersnap died near Bryson's twenty-first birthday in May 2007. My son always knew that if it was his birthday, it was time for his annual party. This was catered with great food every year by AJ's Pizza restaurant in Butler. He also knew that many relatives and friends would turn out for the festivities, singing "happy birthday" as he blew out his candles on the large sheet cake with his name on it. They'd praise him for how far he hit homeruns with his famed "monster" bat. They'd "ooh" and "ah" at his victorious performance in the annual basketball tournament in our basement, dunking over his brother, his cousins, and other hapless opponents (they never stood a *chance*).

Yet, this year, none of these things, not even soda bottles soaring high over telephone wires in the street in front of our house (powered by Diet Coke and Mentos—don't ask me how they came up with this chemical reaction), nor the fizz shooting out of Bryson's nose from ingesting this same concoction (he loved making his friends laugh), nor even games of "knockout" on our trampoline could comfort him for very long without Gingersnap.

In the coming days I searched my files to find the breeder in South Dakota from whom we had purchased Gingersnap thirteen years earlier. Gerry was still in business, and she emailed photos of her latest litter of yellow labs. A few days later Tim and I were on our way to Newark Liberty International Airport to pick up one final birthday present for Bryson: Puppy Dakota. After we arrived home, we asked Bryson to sit down and close his eyes, and then we placed this adorable eight-week-old pup right into his lap. It was love at first sight, and there was little question but that the Milazzo kingdom had found its new queen. Seven years later, as I write these words, Queen Dakota still wakes my now twenty-eight-year-old son each morning by licking his face until he rises.

Gingersnap's framed photos remain on the wall next to Bryson's bed, and he still cries at times when he thinks of her. When he prays to Jesus, he often asks the great King to say "Hello" to Gingersnap for us, as He plays with her, which Bryson knows that Jesus does. Perhaps this makes you smile; and no doubt for some of you, God is far too busy for such matters. Bryson's Friend in heaven is *never* too busy to listen to my childlike son, and I believe He complies with many of my son's simple requests. Lest we forget in our adult arrogance, Jesus is the One who taught us we *must* become as a little child in order to enter the kingdom of heaven (Matt. 18:3).

As I try to grasp something of how the King operates, the best I can do in my adult "maturity" is to envision a mysterious pot stirring in heaven, with every earthly event swirling precisely as He wills. One of the serendipitous blessings He ladled out of that pot was His choice of Dakota to become the new queen in our home. A few years later, she would play an important role in saving the life of this author, as you will see in one of the final snapshots.

Snapshot: Emptying the Nest

The lump in my throat was so large it felt as if it might choke the life out of me. This snapshot is from August 2007, and we had just dropped Tim off for his freshman year at college. Ready or not, this was the end of an era for our struggling family; and oh, how hard it was to let go. I had done the best I could filling the role of mom and dad for him throughout his adolescent years, even as his squeaky wheel brother got most of my grease. Tim was far more ready to jump out of the nest than I was to let go of him. I so *yearned* for more time! Yet, if you think seeing him fly away was hard for *me*, for Bryson this event had doomsday written all over it.

I remembered all the way back to Bryson's reaction when Tim was born, joyfully banging on the glass of the hospital nursery where Tim lay. He was so deeply imprisoned in the darkness of his brain injury then, yet he had somehow understood that a brother is born for adversity (Prov. 17:17). During the ensuing eighteen years, Tim had fulfilled his role better than I could ever have hoped, always being Bryson's defender and best friend. Bryson's instincts were on target once again now. His best friend was leaving him.

Being an emotional Italian, for whom family is closer to godliness than cleanliness, I could have cried for that entire six-hour trip home, but my melancholy mood was brought to a screeching halt. My twenty-one-year-old "tough-guy" rode in the back seat, never thinking he had reached the age when it was appropriate to sit up front. It had been an unusually hot September day, and he had *refused* to get out of the car throughout the *entire* day (the windows were open). Nor would he ingest *any* food or beverages as I accompanied Tim through his orientation program, which lasted for several hours.

I viewed him in the mirror as the car rolled toward home, realizing that lack of food and water was the least of his troubles now. He was completely traumatized; make that terrorized, by what had occurred on this day. But there's no *way* he'd cry, as he had done for Gingersnap. This tough guy was now loaded for bear, and he set his sights squarely on Daddy Bear.

Bullets came flying from that back seat as soon as we pulled from the parking lot, out of the mouth of a tough guy who simply couldn't understand that Daddy was grieving this emptying of our nest as much as he was. A barrage of, "Shut up!" "You're an idiot!" "I hate you!" were among the missiles launched (those clean enough to put in this book) during that *entire* six-hour ride home. This attack sobered me instantly, snapping me right out of my depression. I was reminded that the powers of hell are very real (Eph. 6:12), and that those dark powers had successfully penetrated this tough guy's mind several times in the past. As always, I would be vigilant, watching him closely in the days ahead.

As the car sped along, further and further from Tim, my mind drifted back to another car ride that I will never forget. I peered into the rearview mirror then too, not at an angry man-child in a tough guy's body, but at a tender one-year-old baby boy. We were driving home from a Manhattan hospital where it had just been confirmed how profound and devastating his brain injury was. Glimpse after glimpse his body remained limp, his eyes lifeless and dull. For the first time, it sank in just how excruciatingly painful and difficult his life would permanently be.

Tears filled my eyes on that day long ago, and I found myself *pleading* with God to heal my precious, broken boy. Instead of a reply from heaven, as I grappled for hope, I heard only the rumblings of a cursed rhyme taunting me for the first time: "All the king's horses and all the king's men couldn't put Humpty Dumpty together again." I immediately feared that hellish rhyme, and tried to block it out of my head.

I couldn't conceive of all the events that would unfold in this broken child's life way back then, but I instinctively knew there would be many car rides in the years ahead just as sobering.

SNAPSHOT: A DUMB DAD

During the years when Tim was away at college, Bryson's life was degenerating into fallowness, loneliness, and despondency, and I was feeling more impotent than ever to help him. He had aged out of his extended high school at twenty-one, and from all the recreation and sports programs that had once caused him to thrive. He was almost always alone now, and he was often discouraged, frustrated, and well, sometimes he was just plain ornery.

I knew that underneath all those porcupine quills of horrid behavior was a frightened, lonely child trapped inside a grown man's body. It just *killed* me to see this boy who was once filled with such lofty aspirations and dreams languishing in front of the television, or in front of the video game monitor. I searched out a few programs in our area for special-needs adults, but he *bristled* at the prospect of being involved in *any* social or recreation programs for the disabled. If a group had even the *scent* of being a handicapped group, he ran from it emotionally just as fast as he could, being angry at me for even suggesting that he might find some companionship there.

Ironically, my handicapped son was prejudiced against handicapped people. He just didn't see himself as mentally impaired, which was of course, because he was mentally impaired. Here was a child who couldn't bathe himself or tie his own shoes, yet in his irrepressible, fantasy-filled mind, he was going to date Mila Kunis, not hang out at social events geared toward the handicapped.

We were quite a pair I suppose (I never got a date with Mila Kunis either). In any event, you've heard the saying: "When momma ain't happy, ain't *nobody* happy!" Well, Bryson's fears and loneliness were grating on him *big time* one night, and something pushed his buttons as I was helping him into bed. Oh, momma!

He lit into me, firing insults and abusive missiles that hit the target (me) with the accuracy of an air force drone. Seemingly *every* topic was covered, from the diminutive nature of my intellect, to the foulness of my breath. All that he said was arguably true, but I was so *very* weary on this night, *barely* keeping my composure. This was a tinderbox next to a lit match situation, and I knew if I snapped I could hurt him badly, maybe even kill him.

I reached the point at which I couldn't take *one* more belittling remark. *Enraged*, I started firing missiles back, hollering at him that he had no right to speak to his dad that way, which of course, was true. But it is also true that you simply do not win a confrontation with a mentally impaired individual with anger, especially not this irrepressible, obstinate, never-say-die young man.

Back and forth our verbal rally went, with me gaining the upper hand due to my undamaged intellect, until finally, with his poorly articulated speech pattern he just started screaming, "You a dumb dad! You a dumb dad! You a dumb dad!" No way was I going to let him get away with this now, not after all I had done for him that day, after all I constantly did for him every day. At the top of my lungs I screamed back, "Why would you say such a thing, Bryson? Why am I a dumb dad?

Tell me why? Why am I a dumb dad?" I was yelling so loudly, even Dakota slunk away to hide. Yet, without hesitation, my son glared *right* back into my eyes and screamed just as loudly: "Because you don't see that I'm struggling too!"

I was stunned, jolted into silence. I looked down at him, not seeing an angry man-child sitting on his bed now, but once again, a fragile baby boy in a car seat. After *all* these years, here he was, still struggling so *desperately.*

Ashamed, I said a quick, silent prayer: "Oh, Lord, won't You at long last heal this broken boy?" My prayer was followed only by that old familiar silence from heaven. Exasperated with any notion that God might answer my prayer, or that I'd like His answer even if He did, I focused back to the present. My son was right. I was a "dumb dad" on this night, so dumb that I had failed to remember what he needed me to remember *always.*

He lacked the neurological and emotional equipment to deal with his excruciating disappointment and pain, *especially* the loneliness. My broken boy was struggling *so* badly on this night, even as he had endured endless seasons of struggle and even torture for more than two full decades now. Well, as I'm sure you know, tough guys rarely ever cry; but this dumb dad sure did now, especially as it began to sink in that I needed healing every bit as much as my son. Turning away in hopes that he wouldn't see my tears, I literally started to shake.

I felt like grabbing him and hugging him, as Robin Williams hugged Matt Damon at the end of the feature film, *Good Will Hunting,* when he just keep repeating: "It's not your fault!…It's not your fault!"[2] But this angry tough guy wouldn't let me near him now, nor would he break down and cry the way that even this dumb dad knew he needed to cry. It took a late night bowl of chocolate chip mint ice cream served over pound cake (Bryson's favorite), with faithful Dakota at his side, before he would let me tuck him into bed once again.

But before I tucked him in, we went through a ritual that has been repeated between us every day (several times per day) for many years now. Bryson said, "I love you, Dad; give me a hug." My response, as always, is to teasingly say some variation of what I responded with that night: "There's no need for a hug. I hugged you last week…or maybe it was a few months ago…*definitely* on your last birthday. The point is I *already* hugged you."

Bryson patiently waited, rolling his eyes on this night as always (belying the fact that he *loves* the repetition of Dad's bad jokes), and then I gave him a big hug. Now, finally, he was ready for bed. The three of us, including Dakota, prayed for a good night's sleep. I turned out the lights, leaving my son to dream his dreams.

Back in my room I cried again, and prayed:

> *O Lord! I don't think I can take this anymore. After all these years, the situation is still so painful, and it's beginning to seem more hopeless and impossible than ever! You are in control of all things. I need You to show up now, and grant my son some of his dreams!*

Snapshot: Nyack College and the BCS

> You were tired out by the length of your road, Yet you did not say, "It is hopeless." You found renewed strength, Therefore you did not faint.
>
> —Isaiah 57:10

The serpent knows when we are at our wits' end. Desperately wanting to rob God of glory, he urges us to utter the words, *"It is hopeless,"* and he entices us to turn to him for some idolatrous relief. The half-truth is always Satan's most effective lie. Our circumstances may indeed be "hopeless," but God will *always* provide a way for us to proceed in the face of impossibility if we will trust in Him, and *then* do what we can, in *that* order.[3]

I needed to get my weary carcass "out there," before it *did* become a carcass (not too much of a stretch at this point). I called an old friend, Tom Lane, who met me one morning at Starbucks with two other old friends, Andy Aran and George McGovern, and a new friend, Brian Hanse. These men had formed an awesome ministry called BCS (Bergen County Society) which had as a core value helping Christian men to connect with each other. BCS is the local chapter of a national organization NCS (New Canaan Society) started by Jim Lane, Tom's brother.

Keeping one eye on the clock, knowing that Bryson would arise to take on his day at mid-morning, I poured out my heart to these men, letting them know about my son's frustration, and his despondency. As they began to understand the situation, they discerned that like every man or woman, Bryson needed a reason to get up in the morning. He needed to feel valuable. He needed a job.

I explained Bryson's challenges, including the fact that he is a *very* social being. His emotional disposition, combined with his attention-deficit disorder and visual impairments could not allow him to tolerate isolated piecework, such as on an assembly line. I also mentioned his lack of motor skills and susceptibility to injury. This risk prevented him from being a candidate for stocking store shelves. Beyond this, his limited intellect would not allow him to work a cash register. We had to come up with something unique, ideally having to do with sports.

Ever thoughtful, Tom mentioned he would call Mike Scales, president of Nyack College, which has NCAA Division II sports. Nyack was only thirty minutes away from our Oakland home. Maybe Bryson could become involved with the athletic department in some capacity.

Within a week Tom, Bryson, and I were in the office of the Nyack head basketball coach, Ted Quinn. Ted and his wife, Jackie (a recording star with a wonderful ministry to women), had just moved their family from the Midwest (Ted's previous coaching assignment). He and Bryson hit it off famously, and Bryson became his assistant "coach." In reality, Coach Quinn became like a second father to my son (Bryson's own description of the coach).

Bryson worked two days per week, helping the coach in his office and encouraging the players at practice. He also attended all the home games. Bryson *loved* rubbing shoulders with college level athletes, and those young men (and their trainer Penny Foland) made him feel like an important member of the staff. He often became so excited during those games, it was a miracle that he never got a technical foul as he screamed at the refs from Nyack's bench. I suppose we're fortunate no one ever got arrested.

As noted many times throughout this book, it is often the little things offered through the kindnesses and sacrifices of others that are truly ordained. Those "little" things enable us to persevere in our seemingly hopeless battles, especially when we are tempted to cash in our chips. Tom Lane and the guys were thorough, thinking through some important ancillary issues, such as how Bryson could travel to and from Nyack. Realizing not only that I needed rest due to debilitating health issues, but that I couldn't afford to finance his travel to and from Nyack at this point, the BCS guys established a fund to hire someone to drive Bryson to and from his job.

Bryson had met Jon Muzikowski many years before this, when they were both children. They met during our vacations up at Camp of the Woods, before Bryson was walking independently, when his speech was still very difficult to understand. These limitations never deterred Jon from hanging out with my son, even as others shied away. We had lost touch with Jon for a few years; but if you can believe it, Jon was now a Nyack basketball player! You just can't predict some of the things stirring in heaven's pot. Jon and Bryson renewed their friendship, and had a great time going to and from practices and games with each other.

After four years at Nyack, Coach Quinn moved on to another college, having fulfilled his role in Bryson's life in an *immeasurably* valuable way. I was becoming sicker than I knew during those years, but there was nothing more comforting to my weary soul than to know that this great man was going out of his way to shape my son's character in Christ. I am more grateful to Coach Quinn than I can say here for his godly influence on his life.

As for Nyack College, this awesome institution continued to open its arms to my son, with Dr. Scales remaining generous and kind to both of us. Under the guidance of Keith Davie (the A.D.), Nyack's excellent new coach Jason Crafton picked right up where Coach Quinn left off, as that mysterious pot continued to stir.

Snapshot: Who Said the *Left* Leg?

As soon as I heard the commotion in our basement in January 2010, I knew something was terribly wrong. Bryson's leg had snapped like a pretzel simply by turning in the wrong direction, as he played basketball with Tim and some friends. Tim was home from Liberty University for winter break, and together we carried his brother into the ER, hoping against hope the break wasn't as bad as it appeared. Nonetheless, it was confirmed to be very bad, and the ER doctor couldn't help us. We brought him home, comforting him on pain-killers until I could take him to the best orthopedic surgeon in the world the next morning; our old friend, Dr. Sicherman.

For years, my inside joke with Dr. Sicherman had been that I should have him on retainer, since he patched Bryson up so often. I nearly panicked the next morning when his staff told me he was overbooked. I refused to get off the phone, insisting they let him know Bryson needed him. Dr. Sicherman is a highly regarded professional, but I know him as a man with a heart of gold. I *knew* he'd remember my son, who, honestly, is kind of hard to forget.

I was completely stressed out about an hour later as we sped past numerous patients in Sicherman's overfull waiting room. I blurted some information about the injury to the receptionist as I wheeled him by, and kept right on going into the treatment room. Dr. Sicherman was nearing retirement age, and he could come off a bit gruff at times, especially if the office was busy. He was *woefully* behind schedule on this day, and he had already performed surgery at the hospital early that morning. I'm sure he was tired, and it was clear he was harried.

Well, I'll *never* forget this no-nonsense surgeon looking at the X-ray up on the lighted board, then down at my son lying on the table, and then at his electronic pad. He appeared to be irate. His tone was measured, but his words were forceful and direct. Glaring at his assistant he *demanded* to know, "*Who* said it was his *left* leg!!" All I could think now was, "*Doh!*" I had told the receptionist the *wrong* leg! The assistant in the room began taking a pretty big hit for my mistake now, and I realized I needed to make a quick decision.

As I observed this young woman's plight, it became clear what needed to be done, and there could be no delay. I considered what decency called for, not to mention integrity. My decision was *easy*. I cleared my throat, looked this surgeon straight in the eye and then *zipped* my lips (I mean *tight*)! Listen, I've already told you that I often *felt* as if I had lost my mind, but did you *really* think I was crazy?

Before I left that office a few hours later with Bryson's leg mended and in a cast, Dr. Sicherman had chastised no less than *four* members of his staff as I looked on with an empathetic look on my face as if to convey to the doctor that he ought not to be too hard on them. To this day I laugh myself breathless when I think about that scene, and of course, about my cowardice. And to this day I remain grateful to Dr. Sicherman, who has helped my son out of trouble many more times than I've told you about in this book.

A wonderful therapist named Bladdymir Coronel came to our home later that year to help my son begin his courageous quest toward walking again. A few months after his work with Bladdymir, we went to the office of our old friend, Lynda Eisen, who had taught Bryson to walk again after his knee injury a few years earlier.

It took nearly a full year for my son to walk independently as that leg healed. I have no time to show you snapshots of all the anguish and pain involved in his comeback from this awful injury. But I will tell you that this broken leg was a non-weight bearing injury, and I carried my 155 pound son around the house for much of that year since his cerebral palsy didn't enable him to use crutches.

My back held out *just* long enough, and later that year I spent several months in a back brace. I was reaching new lows in terms of weariness and debilitation. New medical testing ensued in December of 2010, including that notorious piece of me that was sent far away. Yet none of the doctors realized, and I certainly had no clue, how much damage all the years of stress and exhaustion had already done.

Snapshot: Barking up the Right Tree

I was beyond irritated one cold January 2011 night as Dakota began barking loudly in the wee hours of the morning (about 2:00 a.m.). It wasn't normal for her to bark, particularly at night, as she slept solidly on the couch like a queen. I would've crawled out of bed to go downstairs and check things out if I wasn't so *very* weary. I tried to ignore her, thinking she'd heard an animal outside, and that she'd soon stop. But her incessant barking continued, very *loud* barking that seemed intended to wake the dead. I kept drifting back to sleep, and then being awakened, over and over again, by her *ceaseless* barking. Finally, after this went on *forever*, I became so infuriated that I decided: "That's it! I'm going to go downstairs and I'm going to *kill* that dog!"

I slowly began pushing myself up off the bed. Something didn't seem right. I was lying on my back and the bed seemed hard. In fact, the bed was wet. Still in dreamland, I slowly reached my hand toward my head, and then drifted back to sleep. "But oh, that *darn* dog! She just won't quit!" Slowly I opened my eyes, and a blurry Dakota actually began coming into view. Strangely, she seemed to be standing directly *over* me, still barking. Trying hard to wake up from a dream that was turning a bit weird now, the fog began to clear a bit more; and, slowly, eerily, I began to realize I wasn't in bed at all. I was downstairs, lying on the kitchen floor.

I was utterly confused now, and *oh*, my head hurt *so* badly. The light was on and I tried to focus my eyes on the clock, but I seemed to be looking through a tunnel. I finally saw that it was just after 3:00 a.m. In a bit of a panic now, though still dazed, I *vaguely* remembered coming down to the kitchen for a glass of water at about 2:00 a.m. I reached my hand to my head again, this time consciously, and then very, very slowly pushed myself up to a seated position. Finally, I looked around and saw a large pool of blood all over the floor, and I noticed that the oven door had been obliterated. I began to realize that the back of my head had smashed clear through the thick safety glass of that oven door, and I had been lying on the floor, leaning up against that oven.

To this day, I have no recollection of passing out, nor of crashing through that glass. But as the fog cleared a bit more that night, I realized I had been out cold for about an hour, and the dog had been standing over me all that time trying to awaken me, as blood trickled out of my head and neck into the puddle on the floor.

Blood was *everywhere*, and zillions of tiny bits of glass were interspersed throughout the kitchen. To my horror I finally realized that shards of glass were also sticking out of the back of my head and neck. I somehow got to my phone and called my daughter. Miguel answered, and they arrived at my home in about ten minutes, along with the Oakland police and an ambulance. Janelle came in the ambulance, as Miguel stayed to care for Bryson the next morning. Thank God the crash didn't awaken him, or the barking, or he'd have been scared to death!

CT scans at the hospital confirmed I had suffered another bad concussion, and surgery was performed to remove all the glass from my head and neck. Miraculously, my skull was not broken, nor were the main arteries severed in my neck, or obviously, you wouldn't be reading this book right now.

Just as obvious for those with eyes to see, Bryson's queen was called into service that night, in accord with heaven's purpose and will. The King preserved my life, and compelled me to finish this story.

> I will not die, but live, And tell of the works of the LORD.
>
> —PSALM 118:17

RICHES, RAGS AND HIGH PLACES

Between my collapses in 2006 and 2011, a confluence of factors hammered away at my finances with the ferocity of Ray Lewis zeroing in on a receiver daring to catch a ball thrown over the middle. I had done my best to maintain my one-man commercial real estate company while caring for Bryson and writing this book, as I was becoming more and more feeble. The financial books kept registering red ink, even as our family overhead remained enormous.

After the collapse in 2011 my finances spiraled downward like an airplane without an engine, and all bets were off in terms of my being able to purchase a home, ever again. As a real estate man who had owned my first home as a twenty-five-year-old, it is more discouraging than I can say to now lack the means to afford my own home.

As I conclude this book, I now fit somewhere between the categories of the unemployed and the underemployed and certainly within the category of financially distressed. I have been brought to my knees financially; and honestly, I *never* expected to be dealing with such frightening loose ends at this stage of life.

If you are tempted to think I'm alone in this dilemma as an aging parent of an adult handicapped child, think again. An untold number of worn and weary parents are doing our best to care for our vulnerable children as they reach adulthood, even as we struggle with our personal health and finances. Our burden is profound, and I don't lightly say that many of us are afraid even to die for fear of what will become of our broken children.

As mentioned in earlier chapters, I'm convinced that a significant percentage of the brain injuries occurring in recent decades, which seems to be escalating today, is attributable to the childhood vaccination products and procedures currently in force. I also mentioned that I expect to be attacked for sharing this opinion. To the extent that this book plays a role in enlightening the uninitiated to the risks I believe are involved, I will be pleased to take those blows. But irrespective of how you view this epidemic, there should be no mistaking the reality that the burgeoning ranks of autistic and brain-injured children reaching adulthood is on the rise, and a *colossal* bill is coming due for society to pay. For my struggling family, the bill has already come due.

It was a difficult trauma for Bryson when we needed to move to a very modest rented home in Fair Lawn in 2012. This home, from which I am writing these final chapters, has no central air conditioning, which was on my priority list due to the health concerns. Yet it was one of the few homes in this "landlord's" market that would allow us to keep Bryson's queen, which was of course nonnegotiable for us. As the Lord provided the last time we moved, I had a lot of help setting up Bryson's room with his collections of hats, sneakers, necklaces, bracelets, silly bands, posters, and the rest of his treasures. We also set up a cool rec room in the basement. The location is good in terms of getting Bryson where he needs to be, and I have been pleasantly surprised at how well window air conditioners work. The Lord is teaching me to be content, and thankful (Phil. 4:11).

My son Tim generously helped out with the rental expenses as he commuted to Manhattan from this home, until he moved out to marry a sensational young woman, Emily, in September 2013. Since he moved out, I have no longer been able to afford even this modest rented home, and I am desperately attempting to prevent Bryson and me from becoming vagabonds of sorts, moving every few years, knowing this would destroy my vulnerable boy. Throughout this book I've told you that we must proceed by faith, not by sight or by what we *feel* (2 Cor. 5:7). Talk is cheap, and this author must work hard daily to lay aside my feelings now.

I feel like an ocean liner headed toward the rocks, as my remaining assets pour into the sea through a huge hole in the hull. Even if it were more seaworthy, this sluggish vessel still couldn't maneuver quickly enough to avoid the cliffs of financial ruin. A speedboat could skirt this disaster, but the notion of my "vessel" being a speedboat is laughable now. I am so physically and mentally weary that avoiding another collapse, one that I fear may leave Bryson fatherless, must take precedence even over attempting to steer clear of those perilous cliffs.

I am doing things I never *dreamed* when I first began writing this book. I am attempting to complete it on a computer that has no sound, which often freezes and shuts off. I am driving a ten-year-old car that is leaking oil. My last hospital procedure cost me several thousand out of pocket. None of these procedures seem ever to lead toward healing, so I have stopped doing most of them. I've also laid aside all lesser medical issues, such as fixing an injured shoulder and a tooth in the upper *front* of my mouth that has turned black. I wonder, did Richard Gere ever have a black tooth, maybe in *An Officer and a Gentleman*? Oh, never mind!

At an age when most men are thinking retirement, I need to somehow find a way to start over. But my health problems, combined with Bryson's daily care and protection, have kept me bottled up at home, from where the Lord has asked me to finish writing this book. Being "imprisoned" to write this book makes no sense to me at all, especially as I watch my hard earned assets brutally drain away.

As I plead for the Lord to revive my health, or at the very least to give me the strength I need to finish this book, I am often tempted to scream out, "I'm doing what You've asked, Lord! Why aren't You stepping in to help me? You seem even to be intent on hindering my every attempt to follow and obey You!" Even so, as I view my circumstances in the light of God's unchanging Word I am reminded that there is nothing new under the sun.

> He has broken my strength in midcourse; he has shortened my days.
>
> —Psalm 102:23, esv

> He has besieged me and encompassed me with bitterness and hardship. In dark places He has made me dwell, Like those who have long been dead. He has walled me in so that I cannot go out. He has made my chain heavy.... He has blocked my ways with hewn stone; He has made my paths crooked.
>
> —Lamentations 3:5–7, 9

God has indeed broken my strength, and the path laid out for me is as crooked as a jigsaw blade. But I suspect that I am writing this book from *precisely* where God wants me to be.

Most of you have been glad for my transparency throughout this book, and it is a particular comfort to you that I have remained honest about my agonizing experience as I complete it. Not that you're happy to see another human being suffer in a pitiful "misery loves company" way. Rather, your heart yearns for honesty as you attempt to keep standing amidst the frightening loose ends dangling in your own life. You're relieved that this hasn't turned out to be yet *another* "Christian" self-help book from an author with the temerity to toss out a few high sounding platitudes, techniques that promise joy, success, and satisfaction.

If you've learned *anything* from those books, you've come to understand that the behavioral and attitudinal modifications they prescribe, replete with their *endless* humanistic methods, could *never* have caused you to stand against the waves of brutal reality that kept sweeping into your life, threatening to drag you back out to sea. Your experience is far too daily, far too real for empty platitudes. In short, your life is too much like mine. Again, your circumstances differ from mine. But your experiences of suffering are the same in terms of being opportunities for the Lord to accomplish His work in and through you (1 Pet. 5:9), as you trust in Christ alone.

I do not apologize for quoting Paul's introduction from his second letter to the Corinthians so many times in this book. I hope it is indelibly burned into your minds, because you're going to need it in this world.

> For we do not want you to be unaware, brethren, of our affliction which came to us in Asia, that we were burdened excessively, beyond our strength, so that *we despaired even of life*; indeed, we had the sentence of death within ourselves *so that we might not trust in ourselves, but in God.*
>
> —2 Corinthians 1:8–9, emphasis added

I've followed Paul's example in this book, using the afflictions that have caused me to despair of life to urge you readers to trust in God, not in yourselves, nor in the myriad of humanistic, self-help methods Satan has conjured up throughout all human history to exclude God from our minds, and from our hearts.

Yet, even as many of you are relieved by Paul's transparency, and mine too, others of you don't have the *slightest* idea why all these references to "desperation" are necessary. You're satisfied with a faith in which you do good things for God, and He rewards you in kind. He's saved you from your sins, and He'll bring you home after you die. Until then, *you've* got it covered! You're in control of your life, and, of *course*, in control of your faith. You have no real need for Christ, nor any true desire to know Him intimately as Paul did (Phil. 3:7–10), especially if that might disrupt the good life you've got going now.

You're determined to achieve your own "high places" in this world, places that involve wealth and comfort, health and prosperity. Fields that produce no food and flocks being cut off from folds aren't even on your radar screen. You're a positive thinker, and you're not going to allow your optimism to get shot down by *anyone's* sob story, not even this family story. You have neither the time nor the inclination to romanticize about fig trees that don't blossom and all the rest of that jazz. Those prophetic writings are poetic, sure they are; but in your world they are just a mantra for losers! Sentimental drivel! Bring on the next self-help book!

Don't hear me sneering at you if you share this widespread deception. Know that you are walking in *my* shoes! Way back in the beginning of this family story, my life was good too. From a temporal perspective, it was *far* better than it is now. My rocket ship was heading due north, oh yes, and there's no *way* I was looking back. I was a young man in my twenties, blessed with many *fabulous* blessings. I had a beautiful wife and daughter, a lovely home, a great job, good health, and, of course, my firstborn son was just about to enter the world. He was born beautiful, and healthy as can be. A gorgeous child with a button nose! Picture-perfect!

For most babies, traces of perfection linger a while. My precious son had only the briefest dance with it, and then suddenly, he was gone. After he was taken the music in our home stopped, and there was only pin-drop silence for a very long time. Tears, wailings, and pleadings with God sometimes broke the stillness on our side, as heaven remained silent. We scoured the earth, travelling on every yellow brick road, pounding on the door of every emerald palace, yet that picture-perfect baby boy was never to be found again.

A day finally arrived when the music began to play once more, and we accepted the new child heaven sent us to take that perfect baby's place. The child *looked* identical, every bit as perfect as the child who had been taken. But the music was different now; and only as each chapter of our family story unfolded did I truly begin to understand how dissonant and cacophonous the music really was, and how flawed and awkward his dance with life, and ours as a family, would be.

In these chapters you've seen the world's most brilliant professionals rendered completely impotent to restore that once perfect child. Many concluded he was permanently crippled, his mind dormant forever, that he'd never be educable, nor even speak. You've seen hope revived through a "foolish" organization known as NACD, and you've seen that hope take shape through the efforts of a ragtag army of untrained soldiers equipped only with willingness and with love, as that sleeping child was awakened.

You've seen a family fight to fit a square peg child into the round holes of this world, often appearing exceedingly foolish against the forces of self-important arrogance. At every turn they were opposed by those seemingly intent on blocking this child from taking his shot at life, including some supercilious enough even to try to block him from an appropriate education. Time after time you've seen imposing mountains conquered through the courage and tenacity of a broken child, along with the perseverance and faith of those privileged to fight alongside him.

Only by heaven's graces could this child have overcome such enormous odds, fulfilling dreams such as speaking, walking, even learning to run. You've seen him reach some of his cherished fantasies too, including those that came to pass on fields of dreams, and some that took place only on the playgrounds of his childlike mind. Fantasy or real, this irrepressible child worked *excruciatingly* hard for every precious ounce of *joie de vivre*, and for every treasured memory that will *never* be forgotten. Certainly this author, his daddy, will never forget.

You've also seen that irrepressible child stumble and fall, time and again; and you've seen his cherished dreams ebb away as the seasons of his life rolled on. You've winced at the torture of his excruciating injuries, you've cringed as bullies beat him, and you've wept over the senseless brutality of those who dared even to abuse his vulnerable soul. Believe me when I tell you I've spared you the worst of it. Certain things must remain written only upon a father's heart.

You've seen a longsuffering family dragged through the mud by the cruelty and indifference of others, dirtied and bludgeoned, and you've also seen that family stricken down through failures and sins all our own. You've observed a marriage that was ripped apart by divorce, and a seemingly invincible child staggered to the brink of suicide as a serpent bared its vicious fangs. At long last you've seen this author attempt to do for my family what I was ill equipped to do alone, and you've seen a very weary father suffer a game-changing fall.

After reading the chapters of this book and seeing these most recent snapshots from my family album, now you know the *rest* of the story, as revered American storyteller Paul Harvey used to say. Now you know that this author's life is a train wreck by the standards of this world, even as God's love continues to seem absent. But I've written this book to tell you God's love seems absent in everyone's story, for those who lack eyes to see.

My earthly eyes tell me God owes me more, and owes more to my precious, broken son. But if God's love *ever* seemed absent, it was as His firstborn Son was tortured and broken by cruel men, and as His body was nailed to a tree. His brutal murder was the most tragic injustice in history; a victory for evil and a permanent defeat for all that is holy and righteous and good. Or so it seemed…

Yet the rest of this Son's story was not yet written, was it, dear reader? A pot was stirring in heaven precisely in accord with the Father's will; and astonishingly, Jesus rose from the grave. Because His story continues on, my story continues on, even as your story continues on if you are numbered among those who have entrusted your life to Him. How will God choose to deliver me this time? How will He deliver you? God only knows.

But I've heard it said it is more important how a man or a woman finishes their race of faith than how they begin. The race can take unexpected turns, bringing us into dark valleys where fig trees do not blossom, and where there is no fruit on any of the vines. When we find ourselves in so dark a valley, we must refuse the world's self-focused methods of striving to reach the high places on our own without God. To charge up that hill by charting a path of our own is folly. There is only one road to those coveted high places, a narrow road on which we must trustingly, sometimes tearfully, follow a King.

This King can transform even the weakest, most crippled lamb in His fold into a majestic being, giving her (or him) hinds' feet with the strength and dexterity to reach those high places after all. And the King will teach us a secret as we walk with Him way up there. He will cause us to exult, no matter what life may ever bring to us, or cruelly take away, as we realize that the high places we've been seeking have been with us all along, in *Him*.

> The joy of the Lord is your strength.
>
> —Nehemiah 8:10

> The secret of the Lord is for those who fear Him.
>
> —Psalm 25:14

> He makes my feet like hinds' feet, And sets me upon my high places.
>
> —Psalm 18:33

> I have learned to be content in whatever circumstances I am.... I have learned the secret of being filled and going hungry, both of having abundance and suffering need. I can do all things through [Christ].
>
> —Philippians 4:11–13

> Therefore I am well content with weaknesses, with insults, with distresses, with persecutions, with difficulties, for Christ's sake; for when I am weak, then I am strong.
>
> —2 Corinthians 12:10

Chapter 31

FINISHING WELL

I have fought the good fight, I have finished the course, I have kept the faith.
2 TIMOTHY 4:7

Did we imagine that the battle would become easier as the years unfolded? Did we believe that youth was the time of greatest temptation? Did we really think that it was during young manhood and young womanhood that we would have to fight hardest, that as we got older life would become less of a struggle? The fact is, we discover that the battle becomes sterner with the passage of the years.... How few there are who run well to the end![1]
ALAN REDPATH

EVERY GRIDIRON WARRIOR, including this old author who wore a leather helmet during youth football (don't laugh, I'll be taking names), knows there's a "so near, yet so far" dynamic to the very *last* yard of turf before the end zone. With many tasks the Lord assigns to us, including the challenge of remaining useful during our feebler years of older age, and during that final test of trusting Jesus to carry us home when we close our eyes for the last time here, we will face our fiercest, most bloodthirsty opposition *right* at the goal line.

But just imagine if a team simply turned and jogged off the field without even *trying* to get into the end zone, concluding that they had already done their part by driving the ball so beautifully, all the way down the field. How silent that stadium would become. What a disappointment all their efforts would be remembered to be!

God does not sanctify us toward holiness throughout a lifetime so that we can become shiny trophies in our church display cases, bowing before one another and swapping war stories of victories past. We are called to forget what lies behind and press on with Christ for usefulness in His service until the end (Phil. 3:13–14). But again, it would be naïve not to anticipate some of our very hardest battles *right* at the goal line. The question is, will we remain on offense for Christ, persevering in His grace and power until the end, or will we retreat to the bench?

Having had several concussions from collapses now (only a few of which have been described in this book) the diagnosis of post-concussion syndrome, like that of some former football players, was now under consideration. Even now, as I strive to write this final chapter, there are so *many* debilitated days with no rhyme or reason and no pattern I can track, with no productivity whatsoever. Yet one thing I knew in July 2013 is that I was worn down from straining toward the goal of completing this book. Thankfully, it was time for our annual trip up to the little cabin we rent each year in the Adirondack Mountains owned by the wonderful McComb family.

From this modest cabin we go to Camp of the Woods as guest members each day. Camp of the Woods is the quintessential "same time next year" meeting place, and it has always been one of the loves of Bryson's life. The 1980s sitcom *Cheers* got it right. We all need a place where everyone knows our name. Bryson is known and loved at Camp, receiving high fives and "Hey, mans" from friends and staff all day long. Games of dodgeball thrill his soul, as do softball games and campfires at night where he holds court, making his friends laugh with his jokes and stories.

Tim couldn't come this year, needing to save vacation time for his honeymoon in September. This was like not having my right arm with me, but a few of Bryson's friends who come with us now are an *enormous* help. Bryson doesn't know it, but those friends are actually paid companions through a program administered through the New Jersey Division of Developmental Disabilities (DDD). Our sensational case manager, Kristine Elmore, and her supervisors, Christine Broderick and Kathryn Sheldon, along with case manager Rob Miller, have developed a well-conceived "self-directed" program for Bryson as part of an effort by the state to assist aging parents in keeping their adult handicapped children in the family home. I am grateful for this program, and I stagger the hours allotted for Bryson's companions as far as our DDD budget allows each week.

Kristine Elmore is an extremely sharp and smart, wonderfully caring African American young woman who has guided me through the maze of government applications and approvals. She is an intriguing person who has, on occasion, shown up at my home on her motorcycle just to make sure we are okay. She laughs with Bryson, arguing with him about whether Kobe Bryant is better than Dwayne Wade, LeBron James, or Steph Curry, and whether her Giants are better than Bryson's beloved Cowboys. Like my own daughter, she is one of the truly good people involved in social service. No one chooses this field to become rich. They work overloaded caseloads for families with chronically ill or handicapped individuals, straining to make a difference in this world.

Beyond the laughter, I doubt I'd have survived these last few years without Kristine's help. In fact, I may not have survived the very first night of our vacation without the companions she helped to put in place, as you will see. But first, I must tell you about a few other blessings flowing from that DDD program.

Much is written about single moms, and rightly so, for they are often weary, lonely, and beleaguered beyond their ability to describe, not to mention being financially poor. Yet there are many single dads cropping up today who are similarly beleaguered, with far less being written about us, and less support offered. Becoming a single dad more than a decade ago was an absolute game changer. The domestic responsibilities thrust me far under the waterline, along with the challenges of being the sole caregiver of a mentally and physically impaired son.

Grocery shopping took forever, meal preparation was something you might see on a bad sitcom, and my laundry proficiency left us looking significantly less than tailored. No one died from my cooking, though I hold the world record for setting off smoke alarms. And while no one perished, I did carry Tim into the ER one night after one of my famous, out of the can meals (food poisoning). After many years of cruel and intolerable punishment for these kids, and just as my own health was sinking like a rock, a godly woman named Nadene became our home helper, under the auspices of that same DDD program.

Nadene was a veteran at pressing on, having been widowed not once, but *twice*, courageously raising four children on her own. She served us several afternoons per week, taking over our shopping, housecleaning, and most of the cooking. She could have made far more elsewhere than the modest salary she earned through Bryson's DDD program; but as you know, heaven's pot almost always swirls through the sacrifices of others in this world.

Indeed, graces kept flowing from that wondrous pot. The Wyckoff YMCA and its executive director Joy Vottero opened their arms wide to special-needs children and adults under a program known as Personal Partners. This program was conceived by fitness director Mike Morley and dear Amy Jones, a fitness trainer with a heart of pure gold. Patty Karsian and Mary Wright of the membership office have helped this weary dad to keep the funding paperwork on track between the YMCA and the DDD, and through the years they've caused the "Y" to become one of those cherished "Cheers" places not only for Bryson, but for me too.

Steve Verdi, a young man with 90 percent hearing loss is simply the best fitness trainer on the planet. He methodically pushes Bryson to achieve new goals physically, and they have a great time talking about sports, and (ahem) about *girls* during those sessions. Yikes! I'd better bite my tongue! This is a Christian book and I can't let this family story become "unspiritual" *now*! Not when I'm at the goal line! Yet, when you think about it, God is the One who created us with sex drives and other appetites that don't sound all that "spiritual." He made it clear after creating us from dust that it's not good for man to be alone. Obviously, God understands our sex drive (He invented it), and the loneliness of special-needs people has not, somehow, escaped His grasp.

It hasn't escaped mine either, but ready or not (and let me be clear: I'm *not* ready) this subject of my son's sexual awareness makes me want to bury my head—make that my *whole* body—in the sand…*deep*! You may be smiling right now, but I'm not kidding! This issue of wanting a girlfriend and a wife is *always* on Bryson's mind. Perhaps this is a topic for another book one day (I hope not, since writing this one nearly killed me!).

But with so *many* areas of need cropping up in Bryson's life as an adult, I needed to be a regular pleader (a pest really) at a place where I knew I could count on God to dispense what I needed. If you find yourself at one of the "goal lines" of life, facing fierce opposition, you will need to become a pest too.

> Therefore let us draw near with confidence to the throne of grace, so that we may receive mercy and find grace to help in time of need.
>
> —Hebrews 4:16

Making Sense out of Things with a Sensei?

One of the loose ends vexing me for many years was that my son lacked the fine and gross motor skill to become independent in his bathing and toileting. He remained content to have me help him with these tasks, yet these had become more and more difficult through the years due to his size and age, and honestly, due to my age. Even so, since he had suffered so *many* brutal injuries in recent years I was exceedingly cautious each time he went *near* the bathroom. Discouraged, I came to believe that bathroom independence was *never* going to occur.

Year after year, this limitation remained an *absurd* dead-end, one that I couldn't plan or fight my way out of no matter *what* I tried. And believe me, I tried *everything.* I pleaded with God and I brainstormed and pestered therapists, case workers, other parents of handicapped children, and even doctors about what to do. After *years* of anguished effort and prayer, just as we were starting to make a tiny bit of progress, my son went back to square zero in his toileting efforts after he suffered that brutal broken leg I told you about, at twenty-four years old.

After his leg healed late in 2010, it was as if a light went on, and he decided he was going to master this task. If you've learned *anything* about my son during this long family story, you understand that wild horses wouldn't dare to stand in his way once he determines to accomplish something. He *finally* became independent in his toileting at twenty-five years old. Even so, don't get me wrong about this feat; he still needs my help now and then to this day, with occasional mishaps that still require hours of my time. Like a broken shoelace, these accidents always occur at the worst possible time, usually on one of my "down" days physically and mentally. Nonetheless, this achievement was a major milestone in my son's life, and a *huge* daily relief in mine.

The issue of independent bathing was an even thornier problem, not only in view of my son's need for safety, but because he was fully content to have me bathe him, even looking forward to bath time as a comforting event in his daily routine. I finally concluded that the only real shot my son would ever have at independent bathing would be for me to custom build a fully equipped, handicapped bathroom for him. The one I wanted had an upright tub and shower combo that opened like a car door to enable my son to get in and out safely, with a built-in seat to sit in as he showered and to safely dry off on. This bathroom setup would ensure his safety.

I was *very* discouraged when I realized that the cost of installing this bathroom was prohibitive, especially since we are now renters who may need to move again shortly after the completion of this book. This *really* pricked my pride, especially since I had been a multimillionaire, and now I couldn't even provide for my son's needs in terms of something as simple as a *bathroom.* As at so many other junctures throughout this story, this dead-end seemed absolutely impossible. But as

I've told you several times in this book, my old radio friend Dr. Robert A. Cook (now in heaven) often said: "Faith trusts in God, and then does what it can in the face of impossibility."[2] We must proceed in this order, first trusting in God, and *then* doing what we can.

The first act of faith at each dead end requires a decision, a resolution, an absolute *refusal* to give up and give in to despondency, self-pity, and victimhood. God has no victims in His family. He has only dearly loved children. When things are hard and confusing as we come up against dead-ends that seem so random they tempt us to doubt His presence, we *must* choose faith. We don't choose a flimsy, wishful, pixie-dust faith, pretending that things will work out somehow simply because we yearn for this to be so. We accept reality as it is, being willing to surrender to our absurd, despised, dead-end circumstances, knowing that the presence of King Jesus will prove sufficient for us even if He should ask us to endure our "thorn" for the rest of our lives (2 Cor. 8:9; 12:9–10).

However, before we presume that God will never remove our thorn (dead-end), we must not forget the flip side of the coin that is our faith: the perseverance and courage to continue doing what *we* can. But as has been illustrated many times in this book, God's ways are higher and different than ours, and the steps He may require us to take will often seem as foolish as marching around the walls of Jericho, like Joshua, or breaking pitchers to create a discordant sound against well-equipped armies, as Gideon's ragtag troops did in obedience.

The Lord's plan may require steps of obedience that seem *anything* but heroic. They may even appear odd, if not completely insane. Most often, those steps will seem so small and insignificant that they hardly seem to be worth taking. But the longest journey always begins with a single step, followed by another. More important than the apparent efficacy of each step is the posture of total dependence upon God, as we remember that our victory is:

> Not by might nor by power, but by My Spirit, says the LORD of hosts.
>
> —ZECHARIAH 4:6

Since I couldn't afford the bathroom with all the built-in safety features, I installed simple, moveable, plastic handicapped grips that I had seen on an infomercial. I installed them all around our tub and shower area when we moved to our latest rented home in Fair Lawn during the summer of 2012. I had no illusions that my son could use these without a great deal of help, and I installed them with much fear and trembling in view of his propensity to fall. I also bought a shower seat to place in the tub, which our good friend Nate Dorka (Bryson's companion) assembled for us. But once again, when my son determines that he wants to accomplish something, the only "impossible" thing is holding him back. Besides, a heavenly pot had been stirring away, *right* under my nose.

The year before, Bryson had begun mixed martial arts (MMA) training once per week from Sensei Greg Hunko. The sensei is a large, powerful man. "Deadly" would be a more accurate description. Let's just say you wouldn't want to ask for his wallet, even if you had a gun. You get the idea. Yet it wasn't the sensei's size or his years of training, or even his physical power that was his most awesome feature. His heart was.

The sensei insisted that Bryson receive his MMA lessons *without* shoes and socks, forcing him to strain hard just to remain upright during those sessions. He made him jump up and down on pads, do little "fancy dances" (as sensei called them) and many other methods to cause my son to gain higher levels of balance. Sensei called upon Bryson to do so many "impossible" tasks during those sessions, in a very similar way that Bob Doman of the NACD and Bryson's army of volunteers had called upon him to do during his younger years.

I couldn't possibly tell you about all the awesome things Sensei Hunko helped my son to accomplish, both in the gym and in life. There isn't even a question that this MMA training became one of the most significant factors in enabling my son to gain the confidence and balance he needed to begin showering on his *own* (with those plastic grips I installed) for the very *first* time in his life this past year, at twenty-seven years of age.

In fact, Bryson became very angry when he saw the "handicapped seat" Nate had assembled, and he refused to use it. He insisted on climbing into the tub area without any help at all, using those grips to shower while *standing*! As far as the fancy drying area in that built-in bathroom that I couldn't afford, Bryson began using those grips to climb out of the tub area after his shower to steady himself enough to sit down on a towel that I place on the toilet for him (cover down), as he grabs another towel that is placed within reach for him to dry off with.

I was amazed and overjoyed that my son could do these things, and I am in no way exaggerating when I tell you that to the extent this author is still alive when you come to read this book, there will have been no greater relief in my life than the elimination of the stress and strain of bathing (and toileting) my son each day. But I must tell you one more thing about Sensei Hunko.

He knew I couldn't afford Bryson's MMA training, not even in a group setting, and certainly not the more expensive private lessons he needed. Since there was no way to fit the cost of these lessons into our DDD budget, the Sensei *insisted* on providing these to my son *completely free* for *two full years* as I write these words. Not a wealthy man himself, but to provide me with some dignity, the sensei keeps insisting that he receives more benefit from his work with my son than Bryson gets from him. This leaves me speechless, and I can only tell you that this kind, powerful, compassionate man is a reminder to me that mankind was indeed created in God's image.

Not falling for *That* Again, Are You?

The physical collapses I've chronicled in each of the last two chapters seemed to be ancient history now. It had been two full years since I needed to be taken from my home in an ambulance, and I battled hard to complete this book during those years.

As mentioned, I was feeling a bit worn down, and clearly, a vacation was just what the doctor ordered. It was perfect timing for our annual trip to the Adirondacks and Camp of the Woods. Even so, in my mind this was going to be a working vacation. I planned on knocking out a brief epilogue from that little rented cabin before seeking a publisher. Well, a knockout occurred, just not what I had in mind.

It was our *first* night in that cabin, July 13, 2013; and I was deep in dreamland. The *last* thing I needed was to have Bryson's companions, Jon and Frank, banging on my door at 2:00 a.m. "Mr. M, Mr. M! Can you unlock the door?" What were they *thinking*, disturbing me like this? You'd better believe I was irritated. But they just kept on knocking, asking me in more urgent tones to open the door. What in the *world* was up with these guys? I had taken them on this trip to help me to care for Bryson, not to rob me of desperately needed sleep. But they just kept knocking and knocking, literally banging on the door now.

I was *really* ticked off at this point, and thought I'd better get up. Maybe something had happened to Bryson! As I went to get out of bed, I couldn't move. Slowly, I began to grasp the reality that I wasn't in bed. I was face down on the bathroom floor. Then I began to hear loud, involuntary groans coming from deep within me, moaning that I couldn't stop, as those guys kept calling out my name. My neck hurt terribly. I slowly began to remember getting up to use the bathroom, but nothing more. A chilling thought entered my mind that my neck might be broken. It took five more minutes for me to be able to move at all, and believe me, I was grateful for that movement.

Still zoned out, I finally crawled over to unlock the door. Then those young men helped me to my feet, and over to a reclining chair. They filled bags of ice for me to put on my nose, which was bleeding profusely and obviously broken again. In retrospect I realized I should have had my head stabilized in case my neck had been broken. In the days ahead, thank God, this proved not to be the case. Yet I had suffered another serious concussion.

AD HOC

> We say that there ought to be no sorrow, but there is sorrow, and we have to receive ourselves in its fires. If we try and evade sorrow, refuse to lay our account with it, we are foolish. Sorrow is one of the biggest facts in life; it is no use saying sorrow ought not to be. Sin and sorrow and suffering are, and it is not for us to say that God has made a mistake in allowing them.[3]
>
> —OSWALD CHAMBERS

Everything in me *screamed* that this ought not to be happening *now*, just when I was beginning to see a *tiny* bit of daylight in my life! I was so frustrated I could spit!

I had intended to write a brief epilogue from that cabin, thinking that this was my final drive toward the "end zone" in terms of finishing this book. I had no intention *whatsoever* of writing the chapter you are now reading entitled

"Finishing Well." I now understand that the Lord wanted me to experience this most recent collapse and tell you about it, in addition to tying up some of the other loose ends that I've addressed in this ad hoc chapter.

Medical testing ensued after returning home. Some new issues are being considered, but a clear diagnosis is still lacking in terms of the cause of these frightening collapses as I conclude this book. Irrespective of whether anything definitive or new is diagnosed, or it merely becomes clear that all the years of stress, sleeplessness, and weariness have broken me down yet again, believe me when I tell you that I will now take a crack at that epilogue with fear and trembling, praying: "*Please, Lord,* don't give me *anything* more to write about!"

I often think I've seen enough trouble in this world. All the trials and the pain, the unending distresses, the anguish and turmoil involved in caring for a brain-injured child, the loneliness and financial struggles, the battle weariness, the medical challenges, and so *many* other sorrows, well, sometimes these literally make me *yearn* for heaven. Not that I wish for death. It's just that I wonder how much toil and trouble a man or woman can take in this world before we finally become so physically and emotionally spent that we simply *cannot* go on living.

> The years of our life are seventy, or even by reason of strength eighty; yet their span is but toil and trouble; they are soon gone, and we fly away.
>
> —Psalm 90:10, esv

I've written this book having no doubt that many of you reading it right now have yearned for heaven too. Some of you are so weary and discouraged it seems imminently reasonable just to retreat to the bench until the Lord comes to carry you home. Yet something stirs in your heart, does it not, at this notion of finishing well?

One day, it will be clear to every conqueror who has kept the faith that the wounds and scars we've received during our battles here have resulted in more glory accruing to the Father, and more useful and compassionate service flowing through our wounded hearts toward others, than could ever have come from even our loftiest imaginings of an undefeated life on our terms. The times when we are most severely wounded and tempted to give up are the times we *must* press on. Alan Redpath recalled a dramatic instance of such a refusal to surrender:

> I remember in childhood days, during the first World War....I was walking with my father along the pier at Tynemouth, near Newcastle, England. We noticed a crowd of people around and many ships in the harbor. Presently a cloud of smoke appeared in the distance, grew larger, and soon a convoy of battleships came into the river Tyne, and in the center of them there was one battleship heeling over—I wondered how it remained afloat. It was H.M.S. *Lyon,* coming back from the battle of Jutland, a naval battle which turned the attack of Germany on our country at that time. As the ship got nearer the harbor, I saw great holes in her deck. She had no mast, no funnel, no turrets;

> the bridge had gone; the deck was just a shambles. Water was pouring in and out of her as she was being gently nursed home by tugs and an escort of ships. Shall I ever forget the sight of twenty-five sailors and one officer standing rigidly at attention on a pan of the deck, with a tattered bit of the royal ensign flying from the piece of wreckage? Every throat that could cheer, cheered, and every ship that had a siren blew it. These twenty-six were all that were left, a tragic remnant of 1,100 men. But the ship had held on, she had fought through to the end, and she came into harbor victorious, holed and wounded, with hundreds of men killed—but still afloat and undaunted!
>
> In the Christian life we suffer many wounds from Satan, and sometimes from friends. If one day, however, when we get into the heavenly harbor, we get a welcome like that ship received, and hear the Lord say, "Well done, thou good and faithful servant, enter the joy of the Lord," we will care for nothing else, for it will have been worth it all when we see Jesus.[4]

Oh, how I *yearn* to replicate such valor! But in view of my Humpty Dumpty brokenness and the utter depletion of my personal resources, with incoming bombs *still* exploding and smoke rising up from fragments of shattered dreams all around, the concept of finishing well not only seems impossible now, but even laughable as I conclude this book. I need something more than a depiction of courage from the past, more even than glimpses of our glorious future in heaven. Oh wretched, earthen vessel that I am. Where can I *possibly* find the hope and help to fight the good fight here and *now,* in order to finish my course, and keep the faith until the end?

Ah, dear reader, there is indeed a King who has come to put us back together again. I hope you have seen and come to know Him within these pages, since it is for King Jesus that this book has been written. I will now write that epilogue. As you read it, I implore you to understand that there is only *one* name under heaven that has been given by whose grace we must be saved, and by whose mighty power we can indeed live.

> Let it be known to all of you…that by the name of Jesus Christ the Nazarene, whom you crucified, whom God raised from the dead—by this name this man [and this author] stands here before you.…There is salvation in no one else; for there is no other name under heaven that has been given among men by which we must be saved.
>
> —ACTS 4:10, 12

Epilogue

IN JESUS' NAME

When the valley is deep
When the Mountain is steep
When the body is weary
When we stumble and fall
When the choices are hard
When we're battered and scarred
When we've spent our resources
When we've given our all
In Jesus' Name we press on.[1]

DAN BURGESS

I press on toward the goal for the prize of the upward call of God in Christ Jesus.

PHILIPPIANS 3:14

IN THE INTRODUCTION I asked: "What do we do when we've fought our hearts out, given every last ounce of what was in us to give, and we've simply got no fight left? What do we do when all that remains is an overwhelming sense of hopelessness, defeat, and despair?" To the extent that the answer to those questions hasn't been clear within the pages of this book, I will take one last crack at them here. Yet strain as we might, worldly ears will never hear the answer to those questions. Jesus admonished: "He who has an ear, let him hear" (Rev. 3:22).

There's hardly a chapter in this long family story in which I didn't find myself in desperate circumstances of one sort or another. At long last, though I couldn't have planned it this way (nor would I ever have wanted to), I must conclude this book facing one of the most difficult seasons of my life, battling financial insolvency even as I battle for my life and health, devoid of the resources I need to adequately care for my physically and mentally impaired son. That is this author's version of hopelessness and impossibility. What is yours?

I trust it has become clear to you that true, lasting hope does not reside in my personal story. But before you rush off to find it in some other book or story, understand that true hope cannot be found in *any* human story. In the end, we're all just dying individuals on a dying planet. Perhaps that is too morbid to assert in the epilogue of a family story. Yet, if we're honestly grappling with hope, we had better look to something higher than ourselves, something that can never be taken from us through theft or deceit, something even death cannot touch.

My son came into the world a healthy, vibrant baby. In these pages you've seen tragedy radically alter his path, and you've observed his remarkable, sometimes miraculous, progression through the stages of his life. Although he now inhabits an adult body, he will remain a child all his days in this world. Yet in his life I've discovered that even a child, *especially* a child, can have ears that hear (Matt. 18:3).

Bryson knows God created us from dust and breathed life into us. He knows that even though we've been granted such a great gift (not a bad upgrade from dust), we've all turned from God, choosing sin instead of obedience and rebellion instead of faithfulness, and that we are all worthy of death for doing so. Yet he also knows God loved us so much He sent His only begotten Son, Jesus, *right* as we were in the midst of our rebellion, to suffer and die on a cross, taking our sin upon His sinless life, and paying the punishment and death we deserved for our sin.

He knows that Jesus rose from the grave and lives today as an invincible King who walks with all who repent and choose to follow Him, enabling us by His grace and power to press on through every peril we will ever face in this world. He knows a day is coming when Jesus will bring all who have believed in Him home, to a place where there will be no more sin, no more sorrow, no more pain. Yes, my childlike son knows all these things.

And lest I forget, my son knows the correct answer to the questions posed way back in the introduction: "What do we do when we've fought our hearts out, given every last ounce of what was in us to give, and we've simply got no fight left? What do we do when all that remains is an overwhelming sense of hopelessness, defeat, and despair?" His answer simply is: In Jesus' name, we press on.

The above song, "Press On," written by Dan Burgess and sung by Selah, is one of Bryson's favorites, and it's not hard to understand why. All his life he's been forced to press on through *horrendous* anguish and pain. What is harder to understand is *why* he needed to suffer such torment in this world. Indeed, why do we all experience such difficulty and sorrow here? Any honest consideration of these questions points us back to the sin and rebellion we've *all* chosen, sin that wrecked the perfection of God's creation and permanently marred the human race.

Even so, I don't pretend to understand the selectivity of suffering in the world. Who gets cancer, or succumbs to Alzheimer's? Who gets crushed in a car wreck? What winds sweep down to choose a victim, while sparing others *right* next door? What makes Job, or my son, or you, dear reader, the subject of God's showdowns with Satan?

For that matter, what makes Job's declaration, "Though He slay me, yet will I trust Him" (Job 13:15, NKJV), more appropriate or noble than his wife's counsel simply to "curse God and die!" (2:9)? The Bible tells us God loves us, yet who could blame us for becoming cynical, or even bitter? Let's be honest. It's often hard to see God's love here. What we *do* see quite readily is sorrow, pain, and death all around us. I once saw a bumper sticker which read, "Life sucks, and then you die!" How would you answer the occupant of that car?

Religion is full of talk about God's love. Frankly, if God doesn't ever do more than talk, why should we care? Jesus lifts our eyes to a *far* deeper understanding of the love of God than religion will ever grasp. Jesus' love is *fraught* with action. He not only saw our anguish and pain, but He came. He willingly died to grant us forgiveness, eternal life, and genuine hope as we press on in our journey here and now.

Yet let me not wax poetic about the love of Jesus without making this notion of pressing on with Him a bit more practical and real, as I trust I've done throughout this book. In reality, we must press on with Him as if through a war zone, because that's precisely what this world is, and it will continue to be a battleground until Jesus returns.

Every soldier must anticipate becoming battle weary, beleaguered, even wounded from time to time. During times of battle fatigue or woundedness, Satan will not miss his opportunity to taunt us with every step we try to take, pointing out the utter impossibility of victory, tempting us to lay down in defeat. We must understand the serpent's mastery of the half-truth. Our circumstances may indeed be impossible. Give him that part. Being "more than conquerors" in Christ (Rom. 8:37, NKJV) involves a far higher definition of victory than Satan wants us to perceive.

The only victory that overcomes in this battleground world is our faith in Jesus Christ: "This is the victory that has overcome the world—our faith" (1 John 5:4). Let us allow Him to define the terms of our victory, and show us how to press on in the direction He will lead us toward. It is a preposterous understatement to say that Jesus can deal with our impossibilities. Even death couldn't stop Him. *Nothing* can!

Every soldier must also understand there can never be a lost battle, nor a sinful failure, nor even a long wilderness season (even those we know we have caused or contributed to through our own sin), that can ever stop us from pressing on to victory once again, if we keep turning to Christ in repentance to follow Him in obedience, receiving *His* victory by *faith*. The war has already been won by Christ. By faith in His finished work of grace we join Him in His victory, without condemnation, no matter how badly or often we may have failed. Checkmate is *always* to Christ, and *also to us* as we refuse to surrender, but continue to press on in His name.

I'm convinced that the Lord has orchestrated my circumstances so that I now have no choice but to depend upon Christ *alone* as I conclude this book, pressing on in Jesus' name, just as you must do. Indeed, talk is cheap, and so is the written word in many Christian books where there is no life of character to back up what is written. *Please* don't hear me pointing you to my personal character, without Christ. The older I get, the more convinced I become of just how vile, ugly, and in some respects downright dangerous and murderous my potential to sin *still* is. I must continue to work out my salvation with fear and trembling (Phil. 2:12), lest Christ's name be put to shame.

> When a man is getting better he understands more and more clearly the evil that is still left in him. When a man is getting worse he understands his own badness less and less.[2]
>
> —C. S. LEWIS

Yet, while the Lord has given me a clearer grasp of the depravity of my flesh as I've written these pages, He has also reinforced something in my heart that every person needs to take away from this book, in terms of purpose.

STATE YOUR PURPOSE

> I offer neither pay, nor quarters, nor provisions; I offer hunger, thirst, forced marches, battles and death. Let him who loves his country in his heart, and not merely with his lips, follow me.[3]
>
> —GIUSEPPE GARIBALDI

General Giuseppe Garibaldi was credited for unifying Italy during the nineteenth century.[4] He used a rather peculiar invitation, quoted above, in enlisting soldiers for his cause. If I heard only the first sentence of his offer, I'd be tempted to respond: "Hmm! Let me check my calendar. It seems I am busy for the next decade or two. Perhaps we can talk after that?" But when love for country is at the core of the appeal, as Garibaldi wisely added, this sheds a whole different light on the matter.

As I conclude this book from one of the lowest, most broken points of my life, I intend to press on in Jesus' name, to follow Him wherever He may lead me, and obey Him no matter the cost. Again, if you think I state this purpose because I've attained a level of spirituality or holiness that exceeds yours, then perhaps I can interest you in purchasing a very nice bridge that connects Manhattan with Brooklyn.

When Jesus asks for our allegiance, He does so not on the basis of *our* performance, but *His*. He loved us so much that He did not shrink back from torture and death for our sake, nor did He refuse the weight of our sin and shame as it was placed upon His sinless life on a brutal Roman cross. Oh, that we would all see ourselves for who we really are. Oh, that we would be willing to do whatever He may ask of us because He loved us so. And make no mistake in this day of the Christian community's tepid response to His love, the Lord asks *much*.

> If anyone wishes to come after Me, he must deny himself, and take up his cross and follow Me. For whoever wishes to save his life will lose it, but whoever loses his life for My sake and the gospel's will save it. For what does it profit a man to gain the whole world, and forfeit his soul?
>
> —MARK 8:34–36

In this day of wanting our ears to be tickled and of shamelessly watering Christianity down to a temporal, personal success formula, Jesus' command to deny ourselves and take up our cross to follow Him is an utter inconvenience, if not a total embarrassment. Yet, as I conclude this book, I challenge every reader to place something, *anything* you believe to be worthy of inserting, into Paul's declaration of purpose, in the place of Christ:

> For to me, to live is Christ and to die is gain.
>
> —Philippians 1:21

Some would choose "wealth and comfort" as their highest purpose in this world. Others might insert "health" as their ultimate goal. Some may choose "ease" or "fun" or "sex" or "travel" or "power." *Whatever* you believe to be worthy as your overriding purpose, may I ask you a question? What will your chosen purpose be worth to you fifty years from now? How about one hundred years from now?

Please don't close this book without realizing you are a vapor that appears for a little while and then vanishes (James 4:14). A day is *soon* coming when every knee will bow, and every tongue confess that Jesus Christ is Lord (Phil. 2:10–11). What in the world are you waiting for? If you are a follower of Christ, then to deny Him your total surrender is to deny your very identity. We are Christ's ambassadors (2 Cor. 5:20), and He has chosen us to be His letter to others who desperately need Him in this dark world.

You Are a Letter

> You are our letter, written in our hearts, known and read by all men; being manifested that you are a letter of Christ, cared for by us, written not with ink but with the Spirit of the living God, not on tablets of stone but on tablets of human hearts.
>
> —2 Corinthians 3:2–3

Do you really think the King has left us on this planet to enjoy the benefits of His grace without sharing the wealth and light of His presence with others? We are here to be read by others, including many who have no hope of understanding God's written Word, or knowing Jesus as the Living Word, unless they can "read" Truth and Love (Jesus) accurately in our lives, our actions, and our words. I say this not as a burden to be taken upon our shoulders, for this would be too great a load for any man or woman to bear. Our task has everything to do with pointing others to Jesus, even as we desperately cling to Him as broken, needy, earthen vessels ourselves (2 Cor. 4:5–6).

My childlike son will never be able to open His Bible to find scriptures on his own. In light of this, I have become his letter, his Bible, in the same sense that you are a "Bible" for your own young child or grandchild; and by many others, most of whom you will never even realize are "reading" you each day. And you should have no doubt that others are riveted on your pages as you follow in His steps, *especially* as you are called upon to suffer.

> For to you it has been granted for Christ's sake, not only to believe in Him, but also to suffer for His sake.
>
> —Philippians 1:29

> For you have been called for this purpose, since Christ also suffered for you, leaving you an example for you to follow in His steps.
>
> —1 PETER 2:21

As his Bible, I awaken my son each day at mid-morning and read him a brief section of Scripture, which is all his childlike mind can tolerate. I never know what his waking mood will be; and on the worst days I am literally overwhelmed by his obstinacy and mentally-impaired anger, particularly when I am physically debilitated, as is often the case now. But he remains in his bed listening as I talk about Jesus, with Dakota lying quietly alongside.

Like his dad, and like you, my son needs reminders about who Jesus truly is, and who we are in Him. He needs reminders that Jesus will never leave us or forsake us (Heb. 13:5), and that God has separated our sin from us as far as the east is from the west (Ps. 103:12). He needs reinforcement in the truth that although we often fail in our flesh, no condemnation awaits us because of the blood Jesus shed for us on the cross (Rom. 7:24–25; 8:1). He needs reminders that God is a dread warrior (Jer. 20:11, ESV), and since He is for us, *nothing* can stand against us or defeat us (Rom. 8:31). Bottom line: just like you and me, he needs to know that we can always press on in Jesus' name no matter how frightening, discouraging, or impossible our circumstances may ever appear.

It is no less than astonishing how those simple biblical truths put out the fires raging in my son's soul, day after day, even as they douse the flaming arrows that threaten to set my own soul ablaze. On most of those mornings my son's fears subside and his angry disposition turns brighter. Instead of complaints and insults, I will soon hear, "I love you, Dad." My response to my son, who loves endless repetition, is almost always the same: "No you don't, Bryson. I'm the one who loves you. Get it straight, man!" Then he says, "Give me a hug, Dad," to which I say "Nah, not today. I gave you a hug yesterday, or on your birthday, or maybe it was Christmas. I forget exactly *when* it was, but I *know* I gave you a hug." My son rolls his eyes, as always, patiently waiting with queen Dakota looking on. I give him his hug, and on we go.

And on you go, dear reader, as you close this book for the last time. I pray this story has caused you to be evermore determined to press on in Jesus invincible name, abiding in His power, resolved to fulfill your purpose in this world for His glory. Though I am unlikely to meet most of you, I will be praying that this will be true in your life. I ask for your prayers too, as you think of my family from time to time. I'd be especially grateful for prayers lifted up for Bryson.

I mentioned a few chapters ago that many parents of handicapped children are afraid even to die, not knowing how their vulnerable children will manage after we are gone. As a single parent, I feel the immense weight of this burden, and I can relate to the sentiments of Paul, who knew he had but limited time to protect and serve the children the Lord had placed under his care.

> But if I am to live on in the flesh, this will mean fruitful labor for me; and I do not know which to choose. But I am hard-pressed from both directions, having the desire to depart and be with Christ, for that is very much better; yet to remain on in the flesh is more necessary for your sake. Convinced of this, I know that I will remain…for your progress and joy in the faith.
>
> —Philippians 1:22–25

At God's appointed time, my battles will come to an end here, as will yours. Soon enough we will know Paul was right. It will be very much better for us when we see Jesus face-to-face. I eagerly anticipate praising Him for who He is, and for all He has done. I can hardly wait to praise Him for what He will do for my son as he is freed from the constraints of his lifelong bondage to brain injury, and by the exertion of His power, given a body like His.

> For our citizenship is in heaven, from which also we eagerly wait for a Savior, the Lord Jesus Christ; who will transform the body of our humble state into conformity with the body of His glory, by the exertion of the power that He has even to subject all things to Himself.
>
> —Philippians 3:20–21

I will conclude this book on a very personal note. Having been close to death more than once, I realize how temporary life truly is here, and what a gift God has granted me to remain in this world as a "letter" for my severely struggling son. Having been given this gift, I am resolved to battle fiercely against the infirmities that nearly brought my life to an end here, and I am determined to make my son as independent as possible before the day the Lord calls me home. Yet, in another sense, I need to make him even more dependent, not on his Dad, but upon Jesus Christ. As the Baptist declared: "He must increase, but I must decrease" (John 3:30).

Letters can sometimes continue on and have their intended impact, even after we leave this world. In this regard, I will close this book with a letter to be read to my severely struggling son, after I am gone.

> Dear Bryson,
>
> This letter is at the end of a long book your dad has written that describes much of what has happened in your life and in our family since you've been born. I've asked Tim and Janelle to read it to you when I can't be with you in the world anymore. I know that my dying and going to heaven has made you sad, Bryson, but we will only be separated a little while.
>
> Though you are sad, I know you are happy that your dad is now with Jesus, waiting for you in heaven along with Pop Pop, Grammy, and so many others whom you have loved in this world, who are here with Jesus too. It is so clear here that Jesus is the almighty King for whom and by whom the whole world, and the entire universe, was made. Oh, Bryson, Jesus is more awesome than I could describe to you, and He loves you so very much.

Truly, heaven is a place no eye on earth has ever seen, and no one's ears have accurately heard about it, nor has any human mind been able to understand what it's like here. Bryson, it's completely *awesome*!

One thing I *can* tell you is that by the exertion of Christ's power, you are going to have a body just like Jesus' body. Oh, Bryson, this body is more incredible than I can describe, more powerful and faster than the bodies of the athletes you look up to now. It is *way* more powerful than Ray Lewis, LeBron James, Duane Wade, Kobe Bryant, and all the rest of your heroes. You will be able to run, and jump, and even fly. I just can't wait until Jesus blesses you with this gift, because I know all the pain and struggles that your body has put you through on earth.

One more thing; Jesus loves animals! Dakota and Gingersnap will be here too when you get here! They were created for His glory, and in their own way, they glorify Him here, even as they did on earth. Lions even lay down with lambs here! Like I said, it is completely awesome!

Your dad knows, and certainly Jesus knows, that you've suffered much hardship in your life, my son. Your life has been harder than most people in this world will ever have to endure. This letter is not the first time your dad has told you this. I began telling you these things as you were able to hear them, when you became a man. I've told you that you became very ill when you were a young child, and you nearly died. But you surprised everyone by battling back. Against all odds throughout your entire life you've battled victoriously in so many areas, accomplishing amazing things. I was proud of you when you learned to speak, which some people believed you'd never do. I was proud of you when you walked, and when you ran. There were many who doubted you'd do these things too. It was no less than amazing that you became such an inspirational athlete, playing baseball, hockey, basketball, and even football. I've always been proud of you for all these things. Everyone who knows what you've been through and what you've accomplished, those who know who you really are, are proud of you too. But your dad is proud of you for something far more important. You've come to understand what many people never come to understand. You know what is truly important among all the shallow, temporary things people cling to in this world.

I told people in my book that being your dad was one of the greatest privileges Jesus ever granted me in the world. One thing I didn't tell them is that your favorite Bible verse is, "I can do all things through Christ who strengthens me" (Phil. 4:13, NKJV). I hope everyone who reads my book will come to know what you know that in Jesus' strength we can do everything God calls upon us to do always, even the things that are hard.

One of those hard things is to press on without your dad now, my son. This will be very hard for you, but I know you can do anything you set your mind to do. You always have, Bryson. Certainly, you can do anything that

Jesus' calls you to do. Remember, Jesus is not only here. He also lives inside of you.

My boy, there is not a doubt in my mind that you will make me proud as I look down on you from heaven. No, not a doubt in my mind. And remember, Jesus has surrounded you with many people in the world who love you and who will help you, including Tim and Emily, Janelle and Miguel.

Keep praying to Jesus. He loves to hear from you. Whenever you need something, He knows about it already; and it is just like Him to give good gifts to all who belong to Him, both while we are in the world, and forever.

Bryson, because you have believed in Jesus and trusted that He shed His blood for the forgiveness of your sins, you will one day be here with me forever, and with all who have trusted in Him. I ask you to honor Jesus in all you do with your body and with your life until then. Jesus is worth honoring with our lives in the world, my son, because of all He has done to save us, because of all He will do for us in heaven, and most of all, because of who He really is. He is a magnificent God and King, and He loves you far more than you can fully understand.

Bryson, don't ever forget how proud I am of you, how proud I have always been. As you remember this, keep pressing on to follow Jesus. Trust Him to cause you to become more and more like Him as He lives from within you. Though you will sometimes fail and sin as you seek to follow Him, He never fails, and He will certainly complete His work in you.

Remember how much Jesus loves you. Remember how much I love you. It's going to be a great day when we get together again, my son. Yes, my boy, it's going to be a great day.

Thank you for the privilege of being your dad.

Love always,

Dad

A highway will be there, a roadway, And it will be called the Highway of Holiness.... The ransomed of the LORD will return And come with joyful shouting to Zion, With everlasting joy upon their heads. They will find gladness and joy, And sorrow and sighing will flee away.

—ISAIAH 35:8, 10

Therefore we do not lose heart, but though our outer man is decaying, yet our inner man is being renewed day by day. For momentary, light affliction is producing for us an eternal weight of glory far beyond all comparison, while we look not at the things which are seen, but at the things which are not seen; for the things which are seen are temporal, but the things which are not seen are eternal.

—2 CORINTHIANS 4:16–18

DONATION INFORMATION

Tax deductible contributions for the support and care of Bryson Milazzo can be made at: www.AllTheKingsHorsesMinistry.com.

NOTES

Introduction—Sitting on the Wall

1. Henry David Thoreau, *Civil Disobedience and Other Essays* (New York: Dover Publications, 1993).

2. Dan B. Allender and Tremper Longman, *The Cry of the Soul* (Colorado Springs: NavPress, 1994), 142.

3. Horatius Bonar, *When God's Children Suffer* (Grand Rapids MI: Kregel Publications, 1992), 7.

4. Larry Crabb, *Shattered Dreams: God's Unexpected Pathway to Joy* (Colorado Springs: WaterBrook Press, 2001), 23.

5. Bonar, *When God's Children Suffer*, 1992 edition, 11.

Chapter 1—An American Dream

1. Larry Crabb, *The Pressure's Off* (Colorado Springs: WaterBrook Press, 2002), 183.

2. Donald W. McCullough, *Waking from the American Dream* (Downers Grove, IL: InterVarsity Press, 1988), 87.

Chapter 2—Waking from the American Dream

1. Stephen Brown, *When Your Rope Breaks* (Nashville, TN: Thomas Nelson, 1968), 26.

Chapter 3 —The Nightmare

1. Brown, *When Your Rope Breaks*, 27.

Chapter 4—More Than We Can Handle?

1. Bill Gillham, *Lifetime Guarantee: Making Your Christian Life Work and What to Do When It Doesn't* (Eugene, OR: Harvest House, 1993), 188.

2. Greg Laurie, *Hope For Hurting Hearts* (Dana Point, CA: Kerygma Publishing, 2008), 24, 26.

3. Stephen Brown, *When Being Good Isn't Good Enough* (Nashville, TN: Thomas Nelson, 1990), 216; *Key Life Network* Magazine, January–March 1996, 11:11.

4. Nancy Leigh DeMoss, *Revive Our Hearts* radio program, April 22, 2009, excerpted from transcript of *Lessons from the Life of Joshua*, part 8.

5. Charles Haddon Spurgeon, quoted by Nancy Leigh DeMoss, ibid.

6. Hannah Whitall Smith and David Hazard, *Safe Within Your Love* (Minneapolis: Bethany House, 1992), 92.

7. Watchman Nee, *Release of the Spirit* (Indianapolis: Sure Foundation, 1965), 9–10.

8. Stephen Brown, *Jumping Hurdles* (Grand Rapids, MI: Baker Book House, 1997), 55.

CHAPTER 5—WHEN WAVES TURN MINUTES TO HOURS

1. Gordon Lightfoot, "The Wreck of the Edmund Fitzgerald," *Summertime Dream*, released November 20, 1976, Reprise, 45 rpm.
2. Ibid.
3. Bonar, *When God's Children Suffer*, 1992 edition, 106.

CHAPTER 6—A VOICE IN THE DARK

1. John of the Cross, ed. David Hazard, "Inner Sight," *You Set My Spirit Free: A 40-Day Journey in the Company of John of the Cross*, Rekindling the Inner Fire (Minneapolis: Bethany House, 1994), 82.
2. Gary Thomas, *Sacred Marriage* (Grand Rapids, MI: Zondervan, 2000), 115.
3. Ibid., 51.
4. Oswald Chambers, *My Utmost for His Highest* (Grand Rapids, MI: Discovery House, 1992), April 29 entry.

CHAPTER 7—THE YELLOW BRICK ROAD

1. John Eldredge, *The Journey of Desire: Searching for the Life We've Only Dreamed Of* (Nashville, TN: Thomas Nelson, 2000), 2.
2. Bernie S. Siegel, *Love, Medicine, & Miracles* (New York: Harper & Row, 1986), 29.
3. Reinhold Niebuhr, "Serenity Prayer," 1943.
4. Brown, *When Your Rope Breaks*.
5. Ibid., 67–70.
6. Margaret Clarkson, *Grace Grows Best in Winter* (Grand Rapids, MI: Zondervan, 1972), 19–20.
7. G. K. Chesterton, *Heretics* (London: Bodley Head, 1905), 14.
8. Laurie, *Hope for Hurting Hearts*, 92–93.

CHAPTER 8—TOUCHED BY AN ANGEL

1. Philip Yancey, *Disappointment with God* (Grand Rapids, MI: Zondervan, 1968), 235.
2. Robert Boylan, personal conversation with author, 1988.

CHAPTER 9—THE SOUND OF A MIRACLE

1. M. R. DeHaan, *Broken Things* (Grand Rapids, MI: Discovery House, 1988), 13–14.
2. Patsy Clairmont, *Normal Is Just a Setting on Your Dryer* (Colorado Springs: Focus on the Family Publishing, 1998).
3. C. S. Lewis, *A Grief Observed* (New York: Bantam Books, 1976).
4. C. H. Spurgeon, *Lectures to My Students* (London: Marshall, Morgan & Scott, 1969), 161–162.
5. Vince Lombardi, "Vince Lombardi Quotes," *BrainyQuote*, http://www.brainyquote.com/quotes/quotes/v/vincelomba380768.html (accessed November 25, 2014).

6. Theresa of Avila and David Hazard, "The Life of Theresa of Jesus," *Majestic Is Your Name: A 40 Day Journey in the Company of Theresa of Avila*, Rekindling the Inner Fire (Minneapolis: Bethany House, 1993), 86–87.

7. Watchman Nee, *Release of the Spirit*, 35.

Chapter 10—Foolish Things

1. Ben Patterson, *Waiting: Finding Hope When God Seems Silent* (Downers Grove, IL: InterVarsity Press, 1989), 158–159.

2. Will Campbell, *Brother to a Dragonfly* (New York: Continuum International Publishing Group, 1977), in Yancey, *Disappointment with God*.

3. Charles Trumbull, *Victory in Christ* (Fort Washington, PA: Christian Literature Crusade, 1959), 9–10, 31.

4. Andrew Murray, *Abide In Christ* (Fort Washington, PA: Christian Literature Crusade, 1997), 79–80.

5. Hannah Whitall Smith, *The Christian's Secret of a Happy Life* (Westwood, NJ: Fleming H. Revell, 1952), 53, 55.

6. Trumbull, *Victory in Christ*, 53–54.

Chapter 11—The Wings of the Wind

1. William Wallace (Mel Gibson) in the movie *Braveheart*, written by Randall Wallace, produced by Icon Productions, Ladd Company, and B.H. Finance C.V., May 24, 1995.

2. Glenn Doman, *What to Do about Your Brain-Injured Child* (Garden City, NY: Doubleday, 1987), 182.

3. Patterson, *Waiting*, 82–83.

4. Oswald Chambers, February 22 entry.

5. Yogi Berra, "Yogi Berra Quotes," *BrainyQuote*, http://www.brainyquote.com/quotes/authors/y/yogi_berra.html (accessed November 29, 2014).

Chapter 12—The Awakening

1. Eugene Peterson, *Run with the Horses* (Downers Grove, IL: InterVarsity Press, 176, 178.

2. Author's journal entry, August 28, 1989.

3. Dialogue between Anna (Jodie Foster) and Lady Tuptim (Bai Ling) in the movie *Anna and the King*, diaries written by Anna Leonowens and screenplay by Steve Meerson and Peter Krikes, produced by Fox 2000 Pictures and Lawrence Bender, released December 17, 1999.

4. Letter from author to Bryson's Army, November 16, 1989.

Chapter 13—Standing Firm

1. John of the Cross, "Living Flame of Love, Stanza 3," *You Set My Spirit Free*, 28.

2. Brown, *When Being Good Isn't Good Enough*, 27–28.

3. Author's journal entry, November 1989.

CHAPTER 14—THE MIGHTIEST DUCK

1. Charles Stanley, *How to Handle Adversity* (Nashville: Thomas Nelson, 1989).
2. Oswald Chambers, April 14 entry.
3. Neil Armstrong, "Neil Armstrong Quotes," *BrainyQuote*, http://www.brainyquote.com/quotes/quotes/n/neilarmstr101137.html (accessed November 30, 2014).
4. Gillham, *Lifetime Guarantee*, 147.
5. Edward T. Welch, *Addictions: A Banquet in the Grave: Finding Hope in the Power of the Gospel* (Phillipsburg, NJ: P & R Publishing, 2001).
6. Steve Gallagher, *At the Altar of Sexual Idolatry* (Dry Ridge, KY: Pure Life Ministries, 2000).
7. C. S. Lewis, *The Screwtape Letters* (New York: Macmillan, 1944), 47.
8. Crabb, *Shattered Dreams*, 90–91.
9. Smith, *The Christian's Secret of a Happy Life*, 134–135.

CHAPTER 15—THE WASHINGTON CAPER

1. John of the Cross, "Inner Sight," *You Set My Spirit Free*.
2. Andrew Murray and David Hazard, *Mighty Is Your Hand: A 40 Day Journey in the Company of Andrew Murray*, Rekindling the Inner Fire (Minneapolis: Bethany House, 1994), 44.

CHAPTER 16—THE GLADIATOR

1. Letter from author to Bryson's Army, June 1992.

CHAPTER 17—THE GOAL OF OUR INSTRUCTION

1. Oswald Chambers, June 22 entry.
2. Stephen Brown, concepts used frequently in his teaching, especially his students.
3. Watchman Nee, *The Normal Christian Life* (Wheaton, IL: Tyndale House, 1977), 33–34, 52–54, 84–85.
4. Bill Gillham, *What God Wishes Christians Knew about Christianity* (Eugene, OR: Harvest House, 1998), 289–293.

CHAPTER 18—NOTHING WILL BE IMPOSSIBLE

1. TV movie, *A Christmas Carol*, novel written by Charles Dickens and screenplay by Roger O. Hirson, produced by Entertainment Partners Ltd, released December 17, 1984.

CHAPTER 19—THE EYES OF YOUR HEART

1. Jim Elliot, "Jim Elliot Quotes," *BrainyQuote*, http://www.brainyquote.com/quotes/quotes/j/jimelliot189244.html (accessed December 1, 2014).
2. Julian of Norwich and David Hazard, *I Promise You a Crown: 40 Day Journey in the Company of Julian of Norwich*, Rekindling the Inner Fire (Minneapolis: Bethany House, 1995), 145.
3. Watchman Nee, *The Normal Christian Life*, 141–144.

Chapter 20—Next Year in Jerusalem

1. Robert Cook, "In his 23 years as president, [The King's] College grew, became accredited, and had a major impact on hundreds of young people. In 1963, he started The King's Hour radio broadcast. Dr. Cook retired from the presidency in 1985 and served as Chancellor of the College until his death in 1991," "History of The King's College: 1962," The King's College, New York City, https://www.tkc.edu/history (accessed November 25. 2014).
2. Crabb, *The Pressure's Off*, 122–123.
3. Oswald Chambers, September 3 entry.
4. Alan Redpath, *Victorious Christian Living*, (1955; repr., Santa Ana, CA: Calvary Chapel Publishing, 2007), 23–25.

Chapter 21—Field of Dreams

1. Crabb, *The Pressure's Off*, 97.
2. Dialogue between Ray (Kevin Costner) and John (Dwier Brown) in the movie *Field of Dreams*, book written by W. P. Kinsella and screenplay by Phil Alden Robinson, produced by Gordon Company, released May 5, 1989.
3. Crabb, *The Pressure's Off*, 82, 96–97.
4. Oswald Chambers, November 5 entry.

Chapter 22—Born to Run

1. Eric Liddell (Ian Charleson) in the movie *Chariots of Fire*, written by Colin Welland, produced by Twentieth Century Fox, Allied Stars, and Enigma Production, released April 9, 1982.
2. Tom Landry, "Coach Like a Pro," http://www.coachlikeapro.com/basketball-coaching-quotes.html (accessed November 25, 2014).
3. Robert A. Cook (see endnote 1, chapter 20).
4. Shakespeare, *Macbeth*, act 5, scene 5, 19–28.
5. Greg Laurie, "Under Construction," *Harvest Weekend Devotion*, February 28, 2009, Harvest Ministries, http://www.harvest.org/devotional/archive/devotion/2009-02-28.html (accessed December 3, 2014).
6. Greg Laurie, *Discipleship: The Road Less Taken* (Dana Point, CA: Allen David Books, 2009), 32.
7. David Roper, *Psalm 23: The Song of a Passionate Heart* (Grand Rapids, MI: Discovery House, 1994), 88.
8. Mary Kassian, *The Feminist Mistake* (Wheaton IL: Crossway Books), Introduction, 7–8, 12.
9. W. Bradford Wilcox, ed., "Social Indicators of Marital Health & Well-being: Divorce," *State of Our Unions*, The National Marriage Project, http://www.stateofourunions.org/2009/si-divorce.php (accessed January 11, 2015).
10. Peter Benson, ed., "Marriage Strike!" *Unity in the Body of Christ*, http://www.unityinchrist.com/marriage_strike.htm (accessed January 11, 32015).

Chapter 23—You Call *This* Reasonable?

1. Watchman Nee, *The Normal Christian Life*, 106–107.

2. Greg Laurie, "First and Foremost," *Harvest Weekend Devotion*, November 28, 2009.
3. Oswald Chambers, August 14 entry.
4. Murray and Hazard, *Mighty Is Your Hand*, 71.
5. Oswald Chambers, August 29 entry.
6. Author's journal entry, February 1997.
7. Ibid.

CHAPTER 24—THE TIMES THEY ARE A CHANGIN'

1. Bob Dylan, "The Times They Are A-Changin'," song in *The Times They Are A-Changin'* album, released January 13, 1964, Colombia Records.
2. Paul David Tripp, *Instruments in the Redeemer's Hands* (Phillipsburg, NJ: P & R Publishing, 2002), 48.
3. Oswald Chambers, June 26 entry.
4. Robert J. Morgan, *The Red Sea Rules* (Nashville: Thomas Nelson, 32001), 75.
5. Amy Carmichael, *The Edges of His Ways* (London: SPCK, 1955), 147–148; Amy Carmichael, *Thou Givest... They Gather* (Fort Washington, PA: Christian Literature Crusade, 1968), 19–20; Amy Carmichael and David Hazard, *You Are My Hiding Place: A 40 Day Journey in the Company of Amy Carmichael* (Minneapolis: Bethany House, 1991), 68, 70.
6. Dylan, "The Times They Are A-Changin'."
7. Vince Lombardi, "Vince Lombardi Quotes," *BrainyQuote*, http://www.brainyquote.com/quotes/quotes/v/vincelomba115467.html (accessed November 25, 2014).

CHAPTER 25—THE PROVING

1. Oswald Chambers, May 8 entry.
2. Ibid., May 2 entry.
3. Horatius Bonar, *When God's Children Suffer* (London: Evangelical House, 1967), 59–64.
4. Ibid.
5. Ibid.
6. Ibid.
7. Ibid.
8. Ibid.
9. Ibid.
10. Ibid.
11. Ibid.
12. Murray and Hazard, *Mighty Is Your Hand*, 150.

CHAPTER 26—DEATH IN THE POT

1. "Divorce and Children with Disabilities," *Children and Divorce.com*, http://www.children-and-divorce.com/divorce-and-children-with-disabilities.html (accessed December 7. 2014).
2. John Eldredge, *Wild at Heart* (Nashville: Thomas Nelson, 2001), 160–161.

3. Shaunti Feldhahn and Jeff Feldhahn, *For Men Only* (Colorado Springs, CO: Multnomah Publishers, 2006).

4. Shaunti Feldhahn, *For Women Only* (Colorado Springs, CO: Multnomah Books, 2004), 178–180.

5. Dialogue between Erica (Jodie Foster) and Detective Mercer (Terrence Howard) in the movie *The Brave One*, written by Roderick Taylor, Bruce A. Taylor, and Cynthia Mort, produced by Warner Brothers, Village Roadshow Pictures, and Silver Pictures, released September 14, 2007.

6. John Piper, *This Momentary Marriage: A Parable of Permanence* (Wheaton, IL: Crossway Books, 2009), 158.

7. John Piper et al., *Voices of the True Woman Movement: A Call to the Counter-Revolution* (Chicago: Moody Publishers, 2010), 19.

8. Murray and Hazard, *Mighty Is Your Hand*, 36–37.

9. Piper, *This Momentary Marriage*, 159.

10. Ibid., 77.

11. Ibid., 159, 162.

12. John Piper, *A Godward Life* (Sisters, OR: Multnomah Books, 1997), 35, 37.

13. Linda J. Waite et al., "Does Divorce Make People Happy?" *Institute for American Values*, Values,http://americanvalues.org/catalog/pdfs/does_divorce_make_people_happy.pdf (accessed November 28, 2014).

14. Nancy Leigh DeMoss and Tim Grissom, *Seeking Him* (Chicago: Moody Publications, 2009).

15. Murray and Hazard, *Mighty Is Your Hand*, 97–98.

16. Ibid., 124.

17. Oswald Chambers, October 30 entry.

Chapter 27—Worth Fighting For

1. Redpath, *Victorious Christian Living*, 168.

2. Dialogue between Samwise (Sean Astin) and Frodo (Elijah Wood) in the movie *The Lord of the Rings: The Two Towers*, novel written by J. R. R. Tolkien and screenplay by Fran Walsh et al., produced by New Line Cinema, WingNut Films, Tolkien Enterprises, released December 18, 2002.

3. Joni Eareckson Tada, *Pearls of Great Price* (Grand Rapids, MI: Zondervan, 2006).

4. Dialogue between McKnight (Tom Sizemore) and a soldier in the movie *Black Hawk Down*, book written by Mark Bowden and screenplay by Ken Nolan, produced by Revolution Studios, Jerry Bruckheimer Films, and Scott Free Productions, released January 18, 2001.

5. John Wesley in Martin Wells Knapp, *Impressions* (Wheaton, IL: Tyndale House, 1984), 32.

6. Warren W. Wiersbe, *The Strategy of Satan* (Wheaton, IL: Tyndale House, 1979), 132–133.

7. Neil Anderson, "Daily in Christ 10/17," *Freedom in Christ Ministries*, http://www.crosswalk.com/devotionals/dailyinchrist/daily-in-christ-10-or-17-544854.html (accessed November 28, 2014).

Chapter 28—Whatever Kills You Makes You Stronger

1. Billy Joel, "Piano Man," song in the *Piano Man* album, released November 2, 1973, Columbia Records, 45 rpm single.
2. C. S. Lewis, *A Preface to Paradise Lost* (New York: Oxford University Press, 1942), 97.
3. Oswald Chambers, March 3 entry.
4. Stephen Brown, *Three Free Sins* (New York: Howard Books, 2012), 104.
5. Edmund Burke, "Edmund Burke > Quotes," *Goodreads Inc.*, https://www.goodreads.com/author/quotes/17142.Edmund_Burke (accessed November 25, 2014).
6. Winston Churchill, "Winston S. Churchill > Quotes > Quotable Quotes," *Goodreads Inc.*, http://www.goodreads.com/quotes/395356-without-courage-all-other-virtues-lose-their-meaning (accessed November 25, 2014).
7. Friedrich Nietzsche, "Friedrich Nietzsche Quotes," *BrainyQuote*, http://www.brainyquote.com/quotes/quotes/f/friedrichn101616.html (accessed December 9, 2014).
8. Brown, *When Being Good Isn't Good Enough*, 216.
9. Joel, "Piano Man."

Chapter 29—The Expected One

1. Oswald Chambers, August 5 entry.
2. Amy Carmichael, *Experience Worketh Hope* (Edinburgh: T & T Clark, 1944).
3. Jimmy Buffet, "Margaritaville," song in *Changes in Latitudes, Changes in Attitudes* album, released February 14, 1977, by ABC Records.
4. Oswald Chambers, August 10 entry.
5. Ibid., June 16 entry.
6. Bill Murray in the comedy movie *Groundhog Day*, written by Danny Rubin and Harold Ramis, produced by Columbia Pictures, released February 13, 1993
7. William Congreve, *The Mourning Bride: A Tragedy*, act III, scene VIII, 1697.
8. Theodore Roosevelt, "The Man in the Arena," *Citizenship in a Republic*, April 23, 1910, Sorbonne, France, http://www.theodore-roosevelt.com/images/research/speeches/maninthearena.pdf (accessed November 28, 2014).
9. Vince Lombardi, "Vince Lombardi Quotes," *BrainyQuote*, http://www.brainyquote.com/quotes/quotes/v/vincelomba380768.html (accessed November 25, 2014).
10. Rick Blaine (Humphrey Bogart) in the movie *Casablanca*, written by Julius J Epstein and Phillip G. Epstein, produced by Warner Brothers, released January 23, 1942.

Chapter 30—When Fig Trees Don't Blossom

1. Redpath, *Victorious Christian Living*, 30.
2. Dialogue between Sean Maguire (Robin Williams) and Will Hunting (Matt Damon) in the movie *Good Will Hunting*, written by Matt Damon

and Ben Affleck, produced by Be Gentlemen Limited Partnership, Lawrence Bender Productions, Miramax Films, released January 9, 1998.

3. Robert A. Cook, (see note 1, chapter 20).

Chapter 31—Finishing Well

1. Redpath, *Victorious Christian Living*, 203.
2. Robert A. Cook, (see note 1, chapter 20).
3. Oswald Chambers, June 25 entry.
4. Redpath, *Victorious Christian Living*, 43–44.

Epilogue—In Jesus' Name

1. Dan Burgess, "Press On," (sung by Selah and others), Alfred Publishing Co, Inc., 1983.
2. C. S. Lewis, *Mere Christianity* (New York: MacMillan, 1952), 87.
3. Giuseppe Garibaldi, "Giuseppe Garibaldi Quotes," *BrainyQuote*, http://www.brainyquote.com/quotes/quotes/g/giuseppega205832.html (accessed November 18, 2014).
4. John Foot, "Giuseppe Garibaldi," *Encyclopaedia Britannica*, updated July 17, 2014, http://www.britannica.com/EBchecked/topic/225978/Giuseppe-Garibaldi (accessed November 28, 2014).

About the Author

1. William Arthur Ward, "William Arthur Ward Quotes," *BrainyQuote*, http://www.brainyquote.com/quotes/quotes/w/williamart103463.html (accessed January 15, 2015).